ACCA

STUDY TEXT

Paper 2.5

Financial Reporting

IN THIS JUNE 2002 EDITION

- Targeted to the syllabus and study guide
- Quizzes and questions to check your understanding
- Clear layout and style designed to save you time
- Plenty of exam-style questions with NEW detailed guidance from BPP
- Chapter Roundups and summaries to help revision
- Mind Maps to integrate the key points

BPP's **MCQ Cards** and **i-Learn** and **i-Pass** products also support this paper.

NEW IN THIS JUNE 2002 EDITION

- The material on fixed assets, interpretation of accounts, long-term contracts and FRS 18 has been substantially revised

FOR EXAMS IN DECEMBER 2002 AND JUNE 2003

BPP Publishing
June 2002

First edition 2001
Second edition June 2002

ISBN 07517 0236 6 (previous ISBN 07517 0738 4)

British Library Cataloguing-in-Publication Data
A catalogue record for this book is available from the British Library

Published by

BPP Publishing Ltd
Aldine House, Aldine Place
London W12 8AW

www.bpp.com

Printed in Great Britain by Ashford Colour Press

We are grateful to the Association of Chartered Certified Accountants for permission to reproduce past examination questions and questions from the pilot paper. The answers have been prepared by BPP Publishing Limited.

		Page
THE BPP STUDY TEXT		(v)
HELP YOURSELF STUDY FOR YOUR ACCA EXAMS		(vii)
The right approach - suggested study sequence - developing your personal study plan		
SYLLABUS		(xii)
STUDY GUIDE		(xv)
THE EXAM PAPER		(xxii)
OXFORD BROOKES BSC (Hons) IN APPLIED ACCOUNTING		(xx)

PART A: THE REGULATORY FRAMEWORK

1	Review of basic accounting concepts	3
2	The regulatory framework	22

PART B: PREPARING THE FINANCIAL STATEMENTS OF LIMITED LIABILITY COMPANIES

3	Companies Act requirements and the format of accounts	37
4	Fixed assets: tangible assets	77
5	Fixed assets: intangible assets and investments	114
6	Hire purchase and leasing	147
7	Stocks and work in progress	160
8	Taxation in company accounts	180
9	Earnings per share and reporting financial performance	200
10	Cash flow statements	229
11	Liabilities and provisions; reporting the substance of transactions	251
12	Share capital and reserves; financial instruments	278
13	Distributable profits and capital transactions	291
14	Related parties; segmental information	313

PART C: PREPARATION OF CONSOLIDATED FINANCIAL STATEMENTS

15	Constitution of a group	329
16	Consolidated balance sheet: basic principles	344
17	Acquisition of subsidiaries	372
18	Profit and loss account; mergers	391
19	Associates and joint ventures	420

PART D: THE THEORETICAL FRAMEWORK OF ACCOUNTING

20	Theoretical aspects of accounting	449
21	The ASB's Statement of Principles	498

Contents

PART E: ANALYSING AND APPRAISING FINANCIAL AND RELATED INFORMATION

22   Interpretation of financial statements   511

APPENDIX: EXAMINATION QUESTIONS ON PUBLISHED ACCOUNTS   547

EXAM QUESTION BANK   561

EXAM ANSWER BANK   589

INDEX   637

REVIEW FORM & FREE PRIZE DRAW

ORDER FORM

THE BPP STUDY TEXT

Aims of this Study Text

To provide you with the knowledge and understanding, skills and application techniques that you need if you are to be successful in your exams

This Study Text has been written around the **Financial Reporting** syllabus.

- It is **comprehensive**. It covers the syllabus content. No more, no less.

- It is written at the **right level**. Each chapter is written with the ACCA's **study guide** in mind.

- It is targeted to the **exam**. We have taken account of the **pilot paper,** questions put to the examiners at the recent ACCA conference and the assessment methodology.

To allow you to study in the way that best suits your learning style and the time you have available, by following your personal Study Plan (see page (vii))

You may be studying at home on your own until the date of the exam, or you may be attending a full-time course. You may like to (and have time to) read every word, or you may prefer to (or only have time to) skim-read and devote the remainder of your time to question practice. Wherever you fall in the spectrum, you will find the BPP Study Text meets your needs in designing and following your personal Study Plan.

To tie in with the other components of the BPP Effective Study Package to ensure you have the best possible chance of passing the exam (see page (vi))

BPP PUBLISHING

The BPP Effective Study Package

Recommended period of use	Elements of the BPP Effective Study Package
From the outset and throughout	**Learning to learn accountancy** Read this invaluable book as you begin your studies and refer to it as you work through the various elements of the BPP Effective Study Package. It will help you to acquire knowledge, practice and revise, both efficiently and effectively.
Three to twelve months before the exam	**Study Text and i-Learn** Use the Study Text to acquire knowledge, understanding, skills and the ability to use application techniques. Use BPP's **i-Learn** product to reinforce your learning.
Throughout	**Virtual Campus** Study, practice, revise and take advantage of other useful resources with BPP's fully interactive e-learning site with comprehensive tutor support.
Throughout	**MCQ cards and i-Pass** Revise your knowledge and ability to use application techniques, as well as practising this key exam question format, with 150 multiple choice questions. **i-Pass**, our computer-based testing package, provides objective test questions in a variety of formats and is ideal for self-assessment.
One to six months before the exam	**Practice & Revision Kit** Try the numerous examination-format questions, for which there are realistic suggested solutions prepared by BPP's own authors. Then attempt the two mock exams.
From three months before the exam until the last minute	**Passcards** Work through these short, memorable notes which are focused on what is most likely to come up in the exam you will be sitting.
One to six months before the exam	**Success Tapes** These audio tapes cover the vital elements of your syllabus in less than 90 minutes per subject. Each tape also contains exam hints to help you fine tune your strategy.
Three to twelve months before the exam	**Breakthrough Videos** Use a Breakthrough Video to supplement your Study Text. They give you clear tuition on key exam subjects and allow you the luxury of being able to pause or repeat sections until you have fully grasped the topic.

HELP YOURSELF STUDY FOR YOUR ACCA EXAMS

Exams for professional bodies such as ACCA are very different from those you have taken at college or university. You will be under **greater time pressure before** the exam – as you may be combining your study with work as well as in the exam room. There are many different ways of learning and so the BPP Study Text offers you a number of different tools to help you through. Here are some hints and tips: they are not plucked out of the air, but **based on research and experience**. (You don't need to know that long-term memory is in the same part of the brain as emotions and feelings – but it's a fact anyway.)

The right approach

1 The right attitude

Believe in yourself	Yes, there is a lot to learn. Yes, it is a challenge. But thousands have succeeded before and you can too.
Remember why you're doing it	Studying might seem a grind at times, but you are doing it for a reason: to advance your career.

2 The right focus

Read through the Syllabus and Study guide	These tell you what you are expected to know and are supplemented by Exam Focus Points in the text.
Study the Exam Paper section	The pilot paper is likely to be a reasonable guide of what you should expect in the exam.

3 The right method

The big picture	You need to grasp the detail – but keeping in mind how everything fits into the big picture will help you understand better. • The **Introduction** of each chapter puts the material in context. • The **Syllabus content**, **Study guide** and **Exam focus points** show you what you need to **grasp**. • **Mind Maps** show the links and key issues in key topics.
In your own words	To absorb the information (and to practise your written communication skills), it helps **put it into your own words**. • **Take notes.** • Answer the **questions** in each chapter. As well as helping you absorb the information you will practise your written communication skills, which become increasingly important as you progress through your ACCA exams. • Draw **mind maps**. We have some examples. • Try 'teaching' to a colleague or friend.

| Give yourself cues to jog your memory | The BPP Study Text uses **bold** to **highlight key points** and **icons** to identify key features, such as **Exam focus points** and **Key terms.**

• Try **colour coding** with a highlighter pen.
• Write **key points** on cards. |

4   The right review

| Review, review, review | It is a **fact** that regularly reviewing a topic in summary form can **fix it in your memory**. Because **review** is so important, the BPP Study Text helps you to do so in many ways.

• **Chapter roundups** summarise the key points in each chapter. Use them to recap each study session.
• The **Quick quiz** is another review technique to ensure that you have grasped the essentials.
• Go through the **Examples** in each chapter a second or third time. |

Developing your personal Study Plan

One thing that the BPP Learning to learn accountancy book emphasises (see page (iv)) is the need to prepare (and use) a study plan. Planning and sticking to the plan are key elements of learning success.

There are four steps you should work through.

Step 1. **How do you learn?**

First you need to be aware of your style of learning. The BPP Learning to learn accountancy book commits a chapter to this **self-discovery**. What types of intelligence do you display when learning? You might be advised to brush up on certain study skills before launching into this Study Text.

> BPP's **Learning to Learn Accountancy** book helps you to identify what intelligences you show more strongly and then details how you can tailor your study process through your preferences. It also includes handy hints on how to develop intelligences you exhibit less strongly, but which might be needed as you study accountancy.

Are you a **theorist** or are you more **practical**? If you would rather get to grips with a theory before trying to apply it in practice, you should follow the study sequence on page X. If the reverse is true (you like to know why you are learning theory before you do so), you might be advised to flick through Study Text chapters and look at questions, case studies and examples (Steps 7, 8 and 9 in the **suggested study sequence**) before reading through the detailed theory.

Step 2. **How much time do you have?**

Work out the time you have available per week, given the following.

- The standard you have set yourself
- The time you need to set aside later for work on the Practice & Revision Kit and Passcards
- The other exam(s) you are sitting
- Very importantly, practical matters such as work, travel, exercise, sleep and social life

Note your time available in box A.   A [Hours   ]

Step 3. **Allocate your time**

- Take the time you have available per week for this Study Text shown in box A, multiply it by the number of weeks available and insert the result in box B.   B [   ]

- Divide the figure in Box B by the number of chapters in this text and insert the result in box C.   C [   ]

Remember that this is only a rough guide. Some of the chapters in this book are longer and more complicated than others, and you will find some subjects easier to understand than others.

Step 4. **Implement**

Set about studying each chapter in the time shown in box C, following the key study steps in the order suggested by your particular learning style.

This is your personal **Study Plan**. You should try and combine it with the study sequence outlined below. You may want to modify the sequence a little (as has been suggested above) to adapt it to your **personal style**.

BPP PUBLISHING

Suggested study sequence

Tackle the chapters in the order you find them in the Study Text. Taking into account your individual learning style, you could follow this sequence.

Key study steps	Activity
Step 1 **Topic list**	Each numbered topic is a numbered section in the chapter.
Step 2 **Introduction**	This gives you the **big picture** in terms of the **context** of the chapter. The content is referenced to the **Study Guide**, and **Exam Guidance** shows how the topic is likely to be examined. In other words, it sets your **objectives for study.**
Step 3 **Knowledge brought forward boxes**	In these we highlight information and techniques that it is assumed you have 'brought forward' with you from your earlier studies. If there are topics which have changed recently due to legislation for example, these topics are explained in more detail.
Step 4 **Explanations**	Proceed methodically through the chapter, reading each section thoroughly and making sure you understand.
Step 5 **Key terms and Exam focus points**	<ul><li>**Key terms** can often earn you *easy marks* if you state them clearly and correctly in an appropriate exam answer (and they are indexed at the back of the text).</li><li>**Exam focus points** give you a good idea of how we think the examiner intends to examine certain topics.</li></ul>
Step 6 **Note taking**	Take brief notes if you wish, avoiding the temptation to copy out too much.
Step 7 **Examples**	Follow each through to its solution very carefully.
Step 8 **Case examples**	Study each one, and try to add flesh to them from your own experience – they are designed to show how the topics you are studying come alive (and often come unstuck) in the real world.
Step 9 **Questions**	Make a very good attempt at each one.
Step 10 **Answers**	Check yours against ours, and make sure you understand any discrepancies.
Step 11 **Chapter roundup**	Work through it very carefully, to make sure you have grasped the major points it is highlighting.
Step 12 **Quick quiz**	When you are happy that you have covered the chapter, use the **Quick quiz** to check how much you have remembered of the topics covered.
Step 13 **Question(s) in the Question bank**	Either at this point, or later when you are thinking about revising, make a full attempt at the **Question(s)** suggested at the very end of the chapter. You can find these at the end of the Study Text, along with the **Answers** so you can see how you did. We highlight those that are introductory, and those which are of the standard you would expect to find in an exam.

Short of time: *Skim study technique?*

You may find you simply do not have the time available to follow all the key study steps for each chapter, however you adapt them for your particular learning style. If this is the case, follow the **skim study** technique below (the icons in the Study Text will help you to do this).

- Study the chapters in the order you find them in the Study Text.

- For each chapter, follow the key study steps 1-3, and then skim-read through step 4. Jump to step 11, and then go back to step 5. Follow through steps 7 and 8, and prepare outline answers to questions (steps 9/10). Try the Quick quiz (step 12), following up any items you can't answer, then do a plan for the Question (step 13), comparing it against our answers. You should probably still follow step 6 (note-taking), although you may decide simply to rely on the BPP Passcards for this.

Moving on...

However you study, when you are ready to embark on the practice and revision phase of the BPP Effective Study Package, you should still refer back to this Study Text, both as a source of **reference** (you should find the list of key terms and the index particularly helpful for this) and as a **refresher** (the Chapter roundups and Quick quizzes help you here).

And remember to keep careful hold of this Study Text – you will find it invaluable in your work.

> More advice on Study Skills can be found in the BPP **Learning to Learn Accountancy** book

SYLLABUS

Aim

To build on the basic techniques in Paper 1.1 Preparing Financial Statements and to develop knowledge and understanding of more advanced financial accounting concepts and principles. Candidates will be required to apply this understanding by preparing and interpreting financial reports in a practical context.

Objectives

On completion of this paper candidates should be able to:

- Appraise and apply specified accounting concepts and theories to practical work place situations

- Appraise and apply the international regulatory framework of financial reporting

- Prepare financial statements for different entities to comply with the Companies Act and specified Accounting Standards and other related pronouncements

- Prepare group financial statements (excluding group cash flow statements) to include a single subsidiary and possibly an associated company or Joint Venture

- Analyse, interpret and report on financial statements (including cash flow statements) and related information to a variety of user groups

- Discuss and apply the requirements of other specified Accounting Standards

- Demonstrate the skills expected in Part 2.

Position of the paper in the overall syllabus

Paper 2.5 builds on the techniques developed at Paper 1.1 Preparing Financial Statements and tests the conceptual and technical financial accounting knowledge that candidates will require in order to progress to the higher level analytical, judgmental and communication skills of Paper 3.6 Advanced Corporate Reporting.

Paper 2.5 also provides essential financial accounting knowledge and principles that need to be fully understood by auditors, thus it forms some of the prerequisite knowledge of Paper 2.6 Audit and Internal Review, and the option Paper 3.1 Audit and Assurance services.

Prerequisite knowledge of Paper 2.5 is largely the basic knowledge and skills demonstrated at Paper 1.1, but many recent accounting standards require the use of discounting techniques which candidates will have acquired at Paper 2.4 Financial Management and Control.

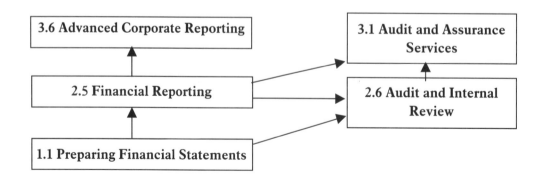

SYLLABUS

1 Accounting principles, concepts and theory

(a) The ASB's Statement of Principles for Financial Reporting.
(b) Agency theory.
(c) Price level changes, capital maintenance.

2 Regulatory framework

(a) Structure of UK regulatory framework

   (i) EC directives
   (ii) Companies Acts

(b) Standard setting process: the Financial Reporting Council and its subsidiary bodies: the role of the International Accounting Standards Committee.

3 Preparation and presentation of financial statements for limited companies and other entities

(a) Accounting for share capital and reserves

   (i) Issue and redemption of shares
   (ii) Distributable profits

(b) Tangible and intangible fixed assets.

(c) Net current assets.

(d) Earning per share.

(e) Tax in company accounting including:

   (i) Current tax
   (ii) Deferred tax

(f) SSAPs, FRSs and UITF abstracts as specified in the examinable documents.

4 Preparation of consolidated financial statements

(a) Definition of subsidiary companies.

(b) Exclusions from consolidations.

(c) Preparation of consolidated profit and loss accounts and balance sheets including:

   (i) Elimination of intra-group transactions
   (ii) Fair value adjustments

(d) Associated companies, joint ventures.

(e) Substance of, and accounting for, mergers.

5   Analysis and interpretation of financial statements and related information

    (a)   Analysis of corporate information.

    (b)   Preparation of reports on financial performance for various user groups.

    (c)   Preparation and analysis of cash flow statements of a single company.

    (d)   Related party transactions.

    (e)   Segmental information.

Excluded topics

The following topics are specifically excluded from the syllabus:

- Partnership and branch financial statements
- Preparing group financial statements involving more than one subsidiary
- Piecemeal acquisitions, disposal of subsidiaries and group reconstructions
- Foreign currency translation/consolidations, hedging
- Group cash flows
- Schemes of reorganisation/reconstruction
- Company/share valuation
- Derivative transactions
- Accounting for pension costs
- The ASB's Financial Reporting Exposure Drafts and Discussion Drafts.

Key areas of the syllabus

The key topic areas are as follows:

Accounting principles and concepts, accounting theory

- Statement of Principles.
- Revenue recognition.
- Substance over form.

Preparation of financial statements of limited companies

- Form and content of published financial statements.
- Accounting and disclosure requirements of the Companies Acts and Accounting Standards.

Preparation of consolidated financial statements

- Definitions of subsidiaries: exclusions from consolidation.
- Simple groups (parent plus a single subsidiary).

Analysis and interpretation of financial statements

- Preparation of reports for various user groups.
- Preparation and analysis of cash flow statements.

Other topic areas

Note these may be examined as part of a question within the above key areas or as a substantial part of a separate optional question:

- Hire purchase and leasing
- Long-term contracts
- Earnings per share
- Impairment of fixed assets, provisions
- Discontinued operations
- Goodwill and other intangibles.

Paper 2.5(U)

Financial Reporting
(United Kingdom)

Study Guide

1   REVIEW OF BASIC CONCEPTS, STATEMENT OF PRINCIPLES FOR FINANCIAL REPORTING

- discuss what is meant by a conceptual framework and GAAP.

- describe the objectives of financial statements and the qualitative characteristics of financial information.

- define the elements of financial statements.

- apply the above definitions to practical situations.

- revision of paper 1.1 - prepare the final accounts of a simple business organisation

2   ACCOUNTING CONCEPTS, ACCOUNTING THEORY

- distinguish between positive and normative accounting concepts.

- outline the principles of agency theory and the efficient markets hypothesis.

- outline the concept of 'comprehensive income'.

- explain the principle of value in use/deprival value.

3   REVENUE RECOGNITION

- outline the principles of the timing of revenue recognition.

- explain the role of the concept of substance over form in relation to recognising sales revenue.

- explain and define realised profits.

- discuss the various points in the production and sales cycle where it may, depending on circumstances, be appropriate to recognise gains and losses - give examples of this.

- describe the ASB's 'balance sheet approach' to revenue recognition within its Statement of Principles.

4   ACCOUNTING FOR PRICE LEVEL CHANGES

- describe the deficiencies of historic cost accounts (HCA) during periods of rising prices.

- explain the concepts of current purchasing power (CPP), current cost accounting (CCA) and real terms accounting, including the concept of capital maintenance.

  (Note: detailed calculations based on CPP and CCA are NOT examinable).

- discuss the advantages and disadvantages of the above accounting systems.

5   THE STRUCTURE OF THE UK REGULATORY FRAMEWORK

- describe the influence of EC directives.

- explain the role of the Companies Acts.

- outline the Standard setting process and the role of the:

  - Financial Reporting Council

  - Accounting Standards Board

  - Urgent Issues Task Force

  - financial reporting

- explain the relationship between UK and international accounting standards (IASs).

6   PREPARATION OF FINANCIAL STATEMENTS FOR LIMITED COMPANIES

- state the requirements of the Companies Act regarding:

- the duty to prepare annual accounts.

- the form and content of the prescribed formats.

- the main provisions of Company Law including accounting rules.

- prepare the financial statements of limited companies in accordance with the prescribed formats and relevant accounting standards.

- distinguish between small and medium companies and outline the disclosure exemptions relating to these companies.

7 REPORTING FINANCIAL PERFORMANCE (FRS 3)

- explain the need for an accounting standard in this area.

- discuss the importance of identifying and reporting the results of discontinuing operations; define discontinuing operation in accordance with FRS 3.

- distinguish between extraordinary and exceptional items, including their accounting treatment and required disclosures.

- prepare a profit and loss account in accordance with the requirements of FRS 3.

8 REPORTING FINANCIAL PERFORMANCE (FRS 3)

- explain the contents and purpose of the statement of recognised gains and losses, linking it to the Statement of Principles and the concept of comprehensive income.

- describe and prepare:
  - A Note of Historical Cost Profits and Losses.
  - reconciliation of movement in shareholders' funds.
  - statement of movement in reserves.

- define prior period adjustments and account for the correction of fundamental errors and changes in accounting policies.

9 SHARE CAPITAL AND RESERVES

- explain the need for an accounting standard on Capital Instruments (FRS 4).

- distinguish between debt and share capital.

- apply the requirements of FRS 4 to the issue and finance costs of:
  - equity and preference shares
  - debt instruments with no conversion rights, and
  - convertible debt.

- explain and apply the general requirements to purchase or redeem shares.

- apply the requirements that allow private companies to redeem shares out of capital.

- discuss the advantages of companies being able to redeem shares.

- define and discuss the Companies Acts rules relating to profits available for distribution.

- calculate the profits available for distribution of public and private companies.

10 FIXED ASSETS - TANGIBLE

- define the initial cost of a fixed asset (including a self-constructed asset) and apply this to various examples of expenditures distinguishing between capital and revenue items.

- describe, and be able to identify, subsequent expenditures that may be capitalised.

- state and appraise the effects of FRS 15's rules for the revaluation of fixed assets.

- account for gains and losses on the disposal of revalued assets.

- calculate depreciation on:
  - revalued assets, and
  - assets that have two or more major components.

- apply the provisions of SSAP 4 Government Grants.

- discuss why the treatment of investment properties should differ from other properties.

- apply the requirements of SSAP 19 'Accounting for Investment Properties'.

11 HIRE PURCHASE AND LEASING

- distinguish between a hire purchase contract and a lease.

- describe and apply the method of determining a lease type (ie an operating or finance lease).

- explain the effect on the financial statements of a finance lease being incorrectly treated as an operating lease.

- account for operating leases in financial statements.

- account for finance leases in the financial statements of lessor and lessees.

- outline the principles of SSAP 21 and its main disclosure requirements.
  Note: the net cash investment method will not be examined.

12 FIXED ASSETS - GOODWILL AND INTANGIBLE ASSETS

- discuss the nature and possible accounting treatments of both internally generated and purchased goodwill.

- distinguish between goodwill and other intangible assets.

- describe the criteria for the initial recognition and measurement of intangible assets.

- describe the subsequent accounting treatment, including the principle of impairment tests in relation to purchased goodwill.

- describe the circumstances in which negative goodwill arises, and its subsequent accounting treatment and disclosure.

- describe and apply the requirements of SSAP 13 'Accounting for Research and Development'.

13 FIXED ASSETS - IMPAIRMENT OF FIXED ASSETS AND GOODWILL

- define the recoverable amount of an asset; define impairment losses.

- give examples of, and be able to identify, circumstances that may indicate that an impairment of fixed assets has occurred.

- describe what is meant by an income generating unit.

- state the basis on which impairment losses should be allocated, and allocate a given impairment loss to the assets of an income generating unit.

14 LIABILITIES - PROVISIONS, CONTINGENT ASSETS AND LIABILITIES

- explain why an accounting standard on provisions is necessary - give examples of previous abuses in this area.

- define provisions, legal and constructive obligations, past events and the transfer of economic benefits.

- state when provisions may and may not be made, and how they should be accounted for.

- explain how provisions should be measured.

- define contingent assets and liabilities - give examples and describe their accounting treatment.

- be able to identify and account for:
  - warranties/guarantees
  - onerous contracts
  - environmental and similar provisions

- discuss the validity of making provisions for future repairs or refurbishment.

15 STOCK AND LONG-TERM CONTRACTS

- review the principles of stock valuation covered in Paper 1.1.

- define a long-term contract and describe why recognising profit before completion is generally considered to be desirable; discuss if this may be profit smoothing.

- describe the ways in which attributable profit may be measured.

- calculate and disclose the amounts to be shown in the financial statements for long-term contracts.

16 EARNINGS PER SHARE (FRS 14)

- explain the importance of comparability in relation to the calculation of earnings per (eps) share and its importance as a stock market indicator.

- explain why the trend of eps may be a more accurate indicator of performance than a company's profit trend.

- define earnings and the basic number of shares.

- calculate the eps in accordance with FRS 14 in the following circumstances:
  - basic eps
  - where there has been a bonus issue of shares during the year, and
  - where there has been a rights issue of shares during the year.

- explain the relevance to existing shareholders of the diluted eps, and describe the circumstances that will give rise to a future dilution of the eps.

- calculate the diluted eps in the following circumstances:
  - where convertible debt or preference shares are in issue; and
  - where share options and warranties exist.

17 TAXATION IN FINANCIAL STATEMENTS

- account for current taxation in accordance with FRS 16.

- record entries relating to corporation tax in the accounting records.

- apply requirements of SSAP 5 Accounting for VAT.

- explain the effect of timing differences on accounting and taxable profits.

- outline the principle of accounting for deferred tax on both the full and the partial provision methods, and discuss their advantages and disadvantages.

- Outline the requirements of FRS 19.

- Calculate and record deferred tax amounts in the financial statements.

18 ACCOUNTING FOR THE SUBSTANCE OF TRANSACTIONS

- explain the importance of recording the substance rather than the legal form of transactions - give examples of previous abuses in this area.

- describe the features which may indicate that the substance of transactions may differ from their legal form.

- explain and apply the principles in FRS 5 for the recognition and derecognition of assets and liabilities.

- be able to recognise the substance of transactions in general, and specifically account for the following types of transactions:

  - stock sold on sale or return/consignment stock.

  - sale and repurchase/leaseback agreements.

  - factoring of debtors.

19-20 GROUP ACCOUNTING - INTRODUCTION

- describe the concept of a group and the objective of consolidated financial statements.

- explain the different methods which could be used to prepare group accounts.

- explain and apply the definition of subsidiary companies in the Companies Acts and FRS 2.

- describe the circumstances and reasoning for subsidiaries to be excluded from consolidated financial statements.

- prepare a consolidated balance sheet for a simple group dealing with pre and post acquisition profits, minority interests and consolidated goodwill.

- explain the need for using coterminous year ends and uniform accounting policies when preparing consolidated financial statements.

- describe how the above is achieved in practice.

- prepare a consolidated profit and loss account for a simple group, including an example where an acquisition occurs during the year and there is a minority interest.

21 GROUP ACCOUNTING - INTRA GROUP ADJUSTMENTS

- explain why intra-group transactions should be eliminated on consolidation.

- explain the nature of a dividend paid out of pre-acquisition profits.

- account for the effects (in the profit and loss account and balance sheet) of intra-group trading and other transactions including:

  - unrealised profits in stock and fixed assets

  - intra-group loans and interest and other intra-group charges, and

  - intra-group dividends including those paid out of pre-acquisition profits.

22 GROUP ACCOUNTING - FAIR VALUE ADJUSTMENTS

- explain why it is necessary for both the consideration paid for a subsidiary and the subsidiary's identifiable assets and liabilities to be accounted for at their fair values when preparing consolidated financial statements.

- prepare consolidated financial statements dealing with the fair value adjustments (including their effect on consolidated goodwill) in respect of:

  - depreciating and non-depreciating fixed assets

  - stocks

  - monetary liabilities (basic discounting techniques may be required)

- assets and liabilities (including contingencies) not included in the subsidiary's own balance sheet.

23 GROUP ACCOUNTING – ASSOCIATES AND JOINT VENTURES

- define associates and joint ventures, including an arrangement that is not an entity (JANE).

- distinguish between equity accounting and proportional consolidation.

- describe the equity and gross equity methods.

- prepare consolidated financial statements to include a single subsidiary and an associated company or a joint venture.

Group Accounting - mergers

- discuss the criteria for determining whether a business combination should be treated as a merger or an acquisition.

- explain why a business combination that is a merger should have a different accounting treatment than that of an acquisition.

- prepare consolidated financial statements applying merger accounting.

- describe and quantify the effect on consolidated financial statements of applying merger accounting compared to acquisition accounting.

25 ANALYSIS AND INTERPRETATION OF FINANCIAL STATEMENTS

- calculate useful financial ratios for single company or group financial statements.

- analyse and interpret ratios to give an assessment of a company's performance in comparison with:

  - a company's previous period's financial statements.

  - another similar company for the same period.

  - industry average ratios.

- discuss the effect that changes in accounting policies or the use of different accounting policies between companies can have on the ability to interpret performance.

- discuss how the interpretation of current cost accounts or current purchasing power accounts would differ to that of historic cost accounts.

- discuss the limitations in the use of ratio analysis for assessing corporate performance, outlining other information that may be of relevance.

Note: the content of reports should draw upon knowledge acquired in other sessions.

These sessions concentrate on the preparation of reports and report writing skills.

26 CASH FLOW STATEMENTS

- prepare a cash flow statement, including

relevant notes, for an individual company in accordance with FRS 1 (revised).

Note: questions may specify the use of the direct or the indirect method.

- appraise the usefulness of, and interpret the information in, a cash flow statement.

27 RELATED PARTIES

- define and apply the definition of related parties in accordance with FRS 8.

- describe the potential to mislead users when related party transactions are included in a company's financial statements.

- adjust financial statements (for comparative purposes) for the effects of non-commercial related party transactions.

- describe the disclosure requirements for related party transactions.

28 SEGMENTAL REPORTING

- discuss the usefulness and problems associated with the provision of segmental information.

- define a reportable segment and the information that is to be reported.

- prepare segmental reports in accordance with SSAP 25.

- assess the performance of a company based on the information contained in its segmental report.

THE EXAM PAPER

The examination is a three hour paper in two sections. It will contain a mix of computational and discursive elements. Some questions will adopt a scenario/case study approach.

The Section A compulsory question will be the preparation of group financial statements, and may include a small related discussion element. Computations will be designed to test an understanding of principles. At least one of the optional questions in Section B will be conceptual/discursive question that may include a simple illustrative numerical element.

An individual question may often involve elements that relate to different areas of the syllabus. For example a published financial statements question could include elements relating to several accounting standards. In scenario questions candidates may be expected to comment on management's chosen accounting treatment and determine a more appropriate one, based on circumstances described in the question.

Questions on topic areas that are also included in Paper 1.1 will be examined at an appropriately greater depth in Paper 2.5. Some Accounting Standards are very detailed and complex, particularly recent ones. At Paper 2.5 candidates need to be aware of the principles and key elements of these Standards. Candidates will also be expected to have an appreciation of the background need for an accounting standard and why it has been introduced.

		Number of Marks
Section A:	One compulsory question	25
Section B:	Choice of 3 from 4 questions (25 marks each)	75
		100

Additional information

Candidates need to be aware that questions involving knowledge of new examinable regulations will not be set until at least six months after the last day of the month in which the regulation was issued.

The Study Guide provides more detailed guidance on the syllabus. Examinable documents are listed in the 'Exam Notes' section of the Students' Newsletter.

Analysis of past papers

Pilot paper

Section A

1   Preparation of consolidated balance sheet and profit and loss account. Discussion of treatment of investment.

Section B

2   Preparation of balance sheet and profit and loss. Discussion on fixed assets
3   Revenue recognition
4   Interpretation of financial statements
5   Loan stock, impairment losses, closure of a division and long term contract

June 2002

Section A

1   Consolidated balance sheet; Associated company status

Section B

2   Preparation of financial statements; EPS calculations
3   Impairment of fixed assets and goodwill; FRS7; R&D expenditure
4   Related party transactions; Interpretation of financial statements
5   Long term contracts; Property transactions

December 2001

Section A

1   Consolidated balance sheet

Section B

2   Preparation of financial statements
3   FRS 15; cost; revaluation
4   Cash flow statement
5   Intangible assets; investment property; stocks

BPP PUBLISHING

OXFORD BROOKES BSc (Hons) IN APPLIED ACCOUNTING

The standard required of candidates completing Part 2 is that required in the final year of a UK degree. Students completing Parts 1 and 2 will have satisfied the examination requirement for an honours degree in Applied Accounting, awarded by Oxford Brookes University.

To achieve the degree, you must also submit two pieces of work based on a **Research and Analysis Project.**

- A 5,000 word **Report** on your chosen topic, which demonstrates that you have acquired the necessary research, analytical and IT skills.

- A 1,500 word **Key Skills Statement,** indicating how you have developed your interpersonal and communication skills.

BPP was selected by the ACCA and Oxford Brookes University to produce the official text *Success in your Research and Analysis Project* to support students in this task. The book pays particular attention to key skills not covered in the professional examinations.

> AN ORDER FORM FOR THE NEW SYLLABUS MATERIAL, INCLUDING THE OXFORD BROOKES PROJECT TEXT, CAN BE FOUND AT THE END OF THIS STUDY TEXT.

OXFORD INSTITUTE OF INTERNATIONAL FINANCE MBA

The ACCA and Oxford Brookes University have set up the Oxford Institute of International Finance to provide an MBA programme. BPP has been appointed the provider of materials and electronic support. This new qualification has been available worldwide from January 2002.

The MBA is available to those who have completed the professional stage of the ACCA qualification (subject to when this was achieved), as the ACCA's Professional exams contribute credits towards the MBA award.

The qualification features an introductory module (*Markets, Management and Strategy*). This is followed by modules on *Global Business Strategy, Managing Self Development* and *Organisational Change and Transformation*. The MBA is completed by a *research dissertation.*

For further information, please see the Oxford Institute's website: www.oxfordinstitute.org

Part A
The regulatory framework

Chapter 1

REVIEW OF BASIC ACCOUNTING CONCEPTS

Topic list	Syllabus reference
1 Desirable characteristics of financial reports	2(a)
2 The regulatory system of accounting	2(b)
3 GAAP and the conceptual framework of accounting	2(a)
4 Revision: basic accounts	2(a)

Introduction

The syllabus for Paper 2.5 is very large and varied. But don't worry. Provided you approach your studies logically and leave plenty of extra time you should get through it. You must not skimp on any area of the syllabus, tempting though it is when faced with so much material.

This first chapter is mainly concerned with revision of those concepts and skills covered in your earlier studies.

If you have any difficulties with the exercises in this chapter, you should go back to your earlier study material and revise; doing a few more exercises should help to jog your memory.

Study guide

- Discuss what is meant by a conceptual framework and GAAP

- Describe the objectives of financial statements and the qualitative characteristics of financial information

- Define the elements of financial statements

- Apply the above definitions to practical situations

- Revision of paper 1.1 – prepare the final accounts of a simple business organisation

Exam guide

You are unlikely to get a full question on the material in this chapter but it is important that you read through and understand the content of this chapter.

1   DESIRABLE CHARACTERISTICS OF FINANCIAL REPORTS

1.1   Financial information, if it is to be useful, should have certain qualities. These qualities were discussed in several documents in the 1970s, notably *The Corporate Report* (issued by the old Accounting Standards Committee). These qualities are listed below. As you can see, they are open to question.

(a)   **Objectivity**. It is not clear to what extent an accounting report can be objective. Some subjective judgements cannot be avoided. The main thing is to make clear where subjective judgement has been used.

(b) **Comparability**. If one purpose of accounting reports is to enable information users to compare one company's performance against another's, the reports of both companies must be prepared by similar methods. Unless accounting practices are made standard, such comparability is unlikely to occur.

(c) **Completeness**. *The Corporate Report* suggested that accounting reports should give 'a rounded picture of the economic activities of the reporting entity'. To be complete, information would need to be provided in 'complex rather than simple documents'. There is a reluctance among many organisations to disclose accounting information which is not required by law or other regulation, and 'completeness' does not really exist.

(d) **Consistency**. This principle cannot be pushed too far. If better accounting techniques are developed, old methods of reporting should be changed.

1.2 The disclosure of accounting information is a vexed question which is still the subject of debate within the accountancy profession and Government. There is a strong body of opinion which favours greater disclosure of accounting information, but the common attitude of reporting companies appears to be that disclosure should be kept to a minimum which conforms with the requirements of law or another regulatory body (SSAPs, FRSs and so forth).

Problems of disclosure

1.3 There are several different problems involved in disclosure.

(a) **What accounting concepts should be applied** in arriving at values for profit and capital?

(b) **What accounting policies should be applied** in the valuation of profit and capital?

(c) Do the profit and loss account, balance sheet, and cash flow statement provide sufficient information for the needs of users, or **are additional statements needed**?

(d) **Should more information be included** in the published balance sheets than is shown at the moment, **or in the case of small 'proprietary' companies, would less information be sufficient** for shareholders than for larger company shareholders?

(e) **Should disclosure requirements be enforced** by statute, accounting standards, or Stock Exchange listing requirements?

1.4 These five issues are all discussed at greater length elsewhere in this Study Text. In the remainder of this chapter, we shall consider the general background, and in particular who the users of information are and what type of information and accounting statements they might need. The most useful reference point for this topic is *The Corporate Report*.

The corporate report

KEY TERM

A **corporate report** is a comprehensive package of information which describes an organisation's *economic* activities. It includes the financial statements required by law (profit and loss account and balance sheet) or by another authority (for example, the cash flow statement, which is described in a later chapter). It also includes information in narrative form, such as the chairman's annual report.

1.5 A working party of the Accounting Standards Committee (ASC) produced a discussion paper in 1975 called *The Corporate Report* in which suggestions were made about:

(a) Which types of organisation should be expected to publish regular financial or economic information.

(b) Who the main users of such information should be.

(c) What type of information and reports would best suit these user needs.

> **Exam focus point**
>
> Although it is in your syllabus, this topic is unlikely to be examined in depth as it is likely to be covered at Paper 1.1. If you are in a hurry, skim through it and memorise the highlighted words.

1.6 In *The Corporate Report*, a distinction was made between:

(a) The responsibility to make general purpose financial information publicly available (this was called 'public accountability').

(b) The obligation to provide some financial information by law.

(c) Special purpose information provided to particular users for specific needs (for example, a bank might want a company to provide a cash flow forecast and a profit forecast before deciding whether to allow the company an overdraft facility).

1.7 The recommendations of the discussion paper were only concerned with public accountability and general purpose information ((a) above). The report stated:

> 'in our view there is an implicit responsibility to report publicly (whether or not required by law or regulation) incumbent on every economic entity whose size or format renders it significant.'

'Significance' means that the organisation controls sufficient human and material resources that its actions would be noticed by the general community. The organisations concerned would include not only medium to large companies but also Central Government, local authorities, trade associations, co-operative societies, trade unions and charities.

Users

1.8 **Users** of corporate reports were defined as those groups which **have a reasonable right to information** about the reporting entity. These were:

(a) **Shareholders** (existing and potential shareholders)
(b) **Loan creditors**
(c) **Employees**
(d) **Analysts and advisers** (journalists, economists, trade unions, stockbrokers)
(e) **Business contacts** (trade creditors, predator companies, competitors)
(f) The **Government** (including tax officials)
(g) The **public** (taxpayers, ratepayers, consumers, political groups, environmentalists)

1.9 Existing and potential **shareholders** need information about a company to help them decide:

(a) Whether to **buy or sell** the company's shares.
(b) Whether to **subscribe for new shares** in the company when a 'rights issue' is made.
(c) How to **vote at annual general meetings** of the company.

1.10 They are **interested in the level of current and future dividends**, and the likely movements up and down in a share's market price. In addition, existing shareholders will want to know whether management has been running the company efficiently.

1.11 It has often been thought that shareholders' interests are confined to the profit and loss account and balance sheet, and to the 'earnings per share' during each year. *The Corporate Report* suggested that, in addition, shareholders would **want to know that**:

(a) **The company is capable of generating sufficient cash from its internal operations** to cope with inflation and the problems of liquidity.

(b) The company's **future prospects** are good.

(c) The company's **shares compare favourably** with others which are available for purchase by investors.

1.12 **Loan creditors** (or potential loan creditors) have a 'right' to financial information about a company, because they will **want to know that interest repayments on the loan** are **secure**. They are concerned with the risk element of default on these repayments. In addition:

(a) If the loan stock is bought and sold on the stock market, investors need financial information to decide whether to buy or sell at a given price.

(b) If the loan is due for redemption (capital repayment) in the near future, investors will want to know that the company will have sufficient cash to pay off the loan.

(c) If the terms of the loan (known as 'covenants') place certain financial restrictions on the company (for instance, by limiting the debt/equity ratios of the company), the loan creditors will need to know that these terms are being upheld.

1.13 **An organisation has a responsibility for the livelihood of its employees.** Since *The Corporate Report* was published, statutory provisions embodied in the Companies Act 1985 have increased the amount of information about employees which must be disclosed in company accounts. CA 1985 also states (s 309) that directors have a duty to show regard for the interests of the company's employees as well as the interests of its shareholders.

1.14 **Employees need information about the security of employment and future prospects** for jobs in the company **and to help with collective bargaining for wage settlements and terms of employment.** *The Corporate Report* suggested that information for collective bargaining might be obtained more usefully from special purpose reports at site or factory level; nevertheless, general purpose reports might provide information about job security, future prospects, management efficiency, and the ability (or otherwise) of the company to pay higher wages.

1.15 **Analysts and advisers need information which is of interest to their clients or audience.** For example, stockbrokers will want information to advise investors in stocks and shares and credit-rating agencies will want information to advise would-be trade creditors.

1.16 *The Corporate Report* suggested that 'the rights of the **business contact group** to information arise from their existing or potential direct relationship with the reporting entity. For example, suppliers, trade creditors and customers are all likely to place trust in the reporting entity to fulfil an implied or explicit responsibility.'

(a) **Suppliers need to know that a company is able to pay its debts,** and whether the company is likely to be a good long-term customer.

(b) **Customers need to know that the company will be able to continue to deliver goods** in the future, and will not close down.

1.17 **Competitors** will also be interested in information about the company, and there is **mutual benefit to be obtained from the exchange of such information** provided that it does not breach confidentiality. In some industries, formal schemes of Interfirm Comparison (IFC) have been operated. The value of such comparisons is in acting as a **spur to greater efficiency in operations.**

1.18 The general purpose information in a corporate report cannot, however, be specially adapted to the needs of competitors; competitors should usually be satisfied with obtaining whatever information about the company is publicly available.

1.19 Another important business contact group is a **company which is planning a merger or takeover**. These groups have **interests similar to those of investors (shareholders).** On the other hand, the employees and management of a company subject to a takeover offer will want to know about the past record and management style of the company making the bid.

1.20 The **Government may have an interest in** a company as creditor or customer. In addition, both national and local government will be interested in the:

(a) Current and prospective **contribution of the company to economic well-being and employment** in the area or country.

(b) Ability of the company to pay **taxes**

(c) **Compliance** of the company **with taxation rules and company law**, as verified by independent auditors.

1.21 The Government is in a position to ask for special purpose information (for example, tax returns and the provision of statistics) but might also benefit from more general purpose financial information as provided by a corporate report.

1.22 **Members of the public** may wish to have financial information about a company; in its role as an employer, as a part of the economy, contributing to national wealth and the balance of trade and so on. However, the term 'general public' covers a wide variety of individuals and groups and it would be impossible to provide general purpose accounting information which was specially designed for the needs of the public. However, the public **should have ready access to general purpose information made available to other groups** (shareholders, loan creditors, business contacts).

The objective of corporate reports

1.23 The discussion paper suggested that:

> 'the fundamental objective of corporate reports is to **communicate economic measurements of and information** about the **resources and performance** of the reporting entity useful to those having reasonable rights to such information.'

1.24 Larger organisations, because they are more influential in society, the economy and employment levels, should be expected to provide more information than smaller organisations. In small organisations, employees have easier access to senior managers, directors and even shareholders; therefore formalised information systems are not so necessary. The benefits of the information provided must be expected to justify the costs of collecting it, and in small organisations information costs are proportionately higher in relation to benefits.

BPP
PUBLISHING

1.25 The ASC discussion paper identified the following **criteria of useful information.**

(a) **Relevance.** The information provided should be that which is required to satisfy the needs of users of reports. Such needs will vary as between user groups and over time.

(b) **Comprehensibility.** Too much detail is just as much a defect as too little.

(c) **Reliability.** This will be enhanced in the case of reports which are independently verified.

(d) **Completeness.** 'Reports should present a rounded picture of the economic activities of the reporting entity.'

(e) **Objectivity.** This will be enhanced by the application of standards which are neutral as between competing interests.

(f) **Timeliness.** The usefulness of information is reduced the later it is produced after the time to which it relates and also if the intervals at which it is produced are unreasonably long.

(g) **Comparability.** This involves consistency in the application of accounting concepts and policies.

1.26 The discussion paper also suggested that although some financial reports were already required by law, or Stock Exchange rules, or by the rules of an accounting standard, there are extra reports which could usefully be provided in addition to these.

1.27 Published financial statements which are currently provided (profit and loss account, balance sheet, cash flow statements) have certain **limitations.**

(a) The **emphasis is put on short-term profit**, and consideration of longer-term objectives or non-profit objectives (such as employee welfare) is excluded.

(b) As a result of (a), management concentrates on achieving the best short-term profits to the exclusion of other objectives.

(c) The measurement of a **profit figure is dependent on the choice of accounting policies,** and is not as meaningful as users of the information might like to think.

(d) There is an **implication that the shareholders are the most important users** of the information provided.

Question 1

Quick memory test:

(a) Who are the users of accounting information? You should be able to think of 7.

(b) What qualities do they think the information should have? You should be able to think of 7.

Answer

See Paragraphs 1.8 and 1.25.

The ASB's *Statement of Principles*

1.28 The needs of users of accounts were considered more recently by the ASB in formulating its *Statement of Principles*. The *Statement* was issued in November 1995 in exposure draft form and finalised in December 1999.

1.29 The *Statement* is discussed in Chapter 21 of this Study Text, and will mean more to you when you have worked through the intervening chapters.

2 THE REGULATORY SYSTEM OF ACCOUNTING

2.1 **Unincorporated businesses in the UK can usually prepare their financial statements in any form they choose** (subject to the constraints of specific legislation, such as the Financial Services Act 1986 for investment businesses, for example). **However, all companies must comply with the provisions of the Companies Act 1985** in preparing their financial statements and are also with the provisions of Statements of Standard Accounting Practice (**SSAPs**) and Financial Reporting Standards (**FRSs**) which are issued by a body called the Accounting Standards Board.

2.2 In its *Foreword to Accounting Standards* the Accounting Standards Board states that **accounting standards are applicable to all financial statements whose purpose is to give a true and fair view** (explained in Chapter 2). This necessarily includes the financial statements of every company incorporated in the UK.

2.3 The regulatory framework over company accounts is therefore based on several sources.

(a) Company law.

(b) Accounting standards and other related pronouncements.

(c) International accounting standards (and the influence of other national standard setting bodies).

(d) The requirements of the Stock Exchange.

Company law

2.4 The Companies Act 1985 (CA 1985) consolidated the bulk of previous company legislation which is relevant to your syllabus. This was substantially amended by the Companies Act 1989 (CA 1989), and all references in this text are to CA 1985 as amended by CA 1989.

The European Union

2.5 Since the United Kingdom became a member of the European Union (EU) it has been obliged to comply with legal requirements decided on by the EU. It does this by enacting UK laws to implement EU directives. For example, the CA 1989 was enacted in part to implement the provisions of the seventh and eighth EU directives, which deal with consolidated accounts and auditors.

> ### Exam focus point
>
> Although your syllabus does not require you to be an expert on EU procedure, you should be aware that the form and content of company accounts can be influenced by international developments.

Accounting standards

2.6 **Some accounting principles** (such as valuation of assets) **are embodied in legislation, while others** (for example cash flow statements) **are regulated by accounting standards.**

> **KEY TERM**
>
> An **accounting standard** is a rule or set of rules which prescribes the method (or methods) by which accounts should be prepared and presented. These 'working regulations' are issued by a national or international body of the accountancy profession.

2.7 In the UK, such standards were called Statements of Standard Accounting Practice (SSAPs) and were until 31 July 1990 formulated by the Accounting Standards Committee (ASC). SSAPs are gradually being replaced by Financial Reporting Standards (FRSs) produced by the successor to the ASC, the Accounting Standards Board (ASB). The structure of the new standard setting process, which includes the ASB, is discussed below.

2.8 **Accounting standards interact with company law** in several ways.

(a) 'Realised' profits and losses are determined by reference to generally accepted accounting practice, ie SSAPs and FRSs: s 262 (3).

(b) The accounts must state whether the provisions of accounting standards have been followed or give reasons for, and disclosures of any material departures (see Paragraph 2.18 below): para 36A, Sch 4.

In addition, the Stock Exchange requires listed companies to comply with accounting standards. Failure to comply will also usually lead to the auditors qualifying their report, which the company will want to avoid.

The standard-setting process in the UK

2.9 We have mentioned the previous standard-setting process in the UK, whereby SSAPs were produced by the ASC. In 1987 the Consultative Committee of Accountancy Bodies (CCAB) established a review committee (the Dearing committee) and its report was published in September 1988. Its conclusions were, in essence, that the arrangements then in operation, where 21 unpaid ASC members met for a half-day once a month to discuss new standards, were no longer adequate to produce timely and authoritative pronouncements. On 1 August 1990 the ASC was disbanded and the following regime took its place.

Financial Reporting Council (FRC)

2.10 The FRC was created to cover a wide constituency of interests at a high level. It **guides the standard setting body on policy and sees that its work is properly financed.** It also funds and oversees the Review Panel (see below). It has about 25 members drawn from users, preparers and auditors of accounts.

Accounting Standards Board (ASB)

2.11 **The task of devising accounting standards is now carried out by the ASB,** with a full-time chairman and technical director. A majority of two thirds of the Board is required to approve a new standard. Previously, each new standard had to be approved by the Councils of each of the six CCAB bodies separately before it could be published. The new ASB now issues standards itself on its own authority. The ASB can produce standards more quickly than the ASC and it has the great advantage of legal backing (see below).

Urgent Issues Task Force (UITF)

2.12   An offshoot of the ASB is the UITF, whose function is:

> 'to **tackle urgent matters** not covered by existing standards, and for which, given the urgency, the normal standard-setting process would not be practicable.'
>
> (Sir Ron Dearing)

2.13   The UITF pronouncements, which are called 'abstracts', are intended to come into effect quickly. They therefore tend to become effective within approximately one month of publication date. The UITF has so far issued several abstracts, some of which have been superseded by a new FRSs and Financial Reporting Exposure Drafts (FREDs). The Abstracts close loopholes as soon as they become apparent, triggered frequently by practices in the accounts of companies, thus halting abuses before they become widespread.

2.14   The *Foreword to UITF Abstracts*, issued in February 1994, sets out the authority, scope and application of UITF abstracts. The authority given is that:

> 'The Councils of the CCAB bodies expect their members who assume responsibilities in respect of financial statements to observe UITF Abstracts until they are replaced by accounting standards or otherwise withdrawn by the ASB.'

The scope of and compliance with the abstracts are similar to those associated with accounting standards (accounts which show a true and fair view, non-compliance must be justified and disclosed etc).

Review Panel

2.15   The Review Panel, chaired by a barrister, is **concerned with the examination and questioning of departures from accounting standards by large companies**. It has about 15 members from which smaller panels are formed to tackle cases as they arise. The Review Panel is alerted to most cases for investigation by the results of the new CA 1985 requirement that companies must include in the notes to the accounts a statement that they have been prepared in accordance with applicable accounting standards or, failing that, give details of material departures from those standards, with reasons.

2.16   Although it is expected that most referrals would be resolved by discussion, the Panel (and the Secretary of State for Trade and Industry) **have the power to apply the court for revision of the accounts,** with all costs potentially payable (if the court action is successful) by the company's directors. The auditors may also be disciplined if the audit report on the defective accounts was not qualified with respect to the departure from standards. Revised accounts, whether prepared voluntarily or under duress, will have to be circulated to all persons likely to rely on the previous accounts.

2.17   Because of the Review Panel, listed companies and their auditors are doubtless becoming far more cautious in their attempts to break or bend the rules laid out by both the Companies Act and accounting standards. The actions of the Review Panel against individual companies to date caused no difficulties: most of the companies obeyed the Review Panel dictates without any real argument.

BPP PUBLISHING

2.18   A summary of the structure of the regulatory framework is shown in the following diagram.

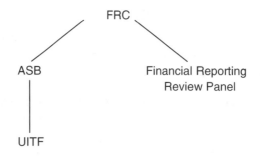

Question 2

Discuss the function of:

(a)   The Accounting Standards Board
(b)   The Review Panel
(c)   The Financial Reporting Council
(d)   The Urgent Issues Task Force

Answer

See Paragraphs 2.9 - 2.18.

International Accounting Standards

2.19   International Accounting Standards (IASs) were originally produced by the **International Accounting Standards Committee (IASC)**, now the **International Accounting Standards Board** (IASB). The IASB **develops accounting standards through an international process that involves the world-wide accountancy profession, the preparers and users of financial statements, and national standard setting bodies.**

2.20   The objectives of the IASB are to:

(a)   **Develop**, in the public interest, a **single set** of high quality, understandable and **enforceable global accounting standards** that require high quality, transparent and comparable information in financial statements and other financial reporting to help participants in the various **capital markets** of the world and other users of the **information** to make **economic decisions**

(b)   **Promote** the use and **rigorous application** of those standards

(c)   Work actively with national standard-setters to bring about **convergence** of national accounting standards and International Financial Reporting Standards (IFRSs) to **high quality solutions**

2.21   The main impact of the IASB on the work of the ASB has involved the IASB's *Framework for the preparation and presentation of financial statements*. The *Framework* was introduced to 'set out the concepts that underlie the preparation and presentation of financial statements for external users'. The ASB has based its own *Statement of Principles* on the IASB's *Framework* (see Section 3). In basic terms, the ASB has adopted the same conceptual approach to financial reporting as the IASB. In its Financial Reporting Standards (FRSs), the ASB states the compliance of the standards with IASs or IAS exposure drafts.

The Stock Exchange

2.22 In the UK there are two different markets on which it is possible for a company to have its securities quoted:

(a) The Stock Exchange
(b) The Alternative Investment Market (AIM)

2.23 **Shares quoted on the main market, the Stock Exchange, are said to be 'listed'** or to have obtained a 'listing'. In order to receive a listing for its securities, a company must conform with Stock Exchange regulations contained in the Listing Rules or Yellow Book issued by the Council of The Stock Exchange. The company commits itself to certain procedures and standards, including matters concerning the disclosure of accounting information, which are more extensive than the disclosure requirements of the Companies Acts. **The requirements of the AIM are less stringent** than the main Stock Exchange. **It is aimed at new, higher risk or smaller companies.**

2.24 Many requirements of the Yellow Book do not have the backing of law, but the ultimate sanction which can be imposed on a listed company which fails to abide by them is the withdrawal of its securities from the Stock Exchange List: the company's shares would no longer be traded on the market.

3 GAAP AND THE CONCEPTUAL FRAMEWORK OF ACCOUNTING

3.1 The Financial Accounting Standards Board, or FASB (the US standards body), has defined a conceptual framework.

> **KEY TERM**
>
> A **conceptual framework** is 'a constitution, a coherent system of interrelated objectives and fundamentals that can lead to consistent standards and that prescribes the nature, function and limits of financial accounting and financial statements.'

The basic idea is therefore to avoid the 'fire fighting' approach which has characterised the development of SSAPs to date, and instead to develop an underlying philosophy as a basis for consistent accounting principles so that the rationale of each SSAP is structured into the whole framework.

3.2 The ASC stated in a consultative document *Setting Accounting Standards* that whilst an agreed framework of accounting would provide a good basis on which to build accounting standards, it believed that no such framework was currently available and that conclusive results would probably not be rapidly achieved. On the other hand, the FASB began a large-scale project in 1973 to develop such a framework, with immense resources committed to this research: several million dollars have been spent each year since the project began. The FASB's publications on the project already amount to over 3,000 pages (of which statements of concepts and standards amount to some 400 pages).

3.3 A great deal of work on the conceptual framework has been carried out by the International Accounting Standards Committee *Framework for the Preparation and Presentation of Financial Statements*, published in July 1989, and by Professor David Solomons in a 1989 discussion paper addressed to the ASC *Guidelines for Financial Reporting Standards* (the Solomons report).

BPP PUBLISHING

3.4   The IASB *Framework* is non-mandatory and it deals with the:

(a) **Objective** of financial statements.

(b) **Qualitative characteristics** that determine the usefulness of information in financial statements.

(c) **Definition, recognition and measurement** of the elements from which financial statements are constructed.

(d) Concepts of **capital and capital maintenance**.

3.5   The IASB believes that further **international harmonisation** of accounting methods can best be **promoted by focusing on these four topics** since they will then lead to published financial statements that meet the common needs of most users.

3.6   The Solomons report proceeds in a similar way. Chapters deal with:

(a) The purpose of financial reporting.
(b) Financial statements and their elements.
(c) The qualitative characteristics of accounting information.
(d) Recognition and measurement.
(e) The choice of a general purpose accounting model.

3.7   Solomons recognised the unsatisfactory nature of the (then) current 'firefighting' approach to UK standard setting, and produces his own set of guidelines which he argues could yield an explicit statement of agreed financial accounting concepts.

Advantages

3.8   The **advantages arising from using a conceptual framework** may be summarised as follows.

(a) **SSAPs were being developed on a 'patchwork quilt' basis** where a particular accounting problem was recognised by the ASC as having emerged, and resources were then channelled into standardising accounting practice in that area, without regard to whether that particular issue was necessarily the most important issue remaining at that time without standardisation.

(b) As stated above, the development of certain SSAPs (for example SSAP 13) has been subject to considerable political interference from interested parties. Where there is a conflict of interest between user groups on which policies to choose, **policies deriving from a conceptual framework will be less open to criticism that the ASC buckled to external pressure.**

(c) Some SSAPs seem to concentrate on the income statement (profit and loss account), some to concentrate on the valuation of net assets (balance sheet). For instance, SSAP 12 (now replaced by FRS 15) ensured that depreciation was charged on a systematic basis through the profit and loss account to comply with the accruals concept, but the net book value figure in the balance sheet had little meaning. Conversely, SSAP 15 requires the balance sheet provision for deferred tax to be the liability currently envisaged, but the profit and loss charge or credit for deferred tax has no meaning other than representing the balancing figure between a provision brought forward and carried forward in the balance sheet. **An unambiguous definition of 'income' and 'value' would ensure all financial statements have equal usefulness to each user group.**

Disadvantages

3.9   A **counter-argument** to supporters of a conceptual framework might be as follows.

(a)   Financial statements are intended for a variety of users, and **it is not certain that a single conceptual framework can be devised which will suit all users**.

(b)   Given the diversity of user requirements, there may be a **need for a variety of accounting standards**, each produced for a different purpose (and **with different concepts as a basis**).

(c)   It is **not clear that a conceptual framework will make the task of preparing and then implementing standards any easier** than it is now.

> ## IMPORTANT!
>
> The ASB has now focused its attention on developing a conceptual framework, based on both the IASB *Framework* and on the recommendations of the Solomons report. The ASB conceptual framework is encompassed in a *Statement of Principles*. The *Statement of Principles* is discussed in detail in Chapter 21. By the time you reach this chapter, you should have a thorough grasp of the problems surrounding asset valuation and profit measurement for various types of transaction, including consolidation which you have not looked at before.

Generally Accepted Accounting Practice (GAAP)

3.10   This term has sprung up in recent years and it **signifies all the rules**, from whatever source, **which govern accounting**. In the UK this is seen primarily as a combination of:

- **Company law** (mainly CA 1985)
- **Accounting standards**
- **Stock exchange requirements**

3.11   Although those sources are the basis for UK GAAP, the concept also includes the effects of non-mandatory sources such as:

(a)   **International accounting standards**
(b)   **Statutory requirements in other countries**, particularly the US.

3.12   In the UK, GAAP does not have any statutory or regulatory authority or definition (unlike other countries, such as the US). The term is mentioned rarely in legislation, and only then in fairly limited terms.

3.13   GAAP is in fact a dynamic concept: it **changes constantly as circumstances alter through new legislation, standards *and* practice.** This idea that GAAP is constantly changing is recognised by the ASB in its *Statement of Aims* where it states that it expects to issue new standards and amend old ones in response to:

> 'evolving business practices, new economic developments and deficiencies identified in current practice.'

The emphasis has shifted from 'principles' to 'practice' in UK GAAP.

3.14   The problem of what is 'generally accepted' is not easy to settle, because new practices will obviously not be generally adopted yet. The criteria for a practice being 'generally accepted' will depend on factors such as whether the practice is addressed by UK accounting standards or legislation, their international equivalents, and whether other companies have adopted the practice. Most importantly perhaps, the question should be whether the practice is consistent with the needs of users and the objectives of financial reporting and whether it is consistent with the 'true and fair' concept.

4 REVISION: BASIC ACCOUNTS

4.1 In the next part of this text we move on to the mechanics of preparing financial statements. It would be useful at this point to refresh your memory of the basic accounting you have already studied and these exercises will help you. Make sure that you understand everything before you go on.

Question 3

A friend has bought some shares in a quoted United Kingdom company and has received the latest accounts. There is one page he is having difficulty in understanding.

Briefly, but clearly, answer his questions.

(a) What is a balance sheet?
(b) What is an asset?
(c) What is a liability?
(d) What is share capital?
(e) What are reserves?
(f) Why does the balance sheet balance?
(g) To what extent does the balance sheet value my investment?

Answer

(a) A *balance sheet* is a statement of the assets, liabilities and capital of a business as at a stated date. It is laid out to show either total assets as equivalent to total liabilities and capital or net assets as equivalent to capital. Other formats are also possible but the top half (or left hand) total will always equal the bottom half (or right hand) total. Some balance sheets are laid out vertically and others horizontally.

(b) An *asset* is owned by a business and is expected to be of some future benefit. Its value is determined as the historical cost of producing or obtaining it (unless an attempt is being made to reflect rising prices in the accounts, in which case a replacement cost might be used). Examples of assets are:

    (i) Plant, machinery, land and other long-term or *fixed* assets.

    (ii) *Current* assets such as stocks, cash and debts owed to the business with reasonable assurance of recovery: these are assets which are not intended to be held on a continuing basis in the business.

(c) A *liability* is an amount owed by a business, other than the amount owed to its proprietors (capital). Examples of liabilities are:

    (i) Amounts owed to the government (VAT or other taxes)
    (ii) Amounts owed to suppliers
    (iii) Bank overdraft
    (iv) Long-term loans from banks or investors

It is usual to differentiate between 'current' and 'long-term' liabilities. The former fall due within a year of the balance sheet date.

(d) *Share capital* is the permanent investment in a business by its owners. In the case of limited company, this takes the form of *shares* for which investors subscribe on formation of the company. Each share has a *nominal* (or face) *value* (say £1). In the balance sheet, total issued share capital is shown at its nominal value.

(e) If a company issues shares for more than their nominal value (at a *premium*) then by law this premium must be recorded separately from the nominal value in a 'share premium account'. This is an example of a reserve. It belongs to the shareholders but cannot be distributed to them, because it is a ca*pital* reserve. Other capital reserves include the revaluation reserve, which shows the surpluses arising on revaluation of assets which are still owned by the company.

Share capital and capital reserves are not distributable except on the winding up of the company, as a guarantee to the company's creditors that the company has enough assets to meet its debts. This is necessary because shareholders in limited companies have 'limited liability'; once they have paid the company for their shares they have no further liability to it if it becomes insolvent. The proprietors of other businesses are, by contrast, personally liable for business debts.

Revenue reserves constitute accumulated profits (less losses) made by the company and can be distributed to shareholders as *dividends*. They too belong to the shareholders, and so are a claim on the resources of the company.

(f) Balance sheets do not always balance on the first attempt, as all accountants know. However, once errors are corrected, all balance sheets balance. This is because in double entry bookkeeping every transaction recorded has a dual effect. Assets are always equal to liabilities plus capital and so capital is always equal to assets less liabilities. This makes sense as the owners of the business are entitled to the net assets of the business as representing their capital plus accumulated surpluses (or less accumulated deficit).

(g) The balance sheet is not intended as a statement of a business's worth at a given point in time. This is because, except where some attempt is made to adjust for the effects of rising prices, assets and liabilities are recorded at historical cost and on a prudent basis. For example, if there is any doubt about the recoverability of a debt, then the value in the accounts must be reduced to the likely recoverable amount. In addition, where fixed assets have a finite useful life, their cost is gradually written off to reflect the use being made of them.

Sometimes fixed assets are *revalued* to their market value but this revaluation then goes out of date as few assets are revalued every year.

The balance sheet figure for capital and reserves therefore bears no relationship to the market value of shares. Market values are the product of a large number of factors, including general economic conditions, alternative investment returns (eg interest rates), likely future profits and dividends and, not least, market sentiment.

Question 4

The accountant of Fiddles plc has begun preparing final accounts but the work is not yet complete. At this stage the items included in the trial balance are as follows.

	£'000
Land	100
Buildings	120
Plant and machinery	170
Depreciation provision	120
Share capital	100
Profit and loss balance brought forward	200
Debtors	200
Creditors	110
Stock	190
Operating profit	80
Debentures (16%)	180
Provision for doubtful debts	3
Bank balance (asset)	12
Suspense	1

Notes (i) to (vii) below are to be taken in to account.

(i) The debtors control account figure, which is used in the trial balance, does not agree with the total of the debtors ledger. A contra of £5,000 has been entered correctly in the individual ledger accounts but has been entered on the wrong side of both control accounts.

A batch total of sales of £12,345 had been entered in the double entry system as £13,345, although the individual ledger accounts entries for these sales were correct. The balance of £4,000 on sales returns account has inadvertently been omitted from the trial balance though correctly entered in the ledger records.

(ii) A standing order of receipt from a regular customer for £2,000, and bank charges of £1,000, have been completely omitted from the records.

(iii) A debtor for £1,000 is to be written off. The provision for doubtful debts balance is to be adjusted to 1% of debtors.

(iv) The opening stock figure had been overstated by £1,000 and the closing stock figure had been understated by £2,000.

(v) Any remaining balance on suspense account should be treated as purchases if a debit balance and as sales if a credit balance.

(vi) The debentures were issued three months before the year end. No entries have been made as regards interest.

(vii) A dividend of 10% of share capital is to be proposed.

Required

(a) Prepare journal entries to cover items in notes (i) to (v) above. You are not to open any new accounts and may use only those accounts included in the trial balance as given.

(b) Prepare final accounts for internal use in good order within the limits of the available information. For presentation purposes all the items arising from notes (i) to (vii) above should be regarded as material.

Answer

(a) JOURNAL ENTRIES FOR ADJUSTMENTS

		Debit £	Credit £
(i)	Creditors	10,000	
	Debtors		10,000
	Operating profit	1,000	
	Debtors		1,000
	Operating profit	4,000	
	Suspense		4,000

		Debit £	Credit £
(ii)	Bank	2,000	
	Debtors		2,000
	Operating profit	1,000	
	Bank		1,000
(iii)	Operating profit	1,000	
	Debtors		1,000
	Provision for doubtful debts (W1)	1,140	
	Operating profit		1,140
(iv)	Stocks	2,000	
	Operating profit		2,000
	Profit and loss brought forward	1,000	
	Operating profit		1,000
(v)	Suspense	3,000	
	Operating profit		3,000

(b) FIDDLES PLC
BALANCE SHEET

	£	£	£
Fixed assets			
Land and buildings		220,000	
Fixtures and fittings		170,000	
		390,000	
Provision for depreciation		(120,000)	
			270,000
Current assets			
Stock (190 + 2)		192,000	
Debtors (W1)	186,000		
Less provision	(1,860)		
		184,140	
Bank (12 + 2 - 1)		13,000	
		389,140	

Current liabilities		
Creditors (110 - 10)	100,000	
Debenture interest payable	7,200	
Dividends proposed	10,000	
	117,200	

	£
Net current assets	271,940
Debentures	(180,000)
Net assets	361,940

	£
Represented by	
Share capital	100,000
Profit and loss account	261,940
	361,940

FIDDLES PLC
PROFIT AND LOSS ACCOUNT

	£
Operating profit (W2)	80,140
Debenture interest (£180,000 × 16% × 3/12)	(7,200)
	72,940
Dividend	(10,000)
	62,940
Profit and loss account brought forward (200,000 - 1,000)	199,000
Profit and loss account carried forward	261,940

Workings

		£
1	Debtors per opening trial balance	200,000
	Contra	(10,000)
	Miscasting	(1,000)
	Standing order	(2,000)
	Written off	(1,000)
		186,000

	£
Provision b/f	3,000
Provision required	1,860
Journal	1,140

		£
2	*Operating profit*	
	Per question	80,000
	Wrong batch total	(1,000)
	Returns	(4,000)
	Bank charges	(1,000)
	Bad debt	(1,000)
	Bad debt provision	1,140
	Stock (2,000 + 1,000)	3,000
	Suspense (sales)	3,000
		80,140

Chapter roundup

- At this stage in your studies, you should be confident in your knowledge of:

    ° **Double entry bookkeeping**
    ° **Basic accounting definitions** (such as those in Question 1 in this chapter)
    ° **Simple balance sheet**
    ° **Simple profit and loss account**

- If you still feel a little rusty, go back to your old study material (which you should still have!) and practise a few questions.

- The regulatory system of accounting involves several bodies including:

    ° The **Financial Reporting Council**
    ° The **Review Panel**
    ° The **Urgent Issues Task Force**
    ° The **Accounting Standards Board**

    You should be able to describe their function.

- You must be able to define a **conceptual framework** and discuss the moves towards a conceptual framework in the UK.

Quick quiz

1   What problems are involved in disclosure in accounts?

2   Define a corporate report.

3   The UK regulatory framework is derived from:

    - ……………… ……….

    - ……………… …………… and other related pronouncements

    - ……………… …………… ……………… (and the influence of other national standard setting bodies)

    - The requirements of the ………….. ……………………..

4   The UK must comply with EU directives. True or false?

5   The Review Panel is concerned with the ,…………. and ………….. of departures from accounting standards by large companies?

6   Define a 'conceptual framework'.

7   One objective of the IASB is to promote the preparation of financial statements using the euro.

    True ☐
    False ☐

Answers to quick quiz

1. - What accounting concepts should be applied
    - What accounting policies should be applied
    - Are additional statements needed
    - How much information should be included
    - Should disclosure requirements be enforced (see para 1.3)

2. A corporate report is a comprehensive package of information which describes and organisation's **economic** activities. (1.4)

3. - Company law
    - Accounting standards
    - IASs
    - Stock exchange. (2.3)

4. True (2.5)

5. **Examination** and **questioning.** (2.15)

6. A coherent system of objectives that can lead to consistent standards and that prescribes the nature, function and limits of financial accounting and financial statements. (3.1)

7. False. (2.20)

Now try the question below from the Exam Question Bank

Number	Level	Marks	Time
1	Introductory	n/a	27 mins

BPP PUBLISHING

Chapter 2

THE REGULATORY FRAMEWORK

Topic list	Syllabus reference
1 The Accounting Standards Committee and SSAPs	2(a)
2 The Accounting Standards Board and FRSs	2(a)
3 The Urgent Issues Task Force	2(a)
4 Big GAAP/little GAAP	2(a)

Introduction

The regulatory framework has been briefly described in Chapter 1.

In this chapter, the current financial reporting environment is examined, including the process leading to the creation of Financial Reporting Exposure Drafts (FREDs) and Financial Reporting Standards (FRSs). The role and structure of the major bodies involved in the financial reporting regime are discussed, particularly the Accounting Standards Board (ASB). In Section 4 we look at the question of whether accounting standards are equally applicable to small and large companies.

Study guide

- Discuss what is meant by a conceptual framework and GAAP

- Outline the Standard setting process and the role of the:

    - Financial Reporting Council
    - Accounting Standards Board
    - Urgent Issues Task Force
    - Financial reporting

- Explain the relationship between UK and international accounting standards (IASs).

- Distinguish between small and medium companies and outline the disclosure exemptions relating to these companies.

Exam guide

Both this chapter and Chapter 3 are extremely important. Make sure that you understand and learn their contents before going on to look at individual items and standards in the following chapters

1   THE ACCOUNTING STANDARDS COMMITTEE AND SSAPS

1.1   We need to discuss briefly the old standard-setting process because some of the standards it produced, the SSAPs, have still not been superseded by FRSs and many are on your syllabus.

1.2   The **ASC** was set up in 1970 as a joint committee of members of the six major accountancy bodies in Britain, the constituent members of the Consultative Committee of Accountancy

Bodies (CCAB). Its terms of reference included the production of **SSAPs** after consultation with all interest parties (companies, government, etc). Consultation with these interest groups was not always satisfactory and **some SSAPs** were criticised for being **unrealistic or 'unfair'**.

1.3 Once issued, **SSAPs were intended to apply to all financial accounts which were 'intended to give a true and fair view of the financial position and profit and loss'**. This included overseas companies incorporated in UK group accounts. A standard could, however, specify (ie restrict) the 'scope' of its application. For example, SSAP 3 (on earnings per share now superseded by FRS 14) applied only to the audited accounts of listed companies (companies whose shares are listed on the Stock Exchange).

1.4 Although there are some areas where the contents of SSAPs overlap with provisions of company law, standards are detailed working regulations within the framework of government legislation, and **they cover areas in which the law is silent**. The accountancy profession prefers to make its own rules for self-regulation, rather than to have rules imposed by law. In addition, standards are not intended to override exemptions from disclosure which are allowed to special cases of companies by law.

1.5 **The Companies Act 1985 states that a departure from its provisions is permissible if that provision is inconsistent with the true and fair view** (see Chapter 3, Section 3). **This may lead to situations in which a SSAP recommends departure from the legal rules.** For example, SSAP 19 *Accounting for investment properties* sanctions such a departure by stating that investment properties need not be depreciated (see Chapter 4). Other areas of possible conflict between SSAPs and statute will be noted in later chapters.

1.6 **Accounting standards (both SSAPs and FRSs) apply mainly to private bodies rather than the public sector** (although SSAPs which are relevant to accounting in the public sector have been applied by organisations in it). A Public Sector Liaison Committee (PSLC) was set up by the ASB to replace the ASC's Public Sector Liaison Group (PSLG) which has led to the establishment of advisory panels on specific parts of the public sector (including health authority, local authority and university accounting).

1.7 A standard will choose one possible treatment (or perhaps two) from many which are available as the **best practice** to be followed. SSAPs are working regulations for practical application and they **have been developed rather haphazardly without a clear, underlying rationale;** without a conceptual framework, as we saw in Chapter 1.

2 THE ACCOUNTING STANDARDS BOARD AND FRSS

2.1 The ASB's consultative process leads to the setting of **Financial Reporting Standards** (FRSs). To produce an FRS, first a working Draft for Discussion (DD) is published to get feedback from people closely involved with or with a direct interest in the standard setting process. The DD, as a result of this process, is converted into a Financial Reporting Exposure Draft (FRED). Candidates should be aware of the contents of FRSs published by the ASB : see below. The ASB has published other documents as Exposure Drafts.

2.2 The standard-setting process can be summarised as follows.

BPP PUBLISHING

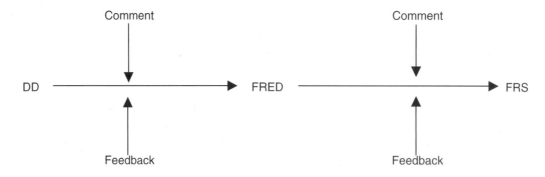

2.3   In July 1991 the ASB published the definitive *Statements of Aims* and, in July 1993, the *Foreword to Accounting Standards*.

Statement of Aims

2.4   The *Statement of Aims* is produced here in full as it is very brief.

Exam focus point

Don't feel you have to learn all of this. Just focus on the highlighted bits.

'*Aims*

The aims of the Accounting Standards Board (the Board) are to **establish and improve standards of financial accounting and reporting**, for the benefit of users, preparers and auditors of financial information.

Achieving the aims

The Board intends to achieve its aims by:

1   **Developing principles** to guide it in establishing standards and to provide a framework within which others can exercise judgement in resolving accounting issues.

2   **Issuing new accounting standards**, or amending existing ones, in response to evolving business practices, new economic developments and deficiencies being identified in current practice.

3   **Addressing urgent issues promptly**.

Fundamental guidelines

1   To be objective and to ensure that the **information** resulting from the application of accounting standards **faithfully represents the underlying commercial activity**. Such information should be neutral in the sense that it is free from any form of bias intended to influence users in a particular direction and should not be designed to favour any group of users or preparers.

2   To ensure that accounting standards are **clearly expressed** and supported by a reasoned analysis of the issues.

3   To determine **what should be incorporated in accounting standards** based on research, public consultation and careful deliberation about the usefulness of the resulting information.

4   To ensure that through a process of **regular communication**, accounting standards are produced with due regard to international developments.

5   To ensure that there is **consistency** both from one accounting standard to another and between accounting standards and company law.

6   To issue accounting standards only when the **expected benefits** exceed the perceived costs. The Board recognises that reliable cost/benefit calculations are seldom possible. However, it will always assess the need for standards in terms of the significance and extent of the problem being addressed and will choose the standard which appears to be most effective in cost/benefit terms.

7   To take account of the desire of the financial community for **evolutionary rather than revolutionary change** in the reporting process where this is consistent with the objectives outlined above.'

Foreword to Accounting Standards

2.5   This document, issued in June 1993, is similar in nature to the foreword used by the ASC in relation to SSAPs. The contents are listed briefly here.

(a) **Introduction.** This is merely background information about the ASB and the documents it will produce.

(b) The **Accounting Standards Board**. Reference is made to the **Statement of Aims**.

(c) **Authority**. This section mentions:

(i)   The legal authority of FRSs in relation to the Act.

(ii)   Directors' responsibilities to prepare accounts showing a true and fair view.

(iii)   The responsibility of members of CCAB bodies in industry and practice in relation to financial statements (as preparers or auditors).

(iv)   CCAB bodies may investigate non-compliance.

(d) **Scope and application.** The standards apply to:

(i)   Financial statements of a reporting entity that are intended to give a true and fair view.

(ii)   Group accounts in the UK (and Ireland) including any overseas entities.

(e) **Compliance with accounting standards**. The following rules and comments are laid down.

(i)   It will normally be necessary to comply with the standards to show a true and fair view.

(ii)   In applying the standards, the user should be guided by their spirit and reasoning.

(iii)   In *rare* cases it may be necessary to depart from a standard to show a true and fair view.

(iv)   Departures should be dealt with objectively according to the 'economic and commercial characteristics of the circumstances'; the departure and its financial effect should be disclosed.

(v)   The Review Panel and the DTI have powers and procedures to investigate departures and to require a restatement through the court.

(f) **The public sector.** 'The prescription of accounting requirements for the public sector in the United Kingdom is a matter for the Government'.

(g) **The issue of an FRS.** This section covers the procedures for discussion, consultation and drafting.

(h) **Accounting standards and the legal framework**. Consistency with UK and EU law is aimed for.

(i) **International Accounting Standards**. An FRS will contain a section explaining how it relates to the IAS dealing with the same topic. 'The Board supports the IASB in its aims to harmonise international financial reporting'.

(j) **Early adoption of FREDs**. The contents of FREDs may change before the FRS stage is reached and therefore early adoption is discouraged unless the information is shown as a supplement.

(k) **Appendix**. A new legal opinion by Mary Arden has been obtained on the true and fair requirement. This opinion endorses the legal force of standards.

> 'Just as a custom which is upheld by the courts may properly be regarded as a source of law, so too, in my view, does an accounting standard which the court holds must be complied with to meet the true and fair requirement become in cases where it is applicable, a source of law in itself in the widest sense of that term.'

2.6 As you can see, the foreword gives the FRSs a context in relation to other standard setting bodies, company law and users and preparers of accounts.

2.7 Note in particular the content of (e) in Paragraph 2.5 above. The spirit of the standards must be followed, but where there is a departure from a standard (to show a true and fair view), this must be disclosed, including full financial effects.

Current accounting standards

2.8 The following standards are extant at the date of writing. The SSAPs which were in force at the date the ASB was formed have been adopted by the Board. They are gradually being superseded by the new Financial Reporting Standards.

UK accounting standards

Title		Issue date
	Foreword to accounting standards	Jun 93
FRS 1	Cash flow statements (revised Oct 96)	Sep 91
FRS 2	Accounting for subsidiary undertakings	July 92
FRS 3	Reporting financial performance	Oct 92
FRS 4	Capital instruments	Dec 93
FRS 5	Reporting the substance of transactions	Apr 94
FRS 6	Acquisitions and mergers	Sep 94
FRS 7	Fair values in acquisition accounting	Sep 94
FRS 8	Related party disclosures	Oct 95
FRS 9	Associates and joint ventures	Nov 97
FRS 10	Goodwill and intangible assets	Dec 97
FRS 11	Impairment of fixed assets and goodwill	Jul 98
FRS 12	Provisions, contingent liabilities and contingent assets	Sep 98
FRS 13	Derivatives and other financial instruments: disclosures	Sep 98
FRS 14	Earnings per share	Oct 98
FRS 15	Tangible fixed assets	Feb 99
FRS 16	Current tax	Dec 99
FRS 17	Retirement benefits	Nov 00
FRS 18	Accounting policies	Dec 00
FRS 19	Deferred tax	Dec 00
FRSSE	Financial Reporting Standard for Smaller Entities	Dec 99
SSAP 4	Accounting for government grants	Jul 90
SSAP 5	Accounting for value added tax	Apr 74
SSAP 9	Stocks and long-term contracts	Sep 88
SSAP 13	Accounting for research and development	Jan 89
SSAP 17	Accounting for post balance sheet events	Aug 80
SSAP 19	Accounting for investment properties	Nov 81
SSAP 20	Foreign currency translation	Apr 83
SSAP 21	Accounting for leases and hire purchase contracts	Aug 84
SSAP 25	Segmental reporting	Jun 90

Question

In between now and your examination, make sure you set aside time *every* week or month to read the *Students' Newsletter* and either the *Financial Times, The Economist* or any other equivalent publication. Look for news about the actions of the Accounting Standards Board and the other bodies we have discussed in this chapter and read about the accounts of individual companies as they are discussed in the press.

3   THE URGENT ISSUES TASK FORCE (UITF)

3.1   The UITF is an offshoot of the ASB. Its function is:

> 'to tackle **urgent matters** not covered by existing standards, and for which, given the urgency, the normal standard-setting process would not be practicable.' (Sir Ron Dearing)

3.2   The UITF pronouncements, which are called '**abstracts**', are intended to come into effect quickly. They therefore tend to become effective within approximately one month of publication date. The UITF has so far issued twenty two abstracts. Abstracts 1, 2, 3, 7, 8 and 14 have all been superseded by new FRSs and Financial Reporting Exposure Drafts (FREDs). Only Abstracts 4, 5 and 7 are included in the ACCA's list of examinable documents. These are discussed briefly here and they are mentioned in the relevant parts of this text when necessary.

Abstract 4 Presentation of long-term debtors in current assets

3.3   Where the figure of debtors due after more than one year is material in the context of the total net current assets then it should be **disclosed on the face of the balance sheet**, rather than just by way of a note (as has been the practice in the past where long-term debtors were included in current assets). The figure would be material in relation to net current assets if its non-disclosure on the balance sheet would cause readers to misinterpret the accounts. You should bear this in mind when considering the Companies Acts formats, given in Chapter 3.

Abstract 5 Transfers from current assets to fixed assets

3.4   This abstract requires transfers from current assets to fixed assets to be made **at the lower of cost and net realisable value**. This prevents the practice of transfers being made at a value higher than NRV. This avoids charging the profit and loss account with any diminution in value of what are, in effect, unsold trading assets. Once transferred to fixed assets, the CA 1985 alternative accounting rules could be used to take the debit reflecting the diminution in value to a revaluation reserve. This abstract follows the statement of Principles and was triggered by a Review Panel Judgement on Trafalgar House's 1991 accounts. In that incidence, commercial properties were transferred out of current assets into tangible fixed assets, thereby avoiding a £102 million hit to pre-tax profits in the original accounts. Fixed assets are dealt with in Chapter 4.

Abstract 15 Disclosure of substantial acquisitions

3.5   This clarifies the threshold for **disclosure of substantial acquisitions** under the Stock Exchange Listing Rules.

3.6   The UITF is currently considering another topic, marking current asset investments to market.

Foreword to UITF Abstracts

3.7   This foreword was issued in February 1994. It is closely associated with the *Foreword to accounting standards* in its scope and application and users are asked to 'be guided by the spirit and reasoning' behind the abstracts.

3.8   Most importantly, the document sets out the following criteria for compliance with the UITF abstracts.

> 'The Councils of the CCAB bodies expect their members who assume responsibilities in respect of financial statements to **observe UITF Abstracts until they are replaced by accounting standards or otherwise withdrawn** by the ASB.'

3.9   The scope of and compliance with the abstracts are similar to those associated with accounting standards (accounts which show a true and fair view, non-compliance must be justified and disclosed etc).

The effectiveness of the UITF

3.10   There is no doubt that the prompt action of the UITF has **closed many loopholes** as soon as they have become apparent. Some of the abstracts have been triggered by the accounts of individual companies, whereas others reflect concern which has arisen over a period of time. Another aspect of the success of the UITF is the **relative speed** with which the abstracts have been included in new standards, or exposure drafts. In other words, the topics were obviously important enough, not only for the attention of the UITF, but also for the ASB.

3.11   In combination with the Review Panel, the UITF can halt abuses in financial reporting as soon as they occur. This will also act as a preventative measure, causing many companies and their auditors to hesitate before breaking (or even bending) the rules.

4   BIG GAAP/LITTLE GAAP

4.1   Most UK companies are **small companies**. They are generally owned and managed by one person or a family. The owners have invested their own money in the business and there are **no outside shareholders to protect**.

4.2   **Large companies**, by contrast, particularly public limited companies may have shareholders who have invested their money, possibly through a pension fund, with no knowledge whatever of the company. These **shareholders need protection and the regulations for such companies need to be more stringent**.

KEY TERM

It could therefore be argued that company accounts should be of two types: 'simple' ones for small companies with fewer regulations and disclosure requirements and 'complicated' ones for larger companies with extensive and detailed requirements. This is the **'big GAAP/little GAAP'** divide.

4.3   In 1994 a working party of the Consultative Committee of Accountancy Bodies was set up to consider whether small companies should be exempt from most of or all accounting standards. In November 1994 the working party concluded that:

> 'the current form of financial reporting may not best serve the needs of some users. Indeed it could be argued that the application of the full range of present requirements may make some information less understandable, or even result in a distorted presentation, compared with figures that users understand.'

4.4   The working party proposed that companies meeting the Companies Act definition of **small** (turnover of less than £2.6m, balance sheet total of £1.4m and an average of 50 employees) would be **exempt from all standards, except for certain core ones**, after taking into account the fact that the accounting regime specified by the Companies Act lays down most of the fundamental principles necessary to produce accounts which show a true and fair. The proposed 'core' standards were as follows.

SSAP 4 *Accounting for government grants*
SSAP 9 *Stocks and long-term contracts*
SSAP 13 *Accounting for research and development*
SSAP 17 *Accounting for post balance sheet events*
SSAP 18 *Accounting for contingencies* (now replaced by FRS 12 *Provisions, contingent liabilities and contingent assets*).

4.5   Initially the proposals met with a **frosty reception** by the profession, with the ACCA, for example, warning that they were 'too radical' and would lead to a 'serious decline in the quality of financial reporting'. It was suggested that small company accounts might not show a true and fair view if they do not follow the majority of standards.

4.6   However, in July 1995 it was reported in *Accountancy* that the proposals were beginning to find favour. Moreover, the Department of Trade and Industry published a consultation paper *Accounting Simplifications* which addressed the legal aspects of small company accounts.

FRS for Smaller Entities

4.7   In December 1995, the debate was significantly accelerated. The working party published its discussion paper *Designed to fit - a reporting standard for smaller entities*. Then in December 1996 the ASB published an Exposure Draft of the *Financial Reporting Standard for Smaller Entities* and this was published in final form in December 1997. It brings together in one brief document all the accounting guidance which UK small businesses will require to draw up their financial statements.

4.8   The **FRSSE retains all of the basic principles of accounting standards while discarding the detailed explanatory notes**. This slims down the volume of accounting standards dramatically. For example, FRS 4 *Capital instruments* and FRS 5 *Reporting the substance of*

transactions have been reduced to just a couple of paragraphs. The original standards are very substantial. Disclosure requirements are greatly reduced.

4.9 The FRSSE is applicable to all companies that satisfy the definition of a small company in companies legislation and is available to other entities that would meet that definition if they were companies. A company that chooses to comply with the FRSSE is exempt from all other accounting standards and UITF Abstracts.

4.10 The FRSSE contains in a simplified form the requirements from existing accounting standards that are relevant to the majority of smaller entities.

4.11 In order to keep the FRSSE as user-friendly as possible some of the requirements in accounting standards relating to more complex transactions, eg the treatment of convertible debt in FRS 4 *Capital instruments*, have not been included in the FRSSE, as they do not affect most smaller entities. Where guidance is needed on a matter not contained in the FRSSE, regard should be paid to existing practice as set out in the relevant accounting standards.

Measurement

4.12 The measurement bases in the FRSSE are the same as, or a simplification of, those in existing accounting standards. For example, under the FRSSE a lessee that is a small company could account for the finance charges on a finance lease on a straight-line basis over the life of the lease, rather than, as in SSAP 21, using a constant periodic rate of return.

Detailed requirements

4.13 The main headings of the FRSSE are listed below with explanatory notes, where appropriate, indicating changes from the original standards or other points of significance. (The FRSSE will not be discussed in detail as many of the standards on which it is based are covered elsewhere in this Study Text.)

(a) **Scope**. The FRSSE is capable of application to smaller **entities** and not just smaller companies. It applies to the companies entitled to the exemptions available in ss 246 and 247 CA 1985 for small companies and which state that they have taken advantage of such exemptions. The FRSSE is also applicable to small groups (as defined by companies legislation) even though there is no statutory requirement for them to prepare consolidated accounts.

(b) **General**. The financial statements should state that they have been prepared in accordance with the FRSSE.

(c) **Profit and loss account**. The requirement of FRS 3 *Reporting financial performance* to **analyse the profit and loss account** into continuing, discontinued and acquired operations has been **lifted**.

(d) **Statement of total recognised gains and losses**. This statement has been **retained**. However, where the only recognised gains and losses are those included in the profit and loss account, no separate statement to that effect is required. This cuts out a large amount of disclosure which, for small companies, was felt to be superfluous. There is no need to show historical cost profits and losses or a reconciliation of movements in shareholders' funds.

(e) **Foreign currency translation**

(f) **Taxation**

(g) **Goodwill**

(h) **Investment properties**

(i) **Depreciation**

(j) **Government grants**

(k) **Research and development**

(l) **Short and long-term contracts**

(m) **Leases**. SSAP 21 *Accounting for leases and hire purchase contracts* is modified such that, for finance leases, charges can normally be spread on a **straight-line basis** and assets and liabilities can normally be recorded at their fair value, rather than the value of the minimum lease payments.

(n) **Pensions**. There is **no requirement to disclose** the accounting policy for pension scheme contributions, or funding policy, or circumstances where the actuary is an employee or officer of the company.

(o) **Capital instruments**. FRS 4 *Capital instruments* has been **simplified** such that arrangement fees can be charged directly to the profit and loss account rather than spread over the term of the debt where they are not considered significant in amount.

(p) **Contingencies**

(q) **Related parties.** The disclosure requirements for related party transactions in the FRSSE represent a useful dispensation for smaller entities compared with those in FRS 8 *Related party disclosures*. Under FRS 8, related party transactions that are material to the related party, where that related party is an individual, are required to be disclosed in the accounts of the reporting entity even if the transaction is not material to the entity. This is not so for smaller entities adopting the FRSSE, as they need disclose only those related party transactions that are material in relation to the reporting entity.

(r) **Definitions**

Cash flow statement

4.14 Since small entities are already exempt from the requirements of FRS 1 *Cash flow statements* the FRSSE does not include a requirement for a cash flow statement. The ASB nevertheless believes that a cash flow statement is an important aid to the understanding of an entity's financial position and performance and the FRSSE therefore includes a 'voluntary disclosures' section, recommending that smaller entities present a simplified cash flow statement using the indirect method (ie starting with operating profit and reconciling it to the total cash generated (or utilised) in the period).

Small groups

4.15 Small groups are not required by law to prepare consolidated accounts, and therefore in practice not many do so, at least on a statutory basis. The Working Party and the Board, however, agreed with respondents that it would be unfair to those small groups that voluntarily prepare group accounts, if they were not able to take advantage of the provisions in the FRSSE. To import all the necessary requirements from accounting standards and UITF Abstracts into the FRSSE to deal with consolidated accounts would have added substantially to its length and complexity, even though it would have been of interest to only a small percentage of entities. Accordingly, the Working Party and the Board preferred to extend the FRSSE in certain areas and then require small groups adopting the FRSSE to follow those accounting standards and UITF Abstracts that deal with consolidated financial statements. This approach was supported by the majority of respondents to the Exposure Draft commenting on the matter.

4.16 The FRSSE has been described by Barry Johnson (*Certified Accountant*, February 1996) as 'a commendable summary of UK GAAP .... succinct and to the point'. The need for and advantages of such a standard have been indicated above.

4.17 *Criticisms of the FRSSE*

(a) The FRSSE is **unlikely to make it easier or cheaper** to prepare financial statements.

(b) The case in favour of relaxing **measurement** GAAP for smaller companies has not yet been made convincingly. The only exemptions are from disclosure, rather than from measurement. Some argue that this could be achieved more easily by simply stating in the individual FRSs and SSAPs what disclosure requirements apply to all companies and what applies only to large ones.

(c) It is questionable whether accounts prepared under the FRSSE would give a **true and fair view** under company law. The true and fair view requirement applies to all companies, whatever their size.

(d) The present document is **not a 'stand-alone' document**. Users would still need to refer to 'mainstream' standards if they are to prepare financial statements which show a true and fair view.

4.18 However, some commentators back the concept of a financial reporting standard for smaller entities; they feel that the FRSSE provides a satisfactory and workable solution to the problems of smaller entities caused by the increasing complexity of accounting standards.

Future developments

4.19 With the assistance of its advisory committee, the Committee on Accounting for Smaller Entities, the ASB will update and revise the FRSSE periodically to reflect future developments in financial reporting. Any changes to the FRSSE, for example as a result of new accounting standards and UITF Abstracts, will be the subject of public consultation.

4.20 The FRSSE attempts to balance the conflicting views of those who commented on the proposals, ranging from those who believe small companies should be exempt from all accounting standards to those who favour retaining virtually the status quo. Given this divergence of views, the ASB believes that it is particularly important that, going forward, the FRSSE is carefully monitored. It is therefore proposed to review how the FRSSE, as a whole, is working in practice after two full years of effective operation and propose amendments as necessary, in addition to the routine periodic revisions of the FRSSE resulting from new accounting standards and UITF Abstracts.

Exam focus point

As with all topical issues, you should aim to read around the subject. Not all comments on the FRSSE have been favourable.

Small companies and the Companies Act 1985

4.21 Small companies are still required to comply with the normal rules, as set out in the Companies Act 1985 and accounting standards, for measurement. They **no longer need to disclose as much information** in their financial statements as larger companies.

4.22 Despite this, the Companies Act specifically states that the financial statements of smaller companies will still be deemed to give **true and fair view** if they have done nothing more than rely on the exemptions that are available to them. The main reason for this seems to be legal: so that the directors will not be held to be in breach of their statutory duties to prepare proper financial statements. However, it still raises the question of how a specific disclosure can be required in order that the financial statements of one enterprise give a true and fair view, but not required in the case of another.

4.23 Where small companies are subject to audit, their auditors are no longer legally required to state that the financial statements give a true and fair view. It appears that two sets of generally accepted accounting practice are developing. Larger companies will continue to be required to comply with all statutory provisions and accounting standard requirements, while smaller companies will only need to comply with a restricted set of rules.

Chapter roundup

- The aims and operating processes of the **FRC, ASB, FRRP** and **UITF** should all be clear now.

- Most UK companies, are small and it is felt that **accounting standards**, being designed for large companies, are **less relevant to smaller companies**.

- A working party of the CCAB was set up to address this big GAAP/little GAAP problem. It produced the **FRSSE**. Published in final form by the ASB in November 1997, this effectively encapsulates UK GAAP with some simplifications from 'mainstream' accounting standards, notably in respect of FRS 3 and 4.

- The FRSSE contains in a simplified form the requirements from existing accounting standards that are relevant to the majority of smaller entities.

Quick quiz

1 Describe the process involved in developing Financial Reporting Standards.

2 Can financial statements not follow an accounting standard?

3 Which UITF Abstracts are the following?

 Presentation of long-term debtors in current assets
 Transfer from current assets to fixed assets
 Disclosure of substantial acquisitions

4 Under FRSSE, small companies need not comply with FRS 3's requirement to analyse the profit and loss account into continuing, discontinued and acquired operations. True or false?

Answers to quick quiz

1 The ASB produce DDs, then FREDs and finally FRSs. You could depict this in a diagram. (See para 2.1)

2 Yes. To show a true and fair view. (2.5(e))

3 4, 5 and 15 (3.3 to 3.6)

4 True (4.13)

Now try the question below from the Exam Question Bank

Number	Level	Marks	Time
2	Full exam	20	36 mins

Part B

Preparing the financial statements of limited liability companies

Chapter 3

COMPANIES ACT REQUIREMENTS AND THE FORMAT OF ACCOUNTS

Topic list		Syllabus reference
1	SSAP 2 Disclosure of accounting policies	3(f)
2	FRS 18 Accounting policies	3(f)
3	True and fair view	3(f)
4	Published accounts	2(a)
5	The format of the accounts	2(a)
6	Notes to the accounts	2(a)
7	Directors' report	2(a)
8	Auditors' report and chairman's report	2(a)

Introduction

This chapter is as important as Chapter 2 and it may look rather daunting. It lays out the Companies Act formats for the balance sheet and profit and loss account as well as the disclosures required in the notes to the accounts. These are fundamental to the study of financial accounting.

Before we look at the Companies Act, we will refresh your memory of the accounting standard which lays out some of the basic premises upon which accounts are based, FRS 18 *Accounting Policies*. You should be familiar with SSAP 2 from your earlier studies, FRS 18 has replaced SSAP 2.

This chapter is predominantly concerned with Companies Act requirements, but you should refer back to this chapter when you get to Chapter 9 because of the way FRS 3 has affected the format of published accounts and the notes required.

We will mention the Companies Act requirements for each of the individual items mentioned in the rest of the chapters in this part of the Study Text. You should refer back to this chapter frequently to remind yourself of the position of each item in the accounts.

Study guide

- Describe the influence of EC directives

- Explain the role of the Companies Acts

- State the requirement of the Companies Act regarding:

    - The duty to prepare annual accounts

    - The form and content of the prescribed formats

    - The main provisions of Company Law including accounting rules

    - Prepare the financial statement of limited companies in accordance with the prescribed formats and relevant accounting standards

- Distinguish between small and medium companies and outline the disclosure exemptions relating to these companies.

Exam guide

FRS 18 is an important standard. Make sure you understand how to use it, as well as the subtle ways it differs from the withdrawn SSAP 2. Practice the format of the accounts until you can quickly lay out a proforma in the exam.

1 SSAP 2 DISCLOSURE OF ACCOUNTING POLICIES

1.1 You should be familiar with SSAP 2 *Disclosure of accounting policies* from your earlier studies. This has been withdrawn and FRS 18 has been issued. A brief summary of SSAP 2 is nevertheless provided here as a point of reference for when SSAP 2 still comes up in discussions.

Knowledge brought forward from earlier studies

SSAP 2 Disclosure of accounting policies

SSAP 2 defines three important terms.

- **Fundamental accounting concepts** are the broad basic assumptions which underlie the periodic financial accounts of business enterprises.

- **Accounting bases** are the methods developed for applying fundamental accounting concepts to financial transactions and items, for the purpose of financial accounts; and in particular:

  ° For determining the accounting periods in which revenue and costs should be recognised in the P & L a/c.

  ° For determining the amounts at which material items should be stated in the B/S.

- **Accounting policies:** a business entity's accounting policies are simply the accounting bases which they have chosen to follow in a situation where there is a choice of accounting bases: eg depreciation of fixed assets.

Fundamental concepts

SSAP deals with the four fundamental concepts.

- The **'going concern' concept:** the enterprise will continue in operational existence for the foreseeable future.

- The **'accruals' concept:** revenue and costs are accrued (that is, recognised as they are earned or incurred, not as money is received or paid).

- The **'consistency' concept:** there is consistency of accounting treatment of like items within each accounting period and from one period to the next.

- The **concept of 'prudence':** revenue and profits are not anticipated, but are recognised by inclusion in the P&L a/c only when realised in the form either of cash or of assets, the ultimate cash realisation of which can be assessed with reasonable certainty

There is always a presumption that these concepts have been observed. If this is not the case, the facts should be explained.

1.2 The CA 1985 and SSAP 2 share the following requirements.

(a) **Accounting policies should be applied consistently** from one financial year to the next.

(b) If accounts are prepared on the basis of assumptions which differ in material respects from any of the generally accepted fundamental accounting concepts (principles) the details, **reasons for and the effect of, the departure from the fundamental concepts must be given in a note to the accounts**.

(c) The **accounting policies** adopted by a company in determining the (material) amounts to be included in the balance sheet and in determining the profit or loss for the year **must be stated by a note to the accounts**.

Exam focus point

For examination purposes, it is useful to give the accounting policy note as the first note to the accounts, making sure that the explanations are clear, fair and as brief as possible.

2 FRS 18 ACCOUNTING POLICIES

Exam focus point

Some aspects of FRS 18 may look like the old SSAP 2 but you need to understand the differences, so that when you use the terminology in your answers it reflects the new flavours of FRS 18 rather than serving up the old SSAP 2 terminology and interpretation we have become accustomed to in the past. FRS 18 is an important standard as it impacts extensively on financial reporting work.

The *Student Accountant* of 17 October 2001 includes an excellent article on FRS 18 written by Mr Paul Robins. The section below draws on his perspective.

2.1 FRS 18 *Accounting policies* replaces SSAP 2 *Disclosure of accounting policies*. It builds on the concepts outlined in SSAP 2 (issued almost 30 years ago) and attempts to align them with the ASB *Statement of Principles*.

2.2 The objective of FRS 18 is to ensure that for all **material items**:

(a) An entity adopts the accounting policies **most appropriate** to its particular circumstances for the purpose of giving a **true and fair view**

(b) The accounting policies adopted are **reviewed regularly** to ensure that they remain appropriate, and are changed when a new policy becomes more appropriate, and are changed when a new policy becomes more appropriate to the entity's particular circumstances

(c) **Sufficient information** is disclosed in the financial statements to enable users to **understand** the accounting policies adopted and how they have been implemented.

Desirable features

2.3 The most obvious change is the relegation of two fundamental accounting concepts

- **Prudence**
- **Consistency**

These concepts are now **desirable features** of financial statements.

Pervasive concepts

2.4 The bedrocks of accounting are

- Accruals
- Going concern

2.5 FRS 18 places great **importance** upon these concepts. Although these are on the face of it, similar to the previously matching and going concern concepts, there are subtle but important differences.

Accruals

2.6 Within FRS 18, the accruals concept goes to the heart of the definition of assets and liabilities, and plays an important role in the way these items are recognised.

Basic requirement

The accruals basis of accounting requires the **non-cash impact** of transactions to be reflected in the financial statements for the **period in which they occur**, and not, for example, in the period any cash involved is received or paid.

2.7 From the above, it can be seen that FRS 18 adopts a slightly different approach to SSAP 2 on the accruals concept. Together with the definitions of assets and liabilities set out in FRS 5, *Reporting the Substance of Transactions*, FRS 18 in effect provides a discipline within which the old SSAP 2 matching process can operate.

KEY TERMS

- Asset: right to **future economic benefits** controlled by an entity as result of past events.

- Liability: entity's **obligation** to **transfer economic benefits** as result of past events.

2.8 FRS 18, like CA 1985, does not refer to matching.

2.9 EXAMPLE

How would you assess whether expenditure such as unexpired advertising or unused stationery should be carried forward to the next year?

2.10 SOLUTION

Under the old SSAP 2 regime, the decision on whether to carry expenditure forward into next year would involve the matching concept and whether there is a reasonable expectation of future revenue.

Under the new FRS 18 regime, the **decision to carry forward** depends on whether the item being considered meets the **definition of an asset**.

FRS 18 effectively updates SSAP 2 within the ambit of the **Statement of Principles** and FRS 5.

2.11 The article written by Mr Paul Robins, in the *Student Accountant* of October 2001 suggests that the concept of accruals is also closely related to the concept of **realisation**. CA 1985 only allows realised profits to be recognised in the **profit and loss account**. However, CA 1985 does not adequately define the expression 'realised'. Neither does FRS 18 define 'realised'. What FRS 18 does do is to link realisation with the **creation of new assets and liabilities** and hence with the **concept of accruals**.

Going concern

Criteria

2.12   FRS 18 requires financial statements to be prepared on a going concern basis, except where:

(a)   An entity is being liquidated and has ceased trading

(b)   The directors have no realistic alternative but to cease trading or liquidate the business.

In these circumstances, the **directors have an option** to prepare its financial statements on a **basis other than that of a going concern**. Remember, where the criteria are met, the **decision is discretionary** rather than mandatory, to prepare the financial statements on a non-going concern basis.

2.13   The going concern hypothesis assumes that the entity will **continue** in **operational existence** for the **foreseeable future**. The justification for this is that financial statements prepared on a **break up basis** do **not provide** users with much **useful information**, such as on financial adaptability and cash generation ability.

Directors responsibilities

2.14   The directors have an obligation to **assess** whether there are **significant doubts** about an entity's ability to continue as a **going concern**, when preparing financial statements.

2.15   FRS 18 suggests that directors should review the following factors:

- History of company's profitability
- Access to financial resources
- Debt repayment schedules

2.16   Such considerations also govern the **length of time** for which the going concern assessment should be made.

Disclosures

2.17   The following information should be disclosed in the financial statements in relation to the going concern assessment required by FRS 18.

(a)   Any material uncertainties, of which the directors are aware in making their assessment, related to events or conditions that may cast significant doubt upon the entity's ability to continue as a going concern.

(b)   Where the foreseeable future considered by the directors has been limited to a period of less than one year from the date of approval of the financial statements, that fact.

(c)   When the financial statements are not prepared on a going concern basis, that fact, together with the basis on which the financial statements are prepared and the reason why the entity is not regarded as a going concern.

Statement of Principles

2.18   As you will have gathered from the above, FRS 18 is designed to sit alongside the *Statement of Principles* framework. This helps explain the downplaying of the previously important prudence and consistency concepts.

BPP PUBLISHING

2.19 FRS 18 can be said to provide a **'bridge'** between the ideas and concepts envisaged by the *Statement of Principles* and the concepts enshrined in SSAP 2 for a long time.

2.20 The preparers of financial statements must now consider the following **objectives** and constraints in **assessing** the appropriateness of **accounting policies:**

- Relevance
- Reliability
- Comparability
- Understandability

Relevance

2.21 Information is **relevant** if it possess **certain qualities**.

(a) Ability to **influence economic decisions** of users
(b) Is sufficiently **timely** to influence the decision
(c) Has **predictive** or **confirmatory** value, or both.

Eg the FRS 3 requirement for separate analyses of the results of discontinued operations can be said to improve the predictive value of a set of financial statements.

Reliability

2.22 Financial information is reliable if:

(a) It can be depended upon by users to **represent faithfully** what it either purports to represent or could reasonably be expected to represent, and therefore reflects the **substance of the transactions** and other events that have taken place

(b) It is **free** from deliberate or systematic **bias** (ie it is **neutral**)

(c) It is **free** from **material error**

(d) It is **complete** within the bounds of **materiality**

(e) Under conditions of **uncertainty**, it has been **prudently prepared**

Prudence

2.23 In terms of FRS 18, **prudence** relates to the **uncertainty** that may be associated with the **recognition** and **measurement** of **assets** and **liabilities**.

2.24 FRS 18 suggest different levels of confirmatory evidence regarding the recognition of assets and liabilities, where uncertainty exists. In such circumstances, the existence of an **asset or gain** requires **stronger confirmatory evidence** than that required to acknowledge the existence of a liability or loss.

2.25 FRS 18 emphasises that prudence may only be called upon to justify setting up a provision if uncertainty exists. **Prudence** should **not** be **invoked** to **justify setting up hidden reserves, excessive provisions** or **understating assets**. Prudence should not be seen as a tool for smoothing profits in financial statements.

2.26 FRS 18 emphasises that **if financial statements are not neutral they cannot be reliable**. Tension often exists between neutrality and prudence. This should be reconciled by finding a balance that ensures that the deliberate and systematic understatement of assets and gains, and overstatement of liabilities and losses, does not occur.

2.27 Several recent FRSs, especially FRS 12, have adopted a more 'even-handed' approach to the challenge of **measuring** and **recognising** income, expenses, assets and liabilities in financial statements.

Comparability

2.28 FRS 18 suggest that this is achieved through:

(a) Consistency
(b) Disclosure

Hence, consistency, no longer a fundamental accounting concept it its own right, is subsumed under the objective of comparability. Under the old SSAP 2 regime, **consistency implied** a *status quo* approach to financial reporting.

2.29 In practice, **comparability** will often be achieved through **consistency**. However, there may be circumstances where a change in the method of presenting financial information increases the usefulness of the financial report for users.

Understandability

2.30 FRS 18 stipulates that information provided by financial statements should be capable of being understood by users who have

(a) A **reasonable knowledge** of business and economic activities.
(b) A willingness and **reasonable diligence** to study the information provided.

2.31 There can be tensions between the different objectives set out above. In particular, sometimes the accounting policy that is most relevant to a particular entity's circumstances is not the most reliable, and vice versa. In such circumstances, the most appropriate accounting policy will usually be that which is the **most relevant of those that are reliable**.

2.32 Generally, FRS 18 encourages an approach that leads to the most appropriate policies for the company. Note also that FRS 18 does not use the word "conflict" but prefers a process of resolving "tensions" between different objectives.

2.33 The relationship between pervasive concepts, desirable features and accounting policy objectives may be summarised briefly in the following diagram.

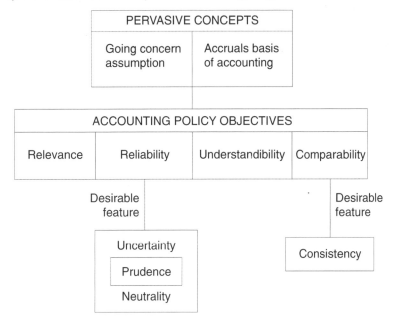

BPP
PUBLISHING

Accounting policies

2.34   FRS 18 prescribes the **regular consideration of the entity's accounting policies**. The **best** accounting policy should be adopted at all times. This is the major reason for downplaying consistency (and to a lesser extent prudence). An entity **cannot retain** an **accounting policy** merely **because** it was **used last** year **or** because it **gives a prudent view**.

2.35   However, the entity should consider how a **change** in accounting policy may affect **comparability**. Essentially a **balance** must be struck between selecting the **most appropriate policies** and presenting **coherent and useful** financial statements. The **overriding guidance** is that the financial statements should give a **true and fair view** of the entity's business. Chopping and changing accounting policies year on year is likely to jeopardise the true and fair view but so too is retaining accounting policies which do not present the most useful information to the users of the accounts.

2.36   FRS 18 suggests that the need to balance the cost of providing information should be balanced with the likely benefit of such information to the users of the entity's financial statements. However, FRS 18 also cautions against the use of cost and benefit considerations to justify the adoption of an accounting policy that is inconsistent with the requirements of accounting standards, UITF Abstracts and CA 1985.

Disclosure

2.37   FRS 18 requires the disclosure of

- A **description of each accounting policy** which is material to the entity's financial statements

- A description of any significant estimation technique

- **Changes** to accounting policies

- The effects of any material change to an estimation technique

Estimation techniques

2.38   An estimation technique is material **only where a large range** of monetary values may be arrived at. The entity should **vary** the **assumptions** it uses, to **assess** how **sensitive** monetary values are under that **technique**. In most cases the range of values will be relatively narrow (consider the useful life of motor vehicles for example).

Changes to accounting policies

2.39   The disclosure of new accounting policies also requires

- An explanation of the **reason for change**

- The **effects of a prior period adjustment** on the previous years results (in accordance with FRS 3)

- The **effects of the change in policy** on the previous year's results

If it is **not possible** to disclose the last two points then the **reason** for this should be disclosed instead.

Exam focus point

You need to be confident about the application of FRS 18. Make sure that you can **identify** a change in accounting policy and the **reason** that it is a change in accounting policy as opposed to a change in estimation technique. You will have to **discuss** the decision you have reached **and justify** your conclusions.

2.40 The most complex aspect to FRS 18 is the **application of the terms and definitions** within the standard. SSAP 2 defined accounting policies and accounting bases. There was some confusion as to what an accounting base was. FRS 18 has dispensed with the term accounting base. However, the term which seems to replace it, **estimation technique**, may prove difficult to apply in practice.

2.41 It is essential that you **understand the following definitions** so you can apply them in an examination situation.

KEY TERM

Accounting policies. The principles, conventions, rules and practices applied by an entity that prescribe how transactions and other events are to be reflected in its financial statements.

2.42 Accounting policies are **not** estimation techniques.

2.43 An accounting policy includes the

- Recognition
- Presentation
- And measurement basis

Of assets, liabilities, gains, losses and changes to shareholders funds.

KEY TERM

Estimation technique. The methods used by an entity to establish the estimated monetary amounts associated with the measurement bases selected for assets, liabilities, gains, losses and changes to shareholder's funds.

2.44 Estimation techniques are used to **implement the measurement basis** of an accounting policy. The accounting policy specifies the measurement basis and the estimation technique is used when there is an uncertainty over this amount.

2.45 The method of **depreciation is an estimation technique**. The accounting policy is to spread the cost of the asset over its useful economic life. **Depreciation** is the **measurement basis**. The **estimation technique** would be, say, **straight line** depreciation as opposed to **reducing balance**.

2.46 A change of estimation technique should **not** be accounted for as a prior period adjustment unless the following apply.

- It is the correction of a fundamental error

- • The Companies Act, an accounting standard or a UITF Abstract **requires the change to be accounted** for as a prior period adjustment.

Application of FRS 18

2.47 FRS 18 gives a number of examples of its application in an appendix to the standard. When a change is required to an accounting policy then **three criteria** must be **considered** to ensure that the change is affecting the accounting policy and not an estimation technique.

1 Recognition
2 Presentation
3 Measurement basis

2.48 If **any one of the criteria apply** then a change has been made to the accounting policy. If they do **not** apply then a change to an estimation technique has taken place.

2.49 You should note that where an **accounting standard gives a choice** of treatments (i.e. SSAP 9 states that stock can be recognised on a FIFO or weighted average cost basis) then adopting the alternative treatment is a **change of accounting policy.** Also note that FRS 15 states that a **change in depreciation method is not** a change in accounting policy.

Example		Recognition	Change to Presentation	Measurement basis?	Change of Accounting Policy
1	Changing from capitalisation of finance costs associated with the construction of fixed assets to charging them through the profit and loss	Yes	Yes	No	Yes
2	A reassessment of an entity's cost centres means that all three will have production overheads allocated to them instead of just two	No	No	No	No
3	Overheads are reclassified from distribution to cost of sales	No	Yes	No	Yes
4	Change from straight-line depreciation to machine hours	No	No	No	No
5	Reallocate depreciation from administration to cost of sales	No	Yes	No	Yes
6	A provision is revised upwards and the estimates of future cash flows are now discounted in accordance with FRS 12. They were not discounted previously as the amounts involved were not material	No	No	No	No

Example	Recognition	Change to Presentation	Change to Measurement basis?	Change of Accounting Policy
7 Deferred tax is now reported on a discounted basis. It was previously undiscounted	No	No	Yes	Yes
8 A foreign subsidiary's profit and loss account is now to be translated at the closing rate. It was previously translated at the average rate	No	No	Yes	Yes
9 Fungible stocks are to be measured on the weighted average cost basis instead of the previously used FIFO basis	No	No	Yes	Yes

Fungible assets

> **KEY TERM**
>
> **Fungible assets** are similar assets which are grouped together as there is no reason to view them separately in economic terms. Shares and items of stock are examples of fungible assets.

2.50 The last example (example 9) is based on a **change to fungible assets**. The standard states that when fungible assets are considered in **aggregate** a change from weighted average cost to FIFO (or vice versa), is a change to the **measurement base**. The standard also recommends that fungible assets should **always be considered in aggregate** in order to enhance **comparability** of financial statements.

Question 1

The board of Sarah plc decide to change the depreciation method they use on their plant and machinery from 30% reducing balance to 20% straight line to better reflect the way the assets are used within the business. Is this a change of accounting policy ?

Answer

No. This is a change to the **estimation technique**. The same measurement basis is used. The historic cost is allocated over the asset's estimated useful life.

Question 2

The board of Sarah plc also decide to change their stock valuation. They replace their FIFO valuation method for an AVCO method to better reflect the way that stock is used within the business. Is this a change in accounting policy?

Answer

Yes. This is a change to the **measurement basis**. The paragraphs on fungible assets discuss this further.

BPP PUBLISHING

Question 3

The board of Sarah plc decide in the following year that the development costs the business incurs should not be capitalised and presented on the balance sheet. Instead they agree that all development expenditure should be expended in the profit and loss account. Is this an accounting policy change?

Answer

Yes. The choice to capitalise or not is given in SSAP 13. The criteria affected by this decision are **recognition and presentation.**

Question 4

Sarah plc's board are also considering reallocating the depreciation charges made on its large fleet of company cars to administration expenses, they were previously shown in cost of sales. Is this an accounting policy change?

Answer

Yes. Sarah plc would be changing the way they **presented** the depreciation figure.

Summary

2.51 FRS 18 requires an entity to conduct a review on an annual basis in order to ensure that it is using the most appropriate accounting policies.

- The three criteria
- Recognition
- Presentation
- Measurement basis

2.52 Are considered in order to establish whether there has been a change of accounting policy or merely a change of measurement basis. The objectives of

- Reliability
- Relevance
- Comparability
- Understandability

2.53 The above must be fulfilled by the accounting policies adopted. This requirement helps prevent entities from changing accounting policies too often.

2.54 FRS 18 introduces subtle changes into the meaning of accruals and going concern. Whereas matching was driven by the need to ensure completeness in the profit and loss account, the accruals basis approaches recognition from the need to ensure the validity of assets and liabilities.

2.55 Prudence and consistency have a lesser role in the accounting policy framework. There may be tension between prudence and neutrality. Prudence should not be used as an excuse for setting up excessive provisions or understating assets. The use of prudence must be linked to uncertainty.

2.56 FRS 18 provides a bridge between the standards setting process and the *Statement of Principles*.

3 TRUE AND FAIR VIEW

Interpretation of true and fair

3.1 Section 226 of CA 1985 states that:

> 'the balance sheet shall give a true and fair view of the state of affairs of the company as at the end of the financial year, and the profit and loss account shall give a true and fair view of the profit or loss of the company for the financial year.'

The balance sheet and profit and loss account should also comply with the requirements of the Fourth Schedule (s 226(3) CA 1985).

> **KEY TERM**
>
> **'True and fair view'** has no set definition. Broadly speaking it means 'reasonably accurate and not misleading'.

3.2 The term 'true and fair view' is **not defined** in the **Companies Acts,** nor in **SSAPs** or **FRSs,** which also claim to be authoritative statements on what is a true and fair view. Moreover, the **courts** have **never tried to define it**.

3.3 In view of the ASB's policy of **reviewing** and, if necessary, **altering** or **replacing existing accounting standards,** a question **arises** as to whether the concept defined by '**true and fair view**' is constant or is **evolving** over a period of years.

3.4 The ASC has sought Counsel's opinion on this question. Very briefly, Counsel's opinion included the following key points:

- **Accuracy** and **completeness** are two key ingredients that contribute to a true and fair view.

- There might **not** be **consensus** amongst reasonable businessman and accountants as to the degree of accuracy and completeness required.

- The concept of **true and fair is dynamic**.

- **Judges** will look for **guidance** to the **ordinary practices** of **professional accountants**.

3.5 A later opinion obtained by the ASB, confirms the above views. This opinion also provides further clues on how to interpret the expression true and fair. The opinion suggests that the courts are **unlikely** to **look for synonyms** for the words '**true**' and '**fair**'. **Instead,** the courts will take an approach of trying to **apply** the **concepts implied** by the expression '**true and fair**'.

3.6 The **Statement of Principles** echos the above, but carefully avoids providing a formal difinition of **true and fair**.

- The true and fair view is a **dynamic concept** and evolves in **response** to changes in **accounting** and **business practice**.

- **Relevance** and **reliability** and **prime indicators** of the **quality** of **financial information**.

True and fair override

> **IMPORTANT!**
>
> S 226 (5) CA 1985 makes an important statement about the need to give a true and fair view. It states that if, in **special circumstances,** compliance with any of the Act's provisions would be inconsistent with the requirement to give a true and fair view, then the directors should depart from that provision to the extent necessary to give a true and fair view. This is the **true and fair override.**

3.7   If a balance sheet or profit and loss account drawn up in compliance with these other requirements of the Act would not provide enough information to give a true and fair view, then any **necessary additional information** must **also** be **given.**

3.8   The overriding priority to give a true and fair view **has in the past been treated as an important 'loophole' in the law,** and has been a cause of some argument or debate within the accounting profession. For example, the CA 1985 permits only realised profits to be recognised in the profit and loss account, whereas SSAP 9 requires unrealised profits on long-term contracts to be credited to profit and loss. Such a policy can only be justified by **invoking** the **overriding requirement** to show a true and fair view.

3.9   If companies do depart from the other requirements of the Act in order to give a true and fair view, they must **explain the particulars of and reasons for the departure, and its effects on the accounts,** in a note to the accounts. As already stated, the **Fourth Schedule** also requires a statement in a **note to the accounts** that the accounts have been prepared in accordance with **applicable accounting standards** and **particulars of any material departure from** those **standards and the reasons** (s 36A Sch 4).

True and fair override disclosures

3.10   As we saw above, where the directors depart from provisions of CA 1985 to the extent necessary to give a true and fair view, the Act required that 'particulars of any such departure, the reasons for it and its effect shall be given in a note to the accounts'. **FRS 18** *Accounting Policies* seeks to clarify the meaning of that sentence. Any **material departure** from the Companies Act, an accounting standard or a UITF abstract should lead to the following information being disclosed.

   (a) **A statement that there has been a departure** from the requirements of companies legislation, an accounting standard or a UITF abstract, and that the departure is **necessary to give a true and fair view.**

   (b) **A description of the treatment normally required** and also a description of the **treatment actually used.**

   (c) An explanation of why the **prescribed treatment would not give a true and fair view.**

   (d) **Its effect:** a description of how the position shown in the accounts is different as a result of the departure, with quantification if possible, or an explanation of the circumstances.

3.11   The disclosures required should either be **included in or cross referenced** to the note required about **compliance with accounting standards, particulars** of any material departure from those standards and the **reasons** for it (Paragraph 36A Sch 4).

3.12 If the departure occurs in **subsequent accounting periods**, the above disclosures should be made in **subsequent financial statements including** the **corresponding amounts** for previous years. If the departure only affects the corresponding amounts then the disclosure should relate to the corresponding amounts.

4 PUBLISHED ACCOUNTS

4.1 Statutory accounts are part of the price to be paid for the benefits of limited liability. **Limited companies must produce such accounts annually and they must appoint an independent person to audit and report on them.** Once prepared, **a copy** of the accounts **must be sent to the Registrar of Companies,** who maintains a separate file for every company. The Registrar's files may be inspected for a nominal fee by any member of the public. This is why the statutory accounts are often referred to as *published accounts*.

4.2 **It is the responsibility of the company's directors to produce accounts which show a true and fair view of the company's results for the period and its financial position at the end of the period** (see Section 3 of this chapter). The board evidence their approval of the accounts by the signature of one director on the balance sheet. Once this has been done, and the auditors have completed their report, the accounts are laid before the members of the company in general meeting. When the members have adopted the accounts they are sent to the Registrar for filing.

4.3 The requirement that the accounts show a true and fair view is paramount; although statute lays down numerous rules on the information to be included in the published accounts and the format of its presentation, any such rule **may be overridden** if compliance with it would prevent the accounts from showing a true and fair view.

Documents included in the accounts

4.4 The documents which **must be included by law** in the accounts laid before a general meeting of the members are:

(a) A **profit and loss account** (or an income and expenditure account in the case of a non-trading company).

(b) A **balance sheet** as at the date to which the profit and loss account is made up.

(c) A **directors' report**.

(d) An **auditors' report** addressed to the members (not to the directors) of the company.

4.5 **In addition, FRS 1 requires a cash flow statement** to be given. This statement is discussed in Chapter 10. FRS 3 has also introduced a new statement and notes, covered in Chapter 9. Here we will look at the legally required accounting statements, the profit and loss account and balance sheet.

The accounting reference period

4.6 The Companies Act 1985 contains the following rules about the length of a company's accounting period and the frequency with which it may be altered (ss 223 to 225).

(a) **Accounts must be prepared for an accounting reference period** (ARP), known as the 'financial year' of the company (whether it is a calendar year or not).

(b) **The profit and loss account should cover the ARP or a period ending not more than seven days before or after the accounting reference date.** Subsequent accounts should cover the period beginning on the day following the last day covered by the previous profit and loss account, and ending as specified above.

(c) **The balance sheet should give a true and fair view** of the state of affairs of the company as at the end of the financial year.

(d) **A company can decide its accounting reference period by giving notice to the Registrar of the date on which the accounting period will end each year.** This date will be the accounting reference date. S 225 makes provisions for the alteration of the accounting reference date.

The laying and delivery of accounts

Exam focus point

You should know paragraphs 4.7 - 4.14 from your earlier studies, so the material is unlikely to come up in the exam.

4.7 S 241 CA 1985 specifies that the directors shall lay before the company in general meeting and also deliver to the Registrar, in respect of each accounting reference period, a copy of every document comprising the accounts for that period. However, the CA 1989 has amended the CA 1985 to allow the members of private companies to elect unanimously to dispense with general meetings. This does *not*, however, exempt the company from providing accounts to members.

4.8 Unlimited companies (with some exceptions) are exempt from the duty to deliver copies of their accounts to the Registrar.

4.9 The **period allowed for laying and delivering accounts** varies, and (s 244):

(a) For **private companies**, it is **ten months** after the end of the accounting reference period.

(b) For **other (public etc) companies**, it is **seven** months.

Accounting records

4.10 S 221 requires that every company's **accounting records must:**

(a) Be sufficient to show and explain the company's transactions.

(b) Disclose with reasonable accuracy at any time the financial position of the company at that time.

(c) Enable the directors to ensure that any profit and loss account or balance sheet gives a true and fair view of the company's financial position.

4.11 S 221 also specifies that accounting records **should contain:**

(a) Day-to-day entries for money received and paid, with an explanation of why the receipts and payments occurred (ie the nature of the transactions).

(b) A record of the company's assets and liabilities.

(c) Where the company deals in goods:

(i) Statements of stocks held at the financial year end.

(ii) Statements of stocktakings on which the figures in (c)(i) are based.

(iii) With the exception of goods sold on retail, statements of all goods bought and sold identifying for each item the suppliers or customers.

4.12 S 222 specifies that the **accounting records are to be kept at the registered office** of the company or at such other place as the directors think fit, and they **should be open to inspection at all times by officers of the company.**

4.13 Also in s 222 is a **requirement for companies to preserve their accounting records:**

(a) **Private** companies, for **3 years**.
(b) **Other** companies, for **6 years**.

The classification of companies

4.14 **A company is considered to be private unless it is registered as a public company.** A major advantage for a public company is that it can raise new funds from the general public by issuing shares or loan stock; s 81 CA 1985 prohibits a private company from offering shares or debentures to the public.

Related party transactions

4.15 It is generally agreed that separate disclosure of transactions between a company and related parties may be needed if the user of the accounts is to be able to gain a full understanding of the results for the accounting period.

4.16 **Two parties are considered to be related when**:

(a) One party is able to exercise control or significant influence over the other party.

(b) Both parties are subject to common control or significant influence from the same source.

For example, companies within the same group will be related parties, or a company and its directors will be related parties.

4.17 The CA 1985 concentrates on requiring disclosure of related party transactions between a company and its directors (or persons 'connected' to directors), including loans and credit transactions.

5   THE FORMAT OF THE ACCOUNTS   Pilot paper

> ### Exam focus point
>
> If you are in a hurry or revising, skip or skim the explanations in Paragraphs 5.1 - 5.8 and go straight to the proformas in Paragraphs 5.8, 5.9 and 6.3.

The form and content of the balance sheet

5.1 The Companies Act 1985 sets out **two formats** for the balance sheet, one **horizontal and** the other **vertical. Once a company has chosen a format it must adhere to it for subsequent financial years** unless, in the opinion of the directors, there are special reasons for a change. Details of any change and the reason for it must be disclosed by note to the accounts.

5.2 Each item on the balance sheet format is referenced by letters and roman and Arabic numbers. These reference labels do not have to be shown in a company's published accounts but are given in the Act for the guidance of companies and are relevant in identifying the:

(a) Extent to which information may be combined or disclosed by note (rather than on the face of the accounts).

(b) Headings and sub-headings which may be adapted or re-arranged to suit the special nature of the company.

(c) Items which do not need to be disclosed in modified accounts for small and medium-sized companies.

5.3 The following points should be borne in mind.

(a) Any item preceded by letters or roman numbers **must** be shown on the face of the balance sheet, unless it has a nil value for both the current and the previous year.

(b) Items preceded by arabic numbers **may** be amalgamated:

(i) If their individual amounts are not material.

(ii) If amalgamation facilitates the assessment of the company's state of affairs (but then the individual items must be disclosed by note).

(c) Items preceded by arabic numbers **may** be:

(i) Adapted (eg title altered)
(ii) Re-arranged (in position)

In any case where the special nature of the company's business requires such an alteration.

(d) Any item required to be shown **may** be shown in greater detail than required by the prescribed format.

(e) A company's balance sheet (or profit and loss account) **may** include an item not otherwise covered by any of the items listed, except that the following must not be treated as assets in any company's balance sheet:

(i) Preliminary expenses.
(ii) Expenses of and commission on any issue of shares or debentures.
(iii) Costs of research.

5.4 Schedule 4 includes the following notes about the balance sheet format.

(a) **Concessions, patents, licences, trademarks,** etc (Item B I 2) may only be shown if:

(i) They were acquired at a purchase cost, and do not consist of goodwill
(ii) Or they are assets created by the company itself.

(b) **Goodwill** (Item B I 3) should be included only to the extent that it is purchased goodwill.

(c) **Own shares** (Item B III 7). CA 1985 allows a company to purchase or acquire its own shares.

(d) **Debtors** (Items C II 1 - 6). Any amounts not falling due until after more than one year should be disclosed separately.

(e) **Debenture loans** (Items E1 and H1). Convertible loans should be shown separately from other debenture loans.

(f) **Payments received (in advance) on account** (Items E3 and H3). These should be shown unless they are accounted for as deductions from the value of stocks (as in the case of progress payments for work in progress on long-term contracts).

The form and content of the profit and loss account

5.5 The Companies Act 1985 sets out two **horizontal and** two **vertical formats** for the profit and loss account. The rules applying to the balance sheet formats described above also apply to the profit and loss account.

5.6 The two different formats are distinguished by the way in which expenditure is analysed. Format 1 analyses costs by type of operation or function, whereas Format 2 analyses costs by items of expense.

5.7 The following points should be borne in mind.

(a) Every profit and loss account **must show the company's profit or loss on ordinary activities before taxation,** no matter what format is used nor how much it might be amended to suit the circumstances of a particular case.

(b) Every profit and loss account must also show, as additional items:

(i) Amounts to be **transferred to reserves,** or amounts to be withdrawn from reserves.

(ii) The amount of **dividends paid and proposed**.

(c) Amounts representing income may not be set off against items representing expenditure (just as assets and liabilities may not be 'netted off' in the balance sheet).

5.8 Below are proforma balance sheets and profit and loss accounts.

PROFORMA BALANCE SHEET (VERTICAL FORMAT)

				£	£	£
A		CALLED UP SHARE CAPITAL NOT PAID*				X
B		FIXED ASSETS				
	I	Intangible assets				
		1	Development costs	X		
		2	Concessions, patents, licences, trade marks and similar rights and assets	X		
		3	Goodwill	X		
		4	Payments on account	X		
					X	
	II	Tangible assets				
		1	Land and buildings	X		
		2	Plant and machinery	X		
		3	Fixtures, fittings, tools and equipment	X		
		4	Payments on account and assets in course of construction	X		
					X	
	III	Investments				
		1	Shares in group undertakings †	X		
		2	Loans to group undertakings †	X		
		3	Participating interest †	X		
		4	Loans to undertakings in which the company has a participating interest †	X		
		5	Other investments other than loans	X		
		6	Other loans	X		
		7	Own shares	X		
					X	
						X
C		CURRENT ASSETS				
	I	Stocks				
		1	Raw materials	X		
		2	Work in progress	X		
		3	Finished goods and goods for resale	X		
		4	Payments on account	X		
					X	
	II	Debtors				
		1	Trade debtors	X		
		2	Amounts owed by group undertakings †	X		
		3	Amounts owed by undertakings in which the company has a participating interest †	X		
		4	Other debtors	X		
		5	Called up share capital not paid*	X		
		6	Prepayments and accrued income**	X		
					X	
	III	Investments				
		1	Shares in group undertakings †	X		
		2	Own shares	X		
		3	Other investments	X		
	IV	Cash at bank and in hand			X	
					X	
D		PREPAYMENTS AND ACCRUED INCOME**			X	
E		CREDITORS: AMOUNTS FALLING DUE WITHIN ONE YEAR				
		1	Debenture loans	X		
		2	Bank loans and overdrafts	X		
		3	Payments received on account	X		

4	Trade creditors	X		
5	Bills of exchange payable	X		
6	Amounts owed to group undertakings †	X		
7	Amounts owed to undertakings in which the company has a participating interest †	X		
8	Other creditors including taxation and social security	X		
9	Accruals and deferred income ***	X		
			(X)	
F	NET CURRENT ASSETS (LIABILITIES)			X
G	TOTAL ASSETS LESS CURRENT LIABILITIES			X
H	CREDITORS: AMOUNTS FALLING DUE AFTER MORE THAN ONE YEAR			
1	Debenture loans	X		
2	Bank loans and overdrafts	X		
3	Payments received on account	X		
4	Trade creditors	X		
5	Bills of exchange payable	X		
6	Amounts owed to group undertakings †	X		
7	Amounts owed to undertakings in which the company has a participating interest †	X		
8	Other creditors including taxation and social security	X		
9	Accruals and deferred income***	X		
			(X)	

PROFORMA BALANCE SHEET (VERTICAL FORMAT)

			£	£	£
I	PROVISIONS FOR LIABILITIES AND CHARGES				
	1	Pensions and similar obligations †	X		
	2	Taxation, including deferred taxation	X		
	3	Other provisions	X		
				(X)	
J	ACCRUALS AND DEFERRED INCOME ***			(X)	
					(X)
					X
K	CAPITAL AND RESERVES				
	I	Called up share capital			X
	II	Share premium account			X
	III	Revaluation reserve			X
	IV	Other reserves			
		1 Capital redemption reserve		X	
		2 Reserve for own shares		X	
		3 Reserves provided for by the articles of association		X	
		4 Other reserves		X	
					X
	V	Profit and loss account			X
					X

(*), (**), (***). These items may be shown in either of the positions indicated.

5.9 Both vertical formats of the profit and loss account are reproduced below.

PROFORMA PROFIT AND LOSS ACCOUNT: FORMAT 1

		£	£
1	Turnover		X
2	Cost of sales ★		(X)
3	Gross profit or loss ★		X
4	Distribution costs ★	(X)	
5	Administrative expenses ★	(X)	
			(X)
			X
6	Other operating income		X
			X
7	Income from shares in group undertakings †	X	
8	Income from shares in undertakings in which the company has a participating interest †	X	
9	Income from other fixed asset investments	X	
10	Other interest receivable and similar income	X	
			X
			X
11	Amounts written off investments	(X)	
12	Interest payable and similar charges	(X)	
			(X)
	Profit or loss on ordinary activities before taxation		X
13	Tax on profit or loss on ordinary activities		(X)
14	Profit or loss on ordinary activities after taxation		X
15	Extraordinary income	X	
16	Extraordinary charges	(X)	
17	Extraordinary profit or loss	X	
18	Tax on extraordinary profit or loss	(X)	
			X
			X

PROFORMA PROFIT AND LOSS ACCOUNT: FORMAT 1 (continued)

		£	£
19	Other taxes not shown under the above items		(X)
20	Profit or loss for the financial year		X

★ These figures will all include depreciation.

PROFORMA PROFIT AND LOSS ACCOUNT: FORMAT 2

		£	£		£
1	Turnover				X
2	Change in stocks of finished goods and work in progress		(X)	or	X
3	Own work capitalised				X
4	Other operating income				X
					X
5	(a) Raw materials and consumables	(X)			
	(b) Other external charges	(X)			
			(X)		
6	Staff costs:				
	(a) wages and salaries	(X)			
	(b) social security costs	(X)			
	(c) other pension costs	(X)			
			(X)		
			(X)		
7	(a) Depreciation and other amounts written off tangible and intangible fixed assets ★★	(X)			
	(b) Exceptional amounts written off current assets	(X)			

			(X)	
8	Other operating charges		(X)	
				(X)
9	Income from shares in group undertakings †	X		
10	Income from shares in undertakings in which the company has a participating interest †	X		
11	Income from other fixed asset investments	X		
12	Other interest receivable and similar income	X		
			X	
			X	
13	Amounts written off investments	(X)		
14	Interest payable and similar charges	(X)		
				(X)
	Profit or loss on ordinary activities before taxation		X	
15	Tax on profit or loss on ordinary activities		(X)	
16	Profit or loss on ordinary activities after taxation		X	
17	Extraordinary income	X		
18	Extraordinary charges	(X)		
19	Extraordinary profit or loss	X		
20	Tax on extraordinary profit or loss	(X)		
			X	
			X	
21	Other taxes not shown under the above items		(X)	
22	Profit or loss for the financial year		X	

★★ This figure will be disclosed by way of a note in Format 1.

Note that because the captions have arabic number references, they do not have to be shown on the face of the profit and loss account but may instead be shown in the notes.

Corresponding amounts for the previous financial year

5.10 Corresponding amounts for the previous financial year **must be given for every item shown in a company's balance sheet or profit and loss account. Where** a corresponding amount for the previous year is **not properly comparable** with an amount disclosed for the current year, **the previous year's amount should be adjusted** (and details of the adjustment given in a note to the accounts).

Some items in more detail

5.11 In the balance sheet, item A and item CII5 are 'called up share capital not paid'. This item is more relevant to other countries in the EU than to Britain (remember that the Fourth Directive applies to all EU countries). However, if at the balance sheet date a company has called up some share capital and not all the called up amounts have been paid, these will be a short-term debt (see Chapter 12 on the issue of shares). This would probably be shown (if material) as item CII5. Item A should not be expected in the accounts of British companies.

5.12 Item BIII7 in the balance sheet, investments in 'own shares', refers to shares which have been bought back by the company, but which have not yet been cancelled.

5.13 'Turnover' is defined by the 1985 Act as 'the amounts derived from the provision of goods and services, falling within the company's ordinary activities, after deduction of:

(a) **Trade discounts.**
(b) **Value added tax.**
(c) **Any other taxes based on the amounts so derived'.**

5.14 **'Cost of sales'** (format 1) is **not defined,** nor are 'distribution costs', nor are 'administrative expenses'. The division of costs between these three categories is based on accepted practice.

5.15 Format 1, unlike Format 2, does not itemise depreciation and wages costs, but:

(a) Provisions for depreciation charged in the year
(b) Wages and salaries, social security costs and other pension costs

Must be disclosed separately in notes to the accounts.

5.16 The Act extends the requirements of FRS 3 about extraordinary profits or losses (see later chapters). The extraordinary profit or loss must be shown as the gross amount, with taxation on it separately disclosed. **Extraordinary items are now extremely rare**.

5.17 The profit and loss account must show profit or loss for the financial year, dividends paid and proposed and transfers to reserves. This means inevitably, that retained profit or loss for the financial year will also be disclosed. There is **no requirement**, however, **to show on the face of the profit and loss account**:

	£
Retained profit for the financial year	X
Profit and loss account brought forward	X
Profit and loss account carried forward	X

However, this well-established practice 'ties together' the information in the profit and loss account with the notes to the balance sheet about movements on reserves and so is often used.

5.18 In itemising staff costs, wages and salaries consist of gross amounts (net pay plus deductions) and social security costs comprise employer's National Insurance contributions.

6 NOTES TO THE ACCOUNTS

6.1 Part III of the Fourth Schedule deals with notes to the balance sheet and profit and loss account. These are sub-divided into:

(a) Disclosure of accounting policies.
(b) Notes to the balance sheet.
(c) Notes to the profit and loss account.

6.2 A note to the accounts must disclose the accounting policies adopted by the company (including the policy used to account for depreciation or the fall in value of assets). This gives statutory backing to the disclosure requirement in FRS 18. Companies must also now state that all relevant accounting standards have been complied with and if not, what the departures are and the reasons for the departure.

6.3 The following example shows a *pro forma* profit and loss account and balance sheet with the required notes covering your syllabus. These notes are expanded in the subsequent chapters on different accounting standards and disclosures.

STANDARD PLC
PROFIT AND LOSS ACCOUNT FOR THE YEAR ENDED
31 DECEMBER 20X5

	Notes	£'000	£'000
Turnover	2		X
Cost of sales			X
Gross profit			X
Distribution costs			X
Administrative expenses			X
Operating profit	3		X
Income from fixed asset investments			X
			X
Interest payable and similar charges	6		X
Profit on ordinary activities before taxation			X
Tax on profit on ordinary activities	7		X
Profit on ordinary activities after taxation			X
Dividend paid and proposed	8	X	
Transfer to general reserve	19	X	
			X
Retained profit for the financial year			X

STANDARD PLC
BALANCE SHEET AS AT 31 DECEMBER 20X5

	Notes	£'000	£'000
Fixed assets			
Intangible assets	9		X
Tangible assets	10		X
Fixed asset investments	11		X
			X
Current assets			
Stocks	12	X	
Debtors	13	X	
Cash at bank and in hand		X	
		X	
Creditors: amounts falling due within one year	14	X	
Net current assets			X
Total assets less current liabilities			X
Creditors: amounts falling due after more than one year	16		X
Accruals and deferred income	17		X
			X
Capital and reserves			
Called up share capital	18		X
Share premium account	19		X
Revaluation reserve	19		X
General reserve	19		X
Profit and loss account	19		X
			X

Approved by the board on ....

.... Director

The notes on pages XX to XX form part of these accounts.

NOTES TO THE ACCOUNTS

1   **Accounting policies**

(a)   These accounts have been prepared under the historical cost convention of accounting and in accordance with applicable accounting standards.

(b)   Depreciation has been provided on a straight line basis in order to write off the cost of depreciable fixed assets over their estimated useful lives. The rates used are:

Buildings	X%
Plant and machinery	X%
Fixtures and fittings	X%

(c)   Stocks have been valued at the lower of cost and net realisable value.

(d)   Development expenditure relating to specific projects intended for commercial exploitation is carried forward and amortised over the period expected to benefit commencing with the period in which related sales are first made. Expenditure on pure and applied research is written off as incurred.

Notes

(a)   Accounting policies are those followed by the company and used in arriving at the figures shown in the profit and loss accounts and balance sheet.

(b)   CA 1985 requires policies in respect of depreciation and foreign currency translation to be included. Others are required by accounting standards insofar as they apply to the company.

2   **Turnover**

Turnover represents amounts derived from the provision of goods and services falling within the company's ordinary activities, after deduction of trade discounts, value added tax and any other tax based on the amounts so derived.

	Turnover	*Profit before tax*
Principal activities	£'000	£'000
Electrical components	X	X
Domestic appliances	X	X
	X	X
Geographical analysis		
UK	X	
America	X	
Europe	X	
	X	

Notes

(a)   Directors are to decide on classification and then apply them consistently.

(b)   Geographical analysis must be by destination of sale.

(c)   If the directors believe this disclosure to be seriously prejudicial to the business the information need not be disclosed.

(d)   The profit after tax figures are only required by SSAP 25 (see Chapter 14) for larger companies.

3 Operating profit

Operating profit is stated after charging:

	£'000
Depreciation	X
Amortisation	X
Hire of plant and machinery (SSAP 21: see Chapter 6)	X
Auditors' remuneration	X
Exceptional items	X
Directors' emoluments (see note 4)	X
Staff costs (see note 5)	X
Research and development	X

Notes

Separate totals are required to be disclosed for:

(a) Audit fees and expenses
(b) Fees paid to auditors for non-audit work

This disclosure is not required for small or medium-sized companies.

Question 1

Alvis Ltd receives an invoice in respect of the current year from its auditors made up as follows.

	£
Audit of accounts	10,000
Taxation computation and advice	1,500
Travelling expenses: audit	1,100
Consultancy fees charged by another firm of accountants	1,600
	14,200

What figure should be disclosed as auditors' remuneration in the notes to the profit and loss account?

Answer

	£
Audit of accounts	10,000
Expenses	1,100
Taxation computation and advice	1,500
	12,600

The consultancy fees are not received by the auditors.

---

4 Directors' emoluments

New requirements for the disclosure of directors' remuneration were introduced by *The Company Accounts (Disclosure of Directors' Emoluments) Regulations 1997* (SI 1997/570). A distinction is made between listed/AIM companies and unlisted companies.

	£'000
Directors	
Aggregate emoluments	X
Gains made on exercise of share options (listed/AIM company only)	X
Amounts receivable (unlisted company: excludes shares) under long-term incentive schemes	X
Company pension contributions	X
Compensation for loss of office	X
Sums paid to third parties for directors' services	X
	X
Highest paid director	
Aggregate emoluments, gains on share options exercised and benefits under long-term incentive schemes (listed/AIM company only)	X
Company pension contributions	X
Accrued pension	X
	X

Notes

(a) All companies must disclose aggregate emoluments paid to/receivable by a director in respect of 'qualifying services'.

(b) **Unlisted companies do not need to disclose:**

(i) The amount of gains made when directors exercise options, only the number of directors who exercised options.

(ii) The net value of any assets that comprise shares, which would otherwise be disclosed in respect of assets received under long-term incentive schemes, but only the number of directors in respect of whose qualifying service shares were receivable under long-term incentive schemes.

(c) For listed companies, the disclosure requirements for share options do not refer to qualifying services, so gains made on the exercise of shares before appointment must therefore be included.

(d) Information about the highest paid director only needs to be given if the aggregate of emoluments, gains on exercise of share options, and amounts receivable by the directors under long-term incentive schemes is > £200,000. For unlisted companies, state whether the highest paid direct or exercised any share options and/or received any shares in respect of qualifying services under a long-term incentive scheme.

(e) The details relating to pensions are beyond the scope of your syllabus.

(f) **Definitions**

(i) **Emoluments.** Salary, fees, bonuses, expense allowances, money value of other benefits, except share options granted, pension amounts and amounts paid under a long-term incentive scheme. Includes 'golden hellos'.

(ii) **Qualifying services.** Services as a director of a company and services in connection with the management of the company's affairs.

(iii) **Listed company.** A company whose securities have been admitted to the Official List of the Stock Exchange (or AIM).

(iv) **Long-term incentive schemes.** Any agreement or arrangement under which money or other assets become receivable by a director and where one or more of the qualifying candidates relating to service cannot be fulfilled in a single financial year. Bonuses relating to an individual year, termination payments and retirement benefits are excluded.

5   **Employee information**

(a)   The **average number of persons** employed during the year was:

By product

Electrical components	X
Domestic appliances	X
	X

By activity

Production	X
Selling	X
Administration	X
	X

(b)   **Employment costs**

	£'000
Aggregate wages and salaries	X
Social security costs	X
Other pension costs	X
	X

Notes

(a)   Classification to be decided by the directors and applied consistently year on year. Must state whether executive directors are included or excluded.

(b)   Social security costs are employer's NI.

(c)   Other pension costs are contributions by the company to a pension scheme.

(d)   **Definitions**

   (i)   **Staff costs.** Costs incurred in respect of persons employed under contract of service. They include part time employees under contract.

   (ii)   **Average number**

      (1)   Ascertain number employed under contracts each week.
      (2)   Aggregate these numbers.
      (3)   Divide by the number of months in the period.

      Include those persons working wholly or mainly overseas.

Question 2

During a 12 month accounting period, the administration department of Azrina Ltd had the following employees.

(a)   12 worked overseas, of whom 1 returned to work in the UK and 2 resigned after 6 months.

(b)   30 UK employees (including 1 executive director).

(c)   20 part-timers who only worked over the three months' summer season and of whom only 8 were employed under a service contract.

Determine the average number of employees (assuming executive directors are included) to be disclosed for the administration department.

Note. The employee information note may include or exclude executive directors and the company must state which option they have chosen.

Answer

Average number

	No
Overseas (12 − (2 × ½))	11
UK employees	30
Contract part-timers	2
(8 for 3 months, which averages out at 2 per year)	
	43

6   Interest payable and similar charges

	£'000
Interest payable on:	
Bank overdrafts and loans	X
Other loans	X
Lease and HP finance charges allocated for the year	X
	X

Note

Similar charges might include arrangement fees for loans.

7   Tax on profits on ordinary activities

	£'000
UK corporation tax (at x% on taxable profit for the year)	X
Transfer to/from deferred taxation	X
Under/over provision in prior years	X
Unrelieved overseas taxation	X
	X

Note

The rate of tax must be disclosed (FRS 16: see Chapter 8).

8   Dividends

			£'000
Preference:	8% paid		X
Ordinary:	interim	3.5p paid	X
	final	7.0p proposed	X
			X

Note

Show for each class of share distinguishing between amounts paid and proposed. Only advisable (and not required) to show amount per share. If the aggregate *proposed* dividend is not shown in the note to the accounts, it must be shown on the face of the P&L a/c.

9   Intangible fixed assets

	Development expenditure £'000
Cost	
At 1 January 20X5	X
Expenditure	X
At 31 December 20X5	**X**
Amortisation	
At 1 January 20X5	X
Charge for year	X
At 31 December 20X5	**X**
Net book value at 31 December 20X5	**X**
Net book value 31 December 20X4	**X**

Note

The above disclosure should be given for each intangible asset.

10 **Tangible fixed assets**

	Freehold land and Buildings £'000	Leasehold land and Buildings Long leases £'000	Leasehold land and Buildings Short leases £'000	Plant and machinery £'000	Fixtures and fittings £'000	Total £'000
Cost (or valuation)						
At 1 Jan 20X5	X	X	X	X	X	X
Additions	X	-	X	-	X	X
Revaluation	X	-	-	-	-	X
Disposals	(X)	-	-	(X)	(X)	(X)
At 31 Dec 20X5	X	X	X	X	X	X
Depreciation						
At 1 Jan 20X5	X	X	X	X	X	X
Charge for year	X	X	X	X	X	X
Revaluation	(X)	-	-	-	-	(X)
Disposals	(X)	-	-	(X)	(X)	(X)
At 31 Dec 20X5	X	X	X	X	X	X
Net book value						
At 31 Dec 20X5	X	X	X	X	X	X
At 31 Dec 20X4	X	X	X	X	X	X

Notes

(a) Long leases are ≥ 50 years unexpired at balance sheet date.

(b) Classification by asset type represents arabic numbers from formats.

(c) Motor vehicles (unless material) are usually included within plant and machinery.

(d) Revaluations in the year: state for each asset revalued:

   (i)   Method of valuation

   (ii) Date of valuation

   (iii) The historical cost equivalent of the above information as if the asset had not been revalued

11 **Fixed asset investments**

	£'000
Shares at cost	
At 1 January 20X5	X
Additions	X
Disposals	(X)
At 31 December 20X5	X

The market value (in aggregate) of the listed investments is £X.

Note

An AIM investment is *not* a listed investment. All stock exchanges of repute allowed. Aggregate market value (ie profits less losses) to be disclosed if material.

12 **Stocks**

	£'000
Raw materials and consumables	X
Work in progress	X
Finished goods	X
	X

The replacement cost of stock is £X higher than its book value.

13 **Debtors**

	£'000
Trade debtors	X
Other debtors	X
Prepayments and accrued income	X
	X

Of this amount £X of recoverable ACT is recoverable after more than one year.

14 **Creditors: amounts falling due within one year**

	£'000
Debenture loans: 8% stock 20X9	X
Bank loans and overdrafts	X
Trade creditors	X
Other creditors including taxation and social security (see note 15)	X
Accruals and deferred income	X
	X

The bank loans and overdraft are secured by a floating charge over the company's assets.

Notes

(a) Give details of security given for all secured creditors.

(b) Include the current portion of instalment creditors here.

15 **Other creditors including taxation and social security**

	£'000
UK corporation tax	X
Social security	X
Proposed dividend	X
	X

Notes

(a) Liabilities for taxation and social security must be shown separately from other creditors.

(b) Dividend liabilities to be disclosed separately.

16 **Creditors: amounts falling due after more than one year**

	£'000
8½% unsecured loan stock 20Y9	X

Notes

(a) Very long-term creditors:

    (i) Disclose the aggregate amount of debentures and other loans:

        (1) Payable after more than five years

        (2) Payable by instalments, any of which fall due after more than five years

(ii)   For (1) and (2) disclose the terms of repayment and rates of interest.

(b)   Debentures during the year, disclose:

(i)   Class issued

(ii)   For each class

(1)   Amount issued

(2)   Consideration received

17   Accruals and deferred income

	£'000
Government grants received	X
Credited to profit and loss account	(X)
	X

Note

Alternative presentation if not included as part of creditors, which saves dividing the accruals or deferred income amount between within and greater than one year.

18   Called up share capital

	£1 ordinary shares £'000	*6.2% preference shares* £'000
Authorised		
Number	X	X
Value	X	X
Allotted		
Number	X	X
Value	X	X

Notes

(a)   Disclose number and nominal value for each class, both authorised and allotted.

(b)   *Shares issued during the year*, disclose:

(i)   Classes allotted

(ii)   For each class

(1)   Number and aggregate nominal value allotted

(2)   Consideration received

19   Reserves

	Share premium £'000	*Revaluation* £'000	*General* £'000	*Profit and loss* £'000
At 1 January 20X5	X	X	X	X
Retained profit for the year	-	-	-	X
Revaluation	-	X	-	-
Transfers	-	-	X	X
At 31 December 2095	X	X	X	X

20   Contingent liabilities

Note: governed by FRS 12 (see Chapter 11).

21   Post balance sheet events

Note: governed by SSAP 17 (see Chapter 11).

BPP
PUBLISHING

22 **Capital commitments**

	£'000
Amounts contracted but not provided for	X

Note

This figure is not included in the balance sheet as it is simply a note of future obligations to warn users of likely future capital expenditure.

Question 3

The best way to learn the format and content of published accounts and notes is to practice questions. However, you must start somewhere, so try to learn the above formats, then close this text and write out on a piece of paper:

(a) A standard layout for a balance sheet and profit and loss account
(b) A list of notes to these accounts which are generally required

Filing exemptions for small and medium-sized companies

6.4 Small and medium-sized companies are allowed certain 'filing exemptions': **the accounts they lodge with the Registrar of companies, and which are available for public inspection, need not contain all the information which must be published by large companies.**

6.5 This concession allows small and medium-sized companies to reduce the amount of information about themselves available to, say, trading rivals. It **does *not* relieve them of their obligation to prepare full statutory accounts, because all companies,** regardless of their size, **must prepare full accounts for approval by the shareholders.**

6.6 Small and medium-sized companies must therefore balance the expense of preparing two different sets of accounts against the advantage of publishing as little information about themselves as possible. Many such companies may decide that the risk of assisting their competitors is preferable to the expense of preparing accounts twice over, and will therefore not take advantage of the filing exemptions.

6.7 A company qualifies as a **small or medium sized** company in a particular financial year **if,** for that year, **two or more** of the following **conditions are satisfied.**

	Small	Medium
(a) **Turnover** (must be adjusted proportionately in the case of an accounting period greater than or less than 12 months)	≤ £2.8m	≤ £11.2m
(b) **Balance sheet total** (total assets before deduction of any liabilities; A-D in the statutory balance sheet format)	≤ £1.4m	≤ £5.6m
(c) **Average number of employees**	≤ 50	≤ 250

6.8 **Public companies can never be entitled to the filing exemptions whatever their size;** nor can banking and insurance companies; nor can companies which are authorised persons under the Financial Services Act 1986; nor can members of groups containing any of these exceptions.

6.9 The form and content of the abbreviated accounts are contained in separate schedules of the Act: Schedule 8A for small companies and Schedule 245A for medium-sized companies. **Small companies may file an abbreviated balance sheet** showing only the items which, in the statutory format, are denoted by a letter or Roman number. They are **not required to file either a profit and loss account or a directors' report. No details need be filed of the emoluments of directors. Only limited notes to the accounts are required.**

6.10 **The only exemptions allowed to medium-sized companies are in the profit and loss account. Turnover need not be analysed between a company's different classes of businesses, or its different geographical markets.** The profit and loss account may begin with the figure of gross profit (or loss) by amalgamation of items 1, 2, 3 and 6 in Format 1, or of items 1 to 5 in Format 2.

6.11 If a small or medium-sized company files 'abbreviated accounts' a statement by the directors must appear above the director's signature on the balance sheet. The statement must be that the financial statements have been prepared in accordance with the special provisions of Part VII of the Act relating to small or (as the case may be) medium-sized companies.

6.12 Abbreviated accounts **must be accompanied by a special report** of the company's auditors stating that, in their opinion, the directors are entitled to deliver abbreviated accounts and those accounts are properly prepared. The text of the auditors' report on the full statutory accounts must be included as a part of this special report. A true and fair view is still required, however; if the shorter-form financial statements fail to give a true and fair view because of the use of exemptions, or for any other reason, the auditors should qualify their audit report in the normal way.

Summary financial statements

6.13 CA 1989 amended CA 1985 so that **listed companies need not send all their members their full financial statements but can instead send them summary financial statements** (SFSs). All members who want to receive full financial statements are still entitled to them, however.

6.14 **An SFS must**:

(a) State that it is only a summary of information in the company's annual accounts and the directors' report.

(b) Contain a statement by the company's auditors of their opinion as to whether the summary financial statement is consistent with those accounts and that report and complies with the relevant statutory requirements.

(c) State whether the auditors' report on the annual accounts was unqualified or qualified, and if it was qualified set out the report in full together with any further material needed to understand the qualification.

6.15 SFSs must be derived from the company's annual accounts and the directors' report and the form and content are specified by regulations made by the Secretary of State.

The key figures from the full statements must be included along with the review of the business and future developments shown in the directors' report. Comparative figures must be shown.

7 DIRECTORS' REPORT

7.1 Attached to every balance sheet there must be a directors' report (s 234 CA 1985). (The Companies Act 1985 allows small companies exemption from delivering a copy of the directors' report to the Registrar of companies.) CA 1985 states specifically what information must be included in the directors' report (as well as what must be shown in the accounts themselves or in notes to the accounts as we saw above).

7.2 The directors' report is **largely a narrative report,** but certain figures must be included in it. **The purpose of the report is to give the users of accounts a more complete picture of the state of affairs of the company**. Narrative descriptions should help to 'put flesh on' the skeleton of details provided by the figures of the accounts themselves. However, in practice the directors' report is often a rather dry and uninformative document, perhaps because it must be verified by the company's external auditors, whereas the chairman's report need not be.

7.3 The directors' report is **expected to contain a fair review of the development of the business of the company during that year and of its position at the end of it.** No guidance is given on the form of the review, nor the amount of detail it should go into.

7.4 S 234 CA 1985 also requires the report to **show the** amount, if any, **recommended** for **dividend**.

7.5 Other disclosure requirements are as follows.

(a) The **principal activities** of the company in the course of the financial year, and any significant changes in those activities during the year.

(b) Where significant, an estimate should be provided of the **difference between the book value of land held as fixed assets and its realistic market value.**

(c) **Disabled persons.** Information about the **company's policy** for:

(i) Giving fair consideration to applications for jobs from disabled persons.

(ii) Continuing to employ (and train) people who have become disabled whilst employed by the company.

(iii) Training, career development and promotion of disabled employees.

(Companies with fewer than 250 employees are exempt from (c).)

(d) The names of persons who were **directors** at any time during the financial year.

(e) For those persons who were directors at the year end, the **interests of each** (or of their spouse or infant children) in shares or debentures of the company:

(i) At the beginning of the year, or at the date of appointment as director, if this occurred during the year.

(ii) At the end of the year.

If a director has no such interests at either date, this fact must be disclosed. (The information in (e) may be shown as a note to the accounts instead of in the directors' report.)

(f) **Political and charitable contributions made,** if these together exceeded more than £200 in the year, giving:

(i) Separate totals for political contributions and charitable contributions.

(ii) The amount of each separate political contribution exceeding £200, and the name of the recipient.

(g) Particulars of any **important events** affecting the company or any of its subsidiaries which have occurred since the end of the financial year (significant 'post-balance sheet events').

(h) An indication of likely **future developments** in the business of the company and of its subsidiaries.

(i) An indication of the activities (if any) of the company and its subsidiaries in the field of **research and development**.

(j) Particulars of **purchases** (if any) of **its own shares** by the company during the year, including reasons for the purchase.

(k) Particulars of **other acquisitions of its own shares** during the year (perhaps because shares were forfeited or surrendered, or because its shares were acquired by the company's nominee or with its financial assistance).

7.6 Note that the 1985 Act requires details of important post balance sheet events to be explained in the directors' report. The requirements of SSAP 17 (see Chapter 11), which should be considered in conjunction with the 1985 Act, are either for the accounts themselves to be altered, or for the amount of the adjustment to results to be disclosed in a note to the accounts.

7.7 A further requirement relating to the directors' report is contained in the Employment Act 1982. The requirement relates to any company **employing on average more than 250 people each week**. The **directors** of such a company **must state in their report what action** has been **taken** during the financial year **to introduce, maintain or develop arrangements aimed at:**

(a) **Employee information**, providing employees systematically with information on matters of concern to them.

(b) **Employee consultation**, consulting employees or their representatives on a regular basis so that the views of employees can be taken into account in making decisions which are likely to affect their interest.

(c) **Employee involvement**, encouraging the involvement of employees in the company's performance through an employees' share scheme or by some other means.

(d) **Company performance**, achieving common **awareness** on the part of all employees of the financial and economic factors affecting the performance of the company.

7.8 It should be noted that **these provisions do not mean that any such action must be taken, only that if it is taken it must be disclosed** in the directors' report. Moreover, wide discretion is granted to the directors in deciding what needs to be disclosed, since no definition is given of such terms as 'matters of concern to them' or 'decisions which are likely to affect their interests'.

Creditor payment policy

7.9 A recent amendment to CA 1985 requires companies to disclose details of the company's policy on the payment of creditors. This **disclosure requirement applies if:**

(a) **The company was at any time during the year a public company.**

    (b) **The company did not qualify as a small or medium-sized company under s 247 and was at any time within the year a member of a group of which the parent company was a public company.**

7.10 The **directors' report needs to state**, with respect to the financial year immediately following that covered by the report:

    (a) Whether in respect of some or all of its suppliers (ie those classified as 'trade creditors') it is the company's policy to follow **any code or standard on payment practice**, and if so, the name of the code or standard, and the place where information about, and copies of, the code or standard can be obtained;

    (b) whether in respect of some or all of its suppliers, it is the company's **policy to:**

        (i)   **Settle the terms of payment** with those suppliers when agreeing the terms of each transaction.

        (ii)   Ensure that those suppliers are **made aware** of the terms of payment.

        (iii) **Abide** by the terms of payment.

    (c) **Where** the company's policy is **not as mentioned** in either of the two paragraphs **above,** in respect of some or all of its suppliers, **what its policy is** with respect to the payment of those suppliers.

If the company's policy is different from different suppliers or classes of suppliers, the directors' must identify the suppliers or classes of suppliers to which the different policies apply.

8   AUDITORS' REPORT AND CHAIRMAN'S REPORT

The auditors' report

8.1 **The annual accounts of a limited company must be audited by persons independent of the company.** In practice, this means that the members of the company appoint a firm of Chartered Accountants or Chartered Certified Accountants to investigate the accounts prepared by the company **and report as to whether or not they show a true and fair** view of the company's results for the year and its financial position at the end of the year. **The audit report is governed by auditing regulations.**

8.2 When the auditors have completed their work they must prepare a report explaining the work that they have done and the opinion they have formed. In simple cases they will be able to report that they have carried out their work in accordance with auditing standards and that, in their opinion, the accounts show a true and fair view and are properly prepared in accordance with the Companies Act 1985. This is described as an **unqualified audit report.**

8.3 Sometimes the auditors may disagree with the directors on a point concerned with the accounts. If they are unable to persuade the directors to change the accounts, and if the item at issue is material, it is the auditors' duty to prepare a **qualified report**, setting out the matter(s) on which they disagree with the directors.

8.4 The financial statements to which the auditors refer in their report comprise the:

    (a) **Profit and loss account.**
    (b) **Balance sheet.**
    (c) **Notes to the accounts.**
    (d) **Cash flow statement.**

In addition they **must consider whether the information given in the directors' report is consistent with the audited accounts**. If they believes it is not consistent then they must state that fact in their report. Note that the cash flow statement is not mentioned outright.

8.5 The auditors' report is included as a part of the company's published accounts. It is **addressed to the members** of the company (not to the directors).

The chairman's report

8.6 Most large companies include a **chairman's report** in their published financial statements. This is **purely voluntary** as there is no statutory requirement to do so.

8.7 The chairman's report is not governed by any regulations and is often unduly optimistic. Listed companies now include an Operating and Financial Review (OFR) in the annual report: see Chapter 22. This has been introduced to encourage more meaningful analysis.

Question 4

In between now and your examination obtain as many sets of company accounts or annual reports as you can. (You may like to use the Financial Times Free Annual Report Service for this purpose – look for the advert on the share price pages of the FT for information.) Read through the whole of each report and compare the format of the accounts and the disclosure of the notes with the contents of this chapter, and with the rest of this Study Text.

Chapter roundup

- This has been a long and detailed chapter but not a conceptually demanding one. You must have a **firm grasp** of its contents before proceeding to the remainder of this second section of the Study Text, in which the statutory and professional requirements of each area of the accounts are discussed in turn.

- You need to learn the *Companies Act formats* and the *notes* required, but remember that the easiest way to do this is to **practise questions**, and read real sets of accounts.

- You will appreciate the *contents* of the auditors' report, the directors' report, the chairman's report if you **read some real annual reports**.

Quick quiz

1 The two bedrocks of accounting are:

    A   Accruals, prudence
    B   Prudence, consistency
    C   Consistency, accruals
    D   Going concern, accruals

2 An estimation technique is the method used to establish the estimated monetary amounts associated with the selected measurement bases.

    True   ☐

    False   ☐

3 What does CA 1985 say about a 'true and fair view'?

4 What points are made by the legal opinions sought regarding a 'true and fair view'?

5 The period allowed for layout and delivery of accounts.

- Private companies .... months
- Public companies............. months

6   Turnover is defined by the Companies Act as the amounts derived from the provision of goods and services falling within the company's ordinary activities after deduction of which of the following.

    A   Carriage inwards
    B   Trade discounts
    C   VAT
    D   Carriage out
    E   Other sales taxes
    F   Stock losses

7

	Small company	*Medium company*
Turnover	....	....
Total assets	....	....
Average number of employees	....	....

8   List eight disclosures required in the directors report.

9   Companies must disclose their creditor payment policy in the financial statements.

    True   ☐

    False   ☐

10   The chairman's report is a statutory requirement.

    True   ☐

    False   ☐

11   Explain the accruals basis of accounting in no more than fifty words.

Quick quiz answers

1   D (See paras 2.3 and 2.4)

2   True (2.37)

3   See para 3.1

4   See para 3.4 and 3.5

5   Ten, seven (4.9)

6   B, C and E (4.13)

7

	Small company	*Medium company*
Turnover	≤£2.8m	≤£11.2m
Total assets	≤£1.4m	≤£5.6m
Average number of employees	≤50	≤250
		(5.7)

8   See paragraphs 7.4 and 7.5

9   False, Only if they are a public company or they fail to meet the requirements for small or medium companies. (6.10)

10   False. (8.6)

11   See para 2.6

Now try the question below from the Exam Question Bank

Number	Level	Marks	Time
3	Full exam	25	45 mins

Chapter 4

FIXED ASSETS: TANGIBLE ASSETS

Topic list	Syllabus reference
1 Statutory provisions relating to all fixed assets	3(b)
2 FRS 15 *Tangible fixed assets*	3(b)
3 Revaluation	3(b)
4 SSAP 19 *Accounting for investment properties*	3(b)
5 SSAP 4 *Accounting for government grants*	3(b)

Introduction

In Section 1, before we look at individual accounting standards, we will review the **Companies Act disclosure requirements** relating to fixed assets. Refer back to Chapter 3 to put these requirements into context. Remember that these provisions apply to *all* fixed assets.

You should already have examined the principles of **depreciation** in your earlier studies. If you are in any doubt about the possible methods of depreciation, refer back to your Paper 1.1 study material.

The other two standards covered in this chapter are on **investment properties** and **government grants**. These are quite straightforward. Develop a sound knowledge of their main provisions and make sure that you can do the relevant exercises.

Study Guide

- Define the initial cost of a fixed asset (including a self-constructed asset) and apply this to various examples of expenditures distinguishing between capital and revenue items.

- Describe, and be able to identify, subsequent expenditures that may be capitalised.

- State and appraise the effects of FRS 15's rules for the revaluation of fixed assets.

- Account for gains and losses on the disposal of revalued assets.

- Calculate depreciation on:

    - Revalued assets, and
    - Assets that have two or more major components.

- Apply the provisions of SSAP 4 Government Grants.

- Discuss why the treatment of investment properties should differ from other properties.

- Apply the requirements of SSAP 19 'Accounting for Investment Properties'.

Exam guide

This is a key area and quite straightforward. Tangible fixed assets may come up as part of a question or subject matter from two or more sections of this chapter may be tested in a full question.

BPP PUBLISHING

1 STATUTORY PROVISIONS RELATING TO ALL FIXED ASSETS

1.1 The standard balance sheet format of CA 1985 divides fixed assets into three categories:

   (a) **Intangible assets** (BI in the CA 1985 format).
   (b) **Tangible assets** (BII).
   (c) **Investments** (BIII).

1.2 In this chapter we will deal with the general rules of the CA 1985 relating to *all* fixed assets. These may be considered under two headings.

   (a) **Valuation:** the amounts at which fixed assets should be stated in the balance sheet.

   (b) **Disclosure:** the information that should be disclosed in the accounts regarding:

   •   valuation of fixed assets
   •   movements on fixed asset accounts during the year.

Valuation of fixed assets

Cost

1.3 The two key ways of acquiring a tangible fixed asset are either by purchase or by self-production.

1.4 **Purchased asset: Its cost is simply the purchase price plus any expenses incidental to its acquisition.**

1.5 **Asset produced by a company for its own use:** This should be included at 'production cost' which *must* include:

   •   **cost of raw materials**

   •   **consumables** used

   •   other **attributable direct costs** (such as labour)

   Production cost **may** additionally **include:**

   •   **a reasonable proportion of indirect costs**

   •   **interest** on any capital borrowed to **finance production** of the asset.

   The amount of capitalised interest must however be disclosed in a note to the accounts.

Depreciation

1.6 The **'cost'** of any fixed asset having a limited economic life, whether purchase price or production cost, **must be reduced by provisions for depreciation** calculated to write off the cost, less any residual value, **systematically over the period of the asset's useful life.** This very general requirement is supplemented by the more detailed provisions of FRS 15 *Tangible fixed assets* which is dealt with in the next section.

1.7 Any provision for **depreciation** should be disclosed on the **face of the profit and loss account or by way of note.** Where a provision becomes **no longer necessary,** because the conditions giving rise to it have altered, it should be **written back**, and again **disclosure** should be made.

Fixed assets valuation: alternative accounting rules

1.8 Although the Companies Act 1985 maintains **historical cost** principles as the **normal basis** for the preparation of accounts, **alternative bases** allowing for **revaluations** and **current cost accounting are permitted provided that**:

(a) The **items affected** and the **basis of valuation** are **disclosed** in a note to the accounts;

(b) The **historical cost** in the current and previous years is **separately disclosed** in the balance sheet or in a note to the accounts. Alternatively, the difference between the revalued amount and historical cost may be disclosed.

> ### KEY TERM
>
> Using the **alternative accounting rules,** the appropriate value of any fixed asset (ie its **current cost or market value**), rather than its purchase price or production cost, **may be included in the balance sheet**.

1.9 Here is a diagram to help clarify the options available under CA 1985, schedule 4.

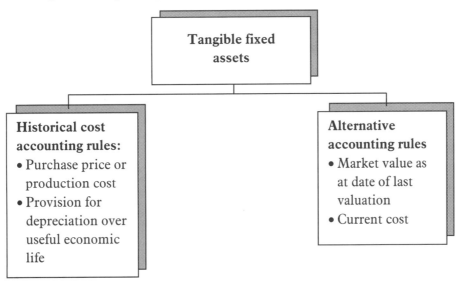

1.10 **Where appropriate, depreciation may be provided on the basis of the new valuation(s),** such depreciation being referred to in the Companies Act 1985 as the '**adjusted amount**' of depreciation. For profit and loss account purposes, **FRS 15** (see below) specifically states that depreciation must be charged on the **revalued amount** and that the *whole* charge must be taken to the **profit and loss account**.

Revaluation reserve

> ### KEY TERM
>
> Where the value of any fixed asset is determined by using the **alternative accounting rules,** the amount of **profit or loss arising** must be credited or (as the case may be) debited to a separate reserve, the **revaluation reserve**.

Uses of revaluation reserve

1.11 The Companies Act 1985 states that an amount may be transferred from the revaluation reserve to the profit and loss account ie debit revaluation reserve and credit profit and loss reserve, if the amount:

- was previously charged to profit and loss account
- represents realised profit
- relates to taxation on a profit or loss taken to the revaluation reserve, or
- is no longer necessary for the valuation method used.

1.12 The revaluation reserve may also be used for a bonus issue of shares. No other debits to revaluation reserve are allowed.

1.13 The amount of a revaluation reserve must be shown under a **separate sub-heading** in **position KIII** on the **balance sheet**. However, the reserve need not necessarily be called a 'revaluation reserve'.

Question 1

Studivation Ltd revalued a freehold building on 31 March 20X5 to £300,000. The original purchase cost 10 years ago was £180,000. Studivation Ltd depreciates freehold buildings over 40 years.

Show the accounting entries for the revaluation and the depreciation charge for the year ended 31 March 20X6.

Answer

(a)	*Revaluation*		£	£
	DEBIT	Fixed asset cost (£300,000 - £180,000)	120,000	
	DEBIT	Accumulated depreciation (£180,000 ÷ 40 × 10)	45,000	
	CREDIT	Revaluation reserve		165,000
(b)	*Depreciation charge*			
	DEBIT	Depreciation (£300,000 ÷ 30)	10,000	
	CREDIT	Accumulated depreciation		10,000

Fixed assets: companies act disclosures

1.14 **Notes to the accounts** must show, for **each class** of **fixed assets**, an analysis of the **movements** on both **costs** and **depreciation provisions**. Refer back to the note on fixed assets in Chapter 3.

1.15 Where any **fixed assets** of a company (other than listed investments) are included in the accounts at an alternative accounting valuation, the **following information** must also be given:

(a) The **years** (so far as they are known to the directors) in which the assets were **severally valued** and the **several values**.

(b) In the case of assets that have been **valued** during the **financial period**, the **names** of the **persons** who valued them or particulars of their **qualifications** for doing so and (whichever is stated) the **bases of valuation** used by them.

1.16 A **note to the accounts** must **classify land and buildings** under the headings of:

(a) **Freehold property**.

(b) **Leasehold property**, distinguishing between:

(i) **Long leaseholds**, in which the **unexpired term** of the lease at the balance sheet date is **not less than 50 years**.

(ii) **Short leaseholds** which are all leaseholds other than long leaseholds.

2 FRS 15 TANGIBLE FIXED ASSETS

> **KEY TERM**
>
> **Tangible fixed assets** have **physical substance** and are held for:
>
> - use in the production or supply of goods or services
> - rental to others
> - administration purposes
>
> on a **continuing basis** in the **reporting entity's activities**.
>
> They are held to **earn revenue** by their **use, not** from their **resale**.

Objective

2.1 FRS 15 deals with accounting for the initial measurement, valuation and depreciation of tangible fixed assets. It also sets out the information that should be disclosed to enable readers to understand the impact of the accounting policies adopted in relation to these issues.

Initial measurement

> **Exam focus point**
>
> Initial measurement and capitalisation of subsequent expenditure were tested in the December 2001 paper.

2.2 A tangible fixed asset should **initially be measured at cost**.

> **KEY TERM**
>
> **Cost** is purchase price plus any costs directly attributable to bringing the asset into working condition for its intended use.

Directly attributable costs

2.3 Directly attributable costs include:

- **Direct labour** costs of using **own employees**

- **Acquisition costs,** eg stamp duty, import duties

- Cost of **site preparation** and clearance

- Initial **delivery and handling** costs

- **Installation** costs

- **Professional fees** eg legal and architect's fees

- The estimated cost of **dismantling and removing** the asset and restoring the site, to the extent that it is recognised as a provision under FRS 12 *Provisions, contingent liabilities and contingent assets* (discussed in Chapter 11).

2.4 Administration and other general overhead costs and employee costs not related to the specific tangible fixed asset are not directly attributable costs.

2.5 In general terms, directly attributable costs can be regarded as incremental costs that would have been avoided only if the tangible fixed asset had not been constructed as required.

Abnormal costs

2.6 Costs such as those arising from design error, wasted materials, industrial disputes, idle capacity or production delays are considered to be **abnormal** and **not directly attributable** to bringing the asset into **working condition** and its **intended use**. This approach is consistent with SSAP 9. They should therefore should **not be capitalised** as part of the cost of the asset.

Time frame for capitalisation

2.7 **Capitalisation** of **directly attributable costs** should **cease** when substantially all the activities that are necessary to get the tangible fixed asset ready for use are complete, even if the asset has not actually been brought into use. A tangible fixed asset is considered to be ready for use when its **physical construction is complete**.

Start-up or commissioning period

2.8 The costs associated with a **start-up** or **commissioning period** should be **included** in the cost of the tangible fixed asset **only where** the **asset is available for use** but **incapable** of operating at **normal levels without** such a **start-up** or **commissioning period**.

2.9 The costs of an **essential commissioning period** are included as part of the **cost of bringing the asset up to its normal operating potential**, and **therefore** as **part** of its **cost**.

However, there is no justification for regarding costs relating to other start-up periods, where the asset is available for use but not yet operating at normal levels.

Question 2

Halliday Inn has been is being built and opens for business in January 20X9. Demand is expected to build up slowly and high levels of room occupancy are only likely to be achieved over a period of several months.

Should any of the costs incurred in the run up to optimal occupancy of hotel be capitalised.

Answer

No. The hotel is able to operate at normal levels immediately on opening without necessarily having to go through a start up period in a slack season.

Question 3

Duncan Donatz Ltd has constructed a high speed machine for making holes of different shapes in doughnuts.

The machine is to be commissioned in two stages:

(a) *Test run phase*. This phase is designed to ensure that the shapes are punched properly and the process operates smoothly and efficiently. During this run in phase, output will be restricted to test runs.

(b) *Demand building phase*. During this phase output is expected to be low because the company is trying to achieve product acceptance of a different innovative type of doughnut. However, the machine is capable of operating at a normal level of output.

How should the costs relating to these two start up phases be treated?

Answer

Phase 1. The relevant costs should be capitalised together with the cost of machine because the machine is **not capable** of operating at normal levels without such a start up or commissioning period.

Phase 2. Costs associated with this period should be written off to profit and loss account. The machine is now capable of operating at normal levels and the low volumes are due to market factors.

2.10 From the above, it is important to be aware of the **practical distinction** between **two phases**:

(a) **Essential start-up** and **commissioning** phase, without which the asset is **incapable** of operating at normal levels.

(b) **Demand building phase** when output is built up to **full utilisation**.

Suspension of a revenue activity during construction

2.11 Operating losses that occur because a revenue activity has been suspended during the construction of a tangible fixed asset are not directly attributable costs. For example, if a restaurant closes for rebuilding, the revenue losses and other costs arising from the suspension of trading are not part of the cost of the new restaurant. Such losses are considered to be **too indirect** and **not linked sufficiently closely** with the **future economic benefits** to be obtained from the new asset.

Question 4

Café Edmondo Ltd has to close its restaurant for rebuilding.

Should the revenue losses and other costs arising from the suspension of trading be capitalised?

Answer

No. These losses are too indirect and not linked sufficiently closely with the economic benefits to be derived from the rebuilt restaurant.

2.12 Remember that the FRS 15 approach differs from the SSAP 9 approach to initial recognition. FRS 15 works on an **incremental cost approach,** whereas **SSAP 9** is based on **total absorption costing basis** and therefore does not prohibit recognition of general overheads.

Finance costs

2.13 Finance costs directly attributable to the construction of a fixed asset **may be capitalised** if it is **company policy** to do so. However, this **policy must be applied consistently**.

2.14 All finance costs that are **directly attributable** to the construction of a tangible fixed asset should be **capitalised** as part of the **cost of the asset**.

> **KEY TERM**
>
> **Directly attributable finance costs** are those that would have been **avoided** if there had been **no expenditure on the asset**.

2.15 If finance costs are capitalised, capitalisation should start when:

- Finance **costs** are being **incurred**
- Expenditure on the **asset** is being **incurred**
- **Activities** necessary to get the **asset ready** for use are **in progress**

2.16 **Capitalisation** of finance costs should **cease** when the asset is **ready for use**.

2.17 Sometimes **construction** of an asset may be **completed in parts** and **each part** is **capable of being used** while construction continues on other parts. An example of such an asset is a retail park consisting of several units. In such cases **capitalisation of borrowing costs relating to a part should cease when substantially all the activities that are necessary to get that part ready for use are completed.**

Question 5

Why would this not apply in the case of a car manufacturing plant?

Answer

This is an industrial plant involving several processes that are carried out **in sequence** at different parts of the plant within the same site.

2.18 Sometimes **active development** on a tangible fixed asset might be **interrupted** for extended periods. During such periods, **capitalisation** of finance costs should be **suspended**.

2.19 The following disclosures are required in respect of capitalisation of borrowing costs.

(a) The accounting policy adopted

(b) The amount of borrowing costs capitalised during the period

(c) The amount of borrowing costs recognised in the profit and loss account during the period

(d) The capitalisation (interest) rate used to determine the amount of capitalised borrowing costs

Recoverable amount

2.20 The **amount recognised** when a tangible fixed asset is acquired or constructed should **not exceed its recoverable amount**. If it does, it should be written down accordingly to its recoverable amount.

2.21 Recoverable amount is defined as being the higher of

(a) Net realisable value (NRV)

(b) Value in use (VU)

2.22 It is not necessary to review tangible fixed assets for **impairment** when they are acquired or constructed. They need to be **reviewed for impairment** only if there is some **indication** that impairment has occurred. Such indications are specified in the current FRS 11 *Impairment of fixed assets and goodwill*. We will look at impairment in more detail later.

Subsequent expenditure

2.23 After a tangible fixed asset has been brought into use, in practice, there is likely to be **further money spent**.

(a) **Revenue expenditure** which should be **written off** to the profit and loss account.

(b) **Captial expenditure** which should be debited to **tangible fixed assets**.

Expenditure to be written off to profit and loss account

> **GENERAL RULE**
>
> Subsequent expenditure to ensure that a tangible fixed asset maintains its previously assessed standard of performance should be written off to profit and loss account as it is incurred.

Question 6

Yummy Foods Ltd has to regularly service and overhaul its labelling machines to ensure that the labels are properly aligned and the tins roll off the production line efficiently, in accordance with the company's production targets.

How should these cost be treated?

Answer

Such expenditure ensures that the machinery sustains its originally assessed standard of performance. Without such expenditure, the useful economic life or residual value is likely to be reduced and in consequence the depreciation charge would increase.

Hence the expenditure is effectively 'repairs and maintenance' to be expensed in the profit and loss account.

Expenditure to be capitalised

2.24 FRS 15 specifies three scenarios where subsequent expenditure should be capitalised.

(a) It **enhances** the **economic benefits** over and **above previously assessed standards of performance**.

(b) A **component** of an asset that has been treated **separately** for **depreciation purposes** (because it has a substantially different useful economic life from the rest of the asset) has been **restored** or **replaced**.

(c) The expenditure related to a **major inspection** or **overhaul** that **restores economic benefits** that have been consumed and reflected in the depreciation charge.

Enhancement of economic benefits

2.25 FRS 15 offers two ways of **enhancing** the **economic benefits** that a tangible fixed asset might deliver:

(a) Mod**ifying the asset** to increase its capacity.

Eg a hotel reduces its non-productive communal areas to give it more bedrooms.

(b) **Upgrading the asset** to achieve a substantial **improvement** in the **quality** of the product or service provided to customers.

Eg a hotel treating its furniture with a special chemical compound that is designed to prolong its condition and serviceable life.

Replacement of separately depreciated component

2.26 In these circumstances, the component is disposed of and replaced by a new asset.

Question 7

Safeair Ltd treats its aircraft engines separately for depreciation purposes. The engine on one of its aircraft caught fire on take off and has had to be replaced.

How should the cost of the replacement engine be treated?

Answer

The new engine should be capitalised as a fixed asset addition with the destroyed engine taken to disposal account and expensed via the profit and loss account.

GENERAL RULE

Each component is depreciated over its **individual** useful life, so that the depreciation profile over the whole asset **more accurately reflects** the **actual** consumption of the asset's economic benefits.

Major overhauls and inspections

2.27 In addition to routine repairs and maintenance, some assets also require substantial expenditure every few years on major overhauls or inspections. Some examples found in practice are aircraft airworthiness inspections, ocean liner refits, theme part ride overhauls, refurbishment of kiln linings and replacing roofs of buildings.

Question 8

Safeair Ltd is required by law to overhaul its aircraft once every three years. Unless the overhauls are done, the aircraft cannot be flown.

How should the costs of the overhauls be treated?

Answer

The cost of the overhaul is capitalised when incurred because it restores the economic benefits flowing from the tangible fixed assets. The carrying amount representing the cost of benefits consumed is removed from the balance sheet.

2.28 The need to undertake an overhaul or inspection is acknowledged in the accounts by depreciating an amount of the asset that is equivalent to the inspection or overhaul costs over the period until the next inspection or overhaul. Hence, a **new asset** is **treated, in affect,** as being made up of **two elements**.

(a) **The core asset.** This is depreciated over its expected useful economic life.

(b) **The built-in overhaul cost.** This is depreciated over the period until the first actual overhaul takes place.

Question 9

Gyant Steps Ltd purchases a new spaceship for taking people on lunar holidays. It costs £200 million and is expected to last 10 years.

The Ministry of Lunar Travel enforces a 3 yearly inspection regime which is expected to cost £6 million in year 3 and £10 million in year 5.

Draw up a schedule showing the costs and depreciation for the lunar spaceship over its 10 year life.

Answer

	Cost			Depreciation			
Year	*b/f*	*Addition*	*c/f*	*b/f*	*Charge*	*c/f*	*NBV*
	£m	£m	£m	£m	£m	£m	£m
1	200		200		21.4 (W1)	21.4	178.6
2	200		200	21.4	21.4 (W1)	42.8	157.2
3	200	6	206	42.8	21.4 (W1)	64.2	141.8
4	206		206	64.2	21.4 (W2)	85.6	120.4
5	206		206	85.6	21.4 (W2)	107.0	99.0
6	206	10	216	107.0	21.4 (W2)	128.4	87.6
7	216		216	128.4	21.9 (W3)	150.3	65.7
8	216		216	150.3	21.9 (W3)	172.2	43.8
9	216		216	172.2	21.9 (W3)	194.1	21.9
10	216		216	194.1	21.9 (W3)	216.0	NIL

Workings

		£m
1.	Depreciation of core asset (194 ÷ 10)	19.4
	Spreading of cost of anticipated overhaul (6 ÷ 3)	2.0
		21.4

The cost of the economic benefits consumed in the first three years takes into consideration the cost of the first anticipated overhaul.

2.	Depreciation of core asset (194 ÷ 10)	19.4
	Spreading of cost of subsequent expenditure which restarts the economic benefits consumed (6 ÷ 3)	2.0
		21.4

Here the actual subsequent expenditure is depreciated over its useful life.

3.	Balance of net book value	87.6
	Remaining life	÷ 4 years
		21.9

Here, there are no further planned overhauls so the book value is written off over its remaining useful life.

Note: Commentators have criticised this FRS 15 approach as being somewhat contrived. See paragraph 2.60 for criticisms of FRS 15.

Decision to identify several economic lives

2.29 The **decision** whether to **identify separate components** or **future expenditures** on **overhauls** or **inspections** for **depreciation** over a **shorter useful economic life** than the rest of the tangible fixed asset is likely to **reflect various factors**.

   (a) Whether the **useful economic lives** of the components are, or the period until the next inspection or overhaul is, **substantially different** from the useful economic life of the remainder of the asset

   (b) The **degree of irregularity** in the **level of expenditures** required to restate the component or asset in different accounting periods

   (c) Their **materiality** in the context of the financial statements.

2.30 The decision may be not to account for each tangible fixed asset as several different asset components or to depreciate part of the asset over a different timescale from the rest of the asset. In these circumstances, the cost of replacing, restoring, overhauling or inspecting the asset or components of the asset is not capitalised, but instead is recognised in the profit and loss account as incurred.

Depreciation

> **Exam focus point**
>
> The pilot paper required a discussion on the subject of a policy of depreciation of fixed assets. You need to have a good working knowledge of FRS 15.
>
> The important point to note was that depreciation is the allocation of cost (or revalued amount), less estimated residual value, over expected useful life. It is not intended as a process of valuing assets.
>
> Regardless of whether or not the asset is revalued, depreciation must be charged over the length of the lease (unless estimated useful life is less than that).

Purpose of depreciation

2.31 As noted earlier, the Companies Act 1985 requires that all fixed assets having a limited economic life should be depreciated. **FRS 15** provides a useful discussion of the **purpose of depreciation** and supplements the statutory requirements in important ways.

> **KEY TERM**
>
> **Depreciation** is defined in FRS 15 as the measure of the cost or revalued amount of the **economic benefits** of the tangible fixed asset that have been **consumed during the period**.
>
> Consumption includes:
>
> * wearing out
> * using up
> * other reduction in the useful economic life
>
> of a tangible fixed asset, whether arising from:
>
> * use
> * effluxion (passage) of time

- obsolescence through either:
    - changes in technology
    - reduction in demand for the goods and services produced by the asset.

2.32 This definition includes

- **amortisation** of **assets** with a **pre-determined life**, such as a **leasehold**
- **depletion** of **wasting assets** such as **mines**.

General requirements

FRS 15 specifies the following general rules regarding depreciation.

(a) The depreciable amount of a tangible fixed asset should be allocated on a **systematic basis** over its **useful economic life**

(b) The depreciation method used should **reflect** as fairly as possible the **pattern** in which the asset's **economic benefits** are **consumed** by the company

(c) The depreciation charge for each period should be recognised as an **expense** in the profit and loss account unless it is permitted to be included in the carrying amount of another asset.

2.33 The general requirements of FRS 15 entail three key issues.

- Selecting a method which reflects the pattern of consumption
- Estimating the useful economic life and residual value
- Dealing with the impact of subsequent expenditure on depreciation

Methods of depreciation

2.34 A **variety of methods** can be used to allocate the depreciable amount of a tangible fixed asset. No specific method is stipulated.

2.35 FRS 15 mentions two common methods of depreciation.

(a) **Straight-line**. This method assumes that equal amounts of economic benefit are consumed in each year of the asset's life. Therefore the asset is written off in **equal instalments** over its **estimated useful economic life**.

(b) **Reducing balance**. Here the **depreciation rate** is applied to the **opening net book value**. This method charges more depreciation in the early years of an asset's life than in later years.

2.36 The closest FRS 15 gets to making a recommunication is to suggest that where the pattern of consumption of an asset's economic benefits is uncertain, straight-line method of depreciation is usually adopted. In practice this is the most widely used method.

Factors affecting depreciation

2.37 FRS 15 outlines the factors to be considered in determining the useful economic life, residual value and depreciation method of an asset.

(a) The **expected usage** of the asset by the entity, assessed by reference to the asset's **expected capacity** or **physical output**

(b) The **expected physical deterioration** of the asset through use or **effluxion of time**; this will depend upon the **repair and maintenance programme** of the entity both when the asset is in **use** and when it is **idle**

(c) **Economic or technological obsolescence**, for example arising from **changes** or **improvements** in **production**, or a change in the **market demand** for the product or **service output** of that asset

(d) **Legal or similar limits** on the **use of the asset**, such as the **expiry dates** of related leases

Changes in estimates

2.38 *Review of useful economic life*

> **GENERAL RULE**
>
> The **useful economic life** of a tangible fixed asset should be **reviewed** at the **end of each reporting period** and revised if expectations are significantly different from previous estimates.

2.39 If **useful economic life** is **revised**, the **carrying amount** (ie book value) of the tangible fixed asset at the date of revision is **depreciated** over the **revised remaining useful economic life** from that point onwards.

2.40 Remember that the useful economic life of a tangible fixed asset is an **accounting estimate**, not an accounting policy. In such cases, the standard accounting practice is **not to restate previous years' figures** when estimates are revised.

2.41 The approach is to depreciate the carrying amount of the tangible fixed asset over the remaining useful economic life, beginning in the period in which the change is made.

However, if future results could be materially distorted, the adjustment to accumulated deprecation should be recognised in the accounts in accordance with FRS 3 (normally as an exceptional item).

Revision of residual value

> **GENERAL RULE**
>
> Where residual value is material, it should be reviewed at the end of each period to take account of **expected technological changes,** but still based on prices prevailing at the date of acquisition (or revaluation).

2.42 A change in estimated residual value is **accounted for prospectively** over the asset's remaining useful economic life, except where the asset is impaired. If an impairment occurs, the asset should be written down immediately. (Impairment will be covered in more detail later in this text.)

2.43 When an asset is revalued, the residual value should also be reassessed, based on prices at the date of revaluation.

Revision of method of depreciation

> **GENERAL RULE**
>
> A change in depreciation method is permissible only on the grounds that the new method will give a **fairer presentation** of the results and of the financial position.

2.44 The depreciation method is an **accounting estimate**. Therefore, a change of method is not a change of accounting policy.

2.45 The carrying amount (ie book value) of the asset is depreciated on the new method over the remaining useful economic life, beginning in the period in which the change is made.

Two or more components of a fixed asset

2.46 A fixed asset may comprise **two or more major components** with **substantially different useful economic lives**. In such cases each component should be **accounted for separately** for depreciation purposes and depreciated over its **individual useful economic life**. Examples include:

- Land and buildings
- The structure of a building and items within the structure, such as general fittings

2.47 Freehold land usually has an indefinite life, unless subject to depletion (eg a quarry). Buildings have a limited life and are therefore depreciated.

Question 10

What about the trading potential associated with a property valued as an operational entity, such as a hotel, pub or club? Should this be treated as a separate component?

Answer

No. The value and life of any trading potential is inherently inseparable from that of the property.

> **GENERAL RULE**
>
> Where the tangible fixed asset comprises two or more major components with substantially different useful economic lives, each component should be accounted for separately for depreciation purposes and depreciated over its useful economic life.

2.48 In effect, the asset is treated as though it were several different assets for depreciation purposes. FRS 15 also requires component depreciation if subsequent expenditure on replacing a component is to be capitalised.

Impact of subsequent expenditure

2.49 In calculating the useful economic life of an asset it is assumed that **subsequent expenditure** will be undertaken to **maintain** the **originally assessed standard of performance** of the asset (for example the cost of servicing or overhauling plant and equipment). Without such expenditure the depreciation expense would be increased

BPP
PUBLISHING

because the useful life and/or residual value of the asset would be reduced. This type of expenditure is **recognised as an expense when incurred**.

2.50   In addition, subsequent expenditure may be undertaken that results in a **restoration** or **replacement** of a component of the asset that has been depreciated or an **enhancement** of **economic benefits** of the asset in excess of the originally assessed standard of performance. This type of expenditure may result in an extension of the **useful economic life of the asset** and represents **capital expenditure**.

> ## IMPORTANT!
> **Subsequent expenditure does not obviate the need to charge depreciation.**

Non-depreciation

> ## GENERAL RULE
> For tangible fixed assets other than non-depreciable land, the **only grounds** for not charging depreciation are that the depreciation charge and accumulated depreciation are **immaterial**.
>
> The depreciation charge and accumulated depreciation are immaterial if they would **not reasonably influence** the **decisions** of a **user** of the accounts.

2.51   An entity must be able to justify that the uncharged depreciation is not material in **aggregate** as well as for **each tangible fixed asset**. Depreciation may be immaterial because of **very long useful economic lives** or **high residual values** (or both). A high residual value will reflect the remaining economic value of the asset at the end of its useful economic life to the entity. These conditions may occur when **all the following are met**:

(a)   The entity has a policy and practice of **regular maintenance and repair** (charges for which are recognised in the profit and loss account) such that the asset is kept to its previously assessed **standard of performance**

(b)   The asset is **unlikely** to **suffer** from economic or technological **obsolescence** (eg due to potential changes in demand in the market following changes in fashion)

(c)   Where **estimated residual values** are **material**:

(i)   The entity has a policy and practice of **disposing** of **similar assets well before** and **end of their economic lives**

(ii)   The **disposal proceeds** of similar assets (after excluding the effect of price changes since the date of acquisition or last revaluation) have **not** been **materially less than** their **carrying amounts**.

2.52   The above rules come into play in relation to what are known as 'trophy assets'.

- **Top quality** buildings in desirable areas
- **Antique** fixtures and fittings
- **Historic** buildings

2.53   This approach was also advocated by the hotel, catering and public house industry on the grounds that their assets were regularly maintained and refurbished and therefore their useful economic life were not restricted.

2.54 However, where entities have avoided changing depreciation on the grounds of immateriality, they will nevertheless be required to perform impairment reviews under FRS 11. In practice, the **impairment review route** may prove **costly** and **counter-productive**, when the profit and loss account has nevertheless and **inevitably to suffer a hit** resulting from an impairment loss.

Impairment requirements

2.55 The application of impairment reviews in relation specifically to trophy assets has been touched as above. **Generally** tangible fixed assets other than non depreciable land, should be **reviewed for impairment** at the **end of the reporting** period where:

- **No depreciation** is charged on the **grounds** that it would be **immaterial**.
- The **estimated remaining useful economic life exceeds 50 years**.

The review should be in accordance with FRS 11 *Impairment of fixed assets and goodwill*, which will be discussed in more detail in the **next chapter**

2.56 Many companies **carry fixed assets** in their balance sheets at **revalued amounts**, particularly in the case of freehold buildings. When this is done, the **depreciation charge** should be calculated **on the basis of the revalued amount** (not the original cost).

2.57 Where the **residual value is material**, it should be **reviewed** at the **end of each reporting period** to take account of reasonably **expected technological changes**. A **change** in the **estimated residual value** should be **accounted for prospectively** over the asset's remaining useful economic life, **except** to the **extent** that the asset has been **impaired** at the **balance sheet date**.

Renewals accounting

> **KEY TERM**
>
> Where **renewals accounting** is adopted, the level of annual expenditure required to maintain the operating capacity of the infrastructure asset is treated as the depreciation charged for the period and is deducted from the carrying amount of the asset (as part of accumulated depreciation). Actual expenditure is capitalised (as part of the cost of the asset) as incurred.

2.58 Definable major assets or components within an infrastructure system or network with determinable finite lives should be treated separately and depreciated over their useful economic lives. For the remaining tangible fixed assets within the system or network, renewals accounting may be used if:

(a) The infrastructure asset is a system that as a whole is intended to be maintained at a specified level of service by the continuing replacement and refurbishment of its components.

(b) The level of annual expenditure required to maintain the operating capacity or service capability of the infrastructure asset is calculated from an asset management plan certified by a qualified, independent person.

(c) The system or network is in a mature or steady state.

BPP
PUBLISHING

Disclosure requirements of FRS 15

2.59 The following information should be disclosed separately in the financial statements for each class of tangible fixed assets.

(a) The depreciation methods used

(b) The useful economic lives or the depreciation rates used

(c) Total depreciation charged for the period

(d) Where material, the financial effect of a change during the period in either the estimate of useful economic lives or the estimate of residual values

(e) The cost or revalued amount at the beginning of the financial period and at the balance sheet date

(f) The cumulative amount of provisions for depreciation or impairment at the beginning of the financial period and at the balance sheet date

(g) A reconciliation of the movements, separately disclosing additions, disposals, revaluations, transfers, depreciation, impairment losses, and reversals of past impairment losses written back in the financial period

(h) The net carrying amount at the beginning of the financial period and at the balance sheet date

Criticisms of FRS 15

2.60 FRS 15 has been largely welcomed, particularly the rules on revaluations (see below). However, some commentators have found problematic the treatment of subsequent expenditure where there is a major overhaul. As mentioned previously, the treatment has been described as 'contrived'.

3 REVALUATION

Policy basis

3.1 Before FRS 15, companies could pick and choose which of their assets they wished to revalue and when. This allowed companies to massage their balance sheet figures through the inclusion of meaningless **out of date valuations**, thereby **hindering comparability** between companies from year to year. FRS 15 puts a stop to this **'cherry picking'**.

> **BASIC REQUIREMENTS**
>
> An entity may adopt a policy of **revaluing tangible fixed assets**. Where this policy is adopted **it must be applied consistently** to all assets of the same class.
>
> Where an asset is revalued its carrying amount should be its **current value** as at the balance sheet date, current value being the **lower of replacement cost and recoverable amount**. The recoverable amount, in turn, is the **higher** of **net realisable value** and **value in use**.

3.2 A **class of fixed assets** is 'a category of tangible fixed assets having a similar nature, function or use in the business of an entity'. (FRS 15)

KEY TERMS

Replacement cost. The cost at which an **identical asset** could be **purchased** or **constructed**.

Depreciated replacement cost. Replacement cost with appropriate **deduction** for **age, condition and obsolescence.**

Recoverable amount. The higher of net realisable value and value in use.

Net realisable value. The **amount** at which an **asset could be disposed of,** less any **direct selling costs.**

Value in use. The **present value** of **future cash flows** obtainable as result of an asset's **continued use, including** those resulting from **ultimate disposal.**

Open market value. The **best price** that could be obtained between a **willing seller** and a **knowledgeable buyer,** assuming **normal market conditions.**

Exiting use value. As for **open market value,** except that value is based on the **assumption** that the property can be used for the **foreseeable future** only for its **existing use.**

3.3   The above basic requirements can be summarised by the following diagram.

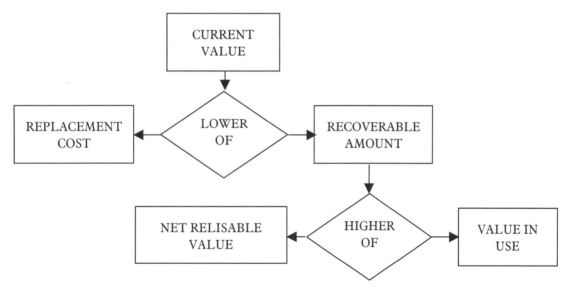

3.4   **Remember the decision to adopt a policy of revaluation of tangible fixed assets is discretionary.** Do not confuse this with other scenarios where the carrying value of a fixed asset should be adjusted:

(a)   **FRS 15 rule** that:

"if the amount recognised when a tangible fixed asset is acquired or constructed exceeds its recoverable amount, it should be written down to its recoverable amount."

(b)   **FRS 11 response to indications of impairment** that requires:

"A review for impairment of a fixed asset (or goodwill) should be carried out if events or circumstances indicate that the carrying amount of the fixed asset (or goodwill) may not be recoverable."

3.5   You may find the following diagram helpful in clarifying the scenarios where, in addition to annual depreciation, the carrying value of a tangible fixed asset needs to be adjusted.

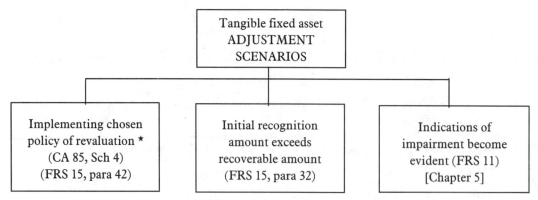

* We shall see later that in certain circumstances, a loss arising on revaluation is effectively tantamount to an impairment loss. However, you must remember that this arises from the revaluation policy route rather than the indications of impairment route.

Frequency of valuation

Specialised properties

3.6 FRS 15 permits three alternative approaches to the valuation of specialised properties, eg schools, hospitals and power stations.

(a) A **full valuation** every **5 years**

(b) An **interim valuation** in **year 3 of the five-year cycle**.

(c) An **interim valuation also in years 1, 2 and 4** of the five-year cycle should also be done where it is likely that there has been a **material change in value**.

Non-specialised properties

3.7 For portfolios of non-specialised properties, eg factories, warehouses, shops and offices, a **full valuation** may be performed on a **rolling basis** designed to cover all the properties over a **five-year cycle**. An **interim valuation** on the **remaining four-fifths** of the portfolio should be done where it is likely that there has been a **material change** in value.

This approach is appropriate only where the property portfolio held by the entity under either of **two specified scenarios**.

(a) The portfolio consists of a number of **broadly similar properties** whose characteristics are such that their values are likely to be affected by the **same market factors**.

(b) The portfolio can be divided on a **continuing basis** into **five groups of a broadly similar spread**.

Valuers

3.8 FRS 15 specifies who may carry out a **full valuation**.

(a) A qualified external valuer (eg a surveyor, who is independent of the company), or
(b) A qualified internal valuer, but subject to review by a qualified external valuer.

3.9 An **interim valuation** may be done by an internal or external, qualified valuer.

Other tangible fixed assets

3.10 For certain types of assets (other than properties) eg company cars, there may be an **active second hand market** for the asset or **appropriate indices** may exist, so that the directors can establish the asset's value with **reasonable reliability** and therefore avoid the need to use the services of a qualified valuer.

3.11 For an index to be appropriate:

  (a) It must be appropriate to the class of asset, its location and conditions.
  (b) It must take into account the impact of technological change.
  (c) It must have a proven track record of regular publication.
  (d) It is expected to be available in the foreseeable future.

3.12 Such valuations must be performed **every five years**, and also in the **intervening years** where there has been a **material change in value**.

Valuation basis

3.13 The following valuation bases should be used for properties that are not impaired.

TYPE		BASIS
Specialised properties	•	These should be valued on the basis of **depreciated replacement cost**.
	•	Specialised properties are those which, due to their **specialised** nature, there is **no general market** in their existing use or condition, except as part of a sale of the business in occupation. Eg oil refineries, hospitals, chemical works, power stations, schools, colleges and universities where there is no competing market demand from other organisations using these types of property in the locality.
	•	The objectives of using depreciated replacement cost is to make a realistic estimate of the current cost of constructing an asset that has the same service potential as the existing asset.
Non-specialised properties	•	These should be valued on the basis of **existing use value** (EUV), plus notional directly attributable acquistion costs where material.
Properties surplus to an entity's requirements	•	These should be valued on the basis of **open market value** (OMV) less expected direct selling costs where these are material. They may be specialised or non-specialised properties.
	•	The **assumption** supporting the specified accounting treatment is that they **will be sold**.

3.14 Where there is an indication of impairment, an impairment review should be carried out in accordance with FRS 11. The asset should be recorded at the lower of revalued amount (as above) and recoverable amount.

3.15 Tangible fixed assets other than properties should be valued using market value or, if not obtainable, depreciated replacement cost.

BPP
PUBLISHING

Reporting gains and losses on revaluations

General points

3.16 A revaluation gain or loss arises when there is a difference between the valuation of a tangible fixed asset when compared to its carrying amount.

3.17 The treatment of revaluation gains and losses involves what is dealt with through either:

- Profit and loss account
- Statement of total recognised gains and losses

and this will depend on the underlying scenarios, which are explored below.

Tangible fixed asset revalued upwards

3.18

Gain	Treatment of gain
Asset not previously revalued	<ul><li>Gain credited to revaluation reserve.</li><li>Reported in STRGL.</li></ul>
Asset previously revalued upwards	<ul><li>Gain credited to revaluation reserve.</li><li>Reported in STRGL.</li></ul>
Asset subjected to previous revaluation loss	<ul><li>Portion of gain that in effect reverses the prior revaluation losses should be credited to profit and loss account, ie restores the asset to its depreciated historical cost.</li><li>Any gain in excess of the above should be credited to revaluation reserve and reported via STRGL.</li></ul>

3.19 The above points are covered in the example 3.22, below.

Tangible fixed asset revalued downwards

3.20

Loss	Treatment of loss
Loss clearly due to consumption of economic benefits eg physical damage or deterioration in quality of goods or services provided by the asset.	All of the loss must be debited to profit and loss account. It does not matter that the asset involved might have been previously revalued upwards. (FRS 15 suggests that this is really an impairment loss)
Losses owing to other causes than the above. Asset previously revalued upwards.	These losses should be recognised in the following order. (a) In STRGL until the carrying amount reaches depreciated historical cost. (b) In the profit and loss account.
Losses owing to other causes than top item above. Asset not previously revalued upwards.	These losses should be recognised in the profit and loss account.

3.21 The above points are demonstrated in the example 3.22.

Depreciation on revalued assets

> **BASIC REQUIREMENTS**
>
> Where an asset has been revalued, the depreciation charge is based on the revaluation amount, less residual value, from the date of revaluation.
>
> The asset's residual value should also be re-estimated on revaluation, based on values prevailing at that date.

3.22 This approach entails two different and conflicting issues.

(a) The profit and loss account bears the cost of the economic benefits consumed, as measured by the enhanced depreciation charge based on the revalued figure for the tangible fixed asset.

(b) Distributable profits should not be prejudiced by the additional depreciation caused by the revaluation.

3.23 The remedy to this problem is to make an annual transfer from revaluation reserve to profit and loss account covering the amount for the addition depreciation caused by the revaluation. This is permitted by Companies Act 1985 and also represents best practice. This is illustrated in the example below.

3.24 EXAMPLE: IMPACT OF REVALUATION ON DEPRECIATION

Kevin Ltd acquires a buffing machine costing £100,000 on 1 July 20X4, which it depreciates at 10% straight line. The company policy is to charge a full year's depreciation in the year of acquisition but none in the year of disposal.

When the directors came to prepare the accounts for the year ended 31 December 20X7, the directors decided to obtain a full professional valuation, to be incorporated into the financial statements.

Yasmin, Nicole and Associates, Chartered Surveyors, valued the asset at £108,000.

It is now 31 December 20X9. Show the entries in the relevant accounts in the book of Kevin Ltd.

3.25 SOLUTION

PLANT AND EQUIPMENT

		£			£
1.7.X4	Cost of buffing machine	100,000	31.12.X7	Balance c/d	108,000
31.12.X7	Revaluation reserve (W3)	8,000			
		108,000			108,000
1.1.X8	Balance b/d	108,000			

PROVISION FOR DEPRECIATION

		£			£
1.7.X7	Revaluation reserve (W3)	40,000	31.12.X4	Charge for year (W1)	10,000
			31.12.X5	Charge for year (W1)	10,000
			31.12.X6	Charge for year (W1)	10,000
			31.12.X7	Charge for year (W1)	10,000
		40,000			40,000
			31.12.X8	Charge for year (W2)	18,000
			31.12.X9	Charge for year (W2)	18,000

DEPRECIATION CHARGE

		£			£
31.12.X4	Provision (W1)	10,000	31.12.X4	Tfr to P+L a/c	10,000
31.12.X5	Provision (W1)	10,000	31.12.X5	Tfr to P+L a/c	10,000
31.12.X6	Provision (W1)	10,000	31.12.X6	Tfr to P+L a/c	10,000
31.12.X7	Provision (W1)	10,000	31.12.X7	Tfr to P+L a/c	10,000
31.12.X8	Provision (W2)	18,000	31.12.X8	Tfr to P+L a/c	18,000
31.12.X9	Provision (W2)	18,000	31.12.X9	Tfr to P+L a/c	18,000

REVALUATION RESERVE

		£			£
31.12.X8	Add'l depn to P+L a/c	8,000	31.12.X7	Adj. On buffing	48,000
31.12.X9	Add'l depn to P+L a/c	8,000		machine (W3)	

Note: These adjustments go directly to P+L reserve, avoiding the current year's P+L account.	*Note:* This adjustment will be done via STRG.

PROFIT AND LOSS RESERVE (depreciation adjustments only)

			£
	31.12.X8	Depn adj	8,000
	31.12.X9	Depn adj	8,000

Workings

1   £100,000 ÷ 10 years = £10,000 per annum.

2   £108,000 ÷ 6 years = 18,000 per annum.

3   *Revaluation of buffing machine*

	£
Cost	100,000
Accumulated depreciation to 31.12.X7	(40,000)
Net book value at 31.12.X7	60,000
Revaluation increase	48,000
Valuation as at 31.12.X7	108,000

3.26   Note that the concept of 'split depreciation' is not acceptable ie. the charge for the year may not be split between a portion based on historical cost and a portion based on the revaluation increase with these being debited to profit and loss account and revaluation reserve, respectively.

3.27   EXAMPLE: REVALUATION MOVEMENTS

The following details relate to Moggy Ltd which has a December year end.

- *Year ended 31 December 20X0:*   Acquired a building for £100 million
  Depreciation; 5% straight line

- *31 December 20X5:*   A professional valuation was obtained in the amount of £42 million.

- *31 December 20X8:*   Due to improved economic circumstances, the value of the building increased to £132 million.

- *31 December 20Y1:*   An interim valuation of £30 million.

Identify the adjustments required and indicate what statements would be affected.

3.28 SOLUTION

20X0 to 20X5

- Annual depreciation charge £5m (£100m × 5%)
- Recognised via the profit and loss account.

31 December 20X5

	£m
Cost	100
Accumulated depreciation (£5m × 6 years)	(30)
Net book value	70
Revalued amount 20X5	42
Revaluation loss charged to profit and loss account	28

20X6 to 20X8

- Annual depreciation of £42m ÷ 14 = £3m
- Processed through the profit and loss account.

31 December 20X8

	£m
Previous revalued amount	42
Accumulated depreciation (£3m × 3 years)	(9)
Carrying value before 20X8 valuation	33
New valuation 20X8	132
Revaluation gain 20X8	99

The portion of the gain that in effect reverses the prior revaluation loss should be credited to profit and loss account, ie restores the asset to depreciated historical cost.

	£m
Historical cost	100
Less depreciation (£5m × 9 years)	(45)
Depreciation historical cost 30.12.X8	55

Hence:

	£m
Depreciated historical cost 30.12.X8	55
Carrying value before 20X8 revaluation	(33)
Portion of gain credited to profit and loss	22
Remainder of gain credited to revaluation reserve via STRGL	77
Revaluation gain 20X8, as above	99

Reconciliation of movements in reserves:

	£m
Depreciation – £5m × 6 years	30
– £3m × 3 years	9
Depreciation 20X0 to 20X8	39
Revaluation loss 31.12.X5	28
Revaluation gain 31.12.X8	(22)
Total debits to profit and loss account 20X0 to 20X8	45
Credit to revaluation reserve 31.21.X8	(77)
Net movement 20X0 to 20X8	(32)

Being:

	£m
Historical cost 20X0	100
Valuation 20X8	(132)
Net amount written up	(32)

20X9 to 20Y1

- Annual depreciation of £12m (£132m ÷ 11 years)
- Debited to profit and loss account.

And

- Annual transfer from revaluation reserve to profit and loss account of £7m. (£77m ÷ 11 years).

- Debit revaluation reserve, credit profit and loss account.

31 December 20Y1

	£m
Previous revalued amount	132
Accumulated depreciation (£12m × 3 years)	(36)
Carrying value before 20Y1 valuation	96
New valuation 20Y1	(30)
Revaluation loss 20Y1	66

The loss should be recognised in the following order:

(a) In the STRGL until the carrying amount reaches depreciated historical cost.

(b) In the profit and loss account.

Historical cost	100
Less Depreciation (£5m × 12 years)	(60)
Depreciated historical cost	40

Hence:

Carrying value before 20Y1 revaluation	96
Depreciated historical cost	(40)
Revaluation loss charged to STRGL	56
Revaluation loss taken to profit and loss account (balancing figure)	10
Revaluation loss 20Y1, as above	66

Proof

REVALUATION RESERVE

		£			£
31.12.X9	Release to P+L a/c	7	31.12.X8	Revaluation gain	77
31.12.Y0	Release to P+L a/c	7			
31.12.Y1	Release to P+L a/c	7			
31.12.Y1	Adj. revaluation 20Y1	56			
		77			77

Gains and losses on disposal

BASIC REQUIREMENTS

Gains or losses on disposal of revalued tangible fixed assets should be accounted for in the profit and loss account of the period in which the disposal occurs.

The profit or loss is calculated as the difference between the

- net sale proceeds
- carrying amount, whether accounted for or
    - the historical cost accounting rules
    - alternative accounting rules

Credit balance on revaluation reserve

3.29 Where this relates to an asset which has been sold, this now becomes realised. It should therefore be transferred to profit and loss account.

Question 11

Refer back to the Moggy Ltd example above in 3.22.

How would you account for the disposal if the building had been sold on 1 January 20X1 for £35 million?

Answer

	£m
Valuation at 31.12.X8	132
Accumulated depreciation (£12m × 2*years)	24
Carrying value at 31.12.Y0	108
Proceeds of sale disposal 1.1.Y1	(35)
Loss on disposal	73

* No charge in year of disposal

- This loss should be processed to disposals account in the usual way.

- In addition, the balance on the revaluation reserve is now realised and can be taken to profit and loss account.

Adjustments

		DEBIT £m	CREDIT £m
DEBIT	Bank – proceeds of sale	35	
DEBIT	Accumulated depreciation	24	
DEBIT	Loss on disposal of fixed assets	73	
CREDIT	Fixed assets		132

Standard journal entry for disposal

		DEBIT £m	CREDIT £m
DEBIT	Revaluation reserve (W1)	63	
CREDIT	Profit and loss reserve		63

Transfer of gain, now realised, to profit and loss reserves.

Workings

1	REVALUATION RESERVE			
		£m		£m
31.12.X9	Release to P+L a/c	7	31.12.X8 Revaluation gain	77
31.12.Y0	Release to P+L a/c	7		
31.12.Y1	Realised gain transferred to P+L a/c	63		
		77		77

Proof:

	£m
Profit realised per revaluation reserve	63
Loss on carrying value	(73)
Net loss	(10)

Being:

	£m
Historical cost	100
Less depreciation (£5m × 11 years)	(55)
Depreciation historical cost 1.1.Y1	45
Proceeds of disposal 1.1.Y1	(35)
Net loss, as above	10

4 SSAP 19 ACCOUNTING FOR INVESTMENT PROPERTIES

4.1 The introduction of SSAP 12, with its requirement that all fixed assets including freehold buildings (though excluding freehold land) should be depreciated, caused a stir amongst property investment companies who feared that their reported profits would be severely reduced. The lobby was sufficiently strong to result in the publication of a separate standard for such properties.

Definition of investment properties

4.2 SSAP 19 defines an investment property as follows.

> **KEY TERM**
>
> '.... An **investment property** is an interest in land and/or buildings:
>
> (a) In respect of which **construction** work and **development** have been **completed**
>
> (b) Which is held for its **investment potential**, any **rental income** being **negotiated** at **arm's length**.
>
> '....The following are **exceptions** from the definition:
>
> (a) A property which is **owned** and **occupied** by a company for its **own purposes** is not an investment property.
>
> (b) A property **let to** and **occupied** by **another group company** is not an investment property for the purposes of its own accounts or the group accounts.'

Question 12

Lucy Limited and its subsidiaries are engaged in manufacturing of sweets and confectionery in Luton. It owns three properties which are held in a different ways.

(a) **Broadacres** is its factory and office building.

(b) **Kandikorna** is a retail premises let to Darren Limited a subsidiary which deals directly with the public.

(c) **High Standards** is an office block which is let to a firm of accountants on an arms length rental basis.

Identify which properties are investment properties.

Answer

(a) Broadacres is **not** an **investment property** because it is owned and **occupied** by Lucy Limited for its **own purposes**.

(b) Kandikorna is **not** an **investment property** because it is let and **occupied** by **another group company**.

(a) High Standards is an **investment company** because it **meets the criteria** for being classified as an investment property.

Justification for special approach to investment properties

4.3 Investment properties, as defined, are **not held** to be **consumed within** the **operations** of an enterprise, but instead for their **investment potential**.

4.4 The sale of an investment property is also unlikely to materially impact on the manufacturing trading operations of an enterprise.

4.5 What is of **prime importance** to users of accounts, regarding investment properties, is their **current value** and any **charges in their current value**, rather than a systematic calculation of annual depreciation.

Accounting treatment

4.6 Per **SSAP 19**, investment properties should not be depreciated. Instead they should be **revalued annually** at their **open market value** and the aggregate **surplus** or **deficit** arising transferred to **investment revaluation reserve** (IRR) via the STRGL.

4.7 There may be circumstances where the **deficit** relating to an **individual investment property** is expected to be **permanent**. In such case, the deficit should be charged in the **profit and loss account** for the period.

4.8 Sometimes an investment property is held on a **lease** with a relatively **short unexpired term**, ie 20 years or less. Here the **carrying value** of lease must be **depreciated** over **useful economic life** in accordance with the approach set out in **FRS 15**. The objective is to avoid the situation whereby the rentals for such short levels are credited to profit and loss accounts whilst on the other hand any annual movements arising from revaluation's are processed to investment revaluation reserve via STRGL.

4.9 SSAP 19 specifies various criteria for determining open market value.

(a) The valuation **need not** be made by **qualified** or **independent valuers**.

(b) However, **disclosure** is required regarding:

- The **names** and **qualifications** of the valuers

- The **basis** of valuation used

- **Whether** the person making the valuation is an **employee** or **officer** of the company.

(c) Sometimes investment properties represent a **substantial proportion** of the **total assets** of a **major enterprise** (eg a listed company). In these instances, their **valuation** would normally be carried out:

(i) **Annually** by a **qualified person** having **recent experience** of valuing **similar properties**

(ii)   At least every **five years** by an **external valuer**.

Question 13

Kikaround Limited acquired two investment properties in Manchester on 31 December 20X6.

	Keegan Towers £'000	Ferguson Towers £'000	Total £'000
Cost 31.12.X6	100	100	200
Valuation			
31.12.X7	70	140	210
31.12.X8	85	145	230
31.12.X9	120	70	190

The deficits on Keegan Towers arising on 31 December 20X7 and 20X8 are expected to be temporary whereas the deficit on Ferguson Towers arising on 31 December 20X9 is expected to be permanent.

Show the investment revaluation reserve for the years ended 31 December 20X7, 20X8 and 20X9.

Answer

INVESTMENT REVALUATION RESERVE

			£'000				£'000
31.12.X7	Keegan Towers		30	31.12.X7	Ferguson Towers		40
31.12.X7	Balance	c/d	10				
			40				40
31.12.X8	Balance	c/d	30	1.1.X8	Balance b/d		10
				31.12.X8	Keegan Towers		15
				31.12.X8	Ferguson Towers		5
			30				30
31.12.X9	Ferguson Towers*		75	1.1.X9	Balance	b/d	30
31.12.X9	Balance	c/d	20	21.12.X9	Keegan Towers		35
				31.12.X9	Transfer to P+L a/c		30
					(Ferguson)		
			95				95

* This could have been debited directly to profit and loss account with a transfer of £45,000 credits from IRR, to give effect to the £30,000 permanent deficit in respect of Ferguson Towers.

4.10   The carrying value of investment properties and investment revaluation reserve should be disclosed prominently in the accounts.

4.11   Investment properties can be owned by ordinary trading companies as well as property investment companies. If the assets of a company consist wholly or mainly of investment properties, this fact should also be disclosed.

4.12   Further points to note about SSAP 19 are as follows.

(a)   SSAP 19 acknowledges that exemption from depreciation for investment property is **contrary** to the depreciation rules in the **Companies Act 1985**. This departure is considered permissible because the Act states that compliance with the rules is a subordinate requirement to the '**overriding purpose of giving a true and fair view**'.

Where the true and fair override is invoked the notes to the accounts must disclose particulars of that departure, the reasons for it, and its effect. (See chapter 3).

(b)   SSAP 19 **does not apply to immaterial items**.

Disposals

4.13 **SSAP 19 does not deal with the problem of accounting for the disposal of investment properties. However, FRS 3** *Reporting financial performance* **states the following** in relation to the disposal of any revalued fixed assets.

    (a) The **profit or loss** on **disposal** of an **asset** should be accounted for as the **difference** between the **sale proceeds** and the **net carrying amount**.

    (b) Any **revaluation surplus** remaining is now **realised**, so FRS 3 requires this to be transferred to the **profit and loss reserve**.

Diminution in value: Amendment to SSAP 19

4.14 Previously, under SSAP 19, any deficit on the IRR had to be taken to the profit and loss account. In other words, where the value of one or more investment property fell so far that the total IRR was insufficient to cover the deficit, then the excess was taken to the profit and loss account. SSAP 19 has now been amended as follows.

    (a) **Any diminution in value which is considered permanent should be charged to the profit and loss account.**

    (b) **Where diminution is temporary, a temporary IRR deficit is allowed.**

Question 14

Compare the accounting treatment of land and buildings as laid down by FRS 15 with the accounting treatment of investment properties as laid down by SSAP 19 and explain why a building owned for its investment potential should be accounted for differently from one which is occupied by its owners.

Answer

FRS 15 requires that all fixed assets should be depreciated, including freehold buildings. The only exception to this is freehold land which need only be depreciated if it is subject to depletion, for example, quarries or mines.

Where a property is revalued, depreciation should be charged so as to write off the new valuation over the estimated remaining useful life of the building.

SSAP 19, by contrast, recognises that there is a **conceptual difference** between *investment properties* and other fixed assets. Such properties are not depreciated and are carried in the balance sheet at open market value, re-assessed every year. An external valuation should be made at least once every five years.

Changes in the value of an investment property should not be taken to the profit and loss account. In other words, a company **cannot claim profit** on the **unrealised gains on revaluation** of such properties. The revaluation should be disclosed as a movement on an 'investment revaluation reserve'. Should this reserve show a **debit balance** (a loss) the **full amount** of the balance should be removed by charging it to the **profit and loss account**.

SSAP 19 acknowledges that there is a difference between investment properties and other fixed assets, including non-investment properties. Investment properties are held 'not for consumption in the business operations but as investments, the disposal of which would not materially affect any manufacturing or trading operations of the enterprise'.

It follows from this that the item of prime importance is the current value of the investment properties and changes in their current value rather than a calculation of systematic annual depreciation should be reported.

Issues relating to SSAP 19

4.15 SSAP 19 may in due course be amended to fit in with FRS 15 from which it is excluded. There are criticisms of the standard, mainly because it does give a clear definition of 'market value'. The Royal Institution of Chartered Surveyors defines *market value* as the best *price at which the sale of an interest in property might reasonably be expected to have been completed unconditionally for cash consideration on the date of valuation, assuming a 'willing seller'*. There is no mention of a 'willing buyer'.

4.16 This definition involves various difficulties.

(a) **A market transaction** cannot take place without **both a seller and a buyer**.

(b) The concept of 'willing seller' (but not a willing buyer) is largely theoretical in **depressed market conditions** where no willing seller really exists, only **unwilling** and even **forced sellers**.

(c) This 'willing seller' concept inevitably leads to an **over-emphasis** on **comparable evidence**, forcing the valuer to **look backwards rather than forwards**.

(d) Following on from (c), such an approach cannot cope with **specialised assets**, such as large regional shopping centres, for which **no ready market** exits.

4.17 The **deficiencies** in the **current definition** of open market value do **not** become **apparent in normal market conditions** where there is a liquid market in actively traded properties. However, at the **extremes of the cycle**, the current **definition** is quite **inadequate**, producing **over-valuation** in times of **boom** and **under-valuation** in times of **slump**, exacerbating market cycles in an extremely damaging way.

5 SSAP 4 ACCOUNTING FOR GOVERNMENT GRANTS

KEY TERM

Government grants are assistance provided by government to an enterprise.

(a) In the form of **cash** or **transfers** of **other assets**.

(b) In **return** for compliance with **certain conditions** relating to the operating activities of the enterprise.

Note: (Items such as free consultancy services are not grants)

5.1 In practice, the range of grants available is quite wide and may change regularly, reflecting changes in policy introduced by various governments. You therefore need to understand the general principles included in SSAP4 and be able to apply them to any scenario you encounter in your exams.

5.2 Note that for these purposes, government includes local, national or international government, agencies and similar bodies.

BASIC REQUIREMENTS

(a) Government grants should be recognised in the profit and loss account so as to match them with the expenditure towards which they are intended to contribute.

> (b) Government grants should not be recognised in the profit and loss account until the conditions for this receipt have been compiled with and there is reasonable assurance that the grant will be received.

Revenue-based grants

5.3 These are given to **cover** some of the costs of various categories of **revenue expenditure**.

5.4 No particular problems arise in respect of revenue grants as they can be **credited** to **revenue** in the **same period** in which the **revenue expenditure** to which they **relate** is charged.

Capital-based grants

5.5 These are given to **cover** a **proportion** of the **costs of certain** items of **capital expenditure** (for example buildings, plant and machinery), and may be **treated** in a **number of ways**.

   (a) **Credit** the **full amount** of the capital grant to **profit and loss account**.

   (b) **Credit** the **full amount** of the capital grant to a **non distributable reserve**.

5.6 In (a) there is an immediate impact on earnings and in (b) there is no impact on earnings. In both cases the concept of matching costs and revenues is not applied. The grant, like the depreciation cost of fixed assets, should apply to the full life of the assets and so should be spread over that period of time.

5.7 **SSAP 4 states that grants relating to fixed assets should be credited to revenue over the expected useful life of the assets and this can be done in one of two ways:**

   (a) **By reducing the acquisition cost of the fixed asset** by the amount of the grant, and providing depreciation on the reduced amount.

   (b) By **treating** the amount of the grant **as a deferred credit and transferring a portion of it to revenue** annually.

5.8 EXAMPLE: ACCOUNTING FOR GOVERNMENT GRANTS

Needham Limited receives a government grant towards the cost of a new grinder.

- Cost £100,000.

- Grant = 20%

- Expected life = four years

- Residual value = Nil.

- Expected profits of the company, before accounting for depreciation on the new machine or the grant = £50,000 per annum over expected life of the grinder.

The two alternative approaches outlined in SSAP 4 would give different accounts presentations.

BPP PUBLISHING

5.9 **SOLUTION**

(a) *Reducing the cost of the asset approach*

	Year 1 £	Year 2 £	Year 3 £	Year 4 £	Total £
Profits					
Profit before depreciation	50,000	50,000	50,000	50,000	200,000
Depreciation*	(20,000)	(20,000)	(20,000)	(20,000)	(80,000)
Profit	30,000	30,000	30,000	30,000	120,000

*The depreciation charge on a straight line basis, for each year, is ¼ of £[100,000 − 20,000 (20%)] = £20,000.

Balance sheet at year end (extract)

	£	£	£	£
Fixed asset at cost	80,000	80,000	80,000	80,000
Accumulated depreciation	(20,000)	(40,000)	(60,000)	(80,000)
Net book value	60,000	40,000	20,000	-

(b) *Treating the grant as a deferred credit approach*

	Year 1 £	Year 2 £	Year 3 £	Year 4 £	Total £
Profits					
Profit before grant & dep'n	50,000	50,000	50,000	50,000	200,000
Depreciation	(25,000)	(25,000)	(25,000)	(25,000)	(100,000)
Grant	5,000	5,000	5,000	5,000	20,000
Profit	30,000	30,000	30,000	30,000	120,000

Balance sheet at year end (extract)

Fixed asset at cost	100,000	100,000	100,000	100,000
Accumulated depreciation	(25,000)	(50,000)	(75,000)	(100,000)
Net book value	75,000	50,000	25,000	-
Deferred income				
Government grant				
deferred credit	15,000	10,000	5,000	-

Assessment of alternative approaches

5.10 **The annual profits under both methods are the same, and both methods apply the matching concept in arriving at the profit figure.** Reducing the cost of the asset is simpler since, by reducing the depreciation charge, the amount of the grant is automatically credited to revenue over the life of the asset.

The **deferred credit method has the advantage of recording fixed assets at their actual cost, which allows for comparability and is independent of government policy.**

However, the netting off **method** may be in **conflict with the Companies Act 1985** in that the asset would no longer be carried at its purchase price or production cost.

5.11 **Legal opinion confirms the unacceptability of the netting off approach and hence the credit method is preferable.**

5.12 Where the second method is used then **the amount of the deferred credit, if material, should be shown separately in the balance sheet**. SSAP 4 states that it should not be shown as part of the shareholders' funds and it is suggested that the amount should appear under the heading of '**Accruals and deferred income**' in the balance sheet.

5.13 The SSAP requires the **disclosure of the accounting policy** adopted for government grants **and** also requires disclosure of:

(a) The impact of government grants on the **company's profits** in the period **and/or** on its **financial position** generally.

(b) Any **potential liability** to repay grants.

(c) The nature of **government aid other than grants** which has materially affected profits in the period and an estimate of the impact, where possible.

5.14 A grant may be awarded to assist the financing of a project as a whole, where both capital and revenue expenditure are combined. In such cases the accounting treatment should be to match the grant with the relative proportions of revenue and capital expenditure incurred in the total project cost. For example, if two thirds of a project's costs are capital in nature and one third is revenue in nature, then any grant awarded against the whole project cost should be treated as one-third revenue-based and two thirds capital-based.

Question 15

Rosemary plc is to receive a relocation grant of 30% of total expenses incurred. In 20X8 the company incurred the following costs associated with the relocation.

	£'000
Capital cost of factory	2,000
Training costs	200
Removal/relocation costs	300
	2,500

Required

Show the treatment of the government grant for 20X8.

Answer

	£'000
Grant received = 30% × 2,500 =	750
Capital expenditure	2,000
Revenue expenditure	500
	2,500

	£'000
Revenue grant = $\dfrac{500}{2,500} \times 750 =$	150
Capital grant = $\dfrac{2,000}{2,500} \times 750 =$	600
	750

		£'000	£'000
DEBIT	Cash	750	
CREDIT	P&L account		150
CREDIT	Deferred income		600

5.15 Section summary

The following accounting treatments apply.

(a) *Revenue-based grants*

DEBIT   Cash
CREDIT   P & L account

In the period in which the revenue expenditure to which the grant relates is charged.

(b) *Capital-based grants*

DEBIT   Cash
CREDIT   Accruals and deferred income

When the grant is received.

DEBIT   Accruals and deferred income
CREDIT   P & L account

Over the useful life of the related fixed asset.

5.16 Disclosure will be as follows.

(a) *Balance sheet: deferred income note*

	£
Balance at 1.1.20X0	X
Grants received during year	X
Transferred to profit and loss account	(X)
Balance at 31.12.20X0	X

(b) *Profit and loss account*: credit under 'other operating income'.

Exam focus point

A full question on tangible fixed assets might combine two or even all three of the standards covered here.

Chapter roundup

- A number of accounting regulations on the valuation and disclosure of fixed assets are contained in the **Companies Act 1985**.

- In the case of tangible fixed assets, these regulations are supplemented by the provisions of **FRS 15** on tangible fixed assets, SSAP 19 on investment properties and SSAP 4 on the accounting treatment of government grants.

- **SSAP 19** conflicts with the statutory requirement to depreciate all fixed assets with a limited economic life, by stating that **investment properties need not ordinarily** be **depreciated**. Companies taking advantage of this provision will need to justify their departure from statute as being necessary to provide a true and fair view.

- Remember that Section 1 of this chapter lists the **statutory requirements** applying to **all fixed assets**, including the intangible assets and investments dealt with in the next chapter.

- You should now go back to Chapter 3 and consider how the accounting treatments and disclosure requirements of these three standards fit in to the published accounts formats and notes and the CA 1985 requirements.

Quick quiz

1   Which of the following elements can be included in the production cost of a fixed asset?

A   Labour
B   Raw materials
C   Electricity and fuel used
D   Interest on loan taken out to finance production of the asset

2   Define depreciation.

3   When the method of depreciation is changed this constitutes a change of accounting policy and an adjustment should be made to the depreciation charged in previous year.

True   ☐

False   ☐

4   When are investment properties (as defined by SSAP 19) subject to depreciation?

5   In which two ways can fixed asset grants be revenue?

Answer to quick quiz

1   All of them. (see paras 2.2 - 2.18)

2   See paragraph 2.31

3   False. (see paras 2.44 and 2.45)

4   When the property is subject to a lease which has 20 years or less to run. (4.8)

5   See paragraph 5.7 as well as paragraphs 5.10 to 5.11

Now try the question below from the Exam Question Bank

Number	Level	Marks	Time
4	Full exam	25	45 mins

Chapter 5

FIXED ASSETS: INTANGIBLE ASSETS AND INVESTMENTS

Topic list	Syllabus reference
1 Intangible assets: Companies Act 1985 requirements	3(b)
2 SSAP 13 *Accounting for research and development*	3(b)
3 Goodwill: introduction	3(b)
4 FRS 10 *Goodwill and intangible assets*	3(b)
5 FRS 11 *Impairment of fixed assets and goodwill*	3(b)
6 Investments	3(b)

Introduction

We will look at intangible assets in this chapter, the main categories of which are R & D costs and goodwill.

Accounting for research and development according to SSAP 13 is relatively straightforward, and has been covered in your Paper 1.1 studies.

The study material on goodwill is closely connected with the later chapters on group accounts. When you reach these chapters you should refer back to the coverage here on goodwill.

The treatment of investments is addressed only briefly here, again because the topic is closely related to group accounts, dealt with in later chapters.

Study guide

- Discuss the nature and possible accounting treatments of both internally generated and purchased goodwill.

- Distinguish between goodwill and other intangible assets.

- Describe the criteria for the initial recognition and measurement of intangible assets.

- Describe the subsequent accounting treatment, including the principle of impairment tests in relation to purchased goodwill.

- Describe the circumstances in which negative goodwill arises, and its subsequent accounting treatment and disclosure.

- Describe and apply the requirements of SSAP 13 'Accounting for Research and Development'.

- Define the recoverable amount of an asset; define impairment losses.

- Give examples of, and be able to identify, circumstances that may indicate that an impairment of fixed assets has occurred.

- Describe what is meant by an income generating unit.

- State the basis on which impairment losses should be allocated.

- Allocate a given impairment loss to the assets of an income generating unit.

Exam guide

Goodwill is certain to feature in the group accounting questions in the exam. You need to be able to account for goodwill but also understand the reasons for its accounting treatment; FRS 11 could come up as the second part of a question.

1 INTANGIBLE ASSETS: COMPANIES ACT 1985 REQUIREMENTS

1.1 The **statutory balance sheet** format lists the following intangible fixed assets (item BI in the format).

(a) **Development costs**
(b) **Concessions, patents, licences, trade marks** and similar rights and assets
(c) **Goodwill**
(d) **Payments on account**

Patents and trade marks

1.2 **Concessions, patents, licences, trade marks etc** should only be **treated,** and **disclosed,** as **assets** if they were **either:**

(a) **Acquired** for **valuable consideration**
(b) **Created** by the **company itself.**

Development costs

1.3 **Development costs, may only be treated as an asset** in the balance sheet (rather than being written off immediately) **in 'special circumstances'**. The Act does not define these circumstances and this is a case where a SSAP goes further than statute. **SSAP 13** (see below) lays down **strict criteria** for determining when such expenditure may be **treated** as an **asset**. The **Act merely states** that, if it is **so treated**, the **following disclosures** must be made by **way of note:**

(a) The **period** over which the amount of the **costs originally capitalised** is **being** or is to be **written off**

(b) The **reasons** for **capitalising** the **development costs**

Goodwill

1.4 The Act implicitly makes a **distinction between inherent goodwill and purchased goodwill.** The distinction will be explained when we review FRS 10 *Goodwill and intangible assets.* For now, please remember that **the Act does not permit inherent goodwill to be included as an asset** in the balance sheet. The **difficulties** of **valuing inherent goodwill** are in any case **so great** that very few companies have ever carried it in their balance sheets. **However,** several **listed companies** have **capitalised brands** which were **developed in-house.**

1.5 **Purchased goodwill may be treated as an asset in the balance sheet.** If it is so treated (rather than being written off immediately):

(a) It must be **written off systematically** over a **period chosen by the directors**
(b) The period chosen must **not exceed** the **useful economic life** of the goodwill

(c) **Disclosure** should be made of the **period chosen** and of the **reasons** for choosing that period.

1.6 **This statutory requirement to amortise any goodwill capitalised does not extend to goodwill arising on consolidation.** Even so, **companies** have to **amortise consolidation** goodwill to comply with the **stricter requirements of FRS 10**. You should note that FRS 10 is stricter than CA 1985 in the case of goodwill on acquisition, as we will see below.

2 SSAP 13 ACCOUNTING FOR RESEARCH AND DEVELOPMENT

2.1 In many companies, especially those which produce food, or 'scientific' products such as medicines, or 'high technology' products, the expenditure on research and development (R & D) is considerable. **When R & D is a large item of cost, its accounting treatment may have a significant influence on the profits of a business and its balance sheet valuation.**

Exam focus point

SSAP 13 might feature in a small way as part of a consolidation question, it is very unlikely to form a major question.

Knowledge brought forward from earlier studies

SSAP 13 Accounting research and development

Definitions

- **Pure/basic research** is experimental/theoretical work with no commercial end in view and no practical application.

- **Applied research** is original investigation directed towards a specific practical aim/objective.

- **Development** is the use of scientific/technical knowledge in order to produce new/substantially improved **materials**, **devices**, **processes** etc.

Accounting treatment

- **Pure and applied research** should be **written off** as incurred.

- **Development expenditure** should be **written off** in year of expenditure, *except* in certain circumstances when it *may* be **deferred to future periods**.

  - **S** Separately defined project
  - **E** Expenditure separately identifiable
  - **C** Commercially viable
  - **T** Technically feasible
  - **O** Overall profit expected
  - **R** Resources exist to complete the project

- Show deferred development costs as an **intangible asset amortised** from the beginning of commercial production, **systematically** by reference to sales, etc.

- Deferred costs should be **reviewed annually**; where the above criteria no longer apply, write off the cost immediately.

- Development expenditure previously written off **can be reinstated** if the **uncertainties** which led to it being written off **no longer apply**.

- **R & D fixed assets** should be **capitalised** and **written off** over their estimated **economic lives**.

- Deferral of costs should be **applied consistently** to all projects.

- SSAP 13 does not apply to:

  - ° Fixed assets used for R&D (except amortisation)
  - ° The cost of locating mineral deposits in extractive industries
  - ° Expenditure where there is a firm contract for reimbursement

Disclosure

- R & D activities should be disclosed in the **directors' report**.

- **Private companies** outside groups which include a plc are **exempt** from disclosing R & D expenditures (except amortisation) if they would meet the **criteria** for a **medium-sized company × 10**.

- *Disclose:*

  ○ **Movements** on deferred development expenditure
  ○ **R & D charged** to the P & L a/c analysed between **current year expenditure** and **amortisation**
  ○ An accounting **policy** note

2.2 The importance of R & D disclosures was emphasised in another **survey** of what **users really needed** in financial statements.

(a) UK institutional investors said the **top requirement** was **future prospects and plans** (84%). R & D is seen to form a crucial quantitative element of prospects and plans.

(b) When specifically asked about R & D, 64% of UK investors said the data was very, or extremely, important to them.

Unfortunately, the top companies analysed failed dismally to provide the information required. There is a wide variety of treatment and information given on R & D and improvements are required in the reporting of R & D.

Question 1

In connection with SSAP 13 *Accounting for research and development*:

(a) Define 'applied research' and 'development'.

(b) Explain why it is considered necessary to distinguish between applied research and development expenditure and how this distinction affects the accounting treatment.

(c) State whether the following items are included within the SSAP 13 definition of research and development, and give your reasons:

   (i) Market research
   (ii) Testing of pre-production prototypes
   (iii) Operational research
   (iv) Testing in search of process alternatives

Answer

(a) *Applied research* expenditure is expenditure on **original investigations** which are carried out in order to gain **new scientific or technical knowledge**, but which also have a specific practical aim or objective. An example might be research into a disease with the intention of finding a cure or a vaccine.

Development expenditure is expenditure on the application of existing scientific or technical knowledge in order to produce **new or substantially improved materials, devices, products, processes, systems or services** prior to the commencement of **commercial production**. The costs of developing a prototype would be development expenditure.

(b) SSAP 13 considers that:

'pure and **applied research** can be regarded as part of a **continuing operation** required to maintain a company's business and its competitive position. In general, **no one particular period** rather than any other will be expected to **benefit** and **therefore** it is appropriate that these **costs** should be **written off** as they are **incurred**.'

This is in accordance with the matching concept which requires that revenue and costs are 'matched with one another *so far as their relationship can be established or justifiably assumed*' and also with the prudence concept.

This has the affect that applied research costs must be written off as incurred but **development expenditure can be deferred** (that is, capitalised as an intangible asset) and **amortised** over the life of the product, service, process or system developed. This treatment is only permissible if the project meets **certain criteria** designed to ensure that deferral is prudent.

(c)   (i)   **Market research** is **not normally** considered to be **research and development** activity. It is **specifically excluded in the SSAP**. This is presumably because it does not depart from routine activity and it does not contain an appreciable element of innovation.

       (ii)   **Testing of prototypes** is included in SSAP 13's list of activities normally to be considered as **research and development**. A prototype must be constructed and tested before full-scale production can be risked and so it is an **essential stage** in the **development process**.

       (iii)   '**Operational research not tied** to a **specific research** and development activity' is an activity which SSAP 13 considers should **not normally** be **included in research and development**. 'Operational research' is presumably used here to denote the **branch of applied mathematics** which includes techniques such as linear programming and network analysis. The implication is that routine use of such techniques (to improve production efficiency, for example) does **not fall within the ambit of SSAP 13**, in spite of the use of the word 'research'.

       (iv)   '**Testing in search for**, or evaluation of, product, service or **process alternatives**' is considered to be **research and development** work by SSAP 13. It would **fall within the definition of applied research**.

Question 2

R.U. Welle Pharmaceuticals plc incurs the following expenditure in years 20X4-20X8.

	Research £'000	Development £'000
20X4	40	65
20X5	45	70
20X6	49	-
20X7	41	-
20X8	43	-

You are told that R.U. Welle Pharmaceuticals plc capitalises development expenditure when appropriate. The item developed in 20X4 and 20X5 goes on sale on 1 January 20X6 and it will be three years from then until any competitor is expected to have a similar product on the market.

Required

Show the profit and loss account and balance sheet extracts for all five years.

Answer

PROFIT AND LOSS ACCOUNT (EXTRACTS)

	20X4 £'000	20X5 £'000	20X6 £'000	20X7 £'000	20X8 £'000
Research expenditure	40	45	49	41	43
Amortisation of development costs	-	-	45	45	45

BALANCE SHEET (EXTRACT)

Intangible fixed assets	20X4 £'000	20X5 £'000	20X6 £'000	20X7 £'000	20X8 £'000
Development costs	65	135	135	135	135
Amortisation	-	-	(45)	(90)	(135)
Net book value	65	135	90	45	-

3   GOODWILL: INTRODUCTION

Nature of goodwill

3.1   By definition, goodwill is an asset which **cannot be realised separately** from the **business as a whole**.

KEY TERM

Goodwill is the difference between:

(a)   the aggregate fair value of the net assets of a business
(b)   the value of the business as a whole.

3.2   There are many factors which may explain why goodwill arises. Examples are:

- skilled management team
- good labour relations
- strategic location
- good customer relations

These factors are **intangible** and it is **difficult** to place a **money value** on them. Until **recently,** it was **not usual** to show **goodwill** as an **asset** in the balance sheet. Any **amount** at which it was valued was **considered** to be **arbitrary** and **subject to fluctuations**.

Potential factors giving rise to goodwill

3.3

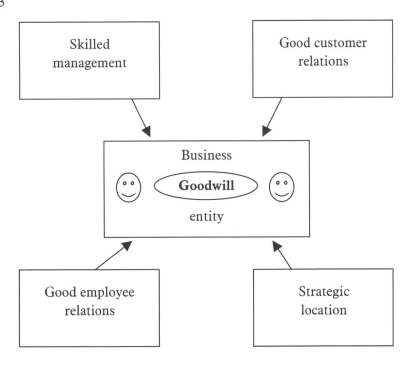

Inherent goodwill and purchased goodwill

3.4 Some form of goodwill is likely to exist in every business. However, the **only circumstances** when **goodwill** is **valued** and may be **disclosed** as an **asset** in the balance sheet is when one **business acquires another as a going concern**. This is because there is then a **positive indication** available of the **value of goodwill acquired**. This is known as **purchased goodwill.**

3.5 **Goodwill which is presumed to exist, but which has not been evidenced in a purchases transaction, is called non purchased or inherent goodwill.**

Possible accounting treatments for inherent goodwill

3.6 There are two possible approaches to accounting for inherent goodwill.

(a) Ignore inherent goodwill and make no entries in the accounting records.

(b) Estimate the value of inherent goodwill and include this in the records and accounts of the business.

3.7 **However,** remember that FRS 10 stipulates that **inherent goodwill** should **not be recognised** in the financial statements. Its **value cannot** be **measured** with sufficient **reliability** because of the **subjectivity** involved. **It should therefore be ignored.**

Possible accounting treatments for purchased goodwill

3.8 A **wide variety of accounting treatments** are possible regarding **purchased goodwill.**

(a) Capitalise goodwill as an **asset** but **amortise** it over its **estimated useful life.**

(b) Capitalise **goodwill** as an **asset** but **write down** the value if **impairment becomes evident.**

(c) **Write off the entire amount** immediately against:

(i) Income

(ii) Reserves

(d) Show goodwill as a **continuing** and **separately identifiable deduction from shareholders' funds** (the 'dangling debit' method).

The case for amortisation approach

3.9 (a) Goodwill is an asset which at the **date of acquisition** has a **definite value to the business.**

(b) This asset is a measure of the extent to which the **earnings** of the **purchased business** will **exceed** those which could be **expected** from the **use of its identifiable assets.** Consequently, it should be **amortised** so as to **match costs against income** (the accruals concept). This is one of the views adopted by FRS 10 *Goodwill and intangible assets.*

The case for immediate write-off approach

3.10 (a) (i) Writing off purchased goodwill immediately would be **consistent with the treatment of inherent goodwill.**

(ii) Alternatively, the purchased goodwill becomes **indistinguishable from the total goodwill** of the group and should therefore be written off.

     (iii)   Goodwill might be treated as an asset, but too much **uncertainty exists** over its **value** and **economic life**, therefore **prudence** dictates that it should be written off.

  (b) (i)   Goodwill is **not an asset** as such and therefore to show it as an asset would be misleading.

     (ii)   Both **inherent** and **purchased** goodwill would be **excluded** (**consistency**, as in (c) above).

     (iii)   **Analysts** may treat goodwill **as they like if it is not amortised.**

BASIC REQUIREMENTS

(a) Purchased goodwill should be capitalised and classified as an asset on the balance sheet.

(b) It should be amortised on a systematic basis over its useful economic life.

Negative goodwill

3.11   Negative goodwill arises when the price paid for a business is less than the fair value of the separable net assets acquired, for example, if the vendor **needed cash quickly** and was forced to sell at a **bargain price.**

4   FRS 10 GOODWILL AND INTANGIBLE ASSETS

Overview

4.1   FRS 10 *Goodwill and intangible assets* was published in December 1997. The requirements of the FRS **apply to all intangible assets except those specifically addressed by another accounting standard**, eg SSAP 13. Oil and gas exploration and development costs are also exempt.

4.2   The FRS 10 applies to **all financial statements except** those entities applying the Financial Reporting Standard for Smaller Entities (**FRSSE**) which do not prepare consolidated accounts.

4.3   Although FRS 10 is framed around the purchase of a subsidiary undertaking, it also applies to the acquisition of unincorporated entities.

Objective of FRS 10

4.4   The objectives stated by FRS 10 are to ensure that:

  (a) **Capitalised goodwill** and **intangible assets** are charged in the **P&L account** as far as possible in the **periods** in which they are **depleted.**

  (b) **Sufficient information** is **disclosed** in the financial statements to enable users to determine the **impact of goodwill** and **intangible assets** on the **financial position** and **performance** of the **reporting entity.**

Definitions

4.5 FRS 10 introduces a variety of new definitions, some of which relate to terms used above.

> **KEY TERMS**
>
> - **Class of intangible assets**: a group of intangible assets that have **similar nature** or **function** in the business of the entity.
>
> - **Identifiable assets and liabilities**: the assets and liabilities of an entity that are capable of being **disposed** of or **settled separately**, without disposing of a business of the entity.
>
> - **Purchased goodwill**: the **difference** between:
>
>   - the fair value of the consideration paid for an acquired entity
>   - the aggregate of the fair values of that entity's identifiable assets and liabilities.
>
> - **Residual value**: the **net realisable value** of an asset at the **end of its useful economic life**. Residual values are based on prices at the date of acquisition (or revaluation) of the asset and **do not take account** of **expected future price changes**.
>
> - **Useful economic life:** the useful economic life of an **intangible asset** is the **period** over which the entity expects to **derive economic benefit** from that asset.
>
>   The useful economic life of **purchased goodwill** is the period over which the **value** of the **underlying business** is expected to **exceed** the values of its **identifiable net assets**.
>
> *(FRS 10)*

Ascertaining goodwill

4.6

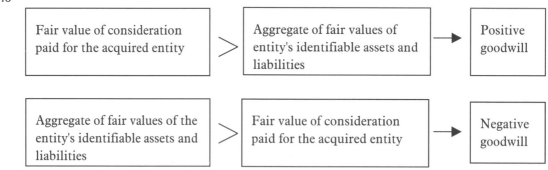

4.7 EXAMPLE

AJ Limited acquires 80% of VJ Limited at 31 December 20X8.

AJ Limited originally made an initial offer of £75,000 which was rejected. A subsequent offer of £95,000 was however accepted. The total value of VJ Limited is £100,000. Identify the goodwill arising under these two scenarios.

4.8 SOLUTION

	Scenario 1 £	Scenario 2 £
Fair value of consideration	75,000	95,000
Fair value of VJ Limited's net assets – 80% of £100,000	(80,000)	80,000
Negative goodwill	5,000	
Positive goodwill		15,000

4.9 FRS 10 also includes definitions of the following terms, which are also defined in FRS 11.

- Impairment
- Intangible assets
- Net realisable value
- Readily ascertainable market value
- Recoverable amount
- Value in use

Purchased goodwill is also defined by FRS 11, but the definition given here is fuller.

Initial recognition and measurement

Goodwill

4.10 **Positive purchased goodwill should be capitalised and classified as an asset on the balance sheet.**

4.11 **Internally generated goodwill should not be capitalised.** This requirement is the same as in the old SSAP 22.

Intangible assets

4.12 An intangible asset **purchased separately** from a business should be **capitalised at cost**. Examples of such assets include patents, copyrights and licences.

4.13 Where an **intangible** asset is **acquired as part of the acquisition of a business** the treatment **depends** on whether its **value** can be **measured reliably** on its initial recognition.

(a) If its value **can be measured reliably**, it should initially be **recorded at its fair value**. (The fair value should **not create** or **increase** any **negative goodwill** arising on the acquisition **unless** the asset has a **readily ascertainable market value**.)

(b) If the value of the asset **cannot be measured reliably**, the intangible asset must be **subsumed within the amount of the purchase price attributed to goodwill.**

Internally developed intangibles

4.14 FRS 10 stipulates that companies may **capitalise non-purchased** ('internally-developed') **intangibles** but **only to the extent that they have a 'readily ascertainable market value'**. This is an important definition that **means that:**

(a) The asset belongs to **a group of homogenous assets** (ie they are all of the same kind), that are **equivalent** in **all material respects.**

(b) There is an **active market** for that **group of assets**, evidenced by **frequent transactions.**

4.15 Examples given by FRS 10 of intangibles that may meet these conditions include certain **operating licences, franchises** and **quotas**.

4.16 FRS 10 also suggests **certain intangibles** that are **not equivalent** in all material aspects, are **indeed unique** and so **do not have readily identifiable market values**.

- Brands
- Publishing titles
- Patented drugs
- Engineering design patents

4.17 Hence, FRS 10 effectively precludes the recognition of most internally developed intangibles in financial accounts.

4.18 Once they have passed the tests for recognition, FRS 10 requires that intangible assets be treated in exactly the way as goodwill.

Approach to amortisation and impairment

4.19 The FRS 10 approach to amortisation reflects the wish to charge the profit and loss account only to the extent that the **carrying value** of the asset is **not supported** by the **current value** of the asset **within the acquired business**.

4.20 The approach is based on a **combination** of:

- **Amortising** over a **limited period** on a **systematic basis**
- An **annual impairment review** (see later coverage)

4.21 The first task is to **decide whether** or not the **goodwill** or **intangible** has a **limited useful economic life**.

4.22 You may find the following diagram helpful in clarifying the approach outlined above.

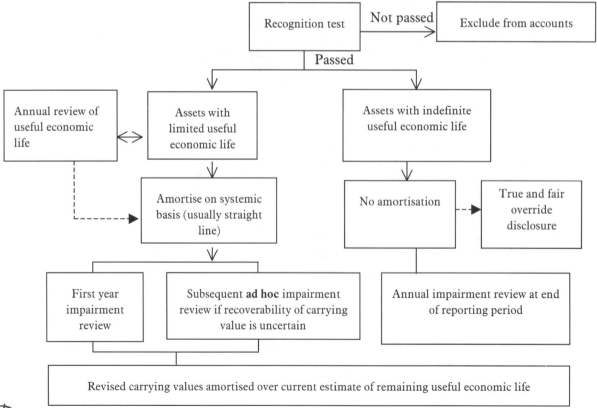

Assets with a limited useful economic life

Amortisation

4.23 FRS 10 states that, where goodwill and intangible assets are regarded as having **limited useful economic lives** they should be **amortised on a systematic basis over those lives**.

4.24 FRS 10 gives **little guidance** on how to **predict** an asset's **useful economic life**, which can be very difficult for goodwill and intangibles as it is **impossible** to **see** them **actually wearing out**. It does, however, give **examples** of **relevant considerations**, which include certain **economic** and **legal factors** relating to the asset. An intangible may, for example, be linked to a product with a **specific lifespan**, or there may be time periods attached to **legal rights** (eg patents).

4.25 There is a **basic assumption** that the **useful economic lives** of **purchased goodwill** and **intangible assets** are limited to periods of **20 years or less**. However, this **presumption** may be **rebutted** and a useful economic life regarded as a longer period or indefinite only if:

(a) The **durability** of the **acquired business** or **intangible asset** can be demonstrated and justifies estimating the **useful economic life** to **exceed 20 years**.

(b) The goodwill or intangible asset is capable of **continued measurement** (so that annual impairment reviews will be feasible).

Question 3

The circumstances where an indefinite useful economic life longer than 20 years may be legitimately presumed are limited. What factors determine the durability of goodwill?

Answer

FRS 10 mentions the following.

(a) The **nature** of the business
(b) The **stability** of the industry in which the acquired business operates
(c) Typical **lifespans** of the products to which the goodwill attaches
(d) The extent to which the acquisition **overcomes** market entry **barriers** that will continue to exist
(e) The expected future **impact** of **competition** on the business

---

4.26 **Uncertainty** about the **length** of the **useful economic** life is **not a good reason** for choosing one that is **unrealistically short** or for adopting a **20 year** useful economic life **by default**.

4.27 In amortising an **intangible asset,** a **residual value** may be assigned to that asset only if such residual value can be **measured reliably**. In practice, the **residual value** of an **intangible asset is often insignificant**.

No residual value may be assigned to **goodwill**.

4.28 The method of amortisation should be chosen to reflect the **expected pattern of depletion** of the goodwill or intangible asset. A **straight-line method should be chosen unless another method can be demonstrated to be more appropriate**.

4.29 Whatever the **useful economic life** chosen, the company should be able to justify it. It **should be reviewed annually and revised if appropriate**.

Impairment review

4.30   In addition to the amortisation, the asset should be reviewed for impairment:

   (a)   At the end of the first full financial year following the acquisition ('**the first year review**').

   (b)   In **other periods** if events or changes in **circumstances** indicate that the **carrying values may not be recoverable**.

4.31   If an impairment is identified at the time of the first year review, this impairment is likely to reflect:

   (a)   An **overpayment**;

   (b)   An **event** that occurred **between** the **acquisition** and the **first year review**.

   (c)   **Depletion** of the acquired goodwill or intangible asset between the acquisition and the first year review that exceeds the amount recognised through amortisation.

4.32   The requirements of FRS 10 are such that the recognition of an **impairment loss** must be **justified** in the same way as the absence of an impairment loss, is by looking at **expected future cash flows**.

4.33   Goodwill and intangible assets that are **amortised** over a period **exceeding 20 years** from the date of acquisition should be **reviewed for impairment at the end of each reporting period**.

4.34   Where the **impairment review** indicates a **diminution** in **value**, the goodwill and intangible assets must be **written down accordingly**. The **revised carrying value** should be **amortised** over the current estimate of the **remaining useful economic life**.

Assets with an indefinite useful economic life

No amortisation

4.35   Where goodwill and intangible assets are regarded as having **indefinite useful economic lives**, they **should not be amortised**.

4.36   'Indefinite' is not the same as 'infinite', it means merely that no limit can be fixed for it.

> **IMPORTANT!**
>
> If the option not to amortise is taken, this constitutes a departure from the Companies Act and will need to be justified by invoking the **true and fair override**.

Impairment review

4.37   Goodwill and intangible assets that are **not amortised** (because their useful economic life is deemed to be indefinite) should be **reviewed for impairment at the end of each reporting period**.

4.38   If an **impairment loss** is **recognised**, the **revised carrying value**, if being amortised, should be **amortised** over the **current estimate** of the **remaining useful economic life**.

4.39 If **goodwill** arising on **consolidation** is found to be **impaired**, the carrying amount of the **investment** held in the accounts of the **parent undertaking** should also be **reviewed for impairment**.

4.40 **The emphasis on impairment reviews is a key feature of FRS 10.** The ASB believes that a formal requirement to monitor the value of acquired goodwill and intangible assets using standardised methods and to report any losses in the financial statements will **enhance** the **quality** of the **information** provided to **users of financial statements**.

Reversal of impairment

4.41 Normally, once an impairment review has identified a loss, this cannot be restored at a later date. However, **if the loss was caused by an *external* event that later reversed in a way that was not foreseen, the original impairment loss may be restored.** An example of this might be: if a direct competitor came on to the market, leading to an impairment loss, and then the competitor did not survive or produced a different product from the one originally envisaged.

Updating of impairment reviews

4.42 After the first period, the reviews need only be updated. If expections of **future cash flows** and **discount rates** have **not changed significantly**, the updating procedure will be **relatively quick** to **perform**.

4.43 If there have been **no adverse changes** in the **key assumptions** and **variables**, or if there was previously substantial leeway between the carrying value and estimated value in use, it **may** even **be possible** to ascertain immediately that an **income-generating unit** is **not impaired**.

Revaluation of goodwill

4.44 **Goodwill may not be revalued, except** in the circumstances described above, ie the **reversal of an impairment**.

If an **intangible asset** has a **readily ascertainable market value**, it may be **revalued** to its **market value**.

4.45 Future amortisation should always be made on the revalued amount, just like depreciation for a revalued tangible fixed asset.

Question 4

Honeybun Ltd has an income-generating unit with the following details:

(a) Carrying value of £4,000,000 at 31 December 20X7. This carrying value comprises £1,000,000 relating to goodwill and £3,000,000 relating to net assets.

(b) The goodwill is not being amortised as its useful life is believed to be indefinite.

(c) In 20X8, changes in the regulatory framework surrounding its business mean that the income-generating unit has a value in use of £3,200,000. As a result of losses, net assets have decreased to £2,800,000 reducing the total carrying value of the unit to £3,800,000 which has thus suffered an impairment loss of £600,000. This is charged to the profit and loss account. The carrying value of goodwill is reduced to £400,000.

(d) In 20X9 the company develops a new product with the result that the value in use of the income-generating unit is now £3,400,000. Net tangible assets have remained at £2,800,000.

BPP PUBLISHING

Can all or any of the impairment loss be reversed?

Answer

No. Despite the value in use of the business unit now being £3,400,000 compared to its carrying value of £3,200,000, it is not possible to reverse £200,000 of the prior year's impairment loss of £600,000 since the reason for the increase in value of the business unit (the launch of the new product) is not the same as the reason for the original impairment loss (the change in the regulatory environment in which the business operates).

Negative goodwill

How negative goodwill arises

4.46 As mentioned earlier, negative goodwill arises when the fair value of the net assets acquired is more than the fair value of the consideration. In other words, the investor has got a bargain.

Subsequent accounting treatment

4.47 FRS 10 states that to ensure that any negative goodwill is justified:

(a) **The investee's assets should be checked for impairment**

(b) **The liabilities checked for understatement**.

If indeed any negative goodwill remains after these tests, it needs to be disclosed consistently with positive goodwill.

4.48 Rather than being shown on the bottom half of the balance sheet as a capital reserve - as was required by SSAP 22 - **it is now disclosed in the intangible fixed assets category, directly under positive goodwill, ie as a 'negative asset'.** A sub-total of the net amount of positive and negative goodwill should be shown on the face of the balance sheet.

4.49 This presentation may seem a little odd. However, the ASB argues that negative goodwill does not meet the definition of a liability under the *Statement of Principles* and that this treatment is consistent with that of positive goodwill.

Transfers to profit and loss account

4.50 Negative goodwill should be **recognised in the profit and loss account in the periods when the non-monetary assets acquired are depreciated or sold.**

4.51 There are two important points to note.

(a) It would be strange for the investor to pay less than its fair value for the monetary items acquired. The value of cash, for example, is pretty universal. Therefore, it is more **likely that the negative goodwill represents a shortfall in the value of the non-monetary items.**

(b) The **benefit** of the 'bargain' of getting these non-monetary items at less than fair value **will only be realised when the non-monetary items themselves are realised**.

[ie it is the non-monetary assets (fixed assets, stock etc) that have been bought on the cheap, effectively at a discount (negative goodwill). Therefore, carry the discount (negative goodwill) in the balance sheet until the relevant assets are sold, or depreciated. Then transfer the relevant chunk of discount (negative goodwill) from the balance sheet to the profit and loss account.]

4.51 Hence, any negative goodwill should be credited to the **profit and loss account** only when the **non-monetary assets themselves** are realised, and this is when they are either **depreciated or sold**.

4.52 FRS 10 also requires any **remaining goodwill** in **excess** of fair values of the non-monetary assets acquired should be recognised in the **profit and loss account** in the **periods expected to be benefitted**.

Question 5

Helena plc acquired its investment in Karen Ltd during the year ended 31 December 20X8. The goodwill on acquisition was calculated as follows.

	£'000	£'000
Cost of investment		400
Fair value of net assets acquired (remaining useful life - 7 years)		
Fixed assets	700	
Stock	100	
Non-monetary assets	800	
Net monetary assets	200	
		(1,000)
Negative goodwill		(600)

Required

Calculate the amount relating to negative goodwill as reflected in the profit and loss account and balance sheet for the year ended 31 December 20X8.

Answer

Amortisation in the profit and loss account for 20X8

Non-monetary assets recognised through the profit and loss account for the year ended 31 December 20X8:

	£'000
Stock (all sold)	100
Depreciation (£700,000 ÷ 7)	100
Non-monetary assets recognised this year	200
Total non-monetary assets at acquisition	800
∴ Proportion recognised this year	¼

Hence:

	£'000
Negative goodwill arising on acquisition	600
Proportion released to profit and loss account for year to 31.12.X8 (¼)	(150)
Balance at 31.12.X8, shown on balance sheet as deduction from positive goodwill	450

The balance of £450,000 will be carried forward and released into the profit and loss account over the next 6 years at £75,000 per annum, ie in the periods expected to be benefitted. (Note: it is assumed that the stock at acquisition was all realised in the year to 31.12.X8.)

Disclosures

4.53 FRS 10 requires various disclosures relating to the following.

- Recognition and measurement
- Amortisation of positive goodwill and intangible assets

- Revaluation
- Negative goodwill
- Impairment (see next section).

4.54 The **disclosure requirements are the same as for any other fixed asset,** including the table showing a reconciliation of movements during the year, for every category of intangible assets (including goodwill), details of revaluations, accounting policies and details of amortisation charged.

4.55 Significant **additional disclosure** requirements include requirements to explain:

- The **bases of valuation** of intangible assets

- The **grounds for believing a useful economic life to exceed 20 years** or to be indefinite

- The **treatment adopted of negative goodwill**

Issues relating to FRS 10

4.56 FRS 10 has involved **significant changes to the accounts of many companies.** Over 95% of companies in the UK had traditionally adopted the 'immediate write off' treatment permitted under now withdrawn SSAP 22.

4.57 The firm Ernst & Young raised issues over the thinking behind the standard.

(a) **FRS 10 still allows a choice of accounting treatments.** Companies can follow a regime that permits the goodwill to be carried as a **permanent asset.** This may allow some **spurious assets** to remain indefinitely in the balance sheet, potentially providing ammunition for challenging of the profession in any likely future wave of accounting scandal.

(b) **The impairment review,** if it is to be based on FRS 11, applies **'labyrinthine methodologies** to very soft numbers'. In other words, it **is subjective,** not least in determining **how** the **business** is to be **segmented. Forecasting cashflows** is also **problematic.**

(c) **The importance of negative goodwill has been underestimated.** It is more likely to arise now that FRS 7 bans reorganisation provisions, thus raising the value of the net assets acquired.

(d) **The treatment of negative goodwill is 'strange'.** It is a **'dangling credit'** in the balance sheet and the profit and loss account treatment simply mirrors that required for depreciation without regard to the fact that this is a **credit** to the profit and loss account.

4.58 **Section summary**

(a) **Purchased goodwill** and **intangible assets** will both be **capitalised** as assets in the balance sheet. The option for goodwill of immediate write off to reserves, by-passing the profit and loss account, will no longer be available as it was under SSAP 22.

(b) Where goodwill and intangible assets have **limited lives** they will be **amortised** to the profit and loss account over their **expected lives.**

(c) Amortisation will not be required for assets that can be justified as having **indefinite lives.** They need to be **written down only if their values drop below those in the balance sheet.**

(d) There is a **general presumption** that the **lives** of goodwill and intangible assets will be **no more than 20 years**. **A longer or indefinite life** may be assigned only if the **durability** of the asset can be demonstrated and if it is **possible to remeasure** its value **each year** to **identify any reduction**.

(e) **Impairment reviews** must be **performed annually** where **lives** of **more than 20 years** are chosen. For **lives of less than 20 years**, they are required only in the **year after acquisition**, and in **other years** if there is some **indication** that the asset's **value might have fallen below its recorded value**.

5   FRS 11 IMPAIRMENT OF FIXED ASSETS AND GOODWILL

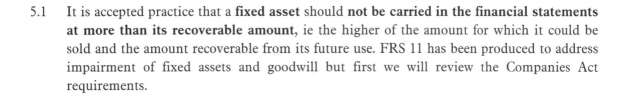

Exam focus point

Impairment is a very examinable area as it ties in well with both FRS 15 and FRS 10. It is likely to be part of a 25 mark question as it was in the pilot paper.

5.1   It is accepted practice that a **fixed asset** should **not be carried in the financial statements at more than its recoverable amount**, ie the higher of the amount for which it could be sold and the amount recoverable from its future use. FRS 11 has been produced to address impairment of fixed assets and goodwill but first we will review the Companies Act requirements.

Companies Act 1985 requirements

5.2   Under CA 85 the treatment of diminutions in value is as follows.

(a) **Assets held at cost**

   (i)   **Temporary diminutions** are **not recognised**.

   (ii) **Permanent diminutions** are **recognised** and **charged to the profit and loss account**.

(b) **Assets held at valuation**

   (i)   **Temporary diminutions** are **recognised** and **debited to reserves**.

   (ii) **Permanent diminutions** are **recognised** and charged to the **asset's previous surplus in reserves** and **then to the profit and loss account** for the year.

5.3   Further points to note are as follows.

(a) Where the increase in value relates to the **reversal of a permanent diminution** in value previously charged to the profit and loss account, the increase will be posted to the profit and loss account for the year.

(b) Any changes in value taken **directly to reserves** must be disclosed in the STRGL.

FRS 11 *Impairment of fixed assets and goodwill*

Overview

5.4   While statute provides some guidance, it provides none on how the **recoverable amount** should be **measured** and **when impairment losses** should be **recognised**. In consequence,

131 *BPP*
PUBLISHING

practice might be **inconsistent** and perhaps some impairments may **not** be **recognised** on a **timely basis**.

5.5 The need for a standard on impairment was increased by the requirement in FRS 10 *Goodwill and intangible assets* (see Section 4) that, where goodwill and intangible assets have a useful life in excess of twenty years or one that is indefinite, the recoverable amount of the goodwill and intangible assets should be reviewed every year.

Objective

5.6 The objective of FRS 11 is to ensure that:

(a) Fixed assets and goodwill are **recorded** in the financial statements at **no more than** their **recoverable amount**.

(b) Any resulting **impairment loss** is **measured** and **recognised** on a **consistent basis**.

(c) **Sufficient information** is **disclosed** in the financial statements to enable users to **understand** the **impact** of the **impairment** on the **financial position** and **performance** of the reporting entity.

Scope

5.7 FRS 11 **excludes**:

(a) Non-purchased goodwill.

(b) Fixed assets which are governed by the ASB's standard on *Derivatives and financial instruments* (FRS 13 see Chapter 12).

(c) Investment properties as defined in SSAP 19.

(d) Shares held by an ESOP.

(e) Cost capitalised pending determination under the Oil Industry Accounting Committee's SORP.

FRS 11 applies to subsidiary undertakings, associates and joint ventures.

BASIC REQUIREMENT

A **review for impairment** of a fixed asset or goodwill should be carried out if **events** or **changes** in **circumstances** indicate that the **carrying amount** of the fixed asset or goodwill **may not be recoverable**.

KEY TERM

Impairment: a **reduction** in the **recoverable amount** of a fixed asset or goodwill **below** its **carrying amount**.   (FRS 11)

5.8 Impairment occurs due to *either*:

(a) Something happening to the **fixed asset** itself.
(b) Something occurring in the **environment** within which the asset operates.

Indicators of impairment

5.9 FRS 11 provides **indicators of impairment** to help determine when an **impairment review** is **required**. Examples of such **events** and **changes** in **circumstances** include the following.

(a) There is a **current period operating loss** or **net cash outflow** from **operating activities,** combined with *either*:

    (i) **Past operating losses** or **net cash outflows** from operating activities

    (ii) An expectation of **continuing operating losses** or **net cash outflows** from operating activities.

(b) A **fixed asset's market value has declined significantly** during the period.

(c) Evidence is available of **obsolescence or physical damage** to the fixed asset.

(d) There is a **significant adverse change** in any of the following.

    (i) Either the **business or the market** in which the fixed asset or goodwill is involved, such as the entrance of a **major competitor**.

    (ii) The **statutory or other regulatory environment** in which the business operates.

    (iii) Any **indicator of value** (eg multiples of turnover) used to measure the fair value of a fixed asset on acquisition.

(e) A **commitment** by management to undertake a **significant reorganisation**.

(f) A major loss of **key employees**.

(g) **Market interest rates** or other market rates of return have **increased significantly,** and these increases are likely to **affect materially** the fixed asset's **recoverable amount**.

5.10 This diagram may help you to visualise the FRS 11 indicators of impairment.

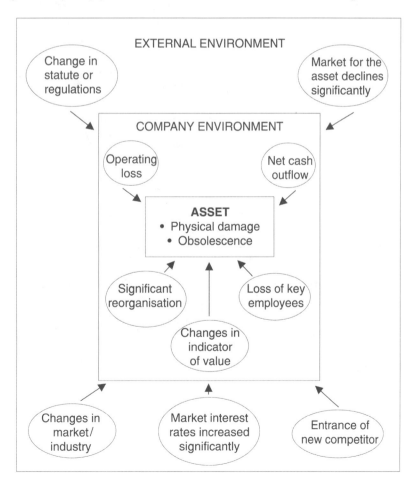

5.11 Where any of the above (or similar) **triggers** occur, then an impairment review should be carried out. In the case of **tangible fixed assets**, if there is **no cause** to suspect **any impairment**, then **no impairment review** is necessary. **Intangible assets** and **goodwill may**, however, **still require review**.

> ### KEY TERMS
>
> **Intangible assets: non-financial** fixed assets that do **not have physical substance** but are **identifiable** and **controlled** by the entity through **custody** or **legal rights**.
>
> **Purchased goodwill**: the **difference** between the **cost** of an acquired entity **and** the aggregate of the **fair values** of that entity's identifiable assets and liabilities.
>
> **Tangible fixed assets**: assets that have **physical substance** and are held for **use** in the **production** or **supply of goods or services**, for **rental** to others, or for **administrative purposes** on a **continuing basis** in the reporting entity's activities.
>
> *(FRS 11)*

Impairment review

> ### BASIC REQUIREMENTS
>
> FRS 11 specifies the process for conducting an impairment review.
>
> - The impairment review will consist of a **comparison** of the **carrying amount** of the fixed asset or goodwill with its **recoverable amount** (the higher of net realisable value, if known, and value in use).
>
> - To the extent that the **carrying amount exceeds** the **recoverable amount**, the fixed asset or goodwill is **impaired** and should be **written down**.
>
> - **The impairment loss should be recognised in the profit and loss account unless it arises on a previously revalued fixed asset.**

> ### KEY TERMS
>
> - **Recoverable amount**: the **higher of net realisable value** and **value in use**.
>
> - **Net realisable value**: the **amount** at which an asset **could be disposed** of, **less** any **direct selling costs**.
>
> - **Value in use**: the **present value** of the **future cash flows** obtainable as a result of an asset's continued use, including those resulting from its **ultimate disposal**.

5.12   The above issues can be summarised by the following diagram.

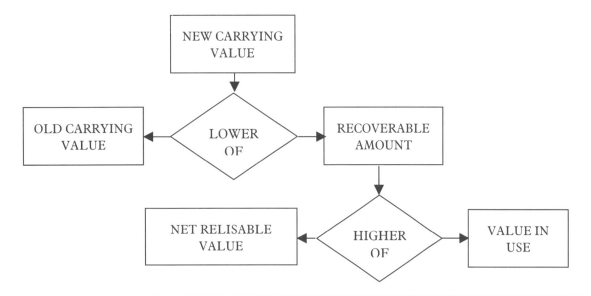

Question 6

Determine the impairment loss relating to one of Goody Goods Limited's fixed assets for the following four scenarios.

	Scenario 1 £'000	Scenario 2 £'000	Scenario 3 £'000	Scenario 4 £'000
• Carrying amount	750	750	900	900
• Net realisable value *	800	600	800	600
• Value in use **	600	800	600	800

Answer

• Recoverable amount	* 800	** 800	* 800	** 800
• Carrying amount	750	750	900	900
• Impairment	Nil	Nil	100	100

5.13   Note the following **rules** here.

(a)   If either NRV *or* value in use is higher than the carrying amount, there is no impairment.

(b)   If a reliable estimate of NRV cannot be made, the recoverable amount is its value in use.

(c)   If NRV is less than the carrying amount, then value in use must be found to see if it is higher still. If it is higher, recoverable amount is based on value in use, not NRV.

BASIC REQUIREMENTS

*   When an **impairment loss** on a fixed asset or goodwill is recognised, the **remaining useful economic life** should be **reviewed** and **revised if necessary.**

*   The **revised carrying amount** should be **depreciated** over the **revised estimate of the useful economic life.**

Calculation of net realisable value

5.14 The net realisable value of an asset that is **traded on an active market** will be based on **market value**. Disposal costs should include **only** the **essential selling costs** of the fixed asset and *not* **any costs** of reducing or **reorganising** the **business**.

Calculation of value in use

5.15 The process for computing value in use has **two basic** steps.

(a) **Develop projections** of future cash flows.

(b) **Discount** projected cash flows to **determine present value**.

5.16 In practice, value in use may **not always easy** to estimate.

(a) The **value in use** of a fixed asset should be estimated **individually** where **reasonably practicable**.

(b) Where it is not reasonably practicable to develop **projected cash flows** arising from an individual fixed asset, value in use should be calculated at the **level of income-generating units**.

(c) The **carrying amount of each income-generating unit** containing the fixed asset or goodwill under review should be compared with the **higher of the value in use and the net realisable value** (if it can be measured reliably) of the unit.

Income generating units

> ### KEY TERM
>
> An **income generating unit** is defined as a **group of assets, liabilities and associated goodwill** that generates **income** that is largely **independent** of the reporting **entity's other income streams**. The assets and liabilities include those already involved in generating the income and an appropriate portion of those used to generate more than one income stream.

5.17 Because it is necessary to **identify only material impairments,** in some cases it may be acceptable to consider a **group of income generating units together** rather than on an individual basis.

5.18 In some cases a detailed calculation of value in use will not be necessary. A **simple estimate** may be **sufficient** to **demonstrate** that either **value in use is higher than carrying value**, in which case there is no impairment, or value in use is lower than net realisable value, in which case impairment is measured by reference to net realisable value.

Identification of income generating units

> ### BASIC REQUIREMENTS
>
> FRS 11 specifies that income generating units should be identified by **dividing** the **total income** of the **entity** into as many largely **independent income streams** as is **reasonably practicable**. Each of the entity's identifiable assets and liabilities should be

attributed to, or apportioned between, one or more income generating unit(s). However, the following are **excluded**.

- Deferred tax balances
- Interest bearing debt
- Dividends payable
- Other financing items

5.19 In general terms, the income streams identified are likely to **follow** the way in which **management** monitors and makes **decisions** about **continuing** or **closing** the **different lines of business** of the entity. **Unique intangible assets**, such as **brands** and **mastheads**, are generally seen to **generate income independently** of each other and are usually **monitored separately**. Hence they can often be used to identify income-generating units. **Other income streams** may be identified by **reference to major products or services**.

5.20 EXAMPLE: IDENTIFICATION OF INCOME GENERATING UNITS

Saferail Limited runs a rail network comprising stations fed by a number of routes. Decisions about continuing or closing the routes are not based on the returns generated by the routes in isolation but on the contribution made to the returns generated by the stations.

5.21 SOLUTION

An income-generating unit comprises a station plus the routes associated with it because the cash inflows generated by the station's activities are not independent of the routes.

Question 7

Identify the income generating unit in the following cases.

(a) Supasheds Limited, manufactures garden sheds at a number of different sites. Not all the sites are used to full capacity and the manufacturer can choose how much to make at each site. However, there is not enough surplus capacity to enable any one site to be closed. The cash inflows generated by any one site therefore depend on the allocation of production across all sites.

(b) Dian Xin Limited has a large number of restaurants across the country. The cash inflows of each restaurants can be individually monitored and sensible allocations of costs to each restaurants can be made.

Answer

(a) The income-generating unit comprises all the sites at which the sheds can be made.

(b) Each restaurant is an income-generating unit by itself. However, any impairment of individual restaurants is unlikely to be material. A material impairment is likely to occur only when a number of restaurants are affected together by the same economic factors. It may therefore be acceptable to consider groupings of restaurants affected by the same economic factors rather than each individual restaurants.

5.22 To perform impairment reviews as accurately as possible:

(a) The **groups of assets and liabilities** that are considered together should be **as small as is reasonably practicable,** but

(b) The **income stream** underlying the **future cash flows** of one group should be **largely independent** of other income streams of the entity and should be **capable** of being **monitored separately**.

5.23 Income-generating units are therefore identified by dividing the total income of the business into as many largely independent income streams as is reasonably practicable in the light of the information available to management.

Central assets

5.24 In practice, businesses may have assets and liabilities that are not directly involved in the production and distribution of individual products therefore not attributed directly to one unit. **Central assets,** such as group or regional **head offices** and **working capital** may have to be **apportioned across** the **units** as on a **logical** and **systematic basis**. In such cases, the **sum of the carrying amounts of the units must equal the carrying amount of the net assets (excluding tax and financing items) of the entity as a whole.**

5.25 There may be circumstances where it is not **possible** to **apportion certain central assets** meaningfully **across the income generating units** to which they contribute. Such assets **may be excluded from** the **individual income generating units**.

(a) An **additional impairment review** should be performed on the **excluded central assets.**

(b) The **income generating units** to which the **central assets contribute** should be combined and their **combined carrying amount** (including that of the central assets) should be **compared** with their **combined value in use.**

Working capital

5.26 If there is any working capital in the balance sheet that will generate cash flows equal to its carrying amount, the carrying amount of the working capital may be excluded from the income-generating units and the cash flows arising from its realisation/settlement excluded from the value in use calculation.

Capitalised goodwill

5.27 This **should be attributed to income generating** units or groups of similar units, in the same way as are the assets and liabilities of the entity.

Cash flows

Basis of cash flows

5.28 The **expected future cash flows** of the income-generating unit, including any allocation of central overheads but excluding cash flows relating to financing and tax, should be:

(a) Based on **reasonable** and **supportable assumptions.**

(b) **Consistent** with the most up-to-date **budgets** and **plans** that have been **formally approved by management**.

(c) Assume a **steady** or **declining growth** rate for the **period beyond** that covered by formal budgets and plans.

Only in **exceptional circumstances** should:

(a) The **period** before the steady or declining growth rate is assumed **extend** to **more than five years**.

(b) The **steady or declining growth rate exceed** the **long-term average growth rate** for the country or **countries** in which the business operates.

Projections of future cash flows

5.29 **Future cash flows** must be estimated for income generating units in their **current condition, ie exclude**:

(a) **Benefits** expected to arise from a **future reorganisation** for which provision has not been made.

(b) **Future capital expenditure** that will improve or **enhance** the income generating units **more than the originally assessed standard of performance**.

Subsequent monitoring of cash flows

5.30 For the **five years** following each impairment review where the recoverable amount has been based on value in use, **actual cash flows should be compared with forecast cash flows**.

5.31 There may be instances where **actual cash flows** are **significantly less** than forecast. This may **suggest** that the **income** generating **unit might** have required recognition of an **impairment** in **previous periods**. In such cases, the original **impairment calculations should be re-performed** using the actual cash flows. Any **impairment** identified should be **recognised** in the **current period** unless the impairment has reversed.

Discount rate

5.32 The **present value** of the income-generating unit under review should be calculated by **discounting** the expected future cash flows of the unit.

(a) The discount rate used should be an **estimate** of the **rate** that the **market would expect** on an **equally risky investment**.

(b) It should **exclude** the **effects** of **any risk** for which the **cash flows** have **been adjusted** and should be calculated on a **pre-tax basis**.

Allocation of impairment loss

5.33 Allocation of any impairment loss calculated (ie where carrying amount exceeds value in use) should be allocated:

(a) First, to any **goodwill** in the unit.
(b) Thereafter to any **capitalised intangible asset** in the unit.
(c) Finally, to the **tangible assets** in the unit (pro-rata or other method).

The rationale behind the above allocation is to write down the assets with the most subjective valuations first.

No intangible asset with a readily ascertainable market value should be written down to below NRV. Similarly, no tangible asset with a reliably measured net realisable value should be written down below its NRV.

Question 8

Nutrinitious Foods Limited has suffered an impairment loss of £90,000 on one of its income generating units because low market entry barriers has enabled competitors to develop and successfully market rival products.

The carrying value of net assets in the income generating unit, before adjusting for the impairment loss are as follows:

	£'000
Goodwill	50
Patent (with no market value)	10
Land and buildings	120
Plant and machinery	60
	240

Demonstrate how the impairment loss of £90,000 should be allocated.

Answer

	£'000
Remember the batting order is:	
• Goodwill	50
• Capitalised intangible fixed assets	10
• Tangible fixed assets, on a pro-rata basis	30
	90

Hence:

	Pre-impairment £'000	Impairment loss £'000	Post-impairment £'000
Goodwill	50	(50)	-
Patent	10	(10)	-
Land and buildings $(30 \times \frac{120}{180})$	120	(20)	100
Plant and machinery $(30 \times \frac{60}{180})$	60	(10)	50
	240	(90)	150

Reversal of past impairments

5.34 Tangible fixed assets and investments are treated differently from goodwill and intangible assets.

Tangible fixed assets and investments

5.35 There may be circumstances where, in subsequent periods after an impairment loss has been recognised, the **recoverable amount** of a tangible fixed asset or investment (in subsidiaries, associates and joint ventures) **increases because of an improvement in economic conditions.**

5.36 In such instances, the resulting **reversal** of the impairment loss should be **recognised in the current period**. However, recognition is *only* **to the extent that it increases the carrying amount of the fixed asset up to the amount that it would have been had the original impairment not occurred.**

The reversal of the impairment loss should be recognised in the **profit and loss account unless** it arises on a **previously revalued fixed asset.**

5.37 The recognition of an increase in the recoverable amount of a tangible fixed asset above the amount that its carrying amount would have been had the original impairment not occurred is a revaluation, not a reversal of an impairment.

5.38 The circumstances we are looking at are those given above (Paragraph 5.9) which would **originally** have **triggered** an **impairment review.** Also, **increases** in value arising as a result of the **passage of time** or through the passing of cash outflows are **not circumstances** that would **give rise** to the **reversal of an impairment loss.**

Goodwill and intangible assets

5.39 The reversal of an impairment loss on intangible assets and goodwill should be **recognised in the current period if, and only if:**

(a) An **external event caused** the **recognition** of the impairment loss in **previous periods,** and **subsequent external events** clearly and demonstrably **reverse** the effects of that event in a way that was **not foreseen in** the **original impairment calculations.**

(b) The impairment loss related to an intangible asset with a **readily ascertainable market value** and the **net realisable value based on that market value** has increased **to above the intangible asset's impaired carrying amount.**

5.40 The reversal of the impairment loss should be **recognised to the extent that it increases the carrying amount of the goodwill or intangible asset up to the amount that it would have been had the original impairment not occurred.**

5.41 The recognition of an increase in the recoverable amount of an intangible asset above the amount that its carrying amount would have been had the original impairment not occurred is a revaluation.

> **KEY TERM**
>
> **Readily ascertainable market value,** in relation to an intangible asset, is the value that is established by reference to a market where:
>
> (a) The asset belongs to a homogeneous population of assets that are equivalent in all material respects.
>
> (b) An active market, evidenced by frequent transactions, exists for that population of assets. *(FRS 11)*

Question 9

Exeler 8 Limited has an income-generating unit comprising a factory, plant and equipment etc and associated purchased goodwill which has become impaired because the product has been overtaken by a technologically more advanced model produced by a competitor. The recoverable amount of the income-generating unit has fallen to £50m, resulting in an impairment loss of £100m, allocated as follows.

	Carrying amounts before impairment £m	Carrying amounts after impairment £m
Goodwill	45	-
Patent (with no market value)	15	-
Tangible fixed assets	90	50
Total	150	50

After three years, Exeler 8 Limited makes a technological breakthrough of its own, and the recoverable amount of the income-generating unit increases to £100m. The carrying amount of the tangible fixed assets had the impairment not occurred would have been £70m.

Required

Calculate the reversal of the impairment loss.

Answer

The reversal of the impairment loss is recognised to the extent that it increases the carrying amount of the tangible fixed assets to what it would have been had the impairment not taken place, ie a reversal of the impairment loss of £20m is recognised and the tangible fixed assets written back to £70m.

Reversal of the impairment is not recognised in relation to the goodwill and patent because the effect of the external event that caused the original impairment has not reversed - the original product is still overtaken by a more advanced model.

Impairment losses on revalued fixed assets

5.42 The general rule is that impairment losses on **revalued fixed assets** should be recognised in the **statement of total recognised gains and losses** until the carrying value of the asset falls **below depreciated historical** cost.

5.43 However, there may be specific circumstances where the impairment is clearly caused by a **consumption of economic benefits** eg damaged, in which case the loss is recognised in the **profit and loss account**. Ie such impairments are regarded as additional depreciation rather than as a decline in value.

5.44 Impairments **below depreciated historical** cost are recognised in the **profit and loss account**.

Question 10

Rollakoastas Limited has a fixed asset with the following details:

	£
• Carrying value at 1 January 20X8 based on its revalued amount	£50,000
• Depreciated historical cost at 1 January 20X8	£36,000
• Impairment loss owing to entry of a new competitor	£20,000

Explain how this impairment loss should be accounted for in the financial statements for the year ended 31 December 20X8.

Answer

	£
• Recognised in statement of total gains and losses	14,000
• Recognised in profit and loss account	6,000

Workings	
Carrying value at 1.1.X8	50,000
Write off to STRGL	(14,000)
Depreciated historical cost	36,000
Write off to profit and loss account	(6,000)
Revised carrying value at 31.12.X8	30,000

Presentation and disclosure

5.45 **Impairment losses recognised in the profit and loss account** should be included within **operating profit** under the **appropriate statutory heading**, and disclosed as an exceptional item if appropriate. Impairment losses recognised in the STRGL should be **disclosed separately** on the face of that statement.

5.46 In **the notes** to the financial statements in **accounting periods after the impairment**, the impairment loss should be treated as follows.

(a) For assets held on a **historical cost basis,** the impairment loss should be included **within cumulative depreciation**: the cost of the asset should not be reduced.

(b) For **revalued assets held at a market value** (eg existing use value or open market value), the impairment loss should be included **within the revalued carrying amount**.

(c) For **revalued assets held at depreciated replacement** cost, an impairment loss **charged to the profit and loss account** should be included **within cumulative depreciation**: the carrying amount of the asset should not be reduced; an **impairment loss charged to the STRGL** should be **deducted from the carrying amount** of the asset.

5.47 If the impairment loss is measured by reference to **value in use** of a fixed asset or income-generating unit, the **discount rate applied to the cash flows should be disclosed**. If a risk-free discount rate is used, some indication of the risk adjustments made to the cash flows should be given.

5.48 Where an impairment loss recognised in a previous period is **reversed** in the current period, the financial statements should **disclose the reason for the reversal,** including any changes in the assumptions upon which the calculation of recoverable amount is based.

5.49 Where an impairment loss would have been recognised in a previous period had the forecasts of future cash flows been more accurate but the impairment has reversed and the reversal of the loss is permitted to be recognised, the impairment now identified and its subsequent reversal should be disclosed.

5.50 Where, in the measurement of value in use, the period before a steady or declining long-term growth rate has been assumed extends to more than five years, the financial statements should **disclose the length of the longer period** and the circumstances justifying it.

5.51 Where, in the measurement of value in use, the long-term growth rate used has exceeded the long-term average growth rate for the country or countries in which the business operates, the financial statements should **disclose the growth rate assumed** and the circumstances justifying it.

5.52 Section summary

The main aspects of FRS 11 to remember are:

- **Indications** of impairment
- Identification of **income-generating** unit
- How an **impairment review** is carried out
- **Restoration of past losses** (tangibles vs intangibles)
- Impairment and restoration of **revalued fixed assets**

6 INVESTMENTS

6.1 The last category of fixed assets we need to consider is investments. Not all investments, however, are held by a company for the long term and it will be convenient to **deal with fixed asset investments and current asset investments together.**

> ### KEY TERM
>
> An **investment** can be defined as an asset that generates **economic benefits** in the form of **distributions** and/or **appreciation in value**.

6.2 Investments intended to be retained by a company on a **continuing basis** (for use in the company's activities) should be treated as **fixed assets**, while any **other investments** should be taken to be **current assets**.

6.3 The categories into which investments should be grouped and separately disclosed are given in the pro-forma balance sheet shown in Chapter 3 under sections BIII and CIII.

Fixed asset investments

6.4 The provisions relating to fixed assets in general, which were given in the previous chapter, embrace investments which are held as fixed assets. But investments will **not normally** have **a limited economic life**, so that **the requirement of systematic depreciation does not apply.** Fixed asset investments will therefore be carried at **cost less provisions** for **permanent diminutions** in value with **revaluations** taken to a **revaluation reserve**

6.5 The **alternative accounting** rules allow the following bases of valuation, other than cost, for fixed asset investments:

(a) **Market value:** if this is higher than the stock exchange value, the latter should also be disclosed.

(b) **Directors' valuation.**

As always when advantage is taken of the alternative accounting rules, **disclosure** must be made of the **items affected**, the **basis** of valuation adopted and the **comparable amounts** determined according to the **historical cost convention**.

Current asset investments

6.6 Current asset investments which are **readily marketable** investments should be shown at **current market value**, with increases or decreases in value taken to the profit and loss account.

6.7 **Other current asset investments** should be shown, in accordance with the prudence concept, at the **lower of purchase price and net realisable value.**

Listed vs unlisted

6.8 Investments, whether fixed assets or current assets, must be **split** between those listed on a recognised stock exchange and those which are unlisted. Shares dealt with on the Alternative Investment Market (**AIM**), are *not* 'listed', but they are '**quoted**'. The amount of income from listed investments need not be shown in the profit and loss account, according to a recent amendment to CA 1985.

6.9   If the **aggregate market value** of investments listed on a recognised stock exchange **differs** from their **carrying value** in the balance sheet, the **market value should be disclosed**.

Chapter roundup

- This chapter has set out the **statutory accounting requirements** relating to **intangible fixed assets** and **investments**. These requirements are supplemented in the case of **development costs** by SSAP 13 and in the case of **goodwill** by FRS 10 and in the case of **impairment** by FRS 11.

- **SSAP 13** is a standard which is generally accepted and well understood. You should ensure that you are very familiar with its provisions. Don't forget to learn the disclosure requirements.

- The treatment of **goodwill and intangibles,** on the other hand, is a controversial and complex area. You must ensure that you can discuss the current thinking on the nature of fixed assets, intangible assets and goodwill and that you can discuss all the possible treatments of **positive** and **negative goodwill** in accounts and the arguments on **brand accounting**. You should be familiar with, and be able to explain, the ASB's requirements as set out in FRS 10 *Goodwill and intangible assets* and FRS 11 *Impairments of fixed assets and goodwill.*

- Go back now to Chapter 3 and consider how the accounting treatments and disclosure requirements discussed in this chapter fit in with the **published accounts formats and notes**.

Quick quiz

1   Patents can only be treated as assets in a company's accounts if they are:

- .... for valuable consideration

- .... by the company itself

2   What are the criteria which must be met before development expenditure can be deferred?

- S......................   • C......................   • O......................

- E......................   • T......................   • R......................

3   Development expenditure written off may be reinstated if the uncertainties which led to the write-off no longer apply.

True   ☐

False ☐

4   How should negative goodwill be accounted for under FRS10?

5   FRS 11 excludes purchased goodwill.

True   ☐

False ☐

6   How is impairment on a revalued fixed asset which has been caused by consumption of economic benefit accounted for?

Answers to quick quiz

1   Acquired, created (see para 1.2)

2   **S**eparately defined project. **E**xpenses identifiable. **C**ommercially viable, **T**echnically feasible, **O**verall profitability, **R**esources to complete it. (2.1)

3   True. (2.1)

4   It should be disclosed in the intangible fixed assets category. (4.48)

5   False. It excludes non-purchased goodwill (5.7)

6   It is disclosed in the profit and loss account (5.43)

Now try the questions below from the Exam Question Bank

Number	Level	Marks	Time
5	Full exam	30	54 mins
6	Full exam	25	45 mins

Chapter 6

HIRE PURCHASE AND LEASING

Topic list	Syllabus reference
1 Types of lease and HP agreement	3(f)
2 Lessees	3(f)
3 Lessors	3(f)

Introduction

Leasing transactions are extremely common so this is an important practical subject. **Lease accounting is regulated by SSAP 21**, which was introduced because of abuses in the use of lease accounting by companies.

These companies effectively 'owned' an asset and 'owed' a debt for its purchase, but showed neither the asset nor the liability on the balance sheet because they were not required to do so. This is called '**off balance sheet finance**', a term which you will meet again later in this Text.

Study guide

- Distinguish between a hire purchase contract and a lease.

- Describe and apply the method of determining a lease type (ie an operating or finance lease).

- Explain the effect on the financial statements of a finance lease being incorrectly treated as an operating lease.

- Account for operating leases in financial statements.

- Account for finance leases in the financial statements of lessor and lessees.

- Outline the principles of SSAP 21 and its main disclosure requirements.

  Note: the net cash investment method will not be examined.

Exam guide

You must learn how to deal with leases. Make sure you can cope with the numbers.

1   TYPES OF LEASE AND HP AGREEMENT

1.1   Where goods are acquired other than on immediate cash terms, arrangements have to be made in respect of the future payments on those goods. In the simplest case of credit sales, the purchaser is allowed a period of time (say one month) to settle the outstanding amount and the normal accounting procedure in respect of debtors/creditors will be adopted. However, **in recent years there has been considerable growth in hire purchase and leasing agreements.**

1.2   **SSAP 21 Accounting for leases and hire purchase contracts standardises the accounting treatment and disclosure of assets held under lease or hire purchase.**

BPP
PUBLISHING

1.3 In a leasing transaction there is a contract between the lessor and the lessee for the hire of an asset. The lessor retains legal ownership but conveys to the lessee the right to use the asset for an agreed period of time in return for specified rentals. **SSAP 21 recognises two types of lease.**

> **KEY TERMS**
>
> A **finance lease** transfers substantially all the risks and rewards of ownership to the lessee. Although strictly the leased asset remains the property of the lessor, in substance the lessee may be considered to have acquired the asset and to have financed the acquisition by obtaining a loan from the lessor.
>
> An **operating lease** is any lease which is not a finance lease. An operating lease has the character of a rental agreement with the lessor usually being responsible for repairs and maintenance of the asset. Often these are relatively short-term agreements with the same asset being leased, in succession, to different lessees.

1.4 A *finance lease* is very similar in substance to a *hire purchase agreement*. (The difference in law is that under a hire purchase agreement the customer eventually, after paying an agreed number of instalments, becomes entitled to exercise an option to purchase the asset. Under a leasing agreement, ownership remains forever with the lessor.)

1.5 In this chapter the **user** of an asset will often be referred to simply as the **lessee**, and the **supplier** as the **lessor**. You should bear in mind that identical requirements apply in the case of hirers and vendors respectively under hire purchase agreements.

1.6 To expand on the definition above, **a finance lease should be presumed if at the inception of a lease the present value of the minimum lease payments amounts to substantially all (normally 90% or more) of the fair value of the leased asset.**

1.7 The present value should be calculated by using the **interest rate implicit in the lease**.

> **KEY TERMS**
>
> The **minimum lease payments** are the minimum payments over the remaining part of the lease term plus any residual amounts guaranteed by the lessee or by a party related to the lessee.
>
> **Fair value** is the price at which an asset could be exchanged in an arm's length transaction.
>
> The **interest rate implicit in the lease** is the discount rate that, at the inception of a lease, when applied to the amounts which the lessor expects to receive and retain, produces an amount equal to the fair value of the leased asset.
>
> The **lease term** is the period for which the lessee has contracted to lease the asset and any further terms for which the lessee has the option to continue to lease the asset, with or without further payment, which option it is reasonably certain at the inception of the lease that the lessee will exercise.

Accounting for leases: lessees and lessors

1.8 **Operating leases** do not really pose an accounting problem. **Payments by the lessee are charged to the lessee's and credited to the lessor's profit and loss account. The lessor treats the leased asset as a fixed asset and depreciates it in the normal way.**

1.9 For assets held **under finance leases or hire purchase** this accounting treatment would not disclose the reality of the situation. If a lessor leases out an asset on a finance lease, the asset will probably never be seen on his premises or used in his business again. It would be inappropriate for a lessor to record such an asset as a fixed asset. In reality, **what the lessor owns is a stream of cash flows receivable from the lessee. The asset is a debtor rather than a fixed asset.**

1.10 Similarly, a lessee may use a finance lease to fund the 'acquisition' of a major asset which he will then use in his business perhaps for many years. **The substance of the transaction is that the lessee has acquired a fixed asset, and this is reflected in the accounting treatment prescribed by SSAP 21,** even though in law the lessee never becomes the owner of the asset.

> ### Exam focus point
>
> Questions on leasing could involve a discussion of the reasons for the different accounting treatments of operating and finance leases, from the perspectives of both the lessor and the lessee. Practical questions could involve preparation of the relevant ledger accounts and/or extracts from the financial statements.

2 LESSEES

Accounting treatment

2.1 In light of the above, **SSAP 21 requires that, when an asset changes hands under a finance lease or HP agreement, lessor and lessee should account for the transaction as though it were a credit sale.** In the lessee's books therefore:

DEBIT   Asset account
CREDIT   Lessor (liability) account

2.2 The amount to be recorded in this way is the capital cost or fair value of the asset. This may be taken as the amount which the lessee might expect to pay for it in a cash transaction.

2.3 A **variant approach** which produces the same net result is to debit the asset account with the fair value, and to debit an interest suspense account with the total amount of interest or finance charges payable under the agreement and to credit a lessor account with the total amount (capital and interest) payable under the agreement. We will see later how this affects the year end accounting entries.

2.4 **The asset should be depreciated over the shorter of:**

(a) The lease term
(b) Its useful life

Apportionment of rental payments

2.5 When the lessee makes **a rental payment** it **will comprise two elements.**

(a) **An interest charge on the finance provided by the lessor**. This proportion of each payment is interest payable and interest receivable in the profit and loss accounts of the lessee and lessor respectively.

(b) **A repayment of part of the capital cost of the asset**. In the lessee's books this proportion of each rental payment must be debited to the lessor's account to reduce the outstanding liability. In the lessor's books, it must be credited to the lessee's account to reduce the amount owing (the debit of course is to cash).

2.6 **The accounting problem is to decide what proportion** of each instalment paid by the lessee **represents interest, and what proportion represents a repayment of the capital** advanced by the lessor. There are **three methods** you may encounter:

(a) The **level spread method**.
(b) The **actuarial method**.
(c) The **sum-of-the-digits method**.

Exam focus point

An examination question would always make it clear which method should be used. In theory, the aim is that the profit and loss account finance charge should produce a constant rate of return on outstanding leasing obligations.

2.7 **The level spread method is based on the assumption that finance charges accrue evenly over the term of the lease agreement.** For example, if an asset with a fair value of £3,000 is being 'acquired' on a finance lease for five payments of £700 each, the total interest is £(3,500 − 3,000) = £500. This is assumed to accrue evenly and therefore there is £100 interest comprised in each rental payment, the £600 balance of each instalment being the capital repayment.

The level spread method is quite **unscientific and takes no account of the commercial realities of the transaction.** You should use it in the examination only if you are specifically instructed to or if there is insufficient information to use another method.

2.8 **The actuarial method is the best and most scientific method.** It derives from the commonsense assumption that the **interest charged by a lessor company will equal the rate of return desired by the company, multiplied by the amount of capital it has invested.**

(a) At the beginning of the lease the capital invested is equal to the fair value of the asset (less any initial deposit paid by the lessee).

(b) This amount reduces as each instalment is paid. It follows that the interest accruing is greatest in the early part of the lease term, and gradually reduces as capital is repaid. In this section, we will look at a simple example of the actuarial method.

2.9 **The sum-of-the-digits method** approximates to the actuarial method, splitting the total interest (without reference to a rate of interest) in such a way that the greater proportion falls in the earlier years. The procedure is as follows.

(a) **Assign a digit to each instalment.** The digit 1 should be assigned to the final instalment, 2 to the penultimate instalment and so on.

(b) **Add the digits.** If there are twelve instalments, then the sum of the digits will be 78. For this reason, the sum of the digits method is sometimes called the *rule of 78*.

(c) **Calculate the interest charge included in each instalment.** Do this by multiplying the total interest accruing over the lease term by the fraction:

$$\frac{\text{Digit applicable to the instalment}}{\text{Sum of the digits}}$$

2.10 EXAMPLE: APPORTIONMENT METHODS

On 1 January 20X0 Bacchus Ltd, wine merchants, buys a small bottling and labelling machine from Silenus Limited on hire purchase terms. The cash price of the machine was £7,710 while the HP price was £10,000. The HP agreement required the immediate payment of a £2,000 deposit with the balance being settled in four equal annual instalments commencing on 31 December 20X0. The HP charge of £2,290 represents interest of 15% per annum, calculated on the remaining balance of the liability during each accounting period. Depreciation on the plant is to be provided for at the rate of 20% per annum on a straight line basis assuming a residual value of nil.

You are required to show the breakdown of each instalment between interest and capital, using in turn each of the apportionment methods described above.

2.11 SOLUTION

In this example, enough detail is given to use any of the apportionment methods. In an examination question, you would normally be directed to use one method specifically.

(a) *Level spread method*

The £2,290 interest charges are regarded as accruing evenly over the term of the HP agreement. Each instalment therefore contains £2,290/4 = £572.50 of interest. The break down is then as follows.

	1st instalment £	*2nd instalment* £	*3rd instalment* £	*4th instalment* £
Interest	572.50	572.50	572.50	572.50
Capital repayment (balance)	1,427.50	1,427.50	1,427.50	1,427.50
	2,000.00	2,000.00	2,000.00	2,000.00

(b) *Sum-of-the-digits method*

Each instalment is allocated a digit as follows.

Instalment	*Digit*
1st (20X0)	4
2nd (20X1)	3
3rd (20X2)	2
4th (20X3)	1
	10

The £2,290 interest charges can then be apportioned.

		£
1st instalment	£2,290 × 4/10	916
2nd instalment	£2,290 × 3/10	687
3rd instalment	£2,290 × 2/10	458
4th instalment	£2,290 × 1/10	229
		2,290

The breakdown is then as follows.

	1st instalment £	2nd instalment £	3rd instalment £	4th instalment £
Interest	916	687	458	229
Capital repayment (balance)	1,084	1,313	1,542	1,771
	2,000	2,000	2,000	2,000

(c) *Actuarial method*

Interest is calculated as 15% of the outstanding *capital* balance at the beginning of each year. The outstanding capital balance reduces each year by the capital element comprised in each instalment. The outstanding capital balance at 1 January 20X0 is £5,710 (£7,710 fair value less £2,000 deposit).

	Total £	Capital £	Interest £
Capital balance at 1 Jan 20X0		5,710	
1st instalment			
(interest = £5,710 × 15%)	2,000	1,144	856
Capital balance at 1 Jan 20X1		4,566	
2nd instalment			
(interest = £4,566 × 15%)	2,000	1,315	685
Capital balance at 1 Jan 20X2		3,251	
3rd instalment			
(interest = £3,251 × 15%)	2,000	1,512	488
Capital balance at 1 Jan 20X3		1,739	
4th instalment			
(interest = £1,739 × 15%)	2,000	1,739	261
	8,000		2,290
Capital balance at 1 Jan 20X4		-	-

Interest suspense account

2.12 Where an interest suspense account is used (see Paragraph 2.3), the double entry for finance lease/HP instalments is as follows (assuming that the actuarial method is used to record the first instalment payable under the lease in the example above).

(a) DEBIT   Asset account   £7,710

               Interest suspense   £2,290

      CREDIT   HP creditor   £10,000

      Being entries required to record acquisition of asset on hire purchase

(b) DEBIT   Lessor/HP creditor   £2,000

      CREDIT   Bank   £2,000

      Being instalment payment recorded in full

(c) DEBIT   Interest payable/finance charges (P&L)   £856

      CREDIT   Interest suspense account   £856

      Being year end adjustment to ensure that the year's interest/finance charges are charged to the profit and loss account

2.13 The equivalent entries where a suspense account is not used might be as follows.

(a) DEBIT   Asset account   £7,710
     CREDIT   HP account   £7,710

(b) DEBIT   HP creditor   £2,000
     CREDIT   Bank   £2,000

(c) DEBIT   Interest payable/finance charges (P & L)   £856
     CREDIT   HP creditor   £856

Entry (c) ensures that the interest element is recorded and is an annual adjustment. It is, of course, possible to make the full correct entry as each instalment is paid:

DEBIT   Interest payable/finance charges (P & L)   £856
     Lessor/HP creditor   £1,144
CREDIT Bank   £2,000

However, in practice in many companies the interest/finance charge calculation is only made annually when preparing published accounts.

2.14 Thus, at the year end, whatever system is used during the year, the balance on the lessor/HP creditor account (where appropriate, less the balance on the interest suspense account) will represent the outstanding capital liability. Future interest/finance charges are not a true liability as the capital could be paid off at any time, thus avoiding these charges.

Repossessions

2.15 Subject to various legal requirements, goods sold on hire purchase (but not credit sale) may be repossessed by the seller **if the hirer fails to maintain his payments.** The ledger accounts in respect of the hire purchase should be closed to **a repossessions account** which **is credited with the value at which the item is brought back into stock and any penalty sums receivable.** Any balance on the repossessions account represents the profit or loss on the repossession.

2.16 EXAMPLE: REPOSSESSIONS

Bacchus, having paid amounts due in 20X0, decided to cease trading in January 20X1. Silenus agreed to cancel the agreement on the payment of a penalty of £1,000 and took the plant into his stock at a value of £4,500. The ledger accounts would be as follows.

HP DEBTORS ACCOUNT

	£		£
Balance b/d	4,566	Repossessions a/c	4,566

REPOSSESSIONS ACCOUNT

	£		£
HP debtors a/c	4,566	Bank: penalty	1,000
P & L a/c: profit on		Purchases:	
repossession	934	Plant taken into stock	
		at valuation *	4,500
	5,500		5,500

* If the question does not give a valuation for the goods repossessed, then they can be taken into stock at the cost element in the outstanding debt:

$$\frac{6,168}{7,710} \times £4,566 = £3,653 \text{ in the above example.}$$

2.17   The total profit Silenus earned from the abortive sale is as follows.

	£
Deposit/instalment received in 20X0	4,000
Penalty received in 20X1	1,000
	5,000
Plant in stock at valuation	4,500
	9,500
Cost of plant	6,168
	3,332

This has been accounted for as follows.

		£
20X0	Gross profit (£1,542) + interest earned (£856)	2,398
20X1	Profit on repossession	934
		3,332

Question 1

Dundas Ltd purchased a machine under a hire purchase agreement on 1 January 20X6. The agreement provided for an immediate payment of £2,000, following by five equal instalments of £3,056, each instalment to be paid on 30 June and 31 December respectively. The cash price of the machine was £10,000. Dundas estimated that it would have a useful economic life of five years, and its residual value would then be £1,000.

In apportioning interest to respective accounting periods, the company uses the 'sum of digits' method.

Required

(a)   Write up the following ledger accounts for each of the three years to 31 December 20X6, 20X7 and 20X8 respectively:

   (i)   Machine hire purchase loan account.
   (ii)   Machine hire purchase interest account.

(b)   Show the following balance sheet extracts relating to the machine as at 31 December 20X6, 20X7 and 20X8 respectively:

   (i)   Fixed assets: machine at net book value.

   (ii)   Creditors: amounts payable within one year - obligation under hire purchase contract.

   (iii) Creditors: amounts falling due after more than one year - obligation under hire purchase contract.

Answer

(a)   (i)

MACHINE HIRE PURCHASE LOAN ACCOUNT

20X6		£	20X6		£
1.1	Bank	2,000	1.1	Machine	10,000
30.6	Bank	3,056	1.1	Machine interest	7,280
31.12	Bank	3,056			
31.12	Balance c/d	9,168			
		17,280			17,280
20X7			20X7		
30.6	Bank	3,056	1.1	Balance b/d	9,168
31.12	Bank	3,056			
31.12	Balance c/d	3,056			
		9,168			9,168
20X8			20X8		
30.6	Bank	3,056	1.1	Balance b/d	3,056

(ii)

MACHINE HIRE PURCHASE INTEREST ACCOUNT

20X6		£	20X6		£
1.1	Machine HP		31.12	Profit and loss a/c	4,368
	loan a/c	7,280	31.12	Balance c/d	2,912
		7,280			7,280
20X7			20X7		
1.1	Balance b/d	2,912	31.12	Profit and loss a/c	2,427
			31.12	Balance c/d	485
		2,912			2,912
20X8			20X8		
1.1	Balance b/d	485	31.12	Profit and loss a/c	485

Working

			£

Sum of the digits = 5 + 4 + 3 + 2 + 1 = 15
(5 half year periods)

Interest charge 19X6	=	$7,280 \times \dfrac{5 + 4}{15}$ =	4,368
Interest charge 19X7	=	$7,280 \times \dfrac{3 + 2}{15}$ =	2,427
Interest charge 19X8	=	$7,280 \times \dfrac{1}{15}$ =	485
			7,280

(b) (i) *Fixed assets: machines at net book value*

		£
At 31.12.X6	Machines at cost	10,000
	Accumulated depreciation	3,600
	Net book value	6,400
At 31.12.X7	Machines at cost	10,000
	Accumulated depreciation	7,200
	Net book value	2,800
At 31.12.X8	Machines at cost	10,000
	Accumulated depreciation	9,000
	Residual value	1,000

Working

Depreciation:	cost	10,000
	residual value	1,000
		9,000
Economic life		2½ years

Annual depreciation charge on a straight line basis $= \dfrac{£9,000}{2\frac{1}{2}}$

= £3,600 per year

(ii) *Creditors: amounts payable within one year - obligation under hire purchase contract*

	£
At 31.12.X6	3,685
At 31.12.X7	2,571
At 31.12.X8	-

Workings

			£
31.12.X6	Balance per loan account		9,168
	Less due in 19X8		(3,056)
	Less interest element		(2,427)
			3,685
31.12.X7	Balance per loan account		3,056
	Less interest element		(485)
			2,571

(iii) *Creditors: amounts falling due after more than one year*

	£
At 31.12.X6	2,571
At 31.12.X7	-
At 31.12.X8	-

For working see (b)(ii) above.

Disclosure requirements for lessees

2.18   SSAP 21 requires lessees to disclose the following information.

(a)   The **gross amounts of assets held under finance leases* together with the related accumulated depreciation, analysed by class of asset**. This information may be consolidated with the corresponding information for owned assets, and not shown separately. In that case, the net amount of assets held under finance leases* included in the overall total should also be disclosed.

(b)   The **amounts of obligations related to finance leases* (net of finance charges allocated to future periods)**. These should be disclosed separately from other obligations and liabilities and should be analysed between amounts payable in the next year, amounts payable in the second to fifth years inclusive from the balance sheet date and the aggregate amounts payable thereafter.

(c)   The **aggregate finance charges allocated for the period** in respect of finance leases.*

* Including the equivalent information in respect of hire purchase contracts.

2.19   These disclosure requirements will be illustrated for Bacchus Ltd (above example). We will assume that Bacchus Ltd makes up its accounts to 31 December and uses the actuarial method to apportion finance charges. The company's accounts for the first year of the HP agreement, the year ended 31 December 20X0, would include the information given below.

BALANCE SHEET AS AT 31 DECEMBER 20X0 (EXTRACTS)

	£	£
Fixed assets		
Tangible assets held under hire purchase agreements		
Plant and machinery at cost	7,710	
Less accumulated depreciation (20% × £7,710)	1,542	
		6,168
Creditors: amounts falling due within one year		
Obligations under hire purchase agreements		1,315
Creditors: amounts falling due after more than one year		
Obligations under hire purchase agreements, falling due		
within two to five years £(1,512 + 1,739)		3,251

(Notice that only the outstanding *capital* element is disclosed under creditors. That is what is meant by the phrase 'net of finance charges allocated to future periods' in Paragraph 2.7(b) above.)

PROFIT AND LOSS ACCOUNT
FOR THE YEAR ENDED 31 DECEMBER 20X0

	£
Interest payable and similar charges	
Hire purchase finance charges	856

2.20 As noted above, SSAP 21 requires that **leased assets should be depreciated over the shorter of the lease term and their useful lives; but assets acquired under HP agreements** resembling finance leases **should be depreciated over their useful lives,** because such assets are legally the debtor's property. Bacchus can therefore depreciate the machine over five years, not four years.

2.21 **For operating leases the disclosure is simpler.**

(a) The **total of operating lease rentals** charged as an expense in the profit and loss account should be disclosed, distinguishing between rentals payable for hire of plant and machinery and other rentals.

(b) Disclosure should be made of **payments to which the lessee is committed** under operating leases, analysed between those in which the commitment expires:

(i) **Within a year** from the balance sheet date
(ii) In the **second to fifth** years inclusive
(iii) **Later than five years** from the balance sheet date

Commitments in respect of land and buildings should be shown separately from other commitments.

3 LESSORS

Accounting treatment

3.1 In principle, accounting for a finance lease by a **lessor** is a **mirror image of the entries for the lessee**. The asset is recorded in the lessor's books as follows.

DEBIT Lessee (debtor) account
CREDIT Sales

3.2 The income derived from the lease is spread over accounting periods so as to give a constant periodic rate of return for the lessor. The complex methods of achieving this are beyond the scope of your syllabus.

FRS 5: SALE AND LEASEBACK TRANSACTIONS

3.3 We will discuss FRS 5 *Reporting the substance of transactions* in Chapter 11. Leases were a common form of off balance sheet finance before SSAP 21 was introduced. Ever since then, businesses have attempted to undertake types of arrangement whereby an asset is 'sold' but in fact the use is still retained.

3.4 **FRS 5 states that where such a transaction is, in effect, a sale and leaseback, no profit should be recognised on entering into the arrangement and no adjustment made to the carrying value of the asset.** As stated in the guidance notes to SSAP 21, **this represents the**

substance of the transactions, 'namely the raising of finance secured on an asset that continues to be held and is not disposed of'.

Disclosure requirements for lessors

3.5 SSAP 21 requires lessors to disclose their **net investments in (a) finance leases and (b) hire purchase contracts at each balance sheet date.**

3.6 The accounts of Silenus Ltd (example above) for the year ended 31 December 20X0 would show the information given below.

BALANCE SHEET AS AT 31 DECEMBER 20X0 (EXTRACTS)

	£
Current assets	
Debtors	
Net investment in finance leases (note)	4,566

NOTES TO THE BALANCE SHEET

Net investment in finance leases	£
Falling due within one year	1,315
Falling due after more than one year	3,251
	4,566

(The Companies Act 1985 requires amounts included as debtors to be separately disclosed if they fall due more than one year after the balance sheet date.)

3.7 SSAP 21 also requires **disclosure by lessors** of the:

(a) **Gross amounts of assets** held for use **in operating leases**, and the related **accumulated depreciation charges.**

(b) **Policy** adopted for accounting for operating leases and finance leases and, in detail, the policy for accounting for finance lease income.

(c) **Aggregate rentals receivable** in respect of an accounting period in relation to finance leases and operating leases separately.

(d) **Cost of assets acquired**, whether by purchase or finance lease, for the purpose of letting under finance leases.

Chapter roundup

- **Finance leases** are like HP contracts. In both cases:
  - Assets acquired should be capitalised
  - Interest element of instalments should be charged against profit.

- **Operating leases** are **rental agreements** and all instalments are charged against profit.

- You must learn (through repeated practice) how to apply the level spread, actuarial and sum-of-the-digits methods of **interest allocation**.

- You must also learn the **disclosure requirements of SSAP 21** for both lessors and lessees.

Quick quiz

1   (a)   ....leases transfer substantially the risks and rewards of ownership.

    (b)   ....leases are usually short-term rental agreements with the lessor being responsible for the repairs and maintenance of the asset.

2   The present value of the minimum lease payments is equal to 89% of the fair value of the leased asset. What type of lease is this likely to be?

3   A business acquires an asset under an HP agreement. What is the double entry?

    DEBIT

    CREDIT

4   Which of the following is the formula for the sum of digits?

    A $\dfrac{n(n-1)}{2}$

    B $\dfrac{n(n+1)}{2}$

    C $\dfrac{2(n-1)}{n}$

    D $\dfrac{2(n+1)}{n}$

5   List the disclosures required under SSAP 21.

6   A lorry has an expected useful life of six years. It is acquired under a four year finance lease. Over which period should it be depreciated?

7   A company leases a photocopier under an operating lease which expires in June 20X2. Its office is leased under an operating lease due to expire in January 20X3. How should past and future operating leases be disclosed in its 31 December 20X1 accounts?

Answers to quick quiz

1   (a)   Finance leases
    (b)   Operating leases (see para 1.3)

2   Per SSAP 21, an operating lease (1.6)

3   DEBIT   Asset account
    CREDIT   Lessor account (2.1)

4   B (2.9)

5   See paragraph 2.8

6   The four year term. (2.9)

7   The total operating lease rentals charged though the profit and loss should be disclosed. The payments committed to should be disclosed analysing them between those falling due in the next year and the second to fifth years. (2.20)

Now try the question below from the Exam Question Bank

Number	Level	Marks	Time
7	Full exam	20	36 mins

Chapter 7

STOCKS AND WORK IN PROGRESS

Topic list	Syllabus reference
1 Stocks and short-term work in progress	3(f)
2 Long-term contract work in progress	3(f)

Introduction

You have encountered stocks and stock valuation in your earlier studies. Stock valuation has a direct impact on a company's gross profit and it is usually a material item in any company's accounts. This is therefore an important subject area. If you have any doubts about accounting for stocks and methods of stock valuation you would be advised to go back to your Paper 1.1 study material and revise this topic.

Section 1 of this chapter goes over some of this ground again, concentrating on the effect of SSAP 9. Section 2 goes on to discuss a new area, long-term contract work in progress.

Study guide

- Review the principles of stock valuation covered in Paper 1.1.

- Define a long-term contract and describe why recognising profit before completion is generally considered to be desirable; discuss if this may be profit smoothing.

- Describe the ways in which attributable profit may be measured.

- Calculate and disclose the amounts to be shown in the financial statements for long-term contracts.

Exam guide

You should find long-term contracts fairly logical as long as you work through the examples and exercise carefully.

1   STOCKS AND SHORT-TERM WORK IN PROGRESS

1.1   In most businesses the value put on stock is an important factor in the determination of profit. Stock valuation is, however, a highly subjective exercise and consequently there is a wide variety of different methods used in practice.

1.2   The Companies Act 1985 regulations and SSAP 9 *Stocks and long-term contracts* requirements were developed to achieve greater uniformity in the valuation methods used and in the disclosure in financial statements prepared under the historical cost convention.

1.3   **SSAP 9 defines stocks and work in progress as:**

(a)   Goods or other assets purchased for resale.

(b)   Consumable stores.

(c)   Raw materials and components purchased for incorporation into products for sale.

(d)   Products and services in intermediate stages of completion.

(e)   Long-term contract balances.

(f)   Finished goods.

1.4   In published accounts, the Companies Act 1985 requires that these stock categories should be grouped and disclosed under the following headings:

(a)   Raw materials and consumables ((c) and (b) above).

(b)   Work in progress ((d) and (e) above).

(c)   Finished goods and goods for resale ((f) and (a) above).

(d)   Payments on account (presumably intended to cover the case of a company which has paid for stock items but not yet received them into stock).

1.5   **A distinction is also made in SSAP 9 between:**

(a)   Stocks and work in progress other than long-term contract work in progress.

(b)   Long-term contract work in progress.

We will look at long-term contracts later in the chapter. Stocks and short-term work in progress are revised briefly here.

Knowledge brought forward from earlier studies

SSAP 9 Stock and long-term contracts (Stock and short-term WIP)

Under the matching concept costs must be allocated between the cost of goods sold (matched against current revenues) and closing stock (matched against future revenues).

*   Stock should be valued at the **lower of cost and net realisable value** (NRV).

*   **Costs** should include those incurred in the **normal course of business** in bringing a product or service to its **present location and condition**.

*   Costs include direct costs (labour, materials), production overheads and other attributable overheads. Exclude all 'abnormal' overheads, eg exceptional spoilage.

*   CA 1985 also allows the inclusion of interest payable on capital borrowed to finance the production of the asset (allowed by SSAP 9 under 'other attributable overheads').

*   **NRV is the actual or estimated selling price less further costs to be incurred in marketing, selling and distribution.**

*   The method used in allocating costs to stock should produce the fairest approximation to the expenditure incurred.

*   Methods include (per CA 1985): average cost, base stock, current cost, FIFO, LIFO, replacement cost, standard cost, unit cost; however, base stock and LIFO are not allowed under SSAP 9.

*   The principle situation where NRV will be less than cost will be where:

    ◦   There have been increases in the costs or falls in selling price
    ◦   Physical deterioration of stock has occurred
    ◦   Products have become obsolescent
    ◦   The company has decided to make and sell a product at a loss
    ◦   There are errors in production or purchasing

1.6 The following question is a very simple reminder of how FIFO and LIFO operate.

Question 1

Digby Pillay, a retailer commenced business on 1 January 20X5, with a capital of £500. He decided to specialise in a single product line and by the end of June 20X5, his purchases and sales of this product were as follows.

	Purchases		Sales	
	Units	Unit price £	Units	Unit price £
January	30	5.00	20	7.00
February	-	-	5	7.20
April	40	6.00	25	8.00
May	25	6.50	30	8.50
June	20	7.00	20	9.00
	115		100	

Required

(a) Ascertain Digby Pillay's gross profit for the period assuming that:

   (i) Stock is valued using FIFO
   (ii) Stock is valued using LIFO

(b) Assuming that all purchases and sales are made for cash and that there are no other transactions for the period, draw up balance sheets as at 30 June 20X5, showing:

   (i) Stock valued on a FIFO basis
   (ii) Stock valued on a LIFO basis

Comment briefly on the significance of these balance sheets.

Answer

(a) (i) *LIFO basis*

	SALES			COST OF SALES		
	Unit	Unit price £	Total £	Unit	Unit price £	Total £
January	20	7.00	140.00	20	5.00	100.00
February	5	7.20	36.00	5	5.00	25.00
April	25	8.00	200.00	25	6.00	150.00
May	30	8.50	255.00	25	6.50	162.50
				5	6.00	30.00
June	20	9.00	180.00	20	7.00	140.00
	100		811.00	100		607.50
Closing stock				10	6.00	60
				5	5.00	25
				15		85

	£
Sales	811.00
Less cost of sales	607.50
Gross profit	203.50

(ii) *FIFO basis*

	£	£
Sales		811.00
Purchases	692.50	
Less closing stock (15 @ £7.00)	105.00	
		587.50
		223.50

(b) BALANCE SHEETS AS AT 30 JUNE 20X5

	(i) LIFO basis £	(ii) FIFO basis £
Original capital	500.00	500.00
Profit	203.50	223.50
	703.50	723.50
Stock	85.00	105.00
Cash	618.50	618.50
	703.50	723.50

In a time of rising prices LIFO (which uses the most current costs) will tend to give a more realistic measure of profit, but results in an outdated stock valuation being disclosed in the balance sheet.

2 LONG-TERM CONTRACT WORK IN PROGRESS

Introduction

2.1 The most controversial aspect of SSAP 9 is its approach to the valuation of work in progress for incomplete long-term contracts.

> **KEY TERM**
>
> A **long-term contract** is defined as: 'a contract entered into for the design, manufacture or construction of a **single substantial asset** or the provision of a service (or of a combination of assets or services which together constitute a **single project**) where the time taken substantially to complete the contract is such that the **contract activity** falls into **different accounting periods**.'

Usually long-term contracts will **exceed one year** in duration, although a **sufficiently material contract** whose activity **straddles a balance sheet date** should still be accounted for as a **long-term contract even if it will last in total less than a year**. This is to ensure that the accounts for **both accounting periods** involved will still give a **true and fair view** of the activities of the company.

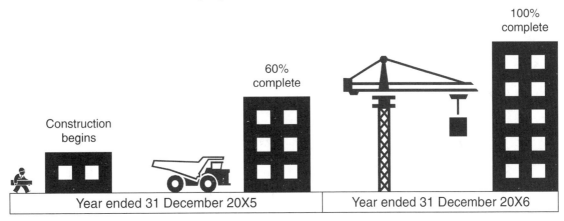

2.2 The existence of a proper **contract** is **important,** because it provides a basis of **reasonable certainty** whereby it is nevertheless **prudent** to **allow recognition** of **profits before completion of work.**

BPP PUBLISHING

The underlying problem

2.3 It is the following requirement which causes the greatest controversy around SSAP 9.

> 'Separate consideration needs to be given to long-term contracts. Owing to the **length of time** taken to complete such contracts, to defer recording turnover and taking profit into account until completion may result in the profit and loss account reflecting not so much a **fair view** of the results of the **activity** of the company **during the year** but rather the results relating to contracts that have been completed in the year. It is therefore appropriate to take **credit** for **ascertainable turnover** and **profit** while contracts are **in progress** ....'

Some companies might prefer to value work in progress on long-term contracts at cost, and to **defer taking any profit** on the contract into the profit and loss account **until the contract had been completed**. This policy may be considered **prudent**, but there may be an **underlying management motive** to **defer profits** and **tax liabilities.**

2.4 EXAMPLE: LONG-TERM CONTRACTS

Jianzhu Construction Ltd started a contract on 1 January 20X5, with an estimated completion date of 31 December 20X6. In the first year, to 31 December 20X5:

(a) Costs incurred amounted to £900,000.

(b) Sixty per cent of the work on the contract was completed.

(c) The final contract price is £2,000,000.

(d) Certificates of work completed have been issued, to the value of £1,200,000. (*Note*. It is usual, in a long-term contract, for a qualified person such as an architect or engineer to inspect the work completed, and if it is satisfactory, to issue certificates. This will then be the notification to the customer that progress payments are now due to the contractor. Progress payments are commonly the amount of valuation on the work certificates issued, minus a precautionary retention of 10%.).

(e) It is estimated with reasonable certainty that further costs to completion in 20X6 will be £600,000.

What is the contract profit in 20X5, and what entries would be made for the contract at 31 December 20X5 if:

(a) Profits are deferred until the completion of the contract?

(b) A proportion of the estimated turnover and profit is credited to the profit and loss account in 20X5?

2.5 SOLUTION

(a) *Profits deferred until completion of contract*

	£
• Turnover and profits recognised on the contract in 20X5	Nil
• Value of work in progress at 31 December 20X5	900,000

SSAP 9 takes the view that this policy is unreasonable, because in 20X6, the total profit of £500,000 [2,000,000 – (900,000 + 600,000)] would be recorded. Since the contract revenues are earned throughout 20X5 and 20X6, a profit of nil in 20X5 and £500,000 in 20X6 would be contrary to the accruals basis of accounting.

(b) It is fairer to recognise turnover and profit throughout the duration of the contract.

164

As at 31 December 20X5 turnover of £1,200,000 should be matched with cost of sales of £900,000 [(900,000 + 600,000) × 60%) in the profit and loss account, leaving an attributable profit for 20X5 of £300,000.

The only balance sheet entry as at 31 December 20X5 is a debtor of £1,200,000 recognising that the company is owed this amount for work done to date. No balance remains for stock, the whole £900,000 having been recognised in cost of sales.

Definitions

2.6 SSAP 9 gives some other important definitions, as well as that of long-term contracts themselves given above.

> ### KEY TERMS
>
> '**Attributable profit**. That part of the **total profit** currently estimated to arise over the **duration** of the **contract**, after allowing for **estimated remedial** and **maintenance costs** and increases in costs so far as **not recoverable** under the terms of the contract, that fairly reflects the profit attributable to that part of the **work performed** at the accounting date. (There can be no attributable profit until the **profitable outcome** of the contract can be assessed with **reasonable certainty**.)
>
> **Foreseeable losses**. Losses which are currently estimated to arise over the **duration** of the **contract** (after allowing for **estimated remedial** and **maintenance costs** and increases in costs so far as **not recoverable** under the terms of the contract). This estimate is required irrespective of:
>
> (a) Whether or not work has yet **commenced** on such contracts
> (b) The **proportion** of work **carried out** at the accounting date
> (c) The amount of **profits expected** to arise on other contracts
>
> **Payments on account**. All amounts **received** and **receivable** at the accounting date in respect of contracts in progress.'

Approach for calculating turnover and profit to be taken

2.7 The SSAP 9 guidelines for calculating the turnover and profit to be taken on incomplete long-term contracts follow directly from the definitions given above.

(a) **Turnover and profit**

  (i) Must reflect the **proportion** of **work carried** out at the **accounting date**.

  (ii) Must take into account any **known inequalities of profitability** in the **various stages** of a contract.

  (iii) Must be ascertained in a **manner appropriate** to the **industry** in which the **company operates**.

(b) **Situations where the outcome of a contract cannot be assessed with reasonable certainty**.

  (i) Generally no profit should be taken up in the profit and loss, especially where the contract is in its early stages.

  (ii) If no loss is expected, it may be appropriate to include in turnover, a proportion of the total contract value using a zero estimate of profit.

(c) **Situations where there is an expected loss on a contract as a whole**

Provision must be made for the whole of the loss as soon as it is foreseen, ie, none of the loss should be deferred.

This has the effect of reducing the value of WIP to its net realisable value. For example, if a contract is 75% complete, and:

(i)   Costs incurred to date are £300,000
(ii)   Further costs to completion are expected to be £100,000
(iii) The contract price is £360,000

In addition to a **suitable proportion of costs incurred**, then the **full expected loss** of **£40,000** should be **charged against profit** in the current period.

This approach must be applied consistently between different contracts over time.

Treatment of other costs

2.8   The **estimated future costs** must take into account **estimated costs of rectification and guarantee work** and any possible increases in wages, prices of raw materials etc, so far as these are **not recoverable** from the **customer** under the terms of the contract.

2.9   **Interest payable** for finance etc must be **excluded** from **costs unless specifically attributable** to the **contract**.

Estimating attributable profit

2.10   There are generally two alternative formulae for determining the estimated attributable profit for the year.

- Work certified basis
- Costs incurred basis

(a) Attributable profit $= \dfrac{\text{Work certified to date}}{\text{Total contract price}} \times \text{Estimated total profit}$

(b) Attributable profit $= \dfrac{\text{Cost of work completed to date}}{\text{Total costs}} \times \text{Estimated total profit}$

2.11   Care should be exercised in adopting a costs incurred basis eg if there is high initial outlay or perhaps the expensive items only go in towards the end of the contract. The examiner may therefore provide a tailored formula for the specific exam question which you will need to interpret and apply on the day.

An extra prudent approach

2.12   Some companies feel that it is more prudent to take credit for profit only in respect of the cash which has been received from the customer. Hence, the figure for attributable profit obtained above, is subjected to a further fraction.

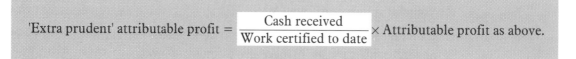

'Extra prudent' attributable profit $= \dfrac{\text{Cash received}}{\text{Work certified to date}} \times \text{Attributable profit as above.}$

2.13 With a little bit of basic maths, the above can be expressed as:

$$\text{'Extra prudent' attributable profit} = \frac{\text{Cash received}}{\text{Total contract price}} \times \text{Estimated total profit}$$

Exam focus point

The extra prudent approach might well not be required by the examiner. It is shown here to demonstrate what some companies use in practice. Read the question carefully to understand the examiner's requirements.

Available guidance

2.14 SSAP 9 does not provide any guidance on how to work out cost of sales, but focuses instead on the approach to determining attributable profit.

2.15 The amount of turnover and profit on a long-term contract to be recognised in an accounting period is found using a cumulative approach ie deduct figure total at end of last year from total at end of this year to get figure for the current year.

	£
Cumulative turnover/attributable profit	X
Less any turnover/attributable profit taken into account in previous years	X
Turnover/profit to be recognised in current period	X

2.16 **Estimates of total profit may change** from one year to another. Therefore, attributable profits have to be **recalculated** at the end of **each period**. Remember that at an **early stage** in the contract, in order to show a **true and fair view** of activity in the period, an **appropriate proportion of turnover** should be recorded in the profit and loss account but, on grounds of **prudence, no profit** should be recorded until the overall result of the contract is more certain.

BPP PUBLISHING

Using a step-by-step approach

2.17 In valuing long-term WIP and implementing the other disclosures required under SSAP 9, you may find a step-by-step approach to be helpful. The following suggested process should assist you to tackle the problem in an ordered way.

STEP 1
Calculate the expected total profit or loss on the contract.

	£
Contract value	X
Less: Costs incurred to date	(X)
Expected further costs to complete	(X)
Expected total profit/(loss)	X/(X)

(a)   If the contract is expected to make a profit, recognise attributable profit, if outcome is reasonably certain.

(b)   If a loss is foreseen (that is, if the costs to date plus estimated costs to completion exceed the contract value) then it must be charged against profits.

(c)   If a loss has already been charged in previous years, then only the difference between the loss as previously and currently estimated need be charged (or credited).

STEP 2
*Using the **percentage certified/completed to date** (or other formula given in the question), calculate **turnover attributable** to the contract for the **period**.*

	£
Total contract value × percentage certified (or formula given in the question)	X
Less Turnover recognised in previous period	(X)
Turnover attributable to current period	X

STEP 3
Calculate the cost of sales attributable to the contract for the period.

	£
Total contract costs × percentage certified (or formula given in question)	X
Less Any costs charged in previous periods	(X)
	X
Add Foreseeable losses in full (not previously charged)	X
Cost of sales attributable to current period	X

STEP 4
Review the balance on work in progress
(a)   A debit balance for WIP will remain on the balance sheet
(b)   A credit balance on WIP should be shown under provision for liabilities and charges.

STEP 5
*Calculate **cumulative** turnover on the contract (the total turnover recorded in respect of the contract in the profit and loss accounts of all accounting periods since the inception of the contract). Compare this with total progress payments to date.*
(a)   If turnover exceeds payments on account (from customers), an 'amount recoverable on contracts' is established and separately disclosed within debtors.
(b)   If payments on account (from customers) exceed cumulative turnover then the excess is:
(i)   First deducted from any remaining balance on work in progress
(ii)   Any balance is disclosed within creditors

2.18 These steps must be done for each contract individually. Only when the amounts under each heading, in respect of contract, have been determined, should they be added together for presentation in the accounts.

Double entry

2.19 The accounting double entry for a long-term contract is as follows.

(a) *During the year*

    (i)   DEBIT   Contract costs account (WIP)
             CREDIT   Bank/creditors

             Being costs incurred on contract

    (ii)   DEBIT   Trade debtors
             CREDIT   Progress payments account

             Being progress payments invoiced to customers

    (iii) DEBIT   Bank
             CREDIT   Trade debtors

             Being cash received from customers

(b) *At year end*

    (i)   DEBIT   Progress payments account
             CREDIT   Turnover (P&L)

             Being turnover recognised in respect of certified work

    (ii)   DEBIT   Cost of sales (P&L)
             CREDIT   Contract costs account (WIP)

             Being costs matched against turnover

    (iii) DEBIT   Provisions on long-term contracts (P&L)
             CREDIT   Provision for future losses (B/S)

             Being a provision for future losses

Summary of accounting treatment

2.20 The following is a handy summary of the accounting treatment for long-term contracts.

Profit and loss account

(a) **Turnover and costs**

    (i)   Turnover and associated costs should be recorded in the profit and loss account 'as contract activity progresses'.

    (ii)   Include an 'appropriate proportion of total contract value as turnover' in the profit and loss account.

    (iii) The costs incurred in reaching that stage of completion are matched with this turnover, resulting in the reporting of results which can be attributed to the proportion of work completed.

    (iv) Turnover is the 'value of work carried out to date'.

(b) **Attributable profit**

    (i)   It must reflect the proportion of work carried out.

    (ii)   It should take into account any known inequalities in profitability in the various stages of a contract.

Balance sheet

(a) **Stocks**

	£
Costs to date	X
Less Transfer to profit and loss account	(X)
	X
Less Foreseeable losses	(X)
	X
Less Payments on account in excess of turnover	(X)
Work in progress	X

(b) **Debtors**

	£
Amounts recoverable on contracts	X
Progress payments receivable (trade debtors)	X

(c) **Creditors.** Where payments on account exceed both cumulative turnover and net WIP the excess should be included in creditors under 'payments on account'.

(d) **Provisions.** To the extent foreseeable future losses exceed WIP, the losses should be provided.

Question 2

The main business of Louise Ltd is construction contracts. At the end of September 20X3 there are two uncompleted contracts on the books, details of which are as follows.

CONTRACT	A	B
Date commenced	1.9.X3	1.4.X1
Expected completed date	23.12.X3	23.12.X3
	£	£
Final contract price	70,000	290,000
Costs to 30.9.X3	21,000	210,450
Value of work certified to 30.9.X3	20,000	230,000
Progress payments invoiced to 30.9.X3	20,000	210,000
Cash received to 30.9.X3	18,000	194,000
Estimated costs to completion at 30.9.X3	41,000	20,600

Required

Prepare calculations showing the amounts to be included in the balance sheet at 30 September 20X3 in respect of the above contracts.

Answer

- *Contract A* is a short-term contract and although it straddles the year end, is not particularly large. It should therefore be included in the balance sheet as work in progress at cost less amounts received and receivable £(21,000 – 20,000) ie £1,000.

- *Contract B* is a long-term contract and will be accounted for using long-term contract accounting.

Estimated final profit

		£
Contract value		290,000
Less:	Costs incurred to date	(210,450)
	Estimated future costs	(20,600)
Expected total profit		58,950

Attributable profit

$$\text{Estimated final profit} \quad \times \quad \frac{\text{Work certified}}{\text{Total contract value}} \quad \times \quad \frac{\text{Cash received *}}{\text{Invoiced amounts}}$$

$$£58,950 \quad \times \quad \frac{230,000}{290,000} \quad \times \quad \frac{194,000}{210,000}$$

Attributable profit   £43,191

* In this instance, the company has adopted the extra prudent approach and applied the cash received fraction. Remember, however, this might not be asked for in your exam.

Profit and loss account (extract)

	£
Turnover	230,000
Cost of sales (W2)	(186,809)
	43,191

Balance sheet (extract)

	£
Stock: long term contracts (W1)	23,641

Debtors:	
Amounts recoverable on contracts (W1)	20,000
Progress payments invoiced less cash received (W1)	16,000

Workings

1

CONTRACT B (WIP)

		£				£
Bank/creditors		210,450	Tfr to cost of sales			186,809
			Balance		c/d	23,641
		210,450				210,450
Balance	b/d	23,641				

TRADE DEBTORS

		£				£
Invoices; progress payments		210,000	Cash received			194,000
			Balance		c/d	16,000
		210,000				210,000
Balance	b/d	16,000				

PROGRESS PAYMENTS – CONTRACT B (Amount recoverable on contracts)

	£			£
Work certified	230,000	Invoices; progress payments		210,000
		Balance	c/d	20,000
	230,000			230,000
Balance c/d	20,000			

TURNOVER

	£		£
		Work certified	230,000

COST OF SALES

	£		£
Tfr from WIP	186,809		

2

	£
Work certified	230,000
Cost of sales (balancing figure)	(186,809)
Attributable profit	43,191

Profitable and loss-making contracts

2.21 Students sometimes find accounting for long-term contracts quite confusing, particularly where contracts are loss-making. We can look at the differences between profitable and loss-making contracts in more depth.

Profitable contracts

2.22 PROFIT AND LOSS ACCOUNT (EXTRACT)

	£
Turnover	X
Cost of sales	(X)
Attributable profit	X

2.23 BALANCE SHEET (EXTRACT)

	£
Current assets	
Stock: Long-term contracts	
Costs to date	X
Less P&L a/c cost of sales	(X)
Less Excess payments on accounts	(X)
	X
Debtors: amounts recoverable on contracts	£
Turnover, work certified	X
Less Progress payments invoiced	(X)
	X
Debtors: trade debtors	£
Progress payments invoiced less cash received	X
Current liabilities	£
Payments on account (when payments received in excess of turnover which cannot be offset against stock balance)	X

Loss-making contracts

2.24 PROFIT AND LOSS ACCOUNT (EXTRACT)

	£
Turnover	X
Cost of sales	(X)
	(X)
Provision for loss (balancing figure to give)	(X)
Total foreseeable loss	(X)

2.25 BALANCE SHEET (EXTRACT)

Current assets	£
Stock: long-term contracts	
Costs incurred	X
Less Cost of sales	(X)
Less Provision for loss	(X)
Less Negative debtors balance	(X)
Positive/nil balance	X
Debtors: amounts recoverable on contracts	£
Turnover; work certified	X
Less Progress payments invoiced	(X)
Positive/nil balance	X
Debtors: trade debtors	£
Progress payments invoiced less cash received	X
Current liabilities	£
Payments on account	
Negative debtor balance not relieved against stock	X
Provision for liabilities and charges	£
Provision for loss not offset against stock balance	X

Exam focus point

A question is more likely to be set on long-term contracts than on stock or short term WIP, simply because stock and short term WIP were covered in depth for Paper 1.1. The pilot paper covered long term contracts for 9 marks of a 25 mark question.

2.26 The following comprehensive question should make things clearer.

Question 3

Znowhyatt plc has two contracts in progress, the details of which are as follows.

	Happy (profitable)	*Grumpy (loss-making)*
	£'000	£'000
Total contract price	300	300
Costs incurred to date	90	150
Estimated costs to completion	110	225
Progress payments invoiced and received	116	116

Required

Show extracts from the profit and loss account and the balance sheet for each contract, assuming they are both:

(a) 40% complete; and
(b) 36% complete.

Answer

(a) *Happy contract*

    (i) *40% complete*

	£'000
Profit and loss account	
Turnover (40% × 300)	120
Cost of sales (40% × 200)	(80)
Gross profit	40
Balance sheet	
Debtors (120 − 116)	4
WIP (90 − 80)	10

    (ii) *36% complete*

	£'000
Profit and loss account	
Turnover (36% × 300)	108
Cost of sales (36% × 200)	(72)
Gross profit	36
Balance sheet	
Debtors (108 − 116 = −8)	-
WIP (90 − 72 − 8*) =	10

    * Set off excess payments on account against WIP.

(b) *Grumpy contract*

    (i) *40% complete*

Working

	£'000	£'000
Total contract price		300
Less: costs to date	150	
estimated costs to completion	225	
		375
Foreseeable loss		(75)

	£'000
Profit and loss account	
Turnover (40% × 300)	120
Cost of sales (40% × 375)	(150)
	(30)
Provision for future losses (bal fig)	(45)
Gross loss	(75)
Balance sheet	£'000
Debtors (120 − 116)	4
WIP (150 − 150)	-
Provision for future losses	(45)

(ii)   *36% complete*

	£'000
Profit and loss account	
Turnover (36% × 300)	108
Cost of sales (36% × 375)	(135)
	(27)
Provision for future losses (balancing figure)	(48)
Gross loss	(75)
Balance sheet	
Debtors (108 – 116 = –8)	-
WIP (150 – 135 – 48* = –33)	-
Creditors: payments on account	8
Provisions: provisions for future losses	33

* Set off provision for losses before excess payments on account.

Scope for profit smoothing

2.27   At the beginning of this section on long term contract accounting, the problems associated with taking profits only on completion of a long term contract were identified.

However, the reference provided by **SSAP 9**, whereby **turnover** and **prudently calculated attributable profit** are **recognised** as the **contract progresses**, might create a **different** set of **financial reporting issues**, particularly in terms of the **scope for profit smoothing**.

(a)   The scope for adopting **various formulae** or methods for calculating attributable profit can provide opportunities for profit smoothing. There is **no prescribed formula** provided in **SSAP 9**.

(b)   Given the adoption of a particular formula for determining attributable profit, a company could '**manage**' the **underlying transactions** to provide the desired year by year profit profile over the duration of a long-term contract.

  (i)   **Cost incurred basis**. Actual expenditure could be incurred in a manner that gives the desired level of profit to be taken for a particular year. Eg. putting in an expensive piece of equipment to accelerate profit recognition.

  (ii)   **Work certified basis**. Here, scope for influencing the level of attributable profits recognised, depends on the arrangements for raising certificates.

  (iii)   **Other basis**. There may be other industry or company specific methods that give a particular outcome. The formula may be a basis that ensures a smooth profile of attributable profit but this does not necessarily accord with the underlying commercial reality. The method should be scrutinised to see whether it will produce figures that meet the true and fair criteria.

(c)   The process of determining attributable profits includes potentially subjective estimates eg. costs to complete the contract.

(d)   SSAP 9 specifies that **profit** on a contract should be recognised only when the **outcome can be foreseen** with **reasonable certainty**. SSAP 9 does not provide any guidance on how this assessment can be quantified. Professional judgement has therefore to be used and commonly used rules of thumb can vary between 25% to 30% of contract completion.

BPP
PUBLISHING

2.28 EXAMPLE

Kikabout Konstruction Ltd is building a new £4,000,000 millennium football stadium for a newly promoted club Shepherds Bush Authorials. The contract commenced on 1 June 20X4 and is planned to be completed by 31 July 20X6 in time for the new 20X6/X7 season.

- Costs incurred by Kikabout Konstruction Ltd on the contract to year end 30 December 20X4 amounted to £1,040,000.

- During the year, Kikabout Konstruction issued two invoices for progress payments:

  Progress payment 1   £600,000
  Progress payment 2   £520,000

- The club has paid the first invoice but the second progress payment will only be met when they complete the sale of their star striker to a South American club.

- Work certified by architects for the year amounts to £1,240,000.

- The estimated costs to completion on 31 July 20X6 are £1,960,000.

Show how the above transactions other than the sale of the player, should be accounted for by Kikabout Konstruction Ltd in the year ended 31 December 20X6.

2.29 SOLUTION

Calculation of contract profitability

		£
Contract value		4,000,000
Costs incurred to date	1,040,000	
Expected further costs to complete	1,960,000	3,000,000
Expected total profit		1,000,000

Percentage completed

$$\frac{\text{Work certified}}{\text{Contract value}} = \frac{£1,240,000}{£4,000,000} = 31\%$$

Percentage cash received on work certified

$$\text{Percentage completed} \times \frac{\text{Cash received}}{\text{Work certified}} = 31\% \times \frac{£1,120,000}{£1,240,000} = 28\%$$

Note: The above can be short-cut by using the alternative formula:

$$\frac{\text{Cash received}}{\text{Contract value}} = \frac{£1,120,000}{£4,000,000} = 28\%$$

	Estimated total £	Collected 28% £	Recognised previous period £	Recognised this period £
Turnover	4,000,000	1,120,000	-	1,120,000
Cost of sales (balancing figure)	3,000,000	840,000	-	840,000
Gross profit	1,000,000	280,000	-	280,000

WIP – Shepherd's Bush Authorials Millennium Stadium

		£			£
Bank/Creditors		1,040,000	Cost of sales		840,000
			Balance	c/d	200,000
		1,040,000			1,040,000
Balance	b/d	200,000			

Trade Debtor - Shepherds Bush Authorials

		£			£
Invoice 1		600,000	Bank		600,000
Invoice 2		520,000	Balance	c/d	520,000
		1,120,000			1,120,000
Balance	b/d	520,000			

Progress payments (Amounts recoverable on contracts)

		£			£
Work certified		1,240,000	Invoice 1		600,000
			Invoice 2		520,000
			Balance	c/d	120,000
		1,240,000			1,240,000
Balance	b/d	120,000			

Turnover

	£		£
		Work certified	1,240,000

Cost of sales

	£		£
Tfr from WIP	840,000		

The WIP account shows costs incurred of £1,040,000 less costs of £840,000 transferred to profit and loss account, via cost of sales. The WIP balance should be disclosed as "long-term contract balances" and disclosed separately under the heading stocks.

The progress payments account provides a record of the extent to which work certified by the architects has been invoiced to the customer. The debit of £1,240,000 is the work certified, with credits of £600,000 and £520,000, in respect of invoices sent to the customer.

The debit balance on the progress payment account reflects unbilled work. The debit balance should be disclosed separately as "Amounts recoverable on contracts" under debtors.

The debtors account is in effect a traditional sales ledger account. The two debits of £600,000 and £520,000 represent invoices billed to the customer in respect of progress payments required. The credit of £600,000 is cash received from the customer. The debit balance on this account should be disclosed separately as 'Progress payments receivable' under debtors.

Note Do not be confused by the disclosures under debtors:

DEBIT BALANCE ON	BALANCE SHEET DESCRIPTION
Progress payments account	Amounts recoverable on contracts
Debtors account	Progress payments receivable

Chapter roundup

- The **Companies Act 1985** requires that the balance sheet should show stocks (CI) sub-divided as follows.

  Stocks
  Raw materials and consumables
  Work in progress
  Finished goods and goods for resale
  Payments on account (of purchases)

- Stocks must be valued at the **lower of cost and net realisable value**.

  ° **NRV** is selling price less all costs to completion and less selling costs.

  ° **Cost** comprises cost of purchase and costs of conversion. You must learn the definitions of these terms.

  ° **FIFO and weighted average costing** are the most widely accepted means of valuing stock in accordance with both CA 1985 and SSAP 9.

- The process of calculating accounting entries on **long-term contracts** can be summarised as follows.

  ° Turnover taken on long-term contracts should be debited to 'Amounts recoverable on contracts' (and credited to the profit and loss account).

  ° The amount at which long-term contract work in progress is stated in accounts should be cost, less cost of sales to date, including any foreseeable losses.

  ° Where the invoicing credited to the amounts recoverable on contracts account exceed the debits in respect of work certified, the credit balance on the account should be applied in the following order:

    (a) Cancelling any balance on contract WIP.

    (b) Shown as a payment on amount separately under creditors.

- At this stage of your studies the most difficult aspect of SSAP 9 to be mastered is the **valuation and disclosure of long-term contracts**.

- You must be able both to calculate all the balances to be included in accounts and make effective points on discursive questions.

Quick quiz

1 Net realisable value = Selling price **less** .... **less** ....

2 Which stock costing methods are permissible under SSAP 9?

   A FIFO, LIFO, average cost, unit cost
   B Unit cost, job cost, batch cost, LIFO
   C Process costing, unit cost LIFO, average cost
   D Job costing, average cost, FIFO, unit cost.

3 Any expected loss on a long-term contract must be recognised, in full, in the year it was identified.

   True ☐

   False ☐

4 List the five steps to be taken when valuing long-term contracts.

5 Which items in the profit and loss and balance sheet are potentially affected by long term contracts?

Answers to quick quiz

1   Net realisable value = selling price **less** costs to completion **less** costs to market, sell and distribute. (see para 1.5)

2   D, LIFO is not an acceptable costing method (1.5)

3   True. (2.7)

4   See paragraph 2.17.

5   Profit and loss: turnover and cost of sales. Balance sheet: stocks, debtors, creditors and provisions (2.20)

Now try the question below from the Exam Question Bank

Number	Level	Marks	Time
8	Full exam	30	54 mins

BPP PUBLISHING

Chapter 8

TAXATION IN COMPANY ACCOUNTS

Topic list	Syllabus reference
1 FRS 16 *Current Tax*	3(e)
2 SSAP 5 *Accounting for value added tax*	3(e)
3 FRS 19 *Deferred tax*	3(e)
4 Taxation in company accounts	3(e)
5 Disclosure requirements	3(e)

Introduction

Tax is a straight forward area. There are plenty of exercises here - make sure that you attempt each one yourself without referring to the solution immediately.

Accounting for VAT is particularly easy and you should be relatively familiar with the workings of the tax. Do not overlook the SSAP 5 requirements.

In relation to corporation tax you must be able to calculate the relevant tax figures *and* know how they should be disclosed in the accounts according to FRS 16.

Deferred taxation is probably the most difficult topic in this chapter. Concentrate on trying to understand the logic behind the tax and the reasons why the FRS 19 approach has been adopted.

Study guide

- Account for current taxation in accordance with FRS 16.
- Record entries relating to corporation tax in the accounting records.
- Apply requirements of SSAP 5 Accounting for VAT.
- Explain the effect of timing differences on accounting and taxable profits.
- Outline the principle of accounting for deferred tax on both the full and the partial provision methods, and discuss their advantages and disadvantages.
- Outline the requirements of FRS 19.
- Calculate and record deferred tax amounts in the financial statements.

Exam guide

Learn the disclosures, they are bound to come up in an accounts preparation question

1   FRS 16 CURRENT TAX

1.1   Companies pay corporation tax, usually nine months after the year end. FRS 16 *Current tax*, which was published in December 1999, specifies how current tax should be reflected in the financial statements. This should be done in a **'consistent and transparent manner'**.

1.2 Specifically, the FRS deals with **tax credits** and **withholding tax**. Consider these definitions.

> **KEY TERMS**
>
> * **Current tax.** The amount of tax estimated to be payable or recoverable in respect of the taxable profit or loss for a period, along with adjustments to estimates in respect of previous periods.
>
> * **Withholding tax.** Tax on dividends or other income that is deducted by the payer of the income and paid to the tax authorities wholly on behalf of the recipient.
>
> * **Tax credit.** The tax credit given under UK tax legislation to the recipient of a dividend from a UK company. The credit is given to acknowledge that the income out of which the dividend has been paid has already been charged to tax, rather than because any withholding tax has been deducted at source. The tax credit may discharge or reduce the recipient's liability to tax on the dividend. Non-taxpayers may or may not be able to recover the tax credit.

1.3 You can see from these definitions that a tax credit is different from a withholding tax.

> * A tax credit **gives credit for** tax paid by a company
> * A **withholding tax withholds** the taxable part of the income

Accordingly, the tax credit and the withholding tax are treated differently in the financial statements.

Treatment in financial statements

1.4 Learn this treatment

> **Outgoing dividends paid and proposed, interest or other amounts payable**
>
> * Include withholding tax
> * Exclude tax credit
>
> **Incoming dividends, interest or other amounts payable**
>
> * Include withholding tax
> * Exclude tax credit
> * Include the effect of withholding tax suffered as part of the tax charge

1.5 EXAMPLE: CURRENT TAX

Taxus Ltd made a profit of £1,000,000. It received a dividend of £80,000 on which there was a tax credit of £20,000. From an overseas company it received a dividend of £3,000 on which 25% withholding tax had been deducted. The corporation tax charge was £300,000.

Required

Show how this information would be presented in the financial statements in accordance with FRS 16 *Current tax*.

1.6 SOLUTION

	£
Operating profit	1,000,000
Income from fixed asset investments	
UK (note 1)	80,000
Foreign (note 2)	4,000
Profit before tax	1,084,000
Taxation (note 3)	301,000
Profit after tax	783,000

Notes

1   Excludes tax credit

2   Includes withholding tax: £3,000 + £1,000 = £4,000. Read the question carefully - 25% had been deducted already

3   Add back withholding tax of £1,000

Other requirements of FRS 16

1.7   Current tax should be recognised in the **profit and loss account**. But it is attributable to a gain or loss that has been recognised in the statement of total recognised gains and losses it should be recognised in that statement.

1.8   Current tax should be measured using tax rates and laws that have been enacted or substantially enacted by the balance sheet date.

1.9   Generally (apart from the treatment of withholding tax) income and expenses are **not adjusted** to reflect a **notional amount** of tax that would have been paid or received if the transaction had been taxable or allowable on a different basis. Income and expenses are included in pre-tax results on the basis of amounts **actually receivable or payable**.

Tax disclosure in the notes

1.10   This example, taken from the appendix to FRS 16, illustrates one method of showing by way of a note the tax items required to be disclosed under CA 1985 and the FRS.

	£'000	£'000
UK corporation tax		
Current tax on income for the period	X	
Adjustments in respect of prior periods	X	
	X	
Double taxation relief*	(X)	
		X
Foreign tax		
Current tax on income for the period	X	
Adjustments in respect of prior periods	X	
		X
Tax on profit on ordinary activities		X

*Don't worry about this - it's unlikely to come up in your exam.

2   SSAP 5 ACCOUNTING FOR VALUE ADDED TAX

2.1   **VAT is a tax on the supply of goods and services**. The tax authority responsible for collecting VAT is HM Customs & Excise. **Tax is collected at each transfer point in the chain from prime producer to final consumer**. Eventually, the consumer bears the tax in full and any tax paid earlier in the chain can be recovered by the trader who paid it.

2.2 EXAMPLE: VAT

A manufacturing company, A Ltd, purchases raw materials at a cost of £1,000 plus VAT at 17½%. From the raw materials A Ltd makes finished products which it sells to a retail outlet, B Ltd, for £1,600 plus VAT. B Ltd sells the products to customers at a total price of £2,000 plus VAT. How much VAT is paid to Customs & Excise at each stage in the chain?

2.3 SOLUTION

	Value of goods sold £	VAT at 17½% £
Supplier of raw materials	1,000	175
Value added by A Ltd	600	105
Sale to B Ltd	1,600	280
Value added by B Ltd	400	70
Sales to 'consumers'	2,000	350

How is VAT collected?

2.4 Although it is the final consumer who eventually bears the full tax of £350, the sum is **collected and paid over to Customs & Excise by the traders who make up the chain.** Each trader must assume that his customer is the final consumer and must collect and pay over VAT at the appropriate rate on the full sales value of the goods sold. He is entitled to reclaim VAT paid on his own purchases (inputs) and so makes a net payment to Customs & Excise equal to the tax on value added by himself.

2.5 In the example above, the supplier of raw materials collects from A Ltd VAT of £175, all of which he pays over to Customs & Excise. When A Ltd sells goods to B Ltd VAT is charged at the rate of 17½% on £1,600 = £280. Only £105, however, is paid by A Ltd to Customs & Excise because the company is entitled to deduct VAT of £175 suffered on its own purchases. Similarly, B Ltd must charge its customers £350 in VAT but need only pay over the net amount of £70 after deducting the £280 VAT suffered on its purchase from A Ltd.

Registered and non-registered persons

2.6 **Traders whose sales (outputs) are below a certain minimum need not register for VAT.** Such traders neither charge VAT on their outputs nor are entitled to reclaim VAT on their inputs. They are in the same position as a final consumer.

2.7 **All outputs of registered traders are either taxable or exempt**. Traders carrying on exempt activities (such as banks) cannot charge VAT on their outputs and consequently cannot reclaim VAT paid on their inputs.

2.8 Taxable outputs are usually (fuel being an exception as it is charged at 5%) chargeable at one of **two rates**:

(a) **Zero per cent (zero-rated items)**
(b) **17½% (standard-rated items)**

Customs & Excise publish lists of supplies falling into each category. **Persons carrying on taxable activities** (even activities taxable at zero per cent) **are entitled to reclaim VAT paid on their inputs.**

2.9 Some traders carry on a **mixture of taxable and exempt activities.** Such traders need to apportion the VAT suffered on inputs and **can only reclaim the proportion relating to taxable outputs.**

Accounting for VAT

2.10 As a general principle the treatment of VAT in the accounts of a trader should reflect his role as a collector of the tax and **VAT should not be included in income or in expenditure whether of a capital or of a revenue nature.**

Irrecoverable VAT

2.11 Where the **trader bears the VAT** himself, as in the following cases, this should be reflected in the accounts.

    (a) **Persons not registered** for VAT will suffer VAT on inputs. This will effectively increase the cost of their consumable materials and their fixed assets and must be so reflected, ie shown **inclusive of VAT.**

    (b) **Registered persons** who also carry on **exempted** activities will have a residue of VAT which falls directly on them. In this situation the costs to which this residue applies will be inflated by the **irrecoverable VAT**.

    (c) **Non-deductible inputs will be borne** by all traders (examples are tax on cars bought which are not for resale, entertaining expenses and provision of domestic accommodation for a company's directors).

Exam focus point

Where VAT is not recoverable it must be regarded as an inherent part of the cost of the items purchased and included in the P&L charge or balance sheet as appropriate.

Further points

2.12 **VAT is charged on the price net of any discount** and this general principle is carried to the extent that where a cash discount is offered, VAT is charged on the net amount **even where the discount is not taken up.**

2.13 Most VAT registered persons are obliged to record VAT when a supply is received or made (effectively when a credit sales invoice is raised or a purchase invoice recorded). This has the effect that **the net VAT liability has on occasion to be paid to Customs & Excise before all output tax has been paid by customers**. If a debt is subsequently written off, the VAT element may not be recovered from Customs & Excise for six months from the date of sale, even if the customer becomes insolvent.

2.14 **Some small businesses can join the cash accounting scheme whereby VAT is only paid to Customs & Excise after it is received from customers.** This delays recovery of input tax but improves cash flow overall, although it may involve extra record keeping. Bad debt relief is automatic under this scheme since if VAT is not paid by the customer it is not due to Customs & Excise.

Question 1

Mussel Ltd is preparing accounts for the year ended 31 May 20X9. Included in its balance sheet as at 31 May 20X8 was a balance for VAT recoverable of £15,000.

Its summary profit and loss account for the year is as follows.

	£'000
Sales (all standard rated)	500
Purchases (all standard rated)	120
Gross profit	380
Expenses	280
Operating profit	100
Interest receivable	20
Profit before tax	120

Note: expenses	£000
Wages and salaries	200
Entertainment expenditure	10
Other (all standard rated)	70
	280

Payments of £5,000, £15,000 and £20,000 have been made in the year and a repayment of £12,000 was received. What is the balance for VAT in the balance sheet as at 31 May 20X9? Assume a 17.5% standard rate of VAT.

Answer

MUSSEL LIMITED: VAT ACCOUNT

	£		£
Balance b/d	15,000	Sales (£500,000 × 17.5%)	87,500
Purchases (£120,000 × 17.5%)	21,000	Bank	12,000
Expenses (£70,000 × 17.5%)	12,250		
Bank	40,000		
Balance c/d	11,250		
	99,500		99,500

Requirements of SSAP 5

2.15 SSAP 5 requires the following accounting rules to be followed.

(a) **Turnover** shown in the profit and loss account should **exclude VAT** on taxable outputs. If gross turnover must be shown then the VAT in that figure must also be shown as a deduction in arriving at the turnover exclusive of VAT.

(b) **Irrecoverable VAT** allocated to fixed assets and other items separately disclosed should be **included in their cost** where material and practical.

(c) The **net amount due to (or from) Customs & Excise** should be **included in the total for creditors** (or **debtors**), and need not be separately disclosed.

2.16 Note that the CA 1985 also requires disclosure of the cost of sales figure in the published accounts. This amount should exclude VAT on taxable inputs.

3 FRS 19 DEFERRED TAX

Exam focus point

This section may seem quite complicated. Do not worry about the numbers too much, but remember that you must be able to **explain** the purpose of the deferred tax balance.

3.1 You may already be aware from your studies of taxation that accounting profits and taxable profits are not the same. There are several reasons for this but they may conveniently be considered under two headings.

(a) **Permanent differences** arise because certain expenditure, such as entertainment of UK customers, is not allowed as a deduction for tax purposes although it is quite properly deducted in arriving at accounting profit. Similarly, certain income (such as UK dividend income) is not subject to corporation tax, although it forms part of accounting profit.

(b) **Timing differences** arise because certain items are included in the accounts of a period which is different from that in which they are dealt with for taxation purposes.

Deferred taxation is the tax attributable to timing differences.

KEY TERM

Deferred tax. Estimated future tax consequences of transactions and events recognised in the financial statements of the current and previous periods.

3.2 Deferred taxation is therefore a means of ironing out the tax inequalities arising from timing differences.

(a) In years when **corporation tax is saved** by timing differences such as accelerated capital allowances, a charge for deferred taxation is made in the P&L account and a provision set up in the balance sheet.

(b) In years when **timing differences reverse**, because the depreciation charge exceeds the capital allowances available, a deferred tax credit is made in the P&L account and the balance sheet provision is reduced.

Deferred tax is the subject of a new standard, FRS 19 *Deferred tax*. Before we look at the detailed requirements of FRS 19, we will explore some of the issues surrounding deferred tax.

3.3 You should be clear in your mind that the tax actually payable to the Inland Revenue is the **corporation tax liability**. The credit balance on the deferred taxation account represents an estimate of tax saved because of timing differences but expected ultimately to become payable when those differences reverse.

3.4 FRS 19 identifies the main categories in which timing differences can occur.

(a) **Accelerated capital allowances.** Tax deductions for the cost of a fixed asset are accelerated or decelerated, ie received before or after the cost of the fixed asset is recognised in the profit and loss account.

(b) **Pension liabilities** are accrued in the financial statements but are allowed for tax purposes only when paid or contributed at a later date (pensions are not in the paper 2.5 syllabus).

(c) **Interest charges or development costs** are capitalised on the balance sheet but are treated as revenue expenditure and allowed as incurred for tax purposes.

(d) **Intragroup profits in stock**, unrealised at group level, are reversed on consolidation.

(e) **Revaluations.** An asset is revalued in the financial statements but the revaluation gain becomes taxable only if and when the asset is sold.

(f) **Unrelieved tax losses.** A tax loss is not relieved against past or present taxable profits but can be carried forward to reduce future taxable profits.

(g) **Unremitted earnings of subsidiaries.** The unremitted earnings of subsidiary and associated undertakings and joint ventures are recognised in the group results but will be subject to further taxation only if and when remitted to the parent undertaking.

3.5 Deferred taxation is therefore an accounting convention which is introduced in order to apply the accruals concept to income reporting where timing differences occur. However, **deferred tax assets** are not included in accounts as a rule, because it would not be prudent, given that the recovery of the tax is uncertain.

Basis of provision

3.6 A comprehensive tax allocation system is one in which deferred taxation is computed for every instance of timing differences: **full provision**. The opposite extreme would be the **nil provision** approach ('**flow through** method'), where only the tax payable in the period would be charged to that period.

SSAP 15

3.7 SSAP 15, the forerunner of FRS 19, rejected both these approaches and prescribe a middle course, called **partial provision**.

> 'Tax deferred or accelerated by the effect of timing differences should be accounted for to the extent that it is probable that a liability or asset will crystallise. Tax deferred or accelerated by the effect of timing differences should not be accounted for to the extent that it is probable that a liability or asset will not crystallise.'

3.8 The **probability** that a liability or asset would crystallise was assessed by the directors on the basis of **reasonable assumptions**. They had to take into account all relevant information available up to the date on which they approved the financial statements, and also their intentions for the future. Ideally, financial projections of future plans had to be made for a number (undefined) of years ahead. The directors' judgement had to be exercised with prudence.

3.9 If a company predicted, for example, that capital expenditure would **continue at the same rate** for the foreseeable future, so that capital allowances and depreciation would remain at the same levels, then no originating or reversing differences of any significance to the continuing trend of the tax charge would arise and so no change to the provision for deferred tax needed to be made (unless there were other significant timing differences).

The three different methods compared

3.10 Under the **flow-through method**, the tax liability recognised is the expected legal tax liability for the period (ie no provision is made for deferred tax). The main **advantages** of the method are that it is straightforward to apply and the tax liability recognised is closer to many people's idea of a 'real' liability than that recognised under either full or partial provision.

3.11 The main **disadvantages** of flow-through are that it can lead to large fluctuations in the tax charge and that it does not allow tax relief for long-term liabilities to be recognised until those liabilities are settled. The method is not used internationally.

3.12 The **full provision method** has the **advantage** that it is consistent with general international practice. It also recognises that each timing difference at the balance sheet date has an effect on future tax payments. If a company claims an accelerated capital allowance on an item of plant, future tax assessments will be bigger than they would have been otherwise. Future transactions may well affect those assessments still further, but that is not relevant in assessing the position at the balance sheet date. The **disadvantage** of full provision is that, under certain types of tax system, it gives rise to large liabilities that may fall due only far in the future. The full provision method is the one prescribed by FRS 19.

3.13 The **partial provision method** addresses this disadvantage by providing for deferred tax only to the extent that it is expected to be paid in the foreseeable future. This has an obvious intuitive appeal, but its effect is that deferred tax recognised at the balance sheet date includes the tax effects of future transactions that have not been recognised in the financial statements, and which the reporting company has neither undertaken nor even committed to undertake at that date. It is difficult to reconcile this with the ASB's *Statement of Principles*, which defines assets and liabilities as arising from past events.

Exam focus point

You need to understand the concept of deferred tax, it is unlikely that you will need to perform detailed calculations.

3.14 It is important that you understand the issues properly so consider the example below.

3.15 EXAMPLE: THE THREE METHODS COMPARED

Suppose that Girdo plc begins trading on 1 January 20X7. In its first year it makes profits of £5m, the depreciation charge is £1m and the capital allowances on those assets is £1.5m. The rate of corporation tax is 33%.

3.16 SOLUTION: FLOW THROUGH METHOD

The tax liability for the year is 33% £(5.0 + 1.0 − 1.5)m = £1.485m. The potential deferred tax liability of 33% × (£1.5m − £1m) is completely ignored and no judgement is required on the part of the preparer.

3.17 SOLUTION: FULL PROVISION

The tax liability is £1.485m again, but the debit in the P&L account is increased by the deferred tax liability of 33% × £0.5m = £165,000. The total charge to the P&L account is therefore £1,650,000 which is an effective tax rate of 33% on accounting profits (ie 33% × £5.0m). Again, no judgement is involved in using this method.

3.18 SOLUTION: PARTIAL PROVISION

Is a deferred tax provision necessary under partial provision? It is now necessary to look ahead at future capital expenditure plans. Will capital allowances exceed depreciation over the next few years? If *yes*, no provision for deferred tax is required. If *no*, then a reversal is expected, ie there is a year in which depreciation is greater than capital allowances. The deferred tax provision is made on the maximum reversal which will be created, and any not provided is disclosed by note.

If we assume that the review of expected future capital expenditure under the partial method required a deferred tax charge of £82,500 (33% × £250,000), we can then summarise the position.

Summary

3.19   The methods can be compared as follows.

Method	Provision £	Disclosure £
Flow-through	-	-
Full provision	165,000	-
Partial provision	82,500	82,500

FRS 19 *Deferred tax*

3.20   In December 2000 the ASB published FRS 19. The FRS replaced SSAP 15 and comes into effect for accounting periods ending on or after 23 January 2002, although earlier adoption is encouraged. It requires entities to provide for tax timing differences on a **full, rather than partial provision basis.**

Objective

3.21   The objective of FRS 19 is to ensure that:

(a)   Future tax consequences of past transactions and events are recognised as liabilities or assets in the financial statements

(b)   The financial statements disclose any other special circumstances that may have an effect on future tax charges.

Scope

3.22   The FRS applies **to all financial statements that are intended to give a true and fair view** of a reporting entity's financial position and profit or loss (or income and expenditure) for a period. The FRS applies to taxes calculated on the basis of taxable profits, including withholding taxes paid on behalf of the reporting entity.

3.23   Reporting entities applying the Financial Reporting Standard for Smaller Entities **(FRSSE)** currently applicable are **exempt** from the FRS.

Recognition of deferred tax assets and liabilities

> **REMEMBER!**
>
> **Deferred tax** should be recognised in respect of **all timing differences that have originated but not reversed by the balance sheet date.**
>
> Deferred tax should **not be recognised on permanent differences.**

Question 2

Can you remember some examples of timing differences?

Answer

- Accelerated capital allowances
- Pension liabilities accrued but taxed when paid

- Interest charges and development costs capitalised but allowed for tax purposes when incurred
- Unrealised intra-group stock profits reversed on consolidation
- Revaluation gains
- Tax losses
- Unremitted earnings of subsidiaries, associates and joint ventures recognised in group results.

KEY TERM

Permanent differences. Differences between an entity's taxable profits and its results as stated in the financial statements that arise because certain types of income and expenditure are non-taxable or disallowable, or because certain tax charges or allowances have no corresponding amount in the financial statements.

Allowances for fixed asset expenditure

3.24 Deferred tax **should be recognised** when the **allowances** for the cost of a fixed asset are **received before or after the cost of the fixed asset is recognised in the profit and loss account.** However, if and when **all conditions** for retaining the allowances have been met, the **deferred tax should be reversed.**

3.25 If an asset is not being depreciated (and has not otherwise been written down to a carrying value less than cost), the timing difference is the amount of capital allowances received.

3.26 Most capital allowances are received on a **conditional basis,** ie they are repayable (for example, via a balancing charge) if the assets to which they relate are sold for more than their tax written-down value. However, some, such as industrial buildings allowances, are repayable only if the assets to which they relate are sold within a specified period. Once that period has expired, all conditions for retaining the allowance have been met. At that point, deferred tax that has been recognised (ie on the excess of the allowance over any depreciation) is reversed.

Question 3

An industrial building qualifies for an IBA when purchased in 20X1. The building is still held by the company in 20Z6. What happens to the deferred tax?

Answer

All the conditions for retaining tax allowances have been met. This means that the timing differences have become permanent and the deferred tax recognised should be reversed. Before the 25 year period has passed, deferred tax should be provided on the difference between the amount of the industrial building allowance and any depreciation charged on the asset.

Measurement – discounting

3.27 Reporting entities are **permitted but not required** to discount deferred tax assets and liabilities to reflect the time value of money.

3.28 The ASB believes that, just as other long-term liabilities such as provisions and debt are discounted, so too in principle should long-term deferred tax balances. The FRS therefore permits discounting and provides guidance on how it should be done. However, the ASB stopped short of making discounting mandatory, acknowledging that there is as yet **no internationally accepted methodology** for discounting deferred tax, and that for some entities **the costs might outweigh the benefits.** Entities are encouraged to select the more appropriate policy, taking account of factors such as materiality and the policies of other entities in their sector.

Question 4

Can you think of a situation where it might be appropriate to discount deferred tax liabilities?

Answer

Where the reversal is fairly slow, for example with industrial buildings allowances.

3.29 Discounting should be **applied consistently** to all tax flows on timing differences where the effect is expected to be **material** and where the **tax flows have not already been discounted.**

3.30 **No account** should be taken of **future timing differences** including future tax losses.

3.31 The **scheduling of the reversals** should take account of the **remaining tax effect of transactions already reflected in the financial statements,** for example tax losses at the balance sheet date.

3.32 The **discount rate** should be the **post tax return** that could be obtained at the balance sheet date on **government bonds** with **similar maturity dates** and in **currencies similar to those of the deferred tax assets or liabilities.** It may be possible to use average rates without introducing material errors.

Presentation

3.33 In the **balance sheet** classify:

- Net deferred tax liabilities as 'provisions for liabilities and charges'

- Net deferred tax assets as debtors, as a separate subhead if material where taxes are levied by the same tax authority or in a group where tax losses of one entity can reduce the taxable profits of another.

3.34 Balances are to be **disclosed separately** on the face of the balance sheet **if** so **material** as to distort the financial statements.

3.35 In the **profit and loss account** classify as part of **tax on profit or loss on ordinary activities.**

Disclosures

3.36 FRS 19 has detailed disclosures relating to deferred tax, which are best learnt by studying the illustrative example below, taken from the Appendix.

> ### IMPORTANT!
>
> Note in particular that the FRS requires information to be disclosed **about factors affecting current and future tax charges. A key element** of this is a requirement to disclose a **reconciliation of the current tax charge for the period to the charge that would arise if the profits reported in the financial statements were charged at a standard rate of tax.**

3.37 EXAMPLE: DISCLOSURES

The following illustrates how the disclosures required by the FRS could be presented in the notes to the accounts. The reconciliation of the tax charge, illustrated as a reconciliation of monetary amounts in note 1 (b) below, could alternatively be given as a reconciliation of the standard rate of tax to the effective rate.

1 TAX ON PROFIT ON ORDINARY ACCOUNTS

(a) *Analysis of charge in period*

	20X6		20X5	
	£m	£m	£m	£m
Current tax				
UK corporation tax on profits of the period	40		26	
Adjustments in respect of previous periods	4		(6)	
		44		20
Foreign tax		12		16
Total current tax (note 1(b))		56		36
Deferred tax				
Origination and reversal of timing differences	67		60	
Effect of increased tax rate on opening liability	12		-	
Increase in discount	(14)		(33)	
Total deferred tax (note 2)		65		27
Tax on profit on ordinary activities		121		63

(b) *Factors affecting the tax charge for period*

The tax assessed for the period is lower than the standard rate of corporation tax in the UK (31 per cent). The differences are explained below.

	20X6	20X5
	£m	£m
Profit on ordinary activities before tax	361	327
Profit on ordinary activities multiplied by standard rate of corporation tax in the UK of 31% (20X0: 30%)	112	98
Effects of		
Expenses not deductible for tax purposes (primarily goodwill amortisation)	22	10
Capital allowances for period in excess of depreciation	(58)	(54)
Utilisation of tax losses	(17)	(18)
Rollover relief on profit on disposal of property	(10)	-
Higher tax rates on overseas earnings	3	6
Adjustments to tax charge in respect of previous periods	4	(6)
Current tax charge for period (note 1 (a))	56	36

(c) *Factors that may affect future tax charges*

Based on current capital investment plans, the group expects to continue to be able to claim capital allowances in excess of depreciation in future years but at a slightly lower level than in the current year.

The group has now used all brought-forward tax losses, which have significantly reduced tax payments in recent years.

No provision has been made for deferred tax on gains recognised on revaluing property to its market value or on the sale of properties where potentially taxable gains have been rolled over into replacement assets. Such tax would become payable only if the property were sold without it being possible to claim rollover relief. The total amount unprovided for is £21 million. At present, it is not envisaged that any tax will become payable in the foreseeable future.

The group's overseas tax rates are higher than those in the UK primarily because the profits earned in country X are taxed at a rate of 45 per cent. The group expects a reduction in future tax rates following a recent announcement that the rate of tax in that country is to reduce to 40 per cent.

No deferred tax is recognised on the unremitted earnings of overseas subsidiaries, associates and joint ventures. As the earnings are continually reinvested by the group, no tax is expected to be payable on them in the foreseeable future.

2 PROVISION FOR DEFERRED TAX

	31.12.20X6	31.12.20X5
	£m	£m
Accelerated capital allowances	426	356
Tax losses carried forward	-	(9)
Undiscounted provision for deferred tax	426	347
Discount	(80)	(66)
Discounted provision for deferred tax	346	281
Provision at start of period	281	
Deferred tax charge in profit and loss account for period (note 1)	65	
Provision at end of period	346	

Problems

3.38 The FRS makes a significant change. It will have the effect of **increasing the liabilities** reported by entities that at present have **large amounts of unprovided deferred tax** arising from capital allowances in excess of depreciation.

3.39 Criticisms that may be made of the FRS 19 approach include the following.

(a) The provisions on **discounting** are somewhat **confusing**.

(b) The standard is **complicated,** and there is **scope for manipulation and inconsistency,** since discounting is optional.

(c) It is **open to question whether deferred tax is a liability** as defined in the *Statement of Principles*. It is not, strictly speaking, a present obligation arising as a result of a past event. However, it is being recognised as such under the FRS.

(d) Arguably the flow-through or **nil provision method is closer to the ASB definition,** but this method, although much simpler, has been rejected to bring the standard closer to the IAS.

3.40 **Section summary**

- Deferred tax is tax relating to timing differences.
- Full provision must be made for tax timing differences.
- Discounting is allowed but not required.

Exam focus point

Questions on deferred tax for Paper 2.5 should be fairly straightforward. It is likely to be tested as part of a larger question rather than a question in its own right.

4 TAXATION IN COMPANY ACCOUNTS

4.1 We have now looked at the 'ingredients' of taxation in company accounts. There are two aspects to be learned:

(a) Taxation on profits in the profit and loss account.
(b) Taxation payments due, shown as a liability in the balance sheet.

Taxation in the profit and loss account

4.2 The tax on profit on ordinary activities is calculated by **aggregating**:

(a) **Corporation tax** on taxable profits

(b) **Transfers to or from deferred taxation**

(c) Any **under provision or overprovision** of corporation tax on profits of previous years

4.3 When corporation tax on profits is calculated for the profit and loss account, **the calculation is only an estimate of what the company thinks its tax liability will be. In subsequent dealings with the Inland Revenue, a different corporation tax charge might eventually be agreed.**

4.4 The difference between the estimated tax on profits for one year and the actual tax charge finally agreed for the year is made as an adjustment to taxation on profits in the following year, **resulting in the disclosure of either an underprovision or an overprovision of tax.**

Question 2

In the accounting year to 31 December 20X3, Ben Nevis Ltd made an operating profit before taxation of £110,000.

Corporation tax on the operating profit has been estimated as £45,000. In the previous year (20X2) corporation tax on 20X2 profits had been estimated as £38,000 but it was subsequently agreed at £40,500 with the Inland Revenue.

A transfer to the deferred taxation account of £16,000 will be made in 20X3.

Required

(a) Calculate the tax on profits for 20X3 for disclosure in the accounts.

(b) Calculate the amount of mainstream corporation tax payable on 30 September 20X4.

Answer

(a)   £

	£
Corporation tax on profits	45,000
Deferred taxation	16,000
Underprovision of tax in previous year £(40,500 – 38,000)	2,500
Tax on profits for 20X3	63,500

(b)

	£
Tax payable on 20X3 profits	45,000
Mainstream corporation tax liability	45,000

Taxation in the balance sheet

4.5   It should already be apparent from the previous examples that the corporation tax charge in the profit and loss account will not be the same as corporation tax liabilities in the balance sheet.

4.6   In the balance sheet, there are several items which we might expect to find.

    (a)   **Income tax may be payable** in respect of (say) interest payments paid in the last accounting return period of the year, or accrued.

    (b)   If no corporation tax is payable (or very little), then there might be an **income tax recoverable asset** disclosed in current assets (income tax is normally recovered by offset against the tax liability for the year).

    (c)   There will usually be a **liability for mainstream corporation tax**, possibly including the amounts due in respect of previous years but not yet paid.

    (d)   We may also find a **liability on the deferred taxation account**. Deferred taxation is shown under 'provisions for liabilities and charges' in the balance sheet.

Question 3

For the year ended 31 July 20X4 Matterhorn Ltd made taxable trading profits of £1,200,000 on which corporation tax is payable at 30%.

(a)   A transfer of £20,000 will be made to the deferred taxation account. The balance on this account was £100,000 before making any adjustments for items listed in this paragraph.

(b)   The estimated tax on profits for the year ended 31 July 20X3 was £80,000, but tax has now been agreed with the Inland Revenue at £84,000 and fully paid.

(c)   Mainstream corporation tax on profits for the year to 31 July 20X4 is payable on 1 May 20X5.

(d)   In the year to 31 July 20X4 the company made a capital gain of £60,000 on the sale of some property. This gain is taxable at a rate of 30%.

Required

(a)   Calculate the tax charge for the year to 31 July 20X4.
(b)   Calculate the tax liabilities in the balance sheet of Matterhorn as at 31 July 20X4.

Answer

(a)   *Tax charge for the year*

		£
(i)	Tax on trading profits (30% of £1,200,000)	360,000
	Tax on capital gain	18,000
	Deferred taxation	20,000
		398,000
	Underprovision of taxation in previous years £(84,000 – 80,000)	4,000
	Tax charge on ordinary activities	402,000

(ii)   *Note.* The profit and loss account will show the following.

	£	£
Operating profit (assumed here to be the same as taxable profits)		1,200,000
Profit from sale of asset (exceptional)		60,000
Profit on ordinary activities before taxation		1,260,000
Tax on profit on ordinary activities		402,000
Retained profits for the year		858,000

	£
Deferred taxation	
Balance brought forward	100,000
Transferred from profit and loss account	20,000
Deferred taxation in the balance sheet	120,000

The mainstream corporation tax liability is as follows.

Payable on 1 May 20X5	£
Tax on ordinary profits (30% of £1,200,000)	360,000
Tax on capital gain (30% of £60,000)	18,000
Due on 1 May 20X5	378,000

Summary	£
Creditors: amounts falling due within one year	
Mainstream corporation tax, payable on 1 May 20X5	378,000
Provisions for liabilities and charges	
Deferred taxation	120,000

Note. It may be helpful to show the journal entries for these items.

			£	£
(a)	DEBIT	Tax charge (profit and loss account)	402,000	
	CREDIT	Corporation tax creditor		*382,000
		Deferred tax		20,000

* This account will show a debit balance of £4,000 until the underprovision is recorded, since payment has already been made: (360,000 + 18,000 + 4,000).

5   DISCLOSURE REQUIREMENTS

5.1   The CA 1985 requires that the 'tax on profit or loss on ordinary activities' is disclosed on the face of the profit and loss account or in a note to the accounts. In addition, the notes to the profit and loss account must state:

(a)   The basis on which the charge for UK corporation tax and UK income tax is computed

(b)   The amounts of the charge for:

(i)   UK corporation tax (showing separately the amount, if greater, of UK corporation tax before any double taxation relief)

(ii)   UK income tax

(iii)   Non-UK taxation on profits, income and capital gains

(*Note.* The same details must be given, if relevant, in respect of the 'tax on extraordinary profit or loss'.)

FRS 16

5.2 FRS 16 *Current Tax* supplements and extends these provisions requiring that a company's *profit and loss account* should disclose separately (if material):

    (a) The **amount of the UK corporation** tax specifying:

        (i) **The current charge for corporation tax** on the income of the year (stating the rate used to make the provision).

        (ii) Adjustments in respect of prior periods.

    (b) The **total foreign taxation** specifying:

        (i) The current foreign tax charge on the income of the year.

        (ii) Adjustments in respect of prior periods.

FRS 19

5.3 FRS 19 requires that **deferred** tax relating to the ordinary activities of the enterprise should be **shown separately** as a part of the tax on profit or loss on ordinary activities, either on the face of the profit and loss account, or by note.

5.4 **Adjustments** to deferred tax arising from changes in tax rates and tax allowances should normally be **disclosed separately** as part of the tax charge for the period.

5.5 The **deferred liabilities and assets,** should be **disclosed in the balance sheet or notes**. They should be disclosed separately on the face of the balance sheet if the amounts are so material that the absence of disclosure would affect interpretation of the Financial Statements.

CA 1985

5.6 Finally, the **Companies Act 1985 requires certain disclosures in respect of deferred tax.**

    (a) Deferred tax should be shown **in the balance sheet under the heading 'provisions for liabilities and charges'** and in the category of provision for 'taxation, including deferred taxation'. The amount of any provision for taxation other than deferred taxation must be disclosed. The provision for taxation is different from tax liabilities which are shown as creditors in the balance sheet.

    (b) **Movements on reserves and provisions** must be disclosed, including provisions for deferred tax:

        (i) The amount of the provision at the beginning of the year and the end of the year

        (ii) The amounts transferred to or from the provision during the year

        (iii) The source/application of any amount so transferred

    (c) Information must be disclosed about any **contingent liability** not provided for in the accounts **(such as deferred tax not provided for) and its legal nature.** It is understood that deferred tax not provided for is a contingent liability within the terms of the Act.

    (d) The **basis on which the charge for UK tax is computed** has to be stated. Particulars are required of any special circumstances affecting the tax liability for the financial year or succeeding financial years.

Chapter roundup

- The **FRS 16 disclosure requirements** relating to company taxation are straight forwards but **must be learned**. The best way is to practise on past exam questions.

- **FRS 19** requires full provision for **deferred** tax.

  ° It is unlikely that complicated numerical questions will be set in the exam so concentrate on **understanding** deferred tax.

- You must also be able to prepare the **notes to the accounts** on tax for publication. This means mastering the disclosure requirements of FRS 16, FRS 19 and the CA 1985.

- Finally, do not forget to revise the provisions of **SSAP 5** on accounting for **VAT**.

Quick quiz

1   The due date of payment of corporation tax is:

    A   Twelve months after the company's financial statements have been filed at Companies House
    B   Nine months after the end of the relevant accounting period
    C   Nine months after the company's financial statements have been filed at Companies House
    D   Twelve months after the end of the relevant accounting period

2   What is the SSAP 5 requirement relating to the disclosure of turnover in company accounts?

3   Temporary differences are the same as timing differences

    True   ☐

    False   ☐

4   What are the three bases under which deferred tax can be computed?

5   Which method does FRS 19 require to be used?

6   Under FRS 19 deferred tax assets and liabilities may/must be discounted. (Delete as applicable.)

7   Tax on profit on ordinary activities is the aggregate of:

    .... + ... + ...

8   List the disclosure requirements set out by the CA 1985.

Answers to quick quiz

1   B (see para 1.3)

2   Generally turnover should exclude VAT (2.15)

3   False. Temporary differences include permanent differences. (3.1)

4   The nil provision basis, the full provision basis and the partial provision basis. (3.10)

5   Full provision. (3.20)

6   May. (3.37)

7   Corporation tax on taxable profits, transfers to/from deferred tax, under/over provisions form previous years. (4.2)

8   See paragraphs 5.1 and 5.7.

Now try the question below from the Exam Question Bank

Number	Level	Marks	Time
9	Full exam	20	36 mins

Chapter 9

EARNINGS PER SHARE AND REPORTING FINANCIAL PERFORMANCE

Topic list	Syllabus reference
1　FRS 14 *Earnings per share*	3(d)
2　FRS 3 *Reporting financial performance*	3(f)

Introduction

Section 1 of this chapter involves the description of EPS, the mechanics of its calculation and the disclosure required by FRS 14. EPS is an important indicator of a company's performance.

FRS 14 is a relatively new standard and therefore topical.

FRS 3 *Reporting financial performance* introduced radical changes to the format of the profit and loss account and the associated notes to the accounts. Of major importance are the definitions of extraordinary and exceptional items and prior year adjustments. You may be asked to produce a statement of total recognised gains and losses.

Remember that you will appreciate the contents of this chapter far more if you obtain and examine some company reports (those of *public companies* are required in this case).

Study guide

- Explain the importance of comparability in relation to the calculation of earnings per (eps) share and its importance as a stock market indicator.

- Explain why the trend of eps may be a more accurate indicator of performance than a company's profit trend.

- Define earnings and the basic number of shares.

- Calculate the eps in accordance with FRS 14 in the following circumstances:

    - basic eps
    - where there has been a bonus issue of shares during the year, and
    - where there has been a rights issue of shares during the year.

- Explain the relevance to existing shareholders of the diluted eps, and describe the circumstances that will give rise to a future dilution of the eps.

- Calculate the diluted eps in the following circumstances:

    - where convertible debt or preference shares are in issue; and
    - where share options and warranties exist.

- Explain the need for an accounting standard in this area.

- Discuss the importance of identifying and reporting the results of discontinuing operations; define discontinuing operation in accordance with FRS 3.

- Distinguish between extraordinary and exceptional items, including their accounting treatment and required disclosures.

FRS 3 REPORTING FINANCIAL PERFORMANCE

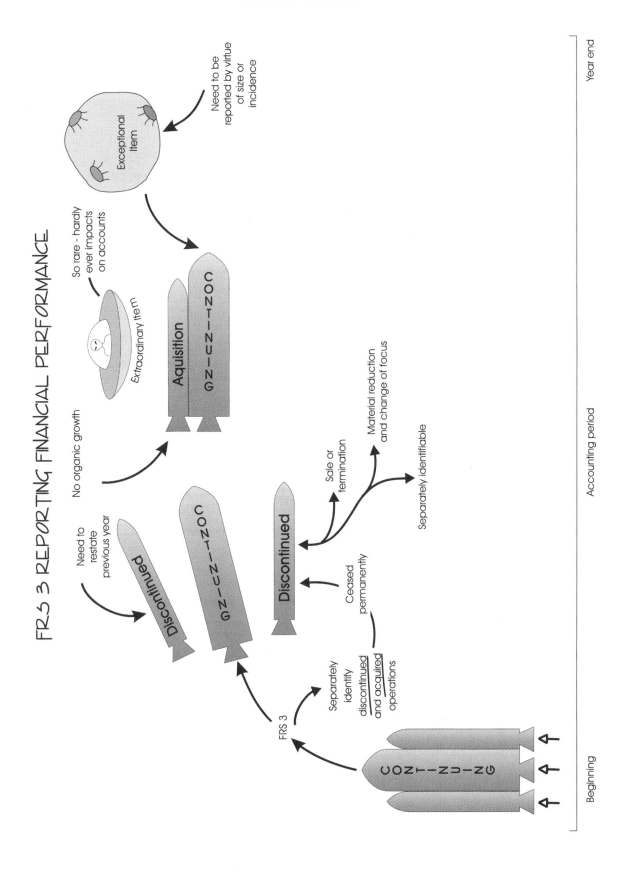

- Prepare a profit and loss account in accordance with the requirements of FRS 3.

- Explain the contents and purpose of the statement of recognised gains and losses, linking it to the Statement of Principles and the concept of comprehensive income.

- Describe and prepare:

  - A Note of Historical Cost Profits and Losses.
  - reconciliation of movement in shareholders' funds.
  - statement of movement in reserves.

- Define prior period adjustments and account for the correction of fundamental errors and changes in accounting policies.

Exam guide

Both of these standards can appear alongside a requirement to interpret financial statements. You not only need to learn the disclosure but also about the information you arrive at.

1 FRS 14 EARNINGS PER SHARE

1.1 Earnings per share (EPS) is widely used by investors as a **measure of a company's performance** and is of particular importance in:

(a) Comparing the results of a company over a period of time.

(b) Comparing the performance of one company's equity shares against the performance of another company's equity, and also against the returns obtainable from loan stock and other forms of investment.

The purpose of any earnings yardstick is to achieve as far as possible clarity of meaning, comparability between one company and another, one year and another, and attributablity of profits to the equity shares. FRS 14 *Earnings per share* goes some way to ensuring that all these aims are achieved.

1.2 FRS 14 applies to all companies who have publicly traded shares or who are in the process of issuing shares publicly. However, where companies present EPS on a voluntary basis, FRS 14 **must** be adopted.

1.3 The ASB stated that earnings per share (EPS) was not a priority, but the development of new **international standards** on the area led to efforts to adopt a similar approach.

1.4 The following key terms may be useful for the remainder of this section.

> ### KEY TERMS
>
> - **Equity instrument:** any contract that evidences a residual interest in the assets of an entity after deducting all of its liabilities.
>
> - **Fair value:** the amount for which an asset could be exchanged, or a liability settled, between knowledgeable, willing parties in an arm's length transaction.
>
> - **Financial instrument:** any contract that gives rise to both a financial asset of one entity and a financial liability or equity instrument of another entity.
>
> - **Ordinary shares:** any equity instrument that is subordinate to all other classes of equity instruments.

> - **Potential ordinary share:** a financial instrument or other contract that may entitle its holder to ordinary shares.
>
> - **Warrants or options:** financial instruments that give the holder the right to purchase ordinary shares. *(FRS 14)*

Basic EPS

1.5 The standard has been developed with the user of the accounts in mind. EPS is a popular measure of profitability. The ASB have actively discouraged reliance on EPS, preferring a more rounded approach. The aim of the standard is to provide a consistent approach to EPS which will allow:

(a) Comparisons between entities' results
(b) And comparison of an entity's results over the years

KEY TERM

EPS is profit in pence attributable to each equity share.

The basic EPS calculation is:

$$\frac{\text{Earnings}}{\text{Issued ordinary shares}}$$

KEY TERMS

Earnings are the net profits after tax, interest, minority earnings and dividends on other classes of shares (also after extraordinary items, but in practice, these are rare).

Issued ordinary shares are all ordinary shares in circulation during the year. The weighted average approach is taken to calculate this amount.

Changes to ordinary share numbers

Share issues at market value

1.6 The following example will show how this issue is treated. Note that:

(a) The weighted average number for the period is used
(b) There is no retrospective effect

1.7 EXAMPLE: WEIGHTED AVERAGE NUMBER OF SHARES

Consider the following issues and buy-backs of shares. What is the weighted average number of shares?

	Issued shares	Shares bought back	Balance
1 January 20X9	20,000	-	20,000
31 March 20X9 Issue of new shares for cash	4,000	-	24,000
1 July 20X9 Purchase of shares for cash	-	8,000	16,000
31 December 20X9 Year end balance	24,000	8,000	16,000

1.8 **SOLUTION**

Weighted average

$(20,000 \times 3/12) + (24,000 \times 3/12) + (16,000 \times 6/12) = 19,000$

or

$20,000 + (4,000 \times 9/12) - (8,000 \times 6/12) = 19,000$

1.9 There are a number of events which will alter the number of ordinary shares issued by a company. These include:

- Bonus issues
- Bonus elements (ie rights issues)
- Share splits
- Share consolidation

1.10 These events must be reflected in the EPS calculations. The basic EPS should reflect issues of ordinary shares from the date consideration is receivable. An event should be included in the diluted EPS calculation even if it occurs after the balance sheet date. All events must be allowed for up to the date of approval of the accounts.

Bonus issues

1.11 A bonus issue involves an increase in the issued shares without a corresponding increase in capital. The adjustment for bonus issues should be made back to the earliest possible period. This means that

(a) The issue is included for the full year.
(b) The issue applies to the prior year.

1.12 The following example shows how a bonus issue should be treated.

1.13 **EXAMPLE: BONUS ISSUE**

	20X8	20X9
Net profit 31 December	£3,000	£4,500
Ordinary shares until 30 June 20X9	500	

Bonus issue 1 July 20X9: one share for every two ordinary shares held at 30 June 20X9

1.14 **SOLUTION**

Bonus issue	$500 \times 1/2 = 250$
EPS for 20X9	$\dfrac{£4,500}{(500 + 250)} = 600\text{p}$
Adjusted EPS for 20X8	$\dfrac{£3,000}{(500 + 250)} = 400\text{p}$

Note that, as the bonus issue involved no consideration, it is treated as though it had occurred at the **earliest period reported**.

Rights issues

1.15 A rights issue usually involves shares issued for an exercise price, that is, less than the fair value of the currently issued shares. The current year's ordinary shares are multiplied by an adjustment factor:

$$\frac{\text{Fair value of current shares}}{\text{Theoretical ex - rights value per share}}$$

1.16 The following example shows how a rights issue should be calculated. Note that fair value is the average price of the ordinary shares during the period.

1.17 EXAMPLE: RIGHTS ISSUE

	20X7	*20X8*	*20X9*
	£	£	£
Net profit as at 31 December	24,000	30,400	36,000
Shares before the rights issue	100,000		

The rights issue is to be one share for every five currently held (giving 20,000 new shares). Exercise price £1.00. The last date to exercise rights is 1 April 20X8.

The fair value of an ordinary share before the issue is £2.20.

1.18 SOLUTION

Theoretical ex-rights value per share is

$$\frac{\text{Fair value of current shares} + \text{Amount received from exercise of rights}}{\text{Number of current shares} + \text{Number of shares issued}}$$

$$\frac{(£2.20 \times 100,000 \text{ shares}) + (£1.00 \times 20,000)}{100,000 \text{ shares} + 20,000 \text{ shares}}$$

Theoretical ex-rights value per share = £2

Adjustment factor

$$\frac{\text{Fair value of current shares}}{\text{Theoretical ex - rights value per share}} = \frac{£2.20}{£2.00} = 1.1$$

Earnings per share

	20X7	*20X8*	*20X9*
20X7 EPS as originally stated:			
£24,000/100,000 shares	24p		
20X7 EPS restated for rights issue:			
£24,000/(100,000 shares × 1.1)	22p		
20X8 EPS allowing for rights issue:			
$\dfrac{£30,400}{(100,000 \times 1.1 \times 3/12) + (120,000 \times 9/12)}$		26p	
20X9 EPS			
£36,000/120,000			30p

Note that the adjustment factor is used on the original number of shares. Once the rights issue has taken place, the new number of shares (in this case 120,000) is included. For 20X8 the weighted average principle is applied.

Contingently issuable shares

1.19 Contingently issuable shares are issued after certain conditions have been fulfilled. They are not included in the basic EPS calculation until all the criteria have been met fully.

Part paid shares

1.20 If shares are part paid, then only the element which has been paid up is included in the calculation.

BPP
PUBLISHING

Alternative EPS

1.21 It should be noted that the adjustments covered so far affect the number of shares in the EPS calculation. This figure is the **denominator.**

> ### KEY TERM
> The **denominator** is the number of shares which are deemed to be entitled to the earnings of the entity.

1.22 The standard's emphasis is strongly upon the weighted average number of ordinary shares as opposed to the earnings figure. Many companies provide alternative EPS figures. The standard is very clear on this.

  (a) The basic EPS and the diluted EPS must have the same prominence as any other EPS figure disclosed.

  (b) The weighted average ordinary shares may only be calculated on the basis prescribed by the standard.

  (c) The reason for the alternative calculation should be disclosed.

  (d) The alternative calculation must be calculated on a consistent basis, year on year.

1.23 Alternative EPS calculations will therefore only have an alternative earnings figure; the **numerator.**

> ### KEY TERM
> The **numerator** is the earnings figure used in the EPS calculation.

1.24 If this amount is different from the reported net profit of the entity then a reconciliation must be provided to show how the numerator has been derived.

1.25 The EPS calculation in simple terms is therefore:

$$\frac{\text{Numerator}}{\text{Denominator}}$$

1.26 A favoured alternative EPS is the **headline EPS.**

'Headline' EPS

1.27 The ASB effectively destroyed the analysts' favourite EPS figure with the publication of FRS 3 and the subsequent publication of FRS 14, making clear that it did not believe anyone should rely on a single earnings figure. FRS 3 did allow for an EPS, but the figure was calculated after every conceivable expense, including extraordinary items if companies are able to identify any in future. The publication of FRS 3 drew loud protests from some investment houses, which felt that the new EPS figure would prove **volatile and confusing** to users. This is the EPS taken up by FRS 14.

1.28 The Institute of Investment Management and Research (IIMR) set up a sub-committee to investigate whether a definition for some kind of maintainable earnings could be developed. The sub-committee concluded that a standard measure for maintainable earnings, which could be used as a basis for forecasts, was not feasible, as too much **conjecture and subjectivity** are involved. This view falls in line with the ASB's.

1.29 Instead, the IIMR defines a **'headline' figure for earnings** which, it acknowledges, 'is inferior to maintainable earnings as a basis for forecasts', but is nevertheless robust and factual. 'The number is justified by its practical usefulness, even if it cannot encapsulate the company's performance in itself.'

1.30 The headline earnings figure **includes** all the trading profits and losses for the year, including interest, and profits and losses arising from operations discontinued or acquired at any point during the year. **Excluded** from the figure are profits or losses from the sale or termination of a discontinued operation, from the sale of fixed assets or businesses or from any permanent diminution in their value or write-off (except for assets acquired for resale). Abnormal trading items (any defined by FRS 3 as extraordinary or exceptional), says the IIMR, should be included in the figure but prominently displayed in a note if they are significant.

1.31 When the IIMR's original ED was published, the *Financial Times* announced that it would use the method to calculate **price/earnings ratios,** and Extel also announced that it would use the figure. The statement was specifically not directed at companies, but many are expected to take up the definition. A large number of listed companies already disclose an EPS figure in addition to the one required by FRS 3 (and 14).

1.32 As with all EPS figures which are offered as an alternative to the FRS 3 and 14 figure, a **reconciliation** of the two EPS figures must be shown. Also, the alternative method must be applied consistently from year to year. No companies are *required* to produce the IIMR figure.

Example of 'headline' EPS

1.33 An **example** of the reconciliation between EPS as calculated under FRS 3 and 14 and 'headline' EPS might be as follows.

	20X6	20X5
	pence	pence
EPS as required by FRS 14	62.5	57.3
Exceptional items		
Classification of restructuring costs	-	4.8
Sale of property adjustments	13.8	3.1
'Headline' EPS	76.3	65.2

Diluted EPS

> **Exam focus point**
>
> You should pay particular attention to this area as it may cause problems in the exam.

1.34 At the end of an accounting period a company may have securities which do not have a claim to equity earnings, but they may do **in the future**. These include:

(a) **Separate classes of equity share** not yet entitled to a share of equity earnings, but becoming so at a future date

(b) **Convertible loan stock** or **convertible preference shares** which enable their holders to exchange their securities at a later date for ordinary shares at a predetermined rate

(c) **Options** or **warrants**

1.35 These securities have the potential effect of increasing the number of equity shares ranking for dividend and so diluting or 'watering down' the EPS. These securities may be **dilutive potential ordinary shares.**

> ### KEY TERM
>
> A **dilutive** potential ordinary share is one which decreases the share of net profit, or increases the loss shared.

1.36 The diluted EPS gives users of the accounts a view on the potential ordinary shares of the entity. There is the potential to forecast the future EPS from the amounts given. Again, the ASB is careful to point out that a number of measures should be used in order to assess the returns from an entity, stating that no one measure is accurate enough to rely on.

Pro forma calculations

1.37 The following are the simple pro forma calculations for the three main sets of securities.

    (a) **Shares not yet ranking for dividend**

        (i) *Earnings*

	£
Earnings	X

        (ii) *Number of shares*

	No
Basic weighted average	X
Add shares that will rank in future periods	X
Diluted number	X

    (b) **Convertible loan stock or preference shares**

        (i) *Earnings*

	£
Earnings	X
Add back loan stock interest net of CT (or preference dividends) 'saved'	X
	X

        (ii) *Number of shares*

	No
Basic weighted average	X
Add additional shares on conversion (using terms giving maximum dilution available after the year end)	X
Diluted number	X

    (c) **Options or warrants**

        (i) *Earnings*

	£
Earnings	X

        (ii) *Number of shares*

	No
Basic weighted average	X
Add additional shares issued at nil consideration	X
Diluted number	X

Share options

1.38 A share option allows the purchase of shares at a favourable amount which is less than the fair value of existing shares. The calculation of diluted EPS includes those shares deemed as issued for no consideration. For this purpose, the following calculation is used.

$$\frac{\text{Shares under option} \times \text{exercise price}}{\text{Fair value of ordinary shares}}$$

1.39 This gives the number of shares that are to be excluded from the EPS calculation. This will become more clear in the following example.

1.40 EXAMPLE: EFFECTS OF SHARE OPTIONS ON DILUTED EARNINGS PER SHARE

Net profit for 20X9	£1,000,000
Weighted average number of ordinary shares for 20X9	10 million
Average fair value of one ordinary share	£2.40
Weighted average number of shares under option during 20X9	3 million
Exercise price for shares under option in 20X9	£2.00

1.41 SOLUTION

	Shares	Net profit	EPS
Net profit for 20X9		£1,000,000	
Weighted average shares for 20X9	10m		
Basic EPS			10p
Number of shares on option	3m		
Number of shares that would have been issued at fair value: (3m × £2)/£2.40	(2.5m)		
Diluted EPS	10.5m	£1,000,000	9.5p

Note that the net profit has not been increased. This is because the calculation only includes shares deemed to be issued for no consideration.

Employee share option schemes

1.42 Employee share option schemes are becoming increasingly popular as an incentive scheme in organisations. Many schemes relate to performance criteria which mean that they are contingent on certain conditions being met. The section on contingently issuable shares further on in this chapter explains how these schemes should be treated when calculating diluted EPS.

1.43 Certain schemes do not have performance measures. As with the share option approach, only those shares deemed as issued for no consideration are included. UITF 17 also affects the calculation as the cost of the scheme is written off to the profit and loss account over its life and these costs are effectively included in the option proceeds. The following example shows how these schemes should be treated.

1.44 EXAMPLE: SHARE OPTION SCHEME (NOT PERFORMANCE RELATED)

A company runs a share option scheme based on the employee's period of service with the company.

As at 31 December 20X7 the provisions of the scheme were:

Date of grant	1 January 20X7
Market price at grant date	£2.24
Exercise price of option	£1.25
Date of vesting	31 December 20X9
Number of shares under option	3 million

Under UITF 17, 33p per option (£2.24 – £1.25/3 years) is charged to the profit and loss in each of the three years 20X7-20X9.

Net profit for the year 20X7	£1,000,000
Weighted average number of ordinary shares	10 million
Average fair value of an ordinary share	£2.50
Assumed proceeds from each option	£1.91 (Exercise price of £1.25 plus the cost relating to future service not recognised of two years at 33p:66p). The following year would be £1.58 (ie £1.25 plus 33p).

1.45 SOLUTION

	Shares	Net profit	EPS
Net profit for 20X7		£1,000,000	
Weighted average shares for 20X7	10m		
Basic EPS			10p
Number of shares on option	3m		
Number of shares that would have been issued at fair value: (3m × £1.91)/£2.50	(2.3m)		
Diluted EPS	10.7m	£1,000,000	9.3p

Contingently issuable shares

1.46 These are shares issued after certain criteria have been met. For the purposes of the diluted EPS calculation these shares are included in full.

1.47 The following example gives two contingent events arising after the acquisition of a business. Most contingent events will be based on target sales or profit. The example includes the opening of new branches. This is also a measure of the entity's successful expansion. Note that many employee share option schemes operate in this manner.

1.48 EXAMPLE: CONTINGENTLY ISSUABLE SHARES

A company has 500,000 ordinary shares in issue at 1 January 20X7. A recent business acquisition has given rise to the following contingently issuable shares.

- 10,000 ordinary shares for every new branch opened in the three years 20X7-20X9

- 1,000 ordinary shares for every £2,000 of net profit in excess of £900,000 over the three years ended 31 December 20X9

(Shares will be issued on 1 January following the period in which a condition is met.)

A new branch was opened on 1 July 20X7, another on 31 March 20X8 and another on 1 October 20X9.

Reported net profits over the three years were £350,000, £400,000 and £600,000 respectively.

1.49 SOLUTION

Basic EPS

	20X7 £		20X8 £		20X9 £	
Numerator	350,000		400,000		600,000	
Denominator						
Ordinary shares	500,000		510,000		520,000	
Branch contingency	5,000	(i)	7,500	(i)	2,500	(i)
Earnings contingency	-	(ii)	-	(ii)	-	(ii)
Total shares	505,000		517,500		522,500	
Basic EPS	69.3p		77.3p		114.8p	

Diluted EPS

	20X7 £		20X8 £		20X9 £	
Numerator	350,000		400,000		600,000	
Denominator						
Ordinary shares in basic EPS	505,000		517,500		522,500	
Additional shares:						
Branch contingency	5,000	(iii)	2,500	(iii)	7,500	(iii)
Earnings contingency	-		-		225,000	(iv)
Total shares	510,000		520,000		755,000	
Diluted EPS	68.6p		76.9p		79.5p	

(i) This figure is simply the shares due for opening a branch pro-rated over the year.

(ii) It is not certain the net profit condition has been satisfied until after the three year period.

(iii) The contingently issuable shares are included from the start of the period they arise so these figures are increasing the denominator by the full 10,000 shares.

(iv) This is (£1,350,000 – £900,000)/£2,000 × 1,000. This figure will be included in the basic EPS figure in the following year 20X0. Note that the £900,000 criteria was not exceeded in the prior year.

1.50 The example highlights FRS 14's emphasis on the denominator as opposed to the numerator. All of the adjustments in this case were to the number of shares.

Convertible bonds

1.51 In cases where the issue of shares will affect earnings, the numerator should be adjusted accordingly. This occurs when bonds are converted. Interest is paid out on the bond. When conversion takes place this interest is no longer payable.

1.52 EXAMPLE: CONVERTIBLE BONDS

Net profit	£500
Ordinary shares in issue	1,000
Basic EPS	50p
Convertible 15% bonds	200

Each block of 5 bonds is convertible to 8 ordinary shares. The tax rate (including any deferred tax) is 40%.

1.53 SOLUTION

Interest expense relating to the bonds 200 @ 15% =	£30
Tax @ 40%	£12
Adjusted net profit £500 + £30 – £12 =	£518
Number of ordinary shares resulting from the bond conversion	320
Number of ordinary shares used for the diluted EPS calculation 1,000 + 320 =	1,320

Diluted EPS $\frac{£518}{1,320} = 39.2p$

1.54 Earnings should be adjusted for savings or expenses occurring as a result of conversion. Other examples of this are:

(a) Preference dividends saved when preference shares are converted.

(b) Additional liability on a profit sharing scheme as a result of higher profits (ie if conversion of bonds increases profit, a higher amount will be payable to members of a profit related pay scheme).

Ranking dilutive securities

1.55 The approach prescribed by FRS 14 involves including only dilutive potential ordinary shares. Antidilutive shares are not to be included. This is a prudent approach which recognises potential reduction of earnings but not increases.

1.56 The following examples show how dilutive potential ordinary shares are identified and included in the calculation of EPS. The standard also states that the dilutive shares should be ranked and taken into account from the most dilutive down to the least dilutive. Potential ordinary shares likely to have a dilutive effect on EPS include options, convertible bonds and convertible preference shares.

1.57 EXAMPLE: RANKING DILUTIVE SECURITIES FOR THE CALCULATION OF WEIGHTED AVERAGE NUMBER OF SHARES

Net profit attributable to ordinary shareholders	£20 million
Net profit from discontinued activities	£5 million
Ordinary shares outstanding	50 million
Average fair value of one ordinary share	£5.00

Potential ordinary shares

Convertible preference shares	500,000 entitled to a cumulative dividend of £5. Each is convertible to 3 shares
3% convertible bond	Nominal amount £50 million. Each £1,000 bond is convertible to 50 shares. There is no amortisation of premium or discounting affecting the interest expense
Options	10 million with exercise price of £4
Tax rate	30%

1.58 SOLUTION

The effect on earnings on conversion of potential ordinary shares

	Increase in earnings £	Increase in ordinary shares Number	Earnings per share £
Convertible preference shares			
Increase in net profit (£5 × 500,000)	2,500,000 (i)		
Incremental shares (3 × 500,000)		1,500,000	1.67
3% convertible bonds			
Increase in net profit			
50,000,000 × 0.03 × (1 – 0.3) (ii)	1,050,000		
Incremental shares (50,000 × 50)		2,500,000	0.42
Options			
Increase in earnings:	nil		
Incremental shares 10 million × (£5 – £4)/£5		2,000,000	nil

Identifying the dilutive shares to include in the diluted EPS

	Net profit from continuing operations £	Ordinary shares Number	Per share £	
Reported	15,000,000	50,000,000	0.30	
Options	-	2,000,000		
	15,000,000	52,000,000	0.29	Dilutive
3% convertible bonds	1,050,000	2,500,000		
	16,050,000	54,500,000	0.29	Antidilutive
Convertible preference shares	2,500,000	1,500,000		
	18,550,000	56,000,000	0.33	Antidilutive

Note that:

- The potential share issues are considered from the most dilutive to the least dilutive.

- The diluted EPS is increased by both the bonds and the preference shares. These are therefore ignored in the diluted EPS calculation.

Basic EPS

Net profit	£20 million
Weighted average number of shares	50 million
Basic EPS	40p

Diluted EPS

Net profit (remains at)	£20 million
Weighted average number of shares	52 million
	38.5p

(i)   The cumulative dividend on the preference shares is not taken into consideration. Only the dividend for the year is included in the increase in earnings.

(ii) It is important to remember the tax element in the bond interest.

1.59 It should be noted that the **numerator,** for the purposes of ranking the dilutive shares, is net profit from continuing operations only. This is net profit after preference share dividends but excluding discontinued operations and extraordinary items. The EPS calculation includes the full amount of net profit attributable to ordinary shareholders.

1.60 The following question is based on the previous example but with dilutive convertible bonds

---

Question 1

Details as above except that the convertible bonds are 1.5% bonds.

Answer

Effect on earnings on conversion of potential ordinary shares

	Increase in earnings £	Increase in ordinary shares Number	Earnings per share £
1.5% Convertible bonds			
Increase in net profit $(50{,}000 \times 0.015 \times (1 - 0.3)$	525,000		
Incremental shares $(50{,}000 \times 50)$		2,500,000	0.21

Identifying the dilutive shares to include in the diluted EPS

	Net profit from continuing operations £	Ordinary shares Number	Per share £	
Reported	15,000,000	50,000,000	0.30	
Options	-	2,000,000		
	15,000,000	52,000,000	0.29	Dilutive
1.5% convertible bonds	525,000	2,500,000		
	15,525,000	54,500,000	0.28	Dilutive

The convertible preference shares will remain antidilutive and basic EPS will remain at 40p.

Diluted EPS

Net profit (20,000,000 + 525,000 bond interest)	£20,525,000
Weighted average number of shares	54.5 million
Diluted EPS	37.7p

1.61 The example in the above question emphasises the adjustments made to earnings and the use of net profit from continuing operations as the numerator.

Disclosure

1.62 Note the following.

(a) FRS 14 requires that **basic EPS** and **diluted EPS** are disclosed on the face of the profit and loss account, even if the amounts are negative. Comparative figures are also required.

(b) A basic and diluted EPS figure is required for every set of ordinary shares with different rights.

(c) The standard requires inclusion of all potential ordinary shares which will have a dilutive effect on the diluted EPS, regardless of materiality.

(d) The nil basis EPS is no longer required as this information can be derived from other disclosures in the financial statements.

(e) EPS need only be presented in the consolidated results of a group where the parent's results are shown as well.

Exam focus point

The purpose of any earnings yardstick is to achieve as far as possible clarity of meaning, comparability between one company and another, one year and another, and attributability of profits to the equity shares. FRS 14 *Earnings per share* goes some way to ensuring that all these aims are achieved.

2   FRS 3 REPORTING FINANCIAL PERFORMANCE

Exam focus point

This is an extremely popular exam topic and it featured in the pilot paper. Make sure that you familiarise yourself fully with the contents of this standard.

2.1   FRS 3 represents an attempt by the ASB to improve the quality of financial information provided to shareholders. In particular it was **an attempt to move away from the high profile of the earnings per share**. The main elements of the FRS are as follows.

(a) New structure of the profit and loss account
(b) Extraordinary items
(c) Statement of total recognised gains and losses
(d) Other new disclosures
(e) Earnings per share

Exam focus point

A key way of developing familiarity with this topic is to look at published financial reports. See FT share page for details of free service.

Exceptional and extraordinary items

2.2   A company may experience events or undertake transactions which are 'out of the ordinary', ie they are not the same as what the company normally does.

2.3   FRS 3 lays down the rules for dealing with 'out of the ordinary' items in the P & L account and restricts the way companies can manipulate these figures.

Exceptional items

KEY TERM

FRS 3 defines **exceptional items** as: 'Material items which derive from events or transactions that fall within the ordinary activities of the reporting entity and which individually or, if of a similar type, in aggregate, need to be disclosed by virtue of their *size or incidence* if the financial statements are to give a true and fair view.'

2.4   The definition of **ordinary activities** is important.

'Any activities which are undertaken by a reporting entity as **part of its business** and such related activities in which the reporting entity engages in furtherance of, incidental to, or arising from these activities. Ordinary activities include the effects on the reporting entity of any event in the various environments in which it operates including the political, regulatory, economic and geographical environments irrespective of the frequency or unusual nature of the event.'

2.5   There are **two** types of exceptional items and their accounting treatment is as follows.

     (a)   Firstly there are **three categories of exceptional items which must be shown separately on the face of the profit and loss account** after operating profit and before interest and allocated appropriately to discontinued and continued activities.

         (i)   **Profit or loss on the sale or termination** of an operation

         (ii)   **Costs of a fundamental reorganisation** or restructuring that has a material effect on the nature and focus of the reporting entity's operations

         (iii)   **Profit or loss on disposal of fixed assets**

         For both items (i) and (iii) profit and losses may not be offset within categories.

     (b)   **All other items should be allocated to the appropriate statutory format heading** and attributed to continuing or discounted operations as appropriate. If the item is sufficiently material that it is needed to show a true and fair view it must be disclosed on the face of the profit and loss account.

2.6   In both (a) and (b) an adequate description must be given in the notes to the accounts to enable its nature to be understood.

2.7   FRS 3 does not give examples of the type of transaction which is likely to be treated as exceptional. However, its predecessor on the subject, SSAP 6, gave a useful list of examples of items which if of a sufficient size might normally be treated as exceptional.

     (a)   Abnormal charges for bad debts and write-offs of stock and work in progress.
     (b)   Abnormal provisions for losses on long-term contracts.
     (c)   Settlement of insurance claims.

Extraordinary items

2.8   **The ASB publicly stated that it does not envisage extraordinary items appearing on a company's profit and loss account after the introduction of FRS 3.** Its decline in importance has been achieved by tightening of the definition of an extraordinary item.

KEY TERM

Extraordinary items are defined as material items possessing a high degree of abnormality which arise from events or transactions that fall outside the ordinary activities of the reporting entity and which are not expected to recur.

2.9   Extraordinary items should be shown on the face of profit and loss account before dividends and other minority interests (for group accounts). Tax and minority interest in the extraordinary item should be shown separately. A description of the extraordinary items should be given in the notes to the accounts.

Structure of the profit and loss account

2.10 **All statutory headings from turnover to operating profit must be subdivided between that arising from continuing operations and that arising from discontinued operations.** In addition, turnover and operating profit must be further analysed between that from existing and that from newly acquired operations.

2.11 **Only figures for turnover and operating profit need be shown on the face of the P & L account;** all additional information regarding costs may be relegated to a note.

PROFIT AND LOSS
EXAMPLE 1 (as shown in FRS 3)

	1993 £m	1993 £m	1992 as restated £m
Turnover			
Continuing operations	550		500
Acquisitions	50		
	600		
Discontinued operations	175		190
		775	690
Cost of sales		(620)	(555)
Gross profit		155	135
Net operating expenses		(104)	(83)
Operating profit			
Continuing operations	50		40
Acquisitions	6		
	56		
Discontinued operations	(15)		12
Less 1992 provision	10		
		51	52
Profit on sale of properties in continuing operations		9	6
Provision for loss on operations to be discontinued			(30)
Loss on disposal of discontinued operations	(17)		
Less 1992 provision	20		
		3	
Profit on ordinary activities before interest		63	28
Interest payable		(18)	(15)
Profit on ordinary activities before taxation		45	13
Tax on profit on ordinary activities		(14)	(4)
Profit on ordinary activities after taxation		31	9
Minority interests		(2)	(2)
Profit before extraordinary items		29	7
Extraordinary items - included only to show positioning		-	-
Profit for the financial year		29	7
Dividends		(8)	(1)
Retained profit for the financial year		21	6
Earnings per share		39p	10p
Adjustments (to be itemised and an adequate description to be given)		Xp	Xp
Adjusted earnings per share		Yp	Yp

Note. Reason for calculating the adjusted earnings per share to be given.

PROFIT AND LOSS ACCOUNT EXAMPLE 2 (to operating profit line)

	Continuing Operations 1993 £m	Acquisitions 1993 £m	Discontinued of operations 1993 £m	Total 1993 £m	Total 1992 as restated £m
Turnover	550	50	175	775	690
Cost of sales	(415)	(40)	(165)	(620)	(555)
Gross profit	135	10	10	155	135
Net operating expenses	(85)	(4)	(25)	(114)	(83)
Less 1992 provision			10	10	
Operating profit	50	6	(5)	51	52
Profit on sale of properties	9			9	6
Provision for loss on operations to be discontinued					(30)
Loss on disposal of the discontinued operations			(17)	(17)	
Less 1992 provision			20	20	
Profit on ordinary activities Before interest	59	6	(2)	63	28

Thereafter example 2 is the same as example 1.

NOTES TO THE FINANCIAL STATEMENTS

Note required in respect of profit and loss account example 1

	1993			1992 (as restated)		
	Continuing £m	Discontinued £m	Total £m	Continuing £m	Discontinued £m	Total £m
Cost of sales	455	165	620	385	170	555
Net operating expenses						
Distribution costs	56	13	69	46	5	51
Administrative expenses	41	12	53	34	3	37
Other operating income	(8)	0	(8)	(5)	0	(5)
	89	25	114	75	8	83
Less 1992 provision	0	(10)	(10)			
	89	15	104			

The total figures for continuing operations in 1993 include the following amounts relating to acquisitions: cost of sales £40 million and net operating expenses £4 million (namely distribution costs £3 million, administrative expenses £3 million and other operating income £2 million).

Note required in respect of profit and loss account example 2

	1993			1992 (as restated)		
	Continuing £m	Discontinued £m	Total £m	Continuing £m	Discontinued £m	Total £m
Turnover				500	190	690
Cost of sales				385	170	555
Net operating expenses						
Distribution costs	56	13	69	46	5	51
Administrative expenses	41	12	53	34	3	37
Other operating income	(8)	0	(8)	(5)	0	(5)
	89	25	114	75	8	83
Operating profit				40	12	52

The total figure of net operating expenses for continuing operations in 1993 includes £4 million in respect of acquisitions (namely distribution costs £3 million, administrative expenses £3 million and other operating income £2 million).

Discontinued operations

2.12 A **discontinued operation** is one which **meets all of the following conditions.**

(a) The sale or termination must have been **completed** before the earlier of 3 months after the year end or the date the financial statements are approved. (Terminations not completed by this date may be disclosed in the notes.)

(b) Former activity must have **ceased permanently**.

(c) The sale or termination has a **material effect** on the nature and focus of the entity's operations and represents a material reduction in its operating facilities resulting either from:

   (i) Its withdrawal from a particular market (class of business or geographical); or from

   (ii) A material reduction in turnover in its continuing markets.

(d) The assets, liabilities, results of operations and activities are **clearly distinguishable**, physically, operationally and for financial reporting purposes.

Accounting for the discontinuation

2.13 (a) **Results**

   The results of the discontinued operation up to the date of sale or termination or the balance sheet date should be shown **under each of the relevant profit and loss account headings**.

(b) **Profit/loss on discontinuation**

   The profit or loss on discontinuation or costs of discontinuation should be **disclosed separately** as an exceptional item after operating profit and before interest.

(c) **Comparative figures**

   Figures for the previous year **must be adjusted for** any **activities** which have become **discontinued in the current year.**

Acquisitions

2.14 Acquisitions include **most holdings acquired by a group** (beyond the scope of your syllabus), **as well as unincorporated businesses purchased**. However, start-ups are not acquisitions.

Question 4

Feelgoode plc's profit and loss account for the year ended 31 December 20X2, with comparatives, is as follows.

	20X2	20X1
	£'000	£'000
Turnover	200	180
Cost of sales	(60)	(80)
Gross profit	140	100
Distribution costs	(25)	(20)
Administration expenses	(50)	(45)
Operating profit	65	35

During the year the company sold a material business operation with all activities ceasing on 14 February 20X3. The loss on the sale of the operation amounted to £2.2m. The results of the operation for 20X1 and 20X2 were as follows.

	20X2	20X1
	£'000	£'000
Turnover	22	26
Profit/(loss)	(7)	(6)

In addition, the company acquired a business which contributed £7m to turnover and an operating profit of £1.5m.

Required

Prepare the profit and loss account and related notes for the year ended 31 December 20X2 complying with the requirements of FRS 3 as far as possible.

Answer

	20X2		20X1	
	£'000	£'000	£'000	£'000
Turnover				
Continuing operations				
(200 – 22 – 7)/(180 – 26)		171.0		154
Acquisitions		7.0		-
		178.0		154
Discontinued		22.0		26
		200.0		180
Cost of sales		(60.0)		(80)
Gross profit		140.0		100
Distribution costs		(25.0)		(20)
Administration expenses (50 – 2.2)		(47.8)		(45)
Operating profit				
Continuing operations* (bal)	72.7		41	
Acquisitions	1.5		-	
	74.2		41	
Discontinued	(7.0)		(6)	
		67.2		35
Exceptional item		(2.2)		-
		65.0		35

* ie 65.0 + 2.2 + 7.0 – 1.5 = 72.7; 35 + 6 = 41

Note to the profit and loss account

	20X2			20X1 (as restated)		
	Continuing	*Discontinued*	*Total*	*Continuing*	*Discontinued*	*Total*
	£'000	*£'000*	*£'000*	*£'000*	*£'000*	*£'000*
Cost of sales	X	X	60.0	X	X	80
Net operating expenses						
Distribution costs	X	X	25.0	X	X	20
Administration expenses	X	X	47.8	X	X	45
	X	X	72.8	X	X	65

FRS 3 statements and notes

2.15   FRS 3 introduced a new statement and a variety of new notes to expand the information required in published accounts which we saw in Chapter 3.

Statement of total recognised gains and losses

2.16   This is required by FRS 3 to be presented with the same prominence as the P & L account, balance sheet and cash flow statement, ie as a **primary statement**.

2.17   The statement will include all gains and losses occurring during the period and so would typically include the following.

	£
Profit for the year (per the profit and loss account)	X
Items taken directly to reserves (not goodwill written off to reserves)	
Surplus on revaluation of fixed assets	X
Surplus/deficit on revaluation of investment properties	X
Total recognised gains and losses for the year	X
Prior period adjustments (see later)	(X)
Total gains and losses recognised since last annual report	X

2.18   At a glance, it seems that all this new statement does is to reconcile the opening and closing net assets of a business. This is, however, not so since FRS 3 requires that **transactions with shareholders are to be excluded**, ie:

(a)   Dividends paid and proposed
(b)   Share issues and redemptions

since these transactions do not represent either gains or losses.

2.19   In the case of goodwill, which is capitalised and amortised under FRS 10, the amortisation charge will appear indirectly (as part of the results for the year) in the statement.

2.20   **Where the profit or loss for the year is the only recognised gain or loss**, a **statement to that effect should be given** immediately below the profit and loss account.

Realised and distributable profits

2.21 At this point it may be worth pointing out that just because gains and losses are 'recognised' in this statement, they are, **not necessarily 'realised'** (described below', or **'distributable'**, ie as a dividend. Realised and distributable profits are covered in Chapter 13.

Reconciliation of movements in shareholders' funds

2.22 This reconciliation is required by FRS 3 to be included in the notes to the accounts. What the statement aims to do is to **pull together financial performance** of the entity as is reflected in:

(a) The profit and loss account.

(b) Other movements in shareholders' funds as determined by the statement of total recognised gains and losses.

(c) All other changes in shareholders funds not recognised in either of the above such as goodwill immediately written off to reserves.

2.23 The typical contents of the reconciliation would be as follows.

	£
Profit for the financial year	X
* Dividends	(X)
	X
Other recognised gains and losses (per statement of total recognised gains and losses)	X
* New share capital	(X)
Net addition to shareholders' funds	X
Opening shareholders' funds	X
Closing shareholders' funds	X

* Items not appearing in the statement of recognised gains and losses

Question 5

Extracts from Zoe Ltd's profit and loss account for the year ended 31 December 20X1 were as follows.

	£'000
Profit after tax	512
Dividend	(120)
Retained profit	392

During the year the following important events took place.

(a) Assets were revalued upward by £110,000.
(b) £300,000 share capital was issued during the year.
(c) Certain stock items were written down by £45,000.
(d) Opening shareholders' funds at 1 January 20X1 were £3,100,000.

Show how the events for the year would be shown in the statement of recognised gains and losses and the reconciliation of movements in shareholders funds.

Answer

STATEMENT OF RECOGNISED GAINS AND LOSSES

	£'000
Profit after tax	512
Asset revaluation	110
	622

RECONCILIATION OF MOVEMENTS IN SHAREHOLDERS' FUNDS

	£'000
Profit after tax	512
Dividend	(120)
	392
Other recognised gains and losses (622 – 512)	110
New share capital	300
Net addition to shareholders' funds	802
Opening shareholders' funds	3,100
Closing shareholders' funds	3,902

Note of historical cost profits and losses

2.24 If a company has adopted any of the alternative accounting rules as regards revaluation of assets then the reported profit figure per the profit and loss account may deviate from the historical cost profit figure. If this deviation is material then the financial statements must include a reconciliation statement after the statement of recognised gains and losses or the profit and loss account. The profit figure to be reconciled is profit before tax; however, the retained profit for the year must also be restated.

2.25 Note that **FRS 3 requires the profit or loss on the disposal of a revalued asset to be calculated by reference to the difference between proceeds and the net carrying amount** (revalued figure less depreciation). The profit or loss based on historical cost will appear in the note of historical cost profits.

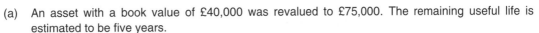

Question 6

Faiza Ltd reported a profit before tax of £162,000 for the year ended 31 December 20X8. During the year the following transactions in fixed assets took place.

(a) An asset with a book value of £40,000 was revalued to £75,000. The remaining useful life is estimated to be five years.

(b) An asset (with a five year useful life at the date of revaluation) was revalued by £20,000 (to carrying value £30,000) was sold one year after revaluation for £48,000.

Show the reconciliation or profit to historical cost profit for the year ended 31 December 20X8.

Answer

RECONCILIATION OF PROFIT TO HISTORICAL COST PROFIT
FOR THE YEAR ENDED 31 DECEMBER 20X8

	£'000
Reported profit on ordinary activities before taxation	162
Realisation of property revaluation gains*	20
Difference between historical cost depreciation charge and the actual depreciation charge of the year calculated on the revalued amount (75,000 - 40,000)/5	7
	189

* By interpretation of the question, the asset was revalued last year with £20,000 being credited to revaluation reserve. With the asset being sold this year, this gain becomes realised. It is assumed that there has been no annual transfer from revaluation reserve to profit and loss account.

Prior period adjustments

2.26 When the financial statements of a company are compiled, certain items (eg accruals, provisions) represent best estimates at a point in time. Further evidence received in the following year may suggest that previous estimates were incorrect. In most cases the 'error' will not be significant in size and so as a result the difference should be dealt with in the current year's accounts.

2.27 There are **two situations where a prior period adjustment is necessary:**

(a) **Fundamental errors** - evidence is found to suggest last year's accounts were wrong.

(b) A **change in accounting policy** (see FRS 18 in Chapter 3).

2.28 **The following accounting treatment should be used.**

(a) Restate prior year profit and loss account and balance sheet.

(b) Restate opening reserves balance.

(c) Include the adjustment in the reconciliation of movements in shareholders' funds.

(d) Include a note at the foot of the statement of total recognised gains and losses of the current period.

2.29 Prior period adjustments are therefore defined by FRS 3 as follows.

KEY TERM

Prior period adjustments are: 'Material adjustments applicable to prior periods arising from changes in accounting policy or from the correction of fundamental errors. They do not include normal recurring adjustments or corrections of accounting estimates made in prior periods.'

2.30 A **fundamental error** is an error which is **so significant that the truth and fairness of the financial statements is not achieved.**

2.31 A **change in accounting policy requires a prior period adjustment based on the accounting concept of consistency.** For users of the financial statements to make meaningful comparisons of a company's results it is important that the current year's and the last year's comparatives are prepared on the same basis. Therefore if for any reason a company changes its accounting policy they must go back and represent last year's accounts on the same basis.

2.32 Reasons for a change in accounting policy are discussed in Chapter 3.

Question 7

Jenny Ltd was established on 1 January 20X0. In the first three years' accounts deferred development expenditure was carried forward as an asset in the balance sheet. During 20X3 the directors decided that for the current and future years, all development expenditure should be written off as it is incurred.

This decision has not resulted from any change in the expected outcome of development projects on hand, but rather from a desire to favour the prudence concept. The following information is available.

(a)   Movements on the deferred development account.

Year	Deferred development expenditure incurred during year £'000	Transfer from deferred development expenditure account to P & L account £'000
20X0	525	-
20X1	780	215
20X2	995	360

(b)   The 20X2 accounts showed the following.

	£'000
Retained reserves b/f	2,955
Retained profit for the year	1,825
Retained profits carried forward	4,780

(c)   The retained profit for 20X3 after charging the actual development expenditure for the year was £2,030,000.

Required

Show how the change in accounting policy should be reflected in the statement of reserves in the company's 20X3 accounts.

Ignore taxation.

Answer

If the new accounting policy had been adopted since the company was incorporated, the additional profit and loss account charges for development expenditure would have been:

	£'000
20X0	525
20X1 (780 – 215)	565
	1,090
20X2 (995 – 360)	635
	1,725

This means that the reserves brought forward at 1 January 20X3 would have been £1,725,000 less than the reported figure of £4,780,000; while the reserves brought forward at 1 January 20X2 would have been £1,090,000 less than the reported figure of £2,955,000.

The statement of reserves in Jenny Ltd's 20X3 accounts should, therefore, appear as follows.

STATEMENT OF RESERVES (EXTRACT)

	20X3 £'000	Comparative (previous year) figures 20X2 £'000	
Retained profits at the beginning of year			
Previously reported	4,780	2,955	
Prior year adjustment (note 1)	1,725	1,090	
Restated	3,055	1,865	
Retained profits for the year	2,030	1,190	(note 2)
Retained profits at the end of the year	5,085	3,055	

Notes

1   The accounts should include a note explaining the reasons for and consequences of the changes in accounting policy. (See above workings for 20X3 and 20X2.)

2   The retained profit shown for 20X2 is after charging the additional development expenditure of £635,000.

Potential problems with FRS 3

2.33   FRS 3 was designed to put an end to various abuses, for example extraordinary items. The latter have now been outlawed. As Sir David Tweedie, Chairman of the ASB, put it:

> **'If the Martians landed and destroyed a company's factory, that could be treated as an extraordinary item.'**

2.34   Other aspects of FRS 3 have remained problematic. Two aspects may be highlighted.

Discontinued operations

2.35   **Companies may** take advantage of the requirement to analyse operations into continuing and discontinued and **use the analysis to hide 'bad news'**. A discontinued operation is likely to be a poor performer so it is in the company's interests to remove it from the rest of the results.

2.36   **Careful consideration should be made as to whether the FRS 3 criteria for classification of an operation as continuing or discontinued have been met.** The following should be singled out for close consideration.

(a)   Have sales and costs relating to the discontinued activity been identified? The directors may wish to include sales in continuing operations if possible and costs in discontinued operation if possible.

(b)   Provisions for profits or (more likely) losses on discontinuance must be considered carefully, as there is scope for manipulation.

Lack of consensus

2.37   FRS 3 was the first manifestation of the ASB's **balance sheet approach** to income recognition as outlined in the Board's *Statement of Principles* (discussed in Chapter 21). This was highlighted through the introduction into UK GAAP of an `additional primary statement of financial performance - the statement of total recognised gains and losses - which focuses on changes in wealth as the means of performance measurement, rather than traditional historical cost profit and loss.

2.38   **Concern has been expressed that the ASB seems to be entrenching into an accounting standard a conceptual approach** which has not been the subject of due process, has no general agreement and which is still only at an early stage of development and discussion. In fact, one of the most crucial chapters of the ASB's framework - that dealing with measurement - had not even been issued in draft form by the time FRS 3 was issued.

Chapter roundup

- You must learn:

  - The effect on EPS of: a new issue of shares; a rights issue; a bonus issue
  - How to calculate **fully diluted EPS**
  - The **disclosure** requirements of FRS 14

  The only way to do this is by working through the examples a number of times and repeated question practice.

- Disclosure of the basic EPS and diluted EPS on the face of the profit and loss is required, along with comparatives for both figures. This is the case even if the figures are negative.

- Other EPS figures can be disclosed in the accounts.

  - These must use the same basis for calculating the denominator
  - The reason for the method used must be disclosed
  - They must be consistent year on year
  - The required EPS figures should have the same prominence within the accounts

- The denominator is calculated by finding the weighted average number of ordinary shares in issue in the year.

- Any effect that conversion to ordinary shares has on the earnings figure must be reflected in the calculation of the diluted EPS.

- Only dilutive shares are included in the diluted EPS. Anti-dilutive shares are ignored.

- FRS 3 *Reporting financial performance* has introduced radical **changes to the profit and loss** account of large and medium sized companies.

- You must know the **FRS 3 definitions** of:

  - **Extraordinary items**
  - **Exceptional items**
  - **Prior year adjustments**
  - **Discontinued operations**
  - **Total recognised gains and losses**

- You must know the format of the **statement of total recognised gains and losses** and understand its contents.

Quick quiz

1 To what companies does FRS 14 apply?

A Companies in the process of issuing shares publicly
B Companies with publicly traded shares
C Any company which discloses an EPS figure
D All of the above

2 Define earnings per share.

3 Following a rights issue, what is the fraction by which the EPS for the corresponding previous period should be multiplied?

4 What is diluted EPS?

5 Ordinary activities are undertaken by a reporting entity as part of its ....

6 Which of the following exceptional items must be shown on the face of the profit and loss account per FRS 3?

A Loss on disposal of manufacturing equipment
B Profit on the sale of a branch

    C   A significant insurance claim settlement

    D   The cost of restructuring the entity so that its focus and the nature of its operations are materially different

    E   A write off of 40% of the year end stock due to unforeseen obsolescence

    F   A provision for a major loss on a long term contract

7   Martians land and promptly destroy a company's factory. Can the company disclose this as an extraordinary event?

8   A company's year end is 31 December 20X1. The financial statements are approved on 10 February 20X2. A large foreign operation is sold on the 11th February. Should the operation be treated as a discontinued operation?

9   How should a discontinued activity be accounted for?

10   Draw up a proforma statement of total recognised gains and losses.

11   The movement in the reconciliation of movements in shareholders funds is:

$$\text{Profit /loss for the financial year} + \text{Other recognised gains/losses} + \text{Dividends} + \text{New share capital}$$

True   ☐

False   ☐

12   The following accounting treatment should be used to make a prior period of adjustment.

- Restate the prior year ………… …………… …………… …………… and ……… …..……… .

- Restate the ………..… ….………… balance.

- Include the adjustment in the …………… …… ………..… ……………… ………… …………..

- Include a ……. at the foot of the statement …… ………… ……………… …………….. …………… ……………

Answers to quick quiz

1   D. (see para 1.2)

2   EPS is profit in pence attributable to each equity share. (1.5)

3    $\dfrac{\text{Fair value of current shares}}{\text{Theoretical ex - rights value per share}}$ (1.15 – 1.18)

4   Diluted EPS gives users of the accounts a view on the potential ordinary shares of the entity. (1.34 – 1.36)

5   Business. (2.4)

6   All of them. (2.5-2.7)

7   Yes. (2.8)

8   No. The sale is after the accounts were approved. Disclosure in a note can be made. (2.12)

9   The **results** of the discontinued activity should be shown along with profit/loss on discontinuation (exceptional item) and comparatives. (2.13)

10   Compare yours to that in paragraph 2.17.

11   True (2.22/2.23)

12   Refer to paragraph 2.30

Now try the question below from the Exam Question Bank

Number	Level	Marks	Time
10	Full exam	25	45 mins

Chapter 10

CASH FLOW STATEMENTS

Topic list	Syllabus reference
1 FRS 1 Cash flow statements	5(c)
2 Preparing a cash flow statement	5(c)
3 Interpretation of cash flow statements	5(c)
4 Cash flow forecasts	5(c)

Introduction

You have already covered basic cash flow accounting in your earlier studies. Here, the study of cash flow statement revolves around FRS 1, which governs the content and disclosure of cash flow statements in company accounts.

FRS 1 was the first standard produced by the Accounting Standards Board and it was revised in October 1996.

This chapter adopts a systematic approach to the preparation of cash flow statements in examinations; you should learn this method and you will then be equipped for any problems in the exam itself.

The third section in the chapter looks at the information which is provided by cash flow statements and how it should be analysed. Finally we look at cash flow forecasts.

Study guide

- Prepare a cash flow statement, including

    ◦   Relevant notes, for an individual company in accordance with FRS 1 (revised).

    ◦   Note: questions may specify the use of the direct or the indirect method.

- Appraise the usefulness of, and interpret the information in, a cash flow statement.

Exam guide

Preparation and analysis of cash flow statements is identified in the syllabus as a key area so make sure you master both techniques.

1   FRS 1 CASH FLOW STATEMENTS

1.1   It has been argued that 'profit' does not always give a useful or meaningful picture of a company's operations. **Readers of a company's financial statements might even be misled by a reported profit figure**.

     (a)   Shareholders might believe that if a company makes a profit after tax of, say, £100,000 then this is the amount which it could afford to **pay as a dividend**. Unless the company has **sufficient cash** available to stay in business and also to pay a dividend, the shareholders' expectations would be wrong.

(b)   Employees might believe that if a company makes profits, it can afford to **pay higher wages** next year. This opinion may not be correct: the ability to pay wages depends on the **availability of cash**.

(c)   Survival of a business entity depends not so much on profits as on its **ability to pay its debts when they fall due**. Such payments might include 'profit and loss' items such as material purchases, wages, interest and taxation etc, but also capital payments for new fixed assets and the repayment of loan capital when this falls due (for example on the redemption of debentures).

1.2   From these examples, it may be apparent that a company's performance and prospects depend not so much on the 'profits' earned in a period, but more realistically on liquidity or **cash flows**.

1.3   The great advantage of a cash flow statement is that it is unambiguous and provides information which is additional to that provided in the rest of the accounts. It also describes to the cash flows of an organisation by activity and not by balance sheet classification.

FRS 1 *Cash flow statements* (revised)

1.4   **FRS 1 sets out the structure of a cash flow statement and it also sets the minimum level of disclosure.** In October 1996 the ASB issued a revised version of FRS 1 *Cash flow statements*. The revision of FRS 1 was part of a normal process of revision, but it also responded to various criticisms of the original FRS 1. Although cash flow statements were found to be useful, some shortcomings were perceived, which we will discuss in Section 3.

Exam focus point

You only need to learn the revised version of the standard. Examination questions are likely to be computational, but some discussion and interpretation may be required.

Objective

1.5   The FRS begins with the following statement.

'The objective of this FRS is to ensure that reporting entities falling within its scope:

(a)   Report their cash generation and cash absorption for a period by highlighting the significant components of cash flow in a way that facilitates comparison of the cash flow performance of different businesses

(b)   Provide information that assists in the assessment of their liquidity, solvency and financial adaptability.'

Scope

1.6   The FRS applies to all financial statements intended to give a true and fair view of the financial position and profit or loss (or income and expenditure), except those of various exempt bodies in group accounts situations or where the content of the financial statement is governed by other statutes or regulatory regimes. In addition, **small entities are excluded** as defined by companies legislation.

Format of the cash flow statement

1.7 An example is given of the format of a cash flow statement for a single company and this is reproduced below.

1.8 A cash flow statement should list its cash flows for the period classified under the following **standard headings**.

> ## STANDARD HEADINGS
>
> (a) Operating activities (using either the direct or indirect method)
> (b) Returns on investments and servicing of finance
> (c) Taxation
> (d) Capital expenditure and financial investment
> (e) Acquisitions and disposals
> (f) Equity dividends paid
> (g) Management of liquid resources
> (h) Financing

The last two headings can be shown in a single section provided a subtotal is given for each heading. Acquisitions and disposals are not on your syllabus; the heading is included here for completeness.

1.9 Individual categories of inflows and outflows under the standard headings should be disclosed separately either in the cash flow statements or in a note to it unless they are allowed to be shown net. Cash inflows and outflows may be shown net if they relate to the management of liquid resources or financing and the inflows and outflows either:

(a) Relate in substance to a single financing transaction (unlikely to be a concern in Paper 2.5)

(b) Are due to short maturities and high turnover occurring from rollover or reissue (for example, short-term deposits).

The requirement to show cash inflows and outflows separately does not apply to cash flows relating to operating activities.

1.10 Each cash flow should be classified according to the substance of the transaction giving rise to it.

Links to other primary statements

1.11 Because the information given by a cash flow statement is best appreciated in the context of the information given by the other primary statements, the FRS requires **two reconciliations**, between:

(a) **Operating profit and the net cash flow from operating activities**.
(b) The **movement in cash in the period and the movement in net debt**.

Neither reconciliation forms part of the cash flow statement but each may be given either adjoining the statement or in a separate note.

1.12 The **movement in net debt** should identify the following components and reconcile these to the opening and closing balance sheet amount:

(a) The **cash flows** of the entity.

    (b) **Other non-cash changes**.

    (c) The recognition of **changes in market value** and **exchange rate movements**.

Definitions

1.13 The FRS includes the following **important definitions** (only those of direct concern to your syllabus are included here). Note particularly the definitions of cash and liquid resources.

    (a) An **active market** is a market of sufficient depth to absorb the investment held without a significant effect on the price. (This definition affects the definition of liquid resources below.)

    (b) **Cash** is cash in hand and deposits repayable on demand with any qualifying financial institution, less overdrafts from any qualifying financial institution repayable on demand. Deposits are repayable on demand if they can be withdrawn at any time without notice and without penalty or if a maturity or period of notice of not more than 24 hours or one working day has been agreed. Cash includes cash in hand and deposit denominated in foreign currencies.

    (c) **Cash flow** is an increase or decrease in an amount of cash.

    (d) **Liquid resources** are current asset investments held as readily disposable stores of value. A readily disposable investment is one that:

        (i) Is disposable by the reporting entity without curtailing or disrupting its business.

        (ii) Is either:

            (1) Readily convertible into known amounts of cash at or close to its carrying amount.

            (2) Traded in an active market.

    (e) **Net debt** is the borrowings of the reporting entity less cash and liquid resources. Where cash and liquid resources exceed the borrowings of the entity reference should be to 'net funds' rather than to 'net debt'.

    (f) **Overdraft** is a borrowing facility repayable on demand that is used by drawing on a current account with a qualifying financial institution.

Classification of cash flows by standard heading

1.14 The FRS looks at each of the cash flow categories in turn.

Exam focus point

If you are in a hurry or revising skim through these definitions, taking in the highlighted words and go straight to the example in paragraph 1.39.

Operating activities

1.15 Cash flows from operating activities are in general the **cash effects of transactions** and other events **relating to operating or trading activities,** normally shown in the profit and loss account in arriving at operating profit. They include cash flows in respect of operating items relating to provisions, whether or not the provision was included in operating profit.

1.16 A **reconciliation** between the operating profit reported in the profit and loss account and the net cash flow from operating activities should be given **either adjoining the cash flow statement or as a note**. The reconciliation is not part of the cash flow statement: if adjoining the cash flow statement, it should be clearly labelled and kept separate. The reconciliation should disclose separately the movements in stocks, debtors and creditors related to operating activities and other differences between cash flows and profits.

Returns on investments and servicing of finance

1.17 These are **receipts resulting from the ownership of an investment and payments to providers of finance and non-equity shareholders** (eg the holders of preference shares).

1.18 **Cash inflows** from returns on investments and servicing of finance include:

(a) **Interest received**, including any related tax recovered.
(b) **Dividends received**, net of any tax credits.

1.19 **Cash outflows** from returns on investments and servicing of finance include:

(a) **Interest paid** (even if capitalised), including any tax deducted and paid to the relevant tax authority.

(b) Cash flows that are treated as **finance costs** (this will include issue costs on debt and non-equity share capital).

(c) The **interest element of finance lease rental** payments.

(d) **Dividends paid on non-equity shares** of the entity.

Taxation

1.20 These are cash flows to or from taxation authorities in respect of the reporting entity's revenue and capital profits. VAT and other sales taxes are discussed later.

(a) Taxation cash **inflows** include **cash receipts** from the relevant tax authority of tax rebates, claims or returns of overpayments.

(b) Taxation cash **outflows** include **cash payments** to the relevant tax authority of tax, including payments of advance corporation tax.

Capital expenditure and financial investment

1.21 These **cash flows** are those **related to the acquisition or disposal of any fixed asset** other than one required to be classified under 'acquisitions and disposals' (discussed below), **and any current asset investment** not included in liquid resources (also dealt with below). If no cash flows relating to financial investment fall to be included under this heading the caption may be reduced to 'capital expenditure'.

1.22 The **cash inflows** here include:

(a) **Receipts from sales or disposals** of property, plant or equipment.
(b) **Receipts from the repayment of** the reporting entity's **loans** to other entities.

1.23 **Cash outflows** in this category include:

(a) **Payments to acquire property,** plant or equipment.
(b) **Loans made** by the reporting entity.

Acquisitions and disposals

1.24 These cash flows are related to the acquisition or disposal of any trade or business, or of an investment in an entity that is either an associate, a joint venture, or a subsidiary undertaking (these group matters are beyond the scope of your syllabus).

(a) Cash **inflows** here include **receipts from sales of trades or businesses**.
(b) Cash **outflows** here include **payments to acquire trades or businesses**.

Equity dividends paid

1.25 The cash outflows are **dividends paid on** the reporting entity's **equity shares**, excluding any advance corporation tax.

Management of liquid resources

1.26 This section should include cash flows in respect of liquid resources as defined above. Each entity should explain what it includes as liquid resources and any changes in its policy. The cash flows in this section can be shown in a single section with those under 'financing' provided that separate subtotals for each are given.

1.27 **Cash inflows** include:

(a) **Withdrawals from short-term deposits** not qualifying as cash.

(b) Inflows from **disposal or redemption** of any other investments held as liquid resources.

1.28 **Cash outflows** include:

(a) **Payments into short-term deposits** not qualifying as cash.
(b) Outflows to **acquire any other investments** held as liquid resources.

Financing

1.29 Financing cash flows comprise receipts or repayments of principal from or to external providers of finance. The cash flows in this section can be shown in a single section with those under 'management of liquid resources' provided that separate subtotals for each are given.

1.30 Financing **cash inflows** include receipts **from issuing**:

(a) **Shares** or other equity instruments.

(b) **Debentures**, loans and from other long-term and short-term borrowings (other than overdrafts).

1.31 Financing cash **outflows** include:

(a) **Repayments of amounts borrowed** (other than overdrafts).
(b) The **capital element of finance lease rental** payments.
(c) Payments to **reacquire or redeem the entity's shares**.
(d) Payments of **expenses or commission on any issue of equity shares**.

Exceptional and extraordinary items and cash flows

1.32 Where cash flows relate to items that are classified as exceptional or extraordinary in the profit and loss account they **should be shown under the appropriate standard headings**

according to the nature of each item. The cash flows relating to exceptional or extraordinary items should be identified in the cash flow statement or a note to it and the relationship between the cash flows and the originating exceptional or extraordinary item should be explained.

1.33   **Where cash flows are exceptional because of their size or incidence** but are not related to items that are treated as exceptional or extraordinary in the profit and loss account, **sufficient disclosure should be given to explain their cause and nature.**

Value added tax and other taxes

1.34   **Cash flows should be shown net of any attributable value added tax or other sale tax unless the tax is irrecoverable by the reporting entity**. The net movement on the amount payable to, or receivable from the taxing authority should be allocated to cash flows from operating activities unless a different treatment is more appropriate in the particular circumstances concerned. Where restrictions apply to the recoverability of such taxes, the irrecoverable amount should be allocated to those expenditures affected by the restrictions. If this is impracticable, the irrecoverable tax should be included under the most appropriate standard heading.

1.35   **Taxation cash flows other than those** in respect of the reporting entity's revenue and capital profits and value added tax, or other sales tax, **should be included within the cash flow statement** under the same standard heading as the cash flow that gave rise to the taxation cash flow, unless a different treatment is more appropriate in the particular circumstances concerned.

Material non-cash transactions

1.36   Material transactions not resulting in movements of cash of the reporting entity **should be disclosed in the notes** to the cash flow statement if disclosure is necessary for an understanding of the underlying transactions.

Comparative figures

1.37   Comparative figures **should be given for all items in the cash flow statement** and such notes thereto as are required by the FRS with the exception of the note to the statement that analyses changes in the balance sheet amount making up net debt.

1.38   EXAMPLE: SINGLE COMPANY

The following example is provided by the standard for a single company.

XYZ LIMITED

CASH FLOW STATEMENT FOR THE YEAR ENDED 31 DECEMBER 20X6

Reconciliation of operating profit to net cash inflow from operating activities

	£'000
Operating profit	6,022
Depreciation charges	899
Increase in stocks	(194)
Increase in debtors	(72)
Increase in creditors	234
Net cash inflow from operating activities	6,889

CASH FLOW STATEMENT

	£'000
Net cash inflow from operating activities	6,889
Returns on investments and servicing of finance (note 1)	2,999
Taxation	(2,922)
Capital expenditure (note 1)	(1,525)
	5,441
Equity dividends paid	(2,417)
	3,024
Management of liquid resources (note 1)	(450)
Financing (note 1)	57
Increase in cash	2,631

Reconciliation of net cash flow to movement in net debt (note 2)

	£'000	£'000
Increase in cash in the period	2,631	
Cash to repurchase debenture	149	
Cash used to increase liquid resources	450	
Change in net debt*		3,230
Net debt at 1.1.96		(2,903)
Net funds at 31.12.96		327

*In this example all change in net debt are cash flows.

The reconciliation of operating profit to net cash flows from operating activities can be shown in a note.

NOTES TO THE CASH FLOW STATEMENT

1 *Gross cash flows*

	£'000	£'000
Returns on investments and servicing of finance		
Interest received	3,011	
Interest paid	(12)	
		2,999
Capital expenditure		
Payments to acquire intangible fixed assets	(71)	
Payments to acquire tangible fixed assets	(1,496)	
Receipts from sales of tangible fixed assets	42	
		(1,525)
Management of liquid resources		
Purchase of treasury bills	(650)	
Sale of treasury bills	200	
		(450)
Financing		
Issue of ordinary share capital	211	
Repurchase of debenture loan	(149)	
Expenses paid in connection with share issues	(5)	
		57

Note. These gross cash flows can be shown on the face of the cash flow statement, but it may sometimes be neater to show them as a note like this.

2   *Analysis of changes in net debt*

	As at 1 Jan 20X6 *£'000*	*Cash flows* *£'000*	*Other changes* *£'000*	*At 31 Dec 20X6* *£'000*
Cash in hand, at bank	42	847		889
Overdrafts	(1,784)	1,784		
		2,631		
Debt due within 1 year	(149)	149	(230)	(230)
Debt due after 1 year	(1,262)		230	(1,032)
Current asset investments	250	450		700
Total	(2,903)	3,230	-	327

Question 1

Close the book for a moment and jot down the format of the cash flow statement.

2   PREPARING A CASH FLOW STATEMENT

Exam focus point

In essence, preparing a cash flow statement is very straightforward. You should therefore simply learn the format given above and apply the steps noted in the example below. Note that the following items are treated in a way that might seem confusing, but the treatment is logical if you think in terms of **cash**.

2.1   (a)   **Increase in stock** is treated as **negative** (in brackets). This is because it represents a cash **outflow**; cash is being spent on stock.

(b)   An **increase in debtors** would be treated as **negative** for the same reasons; more debtors means less cash.

(c)   By contrast an **increase in creditors** is **positive** because cash is being retained and not used to pay off creditors. There is therefore more of it.

2.2   EXAMPLE: PREPARATION OF A CASH FLOW STATEMENT

Kitty Ltd's profit and loss account for the year ended 31 December 20X2 and balance sheets at 31 December 20X1 and 31 December 20X2 were as follows.

BPP
PUBLISHING

KITTY LIMITED
PROFIT AND LOSS ACCOUNT FOR THE YEAR ENDED 31 DECEMBER 20X2

	£'000	£'000
Sales		720
Raw materials consumed	70	
Staff costs	94	
Depreciation	118	
Loss on disposal	18	
		300
Operating profit		420
Interest payable		28
Profit before tax		392
Taxation		124
		268
Dividend		72
Profit retained for year		196
Balance brought forward		490
		686

KITTY LIMITED
BALANCE SHEETS AS AT 31 DECEMBER

	20X2		*20X1*	
	£'000	£'000	£'000	£'000
Fixed assets				
Cost		1,596		1,560
Depreciation		318		224
		1,278		1,336
Current assets				
Stock	24		20	
Trade debtors	76		58	
Bank	48		56	
	148		134	
Current liabilities				
Trade creditors	12		6	
Taxation	102		86	
Proposed dividend	30		24	
	144		116	
Working capital		4		18
		1,282		1,354
Long-term liabilities				
Long-term loans		200		500
		1,082		854
Share capital		360		340
Share premium		36		24
Profit and loss		686		490
		1,082		854

During the year, the company paid £90,000 for a new piece of machinery.

Required

Prepare a cash flow statement for Kitty Ltd for the year ended 31 December 20X2 in accordance with the requirements of FRS 1 (revised).

2.3 SOLUTION

STEP 1

Set out the proforma cash flow statement with all the headings required by FRS 1 (revised). You should leave plenty of space. Ideally, use three or more sheets of paper, one for the main statement, one for the notes (particularly if you have a separate note for the gross cash flows) and one for your workings. It is obviously essential to know the formats very well.

STEP 2

Complete the reconciliation of operating profit to net cash inflow as far as possible. When preparing the statement from balance sheets, you will usually have to calculate such items as depreciation, loss on sale of fixed assets and profit for the year (see Step 4).

STEP 3

Calculate the figures for tax paid, dividends paid, purchase or sale of fixed assets, issue of shares and repayment of loans if these are not already given to you (as they may be). Note that you may not be given the tax charge in the profit loss account. You will then have to assume that the tax paid in the year is last year's year-end provision and calculate the charge as the balancing figure.

STEP 4

If you are not given the profit figure, open up a working for the profit and loss account. Using the opening and closing balances, the taxation charge and dividends paid and proposed, you will be able to calculate profit for the year as the balancing figure to put in the statement.

STEP 5

Complete note 1, the gross cash flows. Alternatively this information may go straight into the statement.

STEP 6

You will now be able to complete the statement by slotting in the figures given or calculated.

STEP 7

Complete note 2 the analysis of changes in net debt.

KITTY LIMITED
CASH FLOW STATEMENT FOR THE YEAR ENDED 31 DECEMBER 20X2

Reconciliation of operating profit to net cash inflow

	£'000	£'000
Operating profit		420
Depreciation charges		118
Loss on sale of tangible fixed assets		18
Increase in stocks		(4)
Increase in debtors		(18)
Increase in creditors		6
Net cash inflow from operating activities		540

CASH FLOW STATEMENT

Net cash flows from operating activities		540
Returns on investment and servicing of finance		
Interest paid		(28)
Taxation		
Corporation tax paid (W1)		(108)
Capital expenditure		
Payments to acquire tangible fixed assets	(90)	
Receipts from sales of tangible fixed assets	12	
Net cash outflow from capital expenditure		(78)
		326
Equity dividends paid (72 – 30 + 24)		(66)
		260
Financing		
Issues of share capital (360 + 36 – 340 – 24)	32	
Long-term loans repaid (500 – 200)	(300)	
Net cash outflow from financing		(268)
Decrease in cash		(8)

NOTES TO THE CASH FLOW STATEMENT

Analysis of changes in net debt

	At 1 Jan 20X2 £'000	Cash flows £'000	At 31 Dec 20X2 £'000
Cash in hand, at bank	56	(8)	48
Debt due after 1 year	(500)	300	(200)
Total	(444)	292	(152)

Workings

1 *Corporation tax paid*

	£'000
Opening CT payable	86
Charge for year	124
Net CT payable at 31.12.X2	(102)
Paid	108

2 *Fixed asset disposals*

COST

	£'000		£'000
At 1.1.X2	1,560	At 31.12.X2	1,596
Purchases	90	Disposals	54
	1,650		1,650

ACCUMULATED DEPRECIATION

	£'000		£'000
At 31.1.X2	318	At 1.1.X2	224
Depreciation on disposals	24	Charge for year	118
	342		342

NBV of disposals	30
Net loss reported	(18)
Proceeds of disposals	12

Alternative methods

2.4 **FRS 1 allows two possible layouts** for cash flow statement in respect of operating activities:

(a) The **indirect method,** which is the one we have used so far

(b) The **direct method.**

2.5 Under the **direct method** the operating element of the cash flow statement should be shown as follows.

	£'000
Operating activities	
Cash received from customers	X
Cash payments to suppliers	(X)
Cash paid to and on behalf of employees	(X)
Other cash payments	(X)
Net cash flow from operating activities	X

2.6 Points to note are as follows.

(a) The **reconciliation** of operating profits and cash flows is **still required** (by note).

(b) **Cash received from customers** represents cash flows received during the accounting period in respect of sales.

(c) **Cash payments to suppliers** represents cash flows made during the accounting period in respect of goods and services.

(d) **Cash payments to and on behalf of employees** represents amounts paid to employees including the associated tax and national insurance. It will, therefore, comprise gross salaries, employer's National Insurance and any other benefits (eg pension contributions).

2.7 **The direct method is, in effect, an analysis of the cash book.** This information does not appear directly in the rest of the financial statements and so many companies might find it difficult to collect the information. Problems might include the need to reanalyse the cash book, to collate results from different cash sources and so on. The indirect method may be easier as it draws on figures which can be obtained from the financial statements fairly easily.

Question 2

The summarised accounts of Rene plc for the year ended 31 December 20X8 are as follows.

RENE PLC
BALANCE SHEET AS AT 31 DECEMBER 20X8

	20X8		20X7	
	£'000	£'000	£'000	£'000
Fixed assets				
Tangible assets		628		514
Current assets				
Stocks	214		210	
Debtors	168		147	
Cash	7		-	
	389		357	
Creditors: amounts falling due				
within one year				
Trade creditors	136		121	
Tax payable	39		28	
Dividends payable	18		16	
Overdraft	-		14	
	193		179	
Net current assets		196		178
Total assets less current		824		692
liabilities				
Creditors: amounts falling due after				
more than one year				
10% debentures		(80)		(50)
		744		642
Capital and reserves				
Share capital (£1 ords)		250		200
Share premium account		70		60
Revaluation reserve		110		100
Profit and loss account		314		282
		744		642

RENE PLC
PROFIT AND LOSS ACCOUNT
FOR THE YEAR ENDED 31 DECEMBER 20X8

	£'000
Sales	600
Cost of sales	(319)
Gross profit	281
Other expenses (including depreciation of £42,000)	(194)
Profit before tax	87
Tax	(31)
Profit after tax	56
Dividends	(24)
Retained profit for the year	32

You are additionally informed that there have been no disposals of fixed assets during the year. New debentures were issued on 1 January 20X8. Wages for the year amounted to £86,000.

Required

Produce a cash flow statement using the direct method suitable for inclusion in the financial statements, as per FRS 1 (revised 1996).

Answer

RENE PLC
CASH FLOW STATEMENT
FOR THE YEAR ENDED 31 DECEMBER 20X8

	£'000	£'000
Operating activities		
Cash received from customers (W1)	579	
Cash payments to suppliers (W2)	(366)	
Cash payments to and on behalf of employees	(86)	
		127
Returns on investments and servicing of finance		
Interest paid		(8)
Taxation		
UK corporation tax paid (W5)		(20)
Capital expenditure		
Purchase of tangible fixed assets (W6)	(146)	
Net cash outflow from capital expenditure		(146)
		(47)
Equity dividends paid (W4)		(22)
Financing		
Issue of share capital	60	
Issue of debentures	30	
Net cash inflow from financing		90
Increase in cash		21

NOTES TO THE CASHFLOW STATEMENT

1 *Reconciliation of operating profit to net cash inflow from operating activities*

	£'000
Operating profit (87 + 8)	95
Depreciation	42
Increase in stock	(4)
Increase in debtors	(21)
Increase in creditors	15
	127

2 *Reconciliation of net cash flow to movement in net debt*

	£'000
Net cash inflow for the period	21
Cash received from debenture issue	(30)
Change in net debt	(9)
Net debt at 1 January 20X8	(64)
Net debt at 31 December 20X8	(73)

3 *Analysis of changes in net debt*

	At 1 January 20X8 £'000	Cash flows £'000	At 31 December 20X8 £'000
Cash at bank	-	7	7
Overdrafts	(14)	14	-
		21	
Debt due after 1 year	(50)	(30)	(80)
Total	(64)	(9)	(73)

Workings

1   *Cash received from customers*

DEBTORS CONTROL ACCOUNT

	£'000		£'000
B/f	147	Cash received (bal)	579
Sales	600	C/f	168
	747		747

2   *Cash paid to suppliers*

CREDITORS CONTROL ACCOUNT

	£'000		£'000
Cash paid (bal)	366	B/f	121
C/f	136	Purchases (W3)	381
	502		502

3   *Purchases*

	£'000
Cost of sales	319
Opening stock	(210)
Closing stock	214
Expenses (194 – 42 – 86 – 8 debenture interest)	58
	381

4   *Dividends*

DIVIDENDS

	£'000		£'000
∴ Dividends paid	22	Balance b/f	16
Balance c/f	18	Dividend for year	24
	40		40

5   *Taxation*

TAXATION

	£'000		£'000
∴ Tax paid	20	Balance b/f	28
Balance c/f	39	Charge for year	31
	59		59

6   *Purchase of fixed assets*

	£'000
Opening fixed assets	514
Less depreciation	(42)
Add revaluation (110 – 100)	10
	482
Closing fixed assets	628
Difference = additions	146

3   INTERPRETATION OF CASH FLOW STATEMENTS

3.1   FRS 1 *Cash flow statements* was introduced on the basis that it would provide better, more comprehensive and more useful information than its predecessor standard. So what kind of information does the cash flow statement, along with its notes, provide?

3.2   Some of the **main areas where FRS 1 should provide information not found elsewhere in the accounts are as follows.**

(a)   The **relationships between profit and cash** can be seen clearly and analysed accordingly.

(b)   **Management of liquid resources** is highlighted, giving a better picture of the liquidity of the company.

(c) **Financing inflows and outflows must be shown, rather than simply passed through reserves.**

3.3 One of the most important things to realise at this point is that, as the ASB is always keen to emphasise, it is wrong to try to assess the health or predict the death of a reporting entity solely on the basis of a single indicator. When analysing cash flow data, the **comparison should not just be between cash flows and profit, but also between cash flows over a period of time** (say three to five years).

3.4 Cash is not synonymous with profit on an annual basis, but you should also remember that the 'behaviour' of profit and cash flows will be very different. **Profit is smoothed out** through accruals, prepayments, provisions and other accounting conventions. This does not apply to cash, so the **cash flow figures are likely to be 'lumpy' in comparison**. You must distinguish between this 'lumpiness' and the trends which will appear over time.

3.5 The **relationship between profit and cash flows will vary constantly**. Note that healthy companies do not always have reported profits exceeding operating cash flows. Similarly, unhealthy companies can have operating cash flows well in excess of reported profit. The value of comparing them is in determining the extent to which earned profits are being converted into the necessary cash flows.

3.6 **Profit is not as important as the extent to which a company can convert its profits into cash on a continuing basis.** This process should be judged over a period longer than one year. The cash flows should be compared with profits over the same periods to decide how successfully the reporting entity has converted earnings into cash.

3.7 Cash flow figures should also be considered in terms of their specific relationships with each other over time. A form of **'cash flow gearing' can** be determined by comparing operating cash flows and financing flows, particularly borrowing, to **establish the extent of dependence of the reporting entity on external funding.**

3.8 **Other relationships** can be examined.

(a) Operating cash flows and investment flows can be related to match cash recovery from investment to investment.

(b) Investment can be compared to distribution to indicate the proportion of total cash outflow designated specifically to investor return and reinstatement.

(c) A comparison of tax outflow to operating cash flow minus investment flow will establish a 'cash basis tax rate'.

3.9 The 'ratios' mentioned above can be monitored inter- and intra-firm and the analyses can be undertaken in monetary, general price-level adjusted, or percentage terms.

The advantages of cash flow accounting

3.10 The advantages of cash flow accounting are as follows.

(a) Survival in business depends on the **ability to generate** cash. Cash flow accounting directs attention towards this critical issue.

(b) Cash flow is **more comprehensive** than 'profit' which is dependent on accounting conventions and concepts.

(c) **Creditors** (long and short-term) **are more interested in an entity's ability to repay them than in its profitability.** Whereas 'profits' might indicate that cash is likely to be available, cash flow accounting is more direct with its message.

(d) Cash flow reporting provides a **better means of comparing the results** of different companies than traditional profit reporting.

(e) Cash flow reporting **satisfies the needs of all users** better.

  (i) For **management,** it provides the sort of information on which decisions should be taken: (in management accounting, 'relevant costs' to a decision are future cash flows); traditional profit accounting does not help with decision-making.

  (ii) For **shareholders and auditors,** cash flow accounting can provide a satisfactory basis for stewardship accounting.

  (iii) As described previously, the information needs of **creditors and employees** will be better served by cash flow accounting.

(f) Cash flow forecasts are **easier to prepare,** as well as more useful, than profit forecasts.

(g) They can in some respects be **audited more easily** than accounts based on the accruals concept.

(h) The accruals concept is confusing, and cash flows are **more easily understood**.

(i) Cash flow accounting should be both retrospective, and also include a forecast for the future. This is of **great information value** to all users of accounting information.

(j) **Forecasts** can subsequently be **monitored** by the publication of variance statements which compare actual cash flows against the forecast.

Question 3

Can you think of some possible disadvantages of cash flow accounting?

Answer

The main disadvantages of cash accounting are essentially the advantages of accruals accounting (proper matching of related items). There is also the practical problem that few businesses keep historical cash flow information in the form needed to prepare a historical cash flow statement and so extra record keeping is likely to be necessary.

Why FRS 1 was revised

3.11 We mentioned at the beginning of this chapter that FRS 1 was revised, at least in part, because of certain criticisms. We will look at these briefly.

3.12 **The original FRS 1 included 'cash equivalents' with cash.** Cash equivalents were highly liquid investments with a maturity date of less than three months from the date of acquisitions (netted off against similar advances from banks). The inclusion of cash equivalents was criticised because it did not reflect the way in which businesses were managed: in particular, the requirement that to be a cash equivalent an investment had to be within three months of maturity was **considered unrealistic. In the revised FRS, only cash in hand and deposits repayable on demand, less overdrafts, are included in 'cash'.**

3.13 To distinguish the management of assets similar to cash (which previously might have been classed as 'cash equivalents') from other investment decisions, the revised FRS has a section dealing separately with the cash flows arising from the management of liquid resources.

3.14 The **new note** required by FRS 1 (revised) **reconciling movement in net debt** gives **additional information** on company performance, solvency and financial adaptability.

4 CASH FLOW FORECASTS

The purpose of forecasts

4.1 Many businesses fail because of cash flow problems. Cash forecasting is vital to ensure that sufficient funds will be available when they are needed at an acceptable cost. Forecasts **provide an early warning of liquidity problems, by estimating:**

(a) **How much cash is required.**
(b) **When it is required.**
(c) **How long it is required for.**
(d) **Whether it will be available** from anticipated sources.

4.2 The timing of cash flows, as well as the amount, is important because a company must know when it might need to borrow and for how long, not just what amount of funding could be required.

4.3 This liquidity information is **of help to creditors and investors as well as to management**, as it assists them in assessing the ability of the company to pay its way. Banks have increasingly insisted that customers provide cash forecasts (or a business plan that includes a cash forecast) as a precondition of lending. A newly-established company wishing to open a bank account will also normally be asked to supply a business plan. The cash and sales forecasts will also allow the bank to monitor the progress of the new company, and control its lending more effectively.

Types of forecast

4.4 There are two broad types of cash forecast.

(a) Cash flow based forecasts (or cash budgets) in **receipts and payments format.**
(b) Balance sheet and **financial statement based forecasts.**

Receipts and payments

4.5 Cash flow based forecasts (receipts and payments) are **forecasts of the amount and timing of cash receipts and payments,** net cash flows and changes in cash balances, for each time period covered by the forecast. Cash flow based forecasts include cash budgets up to a year or so ahead and short-term forecasts of just a few days.

4.6 Forecasting **should have a logical structure based on:**

(a) **Identification** of component cash flows, each component having its own characteristics.

(b) **Assumptions** about the timing and pattern of cash flows.

4.7 The **advantages** of preparing cash flow forecasts in receipt and payments format, which involves forecasting the cash position for a number of individual items, are these.

(a) They are based on the **timings** which might be **identified in the operating cycle.**

(b) They are **straightforward** to prepare.

(c) They **clearly identify the distinction between operational and other cash flows.** Each type of cash flow might have different implications for management.

(d) **Temporary surpluses or deficiencies** within a budget period **are picked up,** as the timing of receipts and payments can be taken into account.

(e) They are likely to be **relevant** to movements in and out of the firm's bank account (subject to clearance delay, see below).

(f) They can **identify any long term trends** in the declining cash balances.

4.8 **However, they do not indicate overall changes in the firm's working capital** such as debtors, creditors or stocks, of which cash is a part. A bias in one figure can, if projected, render further figures unhelpful and wrong. After all, a company's operational cash flows are intimately connected with its levels of stocks, debtors and creditors.

Balance sheet

4.9 A balance sheet based forecast is **an estimate of the company's balance sheet at a future date.** It is used to identify either the cash surplus or the funding shortfall in the company's balance sheet at the forecast date.

(a) **It is not an estimate of cash inflows and outflows.** A number of sequential forecasts can be produced, for example a forecast of the balance sheet at the end of each year for the next five years.

(b) The balance sheet **is produced for management accounting purposes** and so not for external publication or statutory financial reporting.

Uses and limitations of balance sheet-based forecasts

4.10 Balance sheet-based forecasts have two main **uses**:

(a) As **longer-term (strategic) estimates,** to assess the scale of funding requirements or cash surpluses the company expects over time.

(b) **To act as a check on the realism of cash flow-based forecasts.** The estimated balance sheet should be roughly consistent with the net cash change in the cash budget, after allowing for approximations in the balance sheet forecast assumptions.

4.11 Balance sheet-based forecasts have several **limitations.**

(a) Their **practical value is restricted to long-term forecasts and checking the reliability of cash budgets.** Unlike cash budgets, they have no operational or control use.

(b) They will be of **limited accuracy,** given the range of assumptions that must be used and the long timescale of the estimate.

(c) They are **difficult to construct for a multinational group,** especially when several currencies are involved.

Disadvantages of published cash flow forecasts

4.12 Many believe that companies should publish cash flow forecasts. However, published cash flow forecasts have certain disadvantages, which are as follows.

(a) The **information** contained in them **may be manipulated** by unscrupulous managers wishing to show a favourable impression.

(b) They are **only as good as the assumptions on which they are based**. Clearly there is an element of subjectivity and uncertainty involved in preparing them. However, users of cash flow forecasts should be aware of their limitations.

(c) Cash flow forecasts are **very difficult to audit,** because they are **based on subjective prediction**. However, auditors can assess the accounting principles adopted and the consistency with which they are applied.

(d) It is possible that **competitors could make use of the information** disclosed in a cash flow forecast, although if they were compulsory for all companies no single company would benefit from this advantage.

Chapter roundup

- **Cash flow statements** were made compulsory for companies because it was recognised that accounting profit is not the only indicator of a company's performance. FRS 1 *Cash flow statements* was revised in October 1996.

- Cash flow statements concentrate on the **sources** and **uses of cash** and are a useful indicator of a company's **liquidity** and **solvency**.

- You need to learn the **format** of the statement; setting out the format is an essential first stage in preparing the statement but it will only really sink in with more question practice.

- Remember the **step-by-step preparation** procedure and use it for all the questions you practise.

- Cash flow statements provide **useful information** about a company which is not provided elsewhere in the accounts.

- Note that you may be expected to **analyse** or **interpret** a cash flow statement.

- Cash flow forecasts are of two main types

   ◦ Cash budgets in **receipts and payments** form
   ◦ Balance sheet and **financial statements based** forecasts.

Quick quiz

1   List the aims of a cash flow statement.

2   The standard headings in the FRS1 cash flow statement are:

- O................. a.................
- R.................. an i.................. and s.................... of f...................
- T....................
- C.................. e.................... and f.................. i...................
- A.................... and d....................
- E.................... d.................... p.....................
- M.................... of l.................... r....................
- F...................

3   Liquid resources are current asset investments which will mature or can be redeemed within three months of the year end.

True ☐

False ☐

4   Why are you more likely to encounter the indirect method as opposed to the direct method?

5   List five advantages of cash flow accounting.

Answers to quick quiz

1   Comparability and assessment of liquidity, solvency and financial adaptability. (see para 1.5)

2   See paragraph 1.8.

3   False. See the definition in paragraph 1.13(d) if you are not sure about this.

4   The indirect method utilises figures which appear in the financial statements. The figures required for the direct method may not be readily available. (see para 2.7)

5   See paragraph 3.10

Now try the question below from the Exam Question Bank

Number	Level	Marks	Time
11	Full exam	25	45 mins

Chapter 11

LIABILITIES AND PROVISIONS; REPORTING THE SUBSTANCE OF TRANSACTIONS

Topic list	Syllabus reference
1 SSAP 17 and FRS 12	3(f)
2 Creditors	3(f)
3 Provisions and reserves	3(f)
4 Substance over form	3(f)
5 Off balance sheet finance	3(f)

Introduction

SSAP 17 and FRS 12 *Provisions, contingent liabilities and contingent assets* are very important as they can affect many items in the accounts. Make sure you learn all the relevant definitions and understand the standard accounting treatment. You should remember SSAP 17 from your Foundation studies.

There are various disclosures relating to creditors, provisions and reserves, and share capital which it is convenient to mention here. The profit and loss disclosures are additional to the FRS 3 disclosures mentioned in the last chapter.

FRS 5 *Reporting the substance of transactions* is a key standard which you need to understand. Make sure you get to grips with why such a standard was put together.

Study guide

- Explain why an accounting standard on provisions is necessary - give examples of previous abuses in this area.

- Define provisions, legal and constructive obligations, past events and the transfer of economic benefits.

- State when provisions may and may not be made, and how they should be accounted for.

- Explain how provisions should be measured.

- Define contingent assets and liabilities - give examples and describe their accounting treatment.

- Be able to identify and account for:

    - warranties/guarantees
    - onerous contracts
    - environmental and similar provisions

- Discuss the validity of making provisions for future repairs or refurbishment.

- Explain the importance of recording the substance rather than the legal form of transactions - give examples of previous abuses in this area.

- Describe the features which may indicate that the substance of transactions may differ from their legal form.

- Explain and apply the principles in FRS 5 for the recognition and derecognition of assets and liabilities.

- Be able to recognise the substance of transactions in general, and specifically account for the following types of transactions:

  - stock sold on sale or return/consignment stock.
  - sale and repurchase/leaseback agreements.
  - factoring of debtors.

Exam guide

Substance over form has been highlighted as a key area in the syllabus.

1 SSAP 17 AND FRS 12

1.1 SSAP 17 should be familiar to you from your Paper 1 studies. The most important aspects are highlighted in the summary below.

Exam focus point

It is unlikely that a whole question would be based on these standards.

Knowledge brought forward from previous studies

SSAP 17 Accounting for post balance sheet events

- *Post balance sheet event (PBSEs)* are events, both favourable and unfavourable, which occur between the B/S date and the date on which the financial statements are approved by the board of directors.

- *Adjusting events* are PBSEs which provide additional evidence of conditions existing at the B/S date, and therefore need to be incorporated into the financial statements.

- *Non-adjusting events* are PBSEs which concern conditions which did *not* exist at the B/S date.

- *Window dressing* is the arranging of transactions, the substance of which is primarily to alter the appearance of the B/S: it is *not* falsification of accounts. SSAP 17 does allow window dressing but *disclosure* should be made of such transactions

---

FRS 12 Provisions, Contingent Liabilities And Contingent Assets

1.2 As we have seen with regard to post balance sheet events, financial statements must include **all the information necessary for an understanding of the company's financial position**. Provisions, contingent liabilities and contingent assets are 'uncertainties' that must be accounted for consistently if are to achieve this understanding.

Objective

1.3 FRS 12 *Provisions, contingent liabilities and contingent assets* aims to ensure that appropriate **recognition criteria** and **measurement bases** are applied to provisions, contingent liabilities and contingent assets and that **sufficient information** is disclosed in the **notes** to the financial statements to enable users to understand their nature, timing and amount.

Provisions

1.4 You will be familiar with provisions for depreciation and doubtful debts from your earlier studies. The sorts of provisions addressed by FRS 12 are, however, rather different.

1.5 Before FRS 12, there was no accounting standard dealing with provisions. Companies wanting to show their results in the most favourable light used to make large 'one off' **provisions** in years where a high level of underlying profits was generated. These provisions, often known as '**big bath**' provisions, were then available to shield expenditure in future years when perhaps the underlying profits were not as good.

1.6 In other words, **provisions were used for profit smoothing**. Profit smoothing is misleading.

> **IMPORTANT**
>
> The key aim of FRS 12 is to ensure that **provisions are made only where there are valid grounds for them**.

1.7 FRS 12 views a provision as a **liability**.

> **KEY TERMS**
>
> A **provision** is a **liability** of uncertain timing or amount.
>
> A **liability** is an obligation of an entity to transfer economic benefits as a result of past transactions or events. *(FRS 12)*

1.8 The FRS distinguishes provisions from other liabilities such as trade creditors and accruals. This is on the basis that for a provision there is **uncertainty** about the timing or amount of the future expenditure. Whilst uncertainty is clearly present in the case of certain accruals the uncertainty is generally much less than for provisions.

Recognition

1.9 FRS 12 states that a provision should be **recognised** as a liability in the financial statements when:

 (a) An entity has a **present obligation** (legal or constructive) as a result of a past event

 (b) It is probable that a **transfer of economic benefits** will be required to settle the obligation

 (c) A **reliable estimate** can be made of the obligation

Meaning of obligation

1.10 It is fairly clear what a legal obligation is. However, you may not know what a **constructive obligation** is.

> **KEY TERM**
>
> FRS 12 defines a **constructive obligation** as

'An obligation that derives from an entity's actions where:

- By an established pattern of past practice, published policies or a sufficiently specific current statement the entity has indicated to other parties that it will accept certain responsibilities.

- As a result, the entity has created a valid expectation on the part of those other parties that it will discharge those responsibilities.

Question 1

In which of the following circumstances might a provision be recognised?

(a) On 13 December 20X9 the board of an entity decided to close down a division. The accounting date of the company is 31 December. Before 31 December 20X9 the decision was not communicated to any of those affected and no other steps were taken to implement the decision.

(b) The board agreed a detailed closure plan on 20 December 20X9 and details were given to customers and employees.

(c) A company is obliged to incur clean up costs for environmental damage (that has already been caused).

(d) A company intends to carry out future expenditure to operate in a particular way in the future.

Answer

(a) No provision would be recognised as the decision has not been communicated.

(b) A provision would be made in the 20X9 financial statements.

(c) A provision for such costs is appropriate.

(d) No present obligation exists and under FRS 12 no provision would be appropriate. This is because the entity could avoid the future expenditure by its future actions, maybe by changing its method of operation.

Probable transfer of economic benefits

1.11 For the purpose of the FRS, a transfer of economic benefits is regarded as **'probable'** if the event is **more likely than not** to occur. This appears to indicate a probability of more than 50%. However, the standard makes it clear that where there is a number of similar obligations the probability should be based on considering the population as a whole, rather than one single item.

1.12 EXAMPLE: TRANSFER OF ECONOMIC BENEFITS

If a company has entered into a warranty obligation then the probability of transfer of economic benefits may well be extremely small in respect of one specific item. However, when considering the population as a whole the probability of some transfer of economic benefits is quite likely to be much higher. If there is a **greater than 50% probability** of some transfer of economic benefits then a **provision** should be made for the **expected amount**.

Measurement of provisions

> **IMPORTANT**
>
> The amount recognised as a provision should be the best estimate of the expenditure required to settle the present obligation at the balance sheet date.

1.13 The estimates will be determined by the **judgement** of the entity's management supplemented by the experience of similar transactions.

1.14 Allowance is made for **uncertainty**. Where the provision being measured involves a large population of items, the obligation is estimated by weighting all possible outcomes by their discounted probabilities, ie **expected value**.

Question 2

Parker plc sells goods with a warranty under which customers are covered for the cost of repairs of any manufacturing defect that becomes apparent within the first six months of purchase. The company's past experience and future expectations indicate the following pattern of likely repairs.

% of goods sold	Defects	Cost of repairs
		£m
75	None	-
20	Minor	1.0
5	Major	4.0

What is the expected cost of repairs?

Answer

The cost is found using 'expected values' (75% × £nil) + (20% × £1.0m) + (5% × £4.0m) = £400,000.

Future events

1.15 **Future events** which are reasonably expected to occur (eg new legislation, changes in technology) may affect the amount required to settle the entity's obligation and should be taken into account.

Expected disposal of assets

1.16 Gains from the expected disposal of assets should not be taken into account in measuring a provision.

Reimbursements

1.17 Some or all of the expenditure needed to settle a provision may be expected to be recovered form a third party. If so, the **reimbursement should be recognised only when it is virtually certain that reimbursement will be received if the entity settles the obligation.**

(a) The reimbursement should be treated as a separate asset, and the amount recognised should not be greater than the provision itself.

(b) The provision and the amount recognised for reimbursement may be netted off in the profit and loss account.

Changes in provisions

1.18   Provisions should be renewed at each balance sheet date and adjusted to reflect the current best estimate. If it is no longer probable that a transfer of economic benefits will be required to settle the obligation, the provision should be reversed.

Use of provisions

1.19   **A provision should be used only for expenditures for which the provision was originally recognised**. Setting expenditures against a provision that was originally recognised for another purpose would conceal the impact of two different events.

Recognising an asset when recognising a provision

1.20   Normally the setting up of a provision should be charged immediately to the profit and loss account. But **if the incurring of the present obligation recognised as a provision gives access to future economic benefits an asset should be recognised.**

1.21 EXAMPLE: RECOGNISING AN ASSET

An obligation for decommissioning costs is incurred by commissioning an oil rig. At the same time, the commissioning gives access to oil reserves over the years of the oil rig's operation. Therefore an asset representing future access to oil reserves is recognised at the same time as the provision for decommissioning costs.

Future operating losses

1.22   **Provisions should not be recognised for future operating losses.** They do not meet the definition of a liability and the general recognition criteria set out in the standard.

Onerous contracts

1.23   If an entity has a contract that is onerous, the present obligation under the contract **should be recognised and measured** as a provision. An example might be vacant leasehold property.

> **KEY TERM**
>
> An onerous contract is a contract entered into with another party under which the unavoidable costs of fulfilling the terms of the contract exceed any revenues expected to be received from the goods or services supplied or purchased directly or indirectly under the contract and where the entity would have to compensate the other party if it did not fulfil the terms of the contract.

1.24 EXAMPLES OF POSSIBLE PROVISIONS

It is easier to see what FRS 12 is driving at if you look at examples of those items which are possible provisions under this standard. Some of these we have already touched on.

(a)   **Warranties.** These are argued to be genuine provisions as on past experience it is probable, ie more likely than not, that some claims will emerge. The provision must be estimated, however, on the basis of the class as a whole and not on individual claims. There is a clear legal obligation in this case.

(b) **Major repairs**. In the past it has been quite popular for companies to provide for expenditure on a major overhaul to be accrued gradually over the intervening years between overhauls. Under FRS 12 this will no longer be possible as FRS 12 would argue that this is a mere intention to carry out repairs, not an obligation. The entity can always sell the asset in the meantime. The only solution is to treat major assets such as aircraft, ships, furnaces etc as a series of smaller assets where each part is depreciated over shorter lives. Thus any major overhaul may be argued to be replacement and therefore capital rather than revenue expenditure.

(c) **Self insurance**. A number of companies have created a provision for self insurance based on the expected cost of making good fire damage etc instead of paying premiums to an insurance company. Under FRS 12 this provision would no longer be justifiable as the entity has no obligation until a fire or accident occurs. No obligation exists until that time.

(d) **Environmental contamination**. If the company has an environment policy such that other parties would expect the company to clean up any contamination or if the company has broken current environmental legislation then a provision for environmental damage must be made.

(e) **Decommissioning or abandonment costs**. When an oil company initially purchases an oilfield it is put under a legal obligation to decommission the site at the end of its life. Prior to FRS 12 most oil companies applied the SORP on *Accounting for abandonment costs* published by the Oil Industry Accounting Committee and they built up the provision gradually over the field so that no one year would be unduly burdened with the cost.

FRS 12, however, insists that a legal obligation exists on the initial expenditure on the field and therefore a liability exists immediately. This would appear to result in a large charge to profit and loss in the first year of operation of the field. However, the FRS takes the view that the cost of purchasing the field in the first place is not only the cost of the field itself but also the costs of putting it right again. Thus all the costs of abandonment may be capitalised.

(f) **Restructuring**. This is considered in detail below.

Provisions for restructuring

1.25 One of the main purposes of FRS 12 was to target abuses of provisions for restructuring. Accordingly, FRS 12 lays down **strict criteria** to determine when such a provision can be made.

> **KEY TERM**
>
> FRS 12 defines a **restructuring** as:
>
> A programme that is planned and is controlled by management and materially changes either:
>
> - The scope of a business undertaken by an entity
> - The manner in which that business is conducted

1.26 The FRS gives the following **examples** of events that may fall under the definition of restructuring.

- The **sale or termination** of a line of business

- The **closure of business locations** in a country or region or the **relocation** of business activities from one country region to another

- **Changes in management structure**, for example, the elimination of a layer of management

- **Fundamental reorganisations** that have a material effect on the **nature and focus** of the entity's operations

1.27 The question is whether or not an entity has an obligation - legal or constructive - at the balance sheet date.

- An entity must have a **detailed formal plan** for the restructuring.

- It must have **raised a valid expectation** in those affected that it will carry out the restructuring by starting to implement that plan or announcing its main features to those affected by it

IMPORTANT

A mere management decision is not normally sufficient. Management decisions may sometimes trigger off recognition, but only if earlier events such as negotiations with employee representatives and other interested parties have been concluded subject only to management approval.

1.28 Where the restructuring involves the **sale of an operation** then FRS 12 states that no obligation arises until the entity has entered into a **binding sale agreement**. This is because until this has occurred the entity will be able to change its mind and withdraw from the sale even if its intentions have been announced publicly.

Costs to be included within a restructuring provision

1.29 The FRS states that a restructuring provision should include only the **direct expenditures** arising from the restructuring, which are those that are both:

- **Necessarily entailed** by the restructuring; and
- Not associated with the **ongoing activities** of the entity.

1.30 The following costs should specifically **not** be included within a restructuring provision.

- **Retraining** or relocating continuing staff
- **Marketing**
- **Investment in new systems** and distribution networks

Disclosure

1.31 Disclosures for provisions fall into two parts.

(a) Disclosure of details of the **change in carrying value** of a provision from the beginning to the end of the year

(b) Disclosure of the **background** to the making of the provision and the uncertainties affecting its outcome

Contingent liabilities

1.32 Now you understand provisions it will be easier to understand contingent assets and liabilities.

> **KEY TERM**
>
> FRS 12 defines a **contingent liability** as:
>
> - A possible obligation that arises from past events and whose existence will be confirmed only by the occurrence or non-occurrence of one or more uncertain future events not wholly within the entity's control; or
>
> - A present obligation that arises from past events but is not recognised because:
>
>   ° It is not probable that a transfer of economic benefits will be required to settle the obligation
>
>   ° The amount of the obligation cannot be measured with sufficient reliability

1.33 As a rule of thumb, probable means more than 50% likely. **If an obligation is probable, it is not a contingent liability** - instead, a **provision is needed**.

Treatment of contingent liabilities

1.34 Contingent liabilities **should not be recognised in financial statements** but they **should be disclosed**. The required disclosures are:

- A brief description of the nature of the contingent liability
- An estimate of its financial effect
- An indication of the uncertainties that exist
- The possibility of any reimbursement

Contingent assets

> **KEY TERM**
>
> FRS 12 defines a **contingent asset** as:
>
> A possible asset that arises from past events and whose existence will be confirmed by the occurrence of one or more uncertain future events not wholly within the entity's control.

1.35 **A contingent asset must not be recognised.** Only when the realisation of the related economic benefits is **virtually certain** should recognition take place. At that point, **the asset is no longer a contingent asset**!

Disclosure: contingent liabilities

1.36 A **brief description** must be provided of all material contingent liabilities unless they are likely to be remote. In addition, provide

- An estimate of their **financial effect**
- Details of **any uncertainties**

1.37 *Disclosure: contingent assets*

Contingent assets must only be disclosed in the notes if they are **probable**. In that case a brief description of the contingent asset should be provided along with an estimate of its likely financial effect.

'Let out'

1.38 FRS 12 permits reporting entities to avoid disclosure requirements relating to provisions, contingent liabilities and contingent assets if they would be expected to **seriously prejudice** the position of the entity in dispute with other parties. However, this should only be employed in **extremely rare** cases. Details of the general nature of the provision/contingencies must still be provided, together with an explanation of why it has not been disclosed.

1.39 You must practise the questions below to get the hang of FRS 12. But first, study the flow chart, taken from FRS 12, which is a good summary of its requirements.

Exam focus point

If you learn this flow chart you should be able to deal with most of the questions you are likely to meet in the exam.

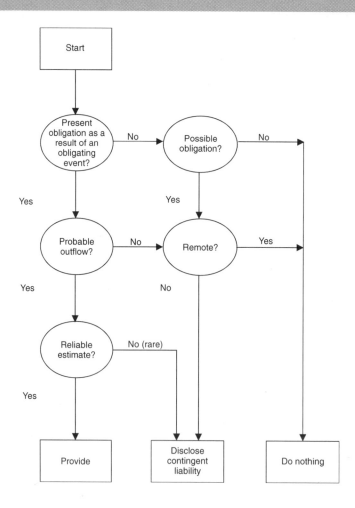

Question 3

During 20X9 Alligator Ltd gives a guarantee of certain borrowings of Crocodile Ltd, whose financial condition at that time is sound. During 20Y0, the financial condition of Crocodile Ltd deteriorates and at 30 June 20Y0 Crocodile Ltd files for protection from its creditors.

What accounting treatment is required:

(a)   At 31 December 20X9?
(b)   At 31 December 20Y0?

Answer

(a)   At 31 December 20X9

There is a present obligation as a result of a past obligating event. The obligating event is the giving of the guarantee, which gives rise to a legal obligation. However, at 31 December 20X9 no transfer of economic benefits is probable in settlement of the obligation.

No provision is recognised. The guarantee is disclosed as a contingent liability unless the probability of any transfer is regarded as remote.

(b)   At 31 December 20Y0

As above, there is a present obligation as a result of a past obligating event, namely the giving of the guarantee.

At 31 December 20Y0 it is probable that a transfer of economic events will be required to settle the obligation. A provision is therefore recognised for the best estimate of the obligation.

Question 4

Super Produx Ltd gives warranties at the time of sale to purchasers of its products. Under the terms of the warranty the manufacturer undertakes to make good, by repair or replacement, manufacturing defects that become apparent within a period of three years from the date of the sale. Should a provision be recognised?

Answer

Super Produx Ltd **cannot avoid** the cost of repairing or replacing all items of product that manifest manufacturing defects in respect of which warranties are given before the balance sheet date, and a provision for the cost of this should therefore be made.

Super Produx Ltd is obliged to repair or replace items that fail within the entire warranty period. Therefore, in respect of **this year's sales**, the obligation provided for at the balance sheet date should be the cost of making good items for which defects have been notified but not yet processed, **plus** an estimate of costs in respect of the other items sold for which there is sufficient evidence that manufacturing defects **will** manifest themselves during their remaining periods of warranty cover.

Question 5

After a wedding in 20X0 ten people died, possibly as a result of food poisoning from products sold by Crippen Ltd. Legal proceedings are started seeking damages from Crippen but it disputes liability. Up to the date of approval of the financial statements for the year to 31 December 20X0, Crippen's lawyers advise that it is probable that it will not be found liable. However, when Crippen prepares the financial statements for the year to 31 December 20X1 its lawyers advise that, owing to developments in the case, it is probable that it will be found liable.

What is the required accounting treatment:

(a)   At 31 December 20X0?
(b)   At 31 December 20X1?

Answer

(a) *At 31 December 20X0*

On the basis of the evidence available when the financial statements were approved, there is no obligation as a result of past events. No provision is recognised. The matter is disclosed as a contingent liability unless the probability of any transfer is regarded as remote.

(b) *At 31 December 20X1*

On the basis of the evidence available, there is a present obligation. A transfer of economic benefits in settlement is probable.

A provision is recognised for the best estimate of the amount needed to settle the present obligation.

Section summary

1.40 • The objective of FRS 12 is to ensure that **appropriate recognition criteria** and measurement bases are applied to **provisions and contingencies** and that **sufficient information** is disclosed.

• The FRS seeks to ensure that provisions are **only recognised** when a **measurable obligation** exists. It includes detailed rules that can be used to ascertain when an obligation exists and how to measure the obligation.

• The standard attempts to **eliminate** the '**profit smoothing**' which has gone on before it was issued.

2   CREDITORS

2.1 If any liabilities included under creditors have been **secured,** the amounts secured and the nature of the security must be **stated.**

2.2 Any amounts included which are **payable** (or repayable) **more than five years** after the balance sheet date must be **specified,** together with the terms of payment or repayment and the rate of any interest payable.

2.3 The amount of any **proposed dividend** should be stated. Details of any arrears of dividends on cumulative preference shares must also be given.

2.4 Where **debentures** have been issued during the year, **details of the issue** (including the reasons why it was made) should be given in a note.

3   PROVISIONS AND RESERVES

3.1 As defined in the CA 1985, **provisions for liabilities and charges** are amounts retained to provide for any liability or loss which is either likely to be incurred or certain to be incurred, but uncertain as to amount or as to the date on which it will crystallise.

3.2 Where a reserve or provision is disclosed as a separate item in a company's balance sheet or in a note, any movements on the account during the year should be specified. The amount of any **provisions for taxation other than deferred taxation must be stated and details must be given of any pension commitments.**

3.3 The pro-forma balance sheet requires that any **share premium account** (KII) **and** any **revaluation reserve** (KIII) be **shown separately**. Any other reserves built up by a company should be disclosed under the appropriate headings (or amalgamated if not material) with the profit and loss account balance (KV) being shown separately.

4   SUBSTANCE OVER FORM

4.1   The phrase '**substance over form**' is described in IAS 1 *Disclosure of accounting policies* as follows.

> 'Transactions and other events should be accounted for and presented in accordance with their substance and financial reality and not merely with their legal form.'

4.2   This is a very important concept and, although it was not used by the ASC, it **has been used to determine accounting treatment in financial statements through accounting standards and so prevent off balance sheet transactions**. The following paragraphs give examples of where the principle of substance over form is enforced, particularly in accounting standards.

SSAP 21 *Accounting for leases and hire purchase* contracts

4.3   In SSAP 21, as we saw in the previous chapter, there is an explicit requirement that if the lessor transfers substantially all the risks and rewards of ownership to the lessee then, even though the legal title has not passed, the item being leased should be shown as an asset in the balance sheet of the lessee and the amount due to the lessor should be shown as a liability.

FRS 8 *Related party disclosures*

4.4   FRS 8 requires financial statements to disclose fully material transactions undertaken with a related party by the reporting entity, regardless of any price charged.

SSAP 9 *Stocks and long-term contracts*

4.5   In SSAP 9 there is a requirement to account for attributable profits on long-term contracts under the accruals convention. However, there may be a problem with realisation, since it is arguable whether we should account for profit which, although attributable to the work done, may not have yet been invoiced to the customer. It is argued that the convention of substance over form is applied to justify ignoring the strict legal position.

FRS 2 *Accounting for subsidiary undertakings*

4.6   This is perhaps the most important area of off balance sheet finance which has been prevented by the application of the substance over form concept.

4.7   The use of quasi-subsidiaries was very common in the 1980s. A **quasi-subsidiary** is defined by FRS 5: in effect it **is a vehicle which does not fulfil the definition of a subsidiary, but it operates just like a subsidiary.**

4.8   The main off balance sheet transactions involving quasi-subsidiaries were as follows.

(a)   **Sale of assets**. The sale of assets to a quasi-subsidiary was carried out to remove the associated borrowings from the balance sheet and so reduce gearing; or perhaps so that the company could credit a profit in such a transaction. The asset could then be rented back to the vendor company under an operating lease (no capitalisation required by the lessee).

(b)   **Purchase of companies or assets**. One reason for such a purchase through a quasi-subsidiary is if the acquired entity is expected to make losses in the near future. Post-acquisition losses can be avoided by postponing the date of acquisition to the date the holding company acquires the purchase from the quasi-subsidiary.

(c) **Business activities conducted outside the group**. Such a subsidiary might have been excluded through a quasi-subsidiary or not consolidated under the 'dissimilar activities' requirement in SSAP 1. Exclusion from consolidation might be undertaken because the activities are high risk and have high gearing.

4.9 CA 1989 introduced a new definition of a subsidiary based on *control* rather than just ownership rights and this definition (along with other related matters) was incorporated into FRS 2, thus substantially reducing the effectiveness of this method of off-balance sheet finance.

Creative accounting

4.10 Creative accounting, the **manipulation of figures for a desired result**, takes many forms. Off balance sheet finance is a major type of creative accounting and it probably has the most serious implications. Before we look at some of the other types of creative accounting, we should consider some important points.

4.11 Firstly, **it is very rare for a company, its directors or employees to manipulate results for the purpose of fraud. The major consideration is usually the effect the results will have on the share price of the company**. If the share price falls, the company becomes vulnerable to takeover.

4.12 Analysts, brokers and economists, whose opinions affect the stock markets, are often perceived as having an outlook which is both short-term and superficial. Consequently, **companies will attempt to produce the results the market expects or wants.** The companies will aim for steady progress in a few key numbers and ratios and they will aim to meet the market's stated expectation.

4.13 Another point to consider, particularly when you approach this topic in an examination, is that the **number of methods** available for creative accounting and the determination and imagination of those who wish to perpetrate such acts are **endless**. It has been seen in the past that, wherever an accounting standard or law closes a loophole, another one is found. This has produced a change of approach in regulators and standard setters, towards general principles rather than detailed rules.

4.14 Let us now examine some examples of creative accounting, the reaction of the standard setters and possible actions in the future which may halt or change such practices. Remember that this list is not comprehensive and that the frequency and materiality of the use of each method will vary a great deal. Remember also that we have already covered several methods in our examination of off balance sheet finance.

Income recognition and cut-off

4.15 **Manipulation of cut-off is relatively straightforward.** A company may issue invoices before the year end and inflate sales for the year when in fact they have not received firm orders for the goods. Income recognition can be manipulated in a variety of ways.

4.16 One example is where a company sells software under contract. The sales contracts will only be realised in full over a period of time, but the company might recognise the full sales value of the contract once it has been secured, even though some payments from clients will fall due over several years. This is clearly imprudent, but the company might justify it by pointing to the irrevocable nature of the contract. But what if a customer should go in to liquidation? No income would be forthcoming from the contract under such circumstances.

Reserves

4.17 **Reserves are often used to manipulate figures, avoiding any impact on the profit and loss account.** This occurs particularly in situations where an accounting standard allows a choice of treatments.

4.18 For example, foreign exchange losses or gains on foreign subsidiaries should be taken as a movement on reserves. If a company states that a foreign currency loan in its books was taken out as a hedge against the investment in the foreign subsidiary, then any losses or gains on that loan can also be taken to reserves and offset against the foreign exchange impact of the investment in the subsidiary. Substantial foreign exchange movements through reserves occurred in the Polly Peck accounts before its collapse.

Revaluations

4.19 **The optional nature of the revaluation of fixed assets leaves such practices open to manipulation.** The choice of whether to revalue can have a significant impact on a company's balance sheet. Companies which carried out such revaluations would expect to suffer a much higher depreciation charge as a result. However, many companies charged depreciation in the profit and loss account based on the historical cost only. The rest of the depreciation charge (on the excess of the revalued amount over cost) was transferred to reserves and offset against the revaluation reserve.

4.20 Again, this is an abuse of the use of reserves and it was outlawed by the revised SSAP 12 (now superseded by FRS 15). Companies must now charge depreciation on the revalued amount and pass the whole charge through the profit and loss account.

Other creative accounting techniques

4.21 The examples given above are some of the major 'abuses' in accounting over recent years. A few more are mentioned here and you should aim to think up as many examples of each as you can. You may also know of other creative accounting techniques which we have not mentioned here.

   (a) **Window dressing**. This is where transactions are passed through the books at the year end to make figures look better, but in fact they have not taken place and are often reversed after the year end. An example is where cheques are written to creditors, entered in the cash book, but not sent out until well after the year end.

   (b) **Taxation**. It has been known for some companies to decide how much they want to pay in taxes for the year and state their profits accordingly! Although the relationship between taxable profits and accounting profits is not straightforward, there is a direct effect on the accounts.

   (c) **Change of accounting policies**. This tends to be a last resort because companies which change accounting policies know they will not be able to do so again for some time. The effect in the year of change can be substantial and prime candidates for such treatment are depreciation, stock valuation, changes from current cost to historical cost (practised frequently by privatised public utilities) and foreign currency losses.

   (d) **Manipulation of accruals, prepayments and contingencies**. These figures can often be very subjective, particularly contingencies. In the case of impending legal action, for example, a contingent liability is difficult to estimate, the case may be far off and the solicitors cannot give any indication of likely success, or failure. In such cases companies will often only disclose the possibility of such a liability, even though the eventual costs may be substantial.

Question 6

Creative accounting, off balance sheet finance and related matters (in particular how ratio analysis can be used to discover these practices) often come up in articles in, for example, the *Financial Times* and *The Economist*. Find a library, preferably a good technical library, which can provide you with copies of back issues of such newspapers or journals and look for articles on creative accounting. Alternatively you may have access to the internet and could therefore search the relevant web sites.

5   OFF BALANCE SHEET FINANCE

KEY TERM

Off balance sheet finance has been described as 'the funding or refinancing of a company's operations in such a way that, under legal requirements and existing accounting conventions, some or all of the finance may not be shown on its balance sheet.'

5.1   **Off balance sheet transactions' is the term used for transactions which meet the above objective.** These transactions may involve the removal of assets from the balance sheet, as well as liabilities, and they are likely to have a significant impact on the profit and loss account.

The off balance sheet finance problem

5.2   The result of the use of increasingly sophisticated off balance sheet finance transactions is a situation where the users of financial statements do not have a proper or clear view of the state of the company's affairs. The disclosures required by company law and current accounting standards do not provide sufficient rules for disclosure of off balance sheet finance transactions and so very little of the true nature of the transaction is exposed.

5.3   Whatever the purpose of such transactions, insufficient disclosure creates a problem. This problem has been debated over the years by the accountancy profession and other interested parties and some progress has been made (see the later sections of this chapter).

5.4   The incidence of company collapses over the last few years has risen due to the recession and a great many of these have revealed much higher borrowings than originally thought, because part of the borrowing was off balance sheet.

5.5   **The main argument used for disallowing off balance sheet finance is that the true substance of the transactions should be shown, not merely the legal form,** particularly when it is exacerbated by poor disclosure.

ASB initiatives

5.6 Although the ASB wanted to give the old exposure draft on this subject priority in its work programme, there were problems. A general problem was how to ensure that any new standard was consistent with the revised *Statement of Principles*. There was also a specific problem with securitisation because of opposition from the banking industry. All these aspects are discussed below.

5.7 Two chapters of the *Statement of Principles* affect the question of off balance sheet finance: *The elements of financial statements* and *The recognition of items in financial statements*.

5.8 The definitions are as follows.

> **KEY TERMS**
>
> (a) **Assets** are defined as 'rights or other access to future economic benefits controlled by an entity as a result of past transactions or events'.
>
> (b) **Liabilities** are defined as 'an entity's obligations to transfer economic benefits as a result of past transactions or events'.

5.9 This chapter also lays out the **criteria for recognition** and derecognition of assets and liabilities.

   (a) An item should be recognised in financial statements if:

      (i) The item meets the definition of an element of financial statements (such as an asset or a liability).

      (ii) There is enough evidence that the change in assets or liabilities inherent in the item has occurred (including evidence that a future inflow or outflow of benefit will occur).

      (iii) The item can be measured in monetary terms with sufficient reliability.

   (b) An item should cease to be recognised as an asset or liability if:

      (i) The item no longer meets the definition of the relevant element of financial statements.

      (ii) There is no longer enough evidence that the enterprise has access to future economic benefits or an obligation to transfer economic benefits.

FRS 5 Reporting the substance of transactions

5.10 After many years' work on the subject of off balance sheet finance (some of it detailed above), the ASB has finally published FRS 5 *Reporting the substance of transactions*. It is a daunting document, running to well over 100 pages, although the standard section itself is relatively short.

Scope and exclusions

5.11 **FRS 5 applies to all entities whose accounts are intended to give a true and fair view, with no exemptions for any particular type or size of companies. However, it excludes a number of transactions from its scope,** unless they are part of a larger series of transactions that is within the scope of the standard. These exclusions are:

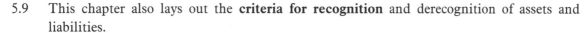

(a) **Forward contracts and futures** (such as those for foreign currencies or commodities).

(b) **Foreign exchange and interest rate swaps**.

(c) contracts where a net amount will be paid or received based on the movement in a price or an index (sometimes referred to as '**contracts for differences**').

(d) **Expenditure commitments** (such as purchase commitments) and orders placed, until the earlier of delivery or payment.

(e) **Employment contracts**.

Relationship to other standards

5.12 The interaction of FRS 5 with other standards and statutory requirements is also an important issue; **whichever rules are the more specific should be applied**. Leasing provides a good example (as we will see in the next chapter): straightforward leases which fall squarely within the terms of SSAP 21 should continue to be accounted for without any need to refer to FRS 5, but where their terms are more complex, or the lease is only one element in a larger series of transactions, then FRS 5 comes into play.

5.13 In addition, the standard requires that its general principle of substance over form should apply to the application of other existing rules.

Exam focus point

A full question on FRS 5, covering both knowledge and application could be set.

Application notes

5.14 FRS 5 deals with certain specific aspects of off balance sheet finance in detailed **application notes**. The topics covered are:

(a) **Consignment stock**
(b) **Sale and repurchase agreements**
(c) **Factoring of debts**
(d) **Securitised assets**
(e) **Loan transfers**

5.15 The application notes explain how to apply the standard to the particular transactions which they describe, and also contain specific disclosure requirements in relation to those transactions. The application notes are not exhaustive and they do not override the general principles of the standard itself, but they are regarded as authoritative insofar as they assist in interpreting it. The notes are discussed in more detail in the next section.

Basic principles

5.16 **FRS 5's fundamental principle is that the substance of an entity's transactions should be reflected in its accounts**. The key considerations are whether a transaction has given rise to new assets and liabilities, and whether it has changed any existing assets and liabilities. Definitions of assets and liabilities and rules for their recognition and derecognition are discussed below.

5.17 Sometimes there will be a series of connected transactions to be evaluated, not just a single transaction. It is necessary to identify and account for the substance of the series of transactions as a whole, rather than addressing each transaction individually.

Definitions of assets and liabilities

5.18 According to the standard:

> '**Assets** are rights or other access to future economic benefits controlled by an entity as a result of past transactions or events.'

> '**Liabilities** are an entity's obligations to transfer economic benefits as a result of past transactions or events.'

5.19 The standard goes on to say that identification of who has the risks relating to an asset will generally indicate who has the benefits and hence who has the asset. It also says that if an entity is in certain circumstances unable to avoid an outflow of benefits, this will provide evidence that it has a liability. The various risks and benefits relating to particular assets and liabilities are discussed in the application notes.

Recognition

5.20 The next key question is deciding **when** something which satisfies the definition of an asset or liability has to be recognised in the balance. sheet. The standard seeks to answer this by saying that:

> 'where a transaction results in an item that meets the definition of an asset or liability, that item should be recognised in the balance sheet if:

> (a) There is sufficient evidence of the existence of the item (including, where appropriate, evidence that a future inflow or outflow of benefit will occur), and

> (b) The item can be measured at a monetary amount with sufficient reliability.'

Derecognition

5.21 As the name suggests, derecognition is the opposite of recognition. It **concerns the question of when to remove from the balance sheet the assets and liabilities which have previously been recognised**. FRS 5 addresses this issue only in relation to assets, not liabilities, and its rules are designed to determine one of three outcomes, discussed below: complete derecognition, no derecognition, and the in-between case, partial derecognition.

5.22 **The issue of derecognition is perhaps one of the most common aspects of off balance sheet transactions; has an asset been sold or has it been used to secure borrowings?** The concept of partial derecognition is a new addition to FRS 5 and attempts to deal with the in-between situation of where sufficient benefits and risks have been transferred to warrant at least some derecognition of an asset.

Complete derecognition

5.23 **In the simplest case, where a transaction results in the transfer to another party of all the significant benefits and risks relating to an asset, the entire asset should cease to be recognised.** In this context, the word 'significant' is explained further: it should not be judged in relation to all the conceivable benefits and risks that could exist, but only in relation to those that are likely to occur in practice. This means that the importance of the risk retained must be assessed in relation to the magnitude of the total realistic risk which exists.

No derecognition

5.24 At the other end of the spectrum, **where a transaction results in no significant change to the benefits or to the risks relating to the asset in question, no sale can be recorded and the entire asset should continue to be recognised.** Retaining *either* the benefits or the risks is sufficient to keep the asset on the balance sheet. This means that the elimination of risk by financing the asset on a non-recourse basis will not remove it from the balance sheet; it would be necessary to dispose of the upside as well in order to justify recording a sale. (A further possible treatment, the special case of a 'linked presentation', is discussed below.)

5.25 The standard says that **any transaction that is 'in substance a financing' will not qualify for derecognition**; the item will therefore stay on the balance sheet, and the finance will be introduced as a liability.

Partial derecognition

5.26 As can be seen, the above criteria are relatively restrictive. The standard therefore goes on to deal with circumstances where, although not all significant benefits and risks have been transferred, the transaction is more than a mere financing and has transferred enough of the benefits and risks to warrant at least some derecognition of the asset. It addresses three such cases.

(a) **Where an asset has been subdivided**

Where an identifiable part of an asset is separated and sold off, with the remainder being retained, the asset should be split and a partial sale recorded. Examples include the sale of a proportionate part of a loan receivable, where all future receipts are shared equally between the parties, or the stripping of interest payments from the principal of a loan instrument.

(b) **Where an item is sold for less than its full life**

This exception arises where the seller retains a residual value risk by offering to buy the asset back at a predetermined price at a later stage in the asset's life. Such an arrangement is sometimes offered in relation to commercial vehicles, aircraft, and so on. The standard says that in such cases the original asset will have been replaced by a residual interest in the asset together with a liability for its obligation to pay the repurchase price.

(c) **Where an item is transferred for its full life but some risk or benefit is retained**

This may arise, for example, where a company gives a warranty or residual value guarantee in relation to the product being sold. Under the standard, this does not preclude the recording of the sale so long as the exposure under the warranty or guarantee can be assessed and provided for if necessary. Companies may also sometimes retain the possibility of an upward adjustment to the sale price of an asset based on its future performance, for example, when a business is sold subject to an earn-out clause, but again this should not preclude the recognition of the sale.

5.27 In all of these cases of partial disposals, the amount of the initial profit or loss may be uncertain. **FRS 5 says that the normal rules of prudence should be applied, but also that the uncertainty should be disclosed if it could have a material effect on the accounts.**

Linked presentation

5.28 The exposure draft, FRED 4, introduced the concept of a 'linked presentation' and this has been carried through into FRS 5. This requires **non-recourse finance** to be **shown on the**

face of the balance sheet as a deduction from the asset to which it relates (rather than in the liabilities section of the balance sheet), provided certain stringent criteria are met. This is really a question of how, rather than whether, to show the asset and liability in the balance sheet, so it is not the same as derecognition of these items, although there are some similarities in the result.

5.29 The standard says the linked presentation should be used when an asset is financed in such a way that:

(a) The finance will be repaid only from proceeds generated by the specific item it finances (or by transfer of the item itself) and there is no possibility whatsoever of a claim on the entity being established other than against funds generated by that item (or against the item itself).

(b) There is no provision whereby the entity may either keep the item on repayment of the finance or reacquire it at any time.

There are also several more specific conditions which elaborate on these principles.

Offset

5.30 FRS 5 makes it clear that **assets and liabilities which qualify for recognition should be accounted for individually, rather than netted off**. Offset is allowed by the standard only where the debit and credit balances are not really separate assets and liabilities, for example where there are amounts due to and from the same third party and there is a legal right of set-off. The key consideration is whether the entity can enforce a right of set-off so that there is no possibility of having to pay the creditor balance without recovering the debtor amount.

5.31 The detailed criteria which **permit offset** are set out in FRS 5:

(a) The **parties owe each other determinable monetary amounts**, denominated either in the same currency or in different but freely convertible currencies.

(b) The **reporting entity has the ability to insist on a net settlement**, which can be enforced in all situations of default by the other party.

(c) The **reporting entity's ability to insist on a net settlement is assured beyond doubt**. This means that the debit balance must be receivable no later than the credit balance requires to be paid, otherwise the entity could be required to pay the other party and later find that it was unable to obtain payment itself. It also means that the ability to insist on a net settlement would survive the insolvency of the other party (which may require detailed examination in group situations).

Consolidation of other entities

5.32 The Companies Act definition of a 'subsidiary undertaking' means that the consolidation of other entities is based largely on *de facto* control. However, FRS 5 takes the view that this is not conclusive in determining which entities are to be included in consolidated accounts. It envisages that there will be occasions where the need to give a true and fair view will require the inclusion of **'quasi subsidiaries'**. FRS 5 defines a quasi subsidiary in these terms.

KEY TERM

'A **quasi subsidiary** of a reporting entity is a company, trust, partnership or other vehicle that, though not fulfilling the definition of a subsidiary, is directly or indirectly controlled by the reporting entity and gives rise to benefits for that entity that are in substance no different from those that would arise were the vehicle a subsidiary.'

5.33 The **key feature of this definition is control, which means the ability to direct the vehicle's financial and operating policies with a view to gaining economic benefit from its activities.** Control is also indicated by the ability to prevent others from exercising those policies or from enjoying the benefits of the vehicle's net assets. A 'deadlock' 50:50 joint venture will still be off balance sheet for both parties, provided the two parties concerned are genuine equals in terms of both their ability to control the venture and their interests in its underlying assets.

5.34 FRS 5 requires that when quasi subsidiaries are included in consolidated accounts, the fact of their inclusion should be disclosed, together with a summary of their own financial statements.

Disclosure

5.35 FRS 5 has a general requirement to **disclose transactions in sufficient detail to enable the reader to understand their commercial effect,** whether or not they have given rise to the recognition of assets and liabilities. This means that where transactions or schemes give rise to assets and liabilities which are *not* recognised in the accounts, disclosure of their nature and effects still has to be considered in order to ensure that the accounts give a true and fair view.

5.36 A second general principle is that an **explanation** should be given **where there are any assets or liabilities whose nature is different from that which the reader might expect** of assets or liabilities appearing in the accounts under that description. The standard also calls for specific disclosures in relation to the use of the linked presentation, the inclusion of quasi subsidiaries in the accounts, and the various transactions dealt with in the application notes.

Common forms of off balance sheet finance

5.37 The application notes attached to FRS 5 are intended to clarify and develop the methods of applying the proposed standard to the particular transactions which they describe and to provide guidance on how to interpret it in relation to other similar transactions. These transactions are the more common types.

Consignment stock

5.38 Consignment stock is an arrangement where stock is **held by one party** (say a distributor) but is **owned by another party** (for example a manufacturer or a finance company). Consignment stock is common in the motor trade and is similar to goods sold on a 'sale or return' basis.

5.39 **To identify the correct treatment, it is necessary to identify the point at which the distributor acquired the benefits of the asset** (the stock) **rather than the point at which**

legal title was acquired. If the manufacturer has the right to require the return of the stock, and if that right is likely to be exercised, then the stock is not an asset of the dealer. If the dealer is rarely required to return the stock, then this part of the transaction will have little commercial effect in practice and should be ignored for accounting purposes. The potential liability would need to be disclosed in the accounts.

Sale and leaseback transactions

5.40   These are arrangements under which the company sells an asset to another person on terms that allow the company to repurchase the assets in certain circumstances. **The key question is whether the transaction is a straightforward sale, or whether it is, in effect, a secured loan.** It is necessary to look at the arrangement to determine who has the rights to the economic benefits that the asset generates, and the terms on which the asset is to be repurchased.

5.41   If the seller has the right to the benefits of the use of the asset, and the repurchase terms are such that the repurchase is likely to take place, the transaction should be accounted for as a loan.

Factoring of debts

5.42   Where debts are factored, the original creditor sells the debts to the factor. The sales price may be fixed at the outset or may be adjusted later. It is also common for the factor to offer a credit facility that allows the seller to draw upon a proportion of the amounts owed.

5.43   In order to determine the correct accounting treatment it is **necessary to consider whether the benefit of the debts has been passed on to the factor, or whether the factor is, in effect, providing a loan on the security of the debtors.** If the seller has to pay interest on the difference between the amounts advanced to him and the amounts that the factor has received, and if the seller bears the risks of non-payment by the debtor, then the indications would be that the transaction is, in effect, a loan. Depending on the circumstances, either a linked presentation or separate presentation may be appropriate.

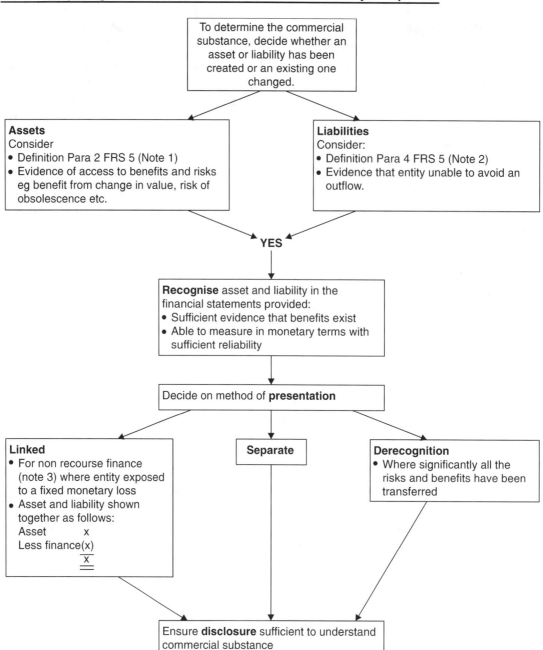

To determine the commercial substance, decide whether an asset or liability has been created or an existing one changed.

Assets
Consider
• Definition Para 2 FRS 5 (Note 1)
• Evidence of access to benefits and risks eg benefit from change in value, risk of obsolescence etc.

Liabilities
Consider:
• Definition Para 4 FRS 5 (Note 2)
• Evidence that entity unable to avoid an outflow.

YES

Recognise asset and liability in the financial statements provided:
• Sufficient evidence that benefits exist
• Able to measure in monetary terms with sufficient reliability

Decide on method of **presentation**

Linked
• For non recourse finance (note 3) where entity exposed to a fixed monetary loss
• Asset and liability shown together as follows:
Asset   x
Less finance(x)
              X̲

Separate

Derecognition
• Where significantly all the risks and benefits have been transferred

Ensure **disclosure** sufficient to understand commercial substance

Securitised assets

5.44   Securitisation is **very common in the financial services industry,** and the **assets** that are **most commonly securitised are mortgages and credit card accounts**, although hire purchase loans, trade debts and even property and stocks are sometimes securitised. Blocks of assets are thus financed, rather than the company's general business.

5.45   The **normal procedure is for the assets to be transferred by the person who held them (the originator) to a special purpose company (the issuer) in exchange for cash**. The issuer will use the proceeds of an issue of debentures or loan notes to pay for the assets. The shares in the issuer are usually held by a third party so that it does not need to be consolidated. The issuer will usually have a very small share capital, and so most of the risk will be borne by the people who lent it the money through the debentures to pay for the assets. For this reason there is usually some form of insurance taken out on the assets to give some security for the lenders.

5.46   **If the originator has retained significant benefits or risks** (say in the event of non-payment) **then the assets should continue to be shown on the originator's balance sheet and the money it received should be shown as a loan creditor.** If the requirements for linked presentation are satisfied, then the two items may be disclosed together on the balance sheet with the loan being subtracted from the asset. If these requirements are not met, then the asset and the liability should be shown under the appropriate headings.

5.47   **Derecognition is only appropriate where the originator has not retained any significant benefits**. In determining this it is necessary to consider whether the originator has access to the benefits of the securitised assets or exposure to their inherent risks, and whether the originator has a liability to repay the proceeds of the debenture or loan note issue. If derecognition is appropriate, then neither the asset nor the loan is shown on the originator's balance sheet.

Loan transfers

5.48   These are arrangements where a loan is transferred to a transferee from an original lender. This will usually be done by the assignment of rights and obligations by the lender, or the creation of a new agreement between the borrower and the transferee. The **same principles apply to loan transfers as apply to debt factoring and securitised assets**.

5.49   The diagram on the previous page will serve as a useful summary.

Chapter roundup

- SSAP 17 amplifies the CA 1985 requirement to take account of **post balance sheet** liabilities and losses.

    - It distinguishes between adjusting and non-adjusting events and gives examples.

    - It also requires disclosure of window dressing transactions.

    - Where an otherwise non-adjusting event indicates that the going concern concept is no longer appropriate, then the accounts may have to be restated on a break-up basis.

    - You should be able to define and discuss all these terms and apply them to practical examples.

- Under FRS 12, a **provision** should be recognised

    - When an entity has a **present obligation**, legal or constructive
    - It is probable that a **transfer of economic benefits** will be required to settle it
    - A **reliable estimate** can be made of its amount

- An entity should not recognise a contingent asset or liability, but they should be disclosed.

- Transactions must be accounted for according to their **substance, not** just their legal **form.**

- There are a number of '**creative accounting**' techniques, the purpose of which is to manipulate figures for a desired result.

- The subject of **off balance sheet finance** is complex and difficult to understand. In practice, off balance sheet finance schemes are often very sophisticated and they are beyond the range of this syllabus.

- Make sure that you have memorised the definitions for **assets and liabilities** and the **criteria** for their **recognition** and **derecognition** given in FRS 5 *Reporting the substance of transactions.*

- You also need to understand the methods of presentation described in FRS 5, particularly **offset** and **linked presentation**.

Quick quiz

1   Define 'post balance sheet events'.

2   A property is valued and a permanent diminution in value is identified.

Adjusting event ☐

Non-adjusting event ☐

3   Stocks are lost in a fire.

Adjusting event ☐

Non-adjusting event ☐

4   A provision is a .... of .... timing or amount.

5   A programme is undertaken by management which converts the previously wholly owned chain of restaurants they ran into franchises. Is this restructuring?

6   Define contingent asset and contingent liability.

7   What are the statutory disclosure requirements in respect of reserves?

8   What is meant by 'substance over form'?

9   How are assets and liabilities defined in the *Statement of Principles*?

10   Describe 'linked presentation' and 'offset' as set out in FRS 5.

11   What topics does FRS 5 discuss in the application notes?

Answers to quick quiz

1   Those events unfavourable and favourable which occur between the balance sheet date and the date of approval. (see knowledge b/f)

2   Adjusting.

3   Non-adjusting.

4   Liability of uncertain timing or amount. (1.7)

5   Yes. The manner in which the business is conducted has changed. (1.25 – 1.28)

6   Refer to paragraphs 1.32 and 1.34 respectively

7   Refer to paragraphs 3.2 and 3.3

8   Transactions should be accounted for in accordance with their substance and financial reality, not their legal form (4.1)

9   Refer to paragraph 5.8

10   Refer to paragraphs 5.28 to 5.31

11   Consignment stock, sale and leaseback transactions, factoring of debts, securities assets and loan transfers.

Now try the question below from the Exam Question Bank

Number	Level	Marks	Time
12	Introductory	n/a	10 mins

BPP PUBLISHING

Chapter 12

SHARE CAPITAL AND RESERVES; FINANCIAL INSTRUMENTS

Topic list	Syllabus reference
1 Called up share capital and FRS 4 *Capital instruments*	3(a)
2 FRS 13 *Derivatives and other financial instruments: disclosures*	3(a)

Introduction

FRS 4 *Capital instruments* covers the accounting for the instruments which a business uses to raise finance. The FRS 5 criteria of substance over form is used in this standard to deal with the issue of debt and equity.

For FRS 13 *Derivatives and other financial instruments* only a general outline of what it covers including what a derivative is and its associated risks, is required.

Study guide

- Explain the need for an accounting standard on Capital Instruments (FRS 4).

- Distinguish between debt and share capital.

- Apply the requirements of FRS 4 to the issue and finance costs of:

    - equity and preference shares
    - debt instruments with no conversion rights, and
    - convertible debt.

Exam guide

Concentrate on FRS 4, FRS 13 is less important.

1   CALLED UP SHARE CAPITAL AND FRS 4 CAPITAL INSTRUMENTS

Pilot paper

1.1   The amount of **allotted share capital and** the amount of **called up share capital** which has been paid up must be **shown separately**.

1.2   The following information must be given by note with respect to a company's share capital:

(a)   The authorised share capital.

(b)   Where shares of more than one class have been allotted, the number and aggregate nominal value of shares of each class allotted.

1.3   In the case of any part of the allotted share capital that consists of **redeemable shares**, the **following information must be given**:

   (a)   The earliest and latest **dates** on which the company has power to redeem those shares.

   (b)   Whether the shares **must be redeemed** in any event **or** are liable to be redeemed **at the option of the company.**

   (c)   Whether any (and if so, what) **premium** is payable on redemption.

1.4   **If** the company has **allotted** any shares **during the financial year**, the **following information must be given:**

   (a)   The **reason** for making the allotment.

   (b)   The **classes** of shares allotted.

   (c)   As respects each class of shares, the **number** allotted, their **aggregate nominal value**, and the **consideration received by** the company for the allotment.

FRS 4 capital instruments

1.5   The ASB issued FRS 4 *Capital instruments* in December 1993.

> **KEY TERM**
>
> **Capital instruments** are instruments which are issued to raise finance. There are many different types. Common ones include bank loans, corporate bonds, convertible debt, ordinary shares, preference shares and options and warrants to subscribe for shares.

1.6   FRS 4 addresses how issuers should account for capital instruments. The standard covers all capital instruments except leases, options or warrants granted under employee share schemes and equity shares issues in a business combination accounted for as a merger.

1.7   The standard **applies to all financial statements** intended to give a true and fair view of a reporting entity's financial position and profit or loss (or income and expenditure). No exemptions have been given on the grounds of size, ownership or industry. Comparative figures may require restatement where the effect on prior years is material.

Distinguishing between debt and equity

1.8   One of the key users' ratios is the gearing ratio, ie the measure of the proportion of debt to equity. In order for this measure to be meaningful there must be consistency in the allocation of financial instruments between these two categories.

1.9   **Capital instruments should be included in one of three categories in the balance sheet: liabilities, shareholders' funds or minority interests.** The rules for distinguishing between debt and equity are based on the accounting model being developed in the ASB's *Statement of Principles*. They require:

   (a)   A company's **shares** to remain **in shareholders' funds**.

   (b)   Capital instruments to be reported as **liabilities if they contain an** 'obligation to transfer economic benefits'.

(c) Capital instruments to be reported as **shareholders' funds if they do not contain an 'obligation to transfer economic benefits'**.

> ### KEY TERM
>
> An 'obligation to transfer economic benefits' means any requirement to make cash payments or transfer other kinds of property even if the requirement is only contingent.

1.10 Some capital instruments have **features of both debt and equity**. The common example of such **'hybrid' instruments** is convertible debt, which is economically equivalent to conventional debt plus a warrant to acquire shares in the future.

1.11 If the individual components of such instruments are physically separable, the FRS requires that they should be accounted for separately. Where the components are inseparable, the instrument should be accounted for as a single instrument. Thus, for example, a convertible bond should not be notionally 'split' into debt and an option to acquire shares.

1.12 The rule for determining whether a capital instrument is a liability is widely drawn. Convertible debt instruments are liabilities.

1.13 The effect of applying these criteria is that **the classification of capital instruments will be consistent with their substance, rather than their legal form**.

Disclosure: general

1.14 A fundamental part of FRS 4's approach on hybrid instruments and other less conventional forms of finance is to require issuers to make **considerable disclosure** about them.

1.15 In order to distinguish shares with debt characteristics from other share capital, the FRS contains a definition of a **'non-equity' shares**. Broadly speaking, these are shares that **contain preferential rights to participate in the company's profits or assets** (for example preference shares) or are redeemable.

1.16 The main new disclosure requirement is the analysis of the following items in the balance sheet.

Item	Analysed between	
Shareholders' funds	Equity interests	Non-equity interests
Minority interests in subsidiaries	Equity interests in subsidiaries	Non-equity interests in subsidiaries
Liabilities	Convertible liabilities	Non-convertible liabilities

1.17 Such analysis is usually to be given on the face of the balance sheet. Dividends to shareholders and the minority interests' share of the results for the year should be analysed similarly in the profit and loss account. Considerable disclosure is also required about the rights and terms of each class of non-equity share and convertible debt.

1.18 The overall effect is to provide the users of financial statements with quite a **detailed analysis of shareholders' funds** showing the amounts pertaining to each separate class of share and a summary of the rights of the holders.

Question 1

A company issues a convertible instrument which does not pay a coupon and is mandatorily convertible into shares of the issuer after 3 years. The holder is compensated through the conversion rights attached to the instrument. Although it is mandatorily convertible, the holders will rank as creditors in the event of insolvency of the issuer.

How should the instrument be classified?

Answer

Under FRS 4, this instrument should be classified in shareholders' funds as there is no 'obligation to transfer economic benefits'. Hence, this will be accounted for like a 'fully-paid' warrant. Its impact will be to dilute shareholders' interests in the future.

(Source: *Capital Instruments: A Guide to FRS 4, Ernst & Young*)

Accounting for debt instruments

1.19 **Debt should be recorded in the balance sheet at the fair value of the consideration received less costs incurred directly in connection with the issue of the instrument.** Such issue costs are narrowly defined and sometimes have to be written off immediately, but otherwise are spread over the life of the debt.

1.20 **The carrying amount of debt should be increased by the finance cost** in respect of the reporting period **and reduced by payments made in respect of the debt** in that period.

KEY TERM

The **finance cost** of debt is the difference between the total payments required to be made and the initial carrying value of the debt (that is the interest cost or the dividends plus any premium payable on redemption or other payments).

1.21 This **should be charged to the profit and loss account over the term of the instrument at a constant rate of interest on the outstanding amount of the debt**. The effective rate of interest implicit in the debt instrument will be required for that purpose.

1.22 Note that under s 130 CA 1985 discounts on the issue of debentures may be taken against the share premium account. This would be shown as a transfer in reserves.

Question 2

On 1 January 20X4, an entity issued a fixed rate debt instrument and received £900,000. Interest is payable annually in arrears at a rate of 5% on the stated principal amount of £1,000,000. The instrument has a 5 year term and the stated principal will be repaid at maturity. Issue costs of £50,000 were incurred.

State the disclosure of the instrument in the profit and loss account and the balance sheet for each year of the term.

Answer

The net proceeds of this issue are £850,000. The finance cost of this instrument is £400,000, being the difference between the total future payments (ie £1,250,000, see column (a) below) and the net proceeds from the issue.

The effective rate of interest implicit in this instrument is the discount rate which equates the present value of future cash flows to the net proceeds received. This is calculated as 8.84% by applying the NPV formula (use interpolation).

The interest charge for the year (column (b) below) is calculated by applying this rate to the carrying value of the debt in the balance sheet during the year.

	(a)	(b)	(c)
			Carrying value
	Cash	Interest	in the balance
	flows	charge	sheet
	£'000	£'000	£'000
At January 20X4	(850)		850.0
At 31 December 20X4	50	75.1	875.1
At 31 December 20X5	50	77.4	902.5
At 31 December 20X6	50	79.8	932.3
At 31 December 20X7	50	82.4	964.7
At 31 December 20X8	1,050	85.3	-
Total	400	400.0	

(Source: *Capital Instruments: A Guide to FRS 4*, Ernst & Young)

1.23 **If debt is repurchased or settled before its maturity, any gains or losses should be recognised immediately** in the profit and loss account.

1.24 In comparison with the Companies Act requirements, a more detailed analysis of maturity of debt is needed as shown below. This should be derived by reference to the earliest date on which the lender could require repayment. The FRS requires committed facilities which satisfy strict conditions to be considered when determining such dates. These conditions will affect some existing practices - for example, commercial paper can no longer be shown as long-term debt.

Convertible debt

1.25 FRS 4 requires that **conversion of debt should not be anticipated** but rather reported in liabilities with the finance cost calculated on the assumption that the debt will never be converted. When the debt is converted, the amount of consideration recognised in respect of shares should be the amount of the liability for the debt at the date of conversion.

Disclosure: debt

1.26 (a) **Maturity of debt**. The financial statements or notes should include an analysis of the maturity of debt showing amount falling due:

(i)   In one year or less, or on demand.
(ii) Between one and two years.
(iii) Between two and five years.

(iv)   In five years or more.

The maturity of the debt should be determined by reference to the earliest date on which the lender can demand repayment.

(b) **Convertible debt should be stated separately** from other liabilities. Details given must include:

(i)   The date of redemption.
(ii)   The amount payable on redemption.
(iii) The number and class of shares into which the debt may be converted.
(iv)   The period in which the conversion may take place.
(v)   Whether conversion is at the option of the issuer or holder.

Repurchase of own debt

1.27   **Any profits or losses arising on the repurchase of debt should be recognised in the year of repurchase.**

Accounting for shares

1.28   **Share issues should be recorded at the fair value of the consideration received less issue costs.** Issue costs should be written off directly to reserves and should not be reported in the statement of total recognised gains and losses, ie those relating directly to the issue of the instrument should be accounted for as a reduction in the proceeds of a capital instrument.

Question 3

A company issues 100 £1 ordinary shares at par. Issue costs of £2 are incurred.

State how this transaction should be recorded and disclosed.

Answer

If there is a share premium account in existence, the share issue may be recorded by increasing share capital by £100 and setting off the issue costs against share premium account. In the analysis of total shareholders' funds, the equity interests will have increased by £98.

If there is no share premium account, share capital will be increased by £100 but the issue costs would be deducted from another reserve (usually profit and loss account reserve) subject to the provisions of the company's articles. Prior to FRS 4, companies in this situation had to charge the issue costs to the profit and loss account. The equity interest within shareholders' funds also increases by £98 in this case.

(Source: *Capital Instruments: A Guide to FRS 4*, Ernst & Young)

1.29   As stated above, under FRS 4 **the balance sheet should show the amount of shareholders' funds attributable to equity interests and the amount attributable to non-equity interests.**

1.30   The **finance cost of non-equity** shares should be **calculated on the same basis as for debt instruments. Dividends in respect of non-equity shares** have to be accounted for **on an accruals basis.** The only exception is where there are insufficient distributable profits and the dividend rights are non-cumulative. Arrears of preference dividends must therefore be provided for rather than simply disclosed.

Warrants

1.31 **Warrants should be included in shareholders' funds at the net proceeds of the issue**. If the warrant lapses unexercised, the amount paid for it becomes a gain and should be taken to the statement of total recognised gains and losses. If the warrant is exercised, the shares issued should be recorded at the aggregate of the net proceeds received when the warrant was issued and the fair value of the consideration received on exercise less issue costs of the shares.

Scrip dividends

1.32 If shares are issued in lieu of dividends, the value of the shares issued, being equal to the value of the dividend payable, should be reflected in the P & L account as an **appropriation of profit**.

Disclosure: shares

1.33 These disclosures should be made.

    (a) Analysis of shares between **equity and non-equity** interests.

    (b) The **rights** of each class of shares should be **summarised** detailing:

        (i) The rights to **dividends**.

        (ii) The dates at which shares are **redeemable** and the amounts payable in respect of redemption.

        (iii) Their **priority and amounts receivable on a winding up**.

        (iv) Their **voting rights**.

    (c) Where warrants or convertible debt are in issue that may require the company to issue shares of a class not currently in issue the details in (b) above must be given.

    (d) The **aggregate dividends** for each class of shares should be disclosed.

Minority interests

1.34 In consolidated financial statements, shares of subsidiary companies which are not owned by the group are accounted for as minority interests. There is one exception to this rule. In some situations (for example where the parent or another group company has guaranteed their dividends or redemption), such shares become liabilities from the perspective of the group and therefore have to be reported as such on consolidation.

> ### Exam focus point
>
> FRS 4 is technically extremely complex. It is unlikely that you would be asked to perform any very difficult calculations, and you should therefore concentrate on the reasons why FRS 4 was considered necessary. You should be able to discuss the main provisions of the standard.

1.35 Generally speaking, FRS 4 was issued to stop companies treating debt as equity and vice versa, on legal form rather than the substance of the transactions. It also forces companies to recognise finance costs.

2 FRS 13 DERIVATIVES AND OTHER FINANCIAL INSTRUMENTS: DISCLOSURES

Objectives

2.1 FRS 13 appeared in September 1998. It's objective of FRS 13 is to ensure that reporting entities falling within its scope provide in their financial statements disclosure necessary to enable users to assess:

(a) The **risk profile** of the entity for each of the main risks that arise in connection with financial instruments, commodity contracts with similar characteristics.

(b) The **significance** of such instruments and contracts, regardless of whether they are on balance sheet (recognised) or off balance sheet (unrecognised), to an entity's reported financial position, performance and cash flows.

Scope

2.2 FRS 13 applies to an entity that:

(a) Has any of its capital instruments **listed** or **publicly traded** on a stock exchange or market.

(b) Prepares financial statements that are intended to give a true and fair view of the entity's financial position and profit or loss (or income and expenditure) for a period.

2.3 The FRS is in three parts:

(a) **Reporting entities other than financial institutions** and financial institution groups
(b) **Banks,** banking groups and similar institutions
(c) **Other financial institutions** and financial institution groups

We will concentrate on Part (a) as this is more relevant to your syllabus.

2.4 There are various **exclusions** encompassing all interests in group companies (except where held exclusively for resale) pensions, share options, obligations under operating leases (see SSAP 21), insurance contracts, equity shares and warrants and options on equity shares issued by the entity.

Definitions

2.5 The following important definitions are given in FRS 13 (among others).

> **KEY TERMS**
> - **Borrowings:** an entity's borrowings are its debt (as defined in FRS 4) together with its obligations under finance leases (as defined in SSAP 21).
> - **Capital instruments:** defined as in FRS 4.
> - **Derivative financial instrument:** a financial instrument that derives its value from the price or rate of some underlying item.
> - **Equity instrument:** any instrument that evidences an ownership interest in an entity, ie a residual interest in the assets of the entity after deducting all of its liabilities.
> - **Fair value:** The amount at which an asset or liability could be exchanged in an arm's length transaction between informed and willing parties, other than in a forced or liquidation sale.

- **Financial asset**: any asset that is:
  - (a) Cash.
  - (b) A contractual right to receive cash or another financial asset from another entity.
  - (c) A contractual right to exchange financial instruments with another entity under conditions that are potentially favourable.
  - (d) An equity instrument of another entity.
- **Financial instrument**: a financial instrument is any contract that gives rise to both a financial asset of one entity and a financial liability or equity instrument of another entity.
- **Financial liability**: any liability that is a contractual obligation:
  - (a) To deliver cash or another financial asset to another entity.
  - (b) To exchange financial instruments with another entity under conditions that are potentially unfavourable.
- **Functional currency**: the currency of the primary economic environment in which an entity operates and generates net cash flows.
- **Short term debtors and creditors**: Financial assets and liabilities which meet all the following criteria.
  - (a) They would be included under one of the following balance sheet headings if the entity was preparing its financial statements in accordance with Schedule 4 to the Companies Act 1985:
    - (i) Debtors.
    - (ii) Prepayments and accrued income.
    - (iii) Creditors: amounts falling due within one year, other than items that would be included under the 'debenture loans' and 'bank loans and overdrafts' subheadings.
    - (iv) Provisions for liabilities and charges.
    - (v) Accruals and deferred income.
  - (b) They mature or become payable within 12 months of the balance sheet date.
  - (c) They are not a derivative financial instrument.
- **Trading in financial assets and financial liabilities**: Buying, selling, issuing or holding financial assets and financial liabilities in order to take advantage of short-term changes in market prices or rates or, in the case of financial institutions and financial institution groups, in order to facilitate customer transactions.

(FRS 13)

Instruments to be dealt with in the disclosures

2.6 The FRS applies to all financial assets and financial liabilities, except those mentioned in Paragraph 2.4 above. Note also:

(a) Short-term debtors and creditors - **either all** of those should be included in the disclosures **or none of these**.

(b) **All non-equity** shares should be dealt with in the disclosures in the same way as financial liabilities except they should be **disclosed separately**.

Types of risks arising from financial instruments

2.7 This FRS is all about the disclosure of risk, so the different aspects of risk are analysed in some depth.

2.8 The two most familiar risks arising from financial instruments are credit risk and liquidity risk.

> **KEY TERMS**
>
> • **Credit risk**: the possibility that a loss may occur from the failure of another party to perform according to the terms of a contract.
> • **Liquidity risk** (also referred to as funding risk): the risk that an entity will encounter difficulty in realising assets or otherwise raising funds to meet commitments associated with financial instruments.
>
> *(FRS 13)*

2.9 These are **familiar** and they tend to be the types of risk disclosed in financial statements, eg debtors' provisions indicate credit risk; borrowing conditions, current ratio and quick ratio indicate liquidity risk.

2.10 Financial instruments, however, entail two other important types of risk: **cash flow risk** and **market price risk**.

> **KEY TERMS**
>
> • **Cash flow risk**: the risk that future cash flows generated by a monetary financial instrument will fluctuate in amount.
> • **Market price risk**: the possibility that future changes in market prices may change the value, or the burden, of a financial instrument.
>
> *(FRS 13)*

2.11 The main components of **market price risk** likely to affect most entities are also defined.

> **KEY TERMS**
>
> • **Interest rate risk**: the risk that the value of a financial instrument will fluctuate because of changes in market interest rates.
>
> • **Currency risk**: the risk that the value of a financial instrument will fluctuate because of changes in foreign exchange rates.
>
> • **Other market price risk**: the risk that the value of a financial instrument will fluctuate as a result of changes in market prices caused by factors other than interest rates or currencies. This category includes risk stemming from commodity prices and share prices.
>
> *(FRS 13)*

2.12 Until now information on these types of risk has been 'scant and often lacking in focus'. The fact that market price risk and cash flow risk are **diametrically opposed** is rarely mentioned; but the relationship between them has a significant impact on the risk profile. This can be illustrated as follows.

BPP PUBLISHING

Financial instrument	Market price risk	Cash flow risk
Fixed rate interest-earning asset	Exposure	No exposure
Floating rate interest-earning asset	No exposure	Exposure

2.13 Depending on **management's attitude** to these particular risks, transactions may be undertaken to reduce one of the risks at the expense of increasing the other. Consequently, the choice of which risk it seeks to reduce will have an important bearing on the entity's financial position, financial results and cash flows.

Summary of requirements

2.14 FRS 13 requires entities that have any of their capital instruments listed or publicly traded on a domestic or foreign stock market, and all other banks and insurance companies, to disclose in their financial statements certain information, including information about **risk** on the derivatives and other financial instruments that they hold or have issued. This is to enable users to understand the major aspects of the risk profile that might affect the entity's performance and financial condition and how this risk profile is being managed.

2.15 The FRS requires **narrative disclosures** that put into context the entity's chosen risk profile. These narrative disclosures set the scene for, and are supplemented by, a range of **numerical disclosures** that show how the entity's objectives and policies were implemented in the period and provide supplementary quantitative information for evaluating significant or potentially significant exposures. Together, these disclosures will provide a broad overview of the financial instruments held or issued and of the risk position created by them, focusing on those risks and instruments that are of greatest significance.

2.16 The **extent** of information disclosed will vary according to the nature of an entity's activities and the relative importance and complexity of transactions involving financial instruments. The vast majority of companies are not involved in complex transactions. The FRS also encourages an appropriate degree of **aggregation** to avoid excessively detailed disclosures.

Exam focus point

The examiner expects a background knowledge only. You need to know what a derivative is, the nature of the risks derivatives have and the disclosure required.

Question 4

Why do you think FRS 13 requires disclosure of the following?

(a) The maturity profile of the carrying amount of financial liabilities

(b) The maturity profile of undrawn committed borrowing facilities

(c) The carrying amount of financial liabilities analysed to show those liabilities at fixed interest rates and those at floating rates

Answer

(a) This will tell us about patterns of cash flow in the foreseeable future - will we have to pay a big loan off soon; how great is our exposure to debt?

(b) An example of 'undrawn committed borrowing facilities' might be an overdraft facility whose limit is, say, three times our actual overdraft. Such a facility provides a **cushion** against other risks, and gives us flexibility, or, in the words of the *Statement of Principles* 'financial adaptability'.

(c) Again, this is about risk - a floating interest rate liability will be more risky than a fixed rate one, although this risk can go in our favour.

Criticisms of FRS 13

2.17 As a disclosure standard applying only to quoted companies, banks and similar institutions, FRS 13 would not appear to present too many implementation problems. However, some criticisms have been voiced about the detail of the disclosures.

(a) Not all companies will have systems which enable data on hedging to be easily collected.

(b) The requirement to fair-value financial assets and liabilities will involve extra time and costs.

(c) Not all the disclosures are particularly meaningful.

2.18 Section summary

Concentrate on getting an overall picture of the FRS 13 disclosures.

- **Definitions**: financial instruments, derivatives, financial assets/liabilities
- **Risk**: understand market price risk and cash flow risk and their relationship
- **Disclosure**: a background knowledge of the disclosure requirements.

Chapter roundup

- FRS 4 *Capital instruments* is a complex standard. It has been issued to halt abuses in the accounting for **debt and equity**.

- **Disclosure matters** relating to derivatives have already been developed in **FRS 13**. You should understand the major definitions and the different types of risk.

Quick quiz

1 What information must be disclosed in relation to a company's share capital?

2 How should debt and equity be distinguished under FRS 4?

3 How should hybrid instruments be disclosed according to FRS 4?

4 How should the finance costs of debt be allocated under FRS 4?

5 What are the objectives of FRS 13?

6 Define a derivative financial instrument.

7 Credit risk and liquidity risk are associated particularly with financial instruments.

   True ☐

   False ☐

8 .... disclosure and .... disclosure are required by FRS 13.

Answers to quick quiz

1   Authorised share capital and the number and aggregate value of each class of share. (see para 1.2)

2   Refer to paragraph 1.9

3   Refer to paragraphs 1.10 to 1.18

4   **The carrying amount of debt should be increased by the finance cost** in respect of the reporting period **and reduced by payments made in respect of the debt** in that period. (1.20)

5   To enable users to assess the risk profile of financial instruments and significance they have. (2.1)

6   A financial instrument which derives its value from the price or rate of same underlying item. (2.5)

7   True. (2.8)

8   Narrative and numerical. (2.15)

Now try the question below from the Exam Question Bank

Number	Level	Marks	Time
13	Full exam	25	45 mins

Chapter 13

DISTRIBUTABLE PROFITS AND CAPITAL TRANSACTIONS

Topic list	Syllabus reference
1 Revenue recognition	1(a)
2 Distributable profits	3(a)
3 Redemption of shares	3(a)

Introduction

The topics in this chapter are relevant to all types of accounting transactions, providing a theoretical framework for the topics already covered and for accounting in general.

This chapter also leads on to the legal aspects of financial reporting in the next two chapters. A great deal of the legislation governing distributions and capital transactions is concerned with protection of creditors; the aim is to prevent companies favouring shareholders over creditors.

Study guide

- Outline the principles of the timing of revenue recognition.

- Explain the role of the concept of substance over form in relation to recognising sales revenue.

- Explain and define realised profits.

- Discuss the various points in the production and sales cycle where it may, depending on circumstances, be appropriate to recognise gains and losses - give examples of this.

- Explain and apply the general requirements to purchase or redeem shares.

- Apply the requirements that allow private companies to redeem shares out of capital.

- Discuss the advantages of companies being able to redeem shares.

- Define and discuss the Companies Acts rules relating to profits available for distribution.

- Calculate the profits available for distribution of public and private companies.

Exam guide

Revenue recognition is a particularly important area. It is fairly straightforward especially if you take time to relate the concepts to real life situations as you work through the material

1 REVENUE RECOGNITION

Pilot paper

1.1 **Accrual accounting is based on the matching of costs with the revenue they generate.** It is crucially important under this convention that we can establish the point at which revenue may be recognised so that the correct treatment can be applied to the related costs. For example, the costs of producing an item of finished goods should be carried as an asset in the balance sheet until such time as it is sold; they should then be written off as a charge to the trading account. Which of these two treatments should be applied cannot be decided until it is clear at what moment the sale of the item takes place.

1.2 The decision has a direct impact on profit since under the prudence concept it would be unacceptable to recognise the profit on sale until a sale had taken place in accordance with the criteria of revenue recognition.

Point of sale

1.3 **Revenue is generally recognised as earned at the point of sale, because at that point four criteria will generally have been met.**

(a) The product or service has been provided to the buyer.

(b) The buyer has recognised his liability to pay for the goods or services provided. The converse of this is that the seller has recognised that ownership of goods has passed from himself to the buyer.

(c) The buyer has indicated his willingness to hand over cash or other assets in settlement of his liability.

(d) The monetary value of the goods or services has been established.

1.4 At earlier points in the business cycle there will not in general be firm evidence that the above criteria will be met. Until work on a product is complete, there is a risk that some flaw in the manufacturing process will necessitate its writing off; even when the product is complete there is no guarantee that it will find a buyer.

1.5 At later points in the business cycle, for example when cash is received for the sale, the recognition of revenue may occur in a period later than that in which the related costs were charged. Revenue recognition would then depend on fortuitous circumstances, such as the cash flow of a company's debtors, and might fluctuate misleadingly from one period to another.

Times other than point of sale

1.6 However, **occasionally revenue is recognised at other times** than at the completion of a sale.

(a) **Recognition of profit on long-term contract work in progress.** Under SSAP 9 *Stocks and long-term contracts*, credit is taken in the profit and loss account for 'that part of the total profit currently estimated to arise over the duration of the contract which fairly reflects the profit attributable to that part of the work performed at the accounting date'.

    (i)   Owing to the length of time taken to complete such contracts, to defer taking profit into account until completion may result in the profit and loss account reflecting not so much a fair view of the activity of the company during the year but rather the results relating to contracts which have been completed by the year end.

    (ii)   Revenue in this case is recognised when production on, say, a section of the total contract is complete, even though no sale can be made until the whole is complete.

(b)   **Sale on hire purchase.** Title to goods provided on hire purchase terms does not pass until the last payment is made, at which point the sale is complete.

    (i)   To defer the recognition of revenue until that point, however, would be to distort the nature of the revenue earned.

    (ii)   The profits of an HP retailer in effect represent the interest charged on finance provided and such interest arises over the course of the HP agreement rather than at its completion. Revenue in this case is recognised when each instalment of cash is received.

1.7   **The determination of whether revenue should be recognised is based partly on the accruals concept, but also on the often conflicting accounting concept of prudence.** Under the prudence concept revenue and profits are not anticipated and anticipated losses are provided for as soon as they are foreseen (preventing costs being deferred if there is doubt as to their recoverability).

1.8   The question of revenue recognition is obviously closely associated with the definition of realised profits, and this is discussed in the next section.

1.9   **In general terms, under the historical cost system, the following general practice has developed.**

(a)   Revenue from the sale of goods is recognised on the date of delivery to the customer.

(b)   Revenue from services is recognised when the services have been performed and are billable.

(c)   Revenue derived from letting others use the resources of the businesses (for example royalty income, rent and interest) is recognised either as the resources are used or on a time basis.

(d)   Revenue from the sale of assets (other than products of the business) is recognised at the date of the sale.

Problem areas

1.10   The problem with revenue recognition is that there are some areas where accounting standards have not (yet) been issued which deal with all types of transaction. We will not go into too much detail here about these situations, but you should be aware of them, and a list is given below (the list is not comprehensive).

(a)   **Receipt of initial fees,** at the beginning of a service, may not have been 'earned' and it is often difficult to determine what they represent.

(b) **Franchise fees** can be incurred in complex franchise agreements and no standard form of agreement has allowed an accepted accounting practice to develop. Each agreement must be dealt with on its own merits.

(c) **Advance royalty or licence receipts** would normally be dealt with as deferred income and released to the profit and loss account when earned under the agreement. In some businesses, however, such advances consist of a number of different components which require different accounting treatments, for example in the record industry.

(d) **Loan arrangement fees** could be recognised in the year the loan is arranged or spread over the life of the loan.

(e) **Credit card fees** charged by credit card companies on their cardholders might be recognised on receipt or spread over the period that the fee allows the cardholder to use the card.

Revenue

1.11   Revenue recognition should be when it is probable that **future economic benefits** will flow to the enterprise and when these benefits can be **measured reliably**.

1.12   Income includes both revenues and gains. Revenue is income arising in the ordinary course of an enterprise's activities and it may be called different names, such as sales, fees, interest, dividends or royalties.

1.13   Interest, royalties and dividends are included as income because they arise from the use of an enterprise's assets by other parties.

KEY TERMS

Interest is the charge for the use of cash or cash equivalents or amounts due to the enterprise.

Royalties are charges for the use of non-current assets of the enterprise, eg patents, computer software and trademarks.

Dividends are distributions of profit to holders of equity investments, in proportion with their holdings, of each relevant class of capital.

Definitions

KEY TERMS

Revenue is the gross inflow of economic benefits during the period arising in the course of the ordinary activities of an enterprise when those inflows result in increases in equity, other than increases relating to contributions from equity participants.

Fair value is the amount for which an asset could be exchanged, or a liability settled, between knowledgeable, willing parties in an arm's length transaction.

1.14   Revenue **does not include** sales taxes, value added taxes or goods and service taxes which are only collected for third parties, because these do not represent an economic benefit flowing to the entity. The same is true for revenues collected by an agent on behalf of a principal. Revenue for the agent is only the commission receive for acting as agent.

Measurement of revenue

1.15 When a transaction takes place, the amount of revenue is usually decided by the **agreement of the buyer and seller**. The revenue is actually measured, however, as the **fair value of the consideration received**, which will take account of any trade discounts and volume rebates.

Identification of the transaction

1.16 Normally, each transaction can be looked at **as a whole**. Sometimes, however, transactions are more complicated, and it is necessary to break a transaction down into its **component parts**. For example, a sale may include the transfer of goods and the provision of future servicing, the revenue for which should be deferred over the period the service is performed.

1.17 At the other end of the scale, **seemingly separate transactions must be considered together** if apart they lose their commercial meaning. An example would be to sell an asset with an agreement to buy it back at a later date. The second transaction cancels the first and so both must be considered together.

Sale of goods

1.18 Revenue from the sale of goods should only be recognised when *all* these conditions are satisfied.

   (a) The enterprise has transferred the **significant risks and rewards** of ownership of the goods to the buyer

   (b) The enterprise has **no continuing managerial involvement** to the degree usually associated with ownership, and no longer has effective control over the goods sold

   (c) The amount of revenue can be **measured reliably**

   (d) It is probable that the **economic benefits** associated with the transaction will flow to the enterprise

   (e) The **costs incurred** in respect of the transaction can be measured reliably

1.19 The transfer of risks and rewards can only be decided by examining each transaction. Mainly, the transfer occurs at the same time as either the **transfer of legal title**, or the **passing of possession** to the buyer - this is what happens when you buy something in a shop.

1.20 **If significant risks and rewards remain with the seller,** then the transaction is *not* a sale and revenue cannot be recognised, for example if the receipt of the revenue from a particular sale depends on the buyer receiving revenue from his own sale of the goods.

1.21 It is possible for the seller to retain only an **'insignificant' risk of ownership** and for the sale and revenue to be recognised. The main example here is where the seller retains title only to ensure collection of what is owed on the goods. This is a common commercial situation, and when it arises the revenue should be recognised on the date of sale.

1.22 The probability of the enterprise receiving the revenue arising from a transaction must be assessed. It may only become probable that the economic benefits will be received when an uncertainty is removed, for example government permission for funds to be received from another country. Only when the uncertainty is removed should the revenue be recognised. This is in contrast with the situation where revenue has already been recognised but where the **collectability of the cash** is brought into doubt. Where recovery has ceased to be probable, the amount should be recognised as an expense, *not* an adjustment of the revenue previously recognised. These points also refer to services and interest, royalties and dividends below.

1.23 **Matching** should take place, ie the revenue and expenses relating to the same transaction should be recognised at the same time. It is usually easy to estimate expenses at the date of sale (eg warranty costs, shipment costs, etc). Where they cannot be estimated reliably, then revenue cannot be recognised; any consideration which has already been received is treated as a liability.

Rendering of services

1.24 When the outcome of a transaction involving the rendering of services can be estimated reliably, the associated revenue should be recognised by reference to the **stage of completion of the transaction** at the balance sheet date. The outcome of a transaction can be estimated reliably when *all* these conditions are satisfied.

   (a) The amount of revenue can be **measured reliably**

   (b) It is probable that the **economic benefits** associated with the transaction will flow to the enterprise

   (c) The **stage of completion** of the transaction at the balance sheet date can be measured reliably

   (d) The **costs incurred** for the transaction and the costs to complete the transaction can be measured reliably

1.25 The parties to the transaction will normally have to agree the following before an enterprise can make reliable estimates.

   (a) Each party's **enforceable rights** regarding the service to be provided and received by the parties

   (b) The **consideration** to be exchanged

   (c) The **manner and terms of settlement**

1.26 There are various methods of determining the stage of completion of a transaction, but for practical purposes, when services are performed by an indeterminate number of acts over a period of time, revenue should be recognised on a **straight line basis** over the period, unless there is evidence for the use of a more appropriate method. If one act is of more significance than the others, then the significant act should be carried out *before* revenue is recognised.

1.27 In uncertain situations, when the outcome of the transaction involving the rendering of services cannot be estimated reliably, then it may be appropriate to adopt a **no loss/no gain approach**. Revenue is recognised only to the extent of the expenses recognised that are recoverable.

1.28 This is particularly likely during the **early stages of a transaction**, but it is still probable that the enterprise will recover the costs incurred. So the revenue recognised in such a period will be equal to the expenses incurred, with no profit.

1.29 Obviously, if the costs are not likely to be reimbursed, then they must be recognised as an expense immediately. **When the uncertainties cease to exist**, revenue should be recognised as laid out in Paragraph 1.24 above.

Interest, royalties and dividends

1.30 When others use the enterprise's assets yielding interest, royalties and dividends, the revenue should be recognised on the bases set out below when:

(a) It is probable that the **economic benefits** associated with the transaction will flow to the enterprise

(b) The amount of the revenue can be **measured reliably**

1.31 The revenue is recognised on the following bases.

(a) **Interest** is recognised on a time proportion basis that takes into account the effective yield on the asset

(b) **Royalties** are recognised on an accruals basis in accordance with the substance of the relevant agreement

(c) **Dividends** are recognised when the shareholder's right to receive payment is established

1.32 It is unlikely that you would be asked about anything as complex as this in the exam, but you should be aware of the basics. The **effective yield** on an asset mentioned above is the rate of interest required to discount the stream of future cash receipts expected over the life of the asset to equate to the initial carrying amount of the asset.

1.33 Royalties are usually recognised on the same basis that they accrue **under the relevant agreement**. Sometimes the true substance of the agreement may require some other systematic and rational method of recognition.

1.34 Once again, the points made above about **probability and collectability** on sale of goods also apply here.

Question 1

Given that prudence is the main consideration, discuss under what circumstances, if any, revenue might be recognised at the following stages of a sale.

(a) Goods are acquired by the business which it confidently expects to resell very quickly.
(b) A customer places a firm order for goods.
(c) Goods are delivered to the customer.
(d) The customer is invoiced for goods.
(e) The customer pays for the goods.
(f) The customer's cheque in payment for the goods has been cleared by the bank.

Answer

(a) A sale must never be recognised before the goods have even been ordered by a customer. There is no certainty about the value of the sale, nor when it will take place, even if it is virtually certain that goods will be sold.

(b) A sale must never be recognised when the customer places an order. Even though the order will be for a specific quantity of goods at a specific price, it is not yet certain that the sale transaction will go through. The customer may cancel the order, the supplier might be unable to deliver the goods as ordered or it may be decided that the customer is not a good credit risk.

(c) A sale will be recognised when delivery of the goods is made only when:

    (i)   The sale is for cash, and so the cash is received at the same time

    (ii)   Or the sale is on credit and the customer accepts delivery (eg by signing a delivery note)

(d) The critical event for a credit sale is usually the despatch of an invoice to the customer. There is then a legally enforceable debt, payable on specified terms, for a completed sale transaction.

(e) The critical event for a cash sale is when delivery takes place and when cash is received; both take place at the same time.

It would be too cautious or 'prudent' to await cash payment for a credit sale transaction before recognising the sale, unless the customer is a high credit risk and there is a serious doubt about his ability or intention to pay.

(f) It would again be over-cautious to wait for clearance of the customer's cheques before recognising sales revenue. Such a precaution would only be justified in cases where there is a very high risk of the bank refusing to honour the cheque.

2 DISTRIBUTABLE PROFITS

Exam focus point

This is an important section which you must look at.

2.1 A **distribution** is defined by s 263(2) CA 1985 as every description of distribution of a company's assets to members (shareholders) of the company, whether in cash or otherwise, with the exceptions of:

(a) An issue of bonus shares.

(b) The redemption or purchase of the company's own shares out of capital (including the proceeds of a new issue) or out of unrealised profits.

(c) The reduction of share capital by:

    (i)   Reducing the liability on shares in respect of share capital not fully paid up

    (ii)   Paying off paid-up share capital

(d) A distribution of assets to shareholders in a winding up of the company.

IMPORTANT!

Companies must not make a distribution except out of profits available for the purpose. These available profits are:

(a) Its **accumulated realised profits,** insofar as these have not already been used for an earlier distribution or for 'capitalisation'.

(b) **Minus its accumulated realised losses,** insofar as these have not already been written off in a reduction or reconstruction scheme.

2.2 Capital profits and revenue profits (if realised) are taken together and capital losses and revenue losses (if realised) are similarly grouped together. *Unrealised profits* cannot be distributed (for example profit on the revaluation of fixed assets); nor must a company apply unrealised profits to pay up debentures or any unpaid amounts on issued shares.

2.3 **Capitalisation of realised profits is the use of profits:**

(a) To issue bonus shares

(b) As a transfer to the capital redemption reserve

2.4 As a point of detail, s 275(2) allows that any **excess depreciation on a revalued fixed asset above the amount of depreciation that would have been charged on its historical cost can be treated as a realised profit for the purpose of distributions.** This is to avoid penalising companies that make an unrealised profit on the revaluation of an asset, and must then charge depreciation on the revalued amount. For example, suppose that a company buys an asset at a cost of £20,000. It has a life of 4 years and a nil residual value. If it is immediately revalued to £30,000, an unrealised profit of £10,000 would be credited to the revaluation reserve. Annual depreciation must be based on the revalued amount, in this case, ¼ of £30,000 or £7,500. This exceeds depreciation which would have been charged on the asset's cost (£5,000 pa) by £2,500 per annum. This £2,500 can be treated as a distributable profit under s 275(2).

2.5 Section 264 imposes **further restrictions on the distributions of public companies**.

IMPORTANT!

A public company cannot make a distribution if at the time:

(a) The amount of its net assets is less than the combined total of its called-up share capital plus its undistributable reserves.

(b) The distribution will reduce the amount of its net assets to below the combined total of its called-up share capital plus its undistributable reserves.

2.6 **'Undistributable reserves' are:**

(a) The share premium account.

(b) The capital redemption reserve.

(c) Any accumulated surplus of unrealised profits over unrealised losses.

(d) Any other reserve which cannot be distributed, whether by statute, or the company's memorandum or articles of association.

2.7 The key feature of s 264 is that all **accumulated distributable profits, both realised and unrealised, must exceed the accumulated realised and unrealised losses of the company before any distribution can be made**. The difference between the profits and losses is the maximum possible distribution.

2.8 In contrast with s 263, s 264 **includes consideration of unrealised profits and losses,** so that if unrealised losses exceed unrealised profits, the amount of distributions which can be made will be reduced by the amount of the 'deficit'.

2.9 EXAMPLE: PRIVATE COMPANY V PUBLIC COMPANY DISTRIBUTIONS

Huddle Ltd is a private company and Publimco plc is a public limited company. Both companies have a financial year ending on 31 December. On 31 December 20X5, the balance sheets of the companies, by a remarkable coincidence, were identical, as follows.

	Huddle Ltd		Publimco plc	
	£'000	£'000	£'000	£'000
Net assets		365		365
Share capital		300		300
Share premium account		60		60
Unrealised losses on asset revaluations		(25)		(25)
Realised profits	50		50	
Realised losses	(20)		(20)	
		30		30
		365		365

What is the maximum distribution that each company can make?

2.10 SOLUTION

(a)   S 263 restricts the distributable profits of Huddle Ltd to £30,000.

(b)   S 264 further restricts the distributable profits of Publimco plc to £30,000 – £25,000 = £5,000 (or alternatively, £365,000 – £300,000 – £60,000 = £5,000. This is the surplus of net assets over share capital plus undistributable reserves, which in this example are represented by the share premium account).

Realised and distributable profits

2.11   Legislation does not define realised profits very clearly. As a **'rule of thumb',** according to the Consultative Committee of Accounting Bodies, **profits in the profit and loss account are realised, while unrealised profits are credited directly to reserves**.

2.12   FRS 18 *Accounting policies* provides a framework for recognising realised profits. If FRS 18, is followed, profit and loss account profits will be realisable.

Exceptions

2.13   In the case of **sale of revalued fixed assets**, the **unrealised profit on revaluation previously credited to the revaluation reserve** does not pass through the profit and loss account. It is nevertheless to be **regarded as distributable.**

2.14   Where an asset has been revalued, the **increase in depreciation charge** can be treated as a realised profit.

2.15   **Development expenditure** is a realised loss in the year in which it is incurred, except when the costs are capitalised within SSAP 13 guidelines, in which case the costs are amortised as realised losses over a number of years.

2.16   **Provisions** are generally treated as realised losses.

The relevant accounts

2.17 S 270 defines the 'relevant accounts' which should be used to determine the distributable profits. These are the most recent audited annual accounts of the company, prepared in compliance with the Companies Acts. If the accounts are qualified by the auditors, the auditors must state in their report whether they consider that the proposed distribution would contravene the Act.

2.18 **Companies may also base a distribution on interim accounts,** which need not be audited. However, in the case of a public company, such interim accounts must be properly prepared and comply with:

(a) s 228(2) (accounts to give a true and fair view)
(b) s 238 (directors to sign the company's balance sheet)

A copy of the interim accounts should be delivered to the Registrar.

Investment and insurance companies

2.19 S 265 makes a **special provision for investment companies which are public companies.** Investment companies may make a distribution out of realised revenue profits (insofar as they have not already been utilised or capitalised) less its realised and unrealised revenue losses (insofar as these have not already been written off in a capital reduction or reconstruction) provided that its assets equal at least one and a half times the aggregate amount of its liabilities.

2.20 S 268 refers to insurance companies which have long-term business. Any surplus of assets over liabilities on long-term business which has been properly transferred to the company's profit and loss account should be regarded as a *realised* profit. (This section makes a specific point of clarification, and is therefore relatively minor in importance.)

The duties of directors

2.21 S 309 CA 1985 states that the directors of a company must have regard to the interests of the company's employees in general, as well as to the interests of shareholders. This is a duty which is owed by directors to the company alone.

Question 2

Explain the implications of the following items to profits available for distribution in a public company:

(a) Research and development activities
(b) Net deficit on revaluation reserve arising from an overall deficit on the revaluation of fixed assets
(c) Excess depreciation
(d) Goodwill

Answer

(a) S 263 of the Companies Act 1985 provides that, for the purposes of calculating realised profits, development expenditure carried forward in the balance sheet should be treated as a realised loss. This means that development expenditure may not be regarded as part of net assets.

If, however, there are special circumstances which, in the opinion of the directors, justify the treatment of development expenditure as an asset and not as a loss, then this requirement need not apply. It is generally considered that, if the development expenditure qualifies for treatment as an asset under the provisions of SSAP 13, then it may be treated as an asset and not a loss for the purposes of calculating distributable profits.

(b)   A revaluation reserve is a non-distributable reserve because it reflects unrealised profits and losses. A public company cannot make a distribution which reduces its net assets to below the total of called-up share capital and non-distributable reserves. Consequently, any reduction in a revaluation reserve (or an increase in a debit balance) reduces the profits available for distribution.

(c)   Excess depreciation is the depreciation on revalued assets in excess of cost. Since excess depreciation is regarded as the realisation (through use) of part of the corresponding revaluation reserve, it is added back to profits available for distribution.

(d)   Under FRS10, goodwill must be capitalised and amortised. The annual amount written off is considered a realised loss and reduces distributable profits.

---

3   REDEMPTION OF SHARES

3.1   **Any limited company is permitted without restriction to cancel unissued shares and in that way to reduce its authorised share capital.** That change does not alter its financial position.

3.2   If a limited company with a share capital wishes to **reduce its issued share capital** (and incidentally its authorised capital of which the issued capital is part) it may do so **provided that**:

(a)   It has power to do so in its **articles** of association
(b)   It passes a **special resolution**
(c)   It obtains **confirmation** of the reduction **from the court**: s 135

Requirement (a) is simply a matter of procedure. Articles usually contain the necessary power. If not, the company in general meeting would first pass a special resolution to alter the articles appropriately and then proceed, as the second item on the agenda of the meeting, to pass a special resolution to reduce the capital.

3.3   There are **three basic methods of reducing share capital** specified in s 35(2).

(a)   **Extinguish or reduce liability on partly paid shares.** A company may have issued £1 (nominal) shares 75p paid up. The outstanding liability of 25p per share may be eliminated altogether by reducing each share to 75p (nominal) fully paid or some intermediate figure, eg 80p (nominal) 75p paid. Nothing is returned to the shareholders but the company gives up a claim against them for money which it could call up whenever needed.

(b)   **Cancel paid up share capital which has been lost or which is no longer represented by available assets.** Suppose that the issued shares are £1 (nominal) fully paid but the net assets now represent a value of only 50p per share. The difference is probably matched by a debit balance on profit and loss account (or provision for fall in value of assets). The company could reduce the nominal value of its £1 shares to 50p (or some intermediate figure) and apply the amount to write off the debit balance or provision wholly or in part. It would then be able to resume payment of dividends out of future profits without being obliged to make good past losses. The resources of the company are not reduced by this procedure of part cancellation of nominal value of shares but it avoids having to rebuild lost capital by retaining profits.

(c)   **Pay off part of the paid up share capital out of surplus assets.** The company might repay to shareholders, say, 30p in cash per £1 share by reducing the nominal value of the share to 70p. This reduces the assets of the company by 30p per share.

Role of court in reduction of capital

Exam focus point

Paragraphs 3.4 - 3.8 are included for completeness, but they are unlikely to be examined.

3.4 When application is made to the court for approval of the reduction, its first concern is the effect of the reduction on the company's ability to pay its debts: s 136. If the reduction is by method (a) or (c) the court must, and where method (b) is used the court may, require that creditors shall be invited by advertisement to state their objections (if any) to the reduction to the court unless the court decides to dispense with this procedure.

3.5 In modern practice the company usually persuades the court to dispense with advertising for creditors' objections (which can be commercially damaging to the company if its purpose is misunderstood since it may suggest to creditors that the company is insolvent). Two possible methods are:

(a) Paying off all creditors before application is made to the court; or, if that is not practicable.

(b) Producing to the court a guarantee, perhaps from the company's bank, that its existing debts will be paid in full.

The statutory procedure itself, if it is followed, provides that if a creditor does object his claim shall be met by providing security for his debt or such part of it (if it is in dispute) as the court may decide.

3.6 The court also considers whether, if there is more than one class of share, the reduction is fair in its **effect on different classes of shareholder**. If, for example, the company has both ordinary and preference shares, the holders of the preference shares may be entitled in a winding up to repayment of their capital in priority to any repayment to ordinary shareholders. If that is the position then:

(a) Under method (c) the preference shares must be repaid in full under a reduction of capital before any reduction of ordinary shares is made. For example, the reduction might provide for repayment of £1 per £1 share to the holders of preference shares and then, say, 10p per £1 share (thereby reduced to 90p) for ordinary shareholders.

(b) When method (b) is used (where the reduction reflects a loss which would in winding up diminish the surplus available to ordinary shareholders), the reduction would be made by cancellation of part of the nominal value of the ordinary shares without altering the value of the preference shares, so as to preserve the priority rights of preference shares to whatever assets are available in a winding up.

3.7 If the court is satisfied that the reduction does not prejudice creditors and is fair in its effect on shareholders, it approves the reduction by making an order to that effect. The court has power to require the company to add the words 'and reduced' to its name at the end or to publish the reasons for or information about the reduction: s 137. But neither condition is ever imposed in modern practice.

3.8 A copy of the court order and of a minute, approved by the court, to show the altered share capital is delivered to the registrar who issues a certificate of registration. The reduction then takes effect and, if method (c) is used, the payment to shareholders may then be made: s 138.

Share premium account

3.9 Whenever a company obtains for its shares a consideration in excess of their nominal value, it must transfer the excess to a share premium account. The general rule is that the **share premium account is subject to the same restriction as share capital. However, a bonus issue can be made using the share premium account** (reducing share premium in order to increase issued share capital).

3.10 Following the decision in *Shearer v Bercain 1980*, there is an exemption from the general rules on setting up a share premium account, in certain circumstances where new shares are issued as consideration for the acquisition of shares in another company (see Chapter 18).

3.11 The **other permitted uses of share premium** are to pay:

    (a) Capital expenses such as preliminary expenses of forming the company.
    (b) Discount on the issue of shares or debentures.
    (c) Premium (if any) paid on redemption of debentures: s 130(2).

Private companies (but not public companies) may also use a share premium account in purchasing or redeeming their own shares out of capital.

Redemption or purchase by a company of its own shares

3.12 There is a **general prohibition** (s 143) against any voluntary acquisition by a company of its own shares, but that prohibition is subject to **exceptions**.

3.13 A company may:

    (a) Purchase its own shares in compliance with an **order of the court**.
    (b) Issue **redeemable shares** and then redeem them.
    (c) Purchase its own shares under certain **specified procedures**.
    (d) **Forfeit** or accept the surrender of its shares.

These restrictions relate to the **purchase** of shares: there is no objection to accepting a gift.

3.14 The **conditions for the issue and redemption of redeemable shares** are set out in ss 159 to 161.

    (a) The articles must give authority for the issue of redeemable shares. Articles do usually provide for it, but if they do not, the articles must be altered before the shares are issued: s 159.

    (b) Redeemable shares may only be issued if at the time of issue the company also has issued shares which are not redeemable: a company's capital may not consist entirely of redeemable shares: s 159.

    (c) Redeemable shares may only be redeemed if they are fully paid: s 159.

    (d) The terms of redemption must provide for payment on redemption: s 159.

    (e) The shares may be redeemed out of distributable profits, or the proceeds of a new issue of shares, or capital (if it is a private company) in accordance with the relevant rules: s 160.

    (f) Any premium payable on redemption must be provided out of distributable profits subject to an exception described below: s 160.

3.15 The 1948 Act provided regulations which prevented companies from redeeming shares except by transferring a sum equal to the nominal value of shares redeemed from distributable profit reserves to a non-distributable 'capital redemption reserve'. This reduction in distributable reserves is an example of the **capitalisation of profits, where previously distributable profits become undistributable.**

3.16 **The purpose of these regulations was to prevent companies from reducing their share capital investment so as to put creditors of the company at risk.**

3.17 EXAMPLE: CAPITALISATION OF PROFITS

Suppose, for example, that Muffin Ltd had £100,000 of preference shares, redeemable in the very near future at par. A balance sheet of the company is currently as follows.

	£	£
Assets		
Cash	100,000	
Other assets	300,000	
		400,000
Liabilities		
Trade creditors		120,000
Net assets		280,000
Capital and reserves		
Ordinary shares	30,000	
Redeemable preference shares	100,000	
		130,000
Profit and loss account		150,000
		280,000

3.18 Now if Muffin Ltd were able to redeem the preference shares without making any transfer from the profit and loss account to a capital redemption reserve, the effect of the share redemption on the balance sheet would be as follows.

	£
Net assets	
Non-cash assets	300,000
Less trade creditors	120,000
	180,000
Capital and reserves	
Ordinary shares	30,000
Profit and loss account	150,000
	180,000

In this example, the company would still be able to pay dividends out of profits of up to £150,000. If it did, the creditors of the company would be highly vulnerable, financing £120,000 out of a total of £150,000 assets of the company.

3.19 The regulations in the 1948 Act were intended to prevent such extreme situations arising. On redemption of the preference shares, Muffin Ltd would have been required to transfer £100,000 from its profit and loss account to a non-distributable reserve, called at that time a capital redemption reserve fund. The effect of the redemption of shares on the balance sheet would have been:

Net assets	£	£
Non-cash assets		300,000
Less trade creditors		120,000
		180,000
Capital and reserves		
Ordinary shares		30,000
Reserves		
Distributable (profit and loss account)	50,000	
Non-distributable (capital redemption reserve fund)	100,000	
		150,000
		180,000

The maximum distributable profits are now £50,000. If Muffin Ltd paid all these as a dividend, there would still be £250,000 of assets left in the company, just over half of which would be financed by non-distributable equity capital.

3.20 When a company redeems some shares, or purchases some of its own shares, they **should be redeemed**:

(a) **Out of distributable profits**

(b) **Out of the proceeds of a new issue of shares**

and if there is any premium on redemption, **the premium must be paid out of distributable profits**, except that if the shares were issued at a premium, then any premium payable on their redemption may be paid out of the proceeds of a new share issue made for the purpose, up to an amount equal to the lesser of:

(a) The aggregate premiums received on issue of the redeemable shares

(b) The balance on the share premium account (including premium on issue of the new shares)

3.21 EXAMPLE: REDEMPTION OF SHARES

A numerical example might help to clarify this point. Suppose that Jingle Ltd intends to redeem 10,000 shares of £1 each at a premium of 5 pence per share. The redemption must be financed out of:

(a) Distributable profits (10,000 × £1.05 = £10,500).

(b) The proceeds of a new share issue (say, by issuing 10,000 new £1 shares at par). The premium of £500 must be paid out of distributable profits.

(c) Combination of a new share issue and distributable profits.

(d) Out of the proceeds of a new share issue where the redeemable shares were issued at a premium. For example, if the redeemable shares had been issued at a premium of 3p per share, then (assuming that the balance on the share premium account after the new share issue was at least £300) £300 of the premium on redemption could be debited to the share premium account and only £200 need be debited to distributable profits.

3.22 (a) Where a company redeems shares or purchases its own shares wholly out of distributable profits, it must transfer to the capital redemption reserve an amount equal to the nominal value of the shares redeemed (s 170 (1)).

In example (a) above the accounting entries would be:

		£	£
DEBIT	Share capital account	10,000	
	Profit and loss account (premium on redemption)	500	
CREDIT	Cash		10,500
DEBIT	Profit and loss account	10,000	
CREDIT	Capital redemption reserve		10,000

(b) Where a company redeems shares or purchases its shares wholly or partly out of the proceeds of a new share issue, it must transfer to the capital redemption reserve an amount by which the nominal value of the shares redeemed exceeds the *aggregate* proceeds from the new issue (ie nominal value of new shares issued plus share premium) (s 170 (2)).

(i) In example (b) the accounting entries would be:

		£	£
DEBIT	Share capital account (redeemed shares)	10,000	
	Profit and loss account (premium)	500	
CREDIT	Cash (redemption of shares)		10,500
DEBIT	Cash (from new issue)	10,000	
CREDIT	Share capital account		10,000

No credit to the capital redemption reserve is necessary because there is no decrease in the creditors' buffer.

(ii) If the redemption in the same example were made by issuing 5,000 new £1 shares at par, and paying £5,500 out of distributable profits:

		£	£
DEBIT	Share capital account (redeemed shares)	10,000	
	Profit and loss account (premium)	500	
CREDIT	Cash (redemption of shares)		10,500
DEBIT	Cash (from new issue)	5,000	
CREDIT	Share capital account		5,000
DEBIT	Profit and loss account	5,000	
CREDIT	Capital redemption reserve		5,000

(iii) In the example (d) above (assuming a new issue of 10,000 £1 shares at a premium of 8p per share) the accounting entries would be:

		£	£
DEBIT	Cash (from new issue)	10,800	
CREDIT	Share capital account		10,000
	Share premium account		800
DEBIT	Share capital account (redeemed shares)	10,000	
	Share premium account	300	
	Profit and loss account	200	
CREDIT	Cash (redemption of shares)		10,500

No capital redemption reserve is required, as in (i) above. The redemption is financed entirely by a new issue of shares.

Redemption of shares out of capital

3.23 There is one further rule, which is a significant departure from the principle that shares must not be purchased or redeemed in a way which reduces non-distributable equity reserves. This rule applies to private companies only (provided that their articles of association authorise them to do so).

> ### RULE TO LEARN
>
> A private company may redeem or purchase its own shares out of *capital* (ie non-redeemable share capital, capital redemption reserve, share premium account or revaluation reserve) but only on condition that the nominal value of shares redeemed (or purchased):
>
> (a) Exceeds the proceeds of any new share issue to finance the redemption (or purchases).
>
> (b) First exhausts the distributable profits of the company entirely.

3.24 In such a situation, a transfer must be made to the capital redemption reserve of the amount by which distributable profits exceed the premium on redemption or purchase. (If the premium on redemption or purchase exceeds the total of distributable profits, the difference must be deducted from non-redeemable share capital, and there will be no capital redemption reserve.)

3.25 EXAMPLE: REDEMPTION OF SHARES OUT OF CAPITAL

Suppose, for example, that Snowflake Ltd has the following capital and reserves.

	£
Fully paid non-redeemable share capital	100,000
Fully paid redeemable share capital	40,000
	140,000
Distributable profits	18,000
	158,000

The redeemable shares are now to be redeemed at a cost of £46,000 (creating a premium of £6,000 on redemption). To partly cover the costs of redemption, a new issue of 25,000 ordinary £1 shares will be made at par.

The **permissible capital payment** under the Companies Act 1985 is:

	£	£
Cost of redemption		46,000
Less: proceeds of new issue	25,000	
distributable profits	18,000	
		43,000
Permissible capital payment		3,000

The distributable profits exceed the premium on redemption by £(18,000 – 6,000) = £12,000. A transfer of £12,000 will be made to the capital redemption reserve, leaving the company's capital and reserves as:

	£
Non-redeemable share capital	100,000
New shares issued	25,000
Capital redemption reserve	12,000
	137,000

The total capital is now £137,000 which is £3,000 less (the capital repayment) than the non-distributable reserves of the company before redemption (£140,000).

3.26 The rules explained above may seem lengthy and difficult to follow. However, you should bear in mind that **the purpose of the regulations is to protect creditors**. If a company pays out money to its shareholders, there may be insufficient 'liquid' funds left within the business to pay its debts. The Companies Act 1985 tries to prevent creditors being 'cheated' out of repayments of the debts owing to them by 'underhand' prior payments to shareholders. (However, a private company is allowed to reduce its non-distributable reserves if it has first of all eliminated all its distributable reserves. This restricts the 'defence' for creditors provided by the Act.)

Commercial reasons for altering capital structure

3.27 These include the following.

- Greater security of finance.
- Better image for third parties.
- A 'neater' balance sheet.
- Borrowing repaid sooner.
- Cost of borrowing reduced.

Question 3

Set out below are the summarised balance sheets of Krumpet plc and Scone Ltd at 30 June 20X5.

	Krumpet plc £'000	Scone plc £'000
Capital and reserves		
Called up share capital £1 ordinary shares	300	300
Share premium account	60	60
Profit and loss account	160	20
	520	380
Net assets	520	380

On 1 July 20X5 Krumpet plc and Scone Ltd each purchased 50,000 of their own ordinary shares as follows.

Krumpet plc purchased its own shares at 150p each. The shares were originally issued at a premium of 20p. The redemption was partly financed by the issue at par of 5,000 10% redeemable preference shares of £1 each.

Scone Ltd purchased its own shares out of capital at a price of 80p each.

Required

Prepare the summarised balance sheets of Krumpet plc and Scone Ltd at 1 July 20X5 immediately after the above transactions have been effected.

Answer

Workings for Krumpet

	£	£
Cost of redemption (50,000 × £1.50)		75,000

Premium on redemption (50,000 × 50p)		25,000

No premium arises on the new issue.

Distributable profits

Profit and loss account before redemption		160,000
Premium on redemption (must come out of distributable profits, no premium on new issue)		(25,000)
		135,000
Remainder of redemption costs	50,000	
Proceeds of new issue 5,000 × £1	(5,000)	
Remainder out of distributable profits		(45,000)
Balance on profit and loss account		90,000

Transfer to capital redemption reserve

Nominal value of shares redeemed		50,000
Proceeds of new issue		(5,000)
Balance on CRR		45,000

BALANCE SHEET OF KRUMPET PLC AS AT 1 JULY 20X5

	£'000
Capital and reserves	
Preference shares	5
Ordinary shares	250
Share premium	60
Capital redemption reserve	45
	360
Profit and loss account	90
	450
Net assets	450

Workings for Scone

	£
Cost of redemption (50,000 × 80p)	40,000

Discount on redemption (50,000 × 20p)	10,000

Cost of redemption	40,000
Distributable profits	(20,000)
Permissible capital payment (PCP)	20,000

Transfer to capital redemption reserve

Nominal value of shares redeemed	50,000
PCP	20,000
Balance on capital redemption reserve	30,000

BALANCE SHEET OF SCONE LIMITED AS AT 1 JULY 20X5

	£'000
Capital and reserves	
Ordinary shares	250
Share premium	60
Capital redemption reserve	30
	340
Net assets	340

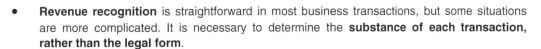

Chapter roundup

- **Revenue recognition** is straightforward in most business transactions, but some situations are more complicated. It is necessary to determine the **substance of each transaction, rather than the legal form**.

- Generally revenue is recognised when the enterprise has transferred to the buyer the **significant risks and rewards of ownership** and when the revenue can be **measured reliably**.

- You should learn the conditions for revenue recognition for all transactions. You should also bear in mind:

  ° The **matching principle**
  ° Probability of revenue receipt vs **collectability of cash**

- You should be able to calculate **maximum distributions available to private and public companies** and to discuss the meaning of distributable and realisable profits.

- You must be able to carry out **simple calculations** showing the amounts to be transferred to the **capital redemption reserve** on purchase or redemption of own shares, how the amount of any **premium** on redemption would be treated, and how much the **permissible capital payment** would be for a private company.

Quick quiz

1   Generally, revenue is recognised at the ………………. …….. ……………… .

2   When will revenue be recognised at other times than on the completion of a sale?

3   What are the general procedures for recognising revenue under the historical cost system?

4   Define 'revenue'.

5   Profits statutorily available for distribution are accumulated realised profits less accumulated realised losses.

   True   ☐

   False   ☐

6   What additional restriction is placed on the distributions of public companies?

7   'Relevant accounts' for the purposes of determining distributable profits are the most …………… …………. …………… …………… of the company.

8   The rules which require the setting up of a capital redemption reserve were put in place to protect which group

   A   Shareholders
   B   The bank
   C   Creditors
   D   Employees

9   When a company redeems or purchases some shares, out of what sources of funds can the shares be redeemed?

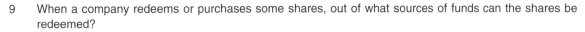

Answers to quick quiz

1   At the point of sales (see para 1.3)

2   Long term contracts and hire purchase (1.6)

3   Refer to paragraph 1.9

4   Refer to paragraph 1.13

5   True. (2.1)

6   Refer to paragraph 2.5

7   Most recent audited accounts (2.17)

8   C (3.16)

9   Distributable profits or proceeds of a new issue (3.20)

Now try the questions below from the Exam Question Bank

Number	Level	Marks	Time
14	Full exam	20	36 mins
15	Full exam	25	45 mins

Chapter 14

RELATED PARTIES; SEGMENTAL INFORMATION

Topic list	Syllabus reference
1 FRS 8 *Related party disclosures*	5(d)
2 SSAP 25 *Segmental reporting*	5(e)

Introduction

FRS 8 is a fairly straightforward standard. Learn the definitions and the disclosures so that you can apply it or discuss it in the exam

SSAP 25 is also a straightforward standard - learn the definitions and formats.

Study guide

- Define and apply the definition of related parties in accordance with FRS 8.

- Describe the potential to mislead users when related party transactions are included in a company's financial statements.

- Adjust financial statements (for comparative purposes) for the effects of non-commercial related party transactions.

- Describe the disclosure requirements for related party transactions.

- Discuss the usefulness and problems associated with the provision of segmental information.

- Define a reportable segment and the information that is to be reported.

- Prepare segmental reports in accordance with SSAP 25.

- Assess the performance of a company based on the information contained in its segmental report.

1 FRS 8 RELATED PARTY DISCLOSURES

1.1 The ASB has produced its most recent FRS on related parties. FRS 8 *Related party disclosures* makes it clear why a standard was required on this subject.

> 'In the absence of information to the contrary, it is assumed that a reporting entity has independent discretionary power over its resources and transactions and pursues its activities independently of the interests of its individual owners, managers and others. Transactions are presumed to have been undertaken on an arm's length basis, ie on terms such as could have obtained in a transaction with an external party, in which each side bargained knowledgeably and freely, unaffected by any relationship between them.
>
> These assumptions may not be justified when related party relationships exist, because the requisite conditions for competitive, free market dealings may not be present. Whilst the parties may endeavour to achieve arm's length bargaining the very nature of the relationship may preclude this occurring.'

1.2   FRS 8 can be summarised as follows.

(a)   FRS 8 *Related party disclosures* requires the **disclosure** of:

(i)   **Information on related party transactions**.

(ii)   The **name of the party controlling** the reporting entity and, if different, that of the ultimate controlling party whether or not any transactions between the reporting entity and those parties have taken place.

Aggregated disclosures are allowed subject to certain restrictions.

Related parties are defined below.

(b)   **No disclosure** is required in consolidated financial statements of **intragroup transactions** and balances eliminated on consolidation. A parent undertaking is not required to provide related party disclosures in its own financial statements when those statements are presented with consolidated financial statements of its group.

(c)   Disclosure is not required in the financial statements of **subsidiary undertakings**, 90% or more of whose voting rights are controlled within the group, of transactions with entities that are part of the group or investees of the group qualifying as related parties provided that the consolidated financial statements in which that subsidiary is included are publicly available.

FRS 8 is not long and the more detailed requirements are as follows.

Objective

1.3   The objective of FRS 8 is to ensure that financial statements contain the disclosures necessary to draw attention to the possibility that the reported financial position and results may have been affected by the existence of related parties and by material transactions with them. In other words, this is a standard which **is primarily concerned with disclosure**.

1.4   The definitions given in FRS 8 are fundamental to the effect of the standard.

DEFINITIONS

(a)   **Close family** are those family members, or members of the same household, who may be expected to influence, or be influenced by, that person in their dealings with the reporting entity.

(b)   **Control** means the ability of an undertaking to direct the financial and operating policies of another undertaking with a view to gaining economic benefits from its activities.

(c)   **Key management** are those persons in senior positions having authority or responsibility for directing or controlling the major activities and resources of the reporting entity.

(d)   **Persons acting in concert** comprise persons who, pursuant to an agreement or understanding (whether formal or informal), actively co-operative, whether through the ownership by any of them of shares in an undertaking or otherwise, to exercise control or influence over that undertaking.

1.5   The most important definitions are of *related parties* and *related party transactions*.

'Related parties

(a)   Two or more parties are related parties when at any time during the financial period:

   (i)   One party has **direct or indirect control** of the other party

   (ii)   The parties are **subject to common control** from the same source

   (iii)   One party has **influence over the financial and operating policies** of the other party to an extent that that other party might be inhibited from pursuing at all times its own separate interests.

   (iv)   The parties, in entering a transaction, are subject to **influence from the same source** to such an extent that one of the parties to the transaction has subordinated its own separate interests.

(b)   For the avoidance of doubt, the following are **related parties** of the reporting entity:

   (i)   Its ultimate and intermediate **parent undertakings**, subsidiary undertakings, and fellow subsidiary undertakings.

   (ii)   Its **associates and joint ventures**.

   (iii)   The **investor or venturer** in respect of which the reporting entity is an associate or a joint venture.

   (iv)   **Directors*** of the reporting entity and the directors of its ultimate and intermediate parent undertakings.

   (v)   Pension funds for the benefit of employees of the reporting entity or of any entity that is a related party of the reporting entity.

   [* Directors include shadow directors, which are defined in companies legislation as persons in accordance with whose directions or instructions the directors of the company are accustomed to act.]

(c)   And the following are **presumed to be related parties** of the reporting entity unless it can be demonstrated that neither party has influenced the financial and operating policies of the other in such a way as to inhibit the pursuit of separate interests:

   (i)   The **key management** of the reporting entity and the key management of its parent undertakings or undertakings.

   (ii)   A person owning or able to exercise control over **20 per cent or more of the voting rights** of the reporting entity, whether directly or through nominees.

   (iii)   Each person **acting in concert** in such a way as to be able to exercise control or influence [in terms of part (a)(iii) of the definition of related party transitions, above] over the reporting entity.

   (iv)   An entity managing or managed by the reporting entity under a **management contract**.

(d)   Additionally, because of their relationship with certain parties that are, or are presumed to be, related parties of the reporting entity, the following are also presumed to be related parties of the reporting entity:

   (i)   **Members of the close family** of any individual falling under parties mentioned in (a) - (c) above.

   (ii)   Partnerships, companies, trusts or other **entities** in which any individual or member of the close family in (a) - (c) above has a **controlling interest**.

Sub-paragraphs (b), (c) and (d) are not intended to be an exhaustive list of related parties.

Related party transaction
The transfer of assets or liabilities or the performance of services by, or for a related party irrespective of whether a price is charged.'

1.6   The most important point is in paragraph (a) of the definition of related parties because it defines in **general terms** what related party transactions are; the succeeding paragraphs of definition only add **some specifics**.

Scope

1.7   FRS 8 applies to all financial statements that are intended to give a true and fair view but it **excludes some transactions**; it does *not* require disclosure:

(a)   In consolidated financial statements, of any transactions or balances between **group entities** that have been **eliminated on consolidation**.

(b)   In a **parent's own financial statements** when those statements are presented together with its consolidated financial statements.

(c)   In the financial statements of **subsidiary undertakings,** 90% per cent or more of whose voting rights are controlled within the group, of transactions with entities that are part of the group or investees of the group qualifying as related parties, provided that the consolidated financial statements in which that subsidiary is included are publicly available.

(d)   Of **pension contributions** paid to a pension fund.

(e)   Of **emoluments** in respect of services as an **employee** of the reporting entity.

Reporting entities taking advantage of the exemption in (c) above are required to state that fact.

1.8   Further types of transaction are also excluded as the FRS does not require disclosure of the relationship and transactions between the reporting entity and the parties listed in (a) to (d) below simply as a result of their role as:

(a)   **Providers of finance** in the course of their business in that regard
(b)   **Utility companies**
(c)   **Government departments** and their sponsored bodies,

Even though they may circumscribe the freedom of action of an entity or participate in its decision-making process.

(d)   A customer, supplier, franchiser, distributor or general agent with whom an entity transacts a significant volume of business.

1.9   **FRS 8 then states the disclosures it requires, under two headings:**

(a)   **Disclosure of control**
(b)   **Disclosure of transactions and balances**

Disclosure of control

1.10   When the reporting entity is controlled by another party, there should be disclosure of the related party relationship and the name of that party and, if different, that of the ultimate controlling party. If the controlling party or ultimate controlling party of the reporting entity is not known, that fact should be disclosed. This information should be disclosed **irrespective of whether any transactions have taken place** between the controlling parties and the reporting entity.

Disclosure of transactions and balances

1.11 Financial statements should **disclose material transactions** undertaken by the reporting entity with a related party. Disclosure should be made **irrespective of whether a price is charged**. The disclosure should include:

(a) The **names** of the transacting parties.

(b) A description of the **relationship** between the parties.

(c) A description of the **transactions**.

(d) The **amounts** involved.

(e) **Any other elements** of the transactions necessary for an understanding of the financial statements.

(f) The **amounts due** to or from related parties **at the balance sheet** date and provisions for doubtful debts due from such parties at that date.

(g) **Amounts written off** in the period in respect of debts due to or from related parties.

Transactions with related parties may be disclosed on an aggregated basis (aggregation of similar transactions by type of related party) unless disclosure of an individual transaction, or connected transactions, is necessary for an understanding of the impact of the transactions on the financial statements of the reporting entity or is required by law.

1.12 Further points of interest are made in the explanatory notes, particularly those on applying the definition of 'related party' given above.

(a) **Common control** is deemed to exist when **both parties are subject to control from boards having a controlling nucleus of directors in common.**

(b) The difference between control and influence is that **control brings with it the ability to cause the controlled party to subordinate its separate interests whereas the outcome of the exercise of influence is less certain.** Two related parties of a third entity are not necessarily related parties of each other.

1.13 Examples of such a situation of 'influence' rather than 'control' are given:

(a) Where two companies are associates of the same investor.

(b) When one party is subject to control and another party is subject to influence from the same source.

(c) Where two parties have a director in common.

In these cases the two parties would not normally be treated as related parties.

Disclosable related party transactions

1.14 The explanatory notes also give examples of related party transactions which would require disclosure:

(a) Purchases or sales of goods (finished or unfinished).
(b) Purchases or sales of property and other assets.
(c) Rendering or receiving of services.
(d) Agency arrangements
(e) Leasing arrangements.
(f) Transfer of research and development.
(g) Licence agreements.

(h) Provision of finance (including loans and equity contributions in cash or in kind).

(i) Guarantees and the provision of collateral security.

(j) Management contracts.

1.15 The *materiality* of related party transactions is also an important question because **only material related party transactions must be disclosed**. You should be familiar with the general definition of materiality, that transactions are material when disclosure might reasonably be expected to influence decisions made by the users of general purpose financial statements. In the case of related party transactions, materiality:

> 'is to be judged, not only in terms of their significance to the reporting entity, but also in relation to the other related party when that party is:
>
> (a) A director, key manager or other individual in a position to influence, or accountable for stewardship of, the reporting entity.
>
> (b) A member of the close family of any individual mentioned in (a) above.
>
> (c) An entity controlled by any individual mentioned in (a) or (b) above.'

Question 1

Which transactions are *excluded* by FRS 8?

Answer

See Paragraphs 1.7 and 1.8.

Current CA 1985 and Stock Exchange requirements

1.16 Some types of related party transactions are covered by existing statutory or Stock Exchange requirements, such as the provisions of the Companies Act 1985 covering transactions by directors and connected persons and 'Class IV' circulars which listed companies are required to send to shareholders when an acquisition or disposal of assets is made from or to a director, substantial shareholder or associate.

2 SSAP 25 SEGMENTAL REPORTING

2.1 SSAP 25 *Segmental reporting* was introduced in June 1990 and builds on the CA 1985 requirements to provide limited segmental analyses.

(a) Where a company has **two or more classes of business, it must show in a note** the amount of **turnover and operating profit attributable to each class** of business; and

(b) where a company operates in **more than one geographical market**, it **must show** in a note the amount of **turnover attributable to each market**.

Any or all of these analyses can be omitted on grounds of commercial sensitivity, but the directors must then state that these analyses would have been published but for these considerations.

2.2 SSAP 25 **applies only to** any entity which:

(a) Is a **public company** or has a public limited company as a subsidiary undertaking, or

(b) Is a **banking or insurance company or group,** or

(c) **Exceeds the criteria, multiplied in each case by 10,** for defining a **medium-sized company** under s 248 of the Companies Act 1985, as amended from time to time by statutory instrument. (The criteria for defining a medium-sized company are given in Chapter 3.)

2.3 The standard adds:

'However, a subsidiary that is not a public limited company or a banking or insurance company need not comply with these provisions if its parent provides segmental information in compliance with this accounting standard.

All entities are encouraged to apply the provisions of this accounting standard in all financial statements intended to give a true and fair view of the financial position and profit or loss.

Where, in the opinion of the directors, the disclosure of any information required by this accounting standard would be seriously prejudicial to the interests of the reporting entity, that information need not be disclosed; but the fact that any such information has not been disclosed must be stated.'

2.4 **SSAP 25 extends the Companies Act requirements** on analysis of turnover and profits as follows:

(a) The **result** as well as turnover **must be disclosed for all segments**.

(b) 'Result' for these purposes is profit or loss before tax, minority interests and extraordinary items.

(c) **Each segment's net assets should be disclosed** (so that return on capital employed can be calculated).

(d) **Segmental turnover must be analysed between sales to customers outside the group and inter-segment sales/transfers** (where material).

Like the CA 1985, SSAP 25 requires analysis by two types of segment, class of business and geographical market.

> **KEY TERM**
>
> The SSAP defines a **class of business** as: 'a distinguishable component of an entity that provides a separate product or service or a separate group of related products or services.'

2.5 Factors to take into account in making this distinction are the nature of the products or services and production processes, markets distribution channels, organisation of activities and legislative framework relating to any part of the business.

2.6 SSAP 25 requires that turnover should be analysed by **geographical market** in two different ways, explained as follows.

> **KEY TERMS**
>
> 'A **geographical segment** is a geographical area comprising an individual country or a group of countries in which an entity operates, or to which it supplies products or services.
>
> A **geographical analysis** should help the user of the financial statements to assess the extent to which an entity's operations are subject to factors such as the following:
>
> (a) Expansionist or restrictive economic climates
> (b) Stable or unstable political regimes
> (c) Exchange control regulations
> (d) Exchange rate fluctuations

2.7 The SSAP amplifies those statements as follows.

'The factors listed above apply both to the geographical locations of the entity's operations and to the geographical locations of its markets. The user of the financial statements gains a fuller understanding of the entity's exposure to these factors if turnover is disclosed according to both location of operations and location of markets. For the purposes of this accounting standard, origin of turnover is the geographical area from which products or services are supplied to a third party or another segment. Destination of turnover is the geographical area to which goods or services are supplied. Because disclosure relating to segment results and net assets will generally be based on location of operations, an analysis of turnover on the same basis will enable the user to match turnover, result and net assets on a consistent basis, and to relate all three to the perceived risks and opportunities of the segments. For these reasons this accounting standard requires the disclosure of sales by origin, but reporting entities should also disclose turnover by destination unless there is no material difference between the two. If there is no material difference, a statement to that effect is required.'

2.8 Identifying segments could be difficult and the SSAP suggests as a **rule of thumb that a segment should normally be regarded as material if its third party turnover is ≥ 10% of the entity's total third party turnover or its profit is ≥ 10% of the combined results of all segments in profit (or its loss is ≥ 10% of the combined results of all loss making segments) or its net assets are ≥ 10% of total net assets of the entity.** The aim is to inform users of the accounts about activities earning a different rate of return from the rest of the business; or subject to different degrees of risk; or experiencing different growth rates; or with different potential for future development.

2.9 Reproduced below is the example given by SSAP 25 in its Appendix. Notice how the segmental results are reconciled to the entity's reported profit before taxation. This is a requirement of the SSAP. The example shows a segmental analysis based on a consolidated profit and loss account. However, SSAP 25 also applies to companies which do not need to prepare group accounts.

2.10 It is quite common for larger companies to operate through divisions or branches, and each of these could qualify as a segment, depending on the circumstances in each case. In both groups of companies and divisionalised single entity companies, there is frequently considerable trade between divisions.

Exam focus point

It is worth memorising this format. A question on SSAP 25 is likely to be quite straightforward.

Notes on the example

2.11 (a) **Common costs should be treated in the way that the directors deem most appropriate** in pursuance of the objectives of segmental reporting. For internal accounting purposes, some companies routinely apportion common costs between divisions, segments and so on and others do not; the same considerations prompting that decision should be applied to segmental reporting.

(b) **For companies in the financial sector it would normally be more sensible to include the net interest income or expense as part of the segment's operating results.** In the majority of cases non-interest bearing operating assets less non-interest bearing liabilities would be the most appropriate measure of capital employed; however, if interest is included in the segment results, then the relevant interest-bearing assets and liabilities should be included in calculating capital employed.

CLASSES OF BUSINESS

	Industry A 20X2 £'000	Industry A 20X1 £'000	Industry B 20X2 £'000	Industry B 20X1 £'000	Other Industries 20X2 £'000	Other Industries 20X1 £'000	Group 20X2 £'000	Group 20X1 £'000
Turnover								
Total sales	33,000	30,000	42,000	38,000	26,000	23,000	101,000	91,000
Inter-segment sales	(4,000)	-	-	-	(12,000)	(14,000)	(16,000)	(14,000)
Sales to third parties	29,000	30,000	42,000	38,000	14,000	9,000	85,000	77,000
Profit before taxation								
Segment profit	3,000	2,500	4,500	4,000	1,800	1,500	9,300	8,000
Common costs							(300)	(300)
Operating profit							9,000	7,700
Net interest							(400)	(500)
							8,600	7,200
Group share of the profit before taxation of associated undertakings	1,000	1,000	1,400	1,200	-	-	2,400	2,200
Group profit before taxation							11,000	9,400
Net assets								
Segment net assets	17,600	15,000	24,000	25,000	19,400	19,000	61,000	59,000
Unallocated assets*							3,000	3,000
							64,000	62,000
Group share of the net assets of associated undertakings	10,200	8,000	8,800	9,000	-	-	19,000	17,000
Total net assets							83,000	79,000

* Unallocated assets consist of assets at the group's head office in London amounting to £2.4 million (20X1: £2.5 million) and at the group's regional office in Hong Kong amounting to £0.6 million (20X1: £0.5 million).

GEOGRAPHICAL SEGMENTS

	United Kingdom 20X2 £'000	United Kingdom 20X1 £'000	North America 20X2 £'000	North America 20X1 £'000	Far East 20X2 £'000	Far East 20X1 £'000	Other 20X2 £'000	Other 20X1 £'000	Group 20X2 £'000	Group 20X1 £'000
Turnover										
Turnover by destination										
Sales to third parties	34,000	31,000	16,000	14,500	25,000	23,000	10,000	8,500	85,000	77,000
Turnover by origin										
Total sales	38,000	34,000	29,000	27,500	23,000	23,000	12,000	10,500	102,000	95,000
Inter-segment sales	-	-	(8,000)	(9,000)	(9,000)	(9,000)	-	-	(17,000)	(18,000)
Sales to third parties	38,000	34,000	21,000	18,500	14,000	14,000	12,000	10,500	85,000	77,000
Profit before taxation										
Segment profit	4,000	2,900	2,500	2,300	1,800	1,900	1,000	900	9,300	8,000
Common costs									(300)	(300)
Operating profit									9,000	7,700
Net interest									(400)	(500)
									8,600	7,200
Group share of the profit before taxation of associated undertakings	950	1,000	1,450	1,200	-	-	-	-	2,400	2,200
Group profit before taxation									11,000	9,400
Net assets										
Segment net assets	16,000	15,000	25,000	26,000	16,000	15,000	4,000	3,000	61,000	59,000
Unallocated assets*									3,000	3,000
									64,000	62,000
Group share of the net assets of associated undertakings	8,500	7,000	10,500	10,000	-	-	-	-	19,000	17,000
Total net assets									83,000	79,000

* Unallocated assets consist of assets at the group's head office in London amounting to £2.4 million (20X1: £2.5 million) and at the group's regional office in Hong Kong amounting to £0.6 million (20X1: £0.5 million).

Arguments against reporting by segment

2.12 Those who argue against this form of disclosure generally emphasise the practical problems, which **include**:

(a) **Identifying segments** for reporting purposes.

(b) **Allocating common income** and costs among the different segments.

(c) **Reporting inter-segment transactions**.

(d) Providing information in such a way as to **eliminate misunderstanding** by investors.

(e) **Avoiding any potential damage** that may be done to the reporting entity by disclosing information about individual segments.

Question 2

The Multitrade Group has three divisions (all based in the UK), A. B and C. Details of their turnover, results and net assets are given below.

	£'000
Division A	
Sales to B	304,928
Other UK sales	57,223
Middle East export sales	406,082
Pacific fringe export sales	77,838
	846,071
Division B	
Sales to C	31,034
Export sales to Europe	195,915
	226,949
Division C	
Export sales to North America	127,003

	Division A £'000	Division B £'000	Division C £'0000
Operational profit/(loss) before tax	162,367	18,754	(8,303)
Re-allocated costs from			
Hear office	48,362	24,181	24,181
Interest costs	3,459	6,042	527

	Head office £'000			
Fixed assets	49,071	200,921	41,612	113,076
Net current assets	47,800	121,832	39,044	92,338
Long-term liabilities	28,636	16,959	6,295	120,841
Deferred taxation	1,024	24,671	9,013	4,028

Required

Prepare a segmental report in accordance with SSAP 25 for publication in Multitrade's group.

Answer

Ignoring comparative figures, Multitrade plc's segmental report would look like this.

CLASSES OF BUSINESS

	Group £'000	Division A £'000	Division B £'000	Division C £'000
Turnover				
Total sales	1,200,023	846,071	226,949	127,003
Inter-segment sales	335,962	304,928	31,034	-
Sales to third parties	864,061	541,143	195,915	127,003
Profit before taxation				
Segment profit/(loss)	172,818	162,367	18,754	(8,303)
Common costs **	96,724			
Operating profit	76,094			
Net interest	10,028			
Group profit before tax	66,066			
Net assets				
Segment net assets	427,016	281,123	65,348	80,545
Unallocated assets	67,211			
Total net assets	494,227			

GEOGRAPHICAL SEGMENTS

	Group	United Kingdom	Middle East	Pacific fringe	Europe	North America
Turnover						
Turnover by destination ***						
Sales to third parties	64,061	57,223	406,082	77,838	195,915	127,003

*   Turnover, profit, net interest and net assets should be the same as those shown in the consolidated accounts.

**   Common costs and unallocated assets are those items in the consolidated accounts which cannot reasonably be allocated to any one segment nor does the group wish to apportion them between segments. An example of a common cost is the cost of maintaining the holding company share register, and an example of an unallocated asset might be the head office building.

***   Turnover by destination must be disclosed in accordance with the Companies Act 1985. If Multitrade's divisions were not all in the UK, then another analysis would be required by SSAP 25 on the same lines as that shown for classes of business but analysed between the geographical origins of turnover.

Chapter roundup

- **FRS 8** is primarily a **disclosure statement**. It is concerned to improve the quality of information provided by published accounts and also to strengthen their stewardship role.

- SSAP 25 is primarily a **disclosure statements** concerned to improve the quality of information provided by published accounts.

- You must be able to prepare a **segmental analysis** and if necessary to use the results to help with interpretation of the accounts, as well as to discuss the **advantages and limitations** of segmental reporting.

Quick quiz

1   Summarise the requirement of FRS 8.

2   Pension funds for the benefit of the employees of the reporting entity are deemed related parties by FRS 8.

    True   ☐
    False ☐

3   How does FRS 8 define related parties?

4   What are the disclosure requirements of FRS 8?

5   What figure prefixes the following as the rule of thumb for identifying a segment under SSAP 25

    •   .... of the entities total third party turnover
    •   .... of the combined profit of all profit making segments
    •   .... of the net assets of the entity

6   How should common costs be allocated in segmental accounts? (2.11)

Answers to quick quiz

1   See paragraph 1.2.

2   True (1.5)

3   Refer to paragraphs 1.5(a)

4   Refer to paragraphs 1.10 and 1.11

5   10   ≥ 10%. (2.8)

6   In the way the directors deem most appropriate in pursuance of the objectives of segmental reporting (2.11)

Now try the questions below from the Exam Question Bank

Number	Level	Marks	Time
16	Introductory	n/a	15 minutes
17	Introductory	n/a	10 minutes

Part C
Preparation of consolidated financial statements

Chapter 15

CONSTITUTION OF A GROUP

Topic list	Syllabus reference
1 Definitions	4(a)
2 Exclusion of subsidiary undertakings from group accounts	4(b)
3 Exemption from the requirement to prepare group accounts	4(b)
4 Content of group accounts	4(c)
5 Group structure	4(c)

Introduction

In this chapter we will look at the major definitions in consolidation and the relevant statutory requirements and accounting standards. These matters are fundamental to your comprehension of group accounts, so make sure you can understand them and then learn them.

The next two chapters deal with the basic techniques of consolidation, and then we move on to more complex aspects in the following chapters.

In all these chapters, make sure that you work through each example and question properly.

Study guide

- Describe the concept of a group and the objective of consolidated financial statements.

- Explain the different methods which could be used to prepare group accounts.

- Explain and apply the definition of subsidiary companies in the Companies Acts and FRS 2.

- Describe the circumstances and reasoning for subsidiaries to be excluded from consolidated financial statements.

- Explain the need for using coterminous year ends and uniform accounting policies when preparing consolidated financial statements.

- Describe how the above is achieved in practice.

Exam guide

Group accounts and consolidation are an extremely important area of your Paper 2.5 syllabus as **you are almost certain to face a large compulsory consolidation question in the examination.**

The key to consolidation questions in the examination is to adopt a logical approach and to practise as many questions as possible beforehand.

BPP PUBLISHING

1   DEFINITIONS

1.1   There are many reasons for businesses to operate as groups; for the goodwill associated with the names of the subsidiaries, for tax or legal purposes and so forth. Company law requires that the results of a group should be presented as a whole. Unfortunately, it is not possible simply to add all the results together and this chapter and those following will teach you how to **consolidate** all the results of companies within a group.

1.2   **In traditional accounting terminology, a group of companies consists of a holding company (or parent company) and one or more subsidiary companies which are controlled by the holding company.** The CA 1989 widened this definition. (The Act amended the CA 1985 and references below are to the amended sections.) As a result, FRS 2 *Accounting for subsidiary undertakings* was published in July 1992 by the ASB, incorporating the CA 1989 changes.

Exam focus point

If you are revising, go straight to the summary at the end of this section.

1.3   There are **two definitions of a group in company law. One** uses the terms 'holding company' and 'subsidiary' and applies **for general purposes. The other** is wider and applies **only for accounting purposes.** It **uses the terms 'parent undertaking' and 'subsidiary undertaking'.** The purpose of this widening of the group for accounting purposes was to curb the practice of structuring a group in such a way that not all companies or ventures within it had to be consolidated. This is an example of off balance sheet financing and has been used extensively to make consolidated accounts look better than is actually justified (see Chapter 11).

1.4   We are only really interested in the accounting definitions of parent and subsidiary undertaking here: they automatically include 'holding companies' and 'subsidiaries' under the general definition.

Parent and subsidiary undertakings: definition

1.5   FRS 2 states that an undertaking is the **parent undertaking** of another undertaking (**a subsidiary undertaking**) if any of the following apply.

KEY TERM

Parent undertaking

(a)   It holds a **majority of the voting rights** in the undertaking.

(b)   It **is a member of the undertaking and has the right to appoint or remove directors** holding a majority of the voting rights at meetings of the board on all, or substantially all, matters.

(c)   **It has the right to exercise a dominant influence over the undertaking**:

(i)   By virtue of provisions contained in the undertaking's memorandum or articles.

(ii)   By virtue of a control contract (in writing, authorised by the memorandum or articles of the controlled undertaking, permitted by law).

(d) **It is a member of the undertaking and controls alone**, under an agreement with other shareholders or members, **a majority of the voting rights in the undertaking.**

(e) It **has a participating interest in the undertaking** and:

   (i) It actually exercises a dominant influence over the undertaking
   (ii) It and the undertaking are managed on a unified basis

(f) A parent undertaking is **also treated as the parent undertaking of the subsidiary undertakings of its subsidiary undertakings.**

1.6 This replaced the previous criterion of owning a majority of equity with one of holding a majority of voting rights. **Also, the board is considered to be controlled if the holding company has the right to appoint directors with a majority of the voting rights on the board** (not just to appoint a simple majority of the directors, regardless of their voting rights).

Exam focus point

The above definition is extremely important and you may be asked to apply it to a given situation in an exam. It depends in turn, however, on the definition of various terms which are included in Paragraph 1.6.

Participating interest

KEY TERM

FRS 2 states that a **participating interest is an interest held by an undertaking in the shares of another undertaking which it holds on a long-term basis for the purpose of securing a contribution to its activities by the exercise of control or influence** arising from or related to that interest.

(a) A holding of **20% or more** of the shares of an undertaking is **presumed** to be a participating interest unless the contrary is shown.

(b) An interest in shares includes an interest which is convertible into an interest in shares, and includes an option to acquire shares or any interest which is convertible into shares.

(c) An interest held on behalf of an undertaking shall be treated as held by that undertaking (ie all group holdings must be aggregated to determine if a subsidiary exists).

1.7 A 'participating interest', like an investment in a 'subsidiary undertaking', **need not be in a company,** because an 'undertaking' means:

(a) A body corporate

(b) A partnership

(c) An unincorporated association carrying on a trade or business, with or without a view to profit

1.8 '**Shares**' therefore **means**:

(a) **Allotted** shares

(b) For undertakings without share capital, **the right to share in the capital and profits and the corresponding liability to meet losses and debts on winding up.**

Dominant influence

> **KEY TERM**
>
> FRS 2 defines **dominant influence** as influence that can be exercised to achieve the operating and financial policies desired by the holder of the influence, notwithstanding the rights or influence of any other party.

1.9 The standard then distinguishes between the two different situations involving dominant influence.

(a) In the context of Paragraph 1.6(c) above, **the right to exercise a dominant influence** means that the holder has **a right to give directions** with respect to the operating and financial policies of another undertaking with which its directors are obliged to comply, whether or not they are for the benefit of that undertaking.

(b) **The actual exercise of dominant influence** is the exercise of an influence that achieves the result that the operating and financial policies of the undertaking influenced are set in accordance with the wishes of the holder of the influence and for the holder's benefit whether or not those wishes are explicit. The actual exercise of dominant influence is identified by its effect in practice rather than by the way in which it is exercised.

1.10 There are four other important definitions.

(a) **Control** is the ability of an undertaking to direct the financial and operating policies of another undertaking with a view to gaining economic benefits from its activities.

(b) An **interest held on a long-term basis** is an interest which is held other than exclusively with a view to subsequent resale.

(c) An **interest held exclusively with a view to subsequent resale** is either:

(i) An interest for which a purchaser has been identified or is being sought, and which is reasonably expected to be disposed of within approximately one year of its date of acquisition.

(ii) An interest that was acquired as a result of the enforcement of a security, unless the interest has become part of the continuing activities of the group or the holder acts as if it intends the interest to become so.

(d) **Managed on a unified basis:** two or more undertakings are managed on a unified basis if the whole of the operations of the undertakings are integrated and they are managed as a single unit. Unified management does not arise solely because one undertaking manages another.

Other definitions from the standard will be introduced where relevant over the next few chapters.

The requirement to consolidate

1.11 FRS 2 requires a parent undertaking to prepare consolidated financial statements for its group unless it uses one of the exemptions available in the standard (see Section 2).

> **KEY TERM**
>
> **Consolidation** is defined as: 'The process of adjusting and combining financial information from the individual financial statements of a parent undertaking and its subsidiary undertaking to prepare consolidated financial statements that present financial information for the group as a single economic entity.'

Associated undertakings

1.12 Another important definition, which applies only for the purposes of preparing group accounts, is that of an 'associated undertaking'. This is not defined by FRS 2, but as CA 1985 (and FRS 9: see Chapter 19).

> **KEY TERM**
>
> 'An "**associated undertaking**" means an undertaking in which an undertaking included in the consolidation has a participating interest and over whose operating and financial policy it exercises a significant influence, and which is not:
>
> (a) A subsidiary undertaking of the parent company
> (b) A joint venture'. (s 20(1) Sch 4A, CA 1985)
>
> 'Where an undertaking holds 20% or more of the voting rights in another undertaking, it shall be presumed to exercise such an influence over it unless the contrary is shown.'
>   (s 20(2) Sch 4A, CA 1985)

1.13 The importance of this definition is that **parent companies are required by law to use equity accounting to account for holdings in 'associated undertakings'**. However, holdings in 'associated companies' (FRS 9 definition: see Chapter 19) are **already accounted for in this way to comply with the SSAP.**

1.14 **Participating interests,** on the other hand, which are not in 'associated undertakings' **have to be disclosed separately from other investments but do not have to be accounted for by the equity method.** Participating interests must be disclosed both in group accounts and in individual company accounts. If you refer back to the statutory accounts formats in Chapter 3, you will see the captions in both the balance sheet and the profit and loss account which refer to 'participating interests'.

1.15 However, in **group accounts** these formats must be amended if necessary as follows.

BPP
PUBLISHING

   (a) Income from interests in associated undertakings   X
       Income from other participating interests   X

      should replace the captions at 8 (format 1) and 10 (format 2) 'Income from participating interests' in the profit and loss account.

   (b) Interests in associated undertakings   X
       Other participating interests   X

      should replace item BIII 3 'Participating interests' in the balance sheet.

1.16   An undertaking **S is a subsidiary undertaking of H if:**

   (a) H is a member of S and *either* holds or **controls > 50% of the voting rights** *or* controls the board; *OR*

   (b) S is a **subsidiary** of H (ie S is a sub-subsidiary); *OR*

   (c) H has the right to exercise a **dominant influence** over S (laid down in the memorandum or articles or a control contract); *OR*

   (d) H has a **participating interest** in S **and** either **actually** exercises a **dominant influence** over S *or* H and S are managed on a unified basis.

   ∴ **Special treatment: consolidate**

1.17   An undertaking A is an **associated undertaking** of H if:

   (a) H and/or one or more of its subsidiary undertakings have a **participating interest** in A and **either** hold more than **20%** of the voting rights **or** can otherwise be demonstrated to exercise a **significant** influence over A's operating and financial policy

   (b) A is not a subsidiary undertaking of H nor is it a joint venture.

   ∴ **Special treatment: equity accounting**

1.18   An investment in an undertaking P is a **participating interest** of H if:

   (a) The H group owns **more than 20%** of P's share capital

   (b) Or the H group has a shareholding or equivalent interest in P **for the long term** and for the purpose of securing a contribution to its activities.

   ∴ **Special treatment: separate disclosure**

2   EXCLUSION OF SUBSIDIARY UNDERTAKINGS FROM GROUP ACCOUNTS

2.1   S 229 CA 1985 (as amended by the CA 1989) provides that a **subsidiary may be omitted** from the consolidated accounts of a group **if:**

   (a) In the opinion of the directors, its inclusion 'is **not material** for the purpose of giving a true and fair view; but two or more undertakings may be excluded only if they are not material taken together'

   (b) There are **severe long-term restrictions** in exercising the parent company's rights eg civil war in the country of an overseas subsidiary

   (c) The holding is **exclusively for resale**

   (d) The information cannot be obtained 'without **disproportionate expense** or undue delay'

2.2   If in the opinion of the directors, a subsidiary undertaking's consolidation is undesirable because the **business of the holding company and subsidiary are so different that they cannot reasonably be treated as a single undertaking, then that undertaking** *must* **be excluded.**

> 'This .... does not apply merely because some of the undertakings are industrial, some commercial and some provide services, or because they carry on industrial or commercial activities involving different products or provide different services.'

2.3   FRS 2 states that a **subsidiary must be excluded** from consolidation if:

(a)   **Severe long-term restrictions are substantially hindering the exercise of the parent's rights** over the subsidiary's assets or management.

(b)   The group's interest in the subsidiary undertaking is **held exclusively with a view to subsequent resale and** the subsidiary has **not been consolidated previously**.

(c)   The subsidiary undertaking's **activities are so different** from those of other undertakings to be included in the consolidation **that its inclusion would be incompatible with the obligation to give a true and fair view.**

The FRS requires the circumstances in which subsidiary undertakings are to be excluded from consolidation to be interpreted **strictly**.

2.4   Where a subsidiary is excluded from group accounts, FRS 2 lays down supplementary provisions on the disclosures and accounting treatment required.

2.5   Where a subsidiary is excluded on grounds of **dissimilar activities** (which should be exceptional), the group accounts should **include separate financial statements for that subsidiary including:**

(a)   A note of the **holding company's interest**.

(b)   Details of **intra-group balances**.

(c)   The **nature of its transactions** with the rest of the group.

(d)   A **reconciliation of the subsidiary's results** (as shown separately) with the value in the consolidated accounts for the 'group's investment in the subsidiary'.

In the consolidated accounts, the excluded subsidiary **should be accounted for by the equity method** of accounting (as though it were an associated company). This is explained in Chapter 20 on accounting for associated companies.

2.6   Subsidiary undertakings **excluded** from consolidation **because of severe long-term restrictions** are to be **treated as fixed asset investments**. They are to be included at their carrying amount when the restrictions came into force, and no further accruals are to be made for profits or losses of those subsidiary undertakings, unless the parent undertaking still exercises significant influence. In the latter case they are to be treated as associated undertakings.

2.7   The following information should be **disclosed** in the group accounts:

(a)   Its **net assets**.

(b)   Its **profit or loss** for the period.

(c)   Any amounts included in the **consolidated profit and loss account** in respect of:

(i)   **Dividends received** by the holding company from the subsidiary.

(ii)   **Writing down the value of the investment.**

2.8 If control is temporary (the investment is **held purely for resale**), the temporary investment **should be included under current assets** in the consolidated balance sheet at the lower of cost and net realisable value.

2.9 In all cases given above, FRS 2 states that the consolidated accounts should show:

(a) The **reasons** for exclusion.
(b) The **names** of subsidiaries excluded.
(c) The **premium or discount on acquisition** not written off.
(d) **Anything else required** by the Companies Acts.

2.10 The CA 1985 requires that when consolidated group accounts are not prepared, or if any subsidiaries are excluded from the group accounts (for any of the reasons given above), **a note to the accounts should be given:**

(a) To explain the reasons why the subsidiaries are not dealt with in group accounts
(b) To disclose any auditors' qualifications in the accounts of the excluded subsidiaries

A note to the (holding) company's accounts (or the consolidated accounts, if any) should also state, for subsidiaries which are not consolidated in group accounts, the aggregate value of the total investment of the holding company in the subsidiaries, by way of the 'equity method' of valuation.

2.11 Section summary

The following table summaries the rules relating to exclusion of a subsidiary.

Reason	Accounting treatment
• Severe long-term restrictions hindering exercise of parent's rights	B/S: equity method up to date of severe restrictions less amounts written off if permanent fall in value
	P&L a/c: dividends received only
• Held exclusively for subsequent resale; has never been consolidated	Current asset at the lower of cost and net realisable value
• Dissimilar activities	Equity method (see Chapter 19)

3 EXEMPTION FROM THE REQUIREMENT TO PREPARE GROUP ACCOUNTS

3.1 The CA 1989 introduced a completely new provision exempting some groups from preparing consolidated accounts. There are two grounds.

(a) **Smaller groups** can claim exemptions on grounds of size (see below).

(b) **Parent companies** (*except* for listed companies) **whose immediate parent is established in an EU member country** need not prepare consolidated accounts. The accounts must give the name and country of incorporation of the parent and state the fact of the exemption. In addition, a copy of the audited consolidated accounts of the parent must be filed with the UK company's accounts. Minority shareholders can, however, require that consolidated accounts are prepared.

FRS 2 adds that exemption may be gained if all of the parent's subsidiary undertakings gain exemption under s 229 CA 1985 (see Paragraph 2.1).

3.2 The **exemption** from preparing consolidated accounts is **not available to:**

(a) Public companies.

(b) Banking and insurance companies.

(c) Authorised persons under the Financial Services Act 1986.

(d) Companies belonging to a group containing a member of the above classes of undertaking.

3.3 Any two of the following **size criteria** for small and medium-sized groups must be met.

	Small	**Medium-sized**
Aggregate turnover	≤ £2.8 million net/ £3.36 million gross	≤ £11.2 million net/ £13.44 million gross
Aggregate gross assets	≤ £1.4 million net/ £1.68 million gross	≤ £5.6 million net/ £6.72 million gross
Aggregate number of employees (average monthly)	≤ 50	≤ 250

3.4 The aggregates can be calculated either before (gross) or after (net) consolidation adjustments for intra-group sales, unrealised profit on stock and so on (see following chapters). The qualifying conditions **must be met:**

(a) **In the case of the parent's first financial year, in that year**
(b) **In the case of any subsequent financial year, in that year and the preceding year**

If the qualifying conditions were met in the preceding year but not in the current year, the exemption can be claimed. If, in the subsequent year, the conditions are met again, the exemption can still be claimed, but if they are not met, then the exemption is lost until the conditions are again met for the second of two successive years.

3.5 When the exemption is claimed, but the auditors believe that the company is not entitled to it, then they must state in their report that the company is in their opinion not entitled to the exemption and this report must be attached to the individual accounts of the company (ie no report is required when the company *is* entitled to the exemption).

4 CONTENT OF GROUP ACCOUNTS

4.1 The information contained in the individual accounts of a holding company and each of its subsidiaries does not give a picture of the group's activities as those of a single entity. To do this, a separate set of accounts can be prepared from the individual accounts. *Note.* **Remember that a group has no separate (legal) existence, except for accounting purposes.**

4.2 There is more than one way of amalgamating the information in the individual accounts into a set of group accounts, but the most common way (and now the legally required way) is to prepare consolidated accounts. **Consolidated accounts are one form of group accounts which combines the information contained in the separate accounts of a holding company and its subsidiaries as if they were the accounts of a single entity.** 'Group accounts' and 'consolidated accounts' are often used synonymously, and now that UK law *requires* group accounts to be consolidated accounts, this tendency will no doubt increase.

4.3 In simple terms a set of consolidated accounts is prepared by **adding together** the assets and liabilities of the holding company and each subsidiary. The **whole of the assets and liabilities of each company** are included, **even though some subsidiaries may be only partly owned**. The 'capital and reserves' side of the balance sheet will indicate how much of the net assets are attributable to the group and how much to outside investors in partly owned subsidiaries. These **outside investors** are known as **minority interests**.

4.4 The CA 1985 requires that group accounts should be prepared whenever a company:

(a) Is a parent company at the end of its financial year

(b) Is not itself a wholly owned subsidiary of a company incorporated in Great Britain

4.5 Most parent companies present their own individual accounts and their group accounts in a single **package**. The package typically comprises a:

(a) **Parent company balance sheet**, which will include 'investments in subsidiary undertakings' as an asset.

(b) **Consolidated balance sheet**.

(c) **Consolidated profit and loss** account.

(d) **Consolidated cash flow statement**.

It is not necessary to publish a parent company profit and loss account (s 230 CA 1985), provided the consolidated profit and loss account contains a note stating the profit or loss for the financial year dealt with in the accounts of the parent company and the fact that the statutory exemption is being relied on.

Exam focus point

If you are in a hurry skim or skip the rest of Section 4.

Co-terminous accounting periods

4.6 S 223 (5) CA 1985 requires that the directors of the holding company **should ensure that the financial year of each of the subsidiaries in the group shall coincide with the financial year of the holding company.** This is to prevent any possible 'window dressing' (although financial years need not coincide if the directors hold the opinion that there are reasons against it).

4.7 If the financial year end of a subsidiary does not coincide with the financial year of the holding company, the appropriate results to include in the group accounts for the subsidiary will be those for its year ending before the year end of the holding company; or if this ended more than three months previously, from interim accounts prepared as at the holding company's year end (s 2(2) Sch 4A CA 1985). These two provisions are included in FRS 2.

4.8 Additionally, FRS 2 requires that a note to the group accounts should disclose the:

(a) Reasons why the directors consider that coinciding dates are not appropriate.
(b) Name(s) of the subsidiary(ies) concerned.
(c) Accounting date and length of the accounting period of each relevant subsidiary.

Disclosure of subsidiaries

4.9 The CA 1985 requires that a parent company disclose, by note:

(a) The name of each subsidiary undertaking.

(b) Its country of incorporation (or, if unincorporated, address of principal place of business).

(c) The identity and proportion of the nominal value of each class of shares held (distinguishing between direct and indirect holdings).

(d) The reason for treating a subsidiary undertaking as such *unless* a majority of the voting rights are held and the proportion is the same as that of shares held.

FRS 2 confirms these provisions and also requires that the nature of each subsidiary's business should be indicated.

(*Note.* A subsidiary company must show, in its own accounts, its ultimate holding company's name and country of incorporation.)

Further provisions of FRS 2

4.10 FRS 2 also requires the following.

(a) **Uniform accounting policies should be applied by all companies in the group,** or if this is not done, appropriate adjustments should be made in the consolidated accounts to achieve uniformity. (If, in exceptional cases, such adjustments are impractical, the different accounting policies used, the effect of the difference on the results and net assets, and the reason for the different treatment should all be disclosed). This is also required by the CA 1985.

(b) **Where there are material additions to the group there should be disclosure of the extent to which the results of the group are affected by profits and losses** of subsidiaries brought in for the first time. This is also now required by the CA 1985.

(c) **Outside or minority interests in the share capital and reserves of companies consolidated should be disclosed separately in the consolidated balance sheet** (also required by the CA 1985). Debit balances should be shown only if there is a binding obligation on minority shareholders to make good any losses. Similarly, the profits and losses of such companies attributable to outside interests should be shown separately in the consolidated profit and loss account after arriving at group profit or loss after tax but before extraordinary items. Minority interests in extraordinary items should be deducted from the relevant amounts.

(d) Changes in membership of a group occur on the date control passes, whether by a transaction or other event. **Changes in the membership of the group during the period should be disclosed.**

(e) When a subsidiary undertaking is acquired the FRS requires its **identifiable assets and liabilities to be brought into the consolidation at their fair values at the date that undertaking becomes a subsidiary** undertaking, even if the acquisition has been made in stages. When a group increases its interest in an undertaking that is already its subsidiary undertaking, the identifiable assets and liabilities of that subsidiary undertaking should be calculated by reference to that fair value. This revaluation is not required if the difference between fair values and carrying amounts of the identifiable assets and liabilities attributable to the increase in stake is not material.

(f) The effect of consolidating the parent and its subsidiary undertakings may be that aggregation obscures useful information about the different undertakings and activities included in the consolidated financial statements. Parent undertakings are encouraged to give **segmental analysis to provide** readers of consolidated financial statements with **useful information on the different risks and rewards, growth and prospects of the different parts of the group.** The specification of such analysis, however, falls outside the scope of the FRS.

Further provisions of the Companies Act 1985

4.11 For each material acquisition in the period, in addition to the above disclosures, a note must state:

(a) The composition and **fair value** of the consideration given.

(b) The name of the undertaking (of the parent undertaking in the case of a newly acquired group).

(c) Whether acquisition or merger accounting has been used (see Chapter 19).

4.12 If **acquisition accounting** was used, a table of the book values and *fair values* as at acquisition of each class of assets and liabilities of the undertaking or group acquired is to be given, including a statement of the amount of any goodwill or negative consolidation difference arising and an explanation of any significant adjustments made.

4.13 If **merger accounting** is used, then an explanation is to be given of any significant adjustments made together with a statement of adjustments to consolidated reserves.

4.14 For each **material disposal** in the period, the name of the subsidiary must be disclosed, along with the FRS 2 requirements (see Section 2).

4.15 Finally, the CA 1985 requirement to disclose cumulative goodwill written off has been amended recently to exclude goodwill written off through the profit and loss account. Consequently, only the **cumulative goodwill that has been written off direct to reserves** in the current year or past years need now be disclosed. Note that negative goodwill does not require disclosure.

5 GROUP STRUCTURE

5.1 With the difficulties of definition and disclosure dealt with, let us now look at group structures. The simplest are those in which a holding company has only a direct interest in the shares of its subsidiary companies. For example:

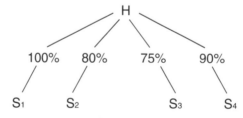

S_1 Ltd is a wholly owned subsidiary of H Ltd. S_2 Ltd, S_3 Ltd and S_4 Ltd are partly owned subsidiaries; a proportion of the shares in these companies is held by outside investors.

5.2 Often a holding company will have indirect holdings in its subsidiary companies. This can lead to more complex group structures.

(a)

H
|
51%
|
S
|
51%
|
SS

H Ltd owns 51% of the equity shares in S Ltd, which is therefore its subsidiary. S Ltd in its turn owns 51% of the equity shares in SS Ltd. SS Ltd is therefore a subsidiary of S Ltd and consequently a subsidiary of H Ltd. SS Ltd would describe S Ltd as its **parent** (or holding) company and H Ltd as its **ultimate parent** (or holding) company.

Note that although H Ltd can control the assets and business of SS Ltd by virtue of the chain of control, its interest in the assets of SS Ltd is only 26%. This can be seen by considering a dividend of £100 paid by SS Ltd: as a 51% shareholder, S Ltd would receive £51; H Ltd would have an interest in 51% of this £51 = £26.01.

(b)

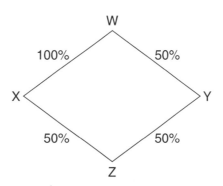

W Ltd owns 100% of the equity of X Ltd and 50% of the equity of Y Ltd. X Ltd and Y Ltd each own 50% of the equity of Z Ltd. Assume that:

(i)   W Ltd does not control the composition of Y Ltd's board; and

(ii)   W Ltd does not hold or control more than 50% of the *voting rights* in Y Ltd; and

(iii) W Ltd does not have the right to exercise a dominant influence over Y Ltd by virtue of its memorandum, articles or a control contract; and

(iv)   W Ltd and Y Ltd are not managed on a unified basis; and

(v)   W Ltd does not actually exercise a dominant influence over Y Ltd; and

(vi)   none of the above apply to either X Ltd's or Y Ltd's holdings in Z Ltd.

In other words, because W Ltd is not in co-operation with the holder(s) of the other 50% of the shares in Y Ltd, neither Y nor Z can be considered subsidiaries.

In that case:

(i)   X Ltd is a subsidiary of W Ltd;

(ii)   Y Ltd is not a subsidiary of W Ltd;

(iii) Z Ltd is not a subsidiary of either X Ltd or Y Ltd. Consequently, it is not a subsidiary of W Ltd.

If Z Ltd pays a dividend of £100, X Ltd and Y Ltd will each receive £50. The interest of W Ltd in this dividend is as follows.

	£
Through X Ltd (100% × £50)	50
Through Y Ltd (50% × £50)	25
	75

Although W Ltd has an interest in 75% of Z Ltd's assets, Z Ltd is not a subsidiary of W Ltd.

(c)

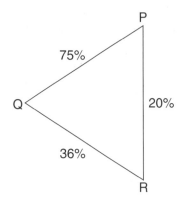

Q Ltd is a subsidiary of P Ltd. P Ltd therefore has indirect control over 36% of R Ltd's equity. P Ltd also has direct control over 20% of R Ltd's equity. R Ltd is therefore a subsidiary of P Ltd, although P Ltd's interest in R Ltd's assets is only 20% + (75% × 36%) = 47%.

Examples (b) and (c) illustrate an important point in company law: in deciding whether a company A holds more than 50% of the equity (or equivalent) of an undertaking B it is necessary to aggregate:

(i) Shares (or equivalent) in B held directly by A
(ii) Shares (or equivalent) in B held by undertakings which are subsidiaries of A

Question 1

During the time until your examination you should obtain as many sets of the published accounts of top quoted companies as possible. Examine the accounting policies in relation to subsidiary and associated companies and consider how these policies are shown in the accounting and consolidation treatment. Consider the effect of any disposals during the year. Also, look at all the disclosures made relating to fair values, goodwill etc and match them to the disclosure requirements outlined in this chapter and in subsequent chapters on FRSs 6 and 7.

Alternatively (or additionally) you should attempt to obtain such information from the financial press.

Chapter roundup

- This chapter has explained the concept of a **group** and introduced several important definitions.

- The principal **regulations** governing the preparation of group accounts have been explained. Many of these are hard to understand and you should re-read this chapter after you have completed your study of this section of the text.

- A number of possible **group structures** have been illustrated to show that a company may hold an interest in the net assets of another company which exceeds 50%, without conferring control of the other company. The converse is also true.

Quick quiz

1 **Fill in the blanks** in the statements below, using the words in the box.

Per FRS 2, A is a parent of B if:

(a) A holds (1) ………………… in B

(b) A can appoint or remove (2) ………………..

(c) A has the right to exercise (3) ……………….. over B

(d) B is a (4) ……………….. of A

• Sub-subsidiary	• Dominant influence
• Directors holding a majority of the voting rights	• A majority of the voting rights

2 If a company holds 20% or more of the shares of another company, it has a participating interest. True or false?

3 What is dominant influence?

4 Sometimes an undertaking **may** be excluded from consolidation. Sometimes it **must** be excluded. Write 'may' or 'must' against the appropriation circumstance.

(a) Inclusion is not material.

(b) The subsidiary is held exclusively for resale and has not been consolidated previously.

(c) The subsidiary's activities are so different from those of other undertakings to be consolidated that its inclusion would be incompatible with the requirement to give a true and fair view.

5 How should a subsidiary excluded on the grounds of temporary control be accounted for in the consolidated balance sheet?

6 What are the size criteria for exemption from preparing group accounts under the CA 1985?

7 It is not necessary for a parent company to publish its profit and loss account.

True   ☐

False   ☐

Answers to quick quiz

1   (a)   A majority of the voting rights
         (b)   Directors holding a majority of the voting rights
         (c)   Significant influence
         (d)   Sub-subsidiary (see para 1.5)

2   False. Significant influence is presumed but the presumption may be rebutted. (1.7)

3   Influence that can be exercised to achieve the operating and financial policies desired by the holder of the influence, notwithstanding the rights or influence of any other party. (1.9)

4   (a)   May
         (b)   Must
         (c)   Must (2.3)

5   It should be included under current assets at the lower of cost and NRV. (2.8)

6   See table on 3.3

7   True (4.5)

Now try the question below from the Exam Question Bank

Number	Level	Marks	Time
18	Full exam	20	36 mins

BPP PUBLISHING

Chapter 16

CONSOLIDATED BALANCE SHEET: BASIC PRINCIPLES

Topic list		Syllabus reference
1	Cancellation and part cancellation	4(c)
2	Minority interests	4(c)
3	Dividends payable by a subsidiary	4(c)
4	Goodwill arising on consolidation	4(c)
5	A technique of consolidation	4(c)
6	Inter-company trading	4(c)
7	Inter-company sales of fixed assets	4(c)
8	Summary: consolidated balance sheet	4(c)

Introduction

This chapter introduces the *basic procedures* required in consolidation and gives a formal step plan for carrying out a balance sheet consolidation. This step procedure should be useful to you as a starting guide for answering any question, but remember that you cannot rely on it to answer the question for you.

The method of consolidation shown here uses schedules for workings (reserves, minority interests etc) rather than the ledger accounts used in some other texts. This is because we believe that ledger accounts lead students to 'learn' the consolidation journals without thinking about what they are doing - always a dangerous practice in consolidation questions.

There are plenty of questions in this chapter - work through *all* of them carefully.

Study guide

- Explain the different methods which could be used to prepare group accounts.

- Prepare a consolidated balance sheet for a simple group dealing with pre and post acquisition profits, minority interests and consolidated goodwill.

- Explain why intra-group transactions should be eliminated on consolidation.

- Account for the effects (in the profit and loss account and balance sheet) of intra-group trading and other transactions including:

    - unrealised profits in stock and fixed assets
    - intra-group loans and interest and other intra-group charges, and
    - intra-group dividends including those paid out of pre-acquisition profits.

Exam guide

Each question must be approached and answered on its own merits. Examiners often put small extra or different problems in because, as they are always reminding students, it is not possible to 'rote-learn' consolidation.

1   CANCELLATION AND PART CANCELLATION

1.1   The preparation of a consolidated balance sheet, in a very simple form, consists of two procedures.

(a)   Take the individual accounts of the holding company and each subsidiary and **cancel out items which appear as an asset in one company and a liability in another.**

(b)   **Add together all the uncancelled assets** and liabilities throughout the group.

1.2   **Items requiring cancellation** may include the following.

(a)   The asset **'shares in subsidiary companies'** which appears in the parent company's accounts will be matched with the liability 'share capital' in the subsidiaries' accounts.

(b)   There may be **inter-company trading** within the group. For example, S Ltd may sell goods to H Ltd. H Ltd would then be a debtor in the accounts of S Ltd, while S Ltd would be a creditor in the accounts of H Ltd.

1.3   EXAMPLE: CANCELLATION

H Ltd regularly sells goods to its one subsidiary company, S Ltd. The balance sheets of the two companies on 31 December 20X6 are given below.

H LIMITED
BALANCE SHEET AS AT 31 DECEMBER 20X6

	£	£	£
Fixed assets			
Tangible assets			35,000
40,000 £1 shares in S Ltd at cost			40,000
			75,000
Current assets			
Stocks		16,000	
Debtors: S Ltd	2,000		
Other	6,000		
		8,000	
Cash at bank		1,000	
		25,000	
Current liabilities			
Creditors		14,000	
			11,000
			86,000
Capital and reserves			
70,000 £1 ordinary shares			70,000
Reserves			16,000
			86,000

S LIMITED
BALANCE SHEET AS AT 31 DECEMBER 20X6

	£	£	£
Fixed assets			
Tangible assets			45,000
Current assets			
Stocks		12,000	
Debtors		9,000	
		21,000	
Current liabilities			
Bank overdraft		3,000	
Creditors: H Ltd	2,000		
Other	2,000		
		4,000	
		7,000	
			14,000
			59,000
Capital and reserves			
40,000 £1 ordinary shares			40,000
Reserves			19,000
			59,000

Prepare the consolidated balance sheet of H Ltd.

1.4 SOLUTION

The cancelling items are:

(a) H Ltd's asset 'investment in shares of S Ltd' (£40,000) cancels with S Ltd's liability 'share capital' (£40,000);

(b) H Ltd's asset 'debtors: S Ltd' (£2,000) cancels with S Ltd's liability 'creditors: H Ltd' (£2,000).

The remaining assets and liabilities are added together to produce the following consolidated balance sheet.

H LIMITED
CONSOLIDATED BALANCE SHEET AS AT 31 DECEMBER 20X6

	£	£
Fixed assets		
Tangible assets		80,000
Current assets		
Stocks	28,000	
Debtors	15,000	
Cash at bank	1,000	
	44,000	
Current liabilities		
Bank overdraft	3,000	
Creditors	16,000	
	19,000	
		25,000
		105,000
Capital and reserves		
70,000 £1 ordinary shares		70,000
Reserves		35,000
		105,000

Notes on the example

1.5   (a)   H Ltd's bank balance is not netted off with S Ltd's bank overdraft. To offset one against the other would be less informative and would conflict with the statutory principle that assets and liabilities should not be netted off.

      (b)   The share capital in the consolidated balance sheet is the share capital of the parent company alone. This must *always* be the case, no matter how complex the consolidation, because the share capital of subsidiary companies must *always* be a wholly cancelling item.

Part cancellation

1.6   **An item may appear in the balance sheets of a parent company and its subsidiary, but not at the same amounts.**

      (a)   **The parent company may have acquired shares in the subsidiary at a price greater or less than their nominal value**. The asset will appear in the parent company's accounts at cost, while the liability will appear in the subsidiary's accounts at nominal value. **This raises the issue of goodwill**, which is dealt with later in this chapter.

      (b)   Even if the parent company acquired shares at nominal value, it **may not have acquired all the shares of the subsidiary** (so the subsidiary may be only partly owned). This **raises the issue of minority interests**, which are also dealt with later in this chapter.

      (c)   The inter-company trading balances may be out of step because of **goods or cash in transit**.

      (d)   One company may have **issued loan stock of which a proportion only is taken up** by the other company.

1.7   The following example illustrates the techniques needed to deal with the second two items. The procedure is to **cancel as far as possible. The remaining uncancelled amounts will appear in the consolidated balance sheet.**

      (a)   Uncancelled loan stock will appear as a liability of the group.

      (b)   Uncancelled balances on inter-company accounts represent goods or cash in transit, which will appear in the consolidated balance sheet.

Question 1

The balance sheets of H Ltd and of its subsidiary S Ltd have been made up to 30 June. H Ltd has owned all the ordinary shares and 40% of the loan stock of S Ltd since its incorporation.

H LIMITED
BALANCE SHEET AS AT 30 JUNE

	£	£
Fixed assets		
Tangible assets		120,000
Investment in S Ltd, at cost		
80,000 ordinary shares of £1 each		80,000
£20,000 of 12% loan stock in S Ltd		20,000
		220,000
Current assets		
Stocks	50,000	
Debtors	40,000	
Current account with S Ltd	18,000	
Cash	4,000	
	112,000	
Creditors: amounts falling due within one year		
Creditors	47,000	
Taxation	15,000	
	62,000	
Net current assets		50,000
		270,000
Creditors: amounts falling due after more than one year		
10% loan stock		75,000
		195,000
Capital and reserves		
Ordinary shares of £1 each, fully paid		100,000
Reserves		95,000
		195,000

S LIMITED
BALANCE SHEET AS AT 30 JUNE

	£	£
Tangible fixed assets		100,000
Current assets		
Stocks	60,000	
Debtors	30,000	
Cash	6,000	
	96,000	
Creditors: amounts falling due within one year		
Creditors	16,000	
Taxation	10,000	
Current account with H Ltd	12,000	
	38,000	
		58,000
		158,000
Creditors: amounts falling due after more than one year		
12% Loan stock		50,000
		108,000
Capital and reserves		
80,000 ordinary shares of £1 each, fully paid		80,000
Reserves		28,000
		108,000

The difference on current account arises because of goods in transit. Prepare the consolidated balance sheet of H Ltd.

Answer

H LIMITED
CONSOLIDATED BALANCE SHEET AS AT 30 JUNE

	£	£
Tangible fixed assets		220,000
Current assets		
Stocks	110,000	
Goods in transit	6,000	
Debtors	70,000	
Cash	10,000	
	196,000	
Creditors: amounts falling due within one year		
Creditors	63,000	
Taxation	25,000	
	88,000	
		108,000
		328,000
Creditors: amounts falling due after more than one year		
10% loan stock	75,000	
12% loan stock	30,000	
		105,000
		223,000
Capital and reserves		
Ordinary shares of £1 each, fully paid		100,000
Reserves		123,000
		223,000

Note especially how:

(a) The uncancelled loan stock in S Ltd becomes a liability of the group
(b) The goods in transit is the difference between the current accounts (£18,000 – £12,000)

2 MINORITY INTERESTS

2.1 It was mentioned earlier that the total assets and liabilities of subsidiary companies are included in the consolidated balance sheet, even in the case of subsidiaries which are only partly owned. A proportion of the net assets of such subsidiaries in fact belongs to investors from outside the group (minority interests).

> ### KEY TERM
>
> FRS 2 defines **minority interest** in a subsidiary undertaking as the 'interest in a subsidiary undertaking included in the consolidation that is attributable to the shares held by or on behalf of persons other than the parent undertaking and its subsidiary undertakings'.

In the consolidated balance sheet it is necessary to distinguish this proportion from those assets attributable to the group and financed by shareholders' funds.

2.2 The net assets of a company are financed by share capital and reserves. The consolidation procedure for dealing with partly owned subsidiaries is to **calculate the proportion of ordinary shares, preference shares and reserves attributable to minority interests.**

2.3 EXAMPLE: MINORITY INTERESTS

H Ltd has owned 75% of the share capital of S Ltd since the date of S Ltd's incorporation. Their latest balance sheets are given below.

H LIMITED - BALANCE SHEET

	£
Fixed assets	
Tangible assets	50,000
30,000 £1 ordinary shares in S Ltd at cost	30,000
	80,000
Net current assets	25,000
	105,000
Capital and reserves	
80,000 £1 ordinary shares	80,000
Reserves	25,000
	105,000

S LIMITED
BALANCE SHEET

	£
Tangible fixed assets	35,000
Net current assets	15,000
	50,000
Capital and reserves	
40,000 £1 ordinary shares	40,000
Reserves	10,000
	50,000

Prepare the consolidated balance sheet.

2.4 SOLUTION

All of S Ltd's net assets are consolidated despite the fact that the company is only 75% owned. The amount of net assets attributable to minority interests is calculated as follows.

	£
Minority share of share capital (25% × £40,000)	10,000
Minority share of reserves (25% × £10,000)	2,500
	12,500

Of S Ltd's share capital of £40,000, £10,000 is included in the figure for minority interest, while £30,000 is cancelled with H Ltd's asset 'investment in S Limited'.

The consolidated balance sheet can now be prepared.

H GROUP
CONSOLIDATED BALANCE SHEET

	£
Tangible fixed assets	85,000
Net current assets	40,000
	125,000
Share capital	80,000
Reserves £(25,000 + (75% × 10,000))	32,500
Shareholders' funds	112,500
Minority interest	12,500
	125,000

2.5 In this example we have shown minority interest on the 'capital and reserves' side of the balance sheet to illustrate how some of S Ltd's net assets are financed by shareholders' funds, while some are financed by outside investors. You may see minority interest as a deduction from the other side of the balance sheet. The second half of the balance sheet will then consist entirely of shareholders' funds. The Companies Act 1985 permits either of the above presentations, but **FRS 4 seems to require the disclosure shown above**.

Exam focus point

In more complicated examples the following technique is recommended for dealing with minority interests.

Step 1 Cancel common items in the draft balance sheets. If there is a minority interest, the subsidiary company's share capital will be a partly cancelled item. Ascertain the proportion of ordinary shares and the proportion (possibly different) of preference shares held by the minority.

Step 2 Produce a working for the minority interest. Add in the amounts of preference and ordinary share capital calculated in step 1: this completes the cancellation of the subsidiary's share capital.

Add also the minority's share of each reserve in the subsidiary company. Reserves belong to equity shareholders; the proportion attributable to minority interests therefore depends on their percentage holding of ordinary shares.

Step 3 Produce a separate working for each reserve (capital, revenue etc) found in the subsidiary company's balance sheet. The initial balances on these accounts will be taken straight from the draft balance sheets of the parent and subsidiary company.2.6

Step 4 The closing balances in these workings can be entered directly onto the consolidated balance sheet.

Question 2

Set out below are the draft balance sheets of H Ltd and its subsidiary S Ltd. You are required to prepare the consolidated balance sheet.

H LIMITED

	£	£
Fixed assets		
Tangible assets		31,000
Investment in S Ltd		
12,000 £1 ordinary shares at cost	12,000	
4,000 £1 preference shares at cost	4,000	
£4,000 10% debentures at cost	4,000	
		20,000
		51,000
Net current assets		11,000
		62,000
Capital and reserves		
Ordinary shares of £1 each		40,000
Revenue reserve		22,000
		62,000

S LIMITED

	£
Tangible fixed assets	34,000
Net current assets	22,000
	56,000
Long-term liability	
10% debentures	10,000
	46,000
Capital and reserves	
Ordinary shares of £1 each	20,000
Preference shares of £1 each	16,000
Capital reserve	6,000
Revenue reserve	4,000
	46,000

Answer

Partly cancelling items are the components of H Ltd's investment in S Ltd, ie ordinary shares, preference shares and loan stock. Minorities have an interest in 75% (12,000/16,000) of S Ltd's preference shares and 40% (8,000/20,000) of S Ltd's equity, including reserves.

You should now product workings for minority interests, capital reserve and revenue reserve as follows.

Workings

1   *Minority interests*

	£
Ordinary share capital (40% of 20,000)	8,000
Reserves: capital (40% × 6,000)	2,400
revenue (40% × 4,000)	1,600
	12,000
Preference share capital (75% × 16,000)	12,000
	24,000

2   *Capital reserve*

	£
H Ltd	-
Share of S Ltd's capital reserve (60% × 6,000)	3,600
	3,600

3   *Revenue reserve*

	£
H Ltd	22,000
Share of S Ltd's revenue reserves (60% × 4,000)	2,400
	24,400

The results of the workings are now used to construct the consolidated balance sheet (CBS).

H GROUP
CONSOLIDATED BALANCE SHEET

	£
Tangible fixed assets	65,000
Net current assets	33,000
	98,000
Long-term liability	
10% debentures	6,000
	92,000
Capital and reserves	
Ordinary shares of £1 each	40,000
Capital reserve	3,600
Revenue reserve	24,400
Shareholders' funds	68,000
Minority interests	24,000
	92,000

Notes

(a)   S Ltd is a subsidiary of H Ltd because H Ltd owns 60% of its equity capital. It is unimportant how little of the preference share capital is owned by H Ltd.

(b)   As always, the share capital in the consolidated balance sheet is that of the parent company alone. The share capital in S Ltd's balance sheet was partly cancelled against the investment shown in H Ltd's balance sheet, while the uncancelled portion was credited to minority interest.

(c)   The figure for minority interest comprises the interest of outside investors in the share capital and reserves of the subsidiary. The uncancelled portion of S Ltd's loan stock is not shown as part of minority interest but is disclosed separately as a liability of the group.

3 DIVIDENDS PAYABLE BY A SUBSIDIARY

3.1 When a subsidiary company pays a dividend during the year the accounting treatment is not difficult. Suppose S Ltd, a 60% subsidiary of H Ltd, pays a dividend of £1,000 on the last day of its accounting period. Its total reserves before paying the dividend stood at £5,000.

(a) £400 of the dividend is paid to minority shareholders. The cash leaves the group and will not appear anywhere in the consolidated balance sheet.

(b) The holding company receives £600 of the dividend, debiting cash and crediting profit and loss account.

(c) The remaining balance of reserves in S Ltd's balance sheet (£4,000) will be consolidated in the normal way. The group's share (60% × £4,000 = £2,400) will be included in group reserves in the balance sheet; the minority share (40% × £4,000 = £1,600) is credited to the minority interest account.

3.2 More care is needed when dealing with **proposed dividends** not yet paid by a subsidiary. The **first step** must be to **ensure that the draft accounts of both subsidiary and parent company are up-to-date and reflect the proposed dividend.**

Exam focus point

A question may state that both companies have accrued for the proposed dividend; alternatively you may be presented with draft balance sheets in which one or other company, or possibly both companies, have omitted to make the necessary entries.

3.3 If neither company has accrued for the proposed dividend you will need to make appropriate adjustments to the draft balance sheets.

(a) If the subsidiary has not yet accrued for the proposed dividend, the adjustment is:

DEBIT   Revenue reserves
CREDIT   Dividends payable

with the full amount of the dividend payable in the subsidiary's books, whether it is due to the parent company or to minority shareholders.

(b) If the parent company has not yet accrued for its share of the proposed dividend, the adjustment is:

DEBIT   Debtors (dividend receivable)
CREDIT   Revenue reserves

with the *parent company's share* of the dividend receivable in the parent's books.

3.4 **On consolidation, the dividend payable in S Ltd's accounts will cancel with the dividend receivable in H Ltd's accounts.** If S Ltd is a wholly owned subsidiary, there will be complete cancellation; if S Ltd is only partly owned, there will be only part cancellation. The uncancelled portion will be the amount of dividend payable to minority shareholders and this will appear in the consolidated balance sheet as a current liability.

3.5 **When preparing the workings for reserves and minority interest, the relevant reserves figures for both companies are the figures** *after* **adjusting for the proposed dividend.**

3.6 EXAMPLE: DIVIDENDS

Set out below are the draft balance sheets of Hug Ltd and its subsidiary Bug Ltd. Hug Ltd has not yet taken account of the dividend proposed by Bug Ltd.

You are required to prepare the consolidated balance sheet.

HUG LIMITED

	£	£
Fixed assets		
Tangible assets		1,350
Investment in Bug Ltd: 1,500 shares at cost		1,500
		2,850
Current assets	700	
Current liabilities		
Creditors	400	
		300
		3,150
Capital and reserves		£
Ordinary shares of £1 each		1,000
Revenue reserves		2,150
		3,150

BUG LIMITED

	£	£
Tangible fixed assets		2,500
Current assets	900	
Current liabilities		
Creditors	200	
Proposed dividend	200	
		500
		3,000
Capital and reserves		
Ordinary shares of £1 each		2,000
Revenue reserves		1,000
		3,000

3.7 SOLUTION

The first step is to bring Hug Ltd's balance sheet up to date by accruing for its share of the dividend receivable from Bug Ltd. Hug Ltd owns 75% (1,500/2,000) of the shares in Bug Ltd. Its share of the proposed dividend is therefore 75% × £200 = £150. Hug Ltd's draft balance sheet should be adjusted as follows.

DEBIT	Debtors: dividend receivable	£150	
CREDIT	Revenue reserves		£150

3.8 Next deal with cancellation. There are two part-cancelling items, the shares of Bug Ltd and the dividend receivable/payable.

3.9 The workings may now be produced. Notice how the relevant reserves figures are the figures after adjusting for the proposed dividend. Because Bug Ltd's accounts are up-to-date, and reflect the proposed figure, the correct reserves figure (£1,000) can be taken straight from the draft balance sheet. In the case of Hug Ltd, it is the adjusted reserves figure (£2,150 + £150 = £2,300) which is used.

Workings

1   *Minority interests*

		£
Share capital (25% × 2,000)		500
Revenue reserves (25% × 1,000)		250
		750

2   *Revenue reserves*

		£
Hug Ltd (as adjusted)		2,300
Share of Bug Ltd's revenue reserves (1,000 × 75%)		750
		3,050

HUG GROUP
CONSOLIDATED BALANCE SHEET

	£	£
Tangible fixed assets		3,850
Current assets	1,600	
Current liabilities		
Creditors	600	
Minority proposed dividend	50	
		950
		4,800
Capital and reserves		
Ordinary shares of £1 each		1,000
Revenue reserves		3,050
Shareholders' funds		4,050
Minority interests		750
		4,800

3.10   If there is a proposed *preference dividend* payable by the subsidiary the same procedure should be applied. Again, the first step is to bring both companies' balance sheets up to date, and again the workings accounts will deal with reserves figures *after* adjusting for the proposed dividends.

3.11 EXAMPLE: PROPOSED PREFERENCE DIVIDEND

Set out below are the draft balance sheets of H Ltd and S Ltd. Neither company has yet provided for any dividend, but you should now provide for:

(a)   The preference dividend of S Ltd
(b)   A proposed ordinary dividend of 10% by S Ltd
(c)   A proposed ordinary dividend of 20% by H Ltd

You are required to prepare the consolidated balance sheet.

H LIMITED

	£	£
Fixed assets		
Tangible assets		72,000
Investment in S Ltd		
30,000 £1 ordinary shares at cost	30,000	
6,000 £1 7% preference shares at cost	6,000	
		36,000
		108,000
Current assets	73,000	
Current liabilities	21,000	
		52,000
		160,000

Capital and reserves		£
Ordinary shares of £1 each		100,000
Revenue reserves		60,000
		160,000

S LIMITED

	£	£
Tangible fixed assets		40,000
Current assets	51,700	
Current liabilities	19,000	
		32,700
		72,700
Capital and reserves		
Ordinary shares of £1 each		40,000
7% preference shares of £1 each		10,000
		50,000
Revenue reserves		22,700
		72,700

3.12 SOLUTION

The draft balance sheet of S Ltd must be adjusted by the following entries.

DEBIT	Revenue reserves	£4,700	
CREDIT	Proposed dividends		
	Preference (7% × £10,000)		£700
	Ordinary (10% × £40,000)		£4,000

The adjusted balance on S Ltd's revenue reserves is now £(22,700 – 4,700)=£18,000.

H Ltd's share in these dividends is:

	£
Preference (60%)	420
Ordinary (75%)	3,000
	3,420

H Ltd's balance sheet must therefore be adjusted as follows.

DEBIT	Debtors: dividends receivable	£3,420	
CREDIT	Revenue reserves		£3,420

A further adjustment to H Ltd's balance sheet is necessary in respect of the company's own proposed dividend of 20% × £100,000 = £20,000.

DEBIT	Revenue reserves	£20,000	
CREDIT	Proposed dividend		£20,000

The adjusted balance on H Ltd's revenue reserve is now £(60,000 + 3,420 – 20,000) = £43,420.

3.13 After S Ltd's share capital and the dividends payable/receivable have been part-cancelled, the workings can be drawn up.

Workings

1   *Minority interests*

		£
Ordinary share capital (25% × 40,000)		10,000
Revenue reserves (25% × 18,000)		4,500
		14,500
Preference share capital (40% × 10,000)		4,000
		18,500

2   *Revenue reserves*

		£
H Ltd's (adjusted balance)		43,420
Share of S Ltd's revenue reserve (75% × 18,000)		13,500
		56,920

H LIMITED CONSOLIDATED BALANCE SHEET

	£	£
Tangible fixed assets		112,000
Current assets	124,700	
Current liabilities		
Sundry	40,000	
Proposed dividend	20,000	
Minority proposed dividend (25% × £4,000) + (40% × £700)	1,280	
		63,420
		175,420
Capital and reserves		
Ordinary shares of £1 each		100,000
Revenue reserves		56,920
Shareholders' funds		156,920
Minority interests		18,500
		175,420

4   GOODWILL ARISING ON CONSOLIDATION

4.1   In the examples we have looked at so far the cost of shares acquired by the parent company has always been equal to the nominal value of those shares. This is seldom the case in practice and we must now consider some more complicated examples. To begin with, **we will examine the entries made by the parent company in its own balance sheet when it acquires shares.**

4.2   When a company H Ltd wishes to **purchase shares** in a company S Ltd it must pay the previous owners of those shares. The most obvious form of payment would be in **cash**. Suppose H Ltd purchases all 40,000 £1 shares in S Ltd and pays £60,000 cash to the previous shareholders in consideration. The entries in H Ltd's books would be:

DEBIT	Investment in S Ltd at cost	£60,000	
CREDIT	Bank		£60,000

4.3   However, the previous shareholders might be prepared to accept some other form of consideration. For example, they might accept an agreed number of **shares** in H Ltd. H Ltd would then issue new shares in the agreed number and allot them to the former shareholders of S Ltd. This kind of deal might be attractive to H Ltd since it avoids the need for a heavy cash outlay. The former shareholders of S Ltd would retain an indirect interest in that company's profitability via their new holding in its parent company.

4.4   Continuing the example, suppose the shareholders of S Ltd agreed to accept one £1 ordinary share in H Ltd for every two £1 ordinary shares in S Ltd. H Ltd would then need to issue and allot 20,000 new £1 shares. How would this transaction be recorded in the books of H Ltd?

4.5   The simplest method would be as follows.

DEBIT	Investment in S Ltd	£20,000
CREDIT	Share capital	£20,000

However, if the 40,000 £1 shares acquired in S Ltd are thought to have a value of £60,000 this would be misleading. The former shareholders of S Ltd have presumably agreed to accept 20,000 shares in H Ltd because they consider each of those shares to have a value of £3. This view of the matter suggests the following method of recording the transaction in H Ltd's books.

DEBIT	Investment in S Ltd	£60,000
CREDIT	Share capital £20,000	
	Share premium account £40,000	

The second method is the one which the Companies Act 1985 requires should normally be used in preparing consolidated accounts.

4.6   The amount which H Ltd records in its books as the cost of its investment in S Ltd may be more or less than the book value of the assets it acquires. Suppose that S Ltd in the previous example has nil reserves, so that its share capital of £40,000 is balanced by net assets with a book value of £40,000. For simplicity, assume that the book value of S Ltd's assets is the same as their market or fair value.

4.7   Now when the directors of H Ltd agree to pay £60,000 for a 100% investment in S Ltd they must believe that, in addition to its tangible assets of £40,000, S Ltd must also have intangible assets worth £20,000. This amount of £20,000 paid over and above the value of the tangible assets acquired is called **goodwill arising on consolidation** (sometimes **premium on acquisition**).

4.8   Following the normal cancellation procedure the £40,000 share capital in S Ltd's balance sheet could be cancelled against £40,000 of the 'investment in S Limited' in the balance sheet of H Ltd. This would leave a £20,000 debit uncancelled in the parent company's accounts and this £20,000 would appear in the consolidated balance sheet under the caption 'Intangible fixed assets. Goodwill arising on consolidation' (although see below for FRS 10's requirements on this type of goodwill).

Goodwill and pre-acquisition profits

4.9   Up to now we have assumed that S Ltd had nil reserves when its shares were purchased by H Ltd. Assuming instead that S Ltd had earned profits of £8,000 in the period before acquisition, its balance sheet just before the purchase would look as follows.

	£
Net tangible assets	48,000
Share capital	40,000
Reserves	8,000
	48,000

4.10 If H Ltd now purchases all the shares in S Ltd it will acquire net tangible assets worth £48,000 at a cost of £60,000. Clearly in this case S Ltd's intangible assets (goodwill) are being valued at £12,000. It should be apparent that **any reserves earned by the subsidiary prior to its acquisition by the parent company must be incorporated in the cancellation process so as to arrive at a figure for goodwill arising on consolidation.** In other words, not only S Ltd's share capital, but also its pre-acquisition reserves, must be cancelled against the asset 'investment in S Ltd' in the accounts of the parent company. The uncancelled balance of £12,000 appears in the consolidated balance sheet.

4.11 The consequence of this is that any pre-acquisition reserves of a subsidiary company are not aggregated with the parent company's reserves in the consolidated balance sheet. **The figure of consolidated reserves comprises the reserves of the parent company plus the post-acquisition reserves only of subsidiary companies. The post-acquisition reserves are simply reserves at the consolidation date less reserves at acquisition.**

4.12 EXAMPLE: GOODWILL AND PRE-ACQUISITION PROFITS

Sing Ltd acquired the ordinary shares of Wing Ltd on 31 March when the draft balance sheets of each company were as follows.

SING LIMITED
BALANCE SHEET AS AT 31 MARCH

	£
Fixed assets	
Investment in 50,000 shares of Wing Ltd at cost	80,000
Net current assets	40,000
	120,000
Capital and reserves	
Ordinary shares	75,000
Revenue reserves	45,000
	120,000

WING LIMITED
BALANCE SHEET AS AT 31 MARCH

	£
Net current assets	60,000
Share capital and reserves	
50,000 ordinary shares of £1 each	50,000
Revenue reserves	10,000
	60,000

Prepare the consolidated balance sheet as at 31 March.

4.13 SOLUTION

The technique to adopt here is to produce a new working: 'Goodwill'. A proforma working is set out below.

Goodwill

	£	£
Cost of investment		X
Share of net assets acquired as represented by:		
Ordinary share capital	X	
Share premium	X	
Reserves on acquisition	X	
Group share	a%	(X)
		X
b% preference shares		(X)
Goodwill		X

4.14 Applying this to our example the working will look like this.

	£	£
Cost of investment		80,000
Share of net assets acquired as represented by:		
Ordinary share capital	50,000	
Revenue reserves on acquisition	10,000	
	60,000	
Group share 100%		60,000
Goodwill		20,000

SING LIMITED
CONSOLIDATED BALANCE SHEET AS AT 31 MARCH

	£
Fixed assets	
Goodwill arising on consolidation	20,000
Net current assets	100,000
	120,000
Capital and reserves	
Ordinary shares	75,000
Revenue reserves	45,000
	120,000

FRS 10 Goodwill and intangible assets

4.15 Goodwill arising on consolidation is one form of **purchased goodwill,** and is therefore governed by FRS 10. As explained in an earlier chapter FRS 10 requires that purchased goodwill should be capitalised and classified as an asset on the balance sheet. It is then eliminated from the accounts by **amortisation** through the profit and loss account.

4.16 **A consolidation adjustment** will be required each year as follows.

DEBIT	Consolidated P&L account
CREDIT	Provision for amortisation of goodwill

The **unamortised portion** will be included in the consolidated balance sheet under **fixed assets.**

4.17 Goodwill arising on consolidation is the difference between the cost of an acquisition and the value of the subsidiary's net assets acquired. This difference can be **negative**: the aggregate of the fair values of the separable net assets acquired may exceed what the holding company paid for them. This 'negative goodwill', also sometimes called 'discount arising on consolidation', is required by FRS 10 to be disclosed in the intangible fixed assets category, directly under positive goodwill, ie as a 'negative asset'

5   A TECHNIQUE OF CONSOLIDATION   Pilot paper

5.1   We have now looked at the topics of cancellation, minority interests and goodwill arising on consolidation. It is time to set out an approach to be used in tackling consolidated balance sheets. The approach we recommend consists of five stages.

Stage 1   Update the draft balance sheets of subsidiaries and parent company to take account of any proposed dividends not yet accrued for.

Stage 2   Agree inter-company current accounts by adjusting for items in transit.

Stage 3   Cancel items common to both balance sheets.

Stage 4   Produce working for minority interests as shown in Paragraph 2.4.

Stage 5   Produce a goodwill working as shown in Paragraph 4.13 above. Then produce a working for capital and revenue reserves.

5.2   You should now attempt to apply this technique to the following question.

Question 3

The draft balance sheets of Ping Ltd and Pong Ltd on 30 June 20X4 were as follows.

PING LIMITED
BALANCE SHEET AS AT 30 JUNE 20X4

	£	£
Fixed assets		
Tangible assets	50,000	
20,000 ordinary shares in Pong Ltd at cost	30,000	
		80,000
Current assets		
Stock	3,000	
Debtors (including £4,000 dividend proposed by Pong Ltd)	20,000	
Cash	2,000	
	25,000	
Creditors: amounts falling due within one year		
Owed to Pong Ltd	8,000	
Trade creditors	10,000	
	18,000	
Net current assets		7,000
		87,000
Capital and reserves		
Ordinary shares of £1 each		45,000
Capital reserves		12,000
Revenue reserves		30,000
		87,000

PONG LIMITED
BALANCE SHEET AS AT 30 JUNE 20X4

	£	£
Tangible fixed assets		40,000
Current assets		
Stock	8,000	
Owed by Ping Ltd	10,000	
Debtors	7,000	
	25,000	
Creditors: amounts falling due within one year		
Trade creditors	7,000	
Proposed dividends	5,000	
	12,000	
Net current assets		13,000
		53,000

Capital and reserves	£
Ordinary shares of £1 each	25,000
Capital reserves	5,000
Revenue reserves	23,000
	53,000

Ping Ltd acquired its investment in Pong Ltd on 1 July 20X1 when the revenue reserves of Pong Ltd stood at £6,000. There have been no changes in the share capital or capital reserves of Pong Ltd since that date. At 30 June 20X4 Pong Ltd had invoiced Ping Ltd for goods to the value of £2,000 which had not been received by Ping Ltd.

Goodwill is deemed to have an indefinite useful life and is therefore to remain in the balance sheet.

Prepare the consolidated balance sheet of Ping Ltd as at 30 June 20X4.

Answer

Stage 1. Ensure parent company and subsidiary balance sheets have correctly taken account of the proposed dividends.

Ping Ltd has £4,000 included in debtors for its share (80%) of Pong Ltd's proposed dividend, so there is no adjustment to make. Similarly, Pong Ltd has correctly accounted for its dividend payable.

Stage 2. Agree current accounts.

Ping Ltd has stock in transit of £2,000 making its total stock £3,000 + £2,000 = £5,000 and its liability to Pong Ltd £8,000 + £2,000 = £10,000.

Stage 3. Cancel common items: these are the current accounts between the two companies of £10,000 each and the dividends payable by Pong to Ping. This leaves a creditor for the dividend owed to the minority in Pong.

Stage 4. Calculate the minority interest.

Minority interest

	£
Ordinary share capital (20% × 25,000)	5,000
Capital reserves (20% × 5,000)	1,000
Revenue reserves (20% × 23,000)	4,600
	10,600

Note. In this particular case, where there are no preference shares or adjustments to Pong Ltd's revenue reserves, the minority interest figure may simply be calculated as 20% of Pong Ltd's net assets, ie 20% × £53,000. Because, however, such adjustments and complications often arise, it is a good idea to get into the habit of producing the working as shown.

Stage 5. Calculate goodwill and reserves.

Goodwill

	£	£
Cost of investment		30,000
Share of assets acquired as represented by:		
Ordinary share capital	25,000	
Capital reserves on acquisition	5,000	
Revenue reserves on acquisition	6,000	
	36,000	
Group share 80%		28,800
Goodwill		1,200

Consolidated capital reserves

	£
Ping Ltd	12,000
Share of Pong Ltd's post acquisition capital reserve	-
	12,000

Consolidated revenue reserves

	£
Ping Ltd	30,000
Share of Pong Ltd's post acquisition	
revenue reserves: 80%(23,000 - 6,000)*	13,600
	43,600

*Note. Post acquisition reserves of Pong Ltd are simply reserves now less reserves at acquisition. The consolidated balance sheet may now be written out.

PING LIMITED
CONSOLIDATED BALANCE SHEET AS AT 30 JUNE 20X4

	£	£
Fixed assets		
Intangible fixed assets: goodwill		1,200
Tangible assets (£50,000 + £40,000)		90,000
		91,200
Current assets		
Stocks (£5,000 + £8,000)	13,000	
Debtors (£16,000 + £7,000)	23,000	
Cash	2,000	
	38,000	
Creditors: amounts falling due within one year		
Trade creditors (£10,000 + £7,000)	17,000	
Minority dividends	1,000	
	18,000	
Net current assets		20,000
		111,200
Capital and reserves		
Ordinary shares of £1 each		45,000
Capital reserves		12,000
Revenue reserves		43,600
Shareholders' funds		100,600
Minority interests		10,600
		111,200

Exam focus point

A consolidated balance sheet will come up as regularly as clockwork. There will nearly always be an adjustment for inter-company trading.

6   INTER-COMPANY TRADING

6.1   We have already come across cases where one company in a group engages in trading with another group company. Any debtor/creditor balances outstanding between the companies are cancelled on consolidation. No further problem arises if all such intra-group transactions are undertaken at cost, without any mark-up for profit.

6.2   However, each company in a group is a separate trading entity and may wish to treat other group companies in the same way as any other customer. In this case, a company (say A Ltd) may buy goods at one price and sell them at a higher price to another group company (B Ltd). The accounts of A Ltd will quite properly include the profit earned on sales to B Ltd; and similarly B Ltd's balance sheet will include stocks at their cost to B Ltd at the amount at which they were purchased from A Ltd.

6.3 This gives rise to **two problems.**

(a) Although A Ltd makes a profit as soon as it sells goods to B Ltd, the group does not make a sale or achieve a profit until an outside customer buys the goods from B Ltd.

(b) Any purchases from A Ltd which remain unsold by B Ltd at the year end will be included in B Ltd's stock. Their balance sheet value will be their cost to B Ltd, which is not the same as their cost to the group.

6.4 The objective of consolidated accounts is to present the financial position of several connected companies as that of a single entity, the group. This means that **in a consolidated balance sheet the only profits recognised should be those earned by the group** in providing goods or services to outsiders; and similarly, stock in the consolidated balance sheet should be valued at cost to the group.

6.5 Suppose that a holding company H Ltd buys goods for £1,600 and sells them to a wholly owned subsidiary S Ltd for £2,000. The goods are in S Ltd's stock at the year end and appear in S Ltd's balance sheet at £2,000. In this case, H Ltd will record a profit of £400 in its individual accounts, but from the group's point of view the figures are:

Cost	£1,600
External sales	nil
Closing stock at cost	£1,600
Profit/loss	nil

6.6 If we add together the figures for retained reserves and stock in the individual balance sheets of H Ltd and S Ltd the resulting figures for consolidated reserves and consolidated stock will each be overstated by £400. A **consolidation adjustment** is therefore necessary as follows.

DEBIT **Group reserves**
CREDIT **Group stock (balance sheet)**

with the amount of profit unrealised by the group.

Question 4

H Ltd acquired all the shares in S Ltd when the reserves of S Ltd stood at £10,000. Draft balance sheets for each company are as follows.

	H Ltd		S Ltd	
	£	£	£	£
Fixed assets				
Tangible assets		80,000		40,000
Investment in S Ltd at cost		46,000		
		126,000		
Current assets	40,000		30,000	
Current liabilities	21,000		18,000	
		19,000		12,000
		145,000		52,000
Capital and reserves				
Ordinary shares of £1 each		100,000		30,000
Reserves		45,000		22,000
		145,000		52,000

During the year S Ltd sold goods to H Ltd for £50,000, the profit to S Ltd being 20% of selling price. At the balance sheet date, £15,000 of these goods remained unsold in the stocks of H Ltd. At the same date, H Ltd owed S Ltd £12,000 for goods bought and this debt is included in the creditors of H Ltd and the debtors of S Ltd.

Note. Goodwill is deemed to have an indefinite useful life and is therefore to remain in the balance sheet.

Required

Prepare a draft consolidated balance sheet for H Ltd.

Answer

1   *Goodwill*

	£	£
Cost of investment		46,000
Share of net assets acquired as represented by		
Share capital	30,000	
Reserves	10,000	
	40,000	
Group share (100%)		40,000
Goodwill		6,000

2   *Reserves*

	£
H Ltd	45,000
Share of S Ltd's post acquisition retained reserves	
£(22,000 – 10,000)	12,000
	57,000
Stock: unrealised profit (20% × £15,000)	3,000
Group reserves	54,000

H LIMITED
CONSOLIDATED BALANCE SHEET

	£	£
Intangible fixed assets: goodwill		6,000
Tangible fixed assets		120,000
		126,000
Current assets (W1)	55,000	
Current liabilities (W2)	27,000	
		28,000
		154,000
Capital and reserves		
Ordinary shares of £1 each		100,000
Reserves		54,000
		154,000

Workings

1   *Current assets*

	£	£
In H Ltd's balance sheet		40,000
In S Ltd's balance sheet	30,000	
Less S Ltd's current account with H Ltd cancelled	12,000	
		18,000
		58,000
Less unrealised profit excluded from stock valuation		3,000
		55,000

2   *Current liabilities*

	£
In H Ltd's balance sheet	21,000
Less H Ltd's current account with S Ltd cancelled	12,000
	9,000
In S Ltd's balance sheet	18,000
	27,000

Minority interests in unrealised inter-company profits

6.7 **A further problem occurs where a subsidiary company which is not wholly owned is involved in inter-company trading within the group**. If a subsidiary S Ltd is 75% owned and sells goods to the holding company for £16,000 cost plus £4,000 profit, ie for £20,000 and if these stocks are unsold by H Ltd at the balance sheet date, the 'unrealised' profit of £4,000 earned by S Ltd and charged to H Ltd will be partly owned by the minority interest of S Ltd. As far as the minority interest of S Ltd is concerned, their share (25% of £4,000) amounting to £1,000 of profit on the sale of goods would appear to have been fully realised. It is only the group that has not yet made a profit on the sale.

6.8 **There are three different possibilities as regards the treatment of these inter-company profits.** Remove:

(a) Only the group's share of the profit loading.

(b) The whole profit loading, charging the minority with their proportion.

(c) The whole of the profit without charging the minority (to reduce group reserves by the whole profit loading).

6.9 **The method most commonly used until recently was the most prudent one, (c).**

DEBIT	Profit and loss account of group	)	with profit loading
CREDIT	Asset account	)	

However, the ASB in its *Interim statement on consolidated accounts* has stated that the minority should be charged or credited with its share of all consolidation adjustments where the adjustment is made in respect of partly owned subsidiaries' profits. If the parent company has made the unrealised profit or loss, then the minority interest is not affected.

6.10 The double entry is therefore as follows.

ENTRIES TO LEARN

DEBIT	Group reserves
DEBIT	Minority interest
CREDIT	Group stock (balance sheet)

6.11 EXAMPLE: MINORITY INTERESTS AND INTER-COMPANY PROFITS

H Ltd has owned 75% of the shares of S Ltd since the incorporation of that company. During the year to 31 December 20X2, S Ltd sold goods costing £16,000 to H Ltd at a price of £20,000 and these goods were still unsold by H Ltd at the end of the year. Draft balance sheets of each company at 31 December 20X2 were as follows.

	H Limited		S Limited	
Fixed assets	£	£	£	£
Tangible assets		125,000		120,000
Investment: 75,000 shares in S Ltd at cost		75,000		-
		200,000		120,000
Current assets				
Stocks	50,000		48,000	
Trade debtors	20,000		16,000	
	70,000		64,000	
Creditors	40,000		24,000	
		30,000		40,000
		230,000		160,000
Capital and reserves				
Ordinary shares of £1 each fully paid		80,000		100,000
Reserves		150,000		60,000
		230,000		160,000

Required

Prepare the draft consolidated balance sheet of H Ltd.

6.12 SOLUTION

The profit earned by S Ltd but unrealised by the group is £4,000 of which £3,000 (75%) is attributable to the group and £1,000 (25%) to the minority.

Remove the whole of the profit loading, charging the minority with their proportion; this is the treatment used here, as required by the ASB.

Reserves	£
H Ltd	150,000
Share of S Ltd's post-acquisition retained reserves	
£(60,000 − 4,000) × 75%	42,000
	192,000

Minority interest	£
Share capital (25% × £100,000)	25,000
Reserves £(60,000 − 4,000) × 25%	14,000
	39,000

H LIMITED
CONSOLIDATED BALANCE SHEET AS AT 31 DECEMBER 20X2

	£	£
Tangible fixed assets		245,000
Current assets		
Stocks £(50,000 + 48,000 − 4,000)	94,000	
Trade debtors	36,000	
	130,000	
Creditors	64,000	
Net current assets		66,000
		311,000
Capital and reserves		
Ordinary shares of £1 each		80,000
Reserves		192,000
Shareholders' funds		272,000
Minority interest		39,000
		311,000

7   INTER-COMPANY SALES OF FIXED ASSETS

7.1   As well as engaging in trading activities with each other, **group companies may on occasion wish to transfer fixed assets. In their individual accounts the companies concerned will treat the transfer just like a sale between unconnected parties:** the selling company will record a profit or loss on sale; while the purchasing company will record the asset at the amount paid to acquire it, and will use that amount as the basis for calculating depreciation.

7.2   **On consolidation, the usual 'group entity' principle applies**. The consolidated balance sheet must show assets at their cost to the group, and any depreciation charged must be based on that cost. **Two consolidation adjustments** will usually be needed to achieve this.

(a)   An **adjustment to alter reserves and fixed assets cost so as to remove any element of unrealised profit or loss**. This is similar to the adjustment required in respect of unrealised profit in stock.

(b)   An **adjustment to alter reserves and accumulated depreciation** is made so that consolidated depreciation is based on the asset's cost to the group.

7.3   **The double entry is as follows.**

(a)   *Sale by holding company*

DEBIT   Group reserves
CREDIT   Fixed assets

with the profit on disposal.

DEBIT   Fixed assets
CREDIT   Group reserves (H's share)
CREDIT   Minority interest (MI's share)

with the additional depreciation.

(b)   *Sale by subsidiary*

DEBIT   Group reserves (H's share)
DEBIT   Minority interest (MI's share)
CREDIT   Fixed assets

with the profit on disposal.

DEBIT   Fixed assets
CREDIT   Group reserves

with the additional depreciation.

7.4   EXAMPLE: INTER-COMPANY SALE OF FIXED ASSETS

H Ltd owns 60% of S Ltd and on 1 January 20X1 S Ltd sells plant costing £10,000 to H Ltd for £12,500. The companies make up accounts to 31 December 20X1 and the balances on their revenue reserves at that date are:

H Ltd	after charging depreciation of 10% on plant	£27,000
S Ltd	including profit on sale of plant	£18,000

Required

Show the revenue reserves account.

7.5 SOLUTION

Revenue reserves

	£
H Ltd	27,000
Share of S Ltd's post-acquisition retained reserves	
£(18,000 – 2,500) × 60%	9,300
Depreciation on plant (10% × £2,500)	250
	36,550

Notes

1   The minority interest in the revenue reserves of S Ltd 40% × £(18,000 – 2,500) = £6,200.

2   The asset is written down to cost and depreciation on the 'profit' element is removed. The group profit and loss account for the year is thus reduced by a net ((£2,500 × 60%) – £250) = £1,250.

8   SUMMARY: CONSOLIDATED BALANCE SHEET

Purpose	To show the net assets which H controls and the ownership of those assets.
Net assets	Always 100% H plus 100% S providing H holds a majority of voting rights.
Share capital	H only.
Reason	Simply reporting to the holding company's shareholders in another form.
Reserves	100% H plus group share of post-acquisition retained reserves of S less consolidation adjustments.
Reason	To show the extent to which the group actually owns net assets included in the top half of the balance sheet.
Minority interest	MI share of S's consolidated net assets.
Reason	To show the extent to which other parties own net assets that are under the control of the holding company.

Chapter roundup

- This chapter has covered the mechanics of preparing simple **consolidated balance sheets**. In particular, procedures have been described for dealing with

  ° Cancellation
  ° Calculation of minority interests
  ° Calculation of goodwill arising on consolidation

- A five-stage drill has been described and exemplified in a comprehensive example.

- The stages are as follows.

  ° Update the draft balance sheets to take account of proposed dividends not accrued for
  ° Agree intercompany current accounts by adjusting for items in transit
  ° Cancel items common to both balance sheets
  ° Minority interests
  ° Goodwill

- We have examined the consolidation adjustments necessary when group companies trade **with or sell fixed assets to each** other.

  ° The guiding principle is that the consolidated balance sheet must show assets at their cost to the group.

  ° Any profit arising on intra-group transactions must be eliminated from the group accounts unless and until it is realised by a sale outside the group.

- It is important that you have a clear understanding of the material in this chapter before you move on to more complicated aspects of consolidation.

Quick quiz

1 What are the components making up the figure of minority interest in a consolidated balance sheet?

2 Fill in the blanks to show the adjustment required before consolidation in cases where a holding company has not accounted for dividends receivable from a subsidiary.

DEBIT
CREDIT
With

3 The following diagram shows the structure of the Alpha group.

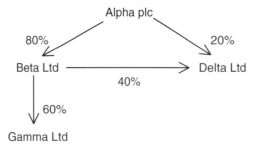

Which are the subsidiaries of Alpha plc?

A Beta Ltd

B Beta Ltd and Gamma Ltd

C Beta Ltd and Delta Ltd

D Beta Ltd, Gamma Ltd and Delta Ltd

4 Goodwill is always positive. True or false?

5   The following figures relate to Sanderstead plc and its subsidiary Croydon Ltd for the year ended 31 December 20X9.

	Sanderstead plc	*Croydon Ltd*
	£	£
Turnover	600,000	300,000
Cost of sales	(400,000)	(200,000)
Gross profit	200,000	100,000

During the year, Sanderstead plc sold goods to Croydon Ltd for £20,000 making a profit of £5,000. These goods were all sold by Croydon Ltd before the year end.

What are the amounts for turnover and gross profit in the consolidated profit and loss accounts of Sanderstead plc for the year ended 31 December 20X9?

Answers to quick quiz

1   The minority's share of ordinary shares, preference shares and reserves. (See para 2.2)

2   DEBIT   Debtors (dividend receivable)
     CREDIT   Revenue reserves
     With the parent company's share of the dividend receivable in the parent's books. (3.3)

3   D   Alpha has control over Beta's 40% holding in Delta and has a 20% direct holding. Thus Delta is a subsidiary.

4   False. Goodwill can be negative if the purchaser has 'got a bargain'. (4.17)

5
	£	
Turnover (1,600 + 300 – 20)	880	
Cost of sales (400 +200 – 20)	580	
Gross profit	300	(Section 6)

To get you started, the question recommended is rather easier than you could expect in an exam

Question to try	Level	Marks	Time
19	Introductory	n/a	36 mins

BPP PUBLISHING

Chapter 17

ACQUISITION OF SUBSIDIARIES

Topic list	Syllabus reference
1 Acquisition of a subsidiary during its accounting period	4(c)
2 Dividends and pre-acquisition profits	4(c)
3 FRS 7 *Fair values in acquisition accounting*	4(c)

Introduction

This chapter deals with the problems associated with the consolidation of a subsidiary acquired during the accounting period (a fairly common occurrence).

The major topic of merger accounting vs acquisition accounting is covered in Chapter 18, along with the consolidated profit and loss account and accounting for associated undertakings.

You should note the interaction of FRS 7 with FRS 2 *Accounting for subsidiary undertakings* (Chapter 15) and FRS 6 *Acquisitions and mergers* (Chapter 18).

Study guide

- Explain the nature of a dividend paid out of pre-acquisition profits.

- Explain why it is necessary for both the consideration paid for a subsidiary and the subsidiary's identifiable assets and liabilities to be accounted for at their fair values when preparing consolidated financial statements.

- Prepare consolidated financial statements dealing with the fair value adjustments (including their effect on consolidated goodwill) in respect of:

  - depreciating and non-depreciating fixed assets

  - stocks

  - monetary liabilities (basic discounting techniques may be required)

  - assets and liabilities (including contingencies) not included in the subsidiary's own balance sheet.

Exam guide

You will not understand the rest of the chapters on consolidation, particularly Chapters 18 and 19, unless you grasp the principles laid out in this chapter. You should pay particular attention to the determination of pre- and post-acquisition profits and the effect of dividends in Section 2.

1 ACQUISITION OF A SUBSIDIARY DURING ITS ACCOUNTING PERIOD

1.1 When a holding company acquires a subsidiary **during its accounting period the only accounting entries will be those recording the cost of acquisition in the holding company's books.** As we have already seen, **at the end of the accounting year** it will be necessary to **prepare consolidated accounts.**

1.2 The subsidiary company's accounts to be consolidated will show the subsidiary's profit or loss for the whole year. **For consolidation** purposes, however, it will be necessary to **distinguish between:**

(a) **Profits earned before acquisition**
(b) **Profits earned after acquisition**

1.3 In practice, a subsidiary company's profit may not accrue evenly over the year; for example, the subsidiary might be engaged in a trade, such as toy sales, with marked seasonal fluctuations. Nevertheless, statute permits the **assumption** to be made **that profits accrue evenly** whenever it is impracticable to arrive at an accurate split of pre- and post-acquisition profits.

1.4 Once the amount of pre-acquisition profit has been established the appropriate consolidation workings (goodwill, reserves) can be produced.

1.5 Bear in mind that **in calculating minority interests the distinction between pre- and post-acquisition profits is irrelevant.** The minority shareholders are simply credited with their share of the subsidiary's total reserves at the balance sheet date.

1.6 It is worthwhile to summarise what happens on consolidation to the reserves figures extracted from a subsidiary's balance sheet. Suppose the accounts of S Ltd, a 60% subsidiary of H Ltd, show reserves of £20,000 at the balance sheet date, of which £14,000 were earned prior to acquisition. The figure of £20,000 will appear in the consolidated balance sheet as follows.

	£
Minority interests working: their share of total reserves at balance sheet date (40% × £20,000)	8,000
Goodwill working: group share of pre-acquisition profits (60% × £14,000)	8,400
Consolidated reserves working: group share of post-acquisition profits (60% × £6,000)	3,600
	20,000

Question 1

Hinge Ltd acquired 80% of the ordinary shares of Singe Ltd on 1 April 20X5. On 31 December 20X4 Singe Ltd's accounts showed a share premium account of £4,000 and revenue reserves of £15,000. The balance sheets of the two companies at 31 December 20X5 are set out below. Neither company has paid or proposed any dividends during the year.

You are required to prepare the consolidated balance sheet of Hinge Ltd at 31 December 20X5.

Note. Goodwill is to be amortised over 25 years. A full year's amortisation is charged in the year of acquisition.

HINGE LIMITED
BALANCE SHEET AS AT 31 DECEMBER 20X5

	£
Fixed assets	
Tangible assets	32,000
16,000 ordinary shares of 50p each in Singe Ltd	50,000
	82,000
Net current assets	65,000
	147,000

I	£
Ordinary shares of £1 each	100,000
Share premium account	7,000
Revenue reserves	40,000
	147,000

SINGE LIMITED
BALANCE SHEET AS AT 31 DECEMBER 20X5

	£
Tangible fixed assets	30,000
Net current assets	23,000
	53,000
Capital and reserves	
20,000 ordinary shares of 50p each	10,000
Share premium account	4,000
Revenue reserves	39,000
	53,000

Answer

Singe Ltd has made a profit of £24,000 (£39,000 − £15,000) for the year. In the absence of any direction to the contrary, this should be assumed to have arisen evenly over the year; £6,000 in the three months to 31 March and £18,000 in the nine months after acquisition. The company's pre-acquisition revenue reserves are therefore as follows.

	£
Balance at 31 December 20X4	15,000
Profit for three months to 31 March 20X5	6,000
Pre-acquisition revenue reserves	21,000

The balance of £4,000 on share premium account is all pre-acquisition.

The consolidation workings can now be drawn up.

1   *Minority interest*

	£
Ordinary share capital (20% × £10,000)	2,000
Revenue reserves (20% × £39,000) (pre-acquisition)	7,800
Share premium (20% × £4,000)	800
	10,600

2   *Goodwill*

	£	£
Cost of investment		50,000
Share of net assets acquired represented by		
Ordinary share capital	10,000	
Revenue reserves (pre-acquisition)	21,000	
Share premium	4,000	
	35,000	
Group share (80%)		28,000
Goodwill		22,000

3   *Revenue reserves*

	£
Hinge Ltd	40,000
Share of Singe Ltd's post acquisition retained reserves	
£(39,000 − 21,000) × 80%	14,400
	54,400
Less: goodwill amortised on consolidation (22,000 ÷ 25)	(880)
	53,520

4   *Share premium account*

		£
Hinge Ltd		7,000
Share of Singe Ltd's post acquisition retained reserve		-
		7,000

HINGE LIMITED
CONSOLIDATED BALANCE SHEET AS AT 31 DECEMBER 20X5

	£
Intangible fixed assets: goodwill	21,120
Tangible fixed assets	62,000
Net current assets	88,000
	171,120
Capital and reserves	
Ordinary shares of £1 each	100,000
Reserves	
Share premium account	7,000
Revenue reserves	53,520
Shareholders' funds	160,520
Minority interest	10,600
	171,120

1.7 EXAMPLE: PRE-ACQUISITION LOSSES OF A SUBSIDIARY

As an illustration of the entries arising when a subsidiary has pre-acquisition *losses*, suppose H Ltd acquired all 50,000 £1 ordinary shares in S Ltd for £20,000 on 1 January 20X1 when there was a debit balance of £35,000 on S Ltd's revenue reserves. In the years 20X1 to 20X4 S Ltd makes profits of £40,000 in total, leaving a credit balance of £5,000 on revenue reserves at 31 December 20X4. H Ltd's reserves at the same date are £70,000. Any goodwill is deemed to have an indefinite useful life and should be held in the balance sheet.

1.8   The consolidation workings would appear as follows.

1   *Goodwill*

	£	£
Cost of investment		20,000
Share of net assets acquired		
as represented by		
Ordinary share capital	50,000	
Revenue reserves	(35,000)	
	15,000	
Group share (100%)		15,000
Goodwill		5,000

2   *Revenue reserve*

	£
H Ltd	70,000
Share of S Ltd's post-acquisition retained reserves	40,000
Group reserves	110,000

2 DIVIDENDS AND PRE-ACQUISITION PROFITS

2.1   **A further problem in consolidation occurs when a subsidiary pays out a dividend soon after acquisition.** The holding company, as a member of the subsidiary, is entitled to its share of the dividends paid but it is necessary to decide whether or not these dividends come out of the pre-acquisition profits of the subsidiary.

2.2 **If the dividends come from post-acquisition profits** there is no problem. **The holding company simply credits the relevant amount to its own profit and loss account,** as with any other dividend income. The double entry is **quite different,** however, **if the dividend is paid from pre-acquisition profits,** being as follows.

DEBIT Cash
CREDIT Investment in subsidiary

The holding company's balance sheet would then disclose the investment as 'Investment in subsidiary at cost less amounts written down'.

2.3 It is **very important that you are clear about the reason for this.** Consider the following balance sheets of S_1 Ltd and S_2 Ltd as at 31 March 20X4.

	S_1 Ltd £	S_2 Ltd £
Current assets	30,000	30,000
Current liabilities	10,000	10,000
Ordinary shareholders' funds	20,000	20,000

Both companies have goodwill, not reflected in the books, valued at £5,000 and are identical in every respect, except that the current liabilities of S_1 Ltd are trade creditors while the current liabilities of S_2 Ltd are a proposed ordinary dividend.

2.4 H_1 Ltd, a prospective purchaser of S_1 Ltd, is willing to pay £25,000 for 100% of S_1, including goodwill. H_2 Ltd, a prospective purchaser of S_2 Ltd, will clearly be willing to pay £35,000 for the acquisition of that company in the knowledge that £10,000 of the cost will immediately be 'refunded' by way of dividend.

2.5 Assume that the two purchases are completed on 31 March 20X4 and on 1 April 20X4 S_1 Ltd and S_2 Ltd pay off their current liabilities as appropriate. H_1 and H_2 will then own identical investments, each consisting of £20,000 of current assets plus £5,000 of goodwill, and it is clearly appropriate that the investment figures in their own balance sheets should be identical. This will be the case if H_2 Ltd sets off the £10,000 dividend receivable against the £35,000 cost of the acquisition, disclosing the investment in S_2 at a net cost of £25,000.

2.6 The point to grasp is that H_2 Ltd cannot credit the dividend to profit because no profit has been made. The correct way of looking at it is to say that H_2 Ltd was willing to pay 'over the odds' for its investment in the presumption that a part of its cost would immediately be repaid. When the dividend is paid, this presumption must be pursued to its conclusion by treating the dividend as a reduction of the cost of the investment.

2.7 **This accounting treatment** used to be a legal requirement but is not *required* by the CA 1985 (or any current SSAP or FRS). However, it **must be considered best practice.**

2.8 EXAMPLE: DIVIDENDS AND PRE-ACQUISITION PROFITS

Hip Ltd acquired 8,000 of the 10,000 £1 ordinary shares of Sip Ltd on 1 January 20X5 for £25,000. Sip Ltd's balance sheet at 31 December 20X4 showed a proposed ordinary dividend of £4,000 and retained reserves of £12,000. The balance sheets of the two companies at 31 December 20X5 are given below.

HIP LIMITED
BALANCE SHEET AS AT 31 DECEMBER 20X5

	£
Fixed assets	
Tangible assets	35,000
Investment in Sip Ltd at cost less	
amounts written down	21,800
	56,800
Net current assets	27,000
	83,800
Capital and reserves	
Ordinary shares of £1 each	50,000
Retained reserves	33,800
	83,800

SIP LIMITED
BALANCE SHEET AS AT 31 DECEMBER 20X5

	£
Tangible fixed assets	14,500
Net current assets	12,500
	27,000
Capital and reserves	
Ordinary shares of £1 each	10,000
Retained reserves	17,000
	27,000

Required

Prepare the consolidated balance sheet of Hip Ltd at 31 December 20X5.

Note. Goodwill is deemed to have a useful life of 10 years and is therefore to be amortised over that period.

2.9 SOLUTION

During the year Sip Ltd has paid the £4,000 proposed dividend in its 20X4 balance sheet. Hip Ltd's share (80% × £4,000 = £3,200) has been correctly credited by that company to its 'investment in Sip Ltd' account. That account appears in the books of Hip Ltd as follows.

INVESTMENT IN SIP LIMITED

	£		£
Bank: purchase of 8,000		Bank: dividend received from	
£1 ordinary shares	25,000	pre-acquisition profits	3,200
		Balance c/f	21,800
	25,000		25,000

If Hip Ltd had incorrectly credited the pre-acquisition dividend to its own profit and loss account, it would have been necessary to make the following adjustments in Hip Ltd's accounts before proceeding to the consolidation.

DEBIT	Retained reserves	£3,200	
CREDIT	Investment in Sip Ltd		£3,200

This procedure is sometimes necessary in examination questions.

The consolidation workings can be drawn up as follows.

1   *Minority interest*

		£
Share capital (20% × £10,000)		2,000
Reserves (20% × £17,000)		3,400
		5,400

2   *Goodwill*

	£	£
Cost of investment		25,000
Less share of pre-acquisition dividend (80% × £4,000)		3,200
		21,800
Share of net assets acquired as represented by		
Ordinary share capital	10,000	
Reserves	12,000	
	22,000	
Group share (80%)		17,600
Goodwill		4,200

3   *Reserves*

	£
Hip Ltd	33,800
Share of Sip Ltd's post acquisition retained reserves	
£(17,000 – 12,000) × 80%	4,000
	37,800
Goodwill amortised on consolidation (4,200 × 1/10)	(420)
	37,380

HIP LIMITED
CONSOLIDATED BALANCE SHEET AS AT 31 DECEMBER 20X5

	£
Intangible fixed assets	3,780
Tangible fixed assets	49,500
Net current assets	39,500
	92,780
Capital and reserves	
Ordinary shares of £1 each	50,000
Retained reserves	37,380
Shareholders' funds	87,380
Minority interest	5,400
	92,780

2.10   The example above included an ordinary dividend paid from pre-acquisition profits. The treatment would be exactly the same if a **preference dividend** had been paid from pre-acquisition profits. Any share of such a preference dividend received by the holding company would be credited not to profit and loss account, but to the investment in subsidiary account.

Is the dividend paid from pre-acquisition profits?

2.11   We need next to consider how it is decided whether a dividend is paid from pre-acquisition profits. In the example above there was no difficulty: Hip Ltd acquired shares in Sip Ltd on the first day of an accounting period and the dividend was in respect of the previous accounting period. Clearly, the dividend was paid from profits earned in the period before acquisition.

2.12 **The position is less straightforward if shares are acquired during the subsidiary's accounting period.** An example will illustrate the point.

2.13 EXAMPLE: ACQUISITION DURING SUBSIDIARY'S ACCOUNTING PERIOD

H Ltd and S Ltd each make up their accounts to 31 December. H Ltd buys 80,000 of the 100,000 £1 ordinary shares of S Ltd for £175,000 on 1 October 20X1. S Ltd's revenue reserves (after deducting proposed dividends) stood at £50,000 on 31 December 20X0. S Ltd's profits after tax for the year to 31 December 20X1 were £20,000. In January 20X2 S Ltd declared a first and final dividend for 20X1 of £10,000. At 31 December 20X1, H Ltd's reserves stood at £110,000; this does not include any adjustment for dividends receivable from S Ltd.

Required

Prepare consolidation workings for revenue reserves, minority interest and cost of control as at 31 December 20X1.

2.14 SOLUTION

The problem is to decide how much of the dividend paid by S Ltd comes from pre-acquisition profits. There are several possible ways of doing this but the method we recommend is based on time-apportionment. The 20X1 dividend eventually declared by S Ltd is deemed to have accrued evenly over the year.

Note. Of the £8,000 dividend receivable by H Ltd, £6,000 is deemed to have come from pre-acquisition profits and is credited to 'Investment in S Ltd'. £2,000 comes from post-acquisition profits and is added to reserves.

1   *Minority interest*

	£
Share capital (20% × £100,000)	20,000
Revenue reserves (20% × £60,000)	12,000
	32,000

The minority also has an interest (£2,000) in the proposed dividend payable by S Ltd. This will appear as a current liability in the consolidated balance sheet.

2   *Goodwill*

	£	£
Cost of investment		175,000
Less pre-acquisition dividend		
£10,000 × 9/12 × 80%		6,000
		169,000
Share of net assets acquired as represented by		
Ordinary share capital	100,000	
Revenue reserves		
£(50,000 + 15,000 − 7,500)	57,500	
	157,500	
Group share (80%)		126,000
Goodwill		43,000

3   *Revenue reserves*

	£
H Ltd	110,000
Dividend receivable	2,000
	112,000
Share of S Ltd's post acquisition	
retained reserves £(60,000 – 57,500) × 80%	2,000
Group reserves	114,000

2.15   It has been argued by some that the question as to whether a dividend from a subsidiary to the holding company is available for onward distribution by the holding company depends on whether receipt of the dividend can be regarded as giving rise to a **realised profit** in the financial statements of the holding company and not simply whether it derives from the pre- or post-acquisition profits of the subsidiary.

2.16   In other words if the subsidiary **recovers in value** after the distribution, the **loss in value is temporary** and need not be deducted from the cost of the investment (only permanent diminutions should be provided).

2.17   Where the investment is carried at fair value, however, it is likely that a dividend which represents a return of pre-acquisition profits would give rise to a **diminution in the value** of investment and thus should be applied in reducing the cost (carrying value) of that investment.

2.18   If this **diminution is not permanent,** this treatment is **not mandatory**. Thus companies could distribute all the subsidiary's pre-acquisition profits as long as the subsidiary could replace them in the future.

2.19   This practice may be legal but it offends good accounting practice. The pre-acquisition dividend is a return of the purchase price and it seems right to deduct it from the cost of the investment.

3   FRS 7 FAIR VALUES IN ACQUISITION ACCOUNTING

3.1   FRS 10 *Goodwill and intangible assets* **defines goodwill as the difference between the purchase consideration paid by the acquiring company and the aggregate of the 'fair values' of the identifiable assets and liabilities acquired.** The balance sheet of a subsidiary company at the date it is acquired may not be a guide to the fair value of its net assets. For example, the market value of a freehold building may have risen greatly since it was acquired, but it may appear in the balance sheet at historical cost less accumulated depreciation.

Fair value adjustment calculations

3.2   Until now we have calculated goodwill as the difference between the cost of the investment and the **book value** of net assets acquired by the group. If this calculation is to comply with the definition in FRS 10 we **must ensure that the book value of the subsidiary's net assets is the same as their fair value.**

3.3   There are **two possible ways** of achieving this.

(a)   **The subsidiary company might incorporate any necessary revaluations in its own books of account.** In this case, we can proceed directly to the consolidation, taking asset values and reserves figures straight from the subsidiary company's balance sheet.

(b) **The revaluations may be made as a consolidation adjustment without being incorporated in the subsidiary company's books**. In this case, we must make the necessary adjustments to the subsidiary's balance sheet as a working. Only then can we proceed to the consolidation.

Note. Remember that when depreciating assets are revalued there may be a corresponding alteration in the amount of depreciation charged and accumulated.

3.4 EXAMPLE: FAIR VALUE ADJUSTMENTS

H Ltd acquired 75% of the ordinary shares of S Ltd on 1 September 20X5. At that date the fair value of S Ltd's fixed assets was £23,000 greater than their net book value, and the balance of retained profits was £21,000. The balance sheets of both companies at 31 August 20X6 are given below. S Ltd has not incorporated any revaluation in its books of account.

H LIMITED
BALANCE SHEET AS AT 31 AUGUST 20X6

	£
Fixed assets	
Tangible assets	63,000
Investment in S Ltd at cost	51,000
	114,000
Net current assets	62,000
	176,000
Capital and reserves	
Ordinary shares of £1 each	80,000
Retained profits	96,000
	176,000

S LIMITED
BALANCE SHEET AS AT 31 AUGUST 20X6

	£
Tangible fixed assets	28,000
Net current assets	33,000
	61,000
Capital and reserves	
Ordinary shares of £1 each	20,000
Retained profits	41,000
	61,000

If S Ltd had revalued its fixed assets at 1 September 20X5, an addition of £3,000 would have been made to the depreciation charged in the profit and loss account for 20X5/X6.

Required

Prepare H Ltd's consolidated balance sheet as at 31 August 20X6.

Note: goodwill is deemed to have a useful life of 5 years and is to be amortised over that period.

3.5 SOLUTION

S Ltd has not incorporated the revaluation in its draft balance sheet. Before beginning the consolidation workings we must therefore adjust the company's balance of profits at the date of acquisition and at the balance sheet date.

S Ltd adjusted balance of retained profits

	£	£
Balance per accounts at 1 September 20X5		21,000
Consolidation adjustment: revaluation surplus		23,000
∴ Pre-acquisition profits for consolidation purposes		44,000
Profit for year ended 31 August 20X6		
Per draft accounts £(41,000 – 21,000)	20,000	
Consolidation adjustment: increase in depreciation charge	(3,000)	
		17,000
Adjusted balance of retained profits at 31 August 20X6		61,000

In the consolidated balance sheet, S Ltd's fixed assets will appear at their revalued amount: £(28,000 + 23,000 – 3,000) = £48,000. The consolidation workings can now be drawn up.

1 *Minority interest*

	£
Share capital (25% × £20,000)	5,000
Revenue reserves (25% × £61,000)	15,250
	20,250

2 *Goodwill*

	£	£
Cost of investment		51,000
Share of net assets acquired as represented by		
Ordinary share capital	20,000	
Revenue reserves		
£(21,000 + 23,000)	44,000	
	64,000	
Group share (75%)		48,000
Goodwill		3,000

3 *Revenue reserves*

	£
H Ltd	96,000
Share of S Ltd's post acquisition retained reserves	
£(41,000 – 21,000 – 3,000) × 75%	12,750
Goodwill amortised on consolidation	(600)
Group reserves	108,150

H LIMITED CONSOLIDATED BALANCE SHEET AS AT 31 AUGUST 20X6

	£
Intangible fixed assets: goodwill	2,400
Tangible fixed assets £(63,000 + 48,000)	111,000
Net current assets	95,000
	208,400
Capital and reserves	
Ordinary shares of £1 each	80,000
Retained profits	108,150
Shareholders' funds	188,150
Minority interest	20,250
	208,400

Question 2

An asset is recorded in S Ltd's books at its historical cost of £4,000. On 1 January 20X1 P Ltd bought 80% of S Ltd's equity. Its directors attributed a fair value of £3,000 to the asset as at that date. It had been depreciated for two years out of an expected life of four years on the straight line basis. There was no expected residual value. On 30 June 20X1 the asset was sold for £2,600. What is the profit or loss on disposal of this asset to be recorded in S Ltd's accounts and in P Ltd's consolidated accounts for the year ended 31 December 20X1?

Answer

S Ltd: NPV at disposal (at historical cost) = £4,000 × 1½/4 = £1,500

∴ Profit on disposal = £1,100 (depreciation charge for the year = £500)

P Ltd: NPV at disposal (at fair value) = £3,000 × 1½/2 = £2,250

∴ Profit on disposal for consolidation = £350 (depreciation for the year = £750). The minority would be credited with 20% of both items as part of the one line entry in the profit and loss account.

FRS 7 *Fair values in acquisition accounting*

3.6   FRS 7 and FRS 6 *Acquisitions and mergers* were published together in September 1994 in order to reform both acquisition and merger accounting practices. Merger accounting and FRS 6 are both discussed in Chapter 18.

> **IMPORTANT!**
>
> The basic principles stated by FRS 7 are that:
>
> (a) **All identifiable assets and liabilities** should be **recognised** which are in existence **at the date of acquisition**.
>
> (b) Such recognised assets and liabilities should be **measured at fair values** which reflect the conditions existing at the date of acquisition.
>
> Fair values should not reflect either the acquirer's intentions or events subsequent to the acquisition.

3.7   In addition any **changes** to the acquired assets and liabilities, and the resulting gains and losses, that arise **after control** of the acquired entity has passed to the acquirer should be reported as part of the **post-acquisition profits** of the group.

3.8   FRS 7 also sets out specific rules on how fair values should be determined for the main categories of asset and liability. The underlying principle remains that **fair values should reflect the price at which an asset or liability could be exchanged in an arm's length transaction.** For long-term monetary assets and liabilities, fair values may be derived by discounting.

3.9   The standard also describes how the value attributed to the consideration given for the acquisition should be determined, and the acquisition expenses that may be included as part of the cost.

Definitions

3.10 The following definitions are given by FRS 7. They are self explanatory except for the highlighted terms.

(a) Acquisition
(b) Business combination
(c) Date of acquisition
(d) **Fair value**
(e) Identifiable assets and liabilities
(f) **Recoverable amount**
(g) **Value in use**

> ### KEY TERMS
>
> (a) In particular note the definition of **fair value**.
>
> 'The amount at which an asset or liability could be exchanged in an arm's length transaction between informed and willing parties, other than in a forced or liquidation sale.'
>
> (b) **Recoverable amount** is the greater of the net realisable value of an asset and, when appropriate, the amount recoverable from its further use.
>
> (c) **Value in use** is the present value of the future cash flows obtainable as a result of an asset's continued use, including those resulting from the ultimate disposal of the asset.

Scope

3.11 FRS 7 applies to all financial statements that are intended to give a true and fair view. Although the FRS is framed in terms of the acquisition of a subsidiary undertaking by a parent company that prepares consolidated financial statements, it **also applies where an individual company entity acquires a business other than a subsidiary undertaking.** This last point means that companies cannot avoid the provisions of FRS 7 when taking over an unincorporated entity or joint venture vehicle.

Determining the fair values of identifiable assets and liabilities acquired

3.12 Most importantly, the FRS lists those **items which do not affect fair values** at the date of acquisition, and **which are therefore to be treated as post-acquisition items:**

(a) Changes resulting from the **acquirer's intentions or future actions.**

(b) **Impairments** or other changes, resulting from events subsequent to the acquisition.

(c) **Provisions or accruals for future operating losses** or for reorganisation and integration costs expected to be incurred as a result of the acquisition, whether they relate to the acquired entity or to the acquirer.

Assessing fair value of major categories

3.13 In general terms, fair values should be determined in accordance with the acquirer's accounting policies for similar assets and liabilities. The standard does, however, go on to describe how the major categories of assets and liabilities should be assessed for fair values.

(a) **Tangible assets: fair value based on:**

    (i)   **Market value**, if similar assets are sold on the open market.

    (ii)   **Depreciated replacement cost**, reflecting normal business practice.

    However, **fair value ≤ replacement cost.**

(b) **Intangible assets**, where recognised: **fair value should be based on replacement costs,** which will normally be estimated market value.

(c) **Stocks and work in progress**

    (i)   For stocks which are replaced by purchasing in a **ready market** (commodities, dealing stock etc), the fair value is **market value**.

    (ii)   For other stocks, with **no ready market** (most manufacturing stocks), fair value is represented by the **current cost** to the acquired company of reproducing the stocks.

(d) **Quoted investments:** value at **market price**, adjusted where necessary for unusual price fluctuations or the size of the holding.

(e) **Monetary assets and liabilities:** fair values should take into account the **amounts expected to be received or paid** and their timing. Reference should be made to market prices (where available) or to the current price if acquiring similar assets or entering into similar obligations, or to the discounted present value.

(f) **Contingencies: reasonable estimates** of the expected outcome may be used.

(g) **Pensions and other post-retirement benefits:** the **fair value of a deficiency, a surplus** (to the extent it is expected to be realised) or accrued obligation should be **recognised** as an asset/liability of the acquiring group. Any changes on acquisition should be treated as post-acquisition items.

(h) **Deferred tax** recognised in a fair value exercise should be measured in accordance with the requirements of FRS 19 (see Chapter 8). Thus deferred tax would not be recognised on an adjustment to recognise a non-monetary asset acquired with the business at its fair value on acquisition.

Business sold or held with a view to subsequent resale

3.14   The fair value exercise for such an entity, 'sold as a single unit, within approximately one year of acquisition', should be carried out on the basis of a **single asset investment**.

> 'Its fair value should be based on the **net proceeds of the sale, adjusted for the fair value of any assets or liabilities transferred** into or out of the business, unless such adjusted net proceeds are demonstrably different from the fair value at the date of acquisition as a result of a post-acquisition event.'

Any relevant part of the business can be treated in this way if it is separately identifiable, ie it does not have to be a separate subsidiary undertaking.

3.15   Where the first financial statements after the date of acquisition come for approval, but the business has not been sold, the above treatment can still be applied if:

(a)   A purchaser has been identified or is being sought.

(b)   The disposal is expected to occur within one year of the date of acquisition.

3.16   The interest (or its assets) should be shown in current assets. On determination of the sales price, the original estimate of fair value should be adjusted to reflect the actual sales proceeds.

BPP
PUBLISHING

Investigation period and goodwill adjustments

3.17 FRS 7 states that:

> 'The recognition and measurement of assets and liabilities acquired should be completed, if possible, by the date on which the first post-acquisition financial statements of the acquirer are approved by the directors.'

Where this has not been possible, provisional valuations should be made, amended if necessary in the next financial statements with a corresponding adjustment to goodwill. Such adjustments should be incorporated into the financial statements in the full year following acquisition. After that, any adjustments (except for the correction of fundamental errors by prior year adjustment) should be recognised as profits or losses as they are identified.

Determining the fair value of purchase consideration

3.18 The cost of acquisition is the amount of cash paid and the fair value of other purchase consideration given by the acquirer, together with the expenses of the acquisition. Where a subsidiary undertaking is acquired in stages, the cost of acquisition is the total of the costs of the interests acquired, determined as at the date of each transaction.

3.19 The main likely components of purchase consideration are as follows.

(a) *Ordinary shares*

(i) **Quoted shares** should be valued at **market price** on the date of acquisition.

(ii) Where there is **no suitable market**, estimate the value using:

(1) The value of **similar quoted securities**
(2) The **present value of the future cash** flows of the instrument used
(3) Any **cash alternative** which was offered

(b) **Other securities:** the value should be based on similar principles to those given in (a).

(c) **Cash or monetary amounts:** value at the **amount paid or payable**.

(d) **Non-monetary assets:** value at **market price**, estimated realisable value, independent valuation or based on other available evidence.

(e) **Deferred consideration: discount** the amounts calculated on the above principles (in (a) to (d)). An appropriate discount rate is that which the acquirer could obtain for a similar borrowing.

(f) **Contingent consideration:** use the **probable** amount. When the actual amount is known, it should be recorded in the financial statements and goodwill adjusted accordingly.

3.20 **Acquisition cost** (the fees and expenses mentioned above) should be **included in the cost of the investment**. Internal costs and the costs of issuing capital instruments should *not* be capitalised, according to the provisions of FRS 4, ie they must be written off to the profit and loss account.

Summary and assessment

3.21 **The most important effect of FRS 7 is the ban it imposes on making provisions for future trading losses** of acquired companies and the costs of any related rationalisation or reorganisation, unless outgoing management had already incurred those liabilities. This is a controversial area, demonstrated by the dissenting view of one member of the ASB.

3.22 **Some commentators argued that the ASB's approach ignores the commercial reality of the transaction** by treating as an expense the costs of reorganisation that the acquirer regards as part of the capital cost of the acquisition; and that within defined limits a provision for planned post-acquisition expenditure should be permitted to be included in the net assets acquired.

Case example

The Hundred Group of finance directors gave an example. If you buy a house for, say £100,000 that you know needs £50,000 spent on it to bring it into good condition and make it equivalent to a property that sells for £150,000, then you would treat the £50,000 renovation expense as part of the cost of the house and not as part of ordinary outgoings. The group states that FRS 7 goes beyond standards set in other countries, including the US. It also recommends that abuses in this area should be dealt with by tightening existing accounting standards and through 'proper policing' by external auditors (the standard is seen to undermine the professional judgement of the auditor) and 'not by distorting accounting concepts'.

3.23 The ASB rejected this view, saying that an intention to incur revenue expenditure subsequent to the acquisition could not properly be regarded as a liability of the acquired business at the date of acquisition.

> 'Acquisition accounting should reflect the business that is acquired as it stands at the date of acquisition and ought not to take account of the changes that an acquirer might intend to make subsequently. Nor could the ASB accept the proposition that some of the inadequacies of the present system could be met by better disclosure. In the ASB's view deficient accounting cannot be put right by disclosure alone.'

3.24 This is still an open area of debate and you should keep track of the arguments in the financial and accountancy press.

Question 3

Tyzo plc prepares accounts to 31 December. On 1 September 20X7 Tyzo plc acquired 6 million £1 shares in Kono plc at £2.00 per share. The purchase was financed by an additional issue of loan stock at an interest rate of 10%. At that date Kono plc produced the following interim financial statements.

	£m		£m
Tangible fixed assets (note 1)	16.0	Trade creditors	3.2
Stocks (note 2)	4.0	Taxation	0.6
Debtors	2.9	Bank overdraft	3.9
Cash in hand	1.2	Long-term loans (note 6)	4.0
		Share capital (£1 shares)	8.0
		Profit and loss account	4.4
	24.1		24.1

Notes

1   The following information relates to the tangible fixed assets of Kono plc at 1 September 20X7.

	£m
Gross replacement cost	28.4
Net replacement cost	16.6
Economic value	18.0
Net realisable value	8.0

The fixed assets of Kono plc at 1 September 20X7 had a total purchase cost to Kono plc of £27.0 million. They were all being depreciated at 25% per annum pro rata on that cost. This policy is also appropriate for the consolidated financial statements of Tyzo plc. No fixed assets of Kono plc which were included in the interim financial statements drawn up as at 1 September 19X7 were disposed of by Kono plc prior to 31 December 20X7. No fixed asset was fully depreciated by 31 December 20X7.

2   The stocks of Kono plc which were shown in the interim financial statements at cost to Kono plc of £4 million would have cost £4.2 million to replace at 1 September 20X7 and had an estimated net realisable value at that date of £4.8 million. Of the stock of Kono plc in hand at 1 September 20X7, goods costing Kono plc £3.0 million were sold for £3.6 million between 1 September 20X7 and 31 December 20X7.

3   The long-term loan of Kono plc carries a rate of interest of 10% per annum, payable on 31 August annually in arrears. The loan is redeemable at par on 31 August 2001. The interest cost is representative of current market rates. The accrued interest payable by Kono plc at 31 December 20X7 is included in the trade creditors of Kono plc at that date.

4   On 1 September 20X7 Tyzo plc took a decision to rationalise the group so as to integrate Kono plc. The costs of the rationalisation (which were to be borne by Tyzo plc) were estimated to total £3.0 million and the process was due to start on 1 March 20X8. No provision for these costs has been made in any of the financial statements given above.

Required

Compute the goodwill on consolidation of Kono plc that will be included in the consolidated financial statements of the Tyzo plc group for the year ended 31 December 20X7, explaining your treatment of the items mentioned above. You should refer to the provisions of relevant accounting standards.

Answer

Goodwill on consolidation of Kono Ltd

	£m	£m
Consideration (£2.00 × 6m)		12.0
Group share of fair value of net assets acquired		
Share capital	8.0	
Pre-acquisition reserves	4.4	
Fair value adjustments		
Tangible fixed assets (16.6 – 16.0)	0.6	
Stocks (4.2 – 4.0)	0.2	
	13.2	
Group share	75%	9.9
Goodwill		2.1

Notes on treatment

(a)   It is assumed that the market value (ie fair value) of the loan stock issued to fund the purchase of the shares in Kono plc is equal to the price of £12.0m. FRS 2 *Accounting for subsidiary undertakings* requires goodwill to be calculated by comparing the fair value of the consideration given with the fair value of the separable net assets of the acquired business or company.

(b)   Share capital and pre-acquisition profits represent the book value of the net assets of Kono plc at the date of acquisition. Adjustments are then required to this book value in order to give the fair value of the net assets at the date of acquisition. For short-term monetary items, fair value is their carrying value on acquisition.

(c)   FRS 7 *Fair values in acquisition accounting* states that the fair value of tangible fixed assets should be determined by market value or, if information on a market price is not available (as is the case here), then by reference to depreciated replacement cost, reflecting normal business practice. The net replacement cost (ie £16.6m) represents the gross replacement cost less depreciation based on that amount, and so further adjustment for extra depreciation is unnecessary.

(d)   FRS 7 also states that stocks which cannot be replaced by purchasing in a ready market (eg commodities) should be valued at current cost to the acquired company of reproducing the stocks. In this case that amount is £4.2m.

(e) The fair value of the loan is the present value of the total amount payable, ie on maturity and in interest. If the quoted interest rate was used as a discount factor, this would give the current par value.

(f) The rationalisation costs must be reported in post-acquisition results under FRS 7 *Fair values in acquisition accounting*, so no adjustment is required in the goodwill calculation.

Chapter roundup

- In this chapter we have looked at certain problems involved in distinguishing between **pre-acquisition** and **post-acquisition profits** of subsidiary companies.

- When a subsidiary is acquired **during its accounting period**, its **pre-acquisition profits** will include a **proportion of its total profits** for the accounting period.

- In the absence of information to the contrary, the profits earned during the period may be assumed to have **accrued evenly** and should be allocated accordingly.

- **Dividends** paid by a subsidiary to its parent company may only be **credited to the parent's profit and loss account** to the extent that they are paid from **post-acquisition profits**.

- **Dividends** received by the holding company **from pre-acquisition profits** should be credited to 'investment in subsidiary' account and treated as **reducing the cost of the shares** acquired.

- **Goodwill arising on consolidation** is the difference between the purchase consideration and the fair value of net assets acquired.

- **Goodwill** should be calculated **after revaluing** the subsidiary company's assets.

- If the subsidiary does not incorporate the revaluation in its own accounts, it should be done as a **consolidation adjustment**.

- The accounting requirements and disclosures of the **fair value exercise** are covered by **FRS 7**, which is controversial as it outlaws the use of provisions for future losses and for reorganisation costs on acquisition of a subsidiary.

Quick quiz

1 A holding company can assume that, for a subsidiary acquired during its accounting period, profits accrue evenly during the year. True or false?

2 What entries are made in the holding company's accounts to record a dividend received from a subsidiary's pre-acquisition profits? Fill in the blanks.

DEBIT
CREDIT

3 How is 'fair value' defined by FRS 7?

4 Which items does FRS 7 state *must* be treated as post-acquisition?

5 How is the cost of an acquisition made up?

6 On 31 March, Vellow Ltd purchased 1,800,000 of the 2,000,000 ordinary shares of £1 each in Yapton Ltd paying £1.20 per share.

At that date the values of the separable net assets of Yapton Ltd were:

Aggregate book value £1,800,000
Aggregate fair value £1,700,000

What is the values of the goodwill on consolidation as at 31 March?

7   On 31 March, Vellow Ltd purchased 1,800,000 of the 2,000,000 ordinary shares of £1 each in Yapton Ltd paying £1.20 per share.

At that date the value of the separable net assets of Yapton Ltd were:

Aggregate book value   £1,800,000
Aggregate fair value   £1,700,000

What is the value of the minority interest as at 31 March?

Answers to quick quiz

1   False in practice, true for the purposes of your exam (unless you are told otherwise). (See para 1.3)

2   DEBIT   Cash
    CREDIT   Investment in subsidiary (1.8)

3   The amount at which an asset or liability could be exchanged in an arm's length transaction between informed and willing parties other than in forced liquidation sale. (3.10)

4   See Para 3.12

5   The amount of cash paid

    The fair value of other purchase consideration given by the acquirer

    The expenses of the acquisition (3.18 to 3.20)

6   £'000
    Cost   2,160
    Fair value of separable net assets acquired
    90% × 1,700,000   1,530
                                                                 630   (Section 3)

7   10% × £1,700,000 = £170,000. (Section 3)

Now try the questions below from the Exam Question Bank

Number	Level	Marks	Time
20	Introductory	n/a	20 mins
21	Full exam	25	45 mins

Chapter 18

PROFIT AND LOSS ACCOUNT; MERGERS

Topic list	Syllabus reference
1 The consolidated profit and loss account	4(c)
2 FRS 6 *Acquisitions and mergers*	4(e)
3 FRS 6 disclosures	4(e)
4 Further practical issues	4(e)

Introduction

The consolidated profit and loss account will appear again in Chapter 19 where we consider the treatment of associated companies and joint ventures.

Merger accounting is a very contentious area. The standard, FRS 6, has drawn criticism for its approach and it is likely to remain controversial for some time. In the future, the use of merger accounting (for 'true' mergers) could be very rare.

The distinction between merger accounting and merger relief is an important one. Make sure you can accurately describe both concepts.

Study guide

- Prepare a consolidated profit and loss account for a simple group, including an example where an acquisition occurs during the year and there is a minority interest.

- Account for the effects (in the profit and loss account and balance sheet) of intra-group trading and other transactions including:

  - unrealised profits in stock and fixed assets
  - intra-group loans and interest and other intra-group charges, and
  - intra-group dividends including those paid out of pre-acquisition profits.

- Discuss the criteria for determining whether a business combination should be treated as a merger or an acquisition.

- Explain why a business combination that is a merger should have a different accounting treatment than that of an acquisition.

- Prepare consolidated financial statements applying merger accounting.

- Describe and quantify the effect on consolidated financial statements of applying merger accounting compared to acquisition accounting.

Exam guide

Generally speaking, the preparation of the consolidated profit and loss account is more straightforward than the preparation of the consolidated balance sheet. Complications do arise, however, usually in the form of inter-company transactions and accounting for pre-acquisition profits.

BPP PUBLISHING

1 THE CONSOLIDATED PROFIT AND LOSS ACCOUNT   Pilot paper

1.1   As always, the source of the consolidated statement is the individual accounts of the separate companies in the group. **It is customary in practice to prepare a working paper (known as a consolidation schedule) on which the individual profit and loss accounts are set out side by side and totalled to form the basis of the consolidated profit and loss account.**

Exam focus point

In an examination it is very much quicker not to do this. Use workings to show the calculation of complex figures such as the minority interest and show the derivation of others on the face of the profit and loss account, as shown in our examples.

1.2 CONSOLIDATED PROFIT AND LOSS ACCOUNT: SIMPLE EXAMPLE

H Ltd acquired 75% of the ordinary shares of S Ltd on that company's incorporation in 20X3. The summarised profit and loss accounts of the two companies for the year ending 31 December 20X6 are set out below.

	H Ltd	S Ltd
	£	£
Turnover	75,000	38,000
Cost of sales	30,000	20,000
Gross profit	45,000	18,000
Administrative expenses	14,000	8,000
Profit before taxation	31,000	10,000
Taxation	10,000	2,000
Retained profit for the year	21,000	8,000
Retained profits brought forward	87,000	17,000
Retained profits carried forward	108,000	25,000

Required

Prepare the consolidated profit and loss account.

1.3 SOLUTION

H LIMITED
CONSOLIDATED PROFIT AND LOSS ACCOUNT
FOR THE YEAR ENDED 31 DECEMBER 20X6

	£
Turnover (75 + 38)	113,000
Cost of sales (30 + 20)	50,000
Gross profit	63,000
Administrative expenses (14 + 8)	22,000
Profit before taxation	41,000
Taxation (10 + 2)	12,000
Profit after taxation	29,000
Minority interest (25% × £8,000)	2,000
Group retained profit for the year	27,000
Retained profits brought forward	
(group share only: 87 + (17 × 75%))	99,750
Retained profits carried forward	126,750

1.4 **Notice how the minority interest is dealt with.**

(a) **Down to the line 'profit after taxation' the whole of S Ltd's results is included without reference to group share or minority share. A one-line adjustment is then inserted to deduct the minority's share of S Ltd's profit after taxation.**

(b) **The minority's share (£4,250) of S Ltd's retained profits brought forward is excluded.** This means that the carried forward figure of £126,750 is the figure which would appear in the balance sheet for group retained reserves.

1.5 This last point may be clearer if we revert to our balance sheet technique and construct the working for group reserves.

Group reserves

	£
H Ltd	108,000
Share of S Ltd's PARR* (75% × £25,000)	18,750
	126,750

The minority share of S Ltd's reserves comprises the minority interest in the £17,000 profits brought forward plus the minority interest (£2,000) in £8,000 retained profits for the year. (*Note. PARR = Post acquisition retained reserves.)

1.6 Notice that a consolidated profit and loss account links up with a consolidated balance sheet exactly as in the case of an individual company's accounts: the figure of retained profits carried forward at the bottom of the profit and loss account appears as the figure for retained profits in the balance sheet.

1.7 We will now look at the **complications introduced by inter-company trading, inter-company dividends and pre-acquisition profits in the subsidiary.**

INTER-COMPANY TRADING

1.8 Like the consolidated balance sheet, the consolidated profit and loss account should deal with the results of the group as those of a single entity. When one company in a group sells goods to another an identical amount is added to the turnover of the first company and to the cost of sales of the second. Yet as far as the entity's dealings with outsiders are concerned no sale has taken place.

The consolidated figures for turnover and cost of sales should represent sales to, and purchases from, outsiders. An adjustment is therefore necessary to reduce the turnover and cost of sales figures by the value of inter-company sales during the year.

1.9 We have also seen in an earlier chapter that any **unrealised profits on inter-company trading should be excluded** from the figure of group profits. This will occur whenever goods sold at a profit within the group remain in the stock of the purchasing company at the year end. The best way to deal with this is to **calculate the unrealised profit** on **unsold stocks at the year end and reduce consolidated gross profit by this amount.** Cost of sales will be the balancing figure

1.10 EXAMPLE: INTER-COMPANY TRADING

Suppose in our earlier example that S Ltd had recorded sales of £5,000 to H Ltd during 20X6. S Ltd had purchased these goods from outside suppliers at a cost of £3,000. One half of the goods remained in H Ltd's stock at 31 December 20X6.

1.11 SOLUTION

The consolidated profit and loss account for the year ended 31 December 20X6 would now be as follows.

	Group
	£
Turnover (75 + 38 – 5)	108,000
Cost of sales (balancing figure)	46,000
Gross profit (45 + 18 – 1★)	62,000
Administrative expenses	(22,000)
Profit before taxation	40,000
Taxation	(12,000)
	28,000
Minority interest (25% × (£8,000 – £1,000★))	1,750
Group retained profit for the year	26,250
Retained profits brought forward	99,750
Retained profits carried forward	126,000

★Provision for unrealised profit: ½ × (£5,000 – £3,000)

A provision will be made for the unrealised profit against the stock figure in the consolidated balance sheet, as explained in Chapter 18.

Inter-company dividends

1.12 In our example so far we have assumed that S Ltd retains all of its after-tax profit. It may be, however, that S Ltd distributes some of its profits as dividends. As before, the minority interest in the subsidiary's profit should be calculated immediately after the figure of after-tax profit. For this purpose, **no account need be taken of how much of the minority interest is to be distributed by S Ltd as dividend.**

1.13 A complication may arise **if the subsidiary** has preference shares and **wishes to pay a preference dividend as well** as an ordinary dividend. In such a case **great care is needed in calculating the minority interest in S Ltd's after-tax profit.**

1.14 EXAMPLE: INTER-COMPANY DIVIDENDS

Sam Ltd's capital consists of 10,000 6% £1 preference shares and 10,000 £1 ordinary shares. On 1 January 20X3, the date of Sam Ltd's incorporation, Ham Ltd acquired 3,000 of the preference shares and 7,500 of the ordinary shares. The profit and loss accounts of the two companies for the year ended 31 December 20X6 are set out below.

	Ham Ltd	*Sam Ltd*
	£	*£*
Turnover	200,000	98,000
Cost of sales	90,000	40,000
Gross profit	110,000	58,000
Administrative expenses	35,000	19,000
Profit before tax	75,000	39,000
Taxation	23,000	18,000
Profit after tax	52,000	21,000
Dividends proposed: preference	-	600
ordinary	14,000	2,000
Retained profit for the year	38,000	18,400
Retained profits brought forward	79,000	23,000
	117,000	41,400

Ham Ltd has not yet accounted for its share of the dividends receivable from Sam Ltd.

Prepare Ham Ltd's consolidated profit and loss account.

1.15 SOLUTION

To calculate the minority interest in Sam Ltd's after-tax profit it is necessary to remember that the first £600 of such profits goes to pay the preference dividend. The balance of after-tax profits belongs to the equity shareholders. The calculation is as follows.

	Total		Minority share
	£		£
Profits earned for preference shareholders	600	(70%)	420
Balance earned for equity shareholders	20,400	(25%)	5,100
Total profits after tax	21,000		5,520

It is irrelevant how much of this is distributed to the minority as dividends: the whole £5,520 must be deducted in arriving at the figure for group profit. The dividends receivable by Ham Ltd, calculated below would cancel with the dividends payable by Sam Ltd to its holding company.

	£
Preference dividend (30% × £600)	180
Ordinary dividend (75% × £2,000)	1,500
	1,680

1.16 HAM LIMITED
CONSOLIDATED PROFIT AND LOSS ACCOUNT
FOR THE YEAR ENDED 31 DECEMBER 20X5

	Group
	£
Turnover (200 + 98)	298,000
Cost of sales (90 + 40)	130,000
Gross profit	168,000
Administrative expenses (35 + 19)	54,000
Profit before tax	114,000
Taxation (23 + 18)	41,000
Profit after tax	73,000
Minority interest (as above)	5,520
Group profit for the year	67,480
Dividend proposed (parent company only)	14,000
Retained profit for the year	53,480
Retained profits brought forward	
(group share only: 79 + (23 × 75%))	96,250
Retained profits carried forward	149,730

Pre-acquisition profits

1.17 As explained above, the figure for retained profits at the bottom of the consolidated profit and loss account must be the same as the figure for retained profits in the consolidated balance sheet. We have seen in previous chapters that **retained profits in the consolidated balance sheet comprise:**

(a) **The whole of the parent company's retained profits,**

(b) Plus a proportion of the subsidiary company's retained profits. The proportion is **the group's share of post-acquisition retained profits in the subsidiary.** From the total retained profits of the subsidiary we must therefore exclude both the minority's share of total retained profits and the group's share of pre-acquisition retained profits.

1.18 A **similar procedure is necessary in the consolidated profit and loss account** if it is to link up with the consolidated balance sheet. Previous examples have shown how the minority share of profits is excluded in the profit and loss account: their share of profits for the year is deducted from profit after tax; while the figure for profits brought forward in the consolidation schedule includes only the group's proportion of the subsidiary's profits.

1.19 In the same way, when considering examples which include pre-acquisition profits in a subsidiary, the figure for profits brought forward should include only the group's share of the post-acquisition retained profits. If the subsidiary is acquired *during* the accounting year, it is therefore necessary to apportion its profit for the year between pre-acquisition and post-acquisition elements. There are two approaches which may be used for this in the consolidated profit and loss account: the whole-year method and the part-year method.

1.20 With the **whole-year method, the whole of the subsidiary's turnover, cost of sales and so on is included and a deduction is then made lower down to exclude the profit accruing prior to acquisition.**

1.21 With the **part-year method, the entire profit and loss account of the subsidiary is split between pre-acquisition and post-acquisition proportions.** Only the post-acquisition figures are included in the profit and loss account. **This method is more usual** than the whole-year method and is the one which will be used in this Study Text.

Question 1

H Ltd acquired 60% of the equity of S Ltd on 1 April 20X5. The profit and loss accounts of the two companies for the year ended 31 December 20X5 are set out below.

	H Ltd £	S Ltd £	S Ltd ($^9/_{12}$) £
Turnover	170,000	80,000	60,000
Cost of sales	65,000	36,000	27,000
Gross profit	105,000	44,000	33,000
Administrative expenses	43,000	12,000	9,000
Profit before tax	62,000	32,000	24,000
Taxation	23,000	8,000	6,000
Profit after tax	39,000	24,000	18,000
Dividends (paid 31 December)	12,000	6,000	
Retained profit for the year	27,000	18,000	
Retained profits brought forward	81,000	40,000	
Retained profits carried forward	108,000	58,000	

H Ltd has not yet accounted for the dividends received from S Ltd.

Prepare the consolidated profit and loss account.

Answer

The shares in S Ltd were acquired three months into the year. Only the post-acquisition proportion (9/12ths) of S Ltd's P & L account is included in the consolidated profit and loss account. This is shown above for convenience.

H LIMITED CONSOLIDATED PROFIT AND LOSS ACCOUNT
FOR THE YEAR ENDED 31 DECEMBER 20X5

	£
Turnover (170 + 60)	230,000
Cost of sales (65 + 27)	92,000
Gross profit	138,000
Administrative expenses (43 + 9)	52,000
Profit before tax	86,000
Taxation (23 + 6)	29,000
Profit after tax	57,000
Minority interest (40% × £18,000)	7,200
Group profit for the year	49,800
Dividends (H Ltd only)	12,000
Retained profit for the year	37,800
Retained profits brought forward*	81,000
Retained profits carried forward	118,800

* All of S Ltd's profits brought forward are pre-acquisition.

Disclosure requirements

1.22 S 230 CA 1985 allows a parent company to dispense with the need to publish its own individual profit and loss account.

(a) Companies taking advantage of this dispensation are obliged to state in their consolidated profit and loss account how much of the group's profit for the financial year is dealt with in the parent company's own profit and loss account.

(b) For internal purposes, of course, it will still be necessary to prepare the parent company's profit and loss account and the profit or loss shown there is the figure to be shown in the note to the group accounts.

(c) This is a point which has been clarified by the CA 1989. In the example above, H Ltd should disclose its own profit after adjustment for its share of the S Ltd dividend (from post-acquisition profits - remember that the pre-acquisition element should be credited to the cost of H's investment in S Ltd).

1.23 Where there are **extraordinary items** (now very rare) in the profit and loss account of a group company the **group share only** of such items should be included, after minority interest and the adjustment for inter-company dividends but before dividends payable by the parent company.

1.24 If you are required to prepare a consolidated profit and loss account in statutory form, you may need to disclose a figure for **directors' emoluments**. The figure should represent the emoluments of **parent company directors only**, whether those emoluments are paid by the parent company or by subsidiary companies. The emoluments of directors of subsidiary companies should be excluded, unless they are also directors of the parent company.

1.25 The movement of reserves statement may be required to show a transfer from the profit and loss account to other reserves. Where this transfer occurs in a subsidiary, only the group's (post-acquisition) share of the transfer will be recorded in the movement of reserves statement. Any minority interest or pre-acquisition profits would be excluded.

MOVEMENT OF RESERVES

	£
Profit and loss account brought forward	X
Add retained profit for the year	X
	X
Less transfer to reserves (all of parent company transfers plus the group share of transfers in a subsidiary)	(X)
Profit and loss account carried forward	X

Question 2

The following information relates to the Brodick group of companies for the year to 30 April 20X7.

	Brodick plc £'000	Lamlash Ltd £'000	Corrie Ltd £'000
Turnover	1,100	500	130
Cost of sales	630	300	70
Gross profit	470	200	60
Administrative expenses	105	150	20
Dividend from Lamlash Ltd	24	-	-
Dividend from Corrie Ltd	6	-	-
Profit before tax	395	50	40
Taxation	65	10	20
Profit after tax	330	40	20
Interim dividend	50	10	-
Proposed dividend	150	20	10
Retained profit for the year	130	10	10
Retained profits brought forward	460	106	30
Retained profits carried forward	590	116	40

Additional information

(a) The issued share capital of the group was as follows.

      Brodick plc   : 5,000,000 ordinary shares of £1 each.
      Lamlash Ltd : 1,000,000 ordinary shares of £1 each.
      Corrie Ltd   : 400,000 ordinary shares of £1 each.

(b) Brodick plc purchased 80% of the issued share capital of Lamlash Ltd in 20X0. At that time, the retained profits of Lamlash amounted to £56,000.

(c) Brodick plc purchased 60% of the issued share capital of Corrie Ltd in 20X4. At that time, the retained profits of Corrie amounted to £20,000.

(d) Brodick plc recognises dividends proposed by other group companies in its profit and loss account.

Required

Insofar as the information permits, prepare the Brodick group of companies' consolidated profit and loss account for the year to 30 April 20X7 in accordance with the Companies Act 1985 and related statements of accounting practice.

Note. Notes to the profit and loss account are not required but you should append a statement showing the make up of the 'retained profits carried forward', and your workings should be submitted.

Answer

You are not asked for notes, but you should know that Brodick would have to state in the notes that it had taken advantage of the provisions of s 230 CA and was not publishing its own profit and loss account. It would then show its own profit for the year, which the Act now states clearly should be the profit shown in its own books (in this case, including dividends received and receivable from Lamlash and Corrie). Brodick's profit for the financial year is £330,000, as shown in the question. An analysis of reserves would also be given as a note to the balance sheet, showing movements on both company and consolidated reserves.

CONSOLIDATED PROFIT AND LOSS ACCOUNT
FOR THE YEAR TO 30 APRIL 20X7

	£'000
Turnover (1,100 + 500 + 130)	1,730
Cost of sales (630 + 300 + 70)	1,000
Gross profit	730
Administrative expenses (105 + 150 + 20)	275
Profit on ordinary activities before taxation	455
Tax on profit on ordinary activities (65 + 10 + 20)	95
Profit on ordinary activities after taxation	360
Minority interests (W1)	16
Profit for the financial year	344
Dividends paid and proposed (parent only)	200
Retained profit for the year	144
Retained profit brought forward 1 May 20X6 (W2)	506
Retained profit carried forward 30 April 20X7	650

Workings

1   *Minority interests*

	£
In Lamlash (20% × profit after tax)	8,000
In Corrie (40% × profit after tax)	8,000
	16,000

2   *Retained profits brought forward*

	£
Brodick plc	460,000
Group share of post-acquisition retained profits brought forward	
Lamlash 80% × £(106,000 - 56,000)	40,000
Corrie 60% × £(30,000 - 20,000)	60,000
	506,000

1.26 Section summary

The table below summaries the main points about the consolidated profit and loss account.

Summary: consolidated P & L account

Purpose	To show the results of the group for an accounting period as if it were a single entity.
Turnover to profit after tax	100% H + 100% S (excluding dividend receivable from subsidiary and adjustments for inter-company transactions).
Reason	To show the results of the group which were controlled by the holding company.
Inter-company sales Unrealised profit on inter-company sales	Strip out inter-company activity from both turnover and cost sales. (a) *Goods sold by H Ltd.* Increase cost of sales by unrealised profit. (b) *Goods sold by S Ltd.* Increase cost of sales by full amount of unrealised profit and decrease minority interest by their share of unrealised profit.
Depreciation	If the value of S Ltd's fixed assets have been subjected to a fair value uplift then any additional depreciation must be charged in the consolidated profit and loss account. The minority interest will need to be adjusted for their share.

Transfer of fixed assets	Expenses must be increased by any profit on the transfer and reduced by any additional depreciation arising from the increased carrying value of the asset.

Minority interests	S's profit after tax (PAT) X
	Less: * unrealised profit (X)
	        * profit on disposal of fixed assets (X)
	        additional depreciation following FV uplift (X)
	Add: ** additional depreciation following
	       disposal of fixed assets X
	                                  X
	
	  MI% X
	
	* Only applicable if sales of goods and fixed assets made by subsidiary.
	
	** Only applicable if sale of fixed assets made by holding company.

Reason	To show the extent to which profits generated through H's control are in fact owned by other parties.
Dividends	H's only.
Reason	S's dividend is due (a) to H; and (b) to MI. H has taken in its share by including the results of S in the consolidated P & L a/c. The MI have taken their share by being given a proportion of S's PAT. Remember: PAT = dividends + retained profit.
Retained reserves	As per the balance sheet calculations.

2   FRS 6 ACQUISITIONS AND MERGERS

2.1   FRS 6 *Acquisitions and mergers* deals with the accounting treatment of business combinations which arise when one or more companies become subsidiaries of another company. Two different methods of accounting for such combinations have evolved in practice.

(a)   **Acquisition accounting is the traditional method of accounting for business combinations** and is the method which has been described in the previous chapters of this section. A company acquires shares in another company (or companies) and either pays for them in cash or issues its own shares or loan stock in exchange for them. If much of the purchase price is paid in cash, there may be a significant outflow of assets from the group.

(b)   **Merger accounting is a method which has become popular more recently.** It is a method of preparing consolidated accounts which may be regarded as appropriate in cases where a business combination is brought about without any significant outflow of funds from the group. This might happen, for example, where one company acquires shares in another company and issues its own shares as consideration for the purchase, rather than paying cash.

2.2   You should be clear in your mind that the term merger accounting refers to a method of preparing consolidated accounts. FRS 6 hardly mentions the problems of how to account for share acquisitions in the individual accounts of the acquiring company. This is a problem to which statutory provisions are relevant; we will discuss it later in this chapter.

Problem with acquisition method

2.3 The **main problem** with using the acquisition method **concerns the effect on the holding company's distributable profits**. Suppose that H Ltd acquires all the shares of S Ltd on day 1 and on day 2 S Ltd pays a dividend equal to the entire amount of its distributable profits. Using the conventional techniques of acquisition accounting described in earlier chapters, H Ltd would not credit the dividend received to its own profit and loss account, so as to increase its own distributable profits; instead, the dividend would be applied to reduce the cost of the investment in S Ltd. The profits available for distribution to members of H Ltd would be unchanged from what they were before the combination.

2.4 If the shares in S Ltd were purchased for cash, this might seem reasonable: cash has been paid out as well as received and so net assets have not increased. The amount of profits available to distribute to the original shareholders of H Ltd remains unchanged, being the distributable profits shown in H Ltd's own individual accounts. On this assumption, conventional acquisition accounting seems to achieve a fair result.

2.5 But what happens if the shareholders in S Ltd are **not bought out for cash**? This would be the case if H Ltd paid for the shares in S Ltd by, say, an issue of new shares in H Ltd. This would mean that members of S Ltd would exchange their shares in that company for a share of the newly-formed group. The **number of shareholders** of H Ltd would now be greatly **increased**. But using acquisition accounting there would be **no corresponding increase in the distributable profits** of H Ltd.

2.6 This **result can be avoided if merger accounting principles are used**. We will come later to the detailed criteria of the Companies Act 1985 and FRS 6, but broadly speaking a **business combination may be accounted for as a merger if payment for the shares acquired is by means of a share exchange; if payment is by cash, conventional acquisition accounting must be used.** An example will illustrate the differences between the two methods. We will show a combination where the purchase consideration is satisfied by means of a share exchange.

2.7 **EXAMPLE: ACQUISITION V MERGER ACCOUNTING**

John Smith and Fred Jones run electrical wholesaling businesses of identical size. Both businesses are incorporated as limited liability companies, the shareholders of which are Smith, Jones and their respective wives.

In 20X1, Smith and Jones decide to combine their businesses and for this purpose they form a new company Smith and Jones Ltd. It is agreed that the new company will acquire all of the shares of John Smith Ltd and Fred Jones Ltd, the consideration in each case being the issue of equal numbers of shares in the new company. The balance sheets of John Smith Ltd and Fred Jones Ltd as at 31 December 20X1 are set out below.

	John Smith Ltd £'000	Fred Jones Ltd £'000
Net assets	100	100
Share capital	20	20
Profit and loss account	80	80
	100	100

The fair value of each business is considered to be £160,000.

2.8 SOLUTION

Using normal acquisition accounting principles, the balance sheet of Smith and Jones Ltd after the share transfers will be as follows.

	Smith and Jones Ltd £'000
Investment in John Smith Ltd	160
Investment in Fred Jones Ltd	160
	320
Share capital	40
Share premium	280
	320

The balance on the share premium account is the difference between the nominal value of the shares issued and the fair value of the assets acquired.

Assuming that the net assets of John Smith Ltd and Fred Jones Ltd are already stated at their fair value, the difference between the book value of the assets (£100,000 in each case) and the fair value of the business (£160,000 in each case) will be goodwill.

The consolidated balance sheet at the date of transfer will therefore be as follows.

	£'000
Goodwill arising on consolidation	120
Net assets	200
	320
Share capital	40
Share premium	280
	320

2.9 From the above, it can be seen that **the new company will have no distributable reserves at the date of the transfer**. Smith and Jones may well consider that this situation is highly unsatisfactory, as from their point of view there is no real change of ownership, merely a pooling of interests. Furthermore there has been no change in the underlying net assets, even though their balance sheet values have increased.

2.10 **It is in the kind of situation outlined above that merger accounting may be appropriate.** In merger accounting, the emphasis is on the continuity of the amalgamated businesses.

Exam focus point

The single most important feature of **merger accounting** is that when a holding company issues shares in consideration for the transfer to it of shares in another company, the shares issued are accounted for at their **nominal value only**. (Under **acquisition accounting** the shares must be accounted for at their **market value**.)

2.11 The other features of merger accounting are demonstrated in the example below.

If we apply merger accounting in the above example, the entry in the books of Smith and Jones Ltd will be:

		£'000	£'000
DEBIT	Investment in John Smith Ltd	20	
	Investment in Fred Jones Ltd	20	
CREDIT	Share capital		40

The investment in the subsidiaries is therefore recorded as the nominal value of the consideration given.

2.12 Under the merger method, the balance sheet of Smith and Jones Ltd would be:

	Smith & Jones Ltd
	£'000
Investment in John Smith Ltd	20
Investment in Fred Jones Ltd	20
	40
Share capital	40

Consolidation would involve cancellation of the 'investment in subsidiary' with the subsidiary's share capital and aggregation of the net assets. The resulting consolidated balance sheet would be:

	£'000
Net assets	200
Share capital	40
Profit and loss account	160
	200

2.13 A **comparison** of the merger balance sheet with the acquisition balance sheet will demonstrate the following features of merger accounting.

> (a) Assets can be recorded at their previous values, as there is no obligation to record them at fair value.
>
> (b) No share premium account will arise in the books of the holding company, as shares issued are recorded at their nominal value only.
>
> (c) A premium on acquisition will never arise under merger accounting.
>
> (d) Previously distributable reserves of the individual companies may remain distributable as there is no enforced freezing of pre-acquisition reserves.
>
> (e) It is simpler than acquisition accounting.

2.14 Point (a) above means that **a ROCE based on a merger balance sheet is usually higher than one based on an acquisition balance sheet.** This, together with point (d), has contributed greatly to the popularity enjoyed by merger accounting with US companies.

> **Exam focus point**
>
> If you are in a hurry or revising, go straight to paragraph 2.23.

2.15 In the UK, merger accounting was not introduced until the Companies Act 1985 removed the barrier imposed by the old s 56 CA 1948. This stated that when a company issued shares for a premium, a sum equal to the value of the premium should be transferred to a share premium account. This provision made merger accounting, in effect, illegal.

2.16 This illegality was emphasised by a legal case *Shearer v Bercain Ltd 1980*. In this case, as well as forcing the creation of a share premium account, the court held that pre-acquisition profits were not available for distribution as dividends to the shareholders of the holding company (under Sch 8, CA 1948).

2.17 The CA 1985 offers relief from creation of a share premium where the issuing company has secured at least 90% of all classes of equity shares in another company in pursuance of an arrangement providing for the allotment of equity shares in the issuing company in consideration for the issue or transfer to the issuing company of equity shares in the other company, or the cancellation of any such shares not held by the issuing company (s 131 CA 1985). This opened the door to merger accounting in the UK. The relief given was fairly wide and this was on the understanding that the accounting profession would produce a more restrictive standard on merger accounting soon after the CA 1981.

2.18 Before we look at FRS 6, which was published in September 1994, let us briefly examine the Companies Act requirements for merger accounting.

Companies Act 1985

2.19 **CA 1985 lays down the following conditions for accounting for acquisition as a merger** (s 10 Sch 4A CA 1985).

   (a) **At least 90%** of the nominal value of the 'relevant shares'* in the undertaking acquired must be held by the group.

   (b) This must be achieved as a result of an arrangement providing for the **issue of equity shares** by the parent company (or one or more of its subsidiaries).

   (c) The **fair value** of any consideration other than equity shares **must not exceed 10% of the nominal value** of the equity shares issued.

   (d) Adoption of the merger method **must accord with generally accepted accounting principles** or standards.

   *'Relevant shares' are 'those carrying unrestricted rights to participate both in distributions and in the assets of the undertaking upon liquidation': usually these will be equity shares.

2.20 If any or all of these conditions were not met, the business combination was an acquisition and the principles of acquisition accounting, as stated in FRS 2, had to be applied.

2.21 If a business combination met all the criteria of CA 1985, and if the holding company elected to use the merger method on consolidation, the **consequences** were as follows.

   (a) It is **not necessary to adjust the carrying values** of the assets and liabilities of the subsidiary **to fair value** either in its own books or as a consolidation adjustment.

   (b) Even if the subsidiary were acquired during the accounting period its **profit or loss should be included for the entire period, without any adjustment in respect of the part year preceding the merger.** Corresponding amounts should be presented as if the companies had been combined throughout the previous period and at the previous balance sheet date.

   (c) The **difference between the carrying value** of the investment in the subsidiary **and the nominal value** of the shares acquired **should be treated as an addition to or deduction from reserves.**

   In fact, these consequences - the mechanics of merger accounting - still apply, **only the conditions for merger accounting and related disclosure have been changed by FRS 6.**

2.22 You should be clear that the CA 1985 requirements still exist. However, **FRS 6 has tightened the requirements for merger accounting by concentrating on the spirit of the transaction**, rather than on mechanical aspects, such as levels of shareholding.

> 'FRS 6 restricts the use of merger accounting to very rare cases of mergers that cannot properly be viewed as the takeover of one company by another; all other business combinations must be accounted for by using acquisition accounting.'

> 'FRS 6 sets out disclosure requirements, for both acquisitions and mergers, to ensure that full explanation of the effect of the combination is disclosed in the financial statements. It also encourages further voluntary disclosure of the acquirer's intended expenditure on the acquired business.'

2.23 Let us now look at FRS 6 in more detail.

FRS 6 *Acquisitions and mergers*

2.24 In general terms **FRS 6 aims to prevent the use of merger accounting for anything other than 'true' mergers, where a partnership is formed, on an equal footing.** Where there is an identifiable 'acquirer', then acquisition accounting *must* be used.

Objective

2.25 The objective of FRS 6 is as follows.

> 'The objective of this FRS is to ensure that **merger accounting is used only for those business combinations that are not**, in substance, the **acquisition** of one entity by another **but** the formation of a new reporting entity as a substantially **equal partnership** where no party is dominant; to ensure the use of acquisition accounting for all other business combinations; and to ensure that in either case the financial statements provide relevant information concerning the effect of the combination.'

Definitions

2.26 The definitions given by the standard are as follows. Note that several definitions are repeated in FRS 7, which we looked at in Chapter 17.

> **'Acquisition**
> A business combination that is not a merger.
>
> **Business combination**
> The bringing together of separate entities into one economic entity as a result of one entity uniting with, or obtaining control over the net assets and operations of, another.
>
> **Equity shares**
> Shares other than non-equity shares.
>
> **Group reconstruction**
> Any of the following arrangements:
>
> (a) The transfer of a shareholding in a subsidiary undertaking from one group company to another.
>
> (b) The addition of a new parent company to a group.
>
> (c) The transfer of shares in one or more subsidiary undertakings of a group to a new company that is not a group company but whose shareholders are the same as those of the group's parent.
>
> (d) The combination into a group of two or more companies that before the combination had the same shareholders.

KEY TERM

Merger. A business combination that results in the creation of a new reporting entity formed from the combining parties, in which the shareholders of the combining entities come together in a partnership for the mutual sharing of the risks and benefits of the combined entity, and in which no party to the combination in substance obtains control over any other, or is otherwise seen to be dominant, whether by virtue of the proportion of its shareholders' rights in the combined entity, the influence of its directors or otherwise.

Non-equity shares
Shares possessing any of the following characteristics:

(a) Any of the rights of the shares to receive payments (whether in respect of dividends, in respect of redemptions or otherwise) are for a limited amount that is not calculated by reference to the company's assets or profits or the dividends on any class of equity share.

(b) Any of the rights to participate in a surplus in a winding up are limited to a specific amount that is not calculated by reference to the company's assets or profits and such limitation had a commercial effect in practice at the time the shares were issued or, if later, at the time the limitation was introduced.

(c) The shares are redeemable, either according to their terms or because the holder, or any party other than the issuer, can require their redemption.'

Scope

2.27 FRS 6 applies to:

'**All financial statements** that are intended to give a true and fair view of a reporting entity's financial position and profit or loss (or income and expenditure) for a period. Although the FRS is framed in terms of an entity becoming a subsidiary undertaking of a parent company that prepares consolidated financial statements, it also applies where an individual company or other reporting entity combines with a business other than a subsidiary undertaking.'

Use of merger accounting

Exam focus point

Merger accounting should be used when:

(a) The use of merger accounting is not prohibited by companies legislation.
(b) The five specific criteria for a merger laid out in FRS 6 are satisfied by the combination.

2.28 The criteria for determining whether the definition of a merger is met are as follows. (Note that convertible share or loan stock should be regarded as equity to the extent that it is converted into equity *as a result of the business combination.*)

Criterion 1   Neither party is portrayed, by either its management or any other party, as either acquirer or acquired.

Criterion 2   All parties take part in setting up a management structure and selecting personnel for the combined entity on the basis of consensus rather than purely by exercise of voting rights.

Criterion 3   The relative sizes of the parties are not so disparate that one party dominates the combined entity by virtue of its relative size.

Criterion 4 A substantial part of the consideration for equity shareholdings in each party will comprise equity shares; conversely, non-equity shares or equity shares with reduced voting rights will comprise only an 'immaterial' part of the consideration. This criterion also covers existing shareholdings.

> 'Where one of the combining entities has, within the period of two years before the combination acquired shares in another of the combining entities, the consideration for this acquisition should be taken into account in determining whether this criterion has been met.'

Note that this criterion states in general terms what is laid out in the Companies Act 1985 in terms of specific shareholdings.

Criterion 5 No equity shareholders of any of the combining entities retains any material interest in the future performance of only part of the combined entity.

2.29 Note that, for the purpose of Criterion 4, the consideration should *not* include:

'(a) An interest in a peripheral part of the business of the entity in which they were shareholders and which does not form part of the combined entity.

(b) The proceeds of the sale of such a business, or loan stock representing such proceeds.

A peripheral part of the business is one that can be disposed of without having a material effect on the nature and focus of the entity's operations.'

Group reconstructions, new parents etc

2.30 Despite the strict criteria which must be met before merger accounting can be used, FRS 6 does allow the use of merger accounting in various **other**, slightly unusual **situations**.

(a) In **group reconstructions**, provided:

(i) The use of merger accounting is not prohibited by companies legislation.

(ii) The ultimate shareholders remain the same, and the rights of each such shareholders, relative to the others, are unchanged.

(iii) No minority's interest in the net assets of the group is altered by the transfer.

(b) In **a combination effected by using a new parent company**, where a direct combination of the parties concerned would have met the FRS 6 criteria for merger accounting. If there *is* an 'acquirer', then the acquirer and new parent should first be combined using merger accounting, then other parties combined using acquisition accounting.

(c) In **various structures of business combination** the FRS should be applied to other transactions which achieve the same results.

Merger accounting

2.31 The main accounting provisions of the merger method are listed by the FRS as follows.

(a) **No fair value exercise** is required, but appropriate **adjustments to achieve uniformity of accounting policies** should be made.

(b) In the group accounts in the year of merger, **results** should be shown **as if the entities had always been combined**, in both that year and the previous year as shown in the corresponding figures.

(c) **Differences** between the nominal value of the shares issued plus the fair value of any other consideration given, and the nominal value of any shares received in exchange should be **shown as a movement on other reserves** in the consolidated financial statements.

(d) Any **existing balance on the new subsidiary's share premium account** or capital redemption reserve should be **shown as a movement on other reserves.** The transactions in (c) and (d) should be shown in the reconciliation of movements in shareholders' funds.

(e) **Merger expenses** should be **charged to the profit and loss account** of the combined entity at the date of the merger (ie *not* as a movement on reserves) in accordance with FRS 3.

2.32 These provisions contrast directly with the requirements of acquisition accounting as we saw earlier.

3 FRS 6 DISCLOSURES

3.1 The disclosure requirements of FRS 6 are lengthy and substantial, but we will try to summarise them here.

Acquisitions and mergers

3.2 The following information should be disclosed for both acquisitions and mergers **in the accounts of the acquirer** or issuing entity, for each combination in the period:

(a) The **names** of the combining entities (other than the reporting entity).
(b) Whether the combination has been accounted for as an **acquisitions or a merger.**
(c) The **date** of the combination.

Mergers

3.3 For each business combination (except group reconstructions) **in the accounts of the combined entity**:

(a) An **analysis** of the principal components of the **current year's profit and loss account and statement of total recognised gains and losses into:**

    (i) **Amounts relating to the merged entity for the period after the date of the merger.**

    (ii) For each party to the merger, amounts relating to that party **for the period up to the date of the merger.**

(b) An analysis between the parties to the merger of the principal components of the profit and loss account and statement of total recognised gains and losses **for the previous financial year.**

(c) The **composition and fair value of the consideration** given by the issuing company and its subsidiary undertakings.

(d) The **aggregate book value of the net assets** of each party to the merger at the **date of the merger.**

(e) The **nature and amount of significant accounting adjustments** made to the net assets of any party to the merger to achieve consistency of accounting policies and an explanation of any other significant adjustments made to the net assets of any party to the merger as a consequence of the merger.

(f)   A statement of the **adjustments to consolidated reserves** resulting from the merger.

3.4   In the case of (a) and (b), at a *minimum* disclosure should be made of turnover, operating profit and exceptional items, split between continuing operations, discontinued operations and acquisitions; profit before taxation; taxation and minority interests; and extraordinary items.

Acquisitions

3.5   In relation to the consideration:

'The composition and fair value of the consideration given by the acquiring company and its subsidiary undertakings should be disclosed. The nature of any deferred or contingent purchase consideration should be stated, including, for contingent consideration, the range of possible outcomes and the principal factors that affect the outcome.'

3.6   We have already discussed the disclosure requirements relating to fair values and goodwill in Chapter 11 when we were looking at goodwill. This is a good opportunity for you to go back to that chapter, look at the disclosure requirements, and consider how FRS 6 interacts with FRS 10.

3.7   FRS 6 also interacts with FRS 3:

'As required by FRS 3, in the period of acquisition the post-acquisition results of the acquired entity should be shown as a component of continuing operations in the profit and loss account, other than those that are also discontinued in the same period; and where an acquisition has a material impact on a major business segment this should be disclosed and explained.'

You should go back to the section in Chapter 9 on FRS 3 and consider the impact FRS 6 has.

3.8   If it is not possible to determine the post-acquisition results to the end of the period of acquisition, an indication of the entity's contribution to turnover and operating results should be given; if not, the reason should be explained.

3.9   Also in relation to FRS 3:

'Any exceptional profit or loss in periods following the acquisition that is determined using the fair values recognised on acquisition should be disclosed in accordance with the requirements of FRS 3, and identified as relating to the acquisition.'

3.10 The FRS then makes it very clear that any **costs incurred post-acquisition** for **reorganising, restructuring and integrating the acquisition should be shown in the profit and loss account of that period (ie post acquisition).** Such costs are described as those that:

(a)   'Would not have been incurred had the acquisition not taken place.

(b)   Relate to a project identified and controlled by management as part of a reorganisation or integration programme set up at the time of acquisition or as a direct consequence of an immediate post-acquisition review.'

In other words, such costs **cannot be treated as movements on reserves.**

3.11 The FRS also lays out disclosure requirements for movements on provisions and accruals made in relation to the acquisition, which should be:

'Disclosed and analysed between the amounts used for the specific purpose for which they were created and the amounts released unused.'

3.12 The cash flow impact of the acquisition should be disclosed according to FRS 1 *Cash flow statements* (see Chapter 10).

3.13 Finally, for a material acquisition:

'The profit after taxation and minority interests of the acquired entity should be given for:

(a) The period from the beginning of the acquired entity's financial year to the date of acquisition, giving the date on which this period began.

(b) Its previous financial year.

Substantial acquisitions

3.14 Extra information should be disclosed for 'substantial acquisitions', which are defined as each business combination accounted for by using acquisition accounting where:

(a) For listed companies, the combination is a Class I or Super Class I transaction under the Stock Exchange Listing Rules (see below).

(b) For other entities, either:

(i) The net assets or operating profits of the acquired entity exceed 15% of those of the acquiring entity.

(ii) The fair value of the consideration given exceeds 15% of the net assets of the acquiring entity.

and should also be made in other exceptional cases where an acquisition is of such significance that the disclosure is necessary in order to give a true and fair view.

3.15 The **extra information** requiring disclosure is a **summarised profit and loss account, and statement of total recognised gains and losses** of the acquired entity from the beginning of the period to the date of acquisition. The **profit after tax and minority interests for the acquired entity's previous financial year** should also be disclosed.

UITF Abstract 15 *Disclosure of substantial acquisitions*

3.16 In relation to Paragraph 3.14 (a) above, in August 1995 the Stock Exchange revised its Listing Rules and they no longer refer to Class 1 transactions.

3.17 The Stock Exchange Listing Rules classify transactions by assessing their size relative to that of the company proposing to make the transaction. It does this by ascertaining whether any of a number of ratios (eg the net assets of the target to the net assets of the offeror) exceeds a given percentage. Class 1 transactions used to be those where the percentage exceeded 15%. Super Class 1 are those where the percentage exceeds 25%. FRS 6 uses the 15% criterion for non-listed entities.

3.18 The UITF reached a consensus that, in order to retain the ASB's original intentions for FRS 6, the reference to Class 1 transactions should be interpreted as meaning those transactions in which any of the ratios set out in the London Stock Exchange Listing Rules defining Super Class 1 transactions exceeds 15%.

Exam focus point

FRS 6 and FRS 7 (which was published at the same time) represent a major revision of the principles and practices of merger and acquisition accounting. They are controversial and arguments are likely to be carried on in the financial and accountancy press for some time. You *must* go back to Chapters 15 and 17 to tie in the disclosure and other requirements of FRS 6 to FRS 2 *Accounting for subsidiary undertakings* and FRS 7 *Fair values in acquisition accounting.* **These three standards are interrelated and you should be able to discuss the relationships between them**.

Question 5

List the criteria for merger accounting given by FRS 6.

Answer

See Paragraph 2.32.

3.19 EXAMPLE: DISCLOSURE OF REORGANISATION COSTS

In an appendix at the end of the standard, the ASB lays out an illustrative example of the disclosure of reorganisation and integration costs. The explanatory part of the standard suggests that management may wish to include these in the notes to the financial statements. The example given below is optional; the best method will depend on individual circumstances.

COSTS OF REORGANISING AND INTEGRATING ACQUISITIONS

	Acquisition of European business (note (a)) £	*Other acquisitions* £	*Total* £
Announced but not charged as at the previous year	-	25	25
Announced in relation to acquisitions during the year	170	-	170
Adjustments to previous year's Estimates	-	(5)	(5)
	170	20	190
Charged in the year:			
Operating profit	55	12	67
Elsewhere	65	-	65
	120	12	132
Announced but still to be charged at 31 December 1995	50	8	58

Note (a): Acquisition of European business

BPP
PUBLISHING

	£	£
Cost of acquisition		400
Reorganisation and integration expenditure announced		
Fundamental restructuring		
Withdrawal from existing US business and related redundancies	65	
Other items (to be charged to operating profit)		
Other redundancy costs	75	
Re branding and redesign costs	30	
Announced reorganisation and integration costs as shown in above table		170
Total investment		570

In addition to the £120 million expenditure shown in the above table, reorganisation and integration costs charged during the year include £30 million in respect of write-downs to fixed assets consequent on the closure of XYZ plant.

4 FURTHER PRACTICAL ISSUES

4.1 The Smith and Jones example in paragraph 2.7 above involved a share for share exchange where the nominal value of the shares issued was equal to the nominal value of the shares acquired. Where this is not the case, or where there is additional consideration in some form other than equity shares, the basic method needs some modification.

Question 6

America plc has decided to combine with Europe plc and has made a successful one for one offer to the ordinary shareholders of Europe plc. Ordinary shares in America plc are quoted on the Stock Exchange at £2.20. The balance sheets of the two companies are set out below.

	America plc £	Europe plc £
Fixed assets	2,800	2,400
Net current assets	1,400	800
	4,200	3,200
Ordinary shares of £1 each	3,000	2,000
Reserves (realised)	1,200	1,200
	4,200	3,200

Required

Prepare a consolidated balance sheet on a merger basis for America plc:

(a) Using the information given above

(b) Assuming that the offer had been 3 shares in America plc for every 2 shares in Europe plc

(c) Assuming that the offer had been 1 share in America plc for every 2 shares in Europe plc

(d) Assuming that America plc had paid 25p per share for Europe plc as well as giving a one for one share exchange

Answer

The investment in Europe plc shown in the accounts of America plc will be as follows.

Under (a)	£2,000
Under (b)	£3,000
Under (c)	£1,000
Under (d) (£2,000 + £500)	£2,500

CONSOLIDATED BALANCE SHEETS

	(a) £	(b) £	(c) £	(d) £
Fixed assets	5,200	5,200	5,200	5,200
Net current assets	2,200	2,200	2,200	1,700
	7,400	7,400	7,400	6,900
Ordinary shares of £1 each	5,000	6,000	4,000	5,000
Unrealised reserve	-	-	1,000	-
Realised reserves	2,400	1,400	2,400	1,900
	7,400	7,400	7,400	6,900

The balance sheet in (a) shows no change in the total realised reserves. This is because the nominal value of the shares acquired exactly matches the nominal value of the shares issued.

The balance sheet in (b) reflects the fact that America plc has issued 3,000 shares, whose nominal value is £1,000 more than the nominal value of the shares taken over. The difference is deducted from realised reserves, since the group has no unrealised reserves.

The balance sheet in (c) includes an unrealised reserve, created because the nominal value of the shares issued is £1,000 less than the nominal value of the shares acquired.

The (d) balance sheet shows net current assets reduced by £500, the amount of cash paid. The difference between America's investment in subsidiary (£2,500) and the nominal value of the shares acquired (£2,000) is again deducted from realised reserves on consolidation.

4.2 It should be obvious from the above that the **total net assets figure never changes** (unless part of the consideration is cash). **Under merger accounting consolidated reserves become in effect a balancing figure.**

Profit and loss account

4.3 Interest in merger accounting generally focuses on the balance sheet. The **profit and loss account aspect** is really **extremely simple**: it involves **aggregation** of the individual company's figures, with **normal consolidation adjustments but no attempt to distinguish between pre- and post-merger profits in the year of merger**. All comparatives are restated as though the companies had always been merged. Note the FRS 3 effects in Section 2.

Minority interest

4.4 Any minority interest (which will never exceed ten per cent under CA 1985, and under FRS 6 will be *very* rare) **is accounted for in the usual way,** namely:

(a) The minority interest in the subsidiary's shareholders' funds is a deferred liability.

(b) Their share of any proposed dividend is a current liability.

(c) Their share of the subsidiary's profits after tax is deducted in the consolidated profit and loss account.

Merger relief

4.5 Although this section of the text is concerned with group accounts it is worthwhile to consider here the way in which a holding company records a share acquisition in its own individual accounts. We are mainly concerned with s 131 CA 1985.

4.6 S 131 CA 1985 provides that **no share premium** account need be created **on an issue of shares provided that:**

BPP
PUBLISHING

(a) **The shares are issued as part of an arrangement to acquire shares in another company.**

(b) **The investing company, after the issue, has managed to secure at least 90% of the equity shares in the other company.** Any shares held by the investing company prior to the new issue may be counted towards the 90% but the relief under s 131 will *only* apply to the shares issued as part of the arrangement.

4.7 The exemption granted by s 131 is often referred to as **merger relief.** This is not the same as merger accounting. You should be clear in your mind that the statutory provisions relate to the recording of a share issue in the **individual accounts** of an investing company **not consolidated accounts.**

4.8 A company taking advantage of merger relief has **a choice of accounting methods when recording the share issue for purposes of its own** (not its consolidated) accounts. Assuming an issue of shares with a nominal value of £50,000 and a market value of £220,000, the choices are as follows.

(a) DEBIT   Investment in subsidiary   £50,000
     CREDIT   Ordinary share capital   £50,000

This method has the disadvantage that it disguises the true value of the investment acquired. The individual balance sheet will be misleading.

(b) DEBIT   Investment in subsidiary   £220,000
     CREDIT   Ordinary share capital   £50,000
               Share premium account   £170,000

This is a most unlikely option in practice. To show a more realistic balance sheet, the company foregoes the relief available under s 131 and creates an unwelcome share premium account.

(c) DEBIT   Investment in subsidiary   £220,000
     CREDIT   Ordinary share capital   £50,000
               Merger reserve   £170,000

This is perhaps the most likely choice. To record the investment at its 'true' cost, the company shows the share issue at its market value by setting up a reserve account; but the restrictions attaching to a share premium account are avoided by labelling the reserve a 'merger reserve'.

4.9 The method chosen from these three options will not affect the decision on the method of consolidation to be adopted. That decision must be taken in the light of the CA 1985 and FRS 6 criteria.

Question 7

You are given the following information.

(a) On 30 June 20X7 Stepney plc obtained acceptance by 100% of the ordinary shareholders of Brennan plc of its offer of one new ordinary share in Stepney plc for every one ordinary share in Brennan plc. The offer was also declared unconditional on 30 June 20X7 and arrangements were made for the share exchange to take place within the next few days. On 30 June 20X7 the ordinary shares of Stepney plc had a market value of £8.50 each. The newly-formed group became known as the Stepney Group plc.

(b) It may be assumed that profits before extraordinary items of both companies accrue evenly over the year. The extraordinary charge in the accounts of Stepney plc relates to an event occurring in March 20X7.

(c) Stepney plc uses the average cost method of stock valuation while Brennan plc has used the FIFO method in preparing its 20X7 financial statements. The directors of the new group have agreed to standardise accounting practice by using average cost throughout the group. This change would have affected Brennan plc's stock values as shown below.

Stock values (Brennan plc)	*FIFO basis*	*Average cost basis*
	£'000	£'000
Stock (31 December 20X6)	2,748	2,528
Stock (31 December 20X7)	3,826	3,014

(d) SUMMARISED BALANCE SHEETS AT 31 DECEMBER 20X7

	Stepney plc	*Brennan plc*
	£'000	£'000
Fixed assets	61,376	24,299
Investment in Brennan plc	2,000	-
Current assets	22,685	8,623
	86,061	32,922
Current liabilities	12,472	5,461
Ordinary share capital	15,000 *	1,000 **
Retained profits	58,589	26,461
	86,061	32,922

* called-up share capital in ordinary shares of £1.00 each
** called-up share capital in ordinary shares of £0.50 each.

(e) SUMMARISED PROFIT AND LOSS ACCOUNTS
FOR THE YEAR ENDED 31 DECEMBER 20X7

	Stepney plc	*Brennan plc*
	£'000	£'000
Turnover	41,456	15,396
Cost of sales	18,221	5,492
Gross profit	23,235	9,904
Administration expenses	2,694	1,063
Selling and distribution costs	4,143	1,824
Profit on ordinary activities before taxation	16,398	7,017
Taxation	5,240	2,076
Profit on ordinary activities after taxation	11,158	4,941
Extraordinary items less taxation	2,616	-
	8,542	4,941
Dividend	2,000	-
Retained profit for year	6,542	4,941
Retained profits at 1 January 20X7	52,047	21,520
Retained profits at 31 December 20X7	58,589	26,461

You are required to prepare, on a merger accounting basis, the consolidated balance sheet at 31 December 20X7 and the consolidated profit and loss account for the year ended 31 December 20X7 of the Stepney Group plc. Assume that the merger requirements of FRS 6 have been met.

Answer

STEPNEY PLC
CONSOLIDATED BALANCE SHEET AS AT 31 DECEMBER 20X7

	£'000	£'000
Fixed assets		85,675
Current assets (W1)	30,496	
Current liabilities	17,933	
Net current assets		12,563
Total assets less current liabilities		98,238
Capital and reserves		
Share capital		15,000
Profit and loss account		83,238
		98,238

CONSOLIDATED PROFIT AND LOSS ACCOUNT
FOR THE YEAR ENDED 31 DECEMBER 20X7

	£'000	£'000
Turnover		56,852
Cost of sales (W3)		24,305
Gross profit		32,547
Distribution costs		5,967
Administrative expenses		3,757
Profit on ordinary activities before taxation		22,823
Tax on profit on ordinary activities		7,316
Profit on ordinary activities after taxation		15,507
Extraordinary losses		2,616
Profit for the financial year		12,891
Dividend		2,000
		10,891
Merger adjustment (W2)		(1,000)
Retained profit for the financial year		9,891
Retained profits brought forward		
As previously reported (52,047 + 21,520)	73,567	
Prior year adjustment (2,748 - 2,528)	(220)	
As restated		73,347
Retained profits carried forward		83,238

Workings

1   *Current assets*

	£'000	£'000
Stepney		22,685
Brennan		8,623
		31,308
Adjustment in respect of Brennan's closing stock		
FIFO cost	3,826	
Average cost	3,014	
		(812)
		30,496

2   *Merger adjustment*

	£'000
Nominal value of shares issued by Stepney	2,000
Nominal value of shares acquired by Stepney	1,000
Difference to be deducted from group reserves	1,000

3   *Cost of sales*

	£'000	£'000
Stepney		18,221
Brennan		
Unadjusted	5,492	
Adjustment in respect of stock valuation		
(3,826 - 3,014) - (2,748 - 2,528)	592	
		6,084
		24,305

Chapter roundup

- This chapter has explained how to prepare a **consolidated profit and loss account** by combining the profit and loss accounts of each group company.

- **Adjustments** must be made:

  - To reduce turnover by the amount of any **intra-group trading**, and to deduct from consolidated gross profit any unrealised profit on stocks thus acquired which are held at the year end. Cost of sales will be the balancing figure.

  - To reduce stock values by the amount of any **unrealised profit** on intra-group trading.

  - To calculate the **minority interest** in subsidiary companies' results for the year.

  - To account for **intra-group dividends**.

  - To **eliminate pre-acquisition** profits.

- **Merger accounting** is a very topical issue. Make sure you know the **criteria** for merger accounting under **FRS 6** and CA 1985 and that you can discuss the differences in approach and the criticisms of merger accounting.

- Make sure also that you can clearly **differentiate acquisitions from mergers** and that you can prepare accounts using both acquisition and merger accounting.

- You should also be able to explain s 131 CA 1985 (**merger relief**) and distinguish it *clearly* from merger accounting.

- FRS 6 represents a major step in **restricting** the practice of businesses who use merger accounting in non-merger situations and therefore distort the true picture of their affairs. The controversy surrounding the standard is bound to continue for some time.

Quick quiz

1   At what stage in the consolidated profit and loss account does the figure for minority interests appear?

2   What dispensation is granted to a parent company by s 230 CA 1985?

3   Barley Ltd has owned 100% of the issued share capital of Oats Ltd for many years. Barley Ltd sells goods to Oats Ltd at cost plus 20%. The following information is available for the year:

    Turnover   - Barley Ltd   £460,000
               - Oats Ltd   £120,000

    During the year Barley Ltd sold goods to Oats Ltd for £60,000 of which £18,000 were still held in stock by Oats at the year end.

    At what amount should turnover appear in the consolidated profit and loss account?

4   Chicken plc owns 80% of Egg plc. Egg plc sells goods to Chicken plc at cost plus 50%. The total invoiced sales to Chicken plc by Egg plc in the year ended 31 December 20X9 were £900,000 and, of these sales, goods which had been invoiced at £60,000 were held in stock by Chicken plc at 31 December 20X9. What is the reduction in aggregate group gross profit?

5   Major Ltd, which makes up its accounts to 31 December, has an 80% owned subsidiary Minor Ltd. Minor Ltd sells goods to Major Ltd at a mark-up on cost of 33.33%. At 31 December 20X8, Major had £12,000 of such goods in stock and at 31 December 20X9 had £15,000 of such goods in stock.

    What is a permissible amount by which the consolidated profit attributable to Major Ltd's shareholders should be adjusted in respect of the above?

BPP
PUBLISHING

Part C: Preparation of consolidated financial statements

Ignore taxation

    A   £1,000 Debit

    B   £800 Credit

    C   £750 Credit

    D   £600 Debit

6   Horace Ltd acquired 75% of the ordinary share capital and 25% of the preference share capital of Sylvia Ltd several years ago. The profit and loss account of Sylvia Ltd for the year ended 28 February 20X0 showed the following:

	£	£
Profit on ordinary activities after tax		4,000
Preference dividend	1,000	
Ordinary dividend	2,000	
		(3,000)
		1,000

What is the minority interest in the consolidated profit and loss account of Horace Ltd for the year ended 28 February 20X0?

7   Saroti plc owns 70% of the ordinary shares and 40% of the preference shares of Macari Ltd. An extract from Macari Ltd's profit and loss account is as follows:

	£
Profit after tax	10,000
Preference dividend paid	(2,000)
Ordinary dividend paid	(5,000)
Retained profit	3,000

What amount for minority interest should be shown in the consolidated profit and loss account of Sartori plc?

8   Describe the effect of acquisition accounting on the distributable profits of a company.

9   Fill in the blank: In merger accounting the investment in the subsidiaries is recorded as the ....

10   Goodwill never arises with merger accounting. True or false?

11   List the five FRS 6 criteria for mergers.

12   Distinguish merger accounting and merger relief.

Answers to quick quiz

1   Down to the line 'profit after taxation', the whole of the subsidiary's results is included. A one line adjustment is then inserted to deduct the minority's share of the subsidiary's PAT. (See para 1.4)

2   See para 1.22.

3   Turnover: 460 + 120 − 60 = 520. (1.8-1.11)

4   $£60,000 \times \dfrac{50}{150} = £20,000$ (1.8-11)

5   D $(15,000 - 12,000) \times \dfrac{33.3}{133.3} \times 80\%$ (1.8-1.11)

6

		£
Preference	75% × 1,000	750
Equity	25% × (4,000 − 1,000)	750
		1,500 (1.12-1.16)

7

		£
Preference	60% × 2,000	1,200
Equity	30% × (10,000 − 2,000)	2,400
Minority interest		3,600 (1.12-1.16)

8   See Para 2.3

9   The nominal value of the consideration given. (2.10)

10 True. (2.13)

11 See Para 2.28

12 Merger accounting is concerned only with methods of preparing consolidated accounts. Merger relief relates to the recording of a share issue in the individual accounts of an investing company. (4.5-46)

Now try the question below from the Exam Question Bank

Number	Level	Marks	Time
22	Full exam	25	45 mins

BPP PUBLISHING

Chapter 19

ASSOCIATES AND JOINT VENTURES

Topic list	Syllabus reference
1 Background	4(d)
2 FRS 9 *Associates and joint ventures*	4(d)
3 Associates	4(d)
4 Incorporated joint ventures and joint arrangements	4(d)
5 Disclosures for associates and joint ventures	4(d)

Introduction

Some investments which do not satisfy the criteria for classification as subsidiaries may nevertheless be much more than trade investments. The most important of these are associates and joint ventures which are the subject of this chapter and of FRS 9 *Associates and joint ventures*.

Study guide

- Define associates and joint ventures, including an arrangement that is not an entity (JANE).

- Distinguish between equity accounting and proportional consolidation.

- Describe the equity and gross equity methods.

- Prepare consolidated financial statements to include a single subsidiary and an associated company or a joint venture.

1   BACKGROUND

1.1   In the 1960s it became increasingly common for companies to trade through companies in which a **substantial but not a controlling interest** was held. Traditionally such companies were accounted for in the same way as trade investments. In other words the income from associated companies was only included in the investing company's accounts to the extent of the dividends received and receivable up to its balance sheet date. However, it was felt that this treatment did not reflect the reality of the investment, not least because the investor could in many cases influence the investee's dividend policy. The need thus arose for an **intermediate form of accounting for those investments which lie between full subsidiary and trade investment status**.

Equity accounting and the Companies Act 1985

1.2   The intermediate form of accounting developed for this purpose is known as **equity accounting.** The full, up-to-date (FRS 9) definition of equity accounting will be given later in this chapter. For now, think of it as follows.

> **KEY TERM**
>
> **Equity accounting** is a modified form of consolidation of the results and assets of the investee where the investor has significant influence but not control. Rather than full, line by line consolidation, it involves incorporating the investor's share of the profit/loss and assets of the investee **in one line** in the investor's profit and loss account and balance sheet.

1.3 Equity accounting was first recognised in UK accounting literature in SSAP 1 *Accounting for associated companies* (now superceded by FRS 9). **Parent companies are also required by law to use equity accounting to account for holdings in associated undertakings, defined as follows.**

> **KEY TERM**
>
> 'An "**associated undertaking**" means an undertaking in which an undertaking included in the consolidation has a participating interest and over whose operating and financial policy it exercises a significant influence, and which is not:
>
> (a) A subsidiary undertaking of the parent company
> (b) A joint venture'. (s 20(1) Sch 4A, CA 1985)
>
> 'Where an undertaking holds 20% or more of the voting rights in another undertaking, it shall be presumed to exercise such an influence over it unless the contrary is shown.'
>   (s 20(2) Sch 4A, CA 1985)

1.4 **Participating interests** which are not in associated undertakings have to be disclosed separately from other investments but do not have to be accounted for by the equity method.

2 FRS 9 ASSOCIATES AND JOINT VENTURES

2.1 FRS 9 *Associates and joint ventures* was issued in November 1997. It sets out the definition and accounting treatments for associates and joint ventures, two types of interests that a reporting entity may have in other entities. The FRS also deals with joint arrangements that are not entities. The definitions and treatments prescribed have been developed to be consistent with the Accounting Standards Board's approach to accounting for subsidiaries (dealt with in FRS 2 *Accounting for subsidiary undertakings*). The requirements are consistent with companies legislation.

Objective

2.2 The objective of FRS 9 is **to reflect the effect on an investor's financial position and performance of** its interest in two special kinds of investments - **associates and joint ventures**. The investor is partly accountable for the activities of these investments because of the closeness of its involvement.

(a) It is closely involved in **associates** as a result of its **participating interest** and **significant influence**.

(b) Its close involvement with **joint ventures** arises as a result of its **long-term interest** and **joint control**.

2.3   The FRS **also deals with joint arrangements that do not qualify as associates or joint ventures because they are not entities.**

Scope

2.4   The FRS applies to all financial statements intending to give a true and fair view. It is **not yet required for those smaller entities adopting the Financial Reporting Standard for Smaller Entities** and preparing consolidated financial statements. However, it is envisaged that a future revision to the FRSSE will require such entities to adopt the FRS. The FRS is effective in respect of financial statements of accounting periods ending on or after 23 June 1998.

Exam focus point

- At this stage, read through the summary and example **for overview only**. Do not expect to understand everything you read.
- **At the end of the chapter**, when you have worked through the detailed sections on associates and joint ventures, **come back to this section to put it in context**.
- When you come to **revise**, look at this section as it contains a clear summary of the requirements of the FRS.

Summary

2.5   The table below, taken from the FRS, describes the **different sorts of interest that a reporting entity may have in other entities or arrangements**. The sections marked with an asterisk (*) are covered by the FRS. The defining relationships described in the table form the basis for the definitions used in the FRS.

Entity/ arrangement	*Nature of relationship*	*Description of the defining relationship - the full definitions are given in the FRS*
Subsidiary	Investor controls its investee	Control is the ability of an entity to direct the operating and financial policies of another entity with a view to gaining economic benefits from its activities. To have control an entity must have both: (a) The ability to deploy the economic resources of the investee or to direct it. (b) The ability to ensure that any resulting benefits accrue to itself (with corresponding exposure to losses) and to restrict the access of others to those benefits.
* Joint arrangement that is not an entity	Entities participate in an arrangement to carry on part of their own trades or businesses	A joint arrangement, whether or not subject to joint control, does not constitute an entity unless it carries on a trade or business of its own.
* Joint venture	Investor holds a long-term interest and shares control under a contractual arrangement	The joint venture agreement can override the rights normally conferred by ownership interests with the effect that: • Acting together, the venturers can control the venture and there are procedures for such joint action. • Each venturer has (implicitly or explicitly) a veto over strategic policy decisions. There is usually a procedure for settling disputes between venturers and, possibly, for terminating the joint venture.

★ Associate	Investor holds a participating interest and exercises significant influence	The investor has a long-term interest and is actively involved, and influential, in the direction of its investee through its participation in policy decisions covering the aspects of policy relevant to the investor, including decisions on strategic issues such as: (i) The expansion or contraction of the business, participation in other entities or changes in products, markets and activities of its investee. (ii) Determining the balance between dividend and reinvestment.
Simple investment		The investor's interest does not quality the investee as an associate, a joint venture or a subsidiary because the investor has limited influence or its interest is not long-term.

2.6 The table below, also taken from the FRS, sets out the **treatments in consolidated financial statements** for the different interests that a reporting entity may have in other entities and for joint arrangements that are not entities - the sections marked with an asterisk (★) are covered by the FRS.

Type of investment	*Treatment in consolidated financial statements*
Subsidiaries	The investor should consolidate the assets, liabilities, results and cash flows of its subsidiaries.
★ Joint arrangements that are not entities	Each party should account for its own share of the assets, liabilities and cash flows in the joint arrangement, measured according to the terms of that arrangement, for example pro rata to their respective interests.
Joint ventures	The venturer should use the gross equity method showing in addition to the amounts included under the equity method, on the face on the balance sheet, the venturer's share of the gross assets and liabilities of its joint ventures, and, in the profit and loss account, the venturer's share of their turnover distinguished from that of the group. Where the venturer conducts a major part of its business through joint ventures, it may show fuller information provided all amounts are distinguished from those of the group.
Associates	The investor should include its associates in its consolidated financial statements using the equity method. In the investor's consolidated profit and loss account the investor's share of its associates' operating results should be included immediately after group operating results. From the level of profit before tax, the investor's share of the relevant amounts for associates should be included within the amounts for the group. In the consolidated statement of total recognised gains and losses the investor's share of the total recognised gains and losses of its associates should be included, shown separately under each heading, if material. In the balance sheet the investor's share of the net assets of its associates should be included and separately disclosed. The cash flow statement should include the cash flows between the investor and its associates. Goodwill arising on the investor's acquisition of its associates, less any amortisation or write-down, should be included in the carrying amount for the associates but should be disclosed separately. In the profit and loss account the amortisation or write-down of such goodwill should be separately disclosed as part of the investor's share of its associates' results.
Simple investments	The investor includes its interests as investments at either cost or valuation.

2.7 EXAMPLE: CONSOLIDATED FINANCIAL STATEMENTS

The following example of consolidated financial statements is taken from Appendix IV of FRS 9. Study it for an overview and come back to it when you have finished the chapter.

2.8 The format is illustrative only. The amounts shown for 'Associates' and 'joint ventures' are subdivisions of the item for which the statutory prescribed heading is 'Income from interests in associated undertakings'. The subdivisions may be shown in a note rather than on the face of the profit and loss account.

CONSOLIDATED PROFIT AND LOSS ACCOUNT

	£m	£m
Turnover: group and share of joint ventures	320	
Less: share of joint ventures' turnover	(120)	
Group turnover		200
Cost of sales		(120)
Gross profit		80
Administrative expenses		(40)
Group operating profit		40
Share of operating profit in		
Joint ventures	30	
Associates	24	
		54
		94
Interest receivable (group)		6
Interest payable		
Group	(26)	
Joint ventures	(10)	
Associates	(12)	
		(48)
Profit on ordinary activities before tax		52
Tax on profit on ordinary activities★		(12)
Profit on ordinary activities after tax		40
Minority interests		(6)
Profit on ordinary activities after taxation and minority interest		34
Equity dividends		(10)
Retained profit for group and its share of associates and joint ventures		24

★Tax relates to the following:
Parent and subsidiaries	(5)	
Joint ventures	(5)	
Associates	(2)	

CONSOLIDATED BALANCE SHEET

	£m	£m	£m
Fixed assets			
Tangible assets		480	
Investments			
Investments in joint ventures:			
Share of gross assets	130		
Share of gross liabilities	(80)		
		50	
Investments in associates		20	
			550
Current assets			
Stock		15	
Debtors		75	
Cash at bank and in hand		10	
		100	
Creditors (due within one year)		(50)	
Net current assets			50
Total assets less current liabilities			600
Creditors (due after more than one year)			(250)
Provisions for liabilities and charges			(10)
Equity minority interest			(40)
			300
Capital and reserves			
Called up share capital			50
Share premium account			150
Profit and loss account			100
Shareholders' funds (all equity)			300

Notes

In the example, there is no individual associate or joint venture that accounts for more than 25 per cent of any of the following for the investor group (excluding any amount for associates and joint ventures).

- Gross assets
- Gross liabilities
- Turnover
- Operating results (on a three-year average)

Additional disclosures for joint ventures (which in aggregate exceed the 15 per cent threshold)

	£m	£m
Share of assets		
Share of fixed assets	100	
Share of current assets	30	
		130
Share of liabilities		
Liabilities due within one year or less	(10)	
Liabilities due after more than one year	(70)	
		(80)
Share of net assets		50

Additional disclosures for associates (which in aggregate exceed the 15 per cent threshold)

	£m	£m
Share of turnover of associates		90
Share of assets		
Share of fixed assets	4	
Share of current assets	28	
		32
Share of liabilities		
Liabilities due within one year or less	(3)	
Liabilities due after more than one year	(9)	
		(12)
Share of net assets		20

3 ASSOCIATES

3.1 Associated undertakings **should be included** by an entity **in** its **consolidated financial statements using the equity method. In the investor's individual statements,** the interest in associates is **shown as a fixed asset investment,** at cost (less any amounts written off) or valuation.

3.2 The most important definitions relate to the **identification** of associates.

> **KEY TERMS**
>
> - **Associate:** an entity (other than a subsidiary) in which another entity (the investor) has a participating interest and over whose operating and financial policies the investor exercises a significant influence.
>
> - **Control** the ability of an entity to direct the operating and financial policies of another entity with a view to gaining economic benefits from its activities.
>
> - **Entity:** a body corporate, a partnership or an unincorporated association carrying on a trade or business with or without a view to profit.
>
> *(FRS 9)*

Participating interest

3.3 FRS 9 defines 'participating interest' in the same way as FRS 2.

> **KEY TERM**
>
> **Participating interest:** an interest held in the shares of another entity on a long-term basis for the purpose of securing a contribution to the investor's activities by the exercise of control or influence arising from or related to that interest.
>
> *(FRS 9)*

3.4 The investor's interest must be **beneficial,** the benefits linked to the exercise of significant influence. An interest convertible to an interest in shares and an option to acquire shares also qualify.

3.5 A participating interest is a **continuing relationship** and the interest does not cease only because the investor sells its interest in the associate.

Long-term interest

3.6   This definition relates to a participating interest.

> **KEY TERM**
>
> **Interest held on a long-term basis**: an interest that is held other than exclusively with a view to subsequent resale. An interest held exclusively with a view to subsequent resale is:
>
> - An interest for which a purchaser has been identified or is being sought, and which is reasonably expected to be disposed or within approximately one year of its date of acquisition.
>
> - An interest that was acquired as a result of the enforcement of a security, unless the interest has become part of the continuing activities of the group or the holder acts as if it intends the interest to become so.   *(FRS 9)*

3.7   This definition is extremely important.

> **KEY TERM**
>
> **Exercise of significant influence**: the exercise of a degree of influence by an investor over the operating and financial policies of its investee that results in the following conditions being fulfilled.
>
> (a) The investor is actively involved and is influential in the direction of its investee through its participation in policy decisions covering all aspects of policy relevant to the investor, including decisions on strategic issues such as:
>
>   (i) The expansion or contraction of the business, participation in other entities, changes in products, markets and activities of its investee.
>
>   (ii) Determining the balance between dividend and reinvestment.
>
> (b) Over time, the investee generally implements policies that are consistent with the strategy of the investor and avoids implementing policies that are contrary to the investor's interests. *(FRS 9)*

3.8   Significant influence is **usually wielded through nomination to the board of directors**, although it may be achieved in other ways. It presupposes an agreement (formal or informal) between the investor and investee.

3.9   **The 20% rule is followed here**, so that a holding of 20% or more of the voting rights suggests (but does not guarantee) that the investor exercises significant influence. At 20% the presumption of the exercise of significant influence can be rebutted if the criteria above are not fulfilled. The holdings of both parent and subsidiaries in the entity should be taken into account.

Accounting for associates

3.10   Following FRS 9, a reporting entity that prepares **consolidated financial statements** should include its associates in those statements using the **equity method in all the primary statements**. In the investor's **individual financial statements**, its interests in associates should be treated as **fixed asset investments** and shown either **at cost less any amounts written off or at valuation**.

3.11 The equity method is discussed here in more detail with regard to each of the primary statements.

Consolidated profit and loss account

3.12 FRS 9 stipulates the following.

(a) The investor's **share of its associates' operating results** should be **included immediately after group operating result** (but after the investor's share of the results of its joint ventures, if any).

(b) Any **amortisation** or write-down **of goodwill** arising on acquiring the associates should be **charged** at this point **and disclosed.**

(c) The **investor's share of any exceptional items** included after operating profit (paragraph 20 of FRS 3) or of interest should be **shown separately** from the amounts for the group.

(d) **At and below the level of profit before tax**, the **investor's share** of the relevant amounts for associates should be **included within the amounts for the group**, although for items **below this level**, such as taxation, the **amounts relating to associates should be disclosed.**

(e) Where it is helpful to give an indication of the size of the business as a whole, a total combining the investor's share of its associates' turnover with **group turnover may be shown as a memorandum item** in the profit and loss account **but** the investor's share of its **associates' turnover should be clearly distinguished** from group turnover.

(f) Similarly, the **segmental analysis of turnover and operating profit** (if given) should clearly **distinguish between** that of the **group and** that of **associates.**

Consolidated balance sheet

3.13 FRS 9 requires the following.

(a) The investor's **consolidated balance sheet should include as a fixed asset investment the investor's share of the net assets of its associates** shown as a separate item.

(b) **Goodwill** arising on the investor's acquisition of its associates, less any amortisation or write-down, should be **included in the carrying amount for the associates but should be disclosed separately**.

Consolidated cash flow statement

3.14 Cash flow statements are covered in Chapter 10. FRS 9 amends the revised version of FRS 1 to reflect the following.

(a) The consolidated cash flow statement should include **dividends received from associates as a separate item** between operating activities and returns on investments and servicing of finance.

(b) Any other cash flows between the investor and its associates should be included under the appropriate cash flow heading for the activity giving rise to the cash flow. None of the other cash flows of the associates should be included.

Consolidated statement of total recognised gains and losses

3.15 The statement of total recognised gains and losses is discussed in Chapter 9 which deals with FRS 3. FRS 9 requires the **investor's share of the total recognised gains and losses of its associates to be included**. If the amounts included are material they should be shown separately under each heading, either in the statement or in a note that is referred to in the statement.

3.16 EXAMPLE: ASSOCIATED COMPANY IN INVESTOR'S OWN ACCOUNTS

H Ltd, a company with subsidiaries, acquires 25,000 of the 100,000 £1 ordinary shares in A Ltd for £60,000 on 1 January 20X0. A Ltd meets the FRS 9 definitions of an associate. In the year to 31 December 20X0, A Ltd earns profits after tax of £24,000, from which it declares a dividend of £6,000.

How will A Ltd's results be accounted for in the individual and consolidated accounts of H Ltd for the year ended 31 December 20X0?

3.17 SOLUTION

In the individual accounts of H Ltd, the investment will be recorded on 1 January 20X0 at cost. Unless there is a permanent diminution in the value of the investment, this amount will remain in the individual balance sheet of H Ltd permanently. The only entry in H Ltd's individual profit and loss account will be to record dividends received. For the year ended 31 December 20X0, H Ltd will:

DEBIT	Cash	£1,500	
CREDIT	Income from shares in associated companies		£1,500

Consolidated profit and loss account

3.18 A consolidation schedule may be used to prepare the consolidated profit and loss account of a group with associates. The treatment of the associate's profits in the following example should be studied carefully.

3.19 EXAMPLE: ASSOCIATE COMPANY IN CONSOLIDATED ACCOUNTS

The following consolidation schedule relates to the H Ltd group, consisting of the holding company, an 80% owned subsidiary (S Ltd) and an associate (A Ltd) in which the group has a 30% interest.

CONSOLIDATION SCHEDULE

	Group £'000	H Ltd £'000	S Ltd £'000		A Ltd £'000
Turnover	1,400	600	800		300
Cost of sales	770	370	400		120
Gross profit	630	230	400		180
Distribution costs and administrative expenses (including depreciation, directors' emoluments etc)	290	110	180		80
Group operating profit	340	120	220		100
Share of operating profit in associate	30	-	-	30%	30
	370	120	220		30
Interest receivable (group)	30	30	-		-
	400	150	220		30
Interest payable (group)	(20)	-	(20)		-
Profit on ordinary activities before tax	380	150	200		30
Taxation					
H Ltd	(150)	(60)	(90)		
Associate	(12)	-	-		(12)
Profit after taxation	218	90	110		18
Minority interest	(22)		(22)		
	196	90	88		18
Inter-company dividends	-	20	(18)		(2)
Group profit	196	110	70		16
Dividends paid and proposed	(45)	(45)	-		-
Retained profits for the financial year	151	65	70		16
Retained profits brought forward	45	30	10		5
Retained profits carried forward	196	95	80		21

Notes

(a) **Group turnover, group gross profit and costs** such as depreciation etc **exclude** the turnover, gross profit and costs etc of **associates**.

(b) The **group share of the associate's operating profit is credited** to the group profit and loss account (here, 30% of £100,000 = £30,000). If the associated company has been acquired during the year, it would be necessary to deduct the pre-acquisition profits.

(c) **Taxation** consists of:

   (i)   Taxation **on the holding company and subsidiaries in total.**

   (ii) Only the **group's share of the tax charge of the associated company**; A Ltd tax would be £40,000, so that the group share is £40,000 × 30% = £12,000.

(d) The **minority interest will only ever apply to subsidiary companies.**

(e) **Inter-company dividends** from subsidiaries and associated companies **should all be recorded.**

(f) **Dividends** paid and proposed **relate to the holding company only.**

Pro-forma consolidated profit and loss account

3.20   The following is a **suggested layout** (using the figures given in the illustration above) for a profit and loss account for a company having subsidiaries as well as associates. It follows the FRS 9 example given in Section 2 of this chapter.

	£'000	£'000
Turnover		1,400
Cost of sales		770
Gross profit		630
Distribution costs and administrative expenses		290
Group operating profit		340
Share of operating profit in associate		30
		370
Interest and similar income receivable (group)		30
		400
Interest payable and similar charges (group)		(20)
Profit on ordinary activities before tax		380
Tax on profit on ordinary activities★		162
Profit after taxation		218
Minority interest (in the current year post tax profits of subsidiary)		(22)
Profit for the financial year attributable to the group		196
(of which £111,000 has been dealt with in the accounts of the holding company)		196
Dividends (of the holding company)		
Paid	20	
Proposed	25	
		45
		151
Earnings per share		Xp
Retained profits for the year		£'000
Holding company		66
Subsidiary		70
Associated company		15
		151
★Tax relates to the following:		
Parent and subsidiaries	150	
Associate	12	

Question 1

'When a subsidiary pays a dividend out of pre-acquisition profits there are different ways of treating the dividend in the accounts of the holding company.'

Discuss.

Answer

Generally, a dividend paid out of pre-acquisition profits should be applied to reduce the cost of the investments in the balance sheet of the holding company. It should not be treated as realised profit.

The thinking behind this is that the holding company cannot credit the dividend to profit because no profit has been made. The holding company was willing to pay 'over the odds' for its investment in the presumption that part of its cost would be immediately re-paid. When the dividend is paid, this presumption must be pursued to its conclusion by treating the dividend as a reduction of the cost of investment or a return of capital.

However, this accounting treatment is no longer a legal requirement, and it is possible to argue that, provided the investment will eventually recover the value that has been removed from it by the distribution, then it is unnecessary to write it down and the dividend to the holding company may be distributed. This implies that, provided the level of profits made by the subsidiary is to be maintained, those profits may be distributed by the holding company.

431

According to FRS 6 *Acquisitions and mergers,* a dividend must be applied to reduce the carrying value of the investment in a subsidiary only to the extent that this is necessary to provide for any diminution in value. Any other amount is realised profit in the hands of the parent company.

Consolidated balance sheet

3.21 As explained earlier, the consolidated balance sheet will contain an **asset 'Investment in associates'.** The amount at which this asset is stated will be its original cost plus the group's share of any **profits earned since acquisition** which have not been distributed as dividends.

3.22 EXAMPLE: CONSOLIDATED BALANCE SHEET

On 1 January 20X6 the net tangible assets of A Ltd amount to £220,000, financed by 100,000 £1 ordinary shares and revenue reserves of £120,000. H Ltd, a company with subsidiaries, acquires 30,000 of the shares in A Ltd for £75,000. During the year ended 31 December 20X6 A Ltd's profit after tax is £30,000, from which dividends of £12,000 are paid.

Show how H Ltd's investment in A Ltd would appear in the consolidated balance sheet at 31 December 20X6.

3.23 SOLUTION

CONSOLIDATED BALANCE SHEET
AS AT 31 DECEMBER 20X6 (extract)

	£
Fixed assets	
Investment in associate	
Cost	75,000
Group share of post-acquisition retained profits	
(30% × £18,000)	5,400
	80,400

3.24 An important point to note is that this figure of £80,400 can be arrived at in a completely different way. It is the sum of:

(a) The group's share of A Ltd's net assets at 31 December 20X6.
(b) The premium paid over net book value for the shares acquired.

3.25 This can be shown as follows.

	£	£
(a) A Ltd's net assets at 31 December 20X6		
Net assets at 1 January 20X6	220,000	
Retained profit for year	18,000	
Net assets at 31 December 20X6	238,000	
Group share (30%)		71,400
(b) Premium on acquisition		
Net assets acquired by group on 1 Jan 20X6		
(30% × £220,000)	66,000	
Price paid for shares	75,000	
Premium on acquisition		9,000
Investment in associate per balance sheet		80,400

3.26 The reason why this is important is because FRS 9 requires the investment in associated companies to be analysed in this way, ie:

(a)   Group share of associate's net assets

(b)   Goodwill arising on acquisition of associate less any amortisation or write down is included in (a) but disclosed separately

3.27 **Fair values should be attributed to the associate's underlying assets and liabilities.** These will provide the basis for subsequent depreciation. Both the consideration paid in the acquisition and the goodwill arising should be calculated in the same way as on the acquisition of a subsidiary. The associate's assets should not include any goodwill earned in the balance sheet of the associate.

3.28 The goodwill should be treated in accordance with the provisions of FRS 10 *Goodwill and intangible assets*. The usual treatment would therefore be to capitalise and amortise. (Our example assumes for simplicity that the goodwill has an indefinite life and there is no amortisation.)

Question 2

How should a holding company treat the following items in the financial statements for an associated company, when preparing group accounts:

(a)   Turnover?
(b)   Inter-company profits?
(c)   Goodwill?

Answer

(a)   The holding company should not aggregate the turnover of an associated company with its own turnover.

(b)   Wherever the effect is material, adjustments similar to those adopted for the purpose of presenting consolidated financial statements should be made to exclude from the investing group's consolidated financial statements such items as unrealised profits on stocks transferred to or from associated companies.

(c)   The investing group's balance sheet should disclose 'interest in associated companies'. The amount disclosed under this heading should include both the investing group's share of any goodwill in the associated companies' own financial statements and any premium paid on acquisition of the interests in the associated companies in so far as it has not already been written off or amortised.

Question 3

Corrie plc has a 75% subsidiary, Brookie plc, of which it also owns 25% of the preference shares. Corrie has an associated company, Eastend Ltd, in which it has a 25% interest. Set out below are the balance sheets of the three companies as at 31 December 20X7. (Investment in subsidiary and associate are shown at cost.)

Part C: Preparation of consolidated financial statements

	Corrie plc	Brookie plc	Eastend Ltd
	£m	£m	£m
Fixed assets			
Tangible assets	4,920	4,350	
Investments			1,500
Shares in Brookie	3,960		
Shares in Eastend	900		
	9,780	4,350	1,500
Current assets			
Stock	780	600	
Debtors	610	360	
Cash at bank and in hand	260	30	
	1,650	990	
Creditors: amounts falling due within one year	610	410	
Net current assets	1,040	580	
Total assets less current liabilities	10,820	4,930	
Creditors: amounts falling due after more than one year	1,730	440	
	9,090	4,490	1,500
Capital and reserves			
Ordinary £1 shares	6,000	2,400	1,500
5% preference shares of £1		1,200	
Share premium account	1,490	100	
Profit and loss account	1,600	790	
	9,090	4,490	1,500

You are the new assistant financial controller of Corrie plc and have been asked to prepare a consolidated balance sheet for the Corrie Group. The following further information is available.

(a) Brookie plc was acquired on 1 January 20X7. Corrie plc paid £3,960m for the ordinary and preference shares. On that date Brookie plc's profit and loss account was £898m (credit balance).

(b) The preference shares of Brookie plc are redeemable on 31 December 20Y6 at a premium of 10%. They were originally issued at par on 1 January 20X7. The premium has not yet been accounted for and provision should be made for the premium on a straight line basis annually.

(c) The balance on the share premium account of Brookie plc represents the premium on the issue of the ordinary shares.

(d) It is the policy of Corrie plc to write off goodwill arising on acquisition against the profit and loss account in the year of acquisition. When Brookie plc was acquired the fair value of its net assets was equal to their book value except for some non-material differences.

(e) Eastend Ltd is an investment company. It has no assets other than a portfolio of investments, the market value of which is £2,200m. In the above balance sheet, the investments are shown at their book value of £1,500m. Corrie plc acquired its interest in Eastend Ltd on 31 December 20X7.

(f) Brookie plc paid a dividend for the year of 2p per ordinary £1 share and also paid the 5% preference dividend. There was no dividend proposed at 31 December 20X7. As assistant financial controller, you have advised the directors of Corrie plc that the dividend payment of Brookie plc should be treated as if it were out of pre-acquisition profits, that is as a deduction from the value of the investment.

(g) Brookie plc manufactures and sells industrial machinery. On 1 January 20X7 it sold a machine to Corrie plc which Corrie plc correctly classified as a fixed asset. The item was sold at a mark up of 25% of cost and is shown in the books of Corrie plc at £720m. Of this amount, £20m is still owed to Brookie plc. Corrie plc has charged a year's depreciation on the machine of 25%.

Required

Prepare the consolidated balance sheet for the Corrie Group plc as at 31 December 20X7. Ignore any additional disclosure requirements of FRS 9.

Answer

(b) CORRIE GROUP PLC
CONSOLIDATED BALANCE SHEET AS AT 31 DECEMBER 20X7

	£m	£m
Fixed assets		
Tangible assets (W4)		9,162
Investment in associate (W6)		550
		9,712
Current assets		
Stocks	1,380	
Debtors (W7)	950	
Cash at bank and in hand	290	
	2,620	
Creditors: amounts falling due within one year (W8)	1,000	
Net current assets		1,620
Total assets less current liabilities		11,332
Creditors: amounts falling due after one year		2,170
		9,162
Capital and reserves		
Share capital		6,000
Share premium		1,490
Profit and loss account (W9)		(21)
		7,469
Minority interest: equity	784	
non-equity	909	
		1,693
		9,162

Workings

1   *Dividends paid*

	Total		Corrie plc
	£m		£m
Ordinary dividend	48	× 75%	36
Preference dividend	60	× 25%	15
	108		51

As these dividends are paid out of pre-acquisition profits, they should be charged against the cost of Corrie plc's investment in Brookie plc.

2   *Goodwill*

	£m	£m
Cost of investment in Brookie plc		3,960
Less dividend from pre-acquisition profits (W1)		51
		3,909
Net assets acquired:		
Share capital	2,400	
Share premium	100	
Profit and loss account	898	
	3,398	
Group share 75%		2,548
		1,361
5% preference shares	1,200	
Group share 25%		300
Goodwill		1,061

3   *Intercompany stock/fixed asset*

	£m	£m
Intercompany profit = 720 × 25/125		144
DEBIT Minority interest P&L 25%	36	
DEBIT Group P&L 75%	108	
CREDIT Fixed assets		144

	£m	£m
Depreciation adjustment		
Excess depreciation: 25% of 144 = £36m		
DEBIT Provision for depreciation	36	
CREDIT Group P&L		36

4   Tangible fixed assets

	£m
Corrie	4,920
Less intercompany profit	(144)
Add back excess depreciation	36
	4,812
Brookie	4,350
	9,162

5   Minority interest

	£m	£m
Equity		784
Share capital	2,400	
Share premium	100	
Profit and loss account (790 – 12)	778	
	3,278	
× 25%		820
Less intercompany profit		36
Non equity		784
Preference shares	1,200	
Premium on redemption	12	
	1,212	
× 75%		909
		1,693

6   Investment in associate

	£m
Cost of investment	900
Share of fair value of investments acquired 25% × 2,200	550
Goodwill	350

As the goodwill has been written off, the investment in associate in the consolidated balance sheet will be the share of net assets at fair value, ie £550m.

7   Debtors

	£m
Corrie	610
Brookie	360
Less intercompany	(20)
	950

8   Creditors: amounts falling due within one year

	£m
Corrie	610
Brookie	410
Less intercompany	(20)
	1,000

9   Profit and loss account

	£m
Corrie	1,600
Less: pre-acquisition dividends wrongly accounted for (15 + 36)	(51)
Plus: over depreciation of FA	36
share of deemed dividend/premium	3
Brookie	
75% × (790 – 12 144 – 898)	(198)
Less goodwill: Eastend	(350)
Brookie	(1,061)
	(21)

Minority interests

3.29 FRS 9 dose not specifically address the situation where an investment in an associate is held by a subsidiary. However, the FRS does stipulate that in calculating the amounts to be included in the consolidated financial statements the same principles should be applied as are applied in the consolidation of subsidiaries. This implies that the **group accounts should include the 'gross' share of net assets, operating profit, interest payable and receivable (if any) and tax, accounting for the minority interest separately**. For example, we will suppose that H Ltd owns 60% of S Ltd which owns 25% of A Ltd, an associate of H Ltd. The relevant amounts for inclusion in the consolidated financial statements would be as follows.

CONSOLIDATED PROFIT AND LOSS ACCOUNT
Operating profit (H 100% + S 100%)
Share of operating profit of associate (A 25%)
Interest receivable (group) (H 100% + S 100% + A 25%)
Interest payable (H 100% + S 100% + A 25%)
Exceptional items (H 100% + S 100% + A 25%)
Tax (H 100% + S 100% + A 25%)
Minority interest (S 40% + A 10%)
Retained profits (H 100% + S 60% + A 15%)

CONSOLIDATED BALANCE SHEET
Investment in associated company (figures based on 25% holding)
Minority interest ((40% × shareholders' funds of S) + (10% × post-acquisition reserves of A))
Unrealised reserves (15% × post-acquisition reserves of A)
Group profit and loss account ((100% × H) + (60% × post-acquisition of S))

4 INCORPORATED JOINT VENTURES AND JOINT ARRANGEMENTS

Joint ventures

4.1 Joint ventures are another form of entity which, while not giving the investor control as with a subsidiary, gives it considerable influence.

4.2 There are three important definitions here.

> **KEY TERMS**
> - **Joint venture**: an entity in which the reporting entity holds an interest on a long-term basis and is **jointly controlled** by the reporting entity and one or more other venturers under a contractual arrangement.
> - **Joint control**: a reporting entity jointly controls a venture with one or more other entities if none of the entities alone can control that entity but all together can do so and decisions on financial and operating policy essential to the activities, economic performance and financial position of that venture require each venturer's consent.
>
> *(FRS 9)*

4.3 **Joint control is exercised by the venturers for their mutual benefit**, each conducting its part of the contractual arrangement with a view to its own advantage. It is possible within the definition for one venturer to manage the joint venture, provided that the venture's principal operating and financial policies are collectively agreed by the venturers and the venturers have the power to ensure that those policies are followed.

4.4 High-level strategic decisions require the consent of each venturer. In effect, each venturer has a veto on such decisions.

Question 4

How is this situation different from that of a minority shareholder in a company? (Think back to your *Legal Framework* studies.)

Answer

A minority shareholder has no veto and is subject to majority rule: *Foss v Harbottle 1843*, except in very limited circumstances.

Accounting aspects: background

4.5 The nature of joint ventures might mean that one line equity accounting is not appropriate. For example, the investor might have a direct interest in certain assets which it has contributed to the venture. Alternatively, it might be considered appropriate to reflect directly in its own financial statements its proportional share of the assets and liabilities of the investee by a form of **proportion consolidation**. This is **a method of accounting where the investor's share of the results, assets and liabilities of its investee is included in its consolidated financial statements on a line-by-line basis.**

4.6 The Companies Act contains provisions which permit proportional consolidation for some joint ventures. This is restricted to unincorporated joint ventures and the joint venture should be managed 'jointly with one or more undertakings not included in the consolidation'.

4.7 FRED 11 *Associates and joint ventures* proposed identifying two classes of joint ventures: those where the venturers shared in common the benefits and risks, which were to be included by the equity method, and those where each venturer had its own separate interest, which were to be included by proportional consolidation.

FRS 9 treatment

4.8 **FRS 9 emphasises the special nature of joint control by identifying joint ventures as a single class of investments wholly separate from associates** to be included by a special method of accounting - the gross equity method.

KEY TERM

Gross equity method: a form of equity method under which the investor's share of the aggregate gross assets and liabilities underlying the net amount included for the investment is shown on the face of the balance sheet and, in the profit and loss account, the investor's share of the investee's turnover is noted. (FRS 9)

PUBLISHING

4.9 The gross equity method is like the equity method except with regard to the following.

(a) In the **consolidated profit and loss** account the investor's share of **joint ventures' turnover** is **shown, but not as part of group turnover.** For example:

	£m	£m
Turnover: group and share of joint ventures	560	
Less: share of joint ventures' turnover	130	
Group turnover		430

(b) In the segmental analysis the investor's share of its joint ventures' turnover should also be distinguished from the turnover of the group.

(c) In the **consolidated balance sheet, the investor's share of the gross assets and liabilities** underlying the net equity amount included for joint ventures should be shown in amplification of that amount. For example:

	£m	£m	£m
Fixed assets			
Tangible assets			700
Investments			
Investments in joint ventures:			
Share of gross assets	250		
Share of gross liabilities	(120)		
		130	
Investment in associates		80	
			910

(d) In both the profit and loss account and the balance sheet **any supplemental information given for joint ventures must be shown clearly separate from amounts for the group** and must not be included in the group totals. An exception is made for items below profit before tax in the profit and loss account.

4.10 In the investor's individual financial statements, investments in joint ventures should be treated as fixed asset investments and shown at cost, less any amounts written off, or at valuation.

Further aspects of FRS 9 applying to both joint ventures and associates

Principles of consolidation

4.11 As has been mentioned, when calculating the amounts to be included in the investor's consolidated financial statements, whether using the equity method for associates or the gross equity method for joint ventures, the **same principles should be applied as are applied in the consolidation of subsidiaries**. This has the following implications.

(a) **Fair values** are to be attributed to assets and liabilities on acquisition. Goodwill should be treated as per FRS 10. This point was dealt with in connection with associates in Paragraphs 3.27 and 3.28. The same applies to joint ventures.

(b) In arriving at the amounts to be included by the equity method, the **same accounting policies** as those of the investor should be applied.

(c) The financial statements of the investor and the associate or joint venture should be prepared to the **same accounting date** and for the **same accounting period**; associates/joint ventures can prepare three months before if necessary with appropriate adjustments and disclosure.

(d) **Profits or losses resulting from transactions between the investor and its associate/joint venture** may be included in the carrying amount of assets in either party. Where this is the case, the part relating to the **investor's share should be eliminated**. Any impairment of those or similar assets must be taken into account if evidence of it is given by the transactions in question.

Investor is a group

4.12 **Where the investor is a group, it share of its associate or joint venture is the aggregate of the holdings of the parent and its subsidiaries in that entity.** The holdings of any of the group's **other associates or joint ventures should be ignored** for this purpose. Where an associate or joint venture itself has subsidiaries, associates or joint ventures, the results and net assets to be taken into account by the equity method are those reported in that investee's consolidated financial statements (including the investee's share of the results and net assets of its associates and joint ventures), after any adjustment necessary to give effect to the investor's accounting policies.

Options, convertibles and non-equity shares

4.13 The investor may hold options, convertibles or non-equity shares in its associate or joint venture. In certain circumstances, the conditions attaching to such holdings are such that the investor should take them into account in reflecting its interest in its investee under the equity or gross equity method. In such cases, the costs of exercising the options or converting the convertibles, or future payments in relation to the non-equity shares, should also be taken into account.

Impairment

4.14 In cases where there is impairment in any goodwill attributable to an associate or joint venture the **goodwill should be written down** and the amount written off in the accounting period separately disclosed.

Commencement and cessation of relationship

4.15 The following points apply with regard to commencement or cessation of an associate or joint venture relationship.

(a) An investment **becomes an associate on the date on which the investor begins to:**
   (i) Hold a **participating interest**.
   (ii) Exercise **significant influence**.

(b) An investment **ceases to be an associate** on the date **when it ceases to fulfil either of the above.**

(c) An investment **becomes a joint venture on the date on which the investor begins to control it jointly** with other investors, provided it has a long-term interest.

(d) On the date when an investor **ceases to have joint control**, the investment **ceases to be a joint venture.**

(e) The **carrying amount** (percentage of investment retained) should be reviewed and, if necessary, written down to the **recoverable amount**.

Joint arrangements that are not entities

4.16 A reporting entity may operate through a structure that has the appearance of a joint venture but not the reality. It may thus be a separate entity in which the participants hold a long-term interest and exercise joint management, but there may be no common interest because each venturer operates independently of the other venturers within that structure. The framework entity acts merely as an agent for the ventures with each venturer able to identify and control its share of the assets, liabilities and cash flows arising within the entity. **Such arrangements have the form but not the substance of a joint venture**.

The accounting treatment for such joint arrangements required by FRS 9 is that **each venturer should account directly for its share of the assets, liabilities and cash flows held within that structure**. This treatment reflects the substance rather than the form of the arrangement.

Investors that do not prepare consolidated accounts

4.17 A reporting entity may have an associate or joint venture, but **no subsidiaries**. It will thus not prepare group accounts. In such cases it **should present the relevant amounts for associates and joint ventures, as appropriate, by preparing a separate set of financial statements** or by showing the relevant amounts, together with the effects of including them, as additional information to its own financial statements. Investing entities that are exempt from preparing consolidated financial statements, or would be exempt if they had subsidiaries, are exempt from this requirement.

Question 5

Ross plc is a long established business in office supplies. The nature of its business has expanded and diversified to take account of technological changes which have taken place in recent years. Now in addition to stationery and office furniture, it also supplies photocopiers, fax machines and more recently new computer based technologies. The expansion has occurred organically but also through acquisition of existing companies and joint ventures. Ross plc's investments are as follows.

(a) *Joey Ltd*. Ross has a 40% interest in the issued share capital of Joey Ltd and representation on the board. Joey Ltd manufactures office furniture and a large proportion of what it produces is sold to Ross. Ross is therefore actively involved in decisions regarding product ranges, designs and pricing to ensure they get the products they want.

(b) *Rachel NRG*. Rachel NRG is a joint venture company which commenced operations on 1 June 19X7. The joint venturers in Rachel are Ross plc and Monica Inc, a company also in office automation, specialising in computer products. The purpose of the joint venture was to distribute their products to Asia Pacific where the demand for office automation is growing rapidly. Ross and Monica have an equal interest in Rachel.

(c) *Phoebe Ltd*. Phoebe Ltd's principal activities is the supply and fitting of bathroom suites. Its managing director is Mrs Janice Chandler, wife of Mr Paul Chandler, a director of Ross plc. Ross plc has a 25% interest in the share capital of Phoebe and the remaining shares are held by various members of the Chandler family. Mr Chandler is on the board of Phoebe as a non-executive director and this was approved at the last AGM by all the voting members of the Chandler family. The activities of Phoebe and Ross are in totally different markets, the share interest is there for historic reasons and Ross has not exercised its voting rights for several years. During the year Ross plc sold one of the company's executive cars to Phoebe Ltd for an agreed open market value of £30,000.

The following are extracts from the financial statements of Joey, Rachel and Phoebe for the year ended 31 March 20X8.

	Joey	Rachel	Phoebe
	£'000	£'000	£'000
Turnover	4,068	17,720	7,640
Operating costs	3,872	16,834	6,980
Operating profit	196	886	660
Interest payable	-	280	30
Profit before tax	196	606	630
Tax	40	152	200
Profit after tax	156	454	430

	Joey	Rachel	Phoebe
	£'000	£'000	£'000
Fixed assets	360	1,720	260
Current assets	2,940	2,130	834
Creditors falling due within one year	(2,214)	(710)	(252)
Creditors falling due after one year	(26)	(1,810)	(400)
	1,060	1,330	442
Cost of investment	600	500	400

Sales of office furniture from Joey to Ross amounted to £160,000 during the year. 10% of the goods remain in the closing stock of Ross. These goods had been sold at a mark up of 25% on cost.

Required

Produce extracts from the consolidated profit and loss account and balance sheet of Ross for the year ended 31 March 20X8 indicating clearly the treatments for Joey, Rachel and Phoebe and where each item would appear.

Answer

EXTRACTS FROM THE CONSOLIDATED PROFIT AND LOSS ACCOUNT
FOR THE YEAR ENDED 31 MARCH 20X8

	£'000	£'000
Turnover	X	
Less share of joint ventures' turnover	(8,860)	
Group turnover		X
Group operating profit		X
Share of operating profit in		
Joint ventures	443	
Associates (W1)	77.2	
Interest payable		
Group	X	
Joint ventures	(140)	
Profit before tax		X
Tax (see below)		X
Profit after tax		X
Tax relates to		
Parent and subsidiary		X
Joint ventures		76
Associates		16

EXTRACTS FROM THE CONSOLIDATED BALANCE SHEET AS AT 31 MARCH 20X8

	£'000	£'000
Fixed assets		
Investments		
Investments in joint ventures		
Share of gross assets	1,925	
Share of gross liabilities	1,260	
		665.0
Investments in associates (W2)		422.8
Other investments		400.0

Workings

1   *Share of associate company profit*

	£'000
Profit of Joey per question	196.0
Less PUP ($160,000 \times 10\% \times {}^{25}/_{125}$)	3.2
	192.8
Group share (40%) (rounded)	77.2

2   *Investment in associates*

	£'000
Net assets per question	1,060.0
Less PUP (W1)	(3.2)
	1,056.8
Group share (40%) (rounded)	422.8

5   DISCLOSURES FOR ASSOCIATES AND JOINT VENTURES

5.1   The disclosures required by FRS 9 are extensive. Some are required for all associates and joint ventures and other additional disclosures are required if certain thresholds are exceeded. These disclosures are to be made in addition to the amounts required on the face of the financial statements under the equity method or the gross equity method.

Exam focus point

A detailed question on disclosures is unlikely to come up in your exam, so a summary table is produced below..

5.2   **FRS 9: Summary of disclosure requirements**

All associates and joint ventures	15% threshold★	25% threshold★
• Names of principal associates/joint venture	• Turnover (associates only)	• Turnover
• Proportion of shares held	• Fixed assets	• Profit before tax
• Accounting date if different	• Current assets	• Taxation
• Nature of business	• Liabilities due within one year	• Profit after tax
• Material differences in accounting policies	• Liabilities due after one year or more	• Fixed assets
• Restrictions on distributions		• Current assets
• Intercompany balances		• Liabilities due within one year
• Reason for rebutting 20% presumption of participating interest/ significant influence		• Liabilities due after one year or more

★Threshold refers to investor's aggregate share of gross assets, gross liabilities, turnover or three year average operating result of investee as compared with the corresponding group figure.

Chapter roundup

- **Associates** and **joint ventures** are entities in which an investor holds a **substantial but not controlling interest**.

- They are the subject of an accounting standard: **FRS 9 *Associates and joint ventures.***

- **Associates** are to be included in the investor's consolidated financial statements using the **equity method**.

  ° The investor's share of its associates' results should be included immediately after group operating profit.

  ° The investor's share of its associates' turnover may be shown as a memorandum item.

- **Joint ventures** are to be included in the venturer's consolidated financial statements by the **gross equity method**.

  ° This requires, in addition to the amounts included under the equity method, disclosure of the venturer's share of its joint ventures' turnover, gross assets and gross liabilities.

- Other **joint arrangements**, such as cost-sharing arrangements and one-off construction projects, are to be included in their participants' individual and consolidated financial statements by **each participant including directly** its share of the assets, liabilities and cash flows arising from the arrangements.

Quick quiz

1   What types of interest does FRS 9 identify?

2   How does FRS 9 define associate?

3   What is meant by 'participating interest'?

4   A group of companies has the following shareholdings.

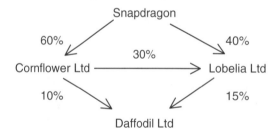

Snapdragon

60%   30%   40%

Cornflower Ltd ──────────> Lobelia Ltd

10%   15%

Daffodil Ltd

For consolidation purposes what, prima facie, is the relationship of Lobelia Ltd and Daffodil Ltd to Snapdragon plc?

5   What **additional** disclosures are required by FRS 9 when the '25% threshold' is reached (ie not also required when the '15% threshold' is reached). Circle any that apply.

(a)   Fixed assets
(b)   Liabilities due within one year
(c)   Profit before tax
(d)   Turnover
(e)   Profit after tax

6   Constable plc owns 40% of Turner plc which it treats as an associated company in accordance with FRS 9. Constable plc also owns 60% of Whistler Ltd. Constable has held both of these shareholdings for more than one year. Turnover of each company for the year ended 30 June 20X0 was as follows.

	£m
Constable	400
Turner	200
Whistler	100

What figure should be shown as turnover in the consolidated profit and loss account of Constable plc?

7   Under the equity method of accounting, the balance sheet of an investing group will disclose, in respect of its associate:

A   Dividends receivable but not share of net assets of the associate

B   Share of net assets of the associate but not dividends receivable

C   Share of net assets of the associate and dividends receivable

D   Cost of investment plus goodwill on acquisition less amounts written off but not dividends receivable

Answers to quick quiz

1   Associates
     Joint ventures
     Joint arrangements that are not entities (see para 2.5)

2   See para 3.2

3   See para 3.3

4   Lobelia Ltd **subsidiary**; Daffodil Ltd **associate**

     Shares held by subsidiary companies count in full. Snapdragon has control of Cornflower's 30% holding in Lobelia. It owns 40% itself, 40 + 30 gives control. Snapdragon therefore controls Lobelia's 15% in Daffodil and Cornflower's 10% in Daffodil (10 + 15 = 25 = associate).

5   (c) and (e) (5.2)

6   Turnover will be 100% H + 100% S only. Associates are introduced in to the consolidated profit and loss account as a share of their operating profits in the first instance.

	£m
Constable	400
Whistler (subsidiary)	100
	500

7   C   Dividends receivable from associates will be included within 'amounts owed by associated companies' and not necessarily disclosed separately. In simple terms, dividends from associates do not 'cancel out' like those from subsidiaries.

Now try the questions below from the Exam Question Bank

Question to try	Level	Marks	Time
23	Exam	50	90 mins
24	Full exam	20	36 mins
25	Full exam	25	45 mins

Part D
The theoretical framework of accounting

Chapter 20

THEORETICAL ASPECTS OF ACCOUNTING

Topic list	Syllabus reference
1 Income and capital	1(c)
2 Entry and exit values	1(c)
3 Current purchasing power (CPP)	1(c)
4 Current cost accounting (CCA)	1(c)
5 Agency theory and the efficient market hypothesis	1(b)
6 Positive and normative accounting concepts	1(c)

Introduction

The topics covered in this chapter fall neatly into three groups.

- Sections 1 and 2 are the first group.
- Sections 3 and 4 are the second group.
- Sections 5 and 6 are the third group.

Study guide

- Distinguish between positive and normative accounting concepts.

- Outline the principles of agency theory and the efficient markets hypothesis.

- Outline the concept of 'comprehensive income'.

- Explain the principle of value in use/deprival value.

- Describe the deficiencies of historic cost accounts (HCA) during periods of rising prices.

- Explain the concepts of current purchasing power (CPP), current cost accounting (CCA) and real terms accounting, including the concept of capital maintenance.

  (Note: detailed calculations based on CPP and CCA are NOT examinable).

- Discuss the advantages and disadvantages of the above accounting systems.

Exam guide

Ideally, you should study all six topics. However, if you are in a hurry, you would be advised to pick two out of the three groups. We recommend Sections 3 -6. In the unlikely event that you get a question on the topics in Sections 1 and 2 there is a limited amount of choice on the paper which will enable you to avoid it.

BPP PUBLISHING

1   INCOME AND CAPITAL

Economic income

1.1   'Income' is used here as a term which **means 'profit' to the accountant, and it is not intended to mean 'revenue'.** The term 'income' is used in preference to 'profit' in order to compare economic and accounting theories.

> ### KEY TERM
>
> In accounting, **income** may be measured as a change in the capital value of a business entity between the beginning and end of a period, if we ignore (for the sake of simplicity) new share or loan capital receipts, dividend payments, loan repayments and inflation.

1.2   **EXAMPLE: INCOME**

Suppose that a company is established on 1 June, with £10,000 in cash financed by ordinary shares (8,000 of £1 each) and £2,000 of 12% loan stock. During the year:

(a)   The company buys fixed assets for cash at a cost of £7,000.

(b)   On 1 June stocks are bought at a cost of £2,000, also for cash.

(c)   During June, all of these stocks are sold for £4,500, £300 of which was unpaid at 30 June.

(d)   Depreciation for June amounted to £100.

(e)   Other expenses for June amounted to £1,000, of which £150 were unpaid at the month end.

(f)   Extra stocks were bought for cash on 30 June, at a cost of £1,500.

1.3   The profit for June would possibly be calculated as follows.

	£	£
Sales	4,500	
Cost of stocks sold	2,000	
Depreciation	100	
Other expenses	1,000	
Loan stock interest ($^1/_{12}$ of 12% of £2,000)	20	
		3,120
Profit in June		1,380

1.4 The balance sheet at 30 June would then be as follows.

	£	£
Fixed assets, net of depreciation		6,900
Current assets		
Stocks	1,500	
Debtors	300	
Cash (note)	2,850	
	4,650	
Current liabilities (accruals, including loan interest)	(170)	
Long-term liability (12% loan stock)	(2,000)	
		2,480
		9,380
Ordinary share capital		8,000
Profit and loss account		1,380
		9,380

Note

Opening cash and revenue	£	Expenditure	£
Sales receipts	4,200	Fixed assets	7,000
Opening cash balance	10,000	Stocks	3,500
	14,200	Other expenses	850
Expenditure	11,350		11,350
Closing cash balance	2,850		

1.5 From this simple example, it can be seen that:

(a) The value of the company's assets at 30 June is partly financed by the profit of £1,380.

(b) Since the opening capital of the business on 1 June was £10,000 we can derive the formula:

$$A_1 + P = A_2$$

where A_1 are assets at the beginning of the period
P is the profit
A_2 are assets at the end of the period.

Note. New capital receipts, capital repayments and dividend payments are ignored in the formula.

1.6 The formula can be re-stated to include dividend payments, so that $A_1 + P - D = A_2$, where D is the dividend payment.

1.7 This means that income, P, can be expressed as $P = D + (A_2 - A_1)$, so income is the sum of dividend payments plus the increase in capital (asset) values between the beginning and end of the period.

1.8 An important conclusion from this formula is that **income is dependent, not only on the amount of cash paid to the owners of the business entity, but also on changes in asset values between the start and end of the period.**

Economic income theories

1.9 Very little has been written about the definition of accounting income, but in contrast economists have evolved a theory of personal income.

1.10 **Fisher** was one of the earliest economists to **define income** in *The Theory of Interest* 1930.

> He suggested that **income** is not the act of receiving money; income is rather the psychological enjoyment which an individual gets from spending the money on the consumption of goods and services. If an individual increases his savings, he is increasing his stock of future consumption and it is the enjoyment from this future consumption that gives a current stock of wealth (the savings or capital) its value.

1.11 Because psychological enjoyment cannot be measured, Fisher said that 'income = consumption' should be measured in terms of the money value of goods and services consumed; however, 'real' economic income is the 'standard of living' which these goods and services provide.

> '[Money income] is most commonly called income, and [enjoyment income] is the most fundamental. But for accounting purposes, real income, as measured by the cost of living, is the most practical.'
> (Fisher)

1.12 Fisher's concept of the value of capital calls for some understanding of the mathematical technique of **discounting** (or discounted cash flow).

1.13 Suppose an individual holds the lease on a property which he rents out for an annual payment of £2,000. The lease has three more years to run.

   (a) The individual's income will be £2,000 per annum for each of the next three years, provided that he spends it all each year and does not save any of it. (If he saves any of the £2,000, these savings will be invested so as to earn more money which in turn will be spent on extra consumption in the future.)

   (b) The **capital value** of the lease:

      (i) **Now** will be the present value of £2,000 per annum for 3 years, discounted at the individual's cost of capital.

      (ii) **In one years' time** will be the present value of £2,000 per annum for 2 years.

      (iii) **In two years' time** will be the present value of £2,000 per annum for 1 year.

      (iv) **In three years' time** the capital value of the lease will be nil, because the lease will have expired.

1.14 **Fisher argued that the cost of capital is the prevailing market rate of interest.** Hicks differed from this view, and argued that the cost of capital should be the rate of return which an individual would obtain by investing his capital in the best alternative investment (perhaps in shares, loan stock, a building society).

1.15 **Fisher's theory is rather unsatisfactory, because equating income with consumption is confusing.** Professor Kaldor (*An Expenditure Tax* 1955) wrote that:

> 'if we reserved the term income for consumption we should still need another term for what would otherwise be called income [money receipts] and we should still be left with the problem of how to define the latter.'

1.16 The economic theorist **Sir John Hicks has described the economic concept of income as being the sum of:**

(a) **Cash flows realised by the individual** during a period of time.

(b) **Changes in the value of the individual's capital** between the beginning and the end of the period.

FORMULA TO LEARN

As a formula: $I = C + (K_2 - K_1)$

where C is the cash flows realised by the individual in the period
K_2 is the value of his capital at the end of a period
K_1 is the value of his capital at the start of a period
$K_2 - K_1$ is therefore the value of the individual's saving.

1.17 To this extent, the accounting definition of profit and the economic concept of personal income are similar.

1.18 **The important difference between accounting and economic income relates to the methods of valuing capital.**

(a) To the accountant, capital is valued in terms of net assets, for example with:

(i) Fixed assets at cost less depreciation, or at a revalued amount.

(ii) Stocks at cost or net realisable value.

(iii) Investments at cost or market value.

(iv) Goodwill at the difference between the cost of assets acquired and their net book value.

and so on.

(b) To the economist, capital is a store of wealth which will be used up in future receipts and therefore future consumption. Capital is only valuable in so far as it provides future benefits; if future benefits did not exist, the individual would spend everything now, and would not bother to save any capital at all. To Hicks, capital could be defined as 'welloffness' and this could be valued as the capitalised money value of prospective future receipts. An important feature of this concept is that value is based on *predictions* of future cash receipts, so cash flows are accounted for as soon as they are predicted rather than when they are realised or even reasonably certain to be realised.

Income and capital maintenance

1.19 Hicks defined income (in *Value and Capital* 1946) as follows.

HICKS' DEFINITION OF INCOME

'the maximum value which (an individual) can consume during a week and still expect to be as well off at the end of the week as he was at the beginning.'

1.20 Thus since $I = C + (K_2 - K_1)$

(a) If $K_2 = K_1$, then $I = C$.

(b)   Similarly, if $K_2 > K_1$ (ie if the amount of the individual's capital increases) then $I > C$.

(c)   If $K_2 < K_1$, the individual will be consuming an amount which is greater than the value of his income. He would be 'eating into his capital'.

1.21   The Sandilands Committee in its *Report of the Inflation Accounting Committee* 1975 described accounting profit in terms of Hicks' definition as follows.

> 'A company's profit for the year is the maximum value which the company can distribute during the year, and still expect to be as well off at the end of the year as it was at the beginning.'

1.22   As a formula: $P = D + (A_2 - A_1)$.

(a)   If $A_2 = A_1$, then $P = D$.

(b)   If $A_2 > A_1$, then $P > D$ and some profits are retained in the business to increase its capital 'value'.

(c)   If $A_2 < A_1$, then $P < D$ and the company would be paying some dividend out of previous years' profits, so that the company would be 'eating into' its reserves.

1.23   **Income and profit are thus associated with the concept of capital maintenance.** The value of income and the value of capital are inextricably related. Using the concept of capital maintenance:

> 'profit is the sum which may be distributed or withdrawn from a business while maintaining intact the capital which existed at the beginning of the period. In other words, the business's capital at the start of a period is used as a bench-mark to determine the business's profit for a period.'
> (*Advanced Financial Accounting* by Lewis, Pendrill and Simon)

The value of capital

1.24   Capital can be valued in a number of ways.

(a)   **Economists might value capital as the present value of future receipts** from an asset, discounted at the individual's cost of capital.

(b)   **Accountants might value assets at:**

   (i)   **Historical cost** (net of depreciation or amounts written off where appropriate).

   (ii)   **Market values** (land and buildings, investments).

   (iii) **Replacement costs** (entry values).

   (iv)   **Net realisable value** (exit values).

   (v)   **Deprival value** or current costs (mixed values).

Each different method of valuing capital must imply a different method of valuing income.

1.25   T A Lee in *Income and Value Measurement: Theory and Practice* made a comparison between the concepts of value and capital maintenance.

> 'The concept of capital maintenance is a vital part of income determination because of the need to incorporate in the income computation a measure of the change in capital during the relevant period. Value, on the other hand, is a necessary ingredient in the computation of capital to which the capital maintenance concept is then applied in determining income. Both are therefore necessary to the income determination process, but neither can of itself measure income.'

1.26   The concepts of valuation and capital maintenance so far described have **ignored the problem of inflation**. It is an axiom of accounting that all assets and liabilities should be measured in money terms, and it is normally assumed that the value of a unit of money (£1)

is stable. However, because of inflation, the 'real' value of £1 (the 'purchasing power' of £1) is continually declining.

1.27 This means that if a company has opening capital of £10,000 on 1 January, earns a recorded historical cost profit of £2,000 and pays a dividend of £2,000, it will have closing capital of £10,000, so that:

$$P = D + (A_2 - A_1), \text{ thus}$$
$$2,000 = 2,000 + (10,000 - 10,000)$$

However, in terms of purchasing power A_2 will be less than A_1, and if $A_2 < A_1$, then in 'real' terms P must be less than D; the 'real' profit is less than £2,000.

1.28 It is possible to develop a convention of accounting which **attempts to value profit and capital in terms of a constant money value.** This was **introduced experimentally in Britain as a provisional statement of standard accounting practice (PSSAP 7) which was subsequently withdrawn.** The accounting convention is known as CPP (current purchasing power) accounting, and is described more fully in Section 3.

Relationship between income measurement and capital measurement

1.29 We have seen that profits or income are related to the concept of capital maintenance, and if we allow for injections of new capital into a business (say a new share issue) then $P = D + (A_2 - A_1) - X$, where X is the amount of new capital introduced during the period.

1.30 A brief study of this formula will suggest that the **measurement of profit depends on the** measurement of A_2 and A_1, the **measurement of capital.** The difference between A_2 and A_1 (the closing and opening balance sheet values) will depend on the methods used to determine how assets in the balance sheet should be valued.

1.31 EXAMPLE: PROFIT AND CAPITAL

For example, suppose that a company has opening stocks of 100 units of finished goods and closing stocks of 200 units. The variable production cost per unit is £5. The increase in capital value over the period in this example would be the difference between opening and closing stock values, and this difference will depend on:

(a) whether marginal costing or full absorption costing is used; and
(b) if absorption costing is used, what overhead recovery rate is applied.

1.32 If variable costing is used, the increase in capital value $(A_2 - A_1)$ is 100 units $\times$ £5 = £500. If absorption costing is used, and the recovery rate is 100% of variable costs, the increase in capital value would be $100 \times £5 \times 200\% = £1,000$. If the overhead recovery rate were 125% of variable costs, the increase in capital value would be $100 \times £5 \times 225\% = £1,125$.

1.33 **Depreciation policy is another example of how capital can be measured in a variety of ways.** For example, if a company buys an asset for £6,000, which has an estimated residual value of nothing, the balance sheet value of the asset will depend on the method of depreciation used (straight line, reducing balance, sum of the digits etc) and also on the number of years over which the asset is depreciated. If the asset is depreciated over 3 years, the loss in capital value in the first year would be £2,000, whereas if it is depreciated over 5 years, the loss in value in the first year would be only £1,200. The choice of 'economic' life would therefore have a direct influence on the reported profit for the year.

1.34 It will have become apparent as you worked through this Study Text that the **choice of accounting policies** for a variety of items **will determine how assets are valued and how much profit can be declared**. These various items include not only stock valuations and depreciation, but also research and development costs, government grants, deferred tax, foreign currency translation and leasing costs.

1.35 There are also several different **conventions** which may be used in accounting **such as historical cost accounting, replacement cost accounting, current cost accounting and current purchasing power accounting**. The choice of convention will help to **determine how assets are valued, and** this in turn will affect **the measurement of profit**. The following sections describe each convention in some detail, but a simple exercise might help to explain the effect of capital measurement on profit measurement.

Question 1

A company has finished goods stocks on 1 January 20X5 which cost £10,000 (using FIFO as a basis for valuation). They were made during 20X4 and at 1 January 20X5 their replacement cost was £12,300. During 20X5 the company produced more goods costing £90,000, and its closing stocks at 31 December (using FIFO) are valued at £8,700. The replacement cost value of the closing stocks is £9,900. Compare the use of historical and replacement cost on the profit and loss account.

Answer

If the historical cost convention is used, and FIFO is the basis of valuation, the cost of sales in 20X5 would be measured as:

	£
Opening stocks	10,000
Production	90,000
	100,000
Less closing stock	8,700
Cost of sales	91,300

If, on the other hand, the 'entry values' or replacement cost convention is used, the cost of sales would be:

	£
Opening stock	12,300
Production	90,000
	102,300
Less closing stock	9,900
Cost of sales	92,400

The difference in the cost of sales (and therefore in profit) by each convention is £(92,400 − 91,300) = £1,100. This difference is due entirely to the method of valuing stocks by each convention.

	Closing stocks (A2) £	Opening stocks (A1) £	Reduction in stocks £
Historical costs	8,700	10,000	1,300
Replacement costs	9,900	12,300	2,400
Difference			1,100

The entity and proprietary concepts of capital

1.36 Before going on to consider different accounting conventions in the following chapters it may be useful to reconsider two different concepts of business capital, the entity concept and the proprietary concept.

1.37   The **entity concept of capital is that a business consists of assets and liabilities**. The assets are owned and the liabilities are owed by the person or people who finance the business, but the **sources of finance are of secondary importance**.

1.38   As a **formula**, the entity concept can be stated as:

$$A - L = C$$

where   A represents assets
         L represents liabilities
         C represents the capital of people financing the business.

Re-arranging the formula, we get:

$$A - L - C = 0$$

If we remember that L must be negative and that if A is greater than L, C will also be negative, then this formula could be re-stated as the accounting identity.

$$A + L + C = 0$$

1.39   'This formulation emphasises the fact that the entity has no legal personality - it cannot own assets, or owe liabilities. It is a mere 'shell' containing a set of assets and liabilities which are legally those of one or more persons, either individuals or corporate bodies ... .'

(G A Lee *Modern Financial Accounting*)

1.40   The entity concept of capital suggests that **before a profit can be made, the value of the 'assets minus liabilities' must be maintained,** regardless of the sources of finance of the business, because the entity should be seen primarily as a set of assets and liabilities which combine to make the business operate.

1.41   In comparison, the **proprietary concept of capital, focuses on the equity ownership of the business.** This concept may be expressed by the **formula**:

$$E = A - L - D$$

where   E is the value of equity
         A is the value of assets
         L is the value of liabilities (excluding debt capital)
         D is debt capital

1.42   A business might be partly financed by debt capital, but it can be argued that the **ultimate purpose of a business is to provide profits for its equity owners after paying interest on debt capital and providing for taxation.**

1.43   The distinction between the entity concept, which concentrates on the business as an operating unit, and the proprietary concept, which concentrates on the purposes of a business to make profits for its owners, may be regarded simply as a matter of differing emphasis when the historical cost accounting convention is used. However, when assets are valued by a different convention, the **differing concepts of capital have important implications for capital maintenance and profit.** A simple example might help to illustrate this point.

BPP PUBLISHING

1.44 Suppose that a new company is formed, financed 50% by equity and 50% by debt capital, so that its balance sheet at the start of operations is as follows.

	£
Cash	8,000
Less debt capital	4,000
	4,000
Equity	4,000

The company buys an asset for £8,000 and pays in cash. It then sells the asset for £11,000 by which time the replacement cost of the asset has risen to £10,000.

1.45 (a) If replacement costing is used to value capital and income, the profit earned by the company, according to the entity concept, would be:

	£
Sale revenue	11,000
Less replacement cost of sale	10,000
Profit	1,000

(b) The balance sheet after the sale might be:

	£
Cash	11,000
Less debt capital	4,000
	7,000

	£
Original equity	4,000
Profit*	1,000
Revaluation reserves (10,000-8,000)	2,000
	7,000

*includes interest payable to debt capital investors, not separately specified here.

1.46 The proprietary concept of capital would be different, because it would take the view that only equity's share of capital needs to be maintained before a profit is made, so that if a company is 50% financed by debt capital, the cost of the sale need only be:

(a) 50% of replacement cost, to protect equity capital; plus
(b) 50% of historical cost, to reflect the share of the asset financed by debt capital.

1.47 Profit would then be:

	£
Sale revenue	11,000
Less cost of sale (50% of £10,000 + 50% of £8,000)	9,000
	2,000

The balance sheet after the sale might be:

	£
Cash	11,000
Less debt capital	4,000
	7,000

Original equity	4,000
Profit (including debt interest as before)	2,000
Revaluation reserve (50% of £10,000 - 8,000)	1,000
	7,000

1.48 The distinction between the entity concept and proprietary concept was apparent in the rules of SSAP 16 on current cost accounting, which distinguished between a current cost operating profit (applying the entity concept of capital maintenance) and a current cost profit attributable to ordinary shareholders (applying the proprietary concept of capital maintenance).

The limitations of economic income models

1.49 There are several disadvantages of these economic theories of income which help to explain perhaps why they do not provide a satisfactory conceptual basis for an accounting theory of profit.

(a) One seeming disadvantage is that **Fisher and Hicks wrote about individuals' income, whereas accountants are concerned with income/profit of a business entity.** It is accepted, however, that Hicks' theory can be applied to business entities without compromising the theory.

(b) A more serious drawback is the **large element of subjective judgement required,** even in the ex post income model. Evaluation of income and capital depends on:

   (i) Predictions of the **size** of future cash flows.
   (ii) Predictions of the **timing** of future cash flows.
   (iii) The choice of an appropriate **discount rate.**

   When predictions turn out to be wrong there will be windfall gains or losses, but the very existence of such unexpected gains or losses means that the measurement of income (I) is haphazard and unsatisfactory.

(c) The **assumption** made by Hicks **that C – (I + W) can be reinvested to earn a single, predictable rate of interest is also questionable.** If a company reinvests some of its revenues (C – (I + W)) it is most unlikely that the rate of return from these re-investments can be predicted with certainty.

(d) If a company plans to achieve capital growth by re-investing some of its income I or windfall profits W, **Hicks' model does not help us to decide how much should be re-invested, and what the largest growth in capital values ought to be.**

Question 2

State and briefly explain Hicks' definition of income and capital.

Answer

Hicks defined income as the maximum amount an individual can consume within a period while remaining as well off at the end of the period as at the beginning. Capital is the discounted present value of the future income stream. Income is thus defined in terms of capital. This contrasts with the accruals model, under which capital is the residue after measuring income. Hicks ignores the distinction made in current financial reporting between realised and unrealised gains.

Hicks' definition of income includes consumption, saving and dis-saving. Sums saved are assumed to be reinvested and to earn interest so as to ensure a constant capital and/or income.

Economic income can be measured only under conditions of certainty. As these normally do not exist, two different models are used as approximations; the ex post model which measures income at the end of the period, and the ex ante model which measures it at the beginning of the period. Both use assumptions about future income streams and capital values and both assume a constant cost of capital. Thus the economic income model is highly subjective and speculative. It is useful as a predictor of future events and for capital investment decisions but not as a method of measuring profit.

Note. This solution extends the Hicks theory a little further than discussed in the text.

BPP PUBLISHING

2 ENTRY AND EXIT VALUES

2.1 **Current value accounting is an attempt to find an alternative accounting convention which combines the advantages of objective reporting with the use of realistic values for assets.** Compare this with the historical cost approach to valuation and revenue recognition in Chapter 13.

Methods of current value accounting

2.2 There are three types of current value accounting, namely the use of:

(a) **Replacement costs**, also known as **current entry values**.

(b) **Realisable values**, also known as **current exit values** (both replacement costs and realisable values are types of market values).

(c) A mixture of realisable values, replacement costs and economic values, in other words, **mixed values**. This system uses the concept of *deprival value*, and has been brought into accounting practice in the UK as *current cost accounting (CCA)*: see Section 4.

2.3 Each of these methods must be described in some detail, but they share certain **common features.**

(a) They **use the transactions basis of accounting, and recognise when profits are realised.** However, income (profit) for the period is computed as the sum of realised profits plus some unrealised profits (or holding gains). In this sense, current value accounting attempts to remain objective, and does not include 'windfall profits' arising from changes in expected future cash flows; as distinct from economic income, which accounts for future cash flows as soon as they are predicted.

(b) They **use current values for assets in the balance sheet**. This is a more meaningful concept of value, because it shows the company's situation more realistically than net book values. At the same time, this means that a company will record a profit when an asset is revalued upwards, and a loss when the current value falls.

> **KEY TERM**
>
> A **holding gain** is a revaluation surplus, arising out of the adjustment of an asset's value upwards from historical cost to current value.

2.4 EXAMPLE: HOLDING GAIN

Suppose that an item of stock is manufactured on 1 April at a cost of £20, and at the end of June it has not been sold, although its current value is now £24. The holding gain is £4, because a balance sheet at the end of June would value the item, not at historical cost, but at current cost. The addition of £4 to assets means that £4 must be added to liabilities, to a 'revaluation surplus' reserve. The holding gain is unrealised, because the asset has not yet been sold.

2.5 At the end of September, the asset is still unsold, but its current value is now £26. For the period 1 July to 30 September, there would be an additional unrealised holding gain of £(26 – 24) = £2. The asset would be valued in the balance sheet at £26, and the revaluation surplus would total £6.

2.6 Finally, suppose that the asset is sold on 10 December for £31, when its current value is £28. The profit would now be realised, but would be measured in current value terms as follows.

	£	£	£
Sales value			31
Current value			28
Operating income★			3
Current value at time of sale	28		
Historical cost	20		
Total holding gain	8		
Attributable to the quarter 1 April - 30 June		4	
Attributable to the quarter 1 July - 30 Sept		2	
Attributable to the quarter 1 Oct - 31 Dec (28-26)		2	
			8
Total profit, as per historical cost accounts			11

(★Operating income is measured as sales value minus current value at the time of sale).

2.7 In a system of historical cost accounts, the total profit of £11 would be credited to the final quarter, the period in which the asset was sold.

In current value accounting, the profits would be distributed amongst three different quarterly periods, as follows:

		£
1 April - 30 June	Unrealised holding gain (UHG)	4
1 July - 30 September	Unrealised holding gain (UHG)	2
1 October - 31 December	Realised holding gain (RHG)	
	plus operating profit (OP)(2+3)	5
		11

The holding gain in the final quarter is realised because the asset has now been sold. Indeed, the unrealised holding gains of the previous two quarterly periods also become 'realised' at this time.

2.8 Holding gains, or revaluation surpluses, were referred to as 'realisable cost savings' by Edwards & Bell in *The theory and measurement of business income* 1961 because they represent savings in the cost of sales achieved by obtaining the asset earlier at a lower cost, rather than at current value on the date of sale, and then selling it straight away.

2.9 In our example, the total holding gain of £8 represents the costs saved by making the asset in April for £20 instead of making it in December for £28.

A brief comparison of current value accounting and HCA

2.10 A simple comparison of current value accounting with historical cost accounting can be made with formulae. **In historical cost accounting, the profit for any period is the sum of:**

(a) **Operating profit** (sales minus the current value of items sold).

(b) **Realised holding gains of the current period.**

(c) **Realised holding gains which arose in previous periods, but were not realised until the current period.**

$$\text{HC profit} = \text{OP} + \text{RHG} + \text{RHG}★$$

where RHG denotes holding gains in the current period, and RHG★ denotes holding gains arising in earlier periods than the current one.

In the numerical analysis above, HCA profit was the sum of:

		£
(a)	Operating profit (OP)	3
(b)	Realised holding gains 1 Oct - 31 Dec (RHG)	2
(c)	Realised holding gains which arose but were unrealised 1 April - 30 Sept (RHG★) (4 + 2)	6
		11

2.11 **In current value accounting, profit is the sum of:**

(a) **Operating profit** (OP).

(b) **Realised holding gains** (RHG).

(c) **Unrealised holding gains** (UHG).

$$\text{Current value profit} = \text{OP} + \text{RHG} + \text{UHG}$$

In our example:

Quarter	OP £	RHG £	UHG £	Total profit £
1 April - 30 June	0	0	4	4
1 July - 30 Sept	0	0	2	2
1 Oct - 31 Dec	3	2	0	5
				11

2.12 Since HCA profit = OP + RHG + RHG★, and
Current value profit = OP + RHG + UHG, then
Current value profit = HCA profit - RHG★ + UHG

By making adjustments to the historical cost profit for RHG★ and UHG, we can derive the current value profit. This ability to make adjustments is now used to apply current cost accounting in practice.

2.13 In current value accounting, a **distinction** is therefore made between:

(a) **Holding gains** (RHG and UHG)

(b) **Current operating gains** (OP)

This distinction will be maintained in the descriptions which follow of the different methods of current value accounting.

2.14 We must now go on to consider the different current value accounting systems in more detail, and the advantages and disadvantages of each will be listed separately later on; however, it will be useful at this stage to list the broad **advantages of all current value systems.**

(a) **They assign a 'true' value to assets** (unfortunately, the 'true' value of assets calls for the subjective judgement of the valuer).

(b) By separating profit into operating profit, realised holding gains and unrealised holding gains, **they present a more informative account of when and why profit has arisen,** unlike historical cost accounting which assigns all profit (as a single value) to the period when the asset is eventually realised.

(c) Current value systems are therefore **more helpful to users,** notably shareholders, and long and short-term creditors. They also provide a more useful basis for management to decide whether the capital of the business has been maintained (or increased).

2.15 A numerical example might help to make this clear. Suppose that a trader buys a piece of land on 1 January 20X2 at a cost of £4,000 and sells it on 30 June 20X3. Owing to a sluggish market for land, its market value on 31 December 20X2 was only £4,200 and on 30 June 20X3 £4,500, although the retail price index has risen from 100 on 1 January 20X2 to 115 on 31 December 20X2 and 125 on 30 June 20X3.

	Current value £		*Price adjusted value* £
1 January 19X2	4,000		4,000
31 December 19X2	4,200	$\left[\times \dfrac{115}{100} \right]$	4,600
30 June 19X3	4,500	$\left[\times \dfrac{125}{100} \right]$	5,000

2.16 The current value at each of the two subsequent dates is higher than historical cost, but it does not allow for the changing value of money, as measured by the retail price index. A collapse in the property market or, in the case of plant and machinery the development of new technology, might cause a *fall* in current values below historical cost, even when there is general price inflation. However, because inflation tends to push most prices up to a greater or lesser degree, it is usual to find that in a period of inflation, current values happen to be higher than historical costs.

2.17 Current value accounting has been given a growing amount of attention from the accountancy profession as a consequence of price-level changes, and the problem of measuring a realistic profit figure in periods of high inflation. This is despite the fact that current value accounting systems are not systems of accounting for inflation. Of the major systems we shall be looking at, **only CPP (current purchasing power accounting) is an inflation accounting system.** It will only be coincidental if current values turn out to be the same as historical costs adjusted for inflation.

Current entry value accounting

2.18 The current entry value of an asset represents the price which would be paid for bringing a similar asset into the business; it **is the replacement cost of the asset.** Two writers who favoured the current entry value system of accounting were Edwards and Bell in *The Theory and Measurement of Business Income* who referred to current entry value 'profit' as 'business income'. Business income, BI, is the sum of:

OP + RHG + UHG

as described previously in Paragraph 2.12. The calculations are based on the replacement cost of the assets.

2.19 **Holding gains** have already been described in Paragraphs 2.4 - 2.9, but we must now look at them again more closely. Three types of holding gain exist, ie **from**:

(a) **Inventory**.
(b) **Depreciable fixed assets**.
(c) **Fixed assets which do not depreciate** (eg land).

Holding gains from inventory

2.20 A company makes two items of product A in 20X3, at a cost of £35 each, and:

(a) Sells one of them during the year for £44 by which time its replacement cost is £40.

(b) Has not sold the second unit by the financial year end (31 December) when its replacement cost has risen to £46.

We would identify:

(a) A realised holding gain of £(40 – 35) = £5 on the first unit.
(b) An unrealised holding gain of £(46 – 35) = £11 on the second unit.

2.21 Total business income for the year ended 31 December 20X3 in respect of these two units would be as follows.

	£	
Current operating profit (£44 – £40)	4	(OP)
Realised holding gain (first unit)	5	(RHG)
Unrealised holding gain (second unit)	11	(UHG)
Total business income	20	

The closing balance sheet would include a value for the second unit still in stock of £46.

Holding gains from depreciable fixed assets

2.22 Depreciable fixed assets present the **most complicated** aspect of holding gains with replacement costs, and a numerical example might help to explain the principles involved.

2.23 EXAMPLE: HOLDING GAINS FROM DEPRECIABLE FIXED ASSETS

Suppose that a company buys a fixed asset at the beginning of year 1 for £9,000. It has an expected life of 3 years, and nil residual value. Straight line depreciation is used. The replacement cost of the asset is £9,900, £10,500 and £12,000 at the end of years 1, 2 and 3 respectively. These are the replacement costs of a brand new asset.

2.24 In year 1, the current operating profit (OP) is calculated after deducting depreciation as $\frac{1}{3}$ of £9,900 = £3,300. Since the asset cost only £9,000, a historical cost depreciation figure would have been only £3,000. This means that in buying the asset one year earlier, the company has made a 'cost saving' or 'holding gain' of £3,300 – £3,000 = £300. This is a realised holding gain (or 'realised cost saving') because the depreciation charge was made against the profits for the current year, year 1.

At the same time, the total holding gain on the asset is £9,900 – £9,000 = £900, of which only £300 has been realised. An additional £600 represents the difference between the written down value of the asset at net replacement cost of £6,600 and net book value, historical cost of £6,000. This saving will be realised in the next two years, but has arisen in year 1; in other words there is an unrealised holding gain (or unrealised cost saving) of £600 in year 1 (which will eventually be 'realised' in year 2 and year 3).

2.25 **Two points must be understood at this stage.**

(a) Depreciation is regarded as a cost which occurs each year, so that a part of the cost of a fixed asset is 'realised' each year.

(b) Replacement cost profit is OP+RHG+UHG, therefore in year 1, both the realised and unrealised holding gains (£300+£600) are added to current operating profit to obtain the total business income for the period (after £3,300 has been deducted in arriving at current operating profit).

2.26 In year 2, the current operating profit (OP) is calculated after deducting depreciation of 2 of £10,500 = £3,500.

By holding the asset between year 1 and 2, there would be a further holding gain. The replacement value of the asset was £9,900 at the end of year 1, and £10,500 at the end of year 2. If we had been dealing with a new asset, the total of RHG and UHG would have been £600. The asset, however, had already had one-third of its life before the start of year 2, and this means that $^1/_3$ of £600 = £200 is irrelevant to the calculation of holding gains, because it relates to depreciation in the first year of the asset's life.

2.27 Holding gains in year 2 would be calculated as follows.

	End of year 1 £	End of year 2 £
Gross replacement cost	9,900	10,500
Assumed (net) replacement cost, based on		
this value: at end of year 1	6,600	7,000
at end of year 2	3,300	3,500

Total holding gain, year 2 = £(7,000 – 6,600) = £400
Unrealised holding gain, year 2 = £(3,500 – 3,300) = £200 (which will be realised over the remaining life of the asset)

The realised holding gain in year 2 is the difference between the depreciation based on the current year's replacement cost (£3,500) and the depreciation which would have been charged based on the previous year's replacement cost (£3,300): £200.

2.28 In year 3, the same principles apply.

(a) The current operating profit would be calculated after deducting depreciation of $^1/3$ of £12,000 = £4,000.

(b) By holding the asset between year 2 and year 3, there was a further holding gain, calculated as follows.

	End of year 2 £	End of year 3 £
Gross replacement cost	10,500	12,000
Assumed (net) replacement cost, based		
on this value: at the end of year 2	3,500	4,000
at the end of year 3	0	0

The total holding gain is £(4,000 – 3,500) = £500, the unrealised holding gain is £0 (which should be expected, since the asset has reached the end of its life and therefore all gains will have been realised).

(c) The realised holding gain in year 3 is the difference between the depreciation charge based on the current year's replacement cost (£4,000) and the charge which would have been applied using the previous year's replacement cost (£3,500).

2.29 The figures may be summarised in the following two tables.

Table 1

	Year 1 £	Year 2 £	Year 3 £	Total £
Increase in gross replacement cost of the asset	900	600	1,500	3,000
Realised holding gain	300	200	500	1,000
	600	400	1,000	2,000
Unrealised holding gain	600	200	0	800
Underprovision of depreciation in previous year	0	200 ★	1,000 ★★	1,200

* ¹/₃ of £600 (GRC increase)   ** ²/₃ of £1,500 (GRC increase)

Table 2

	Year 1 £	Year 2 £	Year 3 £	Total £
Depreciation charge in arriving at current operating profit	(3,300)	(3,500)	(4,000)	(10,800)
Realised holding gain	300	200	500	1,000
Unrealised holding gain	600 *	200 **	0	800
Net charge against business income (current entry value a/cs)	(2,400)	(3,100)	(3,500)	9,000

* Realised in years 2 and 3   ** Realised in year 3

Note. The net charge against business income is less in earlier years than in later years, but the total is £9,000 over 3 years. (£9,000 is the historical cost of the asset.)

2.30 The effect of **using replacement costs** as a basis for charging depreciation is that **holding gains are recognised at an earlier stage than in historical cost accounting, and credited to profit before they are realised**. Thus:

	Depreciation *Historical* *cost a/cs* £	*Net charge* *Replacement* *cost a/cs* £	*Difference* £	
Year 1	3,000	2,400	600	note (a)
Year 2	3,000	3,100	(100)	note (b)
Year 3	3,000	3,500	(500)	note (c)
	9,000	9,000	0	

Notes

(a) The unrealised holding gain of £600 (eventually realised in years 2 and 3).

(b) The unrealised holding gain of £200 (realised in year 3), less the realised holding gain of £300 from year 1.

(c) The realised holding gains of £300 and £200 from years 1 and 2.

Holding gains of non-depreciating assets

2.31 In replacement cost accounting the calculation of holding gains for assets which do not depreciate is more straightforward, and an example should illustrate the principle. Farrar Termer Ltd bought a piece of land on 8 May 20X0 for £15,200. The replacement cost of the land (which was taken to be its market value) was:

£15,900 on 31 December 20X0
£17,000 on 31 December 20X1
£18,200 on 31 December 20X2
£18,400 on 6 March 20X3, when the land was sold for this amount. The company's accounting year ends on 31 December.

2.32 The total gain £(18,400 − 15,200) = £3,200 is realised when the asset is sold in 20X3, and in historical cost accounting the profit would not be recorded until that year (realisation principle). However, in current entry value accounting, unrealised holding gains (capital gains in the case of non-depreciating assets) would be credited to 'business income' in the year they become apparent.

Year	Unrealised holding gain £	Realised holding gain £	Total addition to business income for the year £
20X0	15,900 – 15,200 = 700	-	700
20X1	17,000 – 15,900 = 1,100	-	1,100
20X2	18,200 – 17,000 = 1,200	-	1,200
20X3	-	18,400 – 18,200 = 200	200
			3,200

2.33   The net effect of using current entry value accounting is that profits on fixed assets are accounted for earlier than under the historical cost convention, which is therefore a more prudent system in this respect.

Business income and holding gains

2.34   In this section so far, it has been stressed that business income is the sum of operating profit plus realised and unrealised holding gains for the period.

To complicate the issue a little further, it should be mentioned that there is some **opposition to the idea that holding gains should be included as a part of business income.** The main reasons for this opposition are as follows.

(a)   **Unrealised holding gains** show an increase in the value of assets, but there is **no change in the physical substance of the assets.** To claim a profit when there is no physical change, it can be argued, is unjustifiable.

(b)   Realised holding gains are represented by cash or by cost savings in the case of depreciation. For example, if an item costs £15 cash, and is sold for £25 when its replacement cost is £18, the operating profit (£7) plus the realised holding gain (£3) represent the increase in the company's cash position. However, if the company intends to replace the item it has sold, it will need £18 to do it; therefore only £7, the operating profit, is spare cash. It has therefore been **argued that realised holding gains should be excluded from the profit figure, because the revenue** (or cost savings) **from those gains needs to be kept within the business to maintain its substance or operating capability.**

2.35   This point of view was adopted in the accounting standard SSAP 16 *Current cost accounting*, and we shall now assume that in practice replacement costing would be applied in this way. For example, if a company buys a piece of land on 1 January 20X5 for £20,000 and its value on 31 December is £24,000 and on 2 July 20X6 (when it is sold) is £27,500, the:

(a)   Unrealised gain in the year to 31 December 20X5 is £4,000, but the company's physical asset, the land, is still the same.

(b)   Realised holding gain in 20X6 is £3,500, but if the company intends to replace the land sold with a similar piece of land (and we will assume that this is the case) £27,500 will be needed for the purchase, therefore no profit has been made which could safely have been paid out as a dividend to shareholders.

2.36   It is therefore possible to argue against the inclusion of holding gains in the profit figure, and yet still favour replacement cost accounting to measure operating profit. In other words, it is possible to argue:

(a)   Profit = current entry value OP.

(b)   Holding gains (RHG + UHG) should be credited to a separate reserve account and not treated as profit.

Advantages of replacement costing

2.37   The **advantages of replacement costing** may be summarised as follows.

(a)   It provides management with an **analysis of total profit into operating profit and holding gains,** so that a better assessment can be made about:

(i)   Operational decisions in the past.
(ii)   Decisions in the past to hold assets rather than defer their purchase.

This division of profit therefore provides a measurement of management efficiency in their control over operations.

(b)   If holding gains are excluded from business income, the business income would be the same as the current operating profit; and this would be an **indication of whether the company has maintained its 'physical substance' or 'operating capability',** as described in Paragraphs 2.34 to 2.36.

(c)   **Assets** in the balance sheet are **shown at current values,** which **is less misleading** than the historical cost accounting method of showing assets at net book value.

(d)   Replacement cost **provides accounting information** which enables users to assess the stability of the company, its vulnerability to a takeover or liquidation, its operating capability and future prospects.

(e)   It is **consistent with the concepts of going concern and accruals**; and if holding gains are excluded from profit, it is also a more 'prudent' system of accounting than HCA.

(f)   **It can be used within a double entry bookkeeping system,** although not as easily as HCA.

Disadvantages of replacement costing

2.38   There are some important **disadvantages** of replacement costing, which may be summarised as follows.

(a)   There are **practical difficulties** in estimating replacement costs, and there is scope for different principles to be applied, as well as scope for the subjective judgement of valuers. If replacement costs are the estimated amounts that would have to be paid to replace the asset 'today' but in fact there is no intention on the part of the company to replace the asset, an estimate of the replacement cost will be difficult unless:

(i)   There is an identifiable market (as for property) or available suppliers' list prices.

(ii)   The replacement costs of manufactured finished goods are available from the cost accounting system.

The main problems relate to assets for which there is no identifiable market, such as out-of-date equipment, or specially purpose-built premises (such as oil refineries). These problems will be described in more detail in the later chapter on current cost accounting.

(b)   There is the **conceptual difficulty** of accepting that replacement costing should be applied to assets which may not be replaced at the end of their life. This problem is also discussed more fully in Section 4 on current cost accounting; it is sufficient to note at this point that if business income is to be a measure of capital maintenance, then some form of current value must be assigned to assets, even if they are either obsolete or unlikely to be replaced.

(c) Some businesses operate with long-life plant and machinery and large stocks of slow-moving inventory. Some companies even make their operating profit out of holding stocks (as do wine merchants and whisky distillers). In such cases, **it is debatable whether holding gains are really gains of an operational nature** which should therefore be included as business income.

(d) Replacement costing is **weak in some areas where historical cost accounting is strong.** Two examples of these areas are:

(i)   Assessment of the stewardship of the company by its management.
(ii)   Verifiability of raw data by auditors.

It is perhaps partly for this reason that the accounting profession has tended towards the view embodied in SSAP 16 that accounting procedures in practice should remain based on historical costs, with end of year adjustments made to turn the HCA profit and loss account and balance sheet into current value equivalents.

Question 3

The following extract is taken from the historical cost balance sheet of Rochester Enterprises Ltd.

	31 December 20X0	31 December 20X1
	£'000	£'000
Plant and machinery at cost	200	300
Less aggregate depreciation	40	100
Net book value	160	200

The following facts are relevant.

(a)   Plant costing £200,000 was acquired on 1 January 20X0. The additional items were acquired on 1 January 20X1.

(b)   No plant or machinery was sold or scrapped during 20X0 or 20X1.

(c)   Of the year's depreciation written off in the 20X1 accounts, one-third is related to the items acquired on 1 January 20X1.

(d)   Price index movements were as follows.

	General price index	Index of plant costs for the type of plant owned by Rochester
1 January 20X0	90	80
31 December 20X0	120	100
31 December 20X1	140	110

You are required to show the entries for plant and machinery in the final accounts of Rochester Enterprises Ltd as at 31 December 20X0 and 20X1, on the assumption that the company used a system of replacement cost accounting.

Answer

CURRENT COST BALANCE SHEETS (EXTRACTS)
AS AT 31 DECEMBER

	20X0	20X1
	£'000	£'000
Gross replacement cost	250	385
Accumulated depreciation	50	132
Net replacement cost	200	253

CURRENT COST PROFIT AND LOSS ACCOUNTS
(EXTRACTS) FOR YEAR TO 31 DECEMBER

	20X0	*20X1*
	£'000	£'000
Historical cost depreciation	40	60
Depreciation adjustment (realised holding gain)	10	17
	50	77

(*Note.* In current cost accounts prepared under SSAP 16 the prior year backlog depreciation of £5

(£40 × $\dfrac{110 - 100}{80}$) would not be identified in the balance sheet.)

Workings

					20X0 £'000				*20X1* £'000
1	Gross replacement cost	200 ×	$\dfrac{100}{80}$	=	250	$\dfrac{200}{80}$ ×	$\dfrac{110}{80}$	=	275
						100 ×	$\dfrac{110}{100}$		$\dfrac{110}{385}$
2	Accumulated depreciation	40 ×	$\dfrac{100}{80}$	=	50	80 ×	$\dfrac{110}{80}$	=	110
						20 ×	$\dfrac{110}{100}$	=	$\dfrac{22}{132}$
3	Annual depreciation charge	40 ×	$\dfrac{100}{80}$	=	50	40 ×	$\dfrac{110}{80}$	=	55
						20 ×	$\dfrac{110}{100}$	=	$\dfrac{22}{77}$

Current exit value accounting

2.39 An alternative to current entry value accounting (replacement costs) is current exit value accounting.

> **KEY TERM**
>
> **Exit values** are **net realisable values for assets.** The net realisable value of an asset is the cash which would be obtained if the asset were realised, so that if a building could be sold for £250,000, less £20,000 in sales expenses, the NRV would be £230,000.

2.40 As a very rough guide for company exit values and entry values, we could probably say that for:

(a) Land and buildings, entry values are likely to be higher than exit values.

(b) Plant and equipment, gross replacement cost may be higher than the net realisable value of an asset, but the net replacement cost may be higher or lower than NRV.

(c) Inventory, net realisable value should normally be higher than replacement cost as the selling price of a product should be higher than the cost of its manufacture.

2.41 Several writers have advocated a system of exit value accounting, including in recent times R J Chambers and R R Sterling. The basic principle is that profit or 'realisable income' should be measured as follows:

$$I = D + (R_t - R_{t-1})$$

where

D   is the amount of distributions made during a period
R_t is the net realisable value of the entity's net assets at the end of the period
R_{t-1} is the net realisable value of the entity's net assets at the beginning of the
     period.

2.42   Realisable values imply the sale of assets for cash: in other words 'break-up' values. There has been some debate as to whether realisable values should be estimated on the:

(a)   Assumption that the entity will be liquidated suddenly, or that the assets could be realised in an 'orderly' manner.

(b)   Basis of the existing state of the asset, or on its eventual realisable value minus 'further processing costs'. For example, an item of part-finished work in progress might have a net realisable value of £6 in existing state, but it would eventually have an NRV of £20 when £5 of further processing costs have been spent on it. The exit value could be taken as either £6 or £(20 − 5) = £15.

2.43   It is **generally agreed that exit values should relate to assets in their existing state, on the assumption that assets would be realised in an orderly manner.**

2.44   **Exit values are opportunity costs.**

KEY TERM

An **opportunity cost** could be described as the benefit forgone by holding an asset in its existing form instead of in a next-best-alternative form.

In terms of exit value accounting, the next-best-alternative form of holding an asset is in cash. For example, if an item of machinery has a net realisable value of £500, the opportunity cost of using the machine is the 'sacrifice' of not having the cash from its sale, (£500).

2.45   **Cash** is therefore **a common measure for the opportunity cost of all the net assets of a business entity.** In the theory of exit value accounting, cash provides a common measurement of the alternative goods and services that could be bought if the business entity were liquidated. Chambers wrote that 'realisable income' (ie profit based on the current exit value concept) measures the increase in the potential purchasing power of the owners of the business entity.

2.46   Returning to the formula for realisable income:

$$I = D + (R_t - R_{t-1})$$

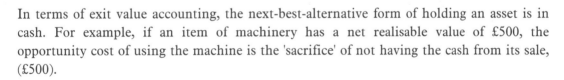

you might be able to see that the difference between R_t and R_{t-1} is the increase or decrease in the potential cash value of an entity's assets, therefore total income will conform to Chambers' definition in the previous paragraph.

2.47   Remember that this concept of potential purchasing power, also called 'the entity's ability to command alternative goods and services' by T A Lee, is not related to the separate issue of price inflation and the declining purchase power of money.

BPP PUBLISHING

2.48 As in the case of entry value accounting, there will be holding gains in exit value accounting. We can again, if required, make a distinction between gains made on assets which are:

(a) Intended for re-sale (operating gains on inventory).

(b) Held for use (non-operating gains on fixed assets).

2.49 There may be realised and unrealised gains on both types of asset during an accounting period, so that total profit is the sum of operating gains and non-operating gains as follows:

$$I = (RG + UG) \text{ operating gains, plus } (RG + UG) \text{ non-operating gains.}$$

2.50 **In the current exit value balance sheet, assets are shown at net realisable value.**

Holding gains as profit

2.51 In **current entry value accounting**, it is usually accepted that **profit should exclude holding gains, both realised and unrealised**, so that the operating capability of the business entity can be maintained (Paragraphs 2.34 - 2.36).

2.52 In **current exit value accounting**, the capital maintenance concept relates to the 'potential purchasing power of owners' or the 'command power over resources in general' as measured by the realisable value of net assets. **All holding gains**, whether unrealised or realised, represent an increase in this potential purchasing power, and are therefore legitimately **included** in the profit figure.

2.53 **Current exit value accounting does not conform to the going concern concept** and for this reason it has not received much support from practising accountants.

2.54 **Current entry value accounting is based on the going concern concept, whereas current exit value accounting is based on the assumption of liquidating assets.** This means that whereas current entry value accounting must attempt to allow for the eventual replacement of assets, there is no such theoretical requirement in current exit value accounting. Realisable profit may therefore fail to provide sufficient funds for the replacement of assets at the end of their lives.

Advantages of current exit value accounting

2.55 The **advantages** of current exit value accounting may be summarised as follows.

(a) It **uses the economic concept of opportunity costs** for the valuation of assets. This acknowledges the current 'sacrifice' which is being made by holding assets instead of converting them into an alternative form.

(b) **Net realisable values provide a common measure** for the value of assets, cash, which in turn represents the potential capability to purchase different goods and services.

(c) There is no reason to assume that a business entity will be a going concern for ever, and **exit values recognise that the entity must come to an end some time.** Exit values are therefore more appropriate 'current value' than entry values.

(d) **It provides an understandable and realistic value for assets.** The 'man in the street' would probably assume that the balance sheet value of an asset is its break-up value, its net realisable value. Creditors would probably find that net realisable values give better information about the security of loans to the entity, and also about the liquidity of the company.

(e) Although accountants are suspicious of net realisable value because it does not adhere to the going concern concept, Chambers has argued that exit values are **applied to some extent in practice, sometimes by legal requirement.**

    (i) **Monetary assets** (cash, debtors, trade creditors etc) are shown at realisable value.

    (ii) **Stocks** are valued at the lower of cost and net realisable value.

    (iii) It is common practice to revalue **land and buildings** in the balance sheet to a current market value.

    (iv) CA 1985 Sch 7 s 1(2) requires that **directors' reports** should include information about the market value of assets consisting in interests in land (property) where this is held by a company, if it differs from the book amount shown in the balance sheet.

Since realisable values are sometimes used in practice, it could be argued that there are good practical reasons why current exit value accounting is a valid concept, in spite of the prejudice of practising accountants against it.

Disadvantages

2.56 There are many **disadvantages** of current exit value accounting, the most important of which lies in the **practical difficulties of implementing it**. The estimation of net realisable values for stocks and work in progress and plant, machinery, fixtures and fittings and so on, would be highly subjective. Replacement costs are comparatively easier to estimate.

3 CURRENT PURCHASING POWER (CPP)

Capital maintenance in times of inflation

3.1 **Profit** can be measured as the **difference between how wealthy a company is at the beginning and at the end of an accounting period.**

(a) This wealth can be expressed in terms of the capital of a company as shown in its opening and closing balance sheets.

(b) A business which maintains its capital unchanged during an accounting period can be said to have broken even.

(c) **Once capital has been maintained, anything achieved in excess represents profit.**

3.2 For this analysis to be of any use, we must be able to draw up a company's balance sheet at the beginning and at the end of a period, so as to place a value on the opening and closing capital. There are particular difficulties in doing this during a period of rising prices.

3.3 In conventional historical cost accounts, assets are stated in the balance sheet at the amount it cost to acquire them (less any amounts written off in respect of depreciation or diminution in value). Capital is simply the difference between assets and liabilities.

IMPORTANT!

If prices are rising, it is possible for a company to show a profit in its historical cost accounts despite having identical physical assets and owing identical liabilities at the beginning and end of its accounting period.

3.4 For example, consider the following opening and closing balance sheets of a company.

	Opening £	Closing £
Stock (100 items at cost)	500	600
Other net assets	1,000	1,000
Capital	1,500	1,600

Assuming that no new capital has been introduced during the year, and no capital has been distributed as dividends, the profit shown in historical cost accounts would be £100, being the excess of closing capital over opening capital. And yet in physical terms the company is no better off: it still has 100 units of stock (which cost £5 each at the beginning of the period, but £6 each at the end) and its other net assets are identical. The 'profit' earned has merely enabled the company to keep pace with inflation.

3.5 **An alternative to the concept of capital maintenance based on historical costs is to express capital in physical terms.** On this basis, no profit would be recognised in the example above because the physical substance of the company is unchanged over the accounting period. In the UK, a system of accounting (called **current cost accounting** or CCA) was introduced in 1980 by SSAP 16 (now withdrawn) and had as its basis a concept of capital maintenance based on 'operating capability'.

> Capital is maintained if at the end of the period the company is in a position to achieve the same physical output as it was at the beginning of the period.

You should bear in mind that financial definitions of capital maintenance are not the only ones possible; in theory at least, there is no reason why profit should not be measured as the increase in a company's *physical* capital over an accounting period.

The unit of measurement

3.6 Another way to tackle the problems of capital maintenance in times of rising prices is to look at the unit of measurement in which accounting values are expressed.

3.7 It is an axiom of **conventional accounting**, as it has developed over the years, that value should be measured in terms of money. It is also **implicitly assumed that money values are stable**, so that £1 at the start of the financial year has the same value as £1 at the end of that year. **But when prices are rising, this assumption is invalid: £1 at the end of the year has less value (less purchasing power) than it had one year previously.**

3.8 This **leads to problems when aggregating amounts which have arisen at different times.** For example, a company's fixed assets may include items bought at different times over a period of many years. They will each have been recorded in £s, but the value of £1 will have varied over the period. In effect the fixed asset figure in a historical cost balance sheet is an aggregate of a number of items expressed in different units. It **could be argued that such a figure is meaningless.**

3.9 Faced with this argument, one possibility would be to re-state all accounts items in terms of a stable monetary unit. There would be difficulties in practice, but in theory there is no reason why a stable unit (£ CPP = £s of current purchasing power) should not be devised. In this section we will look at a system of accounting (current purchasing power accounting, or CPP) based on precisely this idea.

Specific and general price changes

3.10 We can identify two different types of price inflation.

3.11 When prices are rising, it is likely that the current value of assets will also rise, but not necessarily by the general rate of inflation. For example, if the replacement cost of a machine on 1 January 20X2 was £5,000, and the general rate of inflation in 20X2 was 8%, we would not necessarily expect the replacement cost of the machine at 31 December 20X2 to be £5,000 plus 8% = £5,400. The rate of price increase on the machinery might have been less than 8% or more than 8%. (Conceivably, in spite of general inflation, the replacement cost of the machinery might have gone down.)

(a) There is **specific price inflation**, which **measures price changes over time for a specific asset or group of assets.**

(b) There is **general price inflation**, which **is the average rate of inflation, which reduces the general purchasing power of money.**

3.12 To counter the problems of specific price inflation some system of current value accounting may be used (for example, the system of current cost accounting described in the following chapter). The capital maintenance concepts underlying current value systems do not attempt to allow for the maintenance of real value in money terms.

3.13 Current purchasing power (CPP) accounting is based on a different concept of capital maintenance.

> **KEY TERM**
>
> **CPP** measures profits as the increase in the current purchasing power of equity. Profits are therefore stated after allowing for the declining purchasing power of money due to price inflation.

3.14 In Britain attempts to introduce CPP accounting have been in a combination with historical cost accounting, and it is on this aspect that this section will concentrate.

3.15 When applied to historical cost accounting, **CPP is a system of accounting which makes adjustments to income and capital values to allow for the general rate of price inflation.** An attempt to introduce such a system was made in 1974 with the publication of a Provisional Statement of Standard Accounting Practice, PSSAP 7 *Accounting for changes in the purchasing power of money.* Although it was withdrawn after a year, and was then superseded by SSAP 16, it remains a topic of debate and **some knowledge of CPP accounting is necessary to understand the diversity of views currently held on inflation accounting in general.**

The principles and procedures of CPP accounting

3.16 In CPP accounting, profit is measured after allowing for general price changes. It is a fundamental idea of CPP that capital should be maintained in terms of the same monetary purchasing power, so that:

BPP PUBLISHING

$$P_{CPP} = D_{CPP} + (E_{t\,(CPP)} - E_{(t-1)CPP})$$

where P_{CPP} is the CPP accounting profit

D_{CPP} is distributions to shareholders, re-stated in current purchasing power terms

E_t the total value of assets attributable to the owners of the business entity at the end of the accounting period, restated in current purchasing power terms

$E_{(t-1)CPP}$ is the total value of the owners' equity at the beginning of the year re-stated in terms of current purchasing power at the end of the year.

A current purchasing power £ relates to the value of money on the last day of the accounting period.

3.17 **Profit in CPP accounting is** therefore **measured after allowing for maintenance of equity capital.** To the extent that a company is financed by loans, there is no requirement to allow for the maintenance of the purchasing power of the loan creditors' capital. Indeed, as we shall see, the equity of a business can profit from the loss in the purchasing power value of loans.

Monetary and non-monetary items

KEY TERM

A **monetary item** is an asset or liability whose amount is fixed by contract or statute in terms of £s, regardless of changes in general price levels and the purchasing power of the pound.

3.18 The main examples of monetary items are cash, debtors, creditors and loan capital.

KEY TERM

A **non-monetary item** is an asset or liability whose value is not fixed by contract or statute.

3.19 These include land and buildings, plant and machinery and stock.

3.20 In CPP accounting, there is an **important difference** between monetary assets and liabilities.

(a) If a company borrows money in a period of inflation, the amount of the debt will remain fixed (by law) so that when the debt is eventually paid, it will be paid in £s of a lower purchasing power.

For example, if a company borrows £2,000 on 1 January 20X5 and repays the loan on 1 January 20X9, the purchasing power of the £2,000 repaid in 20X9 will be much less than the value of £2,000 in 20X5, because of inflation. Since the company by law must repay only £2,000 of principal, it has gained by having the use of the money from the loan for 4 years. (The lender of the £2,000 will try to protect the value of his loan in a period of inflation by charging a higher rate of interest; however, this does not alter the fact that the loan remains fixed at £2,000 in money value.)

(b) If a company holds cash in a period of inflation, its value in terms of current purchasing power will decline. The company will 'lose' by holding the cash instead of converting it into a non-monetary asset. Similarly, if goods are sold on credit, the amount of the debt is fixed by contract; and in a period of inflation, the current purchasing power of the money from the sale, when it is eventually received, will be less than the purchasing power of the debt, when it was first incurred.

3.21 In CPP accounting, it is therefore argued that **there are gains from having monetary liabilities and losses from having monetary assets.**

(a) In the case of monetary assets, there is a need to make a provision against profit for the loss in purchasing power, because there will be a need for extra finance when the monetary asset is eventually used for operational activities. For example, if a company has a cash balance of £200, which is just sufficient to buy 100 new items of raw material stock on 1 January 20X5, and if the rate of inflation during 20X5 is 10%, the company would need £220 to buy the same 100 items on 1 January 20X6 (assuming the items increase in value by the general rate of inflation). By holding the £200 as a monetary asset throughout 20X5, the company would need £20 more to buy the same goods and services on 1 January 20X6 that it could have obtained on 1 January 20X5. £20 would be a CPP loss on holding the monetary asset (cash) for a whole year.

(b) In the case of monetary liabilities, the argument in favour of including a 'profit' in CPP accounting is not as strong. By incurring a debt, say, on 1 January 20X5, there will not be any eventual cash input to the business. The 'profit' from the monetary liabilities is a 'paper' profit, and T A Lee has argued against including it in the CPP profit and loss account. PSSAP 7, however, noted that

> 'It has been argued that the gain on long-term borrowing should not be shown as profit in the CPP accounts because it might not be possible to distribute it without raising additional finance. This argument, however, confuses the measurement of profitability with the measurement of liquidity. Even in the absence of inflation, the whole of a company's profit may not be distributable without raising additional finance, for example, because it has been invested in, or earmarked for investment in, non-liquid assets.'

PSSAP 7 therefore concluded that all gains and losses from having monetary liabilities or assets should be included in the calculation of CPP profit. The concept of monetary gains and losses is an important one, and it was introduced into current cost accounting practice in Britain (see next section).

3.22 EXAMPLE: CPP ACCOUNTING

Seep Ltd had the following assets and liabilities at 31 December 20X4.

(a) All fixed assets were purchased on 1 January 20X1 at a cost of £60,000, and they had an estimated life of six years. Straight line depreciation is used.

(b) Closing stocks have a historical cost value of £7,900. They were bought in the period November-December 20X4.

(c) Debtors amounted to £8,000, cash to £2,000 and short-term creditors to £6,000.

(d) There is long-term debt capital of £15,000.

(e) The general price index includes the following information:

Year	Date	Price index
20X1	1 January	100
20X4	30 November	158
20X4	31 December	160
20X5	31 December	180

The historical cost balance sheet of Seep Ltd at 31 December 20X4 was as follows.

	£	£
Fixed assets at cost		60,000
Less depreciation		40,000
		20,000
Stocks	7,900	
Debtors	8,000	
Cash	2,000	
Current assets	17,900	
Less creditors	6,000	
		11,900
		31,900
Financed by:		
Equity		16,900
Loan capital		15,000
		31,900

Required

(a) Prepare a CPP balance sheet as at 31 December 20X4.

(b) What was the depreciation charge against CPP profits in 20X4?

(c) What must be the value of equity at 31 December 20X5 if Seep Ltd is to 'break even' and make neither a profit nor a loss in 20X5?

3.23 SOLUTION

(a)

	£c	£c
Fixed assets, at cost 60,000 × 160/100		96,000
Less depreciation 40,000 × 160/100		64,000
		32,000
Stock* 7,900 × 160/158	8,000	
Debtors**		8,000
Cash**	2,000	
	18,000	
Creditors**	6,000	
		12,000
		44,000
Loan stock**		15,000
Equity ***		29,000
		44,000

Notes

*Stocks purchased between 1 November and 31 December are assumed to have an average index value relating to the mid-point of their purchase period, at 30 November.

**Monetary assets and liabilities are not re-valued, because their CPP value is the face value of the debt or cash amount.

***Equity is a mixture of monetary and non-monetary asset values, and is the balancing figure in this example.

(b) Depreciation in 20X4 would be one sixth of the CPP value of the assets at the end of the year, $^1/_6$ of £96,000 = £16,000. Alternatively, it is:

$(^1/_6 \times £60,000) \times 160/100 = £16,000$

(c) To maintain the capital value of equity in CPP terms during 20X5, the CPP value of equity on 31 December 20X5 will need to be:

£29,000 × 180/160 = £32,625

Question 4

Rice and Price set up in business on 1 January 20X5 with no fixed assets, and cash of £5,000. On 1 January they acquired some stocks for the full £5,000 which they sold on 30 June 19X5 for £6,000. On 30 November they obtained a further £2,100 of stock on credit. The index of the general price level gives the following index figures.

Date	Index
1 January 20X5	300
30 June 20X5	330
30 November 20X5	350
31 December 20X5	360

Calculate the CPP profits (or losses) of Rice and Price for the year to 31 December 20X5.

Answer

The approach is to prepare a CPP profit and loss account.

	£c	£c
Sales (6,000 × 360/330)		6,545
Less cost of goods sold (5,000 × 360/300)		6,000
		545
Loss on holding cash for 6 months*	(545)	
Gain by having creditor for 1 month**	60	
		485
CPP profit		60

* (£6,000 × 360/330) - £6,000 = £c 545
**(£2,100 × 360/350) - £2,100 = £c 60

The advantages and disadvantages of CPP accounting

Advantages

3.24 (a) The **restatement of asset values in terms of a stable money value provides a more meaningful basis of comparison** with other companies. Similarly, provided that previous years' profits are re-valued into CPP terms, it is also possible to compare the current year's results with past performance.

(b) Profit is measured in 'real' terms and excludes 'inflationary value increments'. This **enables better forecasts of future prospects to be made.**

(c) CPP **avoids the subjective valuations** of current value accounting, because a single price index is applied to all non-monetary assets.

(d) CPP **provides a stable monetary unit** with which to value profit and capital; ie £c.

(e) Since it is based on historical cost accounting, **raw data is easily verified**, and measurements of value can be readily audited.

Disadvantages

3.25 (a) It is **not clear what £c means**. 'Generalised purchasing power' as measured by the Retail Price Index, or indeed any other general price index, has no obvious practical significance.

> 'Generalised purchasing power has no relevance to any person or entity because no such thing exists in reality, except as a statistician's computation.' (T A Lee)

(b) The use of indices **inevitably involves approximations** in the measurements of value.

(c) **The value of assets in a CPP balance sheet has less meaning than a current value balance sheet**. It cannot be supposed that the CPP value of net assets reflects:

(i) The general goods and services that could be bought if the assets were released.

(ii) The consumption of general goods and services that would have to be forgone to replace those assets.

In this respect, a CPP balance sheet has similar drawbacks to an historical cost balance sheet.

4 CURRENT COST ACCOUNTING (CCA)

Value to the business (deprival value)

4.1 The **conceptual basis of CCA is that the value of assets consumed or sold, and the value of assets in the balance sheet, should be stated at their value to the business** (also known as 'deprival value').

4.2 A system of current cost accounting was introduced into the UK by SSAP 16 *Current cost accounting* in March 1980. This was the culmination of a long process of research into the problems of accounting in times of inflation. One result of this process had been the publication of PSSAP 7 on current purchasing power accounting, described previously. SSAP 16 encountered heavy criticism and was finally withdrawn in April 1988.

4.3 **In CCA, a physical rather than financial definition of capital is used: capital maintenance is measured by the ability of the business entity to keep up the same level of operating capability.**

KEY TERM

The **deprival value** of an asset is the loss which a business entity would suffer if it were deprived of the use of the asset.

4.4 **Value to the business,** or deprival value, can be any of the following values.

(a) **Replacement cost.** In the case of fixed assets, it is assumed that the replacement cost of an asset would be its net replacement cost (NRC), its gross replacement cost minus an appropriate provision for depreciation to reflect the amount of its life already 'used up'.

(b) **Net realisable value** (NRV); what the asset could be sold for, net of any disposal costs.

(c) **Economic value** (EV), or utility; what the existing asset will be worth to the company over the rest of its useful life.

4.5 The choice of deprival value from one of the three values listed will depend on circumstances. The decision tree on the next page illustrates the principles involved in the choice, but in simple terms you should remember that in **CCA deprival value is nearly always replacement cost.**

4.6 If the asset is worth replacing, its deprival value will always be net replacement cost. If the asset is not worth replacing, it might be disposed of straight away, or else it might be kept in operation until the end of its useful life.

4.7 You may therefore come across a statement that deprival value is the **lower of**:

(a) **Net replacement cost**
(b) The **higher of net realisable value and economic value**

4.8 We have already seen that if an asset is not worth replacing at the end of its life, the deprival value will be NRV or EV. However, there are many assets which will not be replaced either:

(a) Because the asset is technologically obsolete, and has been (or will be) superseded by more modern equipment.

(b) Because the business is changing the nature of its operations and will not want to continue in the same line of business once the asset has been used up.

4.9 Such assets, even though there are reasons not to replace them, would still be valued (usually) at net replacement cost, because this 'deprival value' still provides an estimate of the operating capability of the company.

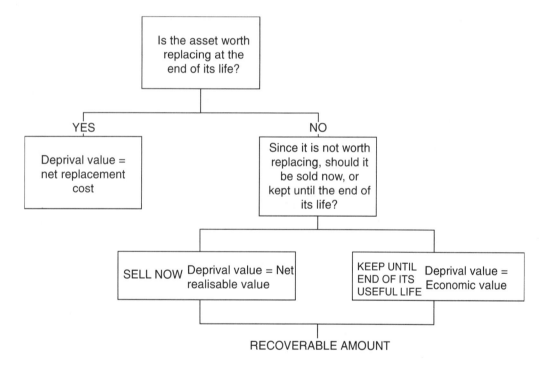

CCA profits and deprival value

4.10 The deprival value of assets is reflected in the CCA profit and loss account by the following means.

(a) **Depreciation** is **charged** on fixed assets **on the basis of gross replacement cost** of the asset (where NRC is the deprival value).

(b) Where **NRV or EV** is the deprival value, the **charge against CCA profits will be the loss in value of the asset during the accounting period**; ie from its previous balance sheet value to its current NRV or EV.

(c) **Goods sold are charged at their replacement cost**. Thus if an item of stock cost £15 to produce, and sells for £20, by which time its replacement cost has risen to £17, the CCA profit would be £3.

	£
Sales	20
Less replacement cost of goods sold	17
Current cost profit	3

4.11 It is useful to explain the distinction here between CCA and accounting for inflation, and a simple example may help to describe the difference. Suppose that Arthur Smith Ltd buys an asset on 1 January for £10,000. The estimated life of the asset is 5 years, and straight line depreciation is charged. At 31 December the gross replacement cost of the asset is £10,500 (5% higher than on 1 January) but general inflation during the year, as measured by the retail price index, has risen 20%.

(a) To maintain the value of the business against inflation, the asset should be revalued as follows.

	£
Gross (£10,000 × 120%)	12,000
Depreciation charge for the year (@ 20%)	2,400
Net value in the balance sheet	9,600

(b) In CCA, the business maintains its operating capability if we revalue the asset as follows.

	£
Gross replacement cost	10,500
Depreciation charge for the year (note)	2,100
NRC; balance sheet value	8,400

	£
Note	
Historical cost depreciation	2,000
CCA depreciation adjustment (5%)	100
Total CCA depreciation cost	2,100

4.12 **CCA preserves the operating capability of the company but does not necessarily preserve it against the declining value in the purchasing power of money** (against inflation). As mentioned in the previous chapter, CCA is a system which takes account of specific price inflation (changes in the prices of specific assets or groups of assets) but not of general price inflation.

4.13 A strict view of current cost accounting might suggest that a set of CCA accounts should be prepared from the outset on the basis of deprival values. In practice that has not been the procedure adopted in the UK. Instead, current cost accounts have been prepared by starting from historical cost accounts and making appropriate adjustments.

Current cost adjustments to historical cost profit

4.14 In current cost accounting profit is calculated as follows

	£	£
Historical cost profit		X
Less: Cost of sales adjustment (COSA)		X
depreciation adjustment	X	
		(X)
Current cost profit		X

The holding gains, both realised and unrealised, are therefore excluded from current cost profit. The double entry for the debits in the current cost profit and loss account is to credit both COSA and depreciation adjustment to a non-distributable revaluation reserve.

The current cost profit and loss account and balance sheet

4.15 The format of the *current cost profit and loss account* would show the following information, although not necessarily in the order given.

	£	£
Historical cost profit (before interest & taxation)		X
Current cost operating adjustments		
Cost of sales adjustment (COSA)	(X)	
Monetary working capital adjustment (loss or gain) (MWCA)	(X) or X	
Depreciation adjustment	(X)	
		(X)
Current cost operating profit (before interest and taxation)		X
Less interest payable and receivable		(X)
Add gearing adjustment		X
Current cost profit attributable to shareholders		X
Less taxation		(X)
Current cost profit after tax		X
Extraordinary items (loss or gain)		(X) or X
Current cost profit or loss for the financial year		X

Cost of sales adjustment (COSA)

4.16 The COSA is **necessary to eliminate realised holding gains on stock**. It **represents the difference between the replacement cost and the historical cost of goods sold.** The exclusion of holding gains from CC profit is a necessary consequence of the need to maintain operating capability. The COSA represent that portion of the HC profit which must be consumed in replacing the stock item sold so that trading can continue. Where practical difficulties arise in estimating replacement cost, a simple indexing system can be used.

Depreciation adjustment

4.17 The depreciation adjustment is **the difference between the depreciation charge on the gross replacement cost of the assets and the historical cost depreciation.** This is (as with the COSA) a realised holding gain which is excluded from the CC profit. Where comparison is made with a different asset for the purposes of calculating replacement cost (because of the obsolescence of the old asset), then allowance must be made for different useful lives and different production capabilities.

Monetary working capital adjustment (MWCA)

4.18 Where a company gives or takes credit for the sale or purchase of goods, the goods are paid for at the end of the credit period at the replacement cost as at the beginning of the credit period. If a company measures profit as the excess of revenue over cost:

(a) **Creditors protect the company** to some extent **from price changes because the company lags behind current prices in its payment.**

(b) **Debtors, in contrast, would be a burden on profits** in a period of rising prices because sales receipts will always relate to previous months' sales at a lower price/cost/profit level.

The MWCA can therefore be either a gain or a loss.

Gearing adjustment

4.19 If a company has **external creditors** who are financing some part of the net assets of the business (stocks, fixed assets and monetary working capital), since the amount owed to these creditors is fixed in monetary terms, and does not rise with inflation, it follows that they are **financing some part of the holding gains represented by COSA, depreciation adjustment and MWCA.** In calculating the amount of current cost profit earned by the shareholders it is **therefore inappropriate to deduct the** *whole* **of these adjustments from historical cost profit.** The deduction **must be abated by the amount of the adjustments** which is **financed by external creditors.**

4.20 In the current cost balance sheet assets will be valued at their 'value to the business' and liabilities at their monetary amount. There will be a current cost reserve to reflect the revaluation surpluses. This has already been described in some detail.

Exam focus point

Although you are not required to produce current cost accounts in your examination, a comprehensive example should help your understanding.

4.21 EXAMPLE: CURRENT COST ACCOUNTS

At the beginning of a period, Arthur Smith Ltd has the following balance sheet.

	£
Fixed assets (newly acquired)	10,000
Stocks (newly acquired)	2,000
	12,000
Financed by	
Equity	8,000
Loan stock (10% interest)	4,000
	12,000

4.22 The company gearing is 33%, in terms of both HC and CCA. During the period, sales of stocks amounted to £15,000, the replacement cost of sales was £13,200 and the historical cost of sales was £12,000. Closing stocks, at replacement cost, were £4,600 and at HC were £4,400. Depreciation is provided for at 10% straight line, and at the end of the period the fixed asset had a gross replacement cost of £11,000. The HC accounts were as follows.

PROFIT AND LOSS ACCOUNT

	£
Sales	15,000
Less cost of sales	12,000
	3,000
Depreciation	1,000
Profit before interest	2,000
Interest	400
Profit	1,600

484

CLOSING BALANCE SHEET

	£
Fixed asset at cost less depreciation	9,000
Stocks	4,400
Cash	200
	13,600
Equity	9,600
Loan stock	4,000
	13,600

Taxation is ignored.

Prepare workings for the CCA accounts. (Depreciation for the period will be based on the end of year value of the fixed asset.)

4.23 SOLUTION

The COSA is (£13,200 – £12,000) = £1,200
The depreciation adjustment is £100
The MWCA is nil (there are no purchases or sales on credit).

Note. The small cash balance in the closing balance sheet would probably be regarded as necessary for business purposes and therefore taken up in the MWCA as monetary working capital. In this example, we will treat the £200 as a cash surplus.

	£	£
Historical cost profit (before interest)		2,000
Current cost adjustments:		
COSA	1,200	
MWCA	0	
Depreciation	100	
		1,300
Current cost operating profit		700

The gearing adjustment is calculated by multiplying the three current cost adjustments (here £1,300) by the gearing proportion (by the proportion of the gains which is financed by borrowing and which therefore provides additional profits for equity, since the real value of the borrowing is declining in a period of rising prices).

The gearing proportion is the ratio:

$$\frac{\text{Net borrowing}}{\text{Average net operating assets in the year}}$$

Net operating assets consist of fixed assets, stocks and monetary working capital. They are financed partly by net borrowings and partly by equity. The gearing proportion can therefore equally well be expressed as:

$$\frac{\text{Average net borrowing in the period}}{\text{Average equity interests plus average net borrowing in the period}}$$

Equity interests include the current cost reserve, and also any proposed dividends. Average figures are taken as being more representative than end of year figures.

	£
Opening figures	
Net borrowing	4,000
Equity interests	8,000
Equity plus net borrowing	12,000

Closing figures: since cash is here regarded as a surplus amount, the company is losing value during a period of inflation by holding cash - just as it is gaining by having fixed loans. If cash is not included in MWC, it is:

(a) Deducted from net borrowings

(b) Excluded from net operating assets

(Net operating assets consist of fixed assets, long term trade investments, stocks and monetary working capital.)

The closing figures are therefore as follows.

	£	£
Fixed assets (at net replacement cost £11,000-£1,100)		9,900
Stocks (at replacement cost)		4,600
Monetary working capital		0
Net operating assets (equals equity interest plus net borrowings)		14,500
Less: net borrowing	4,000	
cash in hand	(200)	
		3,800
Therefore equity interest		10,700

Average figures	*Opening*	*Closing*	*Average*
Net borrowing	£4,000	£3,800	£3,900
Net operating assets	£12,000	£14,500	£13,250

The gearing proportion is $\dfrac{3,900}{13,250} \times 100\% = 29.43\%$

Question 5

Prepare the CCA accounts based on the above example.

Answer

	£	£
Historical cost profit before interest		2,000
Current cost adjustments:		
COSA	1,200	
MWCA	0	
Depreciation	100	
		(1,300)
Current cost operating profit		700
Interest	(400)	
Gearing adjustment (£1,300 × 29.43%)	383	
		(17)
Current cost profit attributable to shareholders		683

CCA BALANCE SHEET (end of year)

	£	£
Fixed assets (net replacement cost)		9,900
Stocks (replacement cost)		4,600
Cash		200
		14,700
Financed by		
Equity at start of year		8,000
Addition to P & L reserve during year		683
Current cost reserve		
Excess of net replacement cost over net book value		
(9,900-9,000)	900	
Depreciation adjustment	100	
COSA	1,200	
MWCA	0	
	2,200	
Less gearing adjustment	(383)	
	1,817	
Add revaluation of year-end stocks	200	
		2,017
		10,700
Loan stock		4,000
		14,700

Summary of double entry: CCA

4.24 It may be useful to summarise the double-entry system in CCA, in which the current cost reserve has a central role.

(a) **For fixed assets, there will be an excess of net replacement cost over (historical cost) net book value**. The increase in this excess amount each accounting period will be recorded as:

DEBIT   net assets (assets account and provision for depreciation account) with the increase in the gross replacement cost minus total extra provision for depreciation;

CREDIT   current cost reserve account

(b) The **various adjustments** will be as follows.

DEBIT   current cost profit and loss account

CREDIT   current cost reserve account;

with the amount of the **COSA**, the depreciation adjustment and the MWCA, if this reduces the current cost profit. If the MWCA increases the current cost profit, the entries would be 'credit P & L account' 'debit current cost reserve'.

(c) The **gearing adjustment** is shown as:

CREDIT   current cost profit and loss account
DEBIT   current cost reserve;

(d) At the end of an accounting period, there may be some **revaluations of closing stocks**:

DEBIT   stocks
CREDIT   current cost reserve account

with the amount of the revaluation.

On the first day of the next accounting period, this entry is **reversed**; ie

CREDIT   stocks (to reduce them to historical cost)
DEBIT   current cost reserve account.

BPP
PUBLISHING

The advantages and disadvantages of current cost accounting

Advantages

4.25 (a) By excluding holding gains from profit, CCA **can be used to indicate whether** the **dividends** paid to shareholders (which by UK law can exceed the size of the CCA profit) **will reduce the operating capability** of the business.

(b) Assets are valued after management has considered the **opportunity cost** of holding them, and the expected benefits from their future use. CCA is therefore **a useful guide for management in deciding whether to hold or sell assets.**

(c) It is **relevant to the needs of information users** in:

(i) Assessing the stability of the business entity.

(ii) Assessing the vulnerability of the business (eg to a takeover), or the liquidity of the business.

(iii) Evaluating the performance of management in maintaining and increasing the business substance.

(iv) Judging future prospects.

(d) It can be **implemented fairly easily** in practice, by making simple adjustments to the historical cost accounting profits. A current cost balance sheet can also be prepared with reasonable simplicity.

Disadvantages

4.26 (a) It is impossible to make valuations of EV or NRV without subjective judgements. The **measurements used are** therefore **not objective.**

(b) There are **several problems to be overcome in deciding how to provide an estimate of replacement costs for fixed assets.**

(i) Depreciation based on replacement costs **does not conform to the traditional accounting view** that depreciation can be viewed as a means of spreading the cost of the asset over its estimated life,

(ii) Depreciation based on replacement costs would appear to be a means of providing that sufficient funds are set aside in the business to ensure that the asset can be replaced at the end of its life. But if it is not certain what technological advances might be in the next few years and how the type of assets required might change between the current time and the estimated time of replacement, it is difficult to argue that depreciation based on today's costs is a valid way of providing for the eventual physical replacement of the asset.

(iii) It is more correct, however, that **depreciation in CCA does not set aside funds for the physical replacement of fixed assets.**

'CCA aims to maintain no more and no less than the facilities that are available at the accounting date ... despite the fact that the fixed assets which provide those facilities might never be replaced in their existing or currently available form ... In simple language, this means charging depreciation on the basis of the current replacement cost of the assets at the time the facilities are used.' (Mallinson)

(iv) It may be argued that depreciation based on **historical cost is more accurate** than replacement cost depreciation, **because the historical cost is known,** whereas replacement cost is simply an estimate. However, replacement costs are re-assessed each year, so that inaccuracies in the estimates in one year can be rectified in the next year.

(c) The **mixed value approach** to valuation **means** that some assets will be valued at replacement cost, but others will be valued at net realisable value or economic value. It is arguable that the **total assets** will, therefore, have an **aggregate value** which is **not particularly meaningful** because of this mixture of different concepts.

(d) It can be argued that **'deprival value' is an unrealistic concept, because the business entity has not been deprived of the use of the asset**. This argument is one which would seem to reject the fundamental approach to 'capital maintenance' on which CCA is based.

5 AGENCY THEORY AND THE EFFICIENT MARKET HYPOTHESIS

5.1 We are now moving on to some more general theories about behaviour within companies and in the stock market.

Agency theory and the 'agency problem'

5.2 **The relationship between management and shareholders is sometimes referred to as an agency relationship**, in which managers act as agents for the shareholders, using delegated powers to run the affairs of the company in the shareholders' best interests.

> **KEY TERM**
>
> **Agency theory** (Fama and Jensen) proposes that, although individual members of the business team act in their own self-interest, the well-being of each individual depends on the well-being of other team members and on the performance of the team in competition with other teams. The firm is seen as constituted by contracts among the different factors of production.

5.3 Agency theory was advanced by two American economists, Jensen and Meckling, in 1976 as a theory to explain relationships within corporations. It has been used to explain management control practices as well as relationships between management and investors: here we are concerned with the latter.

5.4 Jensen and Meckling proposed that corporations be viewed as a set of contracts between management, shareholders and creditors, with management as agents and providers of finance as principals. Financial reports and external audit are two mechanisms by which the agents demonstrate compliance with their obligations to the principals.

5.5 The agency **relationship arising from the separation of ownership from management is sometimes characterised as the 'agency problem'**. For example, if managers hold none or very little of the equity shares of the company they work for, what is to stop them from:

(a) Working inefficiently?
(b) Not bothering to look for profitable new investment opportunities?
(c) Giving themselves high salaries and perks?

5.6 **One power that shareholders possess is the right to remove the directors from office**. But shareholders have to take the initiative to do this, and in many companies, the shareholders lack the energy and organisation to take such a step. Even so, directors will want the company's report and accounts, and the proposed final dividend, to meet with shareholders' approval at the AGM.

5.7 It is the **responsibility of the directors to ensure that management below director level perform well.** Getting the best out of subordinates is one of the functions of management, and directors should be expected to do it as well as they can.

5.8 Another reason why managers might do their best to improve the financial performance of their company is that **managers' pay is often related to the size or profitability of the company.** Managers in very big companies, or in very profitable companies, will normally expect to earn higher salaries than managers in smaller or less successful companies.

5.9 As explained by G Cosserat in an article published in the *Students' Newsletter* (December 1994), **agency theory is based on a number of behavioural and structural assumptions.**

   (a) The most important behavioural assumptions are **individual welfare maximisation, individual rationality,** and the assumption that individuals are **risk-averse.**

   (b) Structural assumptions include the assumption that **investments are not infinitely divisible,** and that **individuals vary in their access to funds and their entrepreneurial ability.** Some criticisms of the theory have attacked these various assumptions. For example, are individuals satisficers rather than maximisers? And are individuals truly 'rational' or perhaps rather gullible?

5.10 The assumptions of the theory **suggest that investors and entrepreneurs have incentives for sharing risks and rewards of entrepreneurial activity,** for example where the entrepreneur, who may enjoy limited liability, borrows from investors at fixed rates of interest.

5.11 The key feature of **an efficient agency contract,** for example within a company, is that it **allows full delegation of decision-making authority over the use of invested funds to management without excessive risk of abuse** of that authority. In the real world, an 'agency cost' arises, being the difference between the return expected if managers truly maximised shareholder wealth and the actual return, given that managers will actually be seeking to maximise their own wealth.

5.12 **'Bonding' and 'monitoring' procedures** help to **act as safeguards** to minimise the risk of investors incurring agency costs. An example of 'bonding' is a condition attached to a loan (eg security over assets, conditions not to raise further loans). A bank lending money to a business will also expect information to be supplied to enable it to *monitor* compliance with the loan agreement.

5.13 Agency theory suggests that audited accounts of limited companies are an important source of 'post-decision' information minimising investors' agency costs, in contrast to alternative approaches which see financial reports as primarily a source of 'pre-decision' information for equity investors. The theory is advanced as an explanation for the continued use of absorption costing and historic costs in management accounts in spite of their apparent lack of relevance in decision making.

The efficient market hypothesis

5.14 It has been argued that the UK and US stock markets are **efficient capital markets,** that is, markets in which:

   (a) The **prices of securities** bought and sold **reflect all the relevant information** which is available to the buyers and sellers. In other words, share prices change quickly to reflect all new information about future prospects.

(b) **No individual dominates** the market.

(c) **Transaction costs** of buying and selling are **not so high** as to discourage trading significantly.

5.15 If the stock market is efficient, **share prices should vary in a rational way.**

   (a) If a company makes a profitable investment, shareholders will get to know about it, and the market price of its shares will rise in anticipation of future dividend increases.

   (b) If a company makes a bad investment shareholders will find out and so the price of its shares will fall.

   (c) If interest rates rise, shareholders will want a higher return from their investments, so market prices will fall.

The definition of efficiency

5.16 The efficiency of a stock market means the ability of a stock market to price stocks and shares fairly and quickly.

> **KEY TERM**
>
> An **efficient market** is one in which the market prices of all the securities traded on it reflect all the available information. There is no possibility of 'speculative bubbles' in which share prices are pushed up or down, by speculative pressure, to unrealistically high or low levels.

Varying degrees of efficiency

5.17 There are three degrees or 'forms' of efficiency:

   (a) Weak form
   (b) Semi-strong form
   (c) Strong form

5.18 Tests can be carried out on the workings of a stock market to establish whether the market operates with a particular form of efficiency.

Weak form tests and weak form efficiency

5.19 The weak form hypothesis of market efficiency states that **current share prices only reflect all information available from past changes in the price.** Share prices do **not** change **in anticipation** of new information being announced.

5.20 Since new information arrives unexpectedly, changes in share prices should occur in a random fashion: **a weak form test seeks to prove the validity of the random walk theory** of share prices. In addition, if the theory is correct then chartist or technical analysis cannot be based on sound principles.

5.21 Research to prove that the stock market displays weak form efficiency has been based on the principle that:

   (a) If share price changes are random
   (b) If there is no connection between past price movements and new share price changes

Then it should be possible to prove statistically there is no correlation between successive changes in the price of a share, that is, that trends in prices cannot be detected.

Proofs of the absence of trends have been claimed in the work of various writers.

Semi-strong form tests and semi-strong form efficiency

5.22 Semi-strong form tests attempt to show that the stock market displays semi-strong efficiency, by which we mean that **current share prices reflect both**:

(a) **All relevant information about past price movements and their implications**.
(b) **All knowledge** which is **available publicly**.

5.23 **Tests to prove semi-strong efficiency have concentrated on the ability of the market to anticipate share price changes before new information is formally announced.** For example, if two companies plan a merger, share prices of the two companies will inevitably change once the merger plans are formally announced. The market would show semi-strong efficiency, however, if it were able to anticipate such an announcement, so that share prices of the companies concerned would change in advance of the merger plans being confirmed.

5.24 **Research** in both Britain and the USA has suggested that market prices anticipate mergers several months before they are formally announced, and the **conclusion drawn is that the stock market in these countries** *do* **exhibit semi-strong efficiency**.

5.25 It has also been argued that the market displays sufficient efficiency for investors to see through 'window dressing' of accounts by companies which use accounting conventions to overstate profits.

5.26 Suppose that a company is planning a rights issue of shares in order to invest in a new project. A semi-strong form efficient market hypothesis (unlike the weak form hypothesis) would predict that if there is public knowledge before the issue is formally announced, of the issue itself and of the expected returns from the project, then the market price (cum rights) will change to reflect the anticipated profits before the issue is announced.

Strong form tests and strong form efficiency

5.27 A strong form test of market efficiency attempts to prove that the stock market displays a strong form of efficiency, by which we mean that **share prices reflect all information available** from:

(a) **Past price changes**.
(b) **Public knowledge or anticipation**.
(c) **Insider knowledge** available to specialists or experts (such as investment managers).

5.28 It would then follow that in order to maximise the wealth of shareholders, management should concentrate simply on maximising the net present value of its investments and it **need not worry**, for example, **about the effect on share prices of financial results in the published accounts because investors will make allowances for low profits or dividends in the current year if higher profits or dividends are expected in the future.**

5.29 In theory an expert, such as an investment manager, should be able to use his privileged access to additional information about companies to earn a higher rate of return than an ordinary investor. Unit trusts should in theory therefore perform better than the average investor. Research to date has suggested, however, that this expert skill does not exist (or at least, that any higher returns earned by experts are offset by management charges).

How efficient are stock markets?

5.30 **Evidence so far collected suggests that stock markets show efficiency that is at least weak form, but tending more towards a semi-strong form.** In other words, current share prices reflect all or most publicly available information about companies and their securities. However, it is very difficult to assess the market's efficiency in relation to shares which are not usually actively traded.

5.31 Fundamental analysis and technical analysis, which are carried out by analysts and investment managers, play an important role in creating an efficient stock market. This is because an efficient market depends on the widespread availability of cheap information about companies, their shares and market conditions, and this is what the firms of market makers and other financial institutions *do* provide for their clients and for the general investing public.

The implications of the efficient market hypothesis

5.32 If the **strong form** of the efficient market hypothesis is correct, **a company's real financial position will be reflected in its share price.** Its real financial position includes both its current position and its expected future profitability.

5.33 If the management of a company attempt to maximise the net present value of their investments and to make public any relevant information about those investments then current share prices will in turn be maximised.

5.34 The implication for an investor is that **if the market shows strong form or semi-strong form efficiency, he can rarely spot shares at a bargain price that will soon rise sharply in value.** This is because the market will already have anticipated future developments, and will have reflected these in the share price. All an investor can do, instead of looking for share bargains, is to concentrate on building up a good spread of shares (a portfolio) in order to achieve a satisfactory balance between risk and return.

The share price crash of October 1987 and the efficient market hypothesis

5.35 The crash of October 1987, in which share prices fell suddenly by 20% to 40% on the world's stock markets, raised serious questions about the validity of random walk theory, the fundamental theory of share values and the efficient market hypothesis.

5.36 If these theories are correct, how can shares that were valued at one level on one day suddenly be worth 40% less the next day, without any change in expectations of corporate profits and dividends?

5.37 On the other hand, a widely feared crash late in 1989 failed to happen, suggesting that stock markets may not be altogether out of touch with the underlying values of companies.

6 POSITIVE AND NORMATIVE ACCOUNTING CONCEPTS

6.1 These two types of concepts are directly opposing and recognise two different approaches to accounting theory.

Exam focus point

Like agency theory, this is most likely to come up as part a question in the examination paper.

Positive accounting concepts

KEY TERM

Positive accounting concepts, or descriptive concepts are based on an approach which is essentially concerned with what accountants do in practice.

6.2 Observations are made and general conclusions are made from these observations to develop a theory. In effect, the observer will look for similarity of treatment. Once sufficient instances have occurred, assurance is gained to the extent that a theory can be developed about the practice in question.

6.3 The theory thus developed **allows explanations and predictions to be made about accountants' behaviour,** particularly about how specified items will be treated.

6.4 The **belief which underlies the positive approach is that the objective of financial statements is to report on the stewardship aspect of the management role,** and thus a report of the utilisation of the assets of the business is required by the directors to the shareholders.

6.5 The basic concepts under this approach define assets, **liabilities,** capital, revenue, expenses, income and transactions. The descriptions are very much based on the way each of these items would arise in practice, for example, **liabilities** are the debts of the business.

6.6 **When it comes to choice of accounting policy, positive accounting theory takes a 'real world' approach,** taking into account such factors as the political sensitivity of the enterprise. For example, it is important for such companies as British Gas not to be seen to be making too much profit, hence the accounting policies chosen will be ones which give a low profit figure or low profitability ratios.

Normative accounting concepts

6.7 The normative approach was developed through the concerns of academic accounting theory. The desire to provide a foundation for the 'science' of accounting led to the search for a 'general theory of accounting'. It was argued that, although various theories and systems operated in accounting, there was no coherent thought governing the whole discipline.

6.8 The first argument was that, instead of describing what accountants did, accounting theory should aim to develop *better* accounting practice.

KEY TERM

The **normative theory** is concerned with 'what should be', not 'what is'.

The theory states that it is possible to develop accounting theory independently of current practice. In fact, this is desirable because of the gap between accounting practice and social and economic reality. In particular, lack of compatibility is a great problem. A theory which imposed standards of quality and relevance of information would improve the situation, as alternative accounting rules would no longer be acceptable: the theory would decide which one was correct.

6.9 The normative approach is **based on imperatives: statements of specific objectives which state that types of transactions 'should be' treated in a certain way.** In order to move from these general statements, **deductive reasoning is required** to reach particular statements. This is compared to the positive approach where inductive reasoning is required to produce general principles from individual practical examples.

6.10 **Criticisms** of the normative approach include the fact that **if assumptions are stated broadly enough to obtain general agreement, they will then be accused of being self-evident, whereas if stated too specifically, no general agreement will be reached.**

Chapter roundup

- **Profit** is an important measure in accounting statements.

  - It measures the efficiency of the company's **management** and helps in decision making.
  - It helps **creditors and investors** to decide whether they can safely lend money .
  - The **government** may use profit as a means of imposing direct taxation.

- **Profit** therefore has a variety of uses and users, but its **measurement depends** on the **methods used to value capital** (assets and liabilities) and on the method, if any, of accounting for price level changes.

- Alternative methods of accounting based on **current value concepts** use **exit values, entry values** or **mixed values**. These principles are developed further in current cost accounting.

- **CPP accounting** is a method of accounting for general (not specific) inflation. It does so by expressing asset values in a stable monetary unit, the £c or £ of current purchasing power.

- In the **CPP balance sheet**, **monetary items** are stated at their **face value**. **Non-monetary items** are stated at their **current purchasing power** as at the balance sheet date.

- **CCA** is an alternative to the historical cost convention which attempts to overcome the problems of accounting for **specific price inflation**. Unlike CPP accounting, it does not attempt to cope with general inflation.

- CCA is based on a **physical concept of capital maintenance**. Profit is recognised after the operating capability of the business has been maintained.

- To recognise **holding gains** as part of current cost profit would conflict with the principle of maintaining operating capability.

- The current cost profit and loss account is constructed by taking **historical cost** profit before interest and taxation as a starting point.

  - Current cost **operating adjustments** in respect of **cost of sales, monetary working capital** and **depreciation** are made so as to arrive at **current cost operating profit**.

  - A **gearing adjustment** is then necessary to arrive at a figure of current cost profit attributable to shareholders.

- **Agency/theory** attempts to explain why companies take decisions which **do not necessarily increase shareholders' wealth.**

- **Positive accounting concepts** are based on what accountants do **in practice**.

- **Normative accounting concepts** aim:

  - to develop **better** accounting practice
  - to develop theory **independent** of practice

BPP PUBLISHING

Part D: The theoretical framework of accounting

Quick quiz

1   How did Fisher define income?

2   How did Hicks define economic income?

3   Distinguish between the entity concept of capital and the proprietary concept of capital.

4   Which methods below relate to current value accounting?

    A   Realisable value
    B   Mixed value
    C   Current exit value
    D   Replacement cost
    E   Current entry value

5   Current value accounting can be described as systems for accounting for inflation?

    True   ☐

    False   ☐

6   List the advantages and disadvantages of replacement cost accounting.

7   Exit values are .... costs.

8   List the advantages and disadvantages of current exit value accounting.

9   You are given an inflation figure of 7% yet the replacement cost of an item of plant bought today for £10,000 is expected to be £10,500 in a years time. Explain why this is so.

10   Stock is a non-monetary item

    True   ☐

    False   ☐

11   List the advantages and disadvantages of CPP as a method of accounting.

12   Fill in the three blanks

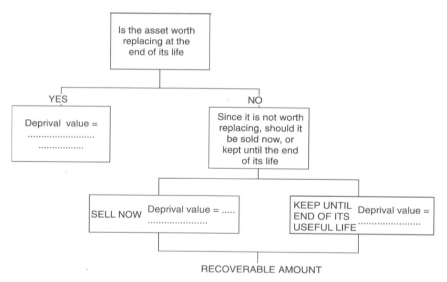

13   List four advantages and four disadvantages of CCA.

14   What are the three forms of efficiency according to the EMH?

Answers to quick quiz

1 Refer to paragraph 1.10

2 The maximum value which (an individual) can consume during a week and still expect to be as well off at the end of the week as he was at the beginning.' (1.19)

3 Entity concept – business as an operating unit. Proprietary concept – business makes profit for owners. (1.43)

4 All of them. (2.2)

5 False (2.17)

6 Refer to paragraphs 2.37 and 2.38

7 Opportunity (2.44)

8 Refer to paragraphs 2.55 and 2.56

9 7% is the general price inflation figure, the plant's specific price inflation figures is 5%. (3.11)

10 True (3.19)

11 Refer to paragraphs 3.24 and 3.25

12 Answers (from left to right) net replacement cost, net realisable value and economic value (4.9)

13 Refer to paragraphs 4.25 and 4.26

14 Weak, semistrong and strong form (5.17)

Now try the question below from the Exam Question Bank

Number	Level	Marks	Time
26	Full exam	25	45 mins

Chapter 21

THE ASB'S STATEMENT OF PRINCIPLES

Topic list	Syllabus reference
1 ASB *Statement of Principles*	1(a)

Introduction

By now you should have acquired a thorough grasp of accounting, both for single companies and for groups. You should therefore have little difficulty with this chapter on the ASB's *Statement of Principles*.

It has been said that in the past the standard-setting body took a 'fire-fighting' approach to developing accounting standards. The old SSAPs were not based on a consistent philosophy and this led to the need for a conceptual framework of accounting.

This chapter deals with the ASB's conceptual framework, the *Statement of Principles*. The *Statement* is designed to provide the basis for all new accounting standards. It is therefore very important and also very topical as you will know from your reading of the financial press.

Study guide

- Describe the ASB's 'balance sheet approach' to revenue recognition within its *Statement of Principles*.

Exam guide

The *Statement of Principles* is a very pervasive document as it provides a framework for standard setters. You should be able to relate the majority of your written answers to the *Statement*, especially when discussing the strengths or weaknesses of a standard.

1   ASB STATEMENT OF PRINCIPLES

1.1   The Accounting Standards Board (ASB) published (in November 1995) an exposure draft of its *Statement of Principles for Financial Reporting*. In March 1999, the text was substantially revised with particular attention being given to the clarity of expression. In December 1999 the *Statement* was finalised. The ASB issued with the revised draft an introductory booklet and a technical supplement. Together these documents respond to the criticisms raised on the 1995 version by exploding myths, rebutting arguments and making technical changes.

1.2   The statement consists of eight chapters.

(1)   The objective of financial statements
(2)   The reporting entity
(3)   The qualitative characteristics of financial information
(4)   The elements of financial statements
(5)   Recognition in financial statements
(6)   Measurement in financial statements

(7) Presentation of financial information

(8) Accounting for interests in other entities

Purpose of the *Statement of Principles*

1.3 The following are the main reasons why the Accounting Standards Board (ASB) developed the *Statement of Principles*.

(a) To assist the ASB by providing a basis for reducing the number of alternative accounting treatments permitted by accounting standards and company law

(b) To provide a framework for the future development of accounting standards

(c) To assist auditors in forming an opinion as to whether financial statements conform with accounting standards

(d) To assist users of accounts in interpreting the information contained in them

(e) To provide guidance in applying accounting standards

(f) To give guidance on areas which are not yet covered by accounting standards

(g) To inform interested parties of the approach taken by the ASB in formulating accounting standards

The role of the *Statement* can thus be summed up as being to provide **consistency, clarity and information**.

Chapter 1 The objective of financial statements

1.4 The main points raised here are as follows.

(a) 'The objective of financial statements is to provide information about the reporting entity's **performance and financial position** that is useful to a wide range of users for assessing the stewardship of management and for making economic decisions.'

(b) It is acknowledged that while all not all the information needs of users can be met by financial statements, there are needs that are common to all users. Financial statements that meet the needs of providers of risk capital to the enterprise will also meet most of the needs of other users that financial statements can satisfy.

Users of financial statements other than investors include the following.

(i) Investors
(ii) Lenders
(iii) Suppliers and other creditors
(iv) Employees
(v) Customers
(vi) Government and their agencies
(vii) The public

(c) The limitations of financial statements are emphasised as well as the strengths.

(d) Investors are the defining choice of user because they focus on the entity's cash-generation ability or financial adaptability.

(d) The information required by investors relates to:

(i) Financial performance
(ii) Financial position
(iii) Generation and use of cash

(iv)   Financial adaptability

The exposure draft discusses the importance of each of these elements and why they are disclosed in the financial statements.

Chapter 2 The reporting entity

1.5   This chapter makes the point that it is important that entities that ought to prepare financial statements, in fact do so. The entity must be a cohesive economic unit. It has a determinable boundary and is held to account for all the things it can control. For this purpose, first direct control and secondly direct plus indirect control are taken into account.

KEY TERM

Control means two things:

(a)   The ability to deploy the economic resources involved
(b)   The ability to benefit (or to suffer) from their deployment

An entity will have control of a second entity if it has the ability to direct that entity's operating and financial policies with a view to gaining economic benefit from its activities.

Control must be distinguished from **management**, where the entity is not exposed to the benefits arising from or risks inherent in the activities of the second entity.

Chapter 3 Qualitative characteristics of financial information

1.6   The ED gives a diagrammatic representation of the discussion, shown below.

(a)   Qualitative characteristics that relate to **content** are **relevance** and **reliability**.

(b)   Qualitative characteristics that relate to **presentation** are **comparability** and **understandability**.

The diagram shown here is reasonably explanatory.

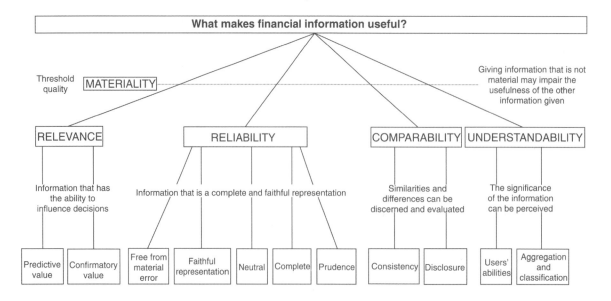

Chapter 4 Elements of financial statements

1.7   The elements of financial statements are listed. They are:

(a)   Assets

(b)   Liabilities

(c)   Ownership interest

(d)   Gains

(e)   Losses

(f)   Contributions from owners

(g)   Distributions to owners

1.8   Any item that does not fall within one of the definitions of elements should not be included in financial statements. The definitions are as follows.

(a)   **Assets** are rights or other access to future economic benefits controlled by an entity as a result of past transactions or events.

(b)   **Liabilities** are obligations of an entity to transfer economic benefits as a result of past transactions or events.

(c)   **Ownership interest** is the residual amount found by deducting all of the entity's liabilities from all of the entity's assets.

(d)   **Gains** are increases in ownership interest, other than those relating to contributions from owners.

(e)   **Losses** are decreases in ownership interest, other than those relating to distributions to owners.

(f)   **Contributions from owners** are increases in ownership interest resulting from investments made by owners in their capacity as owners.

(g)   **Distributions to owners** are decreases in ownership interest resulting from transfers made to owners in their capacity as owners.

Chapter 5 Recognition in financial statements

1.9   If a transaction or other event has created a new asset or liability or added an existing asset or liability, that effect will be recognised if:

(a)   Sufficient evidence exists that the new asset or liability has been created or that there has been an addition to an existing asset or liability.

(b)   The new asset or liability or the addition to the existing asset or liability can be measured at a monetary amount with sufficient reliability.

1.10   In a transaction involving the provision of services or goods for a net gain, the recognition criteria described above will be met on the occurrence of the critical event in the operating cycle involved.

1.11   An asset or liability will be wholly or partly derecognised if:

(a)   Sufficient evidence exists that a transaction or other past event has eliminated a previously recognised asset or liability.

(b)   Although the item continues to be an asset or a liability the criteria for recognition are no longer met.

BPP
PUBLISHING

1.12   The objective of financial statements is achieved to a large extent through the recognition of elements in the primary financial statements - in other words, the depiction of elements both in words and by monetary amounts, and the inclusion of those amounts in the primary financial statement totals. Recognition is a process that has the following stages.

(a)   Initial recognition, which is where an item is depicted in the primary financial statements for the first time.

(b)   Subsequent remeasurement, which involves changing the amount at which an already recognised asset or liability is stated in the primary financial statements.

(c)   Derecognition, which is where an item that was until then recognised ceases to be recognised.

1.13   In practice, entities operate in an uncertain environment and this **uncertainty** may sometimes make it necessary to delay the recognition process. The uncertainty is twofold.

- **Element uncertainty** - does the item exist and meet the definition of elements?
- **Measurement uncertainty** - at what monetary amount should the item be recognised?

1.14   Even though matching is not used by the *Statement* to drive the recognition process, it still plays an important role in the approach described in the draft in allocating the cost of assets across reporting periods and in telling preparers where they may find assets and liabilities.

Question 1

Consider the following situations. In each case, do we have an asset or liability within the definitions given by the *Statement of Principles?* Give reasons for your answer.

(a)   Pat Ltd has purchased a patent for £20,000. The patent gives the company sole use of a particular manufacturing process which will save £3,000 a year for the next five years.

(b)   Baldwin Ltd paid Don Brennan £10,000 to set up a car repair shop, on condition that priority treatment is given to cars from the company's fleet.

(c)   Deals on Wheels Ltd provides a warranty with every car sold.

(d)   Monty Ltd has signed a contract with a human resources consultant. The terms of the contract are that the consultant is to stay for six months and be paid £3,000 per month.

(e)   Rachmann Ltd owns a building which for many years it had let out to students. The building has been declared unsafe by the local council. Not only is it unfit for human habitation, but on more than one occasion slates have fallen off the roof, nearly killing passers-by. To rectify all the damage would cost £300,000; to eliminate the danger to the public would cost £200,000. The building could then be sold for £100,000.

Answer

(a)   This is an asset, albeit an intangible one. There is a past event, control and future economic benefit (through cost savings).

(b)   This cannot be classified as an asset. Baldwin Ltd has no control over the car repair shop and it is difficult to argue that there are 'future economic benefits'.

(c)   This is a liability; the business has taken on an obligation. It would be recognised when the warranty is issued rather than when a claim is made.

(d)   As a firm financial commitment, this has all the appearance of a liability. However, as the consultant has not done any work yet, there has been no past event which could give rise to a liability. Similarly, because there has been no past event there is no asset.

(e)   The situation is not clear cut. It could be argued that there is a liability, depending on the whether the potential danger to the public arising from the building creates a legal obligation to do the repairs. If there is such a liability, it might be possible to set off the sale proceeds of £100,000 against the cost of essential repairs of £200,000, giving a net obligation to transfer economic benefits of £100,000.

The building is clearly not an asset, because although there is control and there has been a past event, there is no expected access to economic benefit.

Chapter 6 Measurement in financial statements

1.15 A monetary carrying amount needs to be assigned so an asset or liability can be recognised. There are two measuring tasks that can be used: **historical cost** or **current value**.

(a) Initially, when an asset is purchased or a liability incurred, the asset/liability is recorded at the transaction cost, that is historical cost, which at that time is equal to current replacement cost.

(b) An asset/liability may subsequently be 'remeasured'. In a historical cost system, this can involve writing down an asset to its recoverable amount. For a liability, the corresponding treatment would be amendment of the monetary amount to the amount ultimately expected to be paid.

(c) Such re-measurements will, however, only be recognised if there is sufficient evidence that the monetary amount of the asset/liability has changed and the new amount can be reliably measured.

Chapter 7 Presentation of financial information

1.16 Aspects of this chapter have also given rise to some controversy. The chapter begins by making the general point that financial statements need to be as simple, straightforward and brief as possible while retaining their relevance and reliability.

Components of financial statements

1.17 The primary financial statements are as follows.

Statement	Measure of
Profit and loss account	Financial performance
Statement of total recognised gains and losses	Financial performance
Balance sheet	Financial position
Cash flow statement	Cash inflows and outflows

1.18 The notes to the financial statements 'amplify and explore' the primary statements; together they form an 'integrated whole'. Disclosure in the notes does not correct or justify non-disclosure or misrepresentation in the primary financial statements.

1.19 'Supplementary information' embraces voluntary disclosures and information which is too subjective for disclosure in the primary financial statement and the notes.

Chapter 8 Accounting for interests in other entities

1.20 Financial statements need to reflect the effect on the reporting entity's financial performance and financial position of its interests in other entities. This involves various measurement, presentation and consolidation issues which are dealt with in this chapter of the *Statement*.

BPP PUBLISHING

Different kinds of investments

1.21 The **classification** of investments should reflect the way in which they are used to further the business of the investor and their effect on the investor's financial position, performance and financial adaptability. The two key factors here are:

(a) The **degree of influence** of the investor

(b) The nature of the **investor's interest** in the results, assets and liabilities of its investee

1.22 The different types of investment are summarised in the following table.

Degree of influence	Nature of interest	Resulting categorisation
Control	The investor controls the investee	Subsidiary
Joint control	The investor does not itself control the investee but shares control through some form of arrangement jointly with others	Joint venture
Significant influence	The investor has neither control nor joint control, but exerts a degree of influence over the investee's operating and financial policies that is at the least a significant influence and at the most just short of joint control	Associate
Lesser or no influence	Any influence that the investor has over the investee's operating and financial policies is less than a significant influence	Simple investment

Parent and subsidiary

1.23 Parent entities prepare **consolidated financial statements** to provide financial information about the group as a single reporting entity. Consolidation is a process that aggregates the total assets, liabilities and results of the parent and its subsidiaries.

1.24 In determining which investments should be consolidated, the principle of control should predominate. However, consolidated financial statements should also reflect the extent of **outside ownership interests** because they are important factors in considering the parent's access and exposure to the results of its subsidiaries.

Associates and joint ventures

1.25 There are interests involving significant influence and joint control respectively. The method used should recognise the reporting entity's share of the results and the changes in net assets of the investee and should not misrepresent the extent of its influence. The **equity method** is therefore used.

Business combinations

1.26 Two types are recognised.

- **Purchases/acquisitions.** The assets and liabilities of the entity acquired are treated as if the transaction was the purchase of a bundle of assets and liabilities on the open market.

- **Uniting of interests/mergers**. The assets and liabilities of one party to the transaction are treated in the same way as the assets and liabilities of all the other parties; none of the assets or liabilities are treated as being purchased as a bundle of assets and liabilities on the open market.

Questions and answers

1.27 The original November 1995 exposure draft of the *Statement of Principles* attracted a great deal of criticism, not least from the firm Ernst & Young. In an attempt to address the criticisms raised, the ASB produced a booklet to go with the *Statement*, called '*Some questions answered*'. Below is an outline of the topics covered.

Status and purpose

1.28 The points made here are as follows.

   (a) The *Statement* is a description of the fundamental approach that should underpin the financial statements. It is intended to be:

   - Comprehensive
   - Internally consistent
   - Consistent with international approaches

   (b) The final version will **not** be an accounting standard.

   (c) Its main influence on accounting practice will be through its influence on the standard-setting process. It is only one of the factors that will be taken into account.

Approach

1.29 The approach encompasses the following.

   (a) There are similarities to existing practice and differences.

   (b) The *Statement* is based on the International Accounting Standard Committee's framework statement and is largely consistent with the framework statements issued in Australia, Canada, New Zealand, the USA and elsewhere. This reflects the view that it will be easier to achieve harmonisation of accounting practice if standard-setters work with a common set of principles.

   (c) The 'true and fair' requirement and the accounting concepts defined in FRS 18 play a central role in the revised draft.

   (d) The *Statement's* development has not been constrained by the requirements of companies legislation because:

   - It does not just apply to companies
   - Legal frameworks change in response to developments in accounting thought

The use of current costs and values and current cost accounting

1.30 These points are made.

   (a) The previous version of the *Statement* was criticised as heralding a move towards **current cost accounting**. However, the finalised *Statement* makes it clear that this is **not on the ASB's agenda**.

   (b) The *Statement* explains that historical cost and current value are **alternative measures**. It also explains that it is envisaged that the approach now adopted by the majority of the larger UK listed companies will continue to be used. This approach involves carrying some categories of balance sheet items at historical cost and others at current value. The *Statement* then goes on to describe a framework that would guide the choice of an appropriate measurement basis for each balance sheet category.

The focus on assets and liabilities and the role of transactions

1.31 These points are made.

(a) The previous draft placed great emphasis on assets and liabilities and even defined the items that are to be included in the profit and loss account in terms of assets and liabilities. This approach has been retained.

(b) The approach does not mean that the P&L is unimportant. The primary source of information provided in financial statements is the transactions undertaken by the reporting entity. The primary focus of the accounting process is to allocate these transactions to accounting periods.

(c) The *Statement* regards the profit or loss for the period as the difference between the opening and closing balance sheets adjusted for capital constructions and distributions.

Accounting standards based on the Statement

1.32 The question was raised as to whether accounting standards published in the future and therefore based on the *Statement of Principles* will be very different from past accounting standards. The ASB's view is that they won't. Some of the principles have already played very significant roles in accounting standards and have found general acceptance. The standards include:

- FRS 2 *Accounting for subsidiary undertakings*, which uses the reporting entity concept described in Chapter 2 of the Statement.

- FRS 4 *Capital instruments* and FRS 5 *Reporting the substance of transactions*, which use the definitions of assets and liabilities set out in Chapter 4.

- FRS 11 *Impairment of fixed assets and goodwill*, which uses the recoverable amount notion described in Chapter 6.

Exam focus point

The *Statement of Principles* is a topical area of the Paper 2.5 syllabus. Keep your eye out for articles on it in the *Student Accountant*.

Question 2

What is the purpose of the ASB's *Statement of Principles?*

Answer

The following are the main reasons why the ASB developed the *Statement of Principles.*

(a) To assist the ASB by providing a basis for reducing the number of alternative accounting treatments permitted by accounting standards and company law

(b) To provide a framework for the future development of accounting standards

(c) To assist auditors in forming an opinion as to whether financial statements conform with accounting standards

(d) To assist users of accounts in interpreting the information contained in them

(e) To provide guidance in applying accounting standards

(f) To give guidance on areas which are not yet covered by accounting standards

(g) To inform interested parties of the approach taken by the ASB in formulating accounting standards

The role of the *Statement* can thus be summed up as being to provide consistency, clarity and information.

Chapter roundup

- A revised version of the *Statement of Principles* has been issued. Key points to note are:

  ○ The *Statement* is **not an accounting standard.**
  ○ It will affect **accounting practice by influencing the standard-setting process.**
  ○ **'True and fair', FRS 18 and matching are important.**
  ○ **Current cost accounting** is **not** on the agenda.
  ○ The **balance sheet** and **P&L** are **equally important.**

Quick quiz

1   Which of the following are chapters in the Statement of Principles

A   Subsidiaries, associates and joint ventures
B   Profit measurement in financial statements
C   The objective of financial statements
D   Accounting for interest in other entities
E   Recognition in financial statements
F   Presentation of financial information
G   Substance of transactions in financial statements
H   The qualitative characteristics of financial information
I   The quantitative characteristics of financial information
J   Measurement in financial statements
K   The reporting entity
L   The elements of financial statements.

2   Name **five** of the **six** user groups identified in the Statement of Principles.

3   A **gain** as defined by the Statement of Principles is an increase in the net assets of the entity.

True ☐

False ☐

4   Financial statements need to be as ...., ... and .... as possible while retaining their .... and ....

5   The *Statement* favours current cost accounting. True or false?

Answers to quick quiz

1   C, D, E, F, H, J, K and L. (see para 1.2)
2   See paragraph 1.4(b)
3   False. (1.8)
4   See para 1.16.
5   False (1.31)

Now try the question below from the Exam Question Bank

Number	Level	Marks	Time
27	Full exam	20	36 mins

Part E

Analysing and appraising financial and related information

Chapter 22

INTERPRETATION OF FINANCIAL STATEMENTS

Topic list	Syllabus reference
1 The broad categories of ratios	5(a),(b)
2 Profitability and return on capital	5(a),(b)
3 Long term solvency and stability	5(a),(b)
4 Short term solvency and liquidity	5(a),(b)
5 Efficiency	5(a),(b)
6 Shareholders' investment ratios	5(a),(b)
7 Accounting policies and the limitations of ratio analysis	5(a),(b)
8 Reports on financial performance	5(a),(b)

Introduction

You may remember some of the basic interpretation of accounts from your earlier studies. This chapter recaps and develops the calculation of ratios and covers more complex accounting relationships. More importantly, perhaps, this chapter looks at how ratios can be analysed, interpreted and how the results should be presented to management.

Wide reading is encouraged in this area. If you want to look at real sets of accounts you could try the Financial Times Free Annual Reports Service - look in the FT at the London Share Service page. In any case, you should read regularly the *Student Accountant* and the *Financial Times at least.*

Study guide

- Calculate useful financial ratios for single company or group financial statements.

- Analyse and interpret ratios to give an assessment of a company's performance in comparison with:

    - a company's previous period's financial statements.
    - another similar company for the same period.
    - industry average ratios.

- Discuss the effect that changes in accounting policies or the use of different accounting policies between companies can have on the ability to interpret performance.

- Discuss how the interpretation of current cost accounts or current purchasing power accounts would differ to that of historic cost accounts.

- Discuss the limitations in the use of ratio analysis for assessing corporate performance, outlining other information that may be of relevance.

Note: the content of reports should draw upon knowledge acquired in other sessions.

These sessions concentrate on the preparation of reports and report writing skills.

Exam guide

You need to master report writing. Ratios are the tools used to interpret financial statements, the most important skill for this area of the syllabus is to develop reasoned arguments which lead to useful and valid conclusions. It is also important to demonstrate real commercial awareness and adopt a holistic perspective in looking at a business.

---

1 THE BROAD CATEGORIES OF RATIOS

Focus on user needs

1.1 An underlying purpose of preparing financial statements is to provide **meaningful information** for **potential users** regarding **financial performance, financial position** and **financial adaptability**. As identified earlier, they fall into a few key categories.

- Shareholders and potential investors
- Management
- Creditors
- Bankers and other providers of finance.

1.2 In general, these users may calculate a range of ratios and performance indicators. However, they are likely to **interpret** them from their **own perspective,** based on their own particular **commercial needs and interests.** In practice, there may well be conflicts of interest between users. For example, **management** will focus on **profitability** whereas a **bank manager** might be more concerned about **solvency. Shareholders** are likely to be interested in how **value** is **generated** and sustained as well as **returns**.

Exam focus point

Ensure you accurately identify who is going to be using the analysis you produce. Your answer must address their specific needs.

1.3 At its most basic, ratio analysis involves **comparing one figure against another** to produce a ratio, and then trying to interpret the meaning of the figure produced.

The broad categories of ratios

1.4 Broadly speaking, basic ratios can be grouped into five categories.

- **Profitability and return**
- **Long-term solvency and stability**
- **Short-term solvency and liquidity**
- **Efficiency (turnover ratios)**
- **Shareholders' investment ratios.**

1.5 Within each heading there are a number of standard measures or ratios that are traditionally calculated and generally accepted as meaningful indicators. However, **each individual business** must be **considered separately,** and a ratio that is meaningful for a manufacturing company may be completely meaningless for a financial institution. Avoid being **too mechanical when working out ratios.** Always be aware of the importance of **user focus.**

1.6 Further **useful insights** might also be gleaned from **companies' financial reports**.

(a) Comments in the **Chairman's report** and **directors' report**.

(b) A review of the **age and nature of the company's assets**.

(c) **Current and future developments** in the company's markets, at home and overseas, recent acquisitions or disposals of a subsidiary by the company.

(d) **Additional statements** and notes such as STRGL, note of historical profits and losses and reconciliation of movements in shareholders funds.

(e) **Exceptional items** in the P&L account.

(f) **Any other noticeable features** of the report and accounts, such as post balance sheet events, contingent liabilities, discontinued activities, qualified auditors' report, the company's taxation position, and so on.

(g) **Notes** dealing with **fixed assets**.

(h) **Notes** dealing with **employee details** and directors' remuneration.

1.7 Remember, the nature and scope of the analysis and the amount and quality of information available will depend on the circumstances and the brief provided. A shareholder may only have access to **published information**, whereas a **bank manager** is likely to be in a position to ask to see not only **financial statements**, but also documents such as **business plans**, periodic **management accounts** and **cash flow projections**.

1.8 In practice, you may be able to actually speak to management to obtain additional information. However, in an exam situation, you may have to identify what additional information might be useful and **explain tactfully** to the examiner how it might impact on your analysis and interpretation.

Industry specific performance indicators

1.9 In practice, businesses may also use a range of **industry and company specific ratios** to help them **manage the business** on a **day to day basis**.

Industry	Performance indicator
Hotels	Room occupancy
Accountants	Chargeable hours utilisation
Farms	Yields per acre
Hospitals	Patient waiting times
Pubs and restaurants	Till overs and unders
Motor manufacturer	Cars produced per worker
Training provider	Exam success rates
Airlines	Daily hours in air per plane

1.10 In practice, accounting firm and banks are developing **benchmarking services** for their clients whereby an individual client's **performance indicators** are shown (anonymously) alongside those of other subscribers to the **benchmarking survey**.

Holistic approach

1.11 Accounting ratios are only one part of the accountants diagnostic kit for analysing and interpreting financial statements. Other useful tools or sources of information, if available may comprise:

(a) The company's business plan
(b) Annual budgets
(c) Cash flow projections
(d) Management accounts
(e) Historic accounts figures (past trends)
(f) SWOT analysis
(g) Industry benchmark surveys
(h) Any other strategy or planning documents
(i) On line company and text search services
(j) Press releases and comments

1.12 The following diagram reinforces the importance of taking a **holistic approach** when reviewing a set of financial statements.

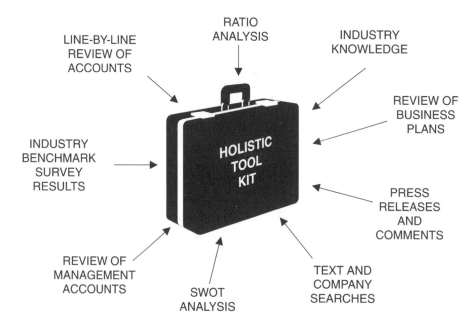

Basic ratios

1.13 The following are the **main accounting ratios** which would **traditionally** be **calculated**. However, in any question that requires you to interpret the financial statements of a company, you should **assess and select** the **most appropriate ratios** to use. Where necessary, you should also **be prepared to apply non-standard industry specific ratios** to support your interpretation.

Accounting ratio	Formula

Profitability and return

(a) Gross margin $\dfrac{\text{Gross profit}}{\text{Turnover}} \times 100$

(b) Net margin $\dfrac{\text{Profit on ordinary activities before interest and taxation (PBIT)}}{\text{Turnover}} \times 100$

(c) Return on capital employed (ROCE) $\dfrac{\text{Profit on ordinary activities before interest and taxation (PBIT)}}{\text{Capital employed}}$

where capital employed = total assets less current liabilities.

(d) Asset turnover $\dfrac{\text{Turnover}}{\text{Capital employed}}$

Long term solvency and stability

(a) Debt ratio $\dfrac{\text{Total debt}}{\text{Total assets}}$

(b) Capital gearing $\dfrac{\text{Prior charge capital}}{\text{Total capital}}$

(c) Debt/equity ratio $\dfrac{\text{Prior charge capital}}{\text{Ordinary share capital and reserves}}$

(d) Interest cover $\dfrac{\text{Profit before interest and tax (PBIT)}}{\text{Interest charges}}$

(e) Cash flow ratio $\dfrac{\text{Net cash inflow}}{\text{Total debts}}$

Short term solvency and liquidity

(a) Current ratio $\dfrac{\text{Current assets}}{\text{Current liabilities}}$

(b) Quick ratio $\dfrac{\text{Current assets less stocks}}{\text{Current liabilities}}$

(c) Creditors turnover $\dfrac{\text{Purchases}}{\text{Trade creditors}}$ or $\dfrac{\text{Trade creditors}}{\text{Purchases}} \times 365$

Efficiency

(d) Stock turnover $\dfrac{\text{Cost of sales}}{\text{Stock}}$ or $\dfrac{\text{Stock}}{\text{Cost of sales}} \times 365$

(e) Debtors turnover $\dfrac{\text{Credit sales}}{\text{Trade debtors}}$ or $\dfrac{\text{Trade debtors}}{\text{Credit sales}} \times 365$

Shareholders' investment ratios

(a) Dividend cover $\dfrac{\text{Earnings per share}}{\text{Net dividend per (ordinary) share}}$

(b) Price earnings (P/E) ratio $\dfrac{\text{Share price}}{\text{Earnings per share}}$

(c) Dividend yield $\dfrac{\text{Dividend on the share for the year}}{\text{Current market value of the share (ex div)}} \times 100$

1.14 EXAMPLE: CALCULATING RATIOS

The balance sheet and profit and loss account figures of Earwigo plc are provided to illustrate the calculation of ratios.

EARWIGO PLC PROFIT AND LOSS ACCOUNT
FOR THE YEAR ENDED 31 DECEMBER 20X8

	Notes	*20X8*	*20X7*
		£	£
Turnover	1	3,095,576	1,909,051
Operating profit	1	359,501	244,229
Interest	2	17,371	19,127
Profit on ordinary activities before taxation		342,130	225,102
Taxation on ordinary activities		74,200	31,272
Profit on ordinary activities after taxation		267,930	193,830
Dividend		41,000	16,800
Retained profit for the year		226,930	177,030
Earnings per share		12.8p	9.3p

EARWIGO PLC BALANCE SHEET
AS AT 31 DECEMBER 20X8

	Notes	*20X8*	*20X7*
		£	£
Fixed assets			
Tangible fixed assets		802,180	656,071
Current assets			
Stocks and work in progress		64,422	86,550
Debtors	3	1,002,701	853,441
Cash at bank and in hand		1,327	68,363
		1,068,450	1,008,354
Creditors: amounts falling due within one year	4	881,731	912,456
Net current assets		186,719	95,898
Total assets less current liabilities		988,899	751,969
Creditors: amounts falling due after more than one year			
10% first mortgage debenture stock 20Y4/20Y9		(100,000)	(100,000)
Provision for liabilities and charges			
Deferred taxation		(20,000)	(10,000)
		868,899	641,969
Capital and reserves			
Called up share capital	5	210,000	210,000
Share premium account		48,178	48,178
Profit and loss account		610,721	383,791
		868,899	641,969

NOTES TO THE ACCOUNTS

			20X8 £	20X7 £
1	*Turnover and profit*			
	(i)	Turnover	3,095,576	1,909,051
		Cost of sales	2,402,609	1,441,950
		Gross profit	692,967	467,101
		Administration expenses	333,466	222,872
		Operating profit	359,501	244,229
	(ii)	Operating profit is stated after charging:		
		Depreciation	151,107	120,147
		Auditors' remuneration	6,500	5,000
		Leasing charges	47,636	46,336
		Directors' emoluments	94,945	66,675
2	*Interest*			
		Payable on bank overdrafts and other loans	8,115	11,909
		Payable on debenture stock	10,000	10,000
			18,115	21,909
		Receivable on short-term deposits	744	2,782
		Net payable	17,371	19,127
3	*Debtors*			
		Amounts falling due within one year		
		Trade debtors	884,559	760,252
		Prepayments and accrued income	97,022	45,729
			981,581	805,981
		Amounts falling due after more than one year		
		Trade debtors	21,120	47,460
		Total debtors	1,002,701	853,441

		20X8 £	20X7 £
4	*Creditors: amounts falling due within one year*		
	Trade creditors	627,018	545,340
	Accruals and deferred income	81,279	280,464
	Corporation tax	108,000	37,200
	Other taxes and social security costs	44,434	32,652
	Dividend	21,000	16,800
		881,731	912,456
5	*Called up share capital*		
	Authorised ordinary shares of 10p each	1,000,000	1,000,000
	Issued and fully paid ordinary shares of 10p each	210,000	210,000

EARWIGO PLC

1.15 Review of year on year movements between 31 December 20X7 and 31 December 20X8

	Increase/(Decrease)
Turnover	62.2%
Operating profit	47.2%
Administration expenses	49.6%
Directors emoluments	42.4%
Net interest payable	(9.1%)
Profit on ordinary activities	52.0%
Taxation	137.3%
Profit on ordinary activities after tax	38.2%
PBIT	45.8%
Dividends	244.1%

1.16 Accounting ratios

Profitability and return	*20X8*	*20X7*
Gross margin	$\dfrac{692,967}{3,095,576} \times 100 = 22.4\%$	$\dfrac{467,101}{1,909,051} \times 100 = 24.5\%$
Net margin	$\dfrac{360,245}{3,095,576} \times 100 = 11.6\%$	$\dfrac{247,011}{1,909,051} \times 100 = 12.9\%$
ROCE	$\dfrac{360,245}{988,899} \times 100 = 36.4\%$	$\dfrac{247,011}{751,969} \times 100 = 32.8\%$
Asset turnover	$\dfrac{3,095,576}{988,899} = 3.1 \text{ times}$	$\dfrac{1.909,051}{751,969} = 2.5 \text{ times}$

Long term stability		
Debt ratio	$\dfrac{981,731}{1,870,630} \times 100 = 52.5\%$	$\dfrac{1,012,456}{1,664,425} \times 100 = 60.8\%$
Capital gearing	$\dfrac{100,000}{988,899} \times 100 = 10.1\%$	$\dfrac{100,000}{751,969} \times 100 = 13.3\%$

Long term solvency		
Debt/equity ratio	$\dfrac{100,000}{868,899} \times 100 = 11.5\%$	$\dfrac{100,000}{641,969} \times 100 = 15.6\%$
Interest cover	$\dfrac{360,245}{18,115} = 19.9 \text{ times}$	$\dfrac{247,011}{21,909} = 11.3 \text{ times}$
Cash flow ratio	$\dfrac{510,608}{981,731} \times 100 = 52.0\%$	$\dfrac{364,376}{1,012,456} \times 100 = 36.0\%$

Short term solvency/liquidity		
Current ratio	$\dfrac{1,068,450}{881,731} \times 100 = 121.2\%$	$\dfrac{1,008,354}{912,456} \times 100 = 110.5\%$
Quick ratio	$\dfrac{1,004,028}{881,731} \times 100 = 113.9\%$	$\dfrac{921,804}{912,456} \times 100 = 101.0\%$
Creditors turnover	$\dfrac{627,018}{2,402,609} \times 365 = 95.3 \text{ days}$	$\dfrac{545,340}{1,441,950} \times 365 = 138.0 \text{ days}$

Efficiency		
Stock turnover	$\dfrac{64,422}{2,402,609} \times 365 = 9.8 \text{ days}$	$\dfrac{86,550}{1,441,950} \times 365 = 21.9 \text{ days}$
Debtors turnover	$\dfrac{1,002,701}{3,095,576} \times 365 = 118.2 \text{ days}$	$\dfrac{853,441}{1,909,051} \times 365 = 163.2 \text{ days}$

Shareholder investment ratios		
Dividend cover	$\dfrac{267,930}{41,000} = 6.5 \text{ times}$	$\dfrac{193,830}{16,800} = 11.5 \text{ times}$

Workings

1   *Profit before interest and tax*

	20X8 £	20X7 £
Profit on ordinary activities before tax	342,130	225,102
Interest payable	18,115	21,909
PBIT	360,245	247,011

2   *Capital employed*

	20X8	20X7
Shareholders funds	868,899	641,969
Creditors: amounts falling due after more than one year	100,000	100,000
Long term provision for liabilities and charges	20,000	10,000
	988,899	751,969

3   *Total debts*

	20X8	20X7
Creditors: amounts falling due within one year	881,731	912,456
Creditors: amounts falling due after more than one year	100,000	100,000
	981,731	1,012,456

4   *Total assets*

	20X8	20X7
Tangible fixed assets	802,180	656,071
Current assets	1,068,450	1,008,354
	1,870,630	1,664,425

5   *Net cash inflow*

	20X8	20X7
Operating profit	359,501	244,229
Depreciation	151,107	120,147
Increase in stocks	★ -	-
Increase in debtors	★ -	-
Increase in creditors	★ -	-
	510,608	364,376

★ Ignored for this purpose, because figures for 20X7 cannot be calculated as 20X6 accounts are not available.

6   *Quick assets*

	20X8	20X7
Current assets	1,068,450	1,008,354
Less Stock and works-in-progress	(64,422)	(86,550)
	1,004,028	921,804

2   PROFITABILITY AND RETURN ON CAPITAL

Gross margin

2.1   Earwigo's plc has increased its turnover significantly from 20X7 to 20X8 by 62.2%. Over this period, the gross margin has fallen from 24.5% to 22.4%.

2.2   Intuitively, there is a relationship between the level of sales and the gross margin. However, it is important to also consider the potential and **independent causes of fluctuations** in both sales levels and gross margins.

Sales levels	Gross profit margin
• Level of marketing effort and expenditure	• Pricing policy, discounts etc
• Product design and quality	• Sales mix
• Relocation of distribution outlets	• Production efficiency
• Service skills training	• Impact of inflation on costs
• Changes in consumer taste or product usage	• Control of waste and spillage
• General economic factors	• Sourcing of supplies, discounts etc
• Impact of legislation	• Stock valuation issues (obsolescence, overhead absorption, NRV etc)
• Competition	

2.3 Generally, the gross margin is an indicator of trading performance. Remember that **achievable margins** will **differ between industries**. In practice, you are likely to try to obtain additional information, such as **relevant industry benchmarking data**.

Net margin

2.4 Earwigo's net margin has fallen from 12.9% in 20X7 to 11.6% in 20X8. PBIT has increased from 20X7 to 20X8 by 45.8%. This is in line with the increase in operating profit for the year by 47.2%. Other items moving along similar lines are administration expenses and directors remuneration with increases of 49.6% and 42.4%, respectively.

2.5 **Net margin** is **not considered** to be **very meaningful** because of its **susceptibility** to **many factors**. In practice, it is difficult to carry out meaningful comparisons of net margins between companies. For example, one company may have purchased its buildings whereas another company prefer to rent its premises.

2.6 Trends in the net margin might provide pointers to the effectiveness of controls over the level of overheads. However, this would seem to be a **blunt tool** because there are **more direct ways** of **financially controlling overheads** for example by monitoring specific overhead accounts.

2.7 In practice, net profit is **more usefully compared** to factors such as **number of employees** or **square footage**.

ROCE

2.8 Earwigo's ROCE has improved from 32.8% in 20X7 to 36.4% in 20X8.

2.9 To assess the acceptability of these ratios **further information** is necessary.

(a) **Benchmark** against the ROCEs of other companies in the **same industry.**

(b) **Cost of servicing finance**. The level of return should be assessed against the returns available from **alternative investments** and should also reflect the level of **business risk** involved.

(c) **Target ROCE**. A comparison with **budgeted ROCE** may reveal whether management is **achieving expected returns**.

2.10 ROCE is probably the **key profitability ratio** in **measuring business performance**. It measures the **return generated** for investors against the **amount invested**. Because of its importance, ROCE is often referred to as the **primary ratio**.

2.11 There are certain **factors** which may **obscure** the **assessment** of ROCE.

(a) **Undervalued fixed assets**, such as property, may depress the capital employed figure and show a **rosier ROCE**.

(b) **Capitalised interest**, will increase capital employee and give a **more conservative ROCE**.

(c) **Aging fixed assets** mean lower capital employed and hence higher ROCE. However, this may indicate a variety of potential operational problems.

 • Impending obsolescence/impairment
 • Inefficiency owing to breakdowns
 • Higher maintenance costs
 • Probable labour intensive operation
 • Competitive inefficiency

Review current carrying values and accumulated depreciation levels for clues of age of fixed assets. Learn to glean meaningful insights about the business from looking at the fixed assets note to the accounts.

(d) **Capitalised development costs**. Like capitalised interest above, will **depress ROCE**. Nevertheless the costs will hit reported profits, but only over a number of years, by way of depreciation or impairment.

(e) **Idle cash balances**. There is a school of thought that advocates these should be removed from capital employed. However, this is likely to give a **misleadingly better** ROCE. The ratio should effectively **measure all aspects of capital employed**.

Asset turnover

2.12 Earwigo plc has improved on its asset utilisation. This went up from 2.5 times in 20X7 to 3.1 times in 20X8.

2.13 Again, it is important to asses this ratio against available industry averages. **Manufacturing industries** are likely to be **capital intensive** and therefore have **low asset turnover**. On the other hand, **service industries** tend to be **human resource intensive** and hence likely to have relatively **high asset turnover**.

2.14 It might be tempting to think that a high profit margin is good, and a low asset turnover means sluggish trading. In broad terms, this is so. But **there is a trade-off between profit margin and asset turnover, and you cannot look at one without allowing for the other.**

(a) A high profit margin means a high profit per £1 of sales, but if this also means that sales prices are high, there is a strong possibility that sales turnover will be depressed, and so asset turnover lower.

(b) A high asset turnover means that the company is generating a lot of sales, but to do this it might have to keep its prices down and so accept a low profit margin per £1 of sales.

2.15 Remember that companies may well arrive at the same ROCE via different routes.

	Company A	Company B
Profit margin	20%	5%
Asset turnover	× 1	× 4
ROCE	20%	20%

3 LONG TERM SOLVENCE AND STABILITY

Debt ratio

3.1 Earwigo's debt ratio has shown an improvement from being 60.8% at the end 20X7 to being 52.5% at the end of 20X8.

3.2 There is no absolute guide to the maximum safe debt ratio, but as a **very general guide**, 50% is commonly regarded as a safe limit. In practice, many companies operate successfully with a higher debt ratio than this, but 50% is nonetheless a **helpful benchmark**. In addition, if the debt ratio is over 50% and getting worse, the company's debt position will be worth looking at more carefully.

3.3 In Earwigo's case, the debt ratio is quite high, mainly because of the large amount of current liabilities. However, the debt ratio has fallen from 60.8% to 52.5% between 20X7 and 20X8, and so the company appears to be improving its debt position.

Capital gearing

3.4 Earwigo plc's capital gearing ratio has fallen from 13.3% for 20X7 to 10.1% for 20X8.

3.5 Gearing **measures** the **relationship** between the **prior charge capital** of a company **and** its **total capital**. It is an indicator of the extent to which a company is reliant on prior charge capital as compared to equity capital.

Preference share capital is normally considered to be **prior charge capital**. Preference dividends must be paid out of profits before ordinary shareholders are entitled to an ordinary dividend. **Debentures** would usually **also** be classified as **prior change capital**.

3.6 **Total capital is ordinary share capital and reserves plus charge capital plus any long-term liabilities or provisions**. In **group accounts** we would also include **minority interests**. Do note that it is easier to identify the same figure for total capital as **total assets less current liabilities**, which you will find given to you in the balance sheet.

3.7 The level of gearing maintained by a company is likely to be part of its **corporate** and **financial strategy**. As with the debt ratio, there is **no absolute limit** to what a gearing ratio ought to be. A company with a gearing ratio of more than 50% is said to be high-geared, whereas low gearing means a gearing ratio of less than 50%.

3.8 In practice, **many companies** are **highly geared**. However, there are **risks** and **potential problems** associated with **high gearing**.

- **Prior changes** can **consume available profits**, leaving **little earnings for equity shareholders**.

- If **earnings** are **volatile**, this will have a consequential **impact** on the company **share price** (**given** a certain **price/earnings ratio**).

- As the company's **borrowing capacity decreases**, lenders will perceive a **greater risk** and hence the company's **marginal cost** of **borrowing** is **likely to rise**.

- If a **loss situation** prevails, the **financial viability** of the company may become **seriously challenged**.

3.9 Here is a little diagram that might help to reinforce your understanding of the implications of different financial structures.

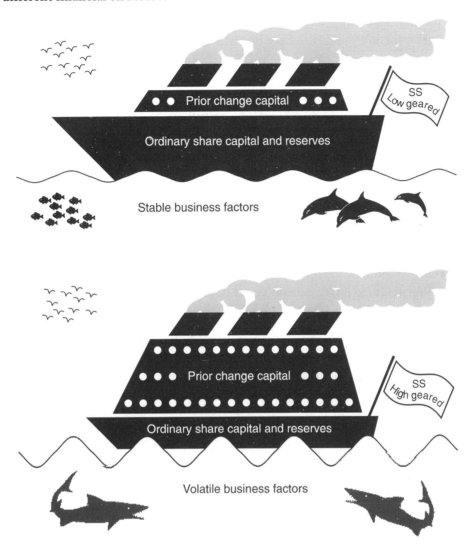

3.10 The two above scenarios can be seen within the context of four theoretical scenarios depicted in the two by two matrix below. This provides another tool which you might find useful in looking at a business.

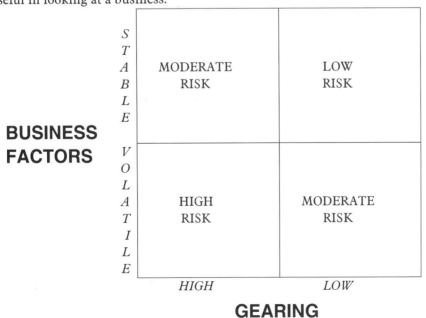

- A business operating with a **highly geared financial structure** and **volatile business factors** is likely to face **high business risk.**

- A business operating with a **lowly geared financial structure** and **stable business factors** structure is likely to have **low business risks**.

- **Moderate business risk** would probably be relevant to businesses with combinations of either:
  - stable business factors and **high gearing**.
  - volatile business factors and **low gearing**.

3.11 **Low geared companies** obviously have **more capacity** to **borrow money**. However increases in prior charge capital will in turn compromise the gearing situation!

3.12 In practice, the **gearing structure** of a company will be influenced by **company policy** as well **nature of the business**. A highly geared structure is likely to rest on three business factors.

- **Stability** of **profits**
- **Suitable assets** to provide **security**
- **Attitude** of **lenders**

3.13 Examples of types of companies likely to satisfy these criteria include property investment companies, hotels and supermarket chains. In general terms, companies in high technology industries are less likely to meet the criteria for sustaining a highly geared structure.

Debt/equity ratio

3.14 Earwigo's debt/equity ratio has improved from 15.6% in 20X7 to 11.5% in 20X8.

This radio provides similar information as the gearing ratio, and here a ratio of 100% or more would indicate high gearing.

Interest cover

3.15 Earwigo's interest cover has improved significantly from 11.3 times in 20X7 to 19.9 times in 20X8.

3.16 Interest cover is an indicator of whether a company is **earning enough profits before interest and tax to pay its interest costs comfortably,** or whether its interest costs are high in relation to the size of its profits, so that a fall in PBIT would then have a **significant effect on profits available for ordinary shareholders.**

3.17 Generally, an interest cover of 2 times or less would be low, and should really exceed 3 times before the company's interest costs are to be considered within acceptable limits.

3.18 Remember that although preference share capital is included as prior charge capital for the gearing ratio, **it is usual to exclude preference dividends from 'interest' charges.** We also look at all interest payments, even interest charges on short-term debt, and so interest cover and gearing do not quite look at the same thing. Interest payments should be taken gross from the **notes to the accounts** and not net of interest receipts as shown on the face of the profit and loss account.

3.19 **Low interest** cover suggests:

(a) Shareholders **dividends may be at risk,** because most profits are required to meet interest charges

(b) **Interest charges themselves** could be at **risk** if **profits decline further**.

3.20 Earwigo plc has more than sufficient interest cover. In view of the company's low gearing, this is not too surprising and so we finally obtain a picture of Earwigo plc as a company that does not seem to have a debt problem, in spite of its high (although declining) debt ratio.

Cash flow ratio

3.21 Earwigo's cash flow ratio has improved from 35.0% in 20X7 to 52.0% in 20X8.

3.22 The cash flow ratio is **the ratio of a company's net cash inflow to its total debts**.

(a) Net cash inflow is the amount of cash which the company has coming into the business from its operations. A suitable figure for net cash inflow can be obtained from the cash flow statement or profit and loss account, with depreciation being added back.

(b) Total debts are short-term and long-term creditors, together with provisions for liabilities and charges. A distinction can be made between debts payable within one year and other debts and provisions.

3.23 Obviously, a company needs to be earning enough cash from operations to be able to meet its foreseeable debts and future commitments, and the cash flow ratio, and changes in the cash flow ratio from one year to the next, provide a useful indicator of a company's cash position.

4 SHORT TERM SOLVENCY/LIQUIDITY

Current ratio

4.1 Earwigo's current ratio has improved from 1.1:1 in 20X7 to 1.2:1 in 20X8.

4.2 The current ratio is the **perennial 'standard' test of liquidity**. It can be obtained from the balance sheet.

4.3 Various books quote a range of acceptable current ratios from 1.0 to 2.0. Obviously 1.0 is a **baseline level** which ensures that the company has sufficient current assets to cover its current liabilities.

4.4 Current ratios are likely to **vary between industries** and may even **vary from company to company** within the same industry.

4.5 In practice, various factors might influence the level of the current rates.

(a) **Seasonal factors**. Many companies have year ends after their busy period to minimise stock counting. The timing of the year end may well impact on the level of a company's current ratio.

Example

Santa Specials Limited is a company which specialises in buying and selling a special brand of Xmas Trees made out of genuine high grade Norwegian plastic.

The trees cost £10 each and are sold for £14 each. Details of its current assets and current liabilities per its monthly management accounts are as follows.

The company stocks up with trees in November. In December it sells the trees and in January it pays off the majority of its suppliers.

	31.11.X6	31.12.X7	31.1.X8
	£'000	£'000	£'000
Current assets			
Stock	100	-	-
Cash	50	190	91
	150	190	91
Current liabilities			
Trade creditors	100	100	1
Current ratio	1.5:1	1.9:1	91:1

This example illustrates how the **positioning of a company's year end** might **influence** the **level of its current ratio**. You could explore for yourself how the current ratio would change if the company were to pay a dividend in February!

The example also demonstrates the **potential for window dressing** by **processing creditors payments** though the accounting system but **not actually mailing the cheque**!

(b) **Timing of payment of long term liabilities**. This is an extension of the principle demonstrated in the Santa Specials example above. For example, consider the impact on the current ratio, if in March the company had to pay a long term liability.

The message here is that you need to **develop a good understanding** of the **business** and the **relevant industry** to help you make high quality comments in your examination.

Quick ratio

4.6 Earwigo's quick ratio has improved from 101.0% in 20X7 to 113.9% in 20X8.

4.7 Otherwise known as the acid test ratio, this indicator **focuses** on only those **current assets** that are **available** to **pay current liabilities when they fall due**.

4.8 Again a quick ratio of 1.0 is desirable but in practice companies might operate effectively at a lower level, depending on the particular business and industry.

4.9 Remembering the **holistic kit approach** suggested earlier. In practice, management is likely to use **cash flow projections** to enable a **proactive approach** to the **management** of its **liquidity**.

4.10 The quick ratio is as susceptible to window dressing as the current ratio, as described above.

Creditor's payment period

4.11 In 20X7, Earwigo took 138.0 days to settle its creditors, but this has accelerated to 95.3 days in 20X8.

4.12 This ratio measure the **average number of days taken to pay creditors**. Published financial statements are unlikely to disclose purchases so you may have to resort the using cost of sales in your calculation.

4.13 Factors to be considered in setting a supplier payment policy may pull in opposite directions.

(a) Delaying payments to creditors represents a source of interest free finance (However, an obvious question is whether suppliers will build this into their prices!)

(b) Slow payments may give an impression, rightly or wrongly, of liquidity problems. Any potential adverse impacts on the company's credit rating should be considered.

4.14 Public companies and members of groups where the parent is a public company, and the company does not qualify as a small or medium sized company under CA 1985, Section 247, must disclose 'creditor days' in respect of amounts due at the year end. This may influence a company's behaviour in relation to how quickly it pays its suppliers.

4.15 In addition, public sector bodies such as local authorities are likely to have publicly responsible credit payment targets. Of course, there may be private sector companies that have ethically driven policies for paying their suppliers quickly. It might be worth considering the converse impact on companies that have debtors who like to pay their creditors quickly.

4.16 In **certain circumstances,** businesses may be required by their **bankers** to **demonstrate their ability to clear their overdraft** on **specific dates** during the year. This will impact on the creditors payment period as well as the current ratio and quick ratio.

4.17 Again, the **creditors payment** period is **susceptible** to being **massaged** by **management.**

5 EFFICIENCY

Stock turnover

5.1 Earwigo has significantly refined its stock turnover rate from once every 21.9 days in 20X7 to once every 9.8 days in 20X8.

5.2 Stock turnover is an indicator of the **average number** of **days** a business takes to **sell an item of stock.** This can be calculated using the **figures** contained in **published accounts.**

5.3 Generally, there is **no universally acceptable level** at which stock should be turned over. A high stock turnover is considered to be better than a low turnover figure. However, in practice several aspects of **stock management policy** have to be balanced in setting a **target stock turnover** for the year.

- Lead times
- Seasonal fluctuations in orders
- Alternative uses of warehouse space
- Bulk buying discounts
- Likelihood of stock perishing or becoming obsolete.
- Minimising of stock holding costs

5.4 The **nature of the product traded** will impact on the stock turnover rate. For example, a **fruit and vegetable shop** is likely turnover its stock more frequently than say a **furniture retailer.**

5.5 A lengthening stock turnover period from one period to the next could indicate a slowdown in trading or build up in stock levels. **Consolidation should be given to both business trading factors as well as stock management issues,** when seeking explanations for movements in stock turnover from one period to the next.

5.6 Also remember that:

(a) Excessively long stock turnover periods tend to increase the **risk of obsolesce**

(b) The computed turnover rate can be affected by the **timing of orders received or dispatched,** especially where these involve relatively **high values.**

5.7   **In practice**, many companies now use a '**just in time**' approach to stock control. This method seeks to **minimise stock holding costs**. Again, its suitability to a company will depend on the nature of the business included such as **alternative sources** and **level of customer loyalty**.

Debtor's turnover

5.8   Earwigo plc took an average of 118.2 days to collect its debtors in 20X8 as compared to 163.2 days in 20X7.

5.9   Debtors turnover is a **rough measure** of the **average length of time for a company's debtors to pay** what they owe the company.

5.10   The figure for sales should be taken as the turnover figure in the P & L account. The trade debtors are not the total figure for debtors in the balance sheet, which includes prepayments and non-trade debtors. The trade debtors figure will be itemised in an analysis of the debtors total, in a note to the accounts.

5.11   The estimate of debtor days is **only approximate**.

(a)   The balance sheet value of debtors might be abnormally high or low compared with the 'normal' level the company usually has.

(b)   Turnover in the P & L account is exclusive of VAT, but debtors in the balance sheet are inclusive of VAT. We are not strictly comparing like with like. (Some companies show turnover inclusive of VAT as well as turnover exclusive of VAT, and the 'inclusive' figure should therefore be used in these cases.)

5.12   Sales are usually made on 'normal credit terms' of payment within 30 days. Debtor days significantly in excess of this might be representative of poor management of funds of a business. However, some companies must allow generous credit terms to win customers. Exporting companies in particular may have to carry large amounts of debtors, and so their average collection period might be well in excess of 30 days.

5.13   The **trend of the collection period (debtor days) over time is probably the best guide.** If debtor days are increasing year on year, this is indicative of a poorly managed credit control function (and potentially therefore a poorly managed company).

5.14   Stock turnover added to debtors turnover indicates how soon stock is converted into cash.

5.15   This is an area where an understanding of the business is important. For example, if you are analysing debtors turnover for a hotel you need to understand and the type of hotel it operates and hence the composition of its sales and debtors mix.

(a)   Accommodation – non corporate guests paying cash for short stays.
(b)   Accommodation – corporate guests staying on credit terms
(c)   Catering – non-corporate guests paying each
(d)   Catering – corporate guests with debtors accounts
(e)   Conference facilities – corporate usage on debtors accounts.

5.16   It may be important to be able to **disaggregate the sale and debtors figures** to enable **meaningful debtors turnover figures** to be calculated. If your calculation can only be done on combined cash and credit sales figures, you should comment accordingly on its limitations and also suggest, in a positive way, what additional information might be useful.

5.17 Be careful over **cash oriented businesses** such as supermarket chains where any **debtors turnover** figure you might be able to calculate **is not likely to be very meaningful**.

5.18 Again when attempting to explain movements in debtors turnover rates between one year to the next, be aware of both **business trading factors** as well as **credit control factors**.

Business trading factors	Credit control factors
• Trying to attract more custom by allowing easier payment terms	• Efficiency of credit control department
• Selling to higher collection risk debtors	• Change in credit terms
• Debtors themselves experiencing financial problems eg because of recession	• Changes in policies on legal action to recover debts
• Acquisition/loss of customers with quick settlement policies eg public sector organisations	• Level of balances already written off.
• General change in customer base	
• Debt factoring	

The cash cycle

5.19 The cash cycle describes the flow of **cash out** of a business and **back into it again** as a result of **normal trading operations**.

5.20 Cash goes out to pay for supplies, wages and salaries and other expenses, although payments can be delayed by taking some credit. A business might hold stock for a while and then sell it. Cash will come back into the business from the sales, although customers might delay payment by themselves taking some credit.

5.21 The main points about the cash cycle are as follows.

(a) The timing of cash flows in and out of a business does not coincide with the time when sales and costs of sales occur. **Cash flows out can be postponed by taking credit. Cash flows in can be delayed by having debtors.**

(b) The **time between making a purchase and making a sale also affects cash flows**. If stocks are held for a long time, the delay between the cash payment for stocks and cash receipts from selling them will also be a long one.

(c) **Holding stocks and having debtors** can therefore be seen as **two reasons why cash receipts are delayed**. Another way of saying this is that if a company invests in working capital, its cash position will show a corresponding decrease.

(d) Similarly, **taking credit** from creditors can be seen as a reason why **cash payments are delayed**. The company's liquidity position will worsen when it has to pay the creditors, unless it can get more cash in from sales and debtors in the meantime.

5.22 The liquidity ratios and working capital turnover ratios are used to test a company's liquidity, length of cash cycle, and investment in working capital.

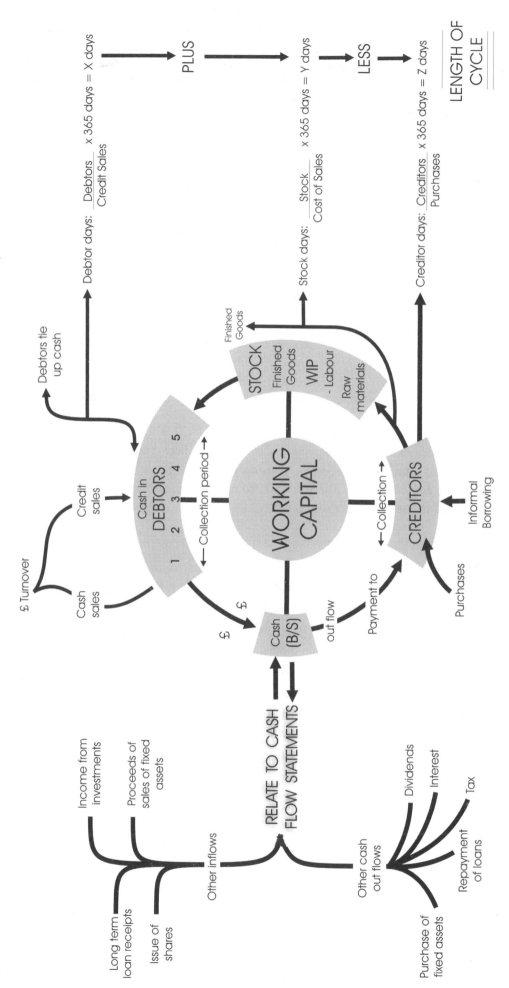

6 SHAREHOLDERS' INVESTMENT RATIOS

6.1 These are the ratios which **help equity shareholders and other investors to assess the value and quality of an investment in the ordinary shares of a company.** The value of an investment in ordinary shares in a listed company is its **market value,** and so investment ratios must have regard not only to information in the company's published accounts, but also to the current price, and **some of these ratios involve using the share price.**

6.2 Earnings per share is a valuable indicator of an ordinary share's performance and is the subject of FRS 14. This was dealt with in Chapter 9.

Dividend cover

6.3 Earwigo's dividend cover has fallen from 11.5 times in 20X7 to 6.5 times in 20X8. This is because the dividend paid has gone up by 244.1% over this period when the net profit after tax has only increased by 38.2%.

6.4 Divided cover is an indicator of how secure shareholders can expect to be in terms of their dividend being paid. It measures the number of times the current dividend could have been paid from available current earnings.

P/E ratio

6.5 A high P/E ratio indicates **strong shareholder confidence** in the company and its future, eg in profit growth, and a lower P/E ratio indicates lower confidence.

6.6 The P/E ratio of one company can be **compared** with the P/E ratios of:

(a) Other **companies** in the **same business sector.**
(b) Other **companies generally.**

The P/E ratio is a generally used stock market ratio.

Dividend yield

6.7 Dividend yield is **the return a shareholder is currently expecting on the shares of a company.**

6.8 **Shareholders look for both dividend yield and capital growth. Obviously, dividend yield is therefore an important aspect of a share's performance.**

Question 3

In the year to 30 September 20X8, Wat-u-like plc declared an interim ordinary dividend of 7.4p per share and a final ordinary dividend of 8.6p per share. Assuming an ex div share price of 315 pence, what is the dividend yield?

Answer

The dividend per share is (7.4 + 8.6) = 16 pence

Dividend yield is $\dfrac{16}{315} \times 100 = 5.1\%$

Earnings yield

6.9 Earnings yield is **a performance indicator** that is not given the same publicity as EPS, P/E ratio, dividend cover and dividend yield. It is **measured as earnings per share, grossed up, as a percentage of the current share price**. It therefore, indicates what the dividend yield could be if:

(a) The company paid out all its profits as dividend and retained nothing in the business.

(b) There were no extraordinary items in the P & L account.

6.10 Some companies retain a bigger proportion of their profits than others, and so the dividend yield between companies can vary for this reason. **Earnings yield overcomes the problem of comparison by assuming that all earnings are paid out as dividends.** *Note.* The earnings yield is equal to the dividend yield multiplied by the dividend cover.

7 ACCOUNTING POLICIES AND THE LIMITATIONS OF RATIO ANALYSIS

7.1 We discussed the disclosure of accounting policies in our examination of FRS 18. The choice of accounting policy and the effect of its implementation are almost as important as its disclosure. This is because the results of a company can be altered significantly by the choice of accounting policy.

The impact of choice of accounting policies

7.2 Where accounting standards allow alternative treatment of items in the accounts, then the accounting policy note should declare which policy has been chosen. It should then be applied consistently.

7.3 The problem of comparability arises where companies with similar business adopt different policies. In recent years, financial reporting standard have restricted the selection of accounting treatments. However, there are a few areas where preparers are allowed significant choice.

Development expenditure

7.4 Although the criteria for capitalising development expenditure are very strict, the **choice** of whether to **capitalise and amortise or write off such costs** can have a significant impact on profit.

7.5 The **capitalisation** of development costs has **various impacts** on the figures used for analysing accounts.

(a) The capitalised development cost will be **amortised annually** and will **hit earnings**, including EPS, **until fully written off**.

(b) The capitalised development costs are included as part of **capital employed** and hence **ROCE will fall**.

(c) The **gearing ratio** will be **reduced** whilst any of the **capitalised development costs** are still **carried in the balance sheet**.

Capitalisation of finance costs

7.6 FRS 15 allows the capitalisation of finance costs that are **directly attributable** to the **construction** of tangible fixed assets. An entity **need not capitalise** finance costs. However, if an entity adopts a **policy of capitalisation** of finance costs, then it should be **applied consistently** to all tangible fixed assets where finance cost fall to be capitalised.

7.7 The impacts of capitalising finance costs in relation to tangible fixed assets on the calculation of accounting ratios is **similar** to those outlined above for **capitalised development costs**.

7.8 Remember that capitalisation of interest does not impact on interest cover because an appropriate adjustment must be made to include capitalised interest in the interest cover calculation.

Leases and the ninety per cent test

7.9 Companies might use the 90% test in such a way that ensures that leases are classified as **operating leases** and thereby kept **off the balance sheet**. This would entail **various impacts** on the accounting ratios.

   (a) The **profit and loss account** would show a **lease charge instead of finance charges and depreciation**.

   (b) The **balance sheet** would **not reflect the asset nor the corresponding liability**. **Capital employed** and **ROCE** would remain **roughly the same**.

   (c) **Long term debt** will be **less** under an **operating lease scenario** with little impact on equity interests. Hence, the **gearing ratio** is **likely** to **fall significantly**.

Tangible fixed asset revaluation

7.10 Revaluation of fixed affects various figures shown in the accounts.

   (a) The total amount of **depreciation written off** through the profit and loss account over the life of the asset **will increase. Reported profits** will therefore be **lower**.

   (b) **Distributable profits** are however **not affected**. A **portion of revaluation reserves** may be **transferred to profit and loss reserves** as they become realised as result of additional depreciation of disposal.

   (c) **Shareholder** funds, **capital employed** and **total net assets** will **increase**.

   (d) **Debt** will be **unaffected**.

7.11 These changes in accounts balances will have consequential impacts on accounting ratios.

   - The **gearing ratio** will **decrease**
   - **ROCE** will **fall**
   - **EPS** will also **fall**.

Areas of judgment and estimation

7.12 The accounting standards specify detailed requirements in many areas of accounting and financial reporting. However, there still remains **significant scope** for the area of **professional judgement** in preparing accounts.

Accounts area	Scope for professional judgement on:
Tangible fixed assets	Depreciation rates and methods
Stocks	Overhead cost inclusion
	Net realisable value estimate
Long-term contracts	Turnover and profit recognition
	Decision to treat as long-term contract
General provisions	Existence of obligation
	Likelihood of transfer of economic benefit
	Measurement of liability

Limitations of ratio analysis

7.13 The consideration of how accounting policies may be used to massage company results leads us to some of the other limitations of ratio analysis. These can be summarised as follows.

(a) **Availability of comparable information.**

(b) **Use of historical/out of date information.**

(c) **Ratios are not definitive - they are only a guide.**

(d) **Interpretation needs careful analysis and should not be considered in isolation.**

(e) **It is a subjective exercise.**

(f) **It can be subject to manipulation and window dressing.**

(g) **Ratios are not defined in standard form.**

(h) **They are a type of tool in a more holistic approach (see section 1.11)**

Exam focus point

In the exam, always bear these points in mind; you may even be asked to discuss such limitations, but in any case they should have an impact on your analysis of a set of results.

Question 1

The following are a selection of accounting ratios for a range of UK listed public companies in various industries ie

- Furniture
- Recruitment and business services
- Supermarket
- Cruise liner holidays
- Bakery shops

Review the table provided, then have a go at trying to identify which ratios relate to which industry. Write your response into the space provided at the foot of the table.

Standard ratios	Company A	Company B	Company C	Company D	Company E
Gross margin	8.0%	61.3%	49.6%	24.0%	-
ROCE	17.4%	26.3%	11.6%	10.1%	29.2%
Asset turnover	2.9 times	3.4 times	2.5 times	0.7 times	2.7 times
Current ratio	0.8:1	0.7:1	1.4:1	0.7:1	1.1:1
Stock turnover	20.4 days	15.7 days	102.2 days	12.0 days	N/A
Debtors turnover	1.1 days	0.5 days	15.0 days	5.8 days	56.2 days
Creditors turnover	40.0 days	54.7 days	53.7 days	30.2 days	-
Non-standard ratio					
Staff costs per employee	£17,566	£9,211	£22,279	£9,672	£24,646
Report date	1999	2000	2001	2000	2001
Industry involved					

Answer

Company	Industry
A	Supermarket chain
B	Bakery shop chain
C	Furniture retailer
D	Cruise holiday operator
E	Recruitment and business services

Operating and Financial Review (OFR)

7.14 The ASB document *Operating and Financial Review* is mentioned in the examinable documents for Paper 2.5. It introduces a statement which is **voluntary rather than mandatory**. It applies mainly to listed companies, but also those large corporations where there is a legitimate public interest. Such companies would be called on to produce an Operating and Financial Review (OFR) in their financial statements.

7.15 The purpose of the OFR is to provide:

'a framework for the directors to discuss and analyse the business's performance and the factors underlying its results and financial position, in order to assist users to assess for themselves the future potential of the business.'

7.16 The OFR should be developed in format and content to suit each organisation, but there would be some **essential features** of an OFR. It should:

(a) **Be written in a clear style and as succinctly as possible,** to be readily understandable by the general reader of annual reports, and should include only matters that are likely to be significant to investors.

(b) **Be balanced and objective,** dealing even-handedly with both good and bad aspects.

(c) **Refer to comments** made **in previous statements** where these have **not** been **borne out by events.**

(d) **Contain analytical discussion** rather than merely numerical analysis.

(e) **Follow a 'top-down' structure,** discussing individual aspects of the business in the context of a discussion of the business as a whole.

(f) Explain the reason for, and effect of any **changes in accounting policies.**

(g) **Make it clear how any ratios or other numerical information given relate to the financial statements.**

BPP PUBLISHING

(h) **Include discussion of:**

 (i) **Trends and factors** underlying the business that have affected the results but are not expected to continue in the future.

 (ii) **Known events, trends and uncertainties** that are expected to have an impact on the business in the future.

7.17 The OFR is in two sections.

(a) **Operating review**

 (i)   Operating results for the period
 (ii)   Dynamics of the business
 (iii) Investments for the future
 (iv) Profit for the year, recognised gains/losses etc
 (v)   Dividends, EPS
 (vi) Accounting policies

(b) **Financial review**

 (i)   Capital structure and treasury policy
 (ii)   Funds
 (iii) Current liquidity
 (iv) Going concern
 (v)   Balance sheet values

7.18 A statement of compliance with the OFR statement is not required, although it might be helpful to the users of the accounts. You can see that the OFR should be of great benefit to less sophisticated users of accounts as it should carry out the analysis of a company's performance on the user's behalf. It should thus highlight the important items in the current year annual report, as well as drawing out 'those aspects of the year under review that are relevant to an assessment of future prospects'.

8 REPORTS ON FINANCIAL PERFORMANCE

8.1 You may have experience already in writing reports within your organisation. Accountants are called upon to write reports for many different purposes. These range from very formal reports, such as those addressed to the board of directors or the audit committee, to one-off reports of a more informal nature.

8.2 The following chart is provided as an aid memoire to help you tackle accounts analysis questions in exams. You, of course, **may have an equally valid approach**, based on your **own practical experience**.

Identify:

- The purpose of your analysis and interpretation.
- The audience to which your comments are to be addressed.

↓

Review the accounts to develop an overall familiarity with the nature of the company, the industry in which it operates, company size, key account balances, significant changes between years etc.

↓

Do a quick brainstorm of the general business issues behind the accounts; market conditions, policies, consumer behaviour, management skills, competition, stability, volatility, risks, etc.

↓

Identify any additional information you might, in practice, have looked at. Recognised any limitations of your ratio analysis (in a positive way in an exam).

↓

Select and calculate an appropriate set of ratios, including any helpful non-standard or industry specific ratios.

↓

Perform comparisons and suggest explanation. Remember the importance of keeping comments constructive.

↓

Ensure your answer or report is relevant and helpful to the needs of the users.

Checklist for report writing

8.3 The following checklist for report writing is provided to help you identify factors that should be considered.

(a) **Purpose or terms of reference**

   (i) Who are the **users** of the report and what are their **interests**?

   (ii) What is the **purpose** of the report? What type of **focus** should it have?

   (iii) What is wanted, **definite recommendations or less specific advice**?

   (iv) What **outcomes** might the report have if its findings or **recommendations** are **implemented**?

   (v) What **previous reviews or reports** have there been on the subject, what did they find or recommend, and what action was taken on these findings, or recommendations?

(b) **Information in the report**

   (i) What is the **source** of each item of information in the report?

   (ii) What is the **age** of the information? Is it **up-to-date**?

   (iii) What **period** does the report **cover** - a month, a year?

   (iv) How can the **accuracy** of the information be checked and **verified**? To what extent might it be subject to error?

   (v) What **other information** might be useful.

(c) **Preparing the report**

   (i) Decide on **structure** of report; headings, sub headings, summary, appendices and other aspects.

BPP
PUBLISHING

      (ii)   Decide on balance between **analysis** and **solution orientation**.

      (iii)   Consider **style** and **tone**.

      (iv)   For exam purposes, use an **easy** to follow **numbering system**.

      (v)   Be aware of putting content over in bite-size (**mark oriented**) chunks!

      (vi)   Beware of tact and diplomacy. Be **constructive**, not **critical**.

  (d) **User-friendliness of the report**

      (i)   What **use** will the report be in its present form? What **action** is it intended to **trigger**?

      (ii)   Does the report meet the requirements of the **terms of reference**?

      (iii)   Will the users who asked for the report be **delighted**?

Format of reports in the examination

Exam focus point

In an examination your time is limited and you are under pressure. To make life a little easier, we suggest that you adopt the following format for any report you are requested to write.

Remember that report writing involves skill – you need to practice it till you can write clearly, positively and quickly under exam conditions.

REPORT (OR MEMORANDUM)

To: Board of Directors (or Chief Accountant, etc)

From: Financial Controller   **Date:**

Subject: Report format

                                Body of report

Signed: Accountant

8.4   If you adopt this style in your practice questions, you should end up producing it automatically. This should ensure that you **do not lose any presentation marks**. Remember if the **question asks specifically for a report**, your **answer must look like a report**.

8.5   Now you have considered the knowledge and skills you will need to produce a report for the examiner. You might like to have a go at doing the following question.

Question 2

The following information has been extracted from the recently published accounts of Seymour Marx plc.

SEYMOUR MARX PLC
EXTRACTS FROM THE PROFIT AND LOSS ACCOUNT

	20X9 £'000	20X8 £'000
Sales	11,200	9,750
Cost of sales	8,460	6,825
Net profit before tax	465	320
This is after charging:		
Depreciation	360	280
Debenture interest	80	60
Interest on bank overdraft	15	9
Audit fees	12	10

SEYMOUR MARX PLC
BALANCE SHEET AS AT 30 APRIL

	20X9 £'000	20X8 £'000
Fixed assets	1,850	1,430
Current assets		
Stock	640	490
Debtors	1,230	1,080
Cash	80	120
	1,950	1,690
Current liabilities		
Bank overdraft	110	80
Creditors	750	690
Taxation	30	20
Dividends	65	55
	955	845
Total assets less current liabilities	2,845	2,275
Long-term capital and reserves		
Ordinary share capital	800	800
Reserves	1,245	875
	2,045	1,675
10% debentures	800	600
	2,845	2,275

The following ratios are those calculated for Seymour Marx plc, based on its published accounts for the previous year, and also the latest industry average ratios:

	Seymour Marx plc 30 April 20X8	Industry average
ROCE (capital employed = equity and debentures)	16.70%	18.50%
Profit/sales	3.90%	4.73%
Asset turnover	4.29	3.91
Current ratio	2.00	1.90
Quick ratio	1.42	1.27
Gross profit margin	30.00%	35.23%
Debtors control	40 days	52 days
Creditors control	37 days	49 days
Stock turnover	13.90	18.30
Gearing	26.37%	32.71%

Required

(a)   Calculate comparable ratios (to two decimal places where appropriate) for Seymour Marx plc for the year ended 30 April 20X9. All calculations must be clearly shown.

(b) Write a report to your board of directors analysing the performance of Seymour Marx plc, comparing the results against the previous year and against the industry average.

Answer

(a)

	20X8	20X9	Industry average
ROCE	$\frac{320+60}{2,275} = 16.70\%$	$\frac{465+80}{2,845} = 19.16\%$	18.50%
Profit/sales	$\frac{320+60}{9,750} = 3.90\%$	$\frac{465+80}{11,200} = 4.87\%$	4.73%
Asset turnover	$\frac{9,750}{2,275} = 4.29x$	$\frac{11,200}{2,845} = 3.94x$	3.91x
Current ratio	$\frac{1,690}{845} = 2.00$	$\frac{1,950}{955} = 2.04$	1.90
Quick ratio	$\frac{1,080+120}{845} = 1.42$	$\frac{1,230+80}{955} = 1.37$	1.27
Gross profit margin	$\frac{9,750-6,825}{9,750} = 30.00\%$	$\frac{11,200-8,460}{11,200} = 24.46\%$	35.23%

	20X8	20X9	Industry average
Debtors turnover	$\frac{1,080}{9,750} \times 365 = 40$ days	$\frac{1,230}{11,200} \times 365 = 40$ days	52 days
Creditors turnover	$\frac{690}{6,825} \times 365 = 37$ days	$\frac{750}{8,460} \times 365 = 32$ days	49 days
Stock turnover	$\frac{6,825}{490} = 13.9x$	$\frac{8,460}{640} = 13.2x$	18.30x
Gearing	$\frac{600}{2,275} = 26.37\%$	$\frac{800}{2,845} = 28.12\%$	32.71%

(b) (i)

REPORT

To: Board of Directors
From: Management accountant   Date: *xx/xx/xx*
Subject: *Analysis of performance of Seymour Marx plc*

This report should be read in conjunction with the appendix attached which shows the relevant ratios (from part (a)).

1   **Trading and profitability**

1.1 Return on capital employed has improved considerably between 20X8 and 20X9 and is now higher than the industry average.

1.2 Net income as a proportion of sales has also improved noticeably between the years and is also now marginally ahead of the industry average. Gross margin, however, is considerably lower than in the previous year and is only some 70% of the industry average.

1.3 The above suggests either that there has been a change in the cost structure of Seymour Marx plc or that there has been a change in the method of cost allocation between the periods. Either way, this is a marked change that requires further investigation.

1.4 The company appears to be in a period of transition as sales have increased by nearly 15% over the year and it would also appear that new fixed assets have been purchased.

1.5 Asset turnover has declined between the periods although the 20X9 figure is in line with the industry average. This reduction might indicate that the efficiency with which assets are used has deteriorated,

(a)   The assets acquired in 20X9 have not yet fully contributed to the business.
(b)   A longer term trend would clarify the picture.

2 **Liquidity and working capital management**

2.1 The current ratio has improved slightly over the year and is marginally higher than the industry average. It is also in line with what is generally regarded as satisfactory (2:1).

2.2 The quick ratio has declined marginally but is still better than the industry average. This suggests that Seymour Marx plc has no short term liquidity problems and should have no difficulty in paying its debts as they become due.

2.3 Debtors as a proportion of sales is unchanged from 20X8 and are considerably lower than the industry average. Consequently, there is probably little scope to reduce this further.

2.4 Consideration should be given to the likelihood that there may be pressure in the future from customers to increase the period of credit given.

2.5 The period of credit taken from suppliers has fallen from 37 days' purchases to 32 days' and is much lower than the industry average.

2.6 The above trends suggest that it may be possible to finance any additional debtors by negotiating better credit terms from suppliers.

2.7 Stock turnover has fallen slightly and is much slower than the industry average and this may partly reflect stocking up ahead of a significant increase in sales.

2.8 The above suggests that there may be some danger that the stock could contain certain obsolete items that may require writing off.

2.9 The relative increase in the level of stock has been financed by an increased overdraft which may reduce if the stock levels can be brought down.

2.10 The high levels of stock, overdraft and debtors compared to that of creditors suggests a labour intensive company or one where considerable value is added to bought-in products.

3 **Gearing**

3.1 The level of gearing has increased only slightly over the year and is below the industry average.

3.2 The return on capital employed is nearly twice the rate of interest on the debentures, hence profitability is likely to be increased by a modest increase in the level of gearing.

Signed: Accountant

Exam focus point

The above is quite a brief and focused answer but clearly includes 17 points (5+10+2). Marks would also be allocated for the heading and the sign off.

You may well find the above numbering system provides a marks-orientated approach for discursive questions generally.

Commercial awareness

8.6 Your interpretation should always demonstrate a **'real world' commercial awareness** sought by examiners. To develop this business acumen may involve a **variety of activities** on your part in addition to your formal academic studies.

(a) **Reading publications** such as the Financial Times, Economist etc.

(b) Watching the **business coverage** on **television** channels

(c) Taking on an **interest** in business of your **employer** or your **clients,** including discussing their **real concerns**

(d) Obtaining **published financial reports** for a range of companies in **different industry** sectors and developing an understanding of their financial structures and the **business factors** they face.

BPP
PUBLISHING

8.7   A useful address in this regard is the free FT annual reports service. Do have a look at the advert on the advert on the FT *'London share service'* page.

Chapter roundup

- This chapter has taken you through basic ratio analysis in a fairly comprehensive fashion. The ratios you should be able to calculate and/or comment on are as follows.

    ° **Profitability and return**
      - Gross margin on sales
      - Return on capital employed
      - Net profit as a percentage of sales
      - Asset turnover ratio

    ° **Long term solvency and stability**
      - Debt ratio
      - Gearing ratio
      - Debt/equity ratio
      - Interest cover
      - Cash flow ratio

    ° **Short term solvency and liquidity**
      - Current ratio
      - Quick ratio (acid test ratio)
      - Creditors turnover

    ° **Efficiency**
      - Stock turnvover
      - Debtors turnover

    ° **Shareholders' investment ratios**
      - Earnings per share
      - Dividend cover
      - P/E ratio
      - Dividend yield
      - Earnings yield

- With the exception of the last three ratios, where the share's market price is required, all of these ratios **can be calculated from information in a company's published accounts**.

- Ratios provide **information through comparison**:

    ° **trends** in a company's ratios from **one year to the next**, indicating an improving or worsening position

    ° in some cases, **against a 'norm', or 'standard'**;

    ° in some cases, **against the ratios of other companies** or **benchmarks**, although differences between one company and another should be taken into consideration.

- You must realise that, however many ratios you can find to calculate, **numbers alone will not answer a question**. You *must* interpret all the information available to you and support your interpretation with ratio calculations.

- Remember that the financial ratios must be viewed in conjunction with the **commercial** and **business issues** that might impact on a business. It is vital that your reports demonstrate **commercial awareness** and not just number crunching ability.

Quick quiz

1   Brainstorm a list of sources of information which would be useful in interpreting a company's accounts.

2   ROCE is $\dfrac{\text{Profit on ordinary activities before interest and tax}}{\text{Capital employed}}$.

    True ☐

    False ☐

3   Company Q has a profit margin of 7%. Briefly comment on this.

4   The debt ratio is a company's long term debt over its net assets.

    True ☐

    False ☐

5   Cash flow ratio is the ratio of:

    A   Gross cash inflow to total debt
    B   Gross cash inflow to net debt
    C   Net cash inflow to total debt
    D   Net cash inflow to net debt

6   List the formulae for:

    (a)   Current ratio   (c)   Debtor days
    (b)   Quick ratio   (d)   Stock turnover

7   List six limitations to ratio analysis.

Answers to quick quiz

1   There are a number of sources (see para 1.6 and para 1.11). Information on competitors and the economic climate are obvious items of information.

2   True (1.13)

3   You should be careful here. You have very little information. This is a low margin but you need to know what industry the company operates in. 7% may be good for a major retailer.

4   False. It is the ratio of total debt to total assets (1.13)

5   C (.1.13)

7   Compare your list to that in paragraph 7.13

Now try the questions below from the Exam Question Bank

Number	Level	Marks	Time
28	Full exam	25	45 mins
29	Full exam	25	45 mins

BPP PUBLISHING

Appendix

Examination questions on published accounts

INTRODUCTION

(a) Before attempting these questions, you should be familiar with the requirements both of statute and of accounting standards (SSAPs and FRSs) in respect of the presentation and content of published accounts.

(b) Provided that you know the legal and accounting regulations, published accounts questions are not difficult to answer. They are, however, very time consuming and almost certainly you will not have time in the examination unless you adopt a clear and systematic approach. In this appendix we suggest an approach which should provide you with a useful guide. However, it is not the only approach, and you might develop your own method and means of answering such questions. Never be put off by the volume of detail given; it provides you with all the information necessary to produce a clear and detailed solution.

(c) Your aim in answering these questions should be to disclose the minimum information required by statute, SSAPs and FRSs. To disclose more than this might suggest to the examiner that you are unclear about what information is *required* to be disclosed and what information is sometimes *voluntarily* disclosed in practice.

(d) In the time available in the examination it is virtually impossible to provide the examiner with all the information normally given in an actual set of accounts, and indeed, the examiner does not expect you to do so. It is only necessary to comply with the statutory and quasi-statutory requirements so far as you are able from the information given. There is generally no need to embellish your solution with made-up information.

SUGGESTED APPROACH

(e) Read the question carefully to ensure you do not do more than the examiner wants. For example, questions often end with a statement that you may ignore the requirement to disclose accounting policies.

(f) It is likely that the examiner will ask you to prepare accounts for presentation to the members (ie the 'full' accounts rather than the modified versions for small and medium-sized companies) and it is suggested that you adopt the 'operational format' profit and loss account (unless otherwise requested) and the vertical balance sheet in your solutions. As far as possible, use the words given in the CA 1985 formats, but remember that certain alternative or additional headings are allowable and may be used in the examination.

(g) Head up a sheet of paper for the profit and loss account, a second sheet for the balance sheet and a third for the notes to the accounts. Keep a fourth sheet ready for your workings. Begin by writing a statement of accounting policies as note 1 to the accounts, unless the question has instructed you to ignore this requirement.

(h) Now, keeping in mind the 1985 Act pro-formas and the FRS 3 requirements, write out the profit and loss account, beginning with turnover and working line by line through the pro-forma. Search through the question for the information relevant to each line as you come to it and mark the question paper to indicate which bits of information have been used.

(i) While you are writing out the profit and loss account you should be building up the notes to the accounts, writing out each in conjunction with the profit and loss caption to which it refers and, of course, entering the cross reference on the face of the profit and loss account. The process of writing out the relevant note will often remove the need to prepare a working and thus save valuable time.

(j) Don't forget to disclose the EPS at the foot of the profit and loss account for a public company, if the figure is given. (You should assume that the company is listed unless told to the contrary.)

(k) Once the profit and loss account and related notes are complete, follow the same procedure to construct the balance sheet, again working line by line through the pro-forma and writing out the relevant notes at the same time as entering the figures on the balance sheet.

(l) Complete the notes to the accounts by considering whether any notes are necessary other than those arising directly from the profit and loss account and balance sheet. Common examples include:

    (i)   Post balance sheet events
    (ii)   Contingent liabilities

(m)   If you *are* asked to produce financial statements which comply with FRS 3, you may be asked to produce:

    (i)   A statement of total recognised gains and losses

    (ii)   A profit and loss account which shows the turnover and operating profit from continuing activities, acquisitions and discontinued activities

    (iii)   A note of historical cost profits and losses, reconciling P & L retained profit to historical cost profit

    (iv)   A reconciliation of movements in shareholders' funds

    (v)   A reserves note

We have ignored the requirements of FRS 3 in the two questions given here, partly because practice is given in those areas elsewhere in the text, but also to avoid distracting you from the main focus of the preparation of the standard CA 1985 pro-formas. Any FRS 3 requirements will be an 'extra' to your questions. Refer back to Chapter 8 to refresh your memory of these formats and notes.

(n)   Finally, do not forget that SSAP 17 requires that the balance sheet should be dated. Indicate at the foot of the balance sheet where the date and director's signature are to appear.

(o)   You should now attempt to apply this approach to the illustrative questions which follow. Do not set yourself any time limit in answering these questions. Published accounts can only be mastered by absorbing the mass of detail required by statute and professional practice.

1   KITCHENTECH

The following list of balances was extracted from the books of Kitchentech Ltd on 31 December 20X8. The company is involved in the retailing of hardware through four shops which it owns in various parts of the country.

	£
Sales	1,875,893
Cost of sales	1,597,777
Administrative expenses	124,723
Directors' salaries	43,352
Debenture interest to 30.6.X8	3,000
Freehold premises at cost (land £100,000)	215,000
Motor vehicles, at cost	37,581
Accumulated depreciation on motor vehicles to 31.12.X7	16,581
Fixtures and fittings at cost	26,550
Accumulated depreciation on fixtures & fittings to 31.12.X7	8,200
Stock	88,452
Debtors	18,550
Creditors and accruals	47,609
Bank overdraft	11,433
Cash in hand	386
Provision for bad debts at 31.12.X7	1,200
Share capital	100,000
Profit and loss account at 31.12.X7	18,455
General reserve	16,000
10% debentures 20X8/Y6 (secured on the freehold buildings)	60,000

The following adjustments are to be made.

(a)   Depreciation is to be provided in the accounts for the year as follows.

> Buildings 2% on cost
> Motor vehicles 25% on written down value
> Fixtures and fittings 10% on cost

(b)   Directors' remuneration is divided amongst the three directors as follows.

	£
Mr Adil - Chairman	4,000
Mr Beane – Marketing director	20,000
Mr Curruthers – Finance director	19,352
	43,352

Fees of £2,000 each are to be provided for the directors.

A pension of £1,900 paid to Mr Dingley-Jones, a former director, is included in the administration expenses.

The salary of Mr Frobisher, the company secretary, is £18,000 and is also included in the administrative expenses.

(c)   Messrs Greene, Penn and partners, the company's auditors, rendered an account in early March 20X8 as follows.

	£
Assistance in preparation of taxation computation for the year ended 31.12.X7	500
Audit of accounts for the year ended 31.12.X7	1,000
	1,500

This bill was the subject of an accrual of £1,200 on 31 December 20X7. A similar bill for £1,500 is expected for the 20X8 accounts in due course.

(d)   The debtors include a balance of £400 owing from Catering Supplies Ltd. This is to be written off as it has proved irrecoverable. The provision for bad debts is to be adjusted to 10% of debtors.

(e)   Corporation tax based upon the profits for the year at the rate of 35% amounting to £40,000 is to be provided.

(f)   A dividend of 14% is to be provided on the ordinary share capital. The authorised ordinary share capital is £200,000 divided into £1 shares. All issued shares are fully paid.

(g)   £30,000 is to be transferred to general reserve.

(h) The basic rate of income tax should be taken as 25%.

Required

Within the limits of the information given, prepare a profit and loss account and balance sheet for the year ended 31 December 20X8 for submission to the members of the company in accordance with statutory requirements and best professional practice.

2   ALPINE

Alpine Athletic Training plc is a manufacturer of sports equipment. Set out below is a trial balance extracted from the books of the company as at 31 December 20X3.

	£	£
Sales		2,925,900
Cost of sales	1,785,897	
Selling expenses	120,000	
Administrative expenses	649,996	
Debtors/creditors	469,332	371,022
Provision for doubtful debts		22,500
Directors' remuneration	181,500	
Audit fee	3,000	
Debenture interest	7,500	
Half year preference dividend paid on 30.6.X3	2,100	
Premises at cost	600,000	
Plant and machinery at cost	135,000	
Provision for depreciation on plant and machinery at 1.1.X3		60,000
Motor vehicles at cost (salesmen's cars)	54,000	
Provision for depreciation on motor vehicles at 1.1.X3		24,000
Stock in trade and work in progress	282,728	
Trade investment at cost	72,000	
Bank overdraft		354,528
Profit and loss account balance at 1.1.X3		65,103
General reserve		30,000
Ordinary share capital		300,000
7% preference share capital		60,000
10% debentures 20X9 secured on premises		150,000
	4,363,053	4,363,053

The following information is also related to the accounts for the year to 31 December 20X3.

(a) The bad debt provision is to be increased to an amount which is equal to 1% of the turnover for the year.

(b) The directors' remuneration is divided amongst the four directors of the company as follows.

	£
Chairman	24,000
Managing director	60,000
Finance director	49,500
Sales director	48,000
	181,500

In addition provision must be made for directors' fees of £5,000 to each of the above directors.

(c) Depreciation is to be provided for the year as follows.

Buildings	2% on cost
Plant and machinery	10% on cost
Motor vehicles	25% on written down value

The only changes in fixed assets during the year were an addition to plant and machinery in early January 20X3 costing £30,000 and the purchase of premises for £600,000 comprising £150,000 for buildings and £450,000 for land.

(d) A provision of £60,000 is to be made for corporation tax at 35% based upon the profits for the year. This will be payable on 30 September 20X4.

(e)   The half year preference dividend to 31 December 20X3 and a final dividend of 6.5 pence a share on the ordinary share capital, are to be provided in the accounts.

(f)   The sum of £15,000 is to be transferred to general reserve.

(g)   The authorised preference share capital is £60,000 in £1 shares.

(h)   The authorised ordinary share capital is £600,000 in 50p shares. All shares in issue are fully paid.

(i)   Assume the basic rate of income tax to be 25%.

(j)   Administrative expenses include £5,244 interest on the overdraft.

(k)   The directors consider the value of the trade investment to be £75,000. It consists of 10,000 20p ordinary shares in Crampon Ltd, a company with an issued share capital of 200,000 ordinary shares.

Required

Within the limits of the above information, prepare the final accounts of Alpine Athletic Training plc for the year ended 31 December 20X3 in a form suitable for presentation to the members and which complies with the requirements of the Companies Act 1985.

The required information should be shown as part of the accounting statements or by way of note, whichever is considered most appropriate.

1   **KITCHENTECH**

PROFIT AND LOSS ACCOUNT FOR THE YEAR ENDED 31 DECEMBER 20X8

	Notes	£	£
Turnover	1		1,875,893
Cost of sales			(1,597,777)
Gross profit			278,116
Distribution costs (W1)		30,920	
Administrative expenses (W1)		156,175	
			(187,095)
Operating profit	2		91,021
Interest payable	3		(6,000)
Profit on ordinary activities before taxation			85,021
Tax on profit on ordinary activities	4		(40,000)
Profit on ordinary activities after taxation			45,021
Dividend: proposed ordinary dividend		14,000	
Transfer to general reserve		30,000	
			44,000
Retained profit for the year			1,021
Earnings per share	5		45.4p

STATEMENT OF RETAINED PROFITS

	£
Retained profit for the year	1,021
Retained profits brought forward	18,455
Retained profits carried forward	19,476

BALANCE SHEET AS AT 31 DECEMBER 20X8

	Notes	£	£
Fixed assets			
Tangible assets	6		244,145
Current assets			
Stock		88,052	
Debtors £(18,550 - 400 - 1,815)		16,735	
Cash in hand		386	
		105,173	
Creditors: amounts falling due within one year			
Bank overdraft		11,433	
Creditors and accruals (W2)		58,409	
Other creditors including taxation	7	54,000	
		123,842	
Net current liabilities			(18,669)
Total assets less current liabilities			225,476
Creditors: amounts falling due after more than one year			
10% debentures 20X8/Y6			(60,000)
			165,476
Capital and reserves			
Called up share capital			
£1 ordinary shares fully paid (authorised: £200,000)			100,000
Reserves			
General reserve		46,000	
Profit and loss account		19,476	
			65,476
			165,476

Approved by the Board of Directors on....................

.............................Director

NOTES TO THE ACCOUNTS

1   *Turnover*

Turnover is the value, net of VAT, of goods sold during the year in a single class of business in the UK.

2   *Operating profit*

	£	£
Operating profit is stated after charging:		
Directors' remuneration		
Salaries	43,352	
Fees	6,000	
Pension to former director	1,900	
		51,252
Depreciation		10,205
Auditors' remuneration		1,000

(*Tutorial note.* No further details are required of directors' remuneration, since in total it is less than £200,000. Note that Mr Frobisher is *not* a director and so his salary is not included in the above total.)

3   *Interest payable*

Interest on 10% debentures 20X8/Y6   £6,000

4   *Tax on profit on ordinary activities*

UK corporation tax at 35% on the profit of the year   £40,000

5   *Earnings per share*

Earnings per share is based on earnings of £45,421 and 100,000 ordinary shares in issue during the year

6   *Fixed assets*

	Land and buildings £	Motor vehicles £	Fixtures & fittings £	Total £
Cost				
At 1 January and 31 December 20X8	215,000	37,581	26,550	279,131
Depreciation				
At 1 January 20X8	-	16,581	8,200	24,781
Charge for year	2,300	5,250	2,655	10,205
At 31 December 20X8	2,300	21,831	10,855	34,986
Net book value				
At 1 January 20X8	215,000	21,000	18,350	254,350
At 31 December 20X8	212,700	15,750	15,695	244,145

7   *Other creditors including taxation*

	£
Corporation tax	40,000
Proposed dividend	14,000
	54,000

Workings

1   *Allocation of costs*

	Distribution costs £	Administrative expenses £
Per list of balances		124,723
Directors' salaries	20,000	23,352
Directors' fees	2,000	4,000
Depreciation:		
Buildings (2% × £115,000)		2,300
Motor vehicles 25% × £(37,581 – 16,581)	5,250	
Fixtures (10% × £26,550)	2,655	
Audit and tax advice; GPP		1,800
(includes £300 under-provided in previous year)		
Bad debt	400	
Provision for doubtful debts		
10% × £(18,550 – 400) – £1,200	615	
	30,920	156,175

(*Note.* The allocation above is somewhat arbitrary, especially as regards the depreciation costs. Other allocations would be acceptable.)

2   *Creditors and accruals*

	£
Per list of balances	47,609
Directors' fees	6,000
Half-year's debenture interest	3,000
20X8 audit and tax fee	1,500
Increase in accrual for 20X7 and audit tax fee	300
	58,409

2   **ALPINE**

PROFIT AND LOSS ACCOUNT FOR THE YEAR ENDED 31 DECEMBER 20X3

	Note	£	£
Turnover (continuing operations)	1		2,925,900
Cost of sales (W1)			(1,799,397)
Gross profit			1,126,503
Distribution costs (W2)		187,259	
Administrative expenses (W3)		799,252	
			(986,511)
Operating profit	2		139,992
Interest payable	3		(20,244)
Profit on ordinary activities before taxation			119,748
Tax on profit on ordinary activities	4		(60,000)
Profit on ordinary activities after taxation			59,748
Dividends	5	43,200	
Transfer to general reserve		15,000	
			(58,200)
Retained profit for the financial year			1,548
Earnings per share	6		9.3p

STATEMENT OF RETAINED PROFITS

	£
Retained profit for the financial year	1,548
Retained profits brought forward	65,103
Retained profits carried forward	66,651

BALANCE SHEET AS AT 31 DECEMBER 20X3

	Note	£	£
Fixed assets			
Tangible assets	7		681,000
Investments (directors' valuation: £75,000)			72,000
			753,000
Current assets			
Stocks and work in progress		282,728	
Debtors £(469,332 – 29,259)		440,073	
		722,801	
Creditors: amounts falling due within one year			
Bank overdraft		354,528	
Trade creditors		371,022	
Other creditors including taxation	8	101,100	
Accruals (£7,500 deb int + £20,000 dir rem)		27,500	
		854,150	
Net current liabilities			(131,349)
Total assets less current liabilities			621,651
Creditors: amounts falling due after more than one year			
10% debentures 20X9			(150,000)
			471,651
Capital and reserves			
Called up share capital			
50p ordinary shares fully paid (authorised: £600,000)		300,000	
£1 7% preference shares fully paid (authorised:£60,000)		60,000	
			360,000
Reserves			
General reserve		45,000	
Profit and loss account (£65,103 + £1,548)		66,651	
			111,651
			471,651

Approved by the Board of Directors on ....

...................Director

NOTES TO THE ACCOUNTS

1   *Turnover*

Turnover represents amounts invoiced, net of VAT, for goods and services supplied during the year in a single class of business in the UK.

2   *Operating profit*

Operating profit is stated after charging:

	£
Depreciation	24,000
Directors' emoluments	201,500
Auditors' remuneration	3,000

Directors' emoluments comprise fees of £20,000 and remuneration of £181,500.

The emoluments of the highest paid director were £63,000. (This information is required because the total of directors' emoluments is over £200,000.)

3   *Interest payable*

	£
On debentures repayable in more than five years	15,000
On bank overdraft	5,244
	20,244

4   *Taxation*

	£
UK corporation tax at 35% on the profits for the year	£60,000

5   *Dividends*

		£
Preference:	interim paid	2,100
	final proposed	2,100
		4,200
Ordinary: final proposed (600,000 × 6.5p)		39,000
		43,200

6   *Earnings per share*

Earnings per share is based on earnings of £(59,748 - 4,200) = £55,548 and 600,000 ordinary shares in issue during the year.

7   *Fixed assets*

	Premises £	*Plant and machinery* £	*Motor vehicles* £	*Total* £
Cost				
At 1 January 20X3	-	105,000	54,000	159,000
Additions in year	600,000	30,000		630,000
At 31 December 20X3	600,000	135,000	54,000	789,000
Depreciation				
At 1 January 20X3	-	60,000	24,000	84,000
Charge for the year	3,000	13,500	7,500	24,000
At 31 December 20X3	3,000	73,500	31,500	108,000
Net book value				
At 1 January 20X3	-	45,000	30,000	75,000
At 31 December 20X3	597,000	61,500	22,500	681,000

8   *Other creditors including taxation*

	£
Corporation tax £(60,000)	60,000
Dividends proposed	41,100
	101,100

Workings

1   *Cost of sales*

	£
Per TB	1,785,897
Add depreciation on plant (10% × £135,000)	13,500
	1,799,397

2	*Distribution costs*	£	£
	Selling expenses		120,000
	Sales director's remuneration £(48,000 + 5,000)		53,000
	Provision for doubtful debts:		
	Provision required (1% × £2,925,900)	29,259	
	Less existing provision	22,500	
	Increase in provision		6,759
	Depreciation on motor vehicles (25% × £30,000)		7,500
			187,259

3	*Administrative expenses*	
		£
	Per TB	649,996
	Directors' remuneration £(24,000 + 60,000 + 49,500 + 15,000)	148,500
	Audit fee	3,000
	Depreciation on buildings (2% × £150,000)	3,000
		804,496
	Less overdraft interest	5,244
		799,252

Exam question bank

Examination standard questions are indicated by the mark and time allocations.

1   REGULATORS   *27 mins*

State three different regulatory influences on the preparation of the published accounts of quoted companies and briefly explain the role of each one. Comment briefly on the effectiveness of this regulatory system.

2   STANDARD SETTERS (20 marks)   *36 mins*

There are those who suggest that any standard setting body is redundant because accounting standards are unnecessary. Other people feel that such standards should be produced, but by the government, so they are legislated.

The old Accounting Standards Committee (ASC) was said by many critics to have failed in its primary objective of achieving greater uniformity and therefore comparability between the financial statements of different entities. Various problems were cited.

(i)   Nearly all the members of the ASC were drawn from the accountancy profession rather than from academia, user groups or other independent bodies.

(ii)   The ASC was not able to react immediately to new problems or controversies.

(iii) The ASC succumbed to political pressures from interested parties on a number of occasions.

(iv)   The ASC adopted a 'fire-fighting' approach, introducing standards as the need arose, rather than adopting an underlying 'conceptual framework' which directly addressed the needs of users.

(v)   The ASC's only method of enforcing accounting standards was to require qualification of the audit report, which many felt was insufficient as deterrent or enforcement.

The dissolution of the ASC and its replacement by the ASB, along with the implementation of all the other Dearing Committee recommendations, was designed to address these criticisms.

Required

(a)   Discuss the statement that accounting standards are unnecessary for the purpose of regulating financial statements.

(b)   Has the ASB (and the other new bodies) remedied all the failings of the ASC listed above? Discuss to what extent the criticisms have been addressed by the new regime.

3   PUBLISHED ACCOUNTS (25 marks)   *45 mins*

(a)   Why is the disclosure of accounting policies required by the Companies Act 1985?

(b)   The Companies Act 1985 regulates the concept of small and medium-sized companies and allows certain 'accounting exemptions' for such entities.

   Required

   (i)   State the criteria which are taken into account to determine whether a company is 'small' or 'medium-sized'.

   (ii)   With regard to small companies only, list the exemptions which are allowed.

(c)   List the contents of the directors' report.

4   D'URBERVILLE (25 marks)   *45 mins*

The financial controller of D'Urberville plc is preparing forecast balance sheets as at 31 December 20X4, 20X5, 20X6 and 20X7.

The 20X4 forecast has been prepared and shows the following figure in respect of motor vehicles.

	£'000
Cost	540
Accumulated depreciation	130
Net book value	410

Depreciation on motor vehicles is charged at 25% on the reducing balance. A full year's depreciation is charged in the year of purchase and none in the year of sale.

The following information has been collated by the assistant accountant in order to help the financial controller prepare his forecast.

FORECAST PURCHASES OF MOTOR VEHICLES
FOR THE YEAR ENDED 31 DECEMBER

	20X5 £'000	20X6 £'000	20X7 £'000
List price			
Cash purchase	180	300	450
Hire purchase	-	400	-
Trade discount (20%)			
Cash purchase	36	60	90
Hire purchase	-	80	-
Cash discount (5% of net price)	7	12	18
Delivery costs (paid to supplier)	10	12	15
Costs of valeting old vehicles to prepare them for sale	2	3	4
Trade-in allowances on old vehicles to be set off against hire purchase deposit or finance lease first year rental		25	20
Hire-purchase deposit	-	85 (110 – 25)	
Finance lease first year rental			90 (110 – 20)
Total cash to be paid to the suppliers of the new vehicles in the year of purchase	147 (180 – 36 – 7 + 10)	97 (85 + 12)	105 (90 + 15)

FORECAST DISPOSALS OF MOTOR VEHICLES (AT COST)
IN THE YEARS ENDED 31 DECEMBER

	20X5 £'000	20X6 £'000	20X7 £'000
Vehicle			
Originally acquired in year ended 31 December			
20X0	30		
20X1	40		
20X2		45	
20X3		65	
20X4			75

The following methods of purchase will be used to acquire the vehicles.

Year ended 31 December 20X5: cash purchase.

Year ended 31 December 20X6: hire purchase. The agreement in question requires an initial deposit of £110,000, then in each of the three years following an instalment of £70,000.

Year ended 31 December 20X7: finance lease agreement. A rental of £110,000 will be payable in arrears for six years.

Required

For the asset motor vehicles in the forecast balance sheets of D'Urberville plc as at 31 December 20X5, 20X6, 20X7, produce a schedule showing cost, accumulated depreciation and net book value. You should show all your workings and make all calculations to the nearest £000.

5   **BLECO (30 marks)**   *54 mins*

The following information relates to the R & D activities of Bleco plc. All projects are given designatory prefixes to indicate their nature.

```
PR = pure research
AR = applied research
D  = development
```

At 1 September 20X0, the balance brought forward as development costs consisted of:

	£
Project: D363	198,300
D367	242,700
D368	nil

During the year ended 31 August 20X1 the following took place.

(a) Project D368 satisfied the SSAP 13 deferment criteria. In previous years, a total of £47,830 expended on this project had been written off to the profit and loss account. The directors have resolved to defer, by capitalisation, the aggregate of the current year's expenditure together with the reinstated figure from previous years.

(b) An applied research project, AR204, was converted into a development project and redesignated D369, but all expenditure up to this point is to be written off.

(c) Two more development projects were instituted, D370 and D371. This latter project was commissioned by Lytax Ltd under a contract for full reimbursement of expenditure; to date, £24,000 has been received from Lytax Ltd.

(d) It has become apparent that the technical feasibility and commercial viability of Project D370 are doubtful.

(e) All other development projects satisfy the SSAP 13 deferment criteria.

(f) (See below)

(g) Project D363 entered full commercial production and is to be amortised on a straight line basis over six years.

Bleco plc depreciates fixed assets on a straight line basis, assuming no residual value, at the following rates.

	% per annum on cost
Laboratory buildings	10
Laboratory equipment	20

A full year's depreciation is charged in the year of acquisition.

Expenditure was incurred as follows.

	PR119 £	AR187 £	AR204 £	D367 £	D368 £	D369 £	D370 £	D371 £	Inallocated £
Wages, salaries and related charges	35,100	27,300	15,260	2,090	16,480	34,070	29,800	27,500	3,300
Materials	810	520	290	340	410	1,560	2,650	3,400	4,070
Direct expenses (other)	250	210	180	170	230	640	690	710	2,240
Production overheads	1,240	3,600	2,950	3,540	4,650	6,980	6,010	6,420	7,070
Fixed assets: Experimental laboratory buildings		200,000							
Testing laboratory buildings						310,000			
Laboratory equipment		170,000				472,000			
Related selling and administrative overheads									76,200
Market research									55,600

Required

Prepare extracts from the profit and loss account of Bleco plc for year ended 31 August 20X1 and from the company's balance sheet at that date, to incorporate the financial effects of the research and development expenditure.

Your answer should comply with the requirements of SSAP 13 *Accounting for research and development*.

Detailed workings for each item must be shown.

6   WINGER (PILOT PAPER – 25 marks)

The following trial balance relates to Winger plc at 31 March 20X1:

	£'000	£'000
Turnover (note i)		358,450
Cost of sales	185,050	
Distribution costs	28,700	
Administration expenses	15,000	
Lease rentals (note ii)	20,000	
Debenture interest paid	2,000	
Interim dividends (note vi)	12,000	
Land and buildings - cost (note iii)	200,000	
Plant and equipment - cost	154,800	
Depreciation 1 April 20X0 - plant and equipment		34,800
Development expenditure (note iv)	30,000	
Profit on disposal of fixed assets		45,000
Trade debtors	55,000	
Stocks - 31 March 20X1	28,240	
Cash and bank	10,660	
Trade creditors		29,400
Taxation - over provision in year to 31 March 20X0		2,200
Ordinary shares of 25p each		150,000
8% Debenture (issued in 20W8)		50,000
Profit and loss reserve 1 April 20X0		71,600
	741,450	741,450

The following notes are relevant:

(i)   Included in the turnover is £27 million, which relates to sales made to customers under sale or return agreements. The expiry date for the return of these goods is 30 April 20X1. Winger plc has charged a mark-up of 20% on cost for these sales.

(ii) A lease rental of £20 million was paid on 1 April 20X0. It is the first of five annual payments in advance for the rental of an item of equipment that has a cash purchase price of £80 million. The auditors have advised that this is a finance lease and have calculated the implicit interest rate in the lease as 12% per annum. Leased assets should be depreciated on a straight-line basis over the life of the lease.

(iii) On 1 April 20X0 Winger plc acquired new land and building at a cost of £200 million. For the purpose of calculating depreciation only, the asset has been separated into the following elements:

Separate asset	Cost	Life
	£'000	
Land	50,000	Freehold
Heating system	20,000	10 years
Lifts	30,000	15 years
Building	100,000	50 years

The depreciation of the elements of the building should be calculated on a straight-line basis. The new building replaced an existing building that was sold on the same date for £95 million. It had cost £50 million and had a carrying value of £80 million at the date of sale. The profit on this building has been calculated on the original cost. It had not been depreciated on the basis that the depreciation charge would not be material.

Plant and machinery is depreciated at 20% on the reducing balance basis.

(iv) The figure for development expenditure in the trial balance represents the amounts capitalised in previous years in respect of the development of a new product. Unfortunately, during the current year, the Government has introduced legislation which effectively bans this type of product. As a consequence of this the project has been abandoned. The directors of Winger plc are of the opinion that writing off the development expenditure, as opposed to its previous capitalisation, represents a change of accounting policy and therefore wish to treat the write off as a prior adjustment.

(v) A provision for corporation tax for the year to 31 March 20X1 of £15 million is required.

(vi) The company has paid an interim ordinary dividend and half of the annual debenture interest. The average annual dividend yield (interim plus final) for companies in Winger plc's market sector is 4%. The current market price of Winger plc's equity shares is £1.25. The directors are to propose a final dividend which will give Winger plc's equity shareholders a return equal to the average gross yield for the sector.

Required

(a) Prepare the profit and loss Account of Winger plc for the year to 31 March 20X1. (9 marks)

(b) Prepare a balance sheet as at 31 March 20X1 in accordance with the Companies Acts and current Accounting Standards so far as the information permits. (11 marks)

Notes to the financial statements are not required.

(c) Discuss the current acceptability of the company's previous policy in respect of non-depreciation of buildings. (5 marks)

---

7 **BULWELL (20 marks)** *36 mins*

Bulwell Aggregates Ltd wish to expand their transport fleet and purchased three heavy lorries with a list price of £18,000 each. Robert Bulwell has negotiated hire purchase finance to fund this expansion, and the company has entered into a hire purchase agreement with Granby Garages plc on 1 January 20X1. The agreement states that Bulwell Aggregates will pay a deposit of £9,000 on 1 January 20X1, and two annual instalments of £24,000 on 31 December 20X1, 20X2 and a final instalment of £20,391 on 31 December 20X3.

Interest is to be calculated at 25% on the balance outstanding on 1 January each year and paid on 31 December each year.

The depreciation policy of Bulwell Aggregates Ltd is to write off the vehicles over a four year period using the straight line method and assuming a scrap value of £1,333 for each vehicle at the end of its useful life.

The cost of the vehicles to Granby Garages is £14,400 each.

Required

(a) Account for the above transactions in the books of Granby Garages plc, showing the entries in the hire purchase trading account for the years 20X1, 20X2 and 20X3. This is the only hire purchase transaction undertaken by this company.

(b) Account for the above transactions in the books of Bulwell Aggregates Ltd showing the entries in the profit and loss account and balance sheet for the years 20X1, 20X2, 20X3. This is the only hire purchase transaction undertaken by this company.

Calculations to the nearest £.

---

8 **SOAP (15 marks)** *27 mins*

Soap plc is working on a number of short-term and long-term contracts. Its policy with regard to attributable profit on the long term contracts is to calculate it as follows.

Degree of completion (%) × total estimated profit (adjusted for known variations in costs accruing in the period)

The directors are sure that their cost calculations for the contracts are accurate, and the auditors concur with them in their belief that the degree of completion is sufficient to accrue profit. It is 31 December 20X7, the company's accounting year end. Further details of the contracts are as follows.

(a) The short term contracts are 7 to 9 months in duration. Some of them will not be completed until 31 March 20X8. It is the directors' policy to accrue profit earned to date on these contracts in the accounts as at 31 December 20X7.

(b) On 1 April 20X7 Soap plc commenced work on a contract with Emmerdale plc. The total contract price was £9 million and the total contract costs were expected to be £7.5 million. The contract is expected to run for two years.

During the year to 31 December 20X7, Soap plc incurred unforeseen additional costs of £500,000 on the contract in the light of which it revised its estimate of the total expected costs to £8 million. The following details are relevant to the position as at 31 December 20X7.

    (i) Costs incurred to date: £4m
    (ii) Payments on account: £3m
    (iii) Percentage complete per independent surveyor: 45%.

(c) On 1 July 20X7 Soap plc entered into a contract with Archers plc. The details of the contract were as follows.

    (i) Duration of contract: 2 years

    (ii) Total contract price: £150,000

    (iii) Estimated total cost: £120,000

    (iv) Percentage of completion (directors' estimate): 20%

      (The terms of the contract did not require an independent valuation by a surveyor.)

    (v) Costs incurred up to 31 December 20X7: £47,500

    (vi) Payments on account received: £40,000

A special machine had been purchased for the purposes of the contract and was being depreciated over the two year period on a straight line basis. The cost of the machine was £20,000, and the depreciation charge to date had been included in the costs incurred figure (v). On 31 December 20X7 it was decided that this machine should be written off. (Assume no residual value.)

(d) On 1 August 20X7, Soap plc entered into a contract with Neighbours Ltd. The details of the contract were as follows.

    (i) Duration: 1½ years
    (ii) Total contract price: £6.4 million
    (iii) Estimated total costs: £5 million
    (iv) Payments on account: £2.5 million
    (v) Costs incurred up to 31 December 20X7: £1.8 million
    (vi) Percentage of completion (independent surveyor's estimate): 25%

Neighbours Ltd was a new customer, so as a precaution, Soap plc had asked for a large deposit.

Required

(a) State whether you think it is good accounting practice to accrue profit on the short term contracts. Give reasons for your view. (4 marks)

(b) For the year ended 31 December 20X7, show the relevant extracts from the profit and loss account and balance sheet of Soap plc as regards the contracts with Emmerdale plc, Archers plc and Neighbours Ltd. You do not need to show the cash and bank balances. (11 marks)

9   **CORAX (20 marks)**   *36 mins*

Corax plc has an allotted capital of £350,000 in fully paid 50p ordinary shares. At 31 December 20X6 the following balances were included in the company's balance sheet.

	£
Agreed corporation tax liability on 20X5 profits	16,300
Estimated corporation tax liability on 20X6 profits	5,000
Deferred taxation account	29,400
Profit and loss account (credit)	43,000

(No dividends had been paid or proposed in respect of 20X6)

The following information relates to the year ended 31 December 20X7.

(a)   Corporation tax liability for 20X5 profits was settled (January).

(b)   Interim dividend of 3p per share was paid (August).

(c)   Corporation tax liability for 20X6 was agreed at £3,800 (December), paid January 20X8.

(d)   Profit for 20X7 (before tax) on ordinary activities was calculated at £100,000.

(e)   Corporation tax based on the 20X7 profits was estimated at £36,000.

(f)   Directors proposed a final dividend of 4.5p per share.

(g)   A transfer to the deferred taxation account of £7,000 for 20X7 is to be made in respect of capital allowances in excess of depreciation charges (the entire balance on the deferred tax account being of a similar nature).

Required

(a)   Make all relevant entries in the ledger accounts (except bank and share capital).

(b)   Complete the profit and loss account for 20X7 and show how the final balances would be included the balance sheet at 31 December 20X7. Show the details given in the notes to the accounts.

Assume income tax at 25%.

10   **CHER (25 marks)**   *45 mins*

Note. To answers parts (b) to (d) of this question, you will need to refer to the profit and loss accounts in the appendix at the end of the question.

(a)   'Reported earnings per share is a very important indicator of performance for a quoted company.'

Why do you think that this is, and do you agree?   (5 marks)

(b)   Cher (Holdings) plc was formed fifteen years ago. As at 1 July 20X3, the issued share capital of the group was as follows, all shares being issued at par.

Ordinary £1 shares fully paid	800,000
Ordinary £1 shares 60p paid	200,000
	1,000,000

On 1 October 20X3, Cher (Holdings) plc received the monies due on the partly paid shares.

Required

Calculate the earnings per share figure for the year ended 30 June 20X4, as it would appear in the financial statements of the group.   (3 marks)

(c)   On 28 February 20X5 Cher (Holdings) plc made a 1 for 4 rights issue at £1.30 per share. The actual *cum rights* price was £1.90 per share on the last day of quotation *cum rights*.

Required

(i)   Calculate earnings per share for the year ended 30 June 20X5. Show the comparative figure for 20X4.   (5 marks)

(ii)   Explain the reasoning behind your calculation in part (c)(i).   (7 marks)

(d)   On 1 January 20X6, a new group Sonny (Holdings) plc was formed. Its purpose was to take over the business of Cher (Holdings) plc, and the need to do so arose from the fact that Cher (Holdings) plc was becoming linked in the mind of the public with an unconnected, somewhat disreputable group, Sheer Moldings plc. Sonny (Holdings) plc was to issue 2 shares for every 1 share in Cher (Holdings) plc. In preparing the financial statements of Sonny (Holdings) plc, which is essentially a continuation of Cher (Holdings) plc, merger accounting principles were adopted.

Required

Calculate earnings per share for the year ended 30 June 20X6. Show the comparative figure for 20X5. (5 marks)

APPENDIX: PROFIT AND LOSS ACCOUNTS

	Cher (Holdings) plc		Sonny (Holdings) plc
Year ended 30 June	20X4	20X5	20X6
	£'000	£'000	£'000
Turnover	2,000	3,400	4,500
Cost of sales	900	800	1,500
Gross profit	1,100	2,600	3,000
Distribution costs	150	240	310
Administrative expenses	260	410	420
Profit on ordinary activities before tax	690	1,950	2,270
Taxation	230	640	750
Profit on ordinary activities after tax	460	1,310	1,520
Dividends	100	200	250
Profit for the financial year	360	1,110	1,270

11 SPICE (25 marks) *45 mins*

The following financial statements relate to Spice plc.

PROFIT AND LOSS ACCOUNT FOR THE YEAR TO 31 MARCH 20X6

	£m	£m
Turnover		710
Cost of sales		(314)
Gross profit		396
Distribution costs	(62)	
Administrative costs	(54)	
		(116)
Operating profit		280
Interest payable	(14)	
Interest receivable	6	
		(8)
Profit before tax		272
Taxation		(64)
Profit for the financial year		208
Dividends		(40)
Retained profit for the year		168

SUMMARISED BALANCE SHEETS

	31 March 20X6		31 March 20X5	
	£m	£m	£m	£m
Tangible fixed assets		550		400
Current assets				
Stock	280		310	
Debtors	260		220	
Interest receivable	2		4	
Short term investments	190		-	
Cash	12		42	
	744		576	
Creditors: amounts falling due within one year	(498)		(344)	
Net current assets		246		232
Total assets less current liabilities		796		632
Creditors: amounts falling due after more than one year		(140)		(164)
Provisions for liabilities and charges - deferred tax		(24)		(16)
Net assets		632		452
Capital and reserves				
Ordinary shares £1 each		220		180
10% £1 preference shares		-		40
		220		220
Reserves				
Share premium account	88		70	
Capital redemption reserve	20		-	
Revaluation reserve	14		-	
Profit and loss account	290		162	
		412		232
		632		452

The following information is relevant.

(a) During the year Spice plc issued 20 million £1 ordinary shares at a premium of 100%, incurring issue costs of £2 million. Subsequent to this a bonus issue of 1 for 10 shares held was made. On 1 September 20X5 Spice plc decided to purchase and cancel all of its preference shares at a premium of 20p per share. The premium has been charged to the profit and loss account as an administrative cost.

(b) Tangible fixed assets include certain properties which were revalued during the year giving a surplus of £14 million. Assets capitalised under finance lease agreements during the year amounted to £56 million. Disposals of assets having a net book value of £38 million realised £42 million. Depreciation for the year was £76 million.

(c) Short term investments of £160 million fall within the definition of 'liquid resources' in FRS 1 (revised). The remainder of the investments is a loan note to a major public company which is repayable on demand. The plc meets the definition of a 'qualifying financial institution' for cash purposes.

(d) *Analysis of creditors as at:*

	31 March 20X6	31 March 20X5
	£m	£m
Repayable within one year:		
Bank overdraft	16	40
Obligations under finance leases	10	6
Trade creditors	426	258
Corporation tax	32	20
Dividends	8	16
Interest payable	6	4
	498	344
Repayable after more than one year:		
Obligations under finance leases	100	84
6% debentures 20X6/20Y1	40	80
	140	164

(e) Some of the debentures were redeemed at par on 31 March 20X6.

(f) Interest on finance leases of £6 million is included in the interest charge in the profit and loss account.

Required

(a) Prepare a cash flow statement for Spice plc for the year ended 31 March 20X6 in compliance with FRS 1 (revised) *Cash flow statements* (indirect method) together with the accompanying notes.

(16 marks)

(b) Prepare an analysis of the movement on share capital and reserves during the year. (5 marks)

(c) The Accounting Standards Board (ASB) would prefer to use the 'direct' (gross) method of presenting cash flow information, yet almost all companies use the 'indirect' (net) method of presentation. Why do the ASB and most listed companies appear to differ on this issue?

(4 marks)

12 JUSTIN CASE

10 mins

One of Justin Case Ltd's employees suffered sever electric shock and nerve damage in trying to install a piece of equipment which was known to be faulty.

The company's solicitors suggest that the employee has a strong case. However, he has to undergo a series of medical tests before likely financial damages can be estimated.

Required

Explain how this matter should be treated in the year-end accounts of Justin Case Ltd in terms of FRS 12.

13 MULTIPLEX (PILOT PAPER – 25 marks)

The following transactions and events have arisen during the preparation of the draft financial statements of Multiplex plc for the year to 31 March 20X1:

(a) On 1 April 20X0 Multiplex plc issued £80 million 8% loan stock at a discount of 10%. The issue costs were £1.4 million made up of apportioned costs of the finance and acquisitions department of £1 million and professional and underwriting costs of £400,000 relating directly to this issue. The loan stock will be redeemed on 31 March 20X5 at a premium of 12%.

Required

Calculate the profit and loss account finance charge for the year to 31 March 20X1 and the balance sheet extracts at 31 March 20X1 in respect of the issue of the loan stock. (5 marks)

Note: you may calculate the finance costs on a straight-line basis.

(b) On 1 January 20X1 Multiplex plc acquired Steamdays Ltd, a company that operates a scenic railway along the coast of a popular tourist area. The summarised balance sheet at fair values of Steamdays Ltd on 1 January 20X1, reflecting the terms of the acquisition was:

	£'000
Goodwill	200
Operating licence	1,000
Property - train stations and land	250
Rail track and coaches	250
Two steam engines	1,000
Other net assets	300
Purchase consideration	3,000

The operating licence is for ten years. It was renewed on 1 January 20X1 by the transport authority and is stated at the cost of its renewal. The carrying values of the property and rail track and coaches are based on their value in use. The engines, and other net assets are valued at their net selling prices.

On 1 February 20X1 the boiler of one of the steam engines exploded, completely destroying the whole engine. Fortunately no one was injured, but the engine was beyond repair. Due to its age a replacement could not be obtained. Because of the reduced passenger capacity the estimated value in use of the whole of the business after the accident was assessed at £2 million.

Passenger numbers after the accident were below expectations even after allowing for the reduced capacity. A market research report concluded that tourists were not using the railway because of their fear of a similar accident occurring to the remaining engine. In the light of this the value in use of the business was re-assessed on 31 March 20X1 at £1.8 million. On this date Multiplex plc received an offer of £600,000 in respect of the operating licence (it is transferable). The realisable value of the other net assets has not changed significantly.

Required

Calculate the carrying value of the assets of Steamdays Ltd (in Multiplex plc's consolidated balance sheet) at 1 February 20X1 and 31 March 20X1 after recognising the impairment losses.

(6 marks)

(c) On 1 January 20X1 the Board of Multiplex plc approved a resolution to close the whole of its loss-making engineering operation. A binding agreement to dispose of the assets was signed shortly afterwards. The sale will be completed on 10 June 20X1 at an agreed value of £30 million. The costs of the closure are estimated at:

- £2 million for redundancy

- £3 million in penalty costs for non-completion of contracted orders

- £1.5 million for associated professional costs

- Losses on the sale of the net assets whose book value at 31 March 20X1 was £46 million

- Operating losses for the period from 1 April 20X1 to the date of sale are estimated at £4.5 million.

Multiplex plc accounts for its various operations on a divisional basis.

Required

Advise the directors on the correct accounting treatment of the closure of the engineering division.

(5 marks)

(d) Multiplex plc is in the intermediate stage of a long-term, construction contract for the building of a new privately owned road bridge over a river estuary. The original details of the contract are:

Approximate duration of contract:	3 years
Date of commencement:	1 October 20W9
Total contract price:	£40 million
Estimated total cost:	£28 million

An independent surveyor certified the value of the work in progress as follows:

- On 31 March 20X0	£12 million
- on 31 March 20X1	£30 million (including the £12 million in 20X0)

Costs incurred at:

- 31 March 20X0	£9 million
- 31 March 20X1	£28.5 million (including the £9 million in 20X0)

Payments received on account by 31 March 20X1 were £25 million

On 1 April 20X0 Multiplex plc agreed to a contract variation that would involve an additional fee of £5 million with associated additional estimated costs of £2 million.

The costs incurred during the year to 31 March 20X1 include £2.5 million relating to the replacement of some bolts which had been made from material that had been incorrectly specified by the firm of civil engineers who were contracted by Multiplex plc to design the bridge. These costs were not included in the original estimates, but Multiplex plc is hopeful that they can be recovered from the firm of civil engineers.

Multiplex plc calculates profit on long-term contracts using the percentage of completion method. The percentage of completion of the contract is based on the value of the work certified to date compared to the total contract price.

Required

Prepare the profit and loss account and balance sheet extracts in respect of the contract for the year to 31 March 20X1 only. (9 marks)

14   DIVIDEND DISTRIBUTION (20 marks)   *36 mins*

(a)   What do you understand by the statement that dividends must not be paid out of the capital of a company?

(b)   What would be the effect on the maximum distributable profits of Donor plc, a public company, of the following transactions:

    (i)   An upward revaluation of a fixed asset by £20,000 on 1 January, and a consequential increase in the depreciation charge of £4,000 in the year to 31 December.

    (ii)   The sale of some land for £500,000, which had a historical cost of £150,000 but which was valued in the balance sheet at £440,000.

15   REVENUE RECOGNITION (PILOT PAPER – 25 marks)

The timing of revenue (income) recognition has long been an area of debate and inconsistency in accounting. Industry practice in relation to revenue recognition varies widely, the following are examples of different points in the operating cycle of businesses that revenue and profit can be recognised.

-    On the acquisition of goods
-    During the manufacture or production of goods
-    On delivery/acceptance of goods
-    When certain conditions have been satisfied after the goods have been delivered
-    Receipt of payment for credit sales
-    On the expiry of a guarantee or warranty

In the past the 'critical event' approach has been used to determine the timing of revenue recognition. The Accounting Standards Board (ASB) in its '*Statement of Principles for Financial Reporting*' has defined the 'elements' of financial statements, and it uses these to determine when a gain or loss occurs.

Required

(a)   Explain what is meant by the critical event in relation to revenue recognition and discuss the criteria used in the Statement of Principles for determining when a gain or loss arises.   (5 marks)

(b)   For each of the stages of the operating cycle identified above, explain why it may be an appropriate point to recognise revenue and, where possible, give a practical example of an industry where it occurs.   (12 marks)

(c)   Jenson plc has entered into the following transactions/agreements in the year to 31 March 20X1:

    (i)   Goods, which had cost £20,000 were sold to Wholesaler plc for £35,000 on 1 June 20X0. Jenson plc has an option to repurchase the goods from Wholesaler plc at any time within the next two years. The repurchase price will be £35,000 plus interest charged at 12% per annum from the date of sale to the date of repurchase. It is expected that Jenson plc will repurchase the goods.

    (ii)   Jenson plc owns the rights to a fast food franchise. On 1 April 20X0 it sold the right to open a new outlet to Mr Cody. The franchise is for five years. Jenson plc received an initial fee of £50,000 for the first year and will receive £5,000 per annum thereafter. Jenson plc has continuing service obligations on its franchise for advertising and product development that amount to approximately £8,000 per annum per franchised outlet. A reasonable profit margin on the provision of the continuing services is deemed to be 20% of revenues received.

    (iii) On 1 September 20X0 Jenson plc received total subscriptions in advance of £240,000. The subscriptions are for 24 monthly publications of a magazine produced by Jenson plc. At the year end Jenson plc had produced and despatched six of the 24 publications. The total cost of producing the magazine is estimated at £192,000 with each publication costing a broadly similar amount.

Required

Describe how Jenson plc should treat each of the above examples in its financial statements in the year to 31 March 20X1.   (8 marks)

16   RELATED PARTY TRANSACTIONS   *15 mins*

(a)   Give ten examples of related party transactions which would require disclosure in terms of FRS 8.

(b)   List what has to be disclosed in the financial statements of a company in respect of related parties.

17   SEGMENTAL REPORTING   *10 mins*

Explain how SSAP 25, *Segmental Reporting*, helps users of financial information to make sensible decisions about the performance and position of a company.

18   GROUP ACCOUNTS (20 marks)   *36 mins*

For many years, under UK law, companies with subsidiaries have been required to publish group accounts, usually in the form of consolidated accounts. You are required to state why you feel the preparation of group accounts is necessary and to outline their limitations, if any.

19   ARLENE AND AMANDA   *36 mins*

Arlene plc acquired 135,000 shares in Amanda Ltd in 20X3. The reserves of Amanda Ltd at the date of acquisition comprised: revenue reserve £20,000; capital reserve £10,000. The draft balance sheets of both companies are given below as at 31 December 20X5.

	Arlene plc		Amanda Ltd	
	£	£	£	£
Fixed assets				
Tangible assets		350,000		210,000
Investments				
Shares in Amanda Ltd at cost		190,000		
		540,000		
Current assets				
Stocks	83,000		42,000	
Debtors	102,000		48,000	
Current account with Amanda Ltd	5,000		-	
Bank and cash	40,000		12,000	
	230,000		102,000	
Current liabilities				
Trade creditors	90,000		37,000	
Current account with Arlene Ltd	-		1,000	
Proposed dividend	30,000		10,000	
	120,000		48,000	
Net current assets		110,000		54,000
Total assets less current liabilities		650,000		264,000
Share capital and reserves				
Ordinary shares of £1 each		400,000		150,000
Revenue reserve		190,000		99,000
Capital reserve		60,000		15,000
		650,000		264,000

Arlene plc has not yet accounted for its share of the dividend proposed by Amanda Ltd.

On 29 December 20X5 Amanda Ltd sent a cheque for £4,000 to Arlene Ltd, which was not received until 3 January 20X6.

You are required to prepare the consolidated balance sheet of Arlene plc as at 31 December 20X5. (Goodwill arising on consolidation is deemed to have an indefinite useful life and is therefore to remain in the balance sheet.)

20   PUCCINI   *20 mins*

Puccini Ltd has just acquired all the share capital of Strauss Ltd, which has significant retained profits. The managing director of Puccini Ltd is considering the payment of a dividend from Strauss Ltd and has asked you to advise him on the financial reporting implications of his idea.

Required

Prepare a set of notes you will need for a meeting with the managing director to discuss the dividend.

21   **HAND (25 marks)**   *45 mins*

The following are the draft balance sheets as at 31 December 20X1 of Hand Ltd and its subsidiary Finger Ltd.

	Hand Limited		Finger Limited	
	£	£	£	£
Fixed assets				
Tangible assets		100,000		76,000
Investment in Finger Ltd at cost				
40,000 £1 ordinary shares		50,000		-
		150,000		76,000
Current assets				
Sundry	195,000		62,000	
Current account with Finger Ltd	8,000		-	
	203,000		62,000	
Current liabilities				
Sundry	163,000		36,000	
Current account with Hand Ltd	-		6,000	
	163,000		42,000	
Net current assets		40,000		20,000
		190,000		96,000
Capital and reserves				
Ordinary shares of £1 each		100,000		60,000
Revenue reserves		90,000		36,000
		190,000		96,000

You ascertain the following information.

(a)   Hand Ltd purchased its shareholding in Finger Ltd on 30 June 20X1.

(b)   The revenue reserves of Finger Ltd consist of the following.

	£
Balance at 31 December 20X0	18,000
Profit for the year	18,000
	36,000

(c)   On 30 June 20X1 the fair value of Finger Ltd's tangible fixed assets exceeded their book value by £3,000. It is group policy to depreciate such assets over five years.

(d)   In July 20X1 Finger Ltd paid an ordinary dividend for 20X0 of £6,000. The dividend had been provided for in Finger Ltd's balance sheet at 31 December 20X0. Hand Ltd has credited its share of the dividend received to profit and loss account.

(e)   The difference in the current account balances represents cash in transit.

Required

Prepare Hand's consolidated balance sheet as at 31 December 20X1.

Note. All goodwill is to be treated in accordance with the provisions of FRS 10.

22   **WAR (25 marks)**   *45 mins*

(a)   When an acquisition takes place, the purchase consideration may be in the form of share capital. Where no suitable market price exists (for example, shares in an unquoted company) how may the fair value of the purchase consideration be estimated?   (4 marks)

(b)   On 1 May 20X7, War plc acquired 70% of the ordinary share capital of Peace Ltd by issuing 500,000 ordinary £1 shares at a premium of 60p per share. The costs associated with the share issue were £50,000.

As at 30 June 20X7, the following financial statements for War plc and Peace Ltd were available.

PROFIT AND LOSS ACCOUNTS
FOR THE YEAR ENDED 30 JUNE 20X7

	War plc £'000	Peace Ltd £'000
Turnover	3,150	1,770
Cost of sales	(1,610)	(1,065)
Gross profit	1,540	705
Distribution costs	(620)	(105)
Administrative expenses	(325)*	(210)
Operating profit	595	390
Interest payable	(70)	(30)
Dividends from Peace plc	42	-
Profit on ordinary activities before taxation	567	360
Tax on profit	(283)	(135)
Profit after tax	284	225
Dividends paid	(38)	(60)
Retained profit for the year	246	165

Note. The issue costs of £50,000 on the issue of ordinary share capital are included in this figure.

BALANCE SHEETS AS AT 30 JUNE 20X7

	War plc £'000	Peace Ltd £'000
Fixed assets		
Tangible fixed assets	1,750	350
Investment in Peace Ltd	800	-
	2,550	350
Current assets		
Stock	150	450
Debtors	238	213
Cash	187	112
	575	775
Creditors: amounts falling due within one year	(400)	(250)
Net current assets	175	525
Total assets less current liabilities	2,725	875
Creditors: amounts falling due after one year	(1,050)	(175)
	1,675	700
Capital and reserves		
Ordinary shares of £1 each	750	100
Share premium	300	150
Profit and loss account	625	450
	1,675	700

You have been asked to prepare the consolidated financial statements, taking account of the following further information.

(i)   Any goodwill arising on acquisition is to be amortised over 5 years on a straight line basis, with a full year's amortisation charged in the year of acquisition. The charge is to be included in administrative expenses.

(ii)   War plc accounts for pre-acquisition dividends by treating them as a deduction from the cost of the investment. Peace Ltd paid an ordinary dividend of 60p per share on 1 June 20X7. No dividends were proposed as at 30 June 20X7.

(iii) The profit of Peace Ltd may be assumed to accrue evenly over the year.

(iv)   The tangible fixed assets of Peace Ltd had a net realisable value of £400,000 at the date of acquisition. Their open market value was £500,000. It has been decided that, as Peace Ltd was acquired so close to the year end, no depreciation adjustment will be made in the group accounts; the year end value will be taken as the carrying value of the tangible fixed assets in the accounts of Peace Ltd. The remaining assets and liabilities of Peace Ltd were all stated at their fair value as at 1 May 20X7.

(v)   Peace Ltd did not issue any shares between the date of acquisition and the year end.

(vi)   There were no intercompany transactions during the year.

Required

Prepare the consolidated balance sheet and the consolidated profit and loss account of the War Group plc for the year ended 30 June 20X7. You should work to the nearest £'000. You do not need to prepare notes to the accounts.
(21 marks)

23   CHIGWELL (50 marks)
90 mins

During the year to 31 December 20X2, before the publication of FRS 6 *Acquisitions and mergers*, Chigwell plc acquired two subsidiaries as follows.

(a)   Chigwell plc had an associated company, Tracy Ltd, of which it owned 25% of the share capital. On 1 September 20X2 it acquired the remainder of the share capital, the consideration being the issue of 200,000 £1 ordinary shares in Chigwell plc. The value of the consideration was £280,000. Goodwill arising on consolidation was £95,000 and should be written off against profit for the year.

The transaction qualified as a merger under the old SSAP 23 because it was effected by a sale of 20% of the original holding to Fiddlers Bank and a subsequent repurchase, all of which was part of the same offer.

(b)   On 1 April 20X2, Chigwell plc offered a share exchange in order to acquire the remainder of Sharon plc's issued share capital. The offer became unconditional on 1 May 20X2. Previous shareholdings of the company had been acquired at a cost of £960,000. The total cost of the acquisition, including the £960,000 previously paid, was £4,425,000.

The difference between the nominal value of the shares issued and their value at the date of issue was £573,000. Goodwill on consolidation amounted to £986,000, and should be written off in full against profit for the year.

Summarised profit and loss accounts for the three companies for the year ended 31 December 20X2 are shown below.

	Chigwell plc £'000	Sharon plc £'000	Tracy Ltd £'000
Turnover	80,946	17,194	3,420
Cost of sales and expenses	62,184	13,592	2,560
Operating profit	18,762	3,602	860
Dividends receivable*	45	-	-
Interest receivable	120	50	-
Profit before tax	18,927	3,652	860
Taxation	6,740	1,525	390
Profit after tax	12,187	2,127	470
Ordinary dividends			
Interim	550	**24	12
Final	50	12	6
Preference dividends	12	-	-
Retained profit for the year	11,575	2,091	452

Notes

* Chigwell plc has credited all dividends, whether pre- or post-acquisition, to the profit and loss account.

** Interim dividends were paid on 1 July 20X2.

Required

(a)   Prepare the consolidated profit and loss account for the Chigwell group for the year ended 31 December 20X2 under the acquisition method. Goodwill written off should be shown separately.
(14 marks)

(b)   Prepare a note showing the amount of the group retained profit for the year (from part (a)) which has been retained by each of the three companies.
(3 marks)

(c)   Prepare the consolidated profit and loss account for the Chigwell group for the year ended 31 December 20X2 using merger accounting.
(10 marks)

(d)   Show in a note the amount of group retained profit (from part (c)) which has been retained by each of the three companies.
(3 marks)

(e)   Prepare a schedule reconciling the retained profit for the year as calculated under the acquisition method with the retained profit for the year as calculated under the merger method.
(5 marks)

(f)   Prepare a schedule showing how the amount shown for investment in subsidiaries under the merger method is calculated.   (5 marks)

(g)   Explain why, under FRS 6 *Acquisitions and mergers*, the purchase of the share capital of Tracy would not qualify as a merger.   (10 marks)

24   ENTERPRISE AND VULCAN (20 marks)

Enterprise plc purchased 30% of Vulcan Ltd on 1 July 20X4. At all times, Enterprise participates fully in Vulcan's financial and operating policy decisions. Goodwill is to be capitalised and amortised over five years.

EXTRACT FROM VULCAN LTD'S BALANCE SHEET AT ACQUISITION

	£'000
Share capital	2,000
Revaluation reserve	200
Profit and loss reserve	900
	3,100

BALANCE SHEETS AS AT 30 JUNE 20X8

	Enterprise plc group		Vulcan Ltd	
	£'000	£'000	£'000	£'000
Fixed assets				
Tangible fixed assets		8,000		7,000
Investment in therapy		2,000		-
		10,000		7,000
Current assets				
Stock	1,340		860	
Debtors	1,000		790	
Cash	260		430	
	2,600		2,080	
Creditors (due within one year)	(1,500)		(1,140)	
		1,100		940
		11,100		7,940
Capital and reserves				
Equity share capital		4,000		2,000
Revaluation reserve		2,000		1,000
Profit and loss reserve		5,100		4,940
		11,100		7,940

PROFIT AND LOSS ACCOUNTS FOR THE YEAR ENDING 30 JUNE 20X8

	Enterprise plc group	Vulcan Ltd
	£'000	£'000
Turnover	10,000	6,0000
Cost of sales	(6,000)	(3,000)
Gross profit	4,000	3,000
Expenses	(1,500)	(880)
Operating profit	2,500	2,120
Interest	(100)	(20)
Profit on ordinary activities before tax	2,400	2,100
Tax on ordinary activities	(800)	(700)
Profit on ordinary activities after tax	1,600	1,400
Dividends	(600)	(100)
Retained profit	1,000	1,300

Required

Prepare the consolidated balance sheet and P&L account for the year ended 30 June 20X8. Ignore any additional disclosure requirements of FRS 9.

25   HEPBURN AND SALTER (PILOT PAPER – 25 marks)

(a)   On 1 October 20X0 Hepburn plc acquired 80% of the ordinary share capital of Salter Ltd by way of a share exchange. Hepburn plc issued five of its own shares for every two shares it acquired in Salter Ltd. The market value of Hepburn plc's shares on 1 October 20X0 was £3 each. The share issue has not yet been recorded in Hepburn plc's books. The summarised financial statements of both companies are:

PROFIT AND LOSS ACCOUNTS FOR THE YEAR TO 31 MARCH 20X1

	Hepburn plc		Salter Ltd	
	£'000	£'000	£'000	£'000
Turnover		1,200		1,000
Cost of sales		(650)		(660)
Gross profit		550		340
Operating expenses		(120)		(88)
Debenture interest		nil		(12)
Operating profit		430		240
Taxation		(100)		(40)
Profit after tax		330		200
Dividends - interim	(40)			
- final	(40)			
		(80)		nil
Retained profit for the year		250		200

BALANCE SHEETS AS AT 31 MARCH 20X1

	Hepburn plc		Salter Ltd	
	£'000	£'000	£'000	£'000
Fixed assets		400		150
Land and Buildings		220		510
Plant and Machinery		20		10
Investments		640		670
Current Assets				
Stock	240		280	
Debtors	170		210	
Bank	20		40	
	430		530	
Creditors: amounts falling due within one year				
Trade creditors	170		155	
Taxation	50		45	
Dividends	40		nil	
	(260)		(200)	
Net current assets		170		330
Creditors: amounts falling after more than one year				
8% Debentures		nil		(150)
Net assets		810		1,000
		810		850
Capital and reserves				
Ordinary shares of £1 each		400		150
Profit and loss account		410		700
		810		850

The following information is relevant.

(i)   The fair value of Salter Ltd's assets were equal to their book values with the exception of its land, which had fair value of £125,000 in excess of its book value at the date of acquisition.

(ii)   In the post acquisition period Hepburn plc sold goods to Salter Ltd at a price of £100,000, this was calculated to give a mark-up on cost of 25% to Hepburn plc. Salter Ltd had half of these goods in stock at the year end.

(iii)   Consolidated goodwill is to be written off as an operating expense over a five-year life. Time apportionment should be used in the year of acquisition.

(iv)   The current accounts of the two companies disagreed due to a cash remittance of £20,000 to Hepburn plc on 26 March 20X1 not being received until after the year end. Before adjusting for this, Salter Ltd's debtor balance in Hepburn plc's books was £56,000.

Required

Prepare a consolidated profit and loss account and balance sheet for Hepburn plc for the year to
31 March 20X1. (20 marks)

(b) At the same date as Hepburn plc made the share exchange for Salter Ltd's shares, it also
acquired 6,000 'A' shares in Woodbridge Ltd for a cash payment of £20,000. The share capital of
Woodbridge Ltd is made up of:

Ordinary voting A shares	10,000
Ordinary non-voting B shares	14,000

All of Woodbridge Ltd's equity shares are entitled to the same dividend rights; however during the
year to 31 March 20X1 Woodbridge Ltd made substantial losses and did not pay any dividends.

Hepburn plc has treated its investment in Woodbridge Ltd as an ordinary fixed asset investment
on the basis that:

(i) It is only entitled to 25% of any dividends that Woodbridge Ltd may pay

(ii) It does not have any directors on the Board of Woodbridge Ltd

(iii) It does not exert any influence over the operating policies or management of Woodbridge
Ltd.

Required

Comment on the accounting treatment of Woodbridge Ltd by Hepburn plc's directors and state
how you believe the investment should be accounted for. (5 marks)

Note. You are not required to amend your answer to part (a) in respect of the information in part
(b). **(25 marks)**

Approaching the answer

(a) On 1 October Hepburn acquired 80% of the equity share capital of Salter by way of a share
exchange. Hepburn issued five of its own shares for every two shares in Salter. The market value
of Hepburn's shares on 1 October 20X0 was £3 each. The share issue has not yet been recorded
in Hepburn's books. The summarised financial statements of both companies are:

You can work out the cost of the investment for the goodwill calculation

PROFIT AND LOSS ACCOUNTS
YEAR TO 31 MARCH 20X1

	Hepburn	Hepburn	Salter	Salter
	£'000	£'000	£'000	£'000
Turnover		1,200		1,000
Cost of sales		(650)		(660)
Gross profit		550		340
Operating expenses		(120)		(88)
Debenture interest		Nil		(12)
Operating profit		430		240
Taxation		(100)		(40)
Profit after tax		330		200
Dividends: interim	(40)			nil
final	(40)			
		(80)		(60)
Retained profit for the year		250		200

BALANCE SHEETS AS AT 31 MARCH 20X1

	Hepburn plc		Salter Ltd	
	£'000	£'000	£'000	£'000
Fixed assets		400		150
Land and Buildings		220		510
Plant and Machinery		20		10
Investments		640		670
Current Assets				
Stock	240		280	
Debtors	170		210	
Bank	20		40	
	430		530	
Creditors: amounts falling due				
within one year				
Trade creditors	170		155	
Taxation	50		45	
Dividends	40		nil	
	(260)		(200)	
Net current assets		170		330
Creditors: amounts falling after				
more than one year				
8% Debentures		nil		(150)
Net assets		810		1,000
		810		850
Capital and reserves				
Ordinary shares of £1 each		400		150
Profit and loss account		410		700
		810		850

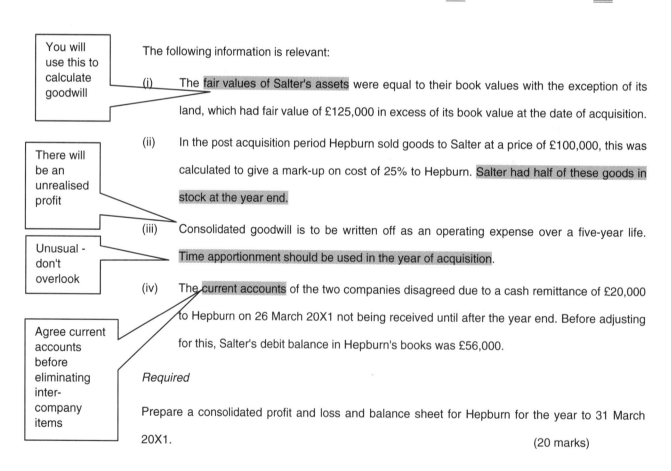

The following information is relevant:

> You will use this to calculate goodwill

(i)   The fair values of Salter's assets were equal to their book values with the exception of its land, which had fair value of £125,000 in excess of its book value at the date of acquisition.

> There will be an unrealised profit

(ii)   In the post acquisition period Hepburn sold goods to Salter at a price of £100,000, this was calculated to give a mark-up on cost of 25% to Hepburn. Salter had half of these goods in stock at the year end.

(iii)   Consolidated goodwill is to be written off as an operating expense over a five-year life.

> Unusual - don't overlook

Time apportionment should be used in the year of acquisition.

(iv)   The current accounts of the two companies disagreed due to a cash remittance of £20,000 to Hepburn on 26 March 20X1 not being received until after the year end. Before adjusting for this, Salter's debit balance in Hepburn's books was £56,000.

> Agree current accounts before eliminating inter-company items

Required

Prepare a consolidated profit and loss and balance sheet for Hepburn for the year to 31 March 20X1.

(20 marks)

(b) At the same date as Hepburn made the share exchange for Salter's shares, it also acquired 6,000 'A' shares in Woodbridge for a cash payment of £20,000. The share capital of Woodbridge is made up of:

Equity voting A shares	10,000
Equity non-voting B shares	14,000

> The % age of shares with voting rights is important

All of Woodbridge's equity shares are entitled to the same dividend rights; however during the year to 31 March 20X1. Woodbridge made substantial losses and did not pay any dividends.

Hepburn has treated its investment in Woodbridge as an ordinary long-term investment on the basis that:

(i) It is only entitled to 25% of any dividends that Woodbridge may pay

(ii) It does not any have directors on the board of Woodbridge

(iii) It does not exert any influence over the operating policies or management of Woodbridge

Required

Comment on the accounting treatment of Woodbridge by Hepburn's directors and state how you believe the investment should be accounted for. (5 marks)

> This is a big hint that the treatment may be wrong

Note. You are not required to amend your answer to part (a) in respect of the information in part (b). (25 marks)

---

26   CPP AND CCA (25 marks)   *45 mins*

(a) 'It is important that managements and other users of financial accounts should be in a position to appreciate the effects of inflation on the business with which they are concerned.'
(PSSAP 7)

Required

Explain how inflation obscures the meaning of accounts prepared by the traditional historical cost convention, and discuss the contribution which CPP accounting could make to providing a more satisfactory system of accounting for inflation.

(b) Compare the general principles underlying CPP and CCA accounting.

(c) Define the term 'realised holding gain'.

(d) Explain briefly the use in CCA accounting of:

(i) The cost of sales adjustment
(ii) The monetary working capital adjustment
(iii) The depreciation adjustment
(iv) The gearing adjustment

---

27   STATEMENT OF PRINCIPLES (20 marks)   *36 mins*

'A major achievement of the ASB was the development of its *Statement of Principles*. However, it is too theoretical to be applied to accounting standards.'

What are the merits of the *Statement of Principles* and do you agree with the criticism that it is too theoretical?

---

28   XYZ GROUP (25 marks)   *45 mins*

A new managing director will soon be taking over the management of the XYZ Group which consists of three companies carrying on similar businesses in the same trade. The group accountant has produced a summary and comparison of the balance sheets, sales and profits for the most recent years to help the new managing director to familiarise himself with the main figures. These are reproduced below.

As the new managing director is essentially a production and marketing expert rather than being from a financial background, he has not had too much experience in reading accounting and financial statements for a group of companies and would find some additional information helpful for use in preliminary discussion with the managers of each of the group companies. However, he has specifically asked that the extra information should not be another extensive statement showing long lists of ratios and percentages which would need yet another statement to interpret the figures. Further, he has managed to obtain a checklist which suggests some 'Criteria for a healthy company' against which the group companies could be compared.

He thinks this checklist could be helpful to the person preparing the report giving the extra information. It suggest the following criteria.

(a) There should be a strong asset base.

(b) There should be adequate control of working capital such as stocks and debtors.

(c) There should be adequate liquidity to ensure that debts can be paid as they arise.

(d) If new funds are likely to be required for any reasons, there should be sufficient borrowing capacity available, or a potential shareholder should be able to invest with confidence.

(e) The operating performance of any individual group company should generally be as good as any other group company, unless there are special reasons otherwise.

(f) A fair commercial return should be earned for the shareholders which covers the risk taken in running the business.

(g) The figures in the accounts should represent accurate valuations of assets and liabilities. Any item of concern should be the subject of further investigations in the context of good account practices.

One immediate problem that the new managing director has to face, when he visits company Y for the first time, is to advise the directors about this year's ordinary dividend. The directors are anxious to keep up good relations with one of the minority shareholders who happens to be a director of their main materials supplier. They therefore wish to pay a dividend of £60,000 as usual, even though a loss was made this particular year. They wish to use the capital redemption reserve to make up any balance not available in general reserve.

SUMMARY AND COMPARISON OF THE BALANCE SHEETS,
SALES AND PROFIT OF THE XYZ GROUP
FOR THE YEAR 20X5/X6

	Company X		Company Y		Company Z		Group	
	£'000	£'000	£'000	£'000	£'000	£'000	£'000	£'000
Fixed assets								
Intangible assets								
Goodwill		-		-		200		866
Research/development		180		-		-		180
Licences/trade marks		140		-		-		140
		320		-		200		1,186
Tangible assets								
Freehold at cost or								
revaluation		300		-		800		1,100
Leasehold at cost	-		-		600		600	
Less amortisation	-		-		580		580	
		-		-		20		20
Plant at cost	1,200		900		1,000		3,100	
Less depreciation	600		400		200		1,200	
		600		500		800		1,900
		1,220		500		1,820		4,206
Investments								
In group companies		2,000		-		-		-
Current assets								
Stock and work in progress	516		250		198		964	
Debtors	468		418		312		1,198	
Bank	100		-		36		136	
	1,084		668		546		2,298	

	Company X		Company Y		Company Z		Group	
	£'000	£'000	£'000	£'000	£'000	£'000	£'000	£'000
Liabilities due within one year								
Bank overdraft	-		172		-		172	
Trade creditors	442		330		86		858	
Customers prepayments	-		106		-		106	
		642		60		460		1,162
		3,862		560		2,280		5,368
Liabilities due after one year								
Debentures (19Y7)		1,000		-		-		1,000
Loan capital		724		-		-		724
Minority interest		-		-		-		620
		2,138		560		2,280		3,024
Capital and reserves								
Share capital		1,300		340		1,500		1,300
Reserves								
Revaluation	-		-		300		300	
Capital redemption	-		200		-		200	
General	838		20		480		1,224	
		838		220		780		1,724
		2,138		560		2,280		3,024
Sales		1,752		1,136		2,316		5,204
Cost of sales		1,488		1,182		1,890		4,560
Net profit (before interest)		264		(46)		426		644
Interest on loans and debentures	108		-		-		108	
Taxation	50		-		98		148	
		158		-		98		256
		106		(46)		328		388
Less minority interest		-		-		-		45
Earnings (loss) after tax		106		(46)		328		343
Extraordinary item		-		-		73		73
Net earnings (loss) available for shareholders		106		(46)		255		270

Required

(a) Prepare a report for the use of the new managing director which highlights any major weaknesses, or other special features, of each of the group companies in the light of the suggested criteria for a healthy company as mentioned above. Use may be made of any appropriate accounting ratios to illustrate specific points.

(b) Identify any items in the summary which you think may require some 'further investigation in the context of good accounting practices' giving reasons for specifying each of these items for special examination and quoting the particular accounting assumption, precept, rule or standard under which it should be examined.

(c) Advise the new managing director as to whether any dividend can be paid by Company Y this year.

---

29   **WEBSTER (PILOT PAPER – 25 marks)**

Webster plc is a diversified holding company that is looking to acquire a suitable engineering company. Two private limited engineering companies, Cole Ltd and Darwin Ltd, are available for sale. The summarised financial statements for the year to 31 March 20X1 of both companies are as follows:

PROFIT AND LOSS ACCOUNTS

	Cole Limited		Darwin Limited	
	£'000	£'000	£'000	£'000
Sales (note (i))		3,000		4,400
Opening stock	450		720	
Purchases (note (ii))	2,030		3,080	
	2,480		3,800	
Closing stock	(540)		(850)	
		(1,940)		(2,950)
Gross profit		1,060		1,450
Operating expenses	480		964	
Debenture interest	80		nil	
Overdraft interest (note (v))	nil		10	
		(560)		(974)
Net profit		500		476

BALANCE SHEETS

	Cole Limited		Darwin Limited	
Fixed assets	£'000	£'000	£'000	£'000
Premises (note iii)		1,140		1,900
Plant (note iv)		1,200		1,200
		2,340		3,100
Current assets				
Stock	540		850	
Debtors	522		750	
Bank	20		nil	
	1,082		1,600	
Current liabilities				
Creditors	438		562	
Overdraft	nil		550	
	(438)		(1,112)	
Net current assets		644		488
		2,984		3,588
10% Debenture		(800)		nil
Net assets		2,184		3,588
Share capital and reserves				
Ordinary share of 1 each		1,000		500
Reserves				
Revaluation reserve		nil		700
Profit and loss - 1 April 20X0	684		1,912	
Profit for year to 31 March 20X1	500		476	
		1,184		2,388
		2,184		3,588

Webster plc bases its preliminary assessment of target companies on certain key ratios. These are listed below together with the relevant figures for Cole Ltd and Darwin Ltd calculated from the above financial statements:

	Cole Limited		Darwin Limited
Return on capital employed (500 + 80)/(2,184 + 800) × 100	19.4%	(476/3,588) × 100	13.3%
Asset turnover (3,000/2,984)	1.01 times	(4,400/3,588)	1.23 times
Gross profit margin	35.3%		33.0%
Net profit margin	16.7%		10.8%
Debtors collection period	64 days		62 days
Creditors payment period	79 days		67 days

Note. Capital employed is defined as shareholders' funds plus long-term, debt at the year end; asset turnover is sales revenues divided by gross assets less current liabilities.

The following additional information has been obtained.

(i)   Cole Ltd is part of the Velox Group. On 1 March 20X1 it was permitted by its holding company to sell goods at a price of £500,000 to Brander Ltd, a fellow subsidiary. Cole Ltd's normal selling price for these goods would have been £375,000. In addition Brander Ltd was instructed to pay for the goods immediately. Cole Ltd normally allows three months credit.

(ii)   On 1 January 20X1 Cole Ltd purchased £275,000 (cost price to Cole Ltd) of its materials from Advent Ltd, another member of the Velox Group. Advent Ltd was also instructed to depart from its normal trading terms that would have resulted in a charge of £300,000 to Cole Ltd for these goods. The Group's finance director also authorised a four-month credit period on this sale. Normal credit terms for this industry are two months credit from suppliers. Cole Ltd had sold all of these goods at the year-end.

(iii)   Fixed assets:

Details relating to the two companies' fixed assets at 31 March 20X1 are:

		Cost/revaluation £'000	Depreciation £'000	Book value £'000
Cole Ltd	- property	3,000	1,860	1,140
	- plant	6,000	4,800	1,200
				2,340
Darwin Ltd	- property	2,000	100	1,900
	- plant	3,000	1,800	1,200
				3,100

Both companies own very similar properties. Darwin Ltd's property was revalued to £2,000,000 at the beginning of the current year (ie. 1 April 20X0). On this date Cole Ltd's property, which is carried at cost less depreciation, had a book value of £1,200,000. Its current value (on the same basis as Darwin Ltd's property) was also £2,000,000. On this date (1 April 20X0) both properties had the same remaining life of 20 years.

(iv)   Darwin Ltd purchased new plant costing £600,000 in February 20X1. In line with company policy a full year's depreciation at 20% per annum has been charged on all plant owned at the year-end. The plant is still being tested and will not come on-stream until next year. The purchase of the plant was largely financed by an overdraft facility that resulted in the interest cost shown in the profit and loss account. Both companies depreciate plant over a five-year life.

(v)   The bank overdraft that would have been required but for the favourable treatment towards Cole Ltd in respect of the items in (i) and (ii) above, would have attracted interest of £15,000 in the year to 31 March 20X1.

Required

(a)   Restate the financial statements of Cole Ltd and Darwin Ltd for the year to 31 March 20X1 in order that they may be considered comparable for decision making purposes. State any assumptions you make.   (10 marks)

(b)   Recalculate the key ratios used by Webster plc and, together with any other relevant points, comment on how the revised ratios may affect the relative assessment of the two companies.

(10 marks)

(c)   Discuss whether the information in notes (i) to (v) above would be publicly available, and if so, describe its source(s).   (5 marks)

Exam answer bank

1 REGULATORS

A listed company is a public limited company whose shares are bought and sold on The Stock Exchange. This involves the signing of a listing agreement which requires compliance with the 'Listing Rules' (formerly known as the Yellow Book). This contains amongst other things The Stock Exchange's detailed rules on the information to be disclosed in listed companies' accounts. This, then, is one regulatory influence on a listed company's accounts. The Stock Exchange enforces compliance by monitoring accounts and reserving the right to withdraw a company's shares from The Stock Exchange List: ie the company's shares would no longer be traded through The Stock Exchange. There is, however, no statutory requirement to obey these rules.

All companies in the UK have to comply with the Companies Acts, which lay down detailed requirements on the preparation of accounts. Company law is becoming more and more detailed, partly because of EU Directives. Another reason to increase statutory regulation is that listed companies are under great pressure to show profit growth and an obvious way to achieve this is to manipulate accounting policies. If this involves breaking the law, as opposed to ignoring professional guidance, company directors may think twice before bending the rules - or, at least, this is the government's hope.

Professional guidance is given by the Accounting Standards Board (ASB), overseen by the Financial Reporting Council. Prescriptive guidance is given in Statements of Standard Accounting Practice (SSAPs) and Financial Reporting Standards (FRSs) which must be applied in all accounts required to show a 'true and fair view' (ie all companies). SSAPs and FRSs are issued after extensive consultation and are revised as required to reflect economic or legal changes. Until fairly recently, companies have been able to disguise non-compliance if their auditors did not qualify the audit report. However, the Companies Act 1989 requires details of non-compliance to be disclosed in the accounts. 'Defective' accounts will in future be revised under court order if necessary and directors signing such accounts can be prosecuted and fined (or even imprisoned). This sanction applies to breach of both accounting standards and company law.

2 STANDARD SETTERS

(a)   The users of financial information - creditors, management, employees, business contacts, financial specialists, government and the general public - are entitled to this information about a business entity to a greater or lesser degree. However, the needs and expectations of these groups will vary.

The preparers of the financial information often find themselves in the position of having to reconcile the interests of different groups in the best way for the business entity. For example whilst shareholders are looking for increased profits to support higher dividends, employees will expect higher wage increases; and yet higher profits without corresponding higher tax allowances (increased capital allowances for example) will result in a larger corporation tax bill.

Without accounting standards to prescribe how certain transactions should be treated, preparers would be tempted to produce financial information which meets the expectations of the favoured user group. For example creative accounting method, such as off balance sheet finance were used to enhance a company's balance sheet to make it more attractive to investors/lenders.

The aim of accounting standards is that they should regulate financial information in order that it shows the following characteristics.

(i)   Objectivity
(ii)   Comparability
(iii) Completeness
(iv)   Consistency

(b)   (i)   *Composition of the ASC*

The ASB membership is still drawn from the accounting profession who act on a voluntary part-time basis, but the Board now has a full-time chairman and technical director. This, it could be argued, shows very little change from the ASC. Unlike the ASC, however, which was controlled by the CCAB and hence the accounting profession, the ASB is controlled by the Financial Reporting Council (FRC) which has 25 members drawn from a wider sphere and includes users, preparers and auditors of accounts.

(ii)   *Emerging issues*

The ASC could only react to emerging issues by going through the long- drawn out process of producing an exposure draft which in due course and after some amendment would become an accounting standard. The effective date of the standard coming in to force was usually some months after its publication.

Under the new regime the Urgent Issues Task Force has been set up as an offshoot of the ASB. It deals with urgent issues not covered by existing standards. Its pronouncements, called abstracts, are intended to come into effect quickly, usually within one month of publication. They may later become incorporated into accounting standards, but in some cases a standard will not be necessary.

(iii)   *ASC too open to pressure*

The ASC was open to political pressure in two ways. Firstly, its members, all being from the accounting profession, were reluctant to produce standards that would act to the detriment of their clients. Secondly, the ASC was pressurised via the government, which was subject to lobbying by large companies with vested interests.

(iv)   *Failure to develop an agreed conceptual framework and to specify user needs*

The need for a conceptual framework is demonstrated by the way UK standards have developed over recent years, haphazardly and in response to perceived problems. The lack of a conceptual framework also meant that fundamental principles were tackled more than once in different standards, thereby producing contradictions and inconsistencies in basic concepts such as those of prudence and matching. Towards the end of its life the ASC realised the need for a conceptual framework and recognised the IASC's *Framework* as a set of guidelines.

In contrast, the ASB identified a need for a conceptual framework at an early stage in its work. In its *Statement of Aims* issued in July 1991 it states that it intends to achieve its aims by 'developing principles to guide it in establishing standards and to provide a framework within which others can exercise judgement in resolving accounting issues'. The framework has been formulated within the *Statement of Principles*, which consists of eight chapters which cover the fundamental principles of accounting and the content of accounts. The ASB used the IASC *Framework* to a large extent as the basis for the *Statement of Principles*, adding material where necessary.

With regard to users, they were not consulted directly under the ASC regime, merely asked to comment on exposure drafts. A variety of user groups are now represented on the FRC which controls the work of the ASB.

(v)   *Inadequate enforcement of standards*

The enforcement of accounting standards, particularly for the large public companies has been enhanced in two ways.

(1)   The CA 1989 requirement that financial statements must state that they have been prepared in accordance with accounting standards. Where there are any significant departures these must be explained and justified.

(2)   The setting up of a Review Panel under the control of the FRC. Its brief is to examine the accounts of large companies and question the departure from accounting standards. The Panel has the power, as its ultimate weapon, to apply to the court for revision of the accounts. The experience to date however is that most companies prefer to resolve any issues by discussion.

3   PUBLISHED ACCOUNTS

(a)   Before the development of accounting standards it was argued that a 'credibility gap' had developed in financial reporting. Some companies were producing accounts based on the principle of prudence; others were selecting from the range of accounting bases available in such a way as to achieve the most favourable profit figure. Users of accounts could not tell which were which.

The range of profit figures which a single enterprise can present by choosing different accounting policies in respect of, say, depreciation, research and development expenditure and deferred taxation is very wide. Investors are unable to take rational decisions if the information presented to them may be interpreted with such latitude. Loan creditors and potential loan creditors cannot decide on the security of their investment unless they are aware of the basis adopted in valuing the assets of the enterprise.

These problems are more serious in the case of quoted companies because of the far greater number of people who have an interest in the activities of such companies. People who may in some degree rely on the accounts of quoted companies, apart from investors and loan creditors, include the companies' employees and business contacts, all kinds of investment analysts and advisers, and the government. Many (particularly investors and employees) will be interested primarily in the future prospects of the company, but others (particularly loan creditors and the government) will be more concerned about the degree of reliance they can place on reported figures.

There are several ways in which disclosure of accounting policies can help to achieve these aims.

(i)   It enables a comparison to be made between companies with different policies. This is useful not only for investment and lending decisions, but also for the purpose of collecting statistics, for example, by government agencies.

(ii)   It prevents possible abuse of the range of accounting bases available so as to distort a company's results and financial position.

(iii)   It enables a proper computation to be made of certain figures important for legal reasons (for example, the amount of corporation tax due; the amount which may be distributed by way of dividend).

(b)   (i)   A company which qualifies to be treated as a *small or medium-sized company* is exempted from delivering its full accounts to the registrar of companies. Full accounts must still be presented to and approved by the members of the company, but the exemptions allow for a reduction in the information which must be published and available (through the registrar) to the general public.

A company cannot benefit from the relevant exemptions for individual accounts in respect of any accounting reference period if it is (or was at any time within the financial year to which the accounts relate):

(1)   A public company.

(2)   A banking company or insurance company.

(3)   An authorised person under the Financial Services Act 1986.

(4)   A member of an ineligible group (which is one in which any of its members is a public company, banking company, insurance company or authorised under the Financial Services Act 1986).

An eligible company or group will qualify for treatment as a small or medium sized company (or group) if it satisfies any two or more of the qualifying conditions for both the current and the previous year. (*Note*. Once qualified, a company will not cease to be so, unless the conditions are not satisfied for two successive years.)

The conditions (which relate to company size) in respect of each company category may be summarised in tabular form.

Category	Turnover	Gross assets	Average employees per week
Small company	Up to £2.8m	Up to £1.4m	Up to 50
Medium company	Up to £11.2m	Up to £5.6m	Up to 250

(ii)   The directors of a company which is entitled to the benefit of a small company exemption (for individual accounts in respect of any accounting reference period) may file, with the registrar of companies, 'abbreviated accounts' (formerly 'modified accounts') as follows:

(1)   A summarised balance sheet.

(2)   Notes only on accounting policies, fixed assets (aggregate movements for tangible and intangible fixed assets and fixed asset investments), share capital, allotments, debts, foreign currency translation and corresponding amounts.

(3)   No profit and loss account.

(4)   No information on directors' emoluments or auditors' remuneration.

(5)   No directors' report.

(c) The directors' report is expected to contain the following information.

(i) A fair review of the development of the business of the company and its subsidiary undertakings during that year and of their position at the end of it. No guidance is given on the form of the review, nor the amount of detail it should go into.

(ii) The amount, if any, recommended for dividend.

(iii) The principal activities of the company and its subsidiaries in the course of the financial year, and any significant changes in those activities during the year.

(iv) Where significant, an estimate should be provided of the difference between the book value of land held as fixed assets and its realistic market value.

(v) Information about the company's policy for the employment for disabled persons.

(vi) The names of persons who were directors at any time during the financial year.

(vii) For those persons who were directors at the year end, the interests of each (or of their spouse or infant children) in shares or debentures of the company or subsidiaries:

(1) At the beginning of the year, or at the date of appointment as director, if this occurred during the year.

(2) At the end of the year.

If a director has no such interests at either date, this fact must be disclosed. (The information in (e) may be shown as a note to the accounts instead of in the directors' report.)

(viii) Political and charitable contributions made, if these together exceeded more than £200 in the year, giving:

(1) Separate totals for political contributions and charitable contributions.

(2) The amount of each separate political contribution exceeding £200, and the name of the recipient.

Wholly owned British subsidiaries are exempt from requirement (g) because the information will be disclosed in the directors' report of the holding company.

(ix) Particulars of any important events affecting the company or any of its subsidiaries which have occurred since the end of the financial year (significant 'post-balance sheet events').

(x) An indication of likely future developments in the business of the company and of its subsidiaries.

(xi) An indication of the activities (if any) of the company and its subsidiaries in the field of research and development.

(xii) Particulars of purchases (if any) of its own shares by the company during the year, including reasons for the purchase.

(xiii) Particulars of other acquisitions of its own shares during the year (perhaps because shares were forfeited or surrendered, or because its shares were acquired by the company's nominee or with its financial assistance).

(xiv) Details of any measures taken by the company directed at increasing employee participation and information.

(xv) Details of the company's creditor payment policy.

4 D'URBERVILLE

SCHEDULE OF MOTOR VEHICLES
FOR THE YEARS ENDED 31 DECEMBER 20X5, 20X6, 20X7

	£'000
20X5	
Cost: At 1 January 20X5	540
Additions	147
Disposals	70
At 31 December 20X5	617

	£'000
Accumulated depreciation: At 1 January 20X5	130
Disposals (W1)	50
Charge for year 25% × (617 − (130 − 50))	134
At 31 December 20X5	214
Net book value at 31 December 20X5	403

	£'000
20X6	
Cost: At 1 January 20X6	617
Additions*	252
Disposals	110
At 31 December 20X6	759
Accumulated depreciation: At 1 January 20X6	214
Disposals (W2)	68
Charge for year 25% (759 − (214 − 68))	153
At 31 December 20X6	299
Net book value at 31 December 20X6	460

*Note. The acquisitions in 20X6 are capitalised at cash price less trade discount (for cash purchases), plus delivery costs £(300 − 60 + 12) = £252,000.

20X7	£'000
Cost: At 1 January 20X7	759
Additions**	375
Disposals	75
At 31 December 20X7	1,059

20X7	£'000
Accumulated depreciation: At 1 January 20X7	299
Disposals (W3) (1,059 − (299 − 43)) × 25%	43
Charge for year 25%	201
At 31 December 20X7	457
Net book value at 31 December 20X5	602

** Note. The acquisitions in 20X7 are capitalised at cash price less trade discount (for cash purchase) plus delivery cost: £(450 − 90 + 15) = £375.

Workings

1   *Accumulated depreciation on 20X5 disposals*

Vehicles acquired in 20X0:

		£
20X0	25% × £30,000	7,500
20X1	25% × £(30,000 − 7,500)	5,625
20X2	25% × £(30,000 − (7,500 + 5,625))	4,219
20X3	25% × £(30,000 − (7,500 + 5,625 + 4,219))	3,164
20X4	25% × £(30,000 − (7,500 + 5,625 + 4,219 + 3,164))	2,373
Total		22,881

Vehicles acquired in 20X1:

		£
20X1	25% × £40,000	10,000
20X2	25% × £(40,000 − 10,000)	7,500
20X3	25% × £(40,000 − (10,000 + 7,500))	5,625
20X4	25% × £(40,000 − (10,000 + 8,500 + 5,625))	4,219
Total		27,344

Total accumulated depreciation on disposals: £(22,881 + 27,344) = £50,225.

2 *Accumulated depreciation on 20X6 disposals*

Vehicles acquired in 20X2:

		£
20X2	25% × £45,000	11,250
20X3	25% × £(45,000 − 11,250)	8,438
20X4	25% × £(45,000 − (11,250 + 8,438))	6,328
20X5	25% × £(45,000 − (11,250 + 8,438 + 6,328))	4,746
Total		30,762

Vehicles acquired in 20X3:

		£
20X3	25% × £65,000	16,250
20X4	25% × £(65,000 − 16,250)	12,188
20X5	25% × £(65,000 − (16,250 + 12,188))	9,141
Total		37,579

Total accumulated depreciation on 20X6 disposals £(30,762 + 37,579) = £68,341

3 *Accumulated depreciation on 20X7 disposals*

Vehicles acquired in 20X2:

		£
20X4	25% × £75,000	18,750
20X5	25% × £(75,000 − 18,750)	14,063
20X6	25% × £(75,000 − (18,750 + 14,063))	10,547
Total		43,360

Note. The hire purchase was treated as though it was an operating lease as the finance leases were already separately identified in the question. If in doubt, always explain your assumptions in your answer.

5 **BLECO**

Notes

(a) Under the original SSAP 13, development expenditure written off could not be reinstated if it subsequently met the SSAP's criteria for capitalisation. The revised SSAP permits such expenditure to be reinstated.

(b) Project D371 is contract WIP, not a development project, because costs are being reimbursed in full and so Bleco is taking no risk itself.

(c) SSAP 13 requires that depreciation on assets used in R & D should be included in the expenditure on R & D to be disclosed and it should also be disclosed separately in accordance with FRS 15.

(d) It is possible (but not obligatory) to capitalise depreciation, just like the other expenses deferred.

(e) Common errors in this question include capitalisation of pure and applied research projects, omission of opening balances, treating the contract WIP as an intangible asset and taking individual expenses to P & L rather than a global figure for R & D written off.

BLECO PLC
PROFIT AND LOSS ACCOUNT
FOR THE YEAR ENDED 31 AUGUST 20X1 (EXTRACT)

	£
Included in cost of sales (or other appropriate category):	
Research and development costs written off (W2)	329,340
Amortisation of development costs (W1)	33,050
	362,390

BLECO PLC
BALANCE SHEET AS AT 31 AUGUST 20X1 (EXTRACTS)

	£
Fixed assets	
Intangible assets	
Deferred development expenditure	652,340
Current assets	
Stocks	
Contract work in progress	14,030
Profit and loss account	
At 1 September 20X0:	
As previously reported	X
Development expenditure previously written off,	
now reinstated	47,830
As restated	X + 47,830

Workings

1   *Deferred development expenditure/long-term contract*

	D369 £	D368 £	D363 £	D367 £	Total £	D371 £
Brought forward	-		198,300	242,700	488,830	-
Reinstated		47,830				
Current year expenditure						
Staff costs	34,070	16,480	-	2,090	52,640	27,500
Materials	1,560	410	-	340	2,310	3,400
Other direct expenses	640	230	-	170	1,040	710
Production overheads	6,980	4,650	-	3,540	15,170	6,420
Depreciation (W3):						
buildings	31,000	-	-	-	31,000	
equipment	94,400	-	-	-	94,400	-
	168,650	21,770	-	6,140	196,560	
Reimbursed						(24,000)
Contract WIP						14,030
Amortisation (1/6)		-	33,050	-	33,050	
Carried forward	168,650	69,600	165,250	248,840	652,340	

2   *Expenditure to be written off*

	Total £	PR119 £	AR187 £	AR204 £	D370 £	Unallocated £
Staff costs	110,760	35,100	27,300	15,260	29,800	3,300
Materials	8,340	810	520	290	2,650	4,070
Direct expenses	3,570	250	210	180	690	2,240
Production overheads	20,870	1,240	3,600	2,950	6,010	7,070
	143,540	37,400	31,630	18,680	39,150	16,680
Sales/admin o'hds	76,200					76,200
Market research	55,600					55,600
Depreciation:						
buildings (W3)	20,000		20,000		-	
equipment (W3)	34,000		34,000		-	
	329,340	37,400	85,630	18,680	39,150	148,480

3   *Depreciation*

	AR187 £	D369 £
Buildings		
£200,000 × 10%	20,000	
£310,000 × 10%		31,000
Equipment		
£170,000 × 20%	34,000	
£472,000 × 20%		94,400

6   WINGER

(a)   WINGER PLC
PROFIT AND LOSS ACCOUNT FOR THE
YEAR ENDED 31 MARCH 20X1

	£'000	£'000
Turnover (358,450 – 27,000)		331,450
Cost of sales (W1)		(208,550)
Gross profit		122,900
Distribution expenses		(28,700)
Administration expenses		(15,000)
Operating profit		79,200
Exceptional items		
Profit on disposal of land and buildings		
(95,000 - 80,000)		15,000
Loss on abandonment of research project		(30,000)
Profit on ordinary activities before interest		64,200
Interest expense (W3)		(11,200)
Profit before tax		53,000
Taxation (15,000 - 2,200)		(12,800)
Profit after tax		40,200
Dividends: interim	12,000	
final (W4)	18,000	
		(30,000)
Retained profit for the period		10,200
Retained profit b/f (71,600 + 30,000)		101,600
Profit and loss account reserve		111,800

(b)   BALANCE SHEET AS AT 31 MARCH 20X1

	£'000	£'000
Fixed assets: tangible		
Land and buildings (200,000 - 6,000 (W2))		194,000
Plant and machinery (W5)		160,000
		354,000
Current assets		
Stock (28,240 + 22,500 (W1))	50,740	
Debtors (55,000 – 27,000 (W1))	28,000	
Cash	10,660	
	89,400	
Creditors due within one year		
Trade and other creditors (W6)	51,400	
Taxation	15,000	
Proposed dividends (W4)	18,000	
	84,400	
Net current assets		5,000
Total assets less current liabilities		359,000
Creditors due after one year		
Lease creditor (W7)		(47,200)
8% debentures		(50,000)
Net assets		261,800
Capital and reserves		
Ordinary shares 25p each		150,000
Profit and loss account (see (a))		111,800
Shareholders' funds		261,800

Workings

1 Cost of sales		£'000
Per question		185,050
Less sale/return goods (27,000 × 100/120)		(22,500)
Add depreciation (W2)		46,000
		208,550

2	*Depreciation*	£'000
	Building (100,000 ÷ 50)	2,000
	Heating system (20,000 ÷ 10)	2,000
	Lifts (30,000 ÷ 15)	2,000
		6,000
	Leased plant (80,000 × 20%)	16,000
	Owned plant (154,800 - 34,800) × 20%	24,000
		46,000

3	*Interest expense*	£'000
	Debenture interest (50,000 × 8%)	4,000
	Finance lease (80,000 - 20,000) × 12%	7,200
		11,200

4	*Final dividend*	£'000
	Total dividend required £1.25 × 4% × (150,000 × 4)	30,000
	Interim dividend paid	(12,000)
	Final dividend required	18,000

5	*Plant and machinery*	£'000
	Cost: owned plant	154,800
	leased plant	80,000
		234,800
	Depreciation: owned plant (34,800 + 24,000 (W2))	(58,800)
	leased plant (80,000 × 20%)	(16,000)
		160,000

6	*Trade and other creditors*	£'000
	Trial balance	29,400
	Lease creditor (W7)	20,000
	Accrued debenture interest	2,000
		51,400

7	*Lease creditor*	£'000
	Total payments due	80,000
	Less amount paid	(20,000)
		60,000
	Add accrued interest (60,000 × 12%)	7,200
	Total creditor	67,200
	Due within one year	20,000
	Due after one year	47,200

(c) Prior to the issue of FRS 15 *Tangible fixed assets*, companies often used to justify the non-depreciation of buildings on several grounds, including:

(i) That the current value of the buildings was **higher than cost**.

(ii) That the level of **maintenance** meant that no deterioration or consumption had taken place.

(iii) That the depreciation charge would **not be material**.

FRS 15 dismisses the first two of them as being **insufficient grounds** for a policy of non-depreciation. Depreciation is **not** a valuation model; rather it is a means of **allocating the depreciable amount** of the asset to accounting periods.

However, it is still permissible not to charge depreciation on the grounds of non-materiality, but only when **both** the depreciation charge for the period **and** the accumulated depreciation that would have been charged against the value of the asset at that point in time, are immaterial. Thus assets with very long lives and/or high residual values may fall not to be depreciated. FRS 15 also requires that, for depreciation to be classed as immaterial:

(i) There must be a policy of **regular maintenance**.

(ii) The asset is unlikely to **suffer obsolescence**.

(iii)   There is a policy **and** practice of disposing of similar assets long **before** the **end of their useful lives** at proceeds not materially less than their carrying amounts.

An annual **test for impairment** is also required (except for land).

On the facts given, Winger's policy may have complied with FRS 15.

7   BULWELL

(a)   BOOKS OF BULWELL AGGREGATES LIMITED

LORRIES ACCOUNT

20X1		£			£
1 Jan	Granby Garages	54,000			

PROVISION FOR DEPRECIATION ON LORRIES

20X1		£	20X1		£
			31 Dec	P & L account: ¼ ×	
31 Dec	Balance c/d	12,500		£(54,000 − (3 × 1,333))	12,500
20X2			20X2		
31 Dec	Balance c/d	25,000	1 Jan	Balance b/d	12,500
			31 Dec	P & L account	12,500
		25,000			25,000
20X3			20X3		
31 Dec	Balance c/d	37,500	1 Jan	Balance b/d	25,000
			31 Dec	P & L account	12,500
		37,500			37,500
20X4			20X4		
31 Dec	Balance c/d	50,000	1 Jan	Balance b/d	37,500
			31 Dec	P & L account	12,500
		50,000			50,000
			20X5		
			1 Jan	Balance b/d	50,000

HP INTEREST PAYABLE

20X1		£	20X1		£
31 Dec	Bank (W)	11,250	31 Dec	P & L account	11,250
20X2			20X2		
31 Dec	Bank (W)	8,063	31 Dec	P & L account	8,063
20X3			20X3		
31 Dec	Bank (W)	4,078	31 Dec	P & L account	4,078

GRANBY GARAGES PLC

20X1		£	20X1		£
1 Jan	Bank - deposit	9,000	1 Jan	Lorries a/c	54,000
31 Dec	Bank (W)	12,750			
	Balance c/d	32,250			
		54,000			54,000
20X2			20X2		
31 Dec	Bank (W)	15,937	1 Jan	Balance b/d	32,250
	Balance c/d	16,313			
		32,250			32,250
20X3			20X3		
31 Dec	Bank (W)	16,313	1 Jan	Balance b/d	16,313

PROFIT AND LOSS ACCOUNTS (EXTRACTS)

	20X1 £	20X2 £	20X3 £	20X4 £
HP interest	11,250	8,063	4,078	
Depreciation on lorries	12,500	12,500	12,500	12,500

BALANCE SHEETS AT 31 DECEMBER (EXTRACTS)

	20X1 £	20X2 £	20X3 £	20X4 £
Fixed assets				
Lorries: at cost	54,000	54,000	54,000	54,000
depreciation	12,500	25,000	37,500	50,000
	41,500	29,000	16,500	4,000
Current liabilities				
HP obligations	15,937	16,313	-	-
Long-term liabilities				
HP obligations	16,313	-	-	-

(b) BOOKS OF GRANBY GARAGES PLC

BULWELL AGGREGATES LIMITED

20X1		£	20X1		£
1 Jan	Sales	54,000	1 Jan	Bank	9,000
			31 Dec	Bank	12,750
				Balance c/d	32,250
		54,000			54,000
20X2			20X2		
1 Jan	Balance b/d	32,250	31 Dec	Bank	15,937
				Balance c/d	16,313
		32,250			32,250
20X3			20X3		
1 Jan	Balance b/d	16,313	31 Dec	Bank	16,313

HP INTEREST RECEIVABLE

20X1		£	20X1		£
31 Dec	P & L account	11,250	31 Dec	Bank	11,250
20X2			20X2		
31 Dec	P & L account	8,063	31 Dec	Bank	8,063
20X3			20X3		
31 Dec	P & L account	4,078	31 Dec	Bank	4,078

TRADING AND PROFIT AND LOSS ACCOUNTS (EXTRACTS)

	£	20X1 £	20X2 £	20X3 £
Sales	54,000		-	-
Cost of sales on HP	43,200		-	-
Gross profit on HP sales		10,800	-	-
HP interest receivable		11,250	8,063	4,078

Working

Apportionment of HP instalments between interest and capital repayment.

	20X1 £	20X2 £	20X3 £
Opening liability (after deposit)	45,000	32,250	16,313
Add interest at 25%	11,250	8,063	4,078
	56,250	40,313	20,391
Less instalment	24,000	24,000	20,391
Closing liability	32,250	16,313	Nil
Interest element as above	11,250	8,063	4,078
∴Capital repayment	12,750	15,937	16,313
Total instalment	24,000	24,000	20,391

8 SOAP

> *Tutorial note.* The key to avoiding getting muddled in part (b) of this question is to set out the proformas (including those for workings) and present your workings logically. Remember, only 11 out of a total of 30 marks are available for the computational aspects of this question.

(a) The definition of a long term contract in SSAP 9 *Stocks and long term contracts* generally applies to contracts which last for more than one year, but does not exclude contracts of less than one year which fall into different accounting periods. The relevant wording of the definition is as follows.

> '(A long term contract is) one where the time taken substantially to complete the contract is such that the contract activity falls into different accounting periods. A contract that is required to be accounted for as long term . . . will usually extend for a period exceeding one year . . . Some contracts with a shorter duration than one year should be accounted for as long term contracts if they are sufficiently material . . . that not to record turnover and attributable profit would lead to distortion'.

The accounting treatment adopted by Soap plc for the shorter contracts would appear to be consistent with this SSAP 9 definition. It is also consistent with the treatment of the other contracts. It is important, however, that the same accounting treatment is used every year, even if the results are not as favourable, unless there are good reasons for changing it.

(b) SOAP PLC
PROFIT AND LOSS ACCOUNT
FOR THE YEAR ENDED 31 DECEMBER 20X7 (EXTRACT)

	£'000
Turnover	5,680
Cost of sales	(5,165)
Gross profit on long term contracts	515

SOAP PLC
BALANCE SHEET AS AT 31 DECEMBER 20X7

	£'000
Current assets	
Stock	
Long term contract balances	137.5
Debtors	
Amounts recoverable on contracts	1,050
Current liabilities	
Payments on account	(350)

Workings

1   *Archers plc*

	£
Costs incurred to date	47,500
Machine write-off $(20,000 - (^6/_{12} \times 10,000))$	15,000
	62,500
Less cost of sales (W4)	(40,000)
Long term contract balance	22,500
Excess of payments on account over turnover $(40 - 30)$	(10,000)
	12,500

2   *Neighbours Ltd*

	£'000
Costs incurred to date	1,800
Cost of sales (W4)	(1,250)
Long term contract balance	550
Less excess of payments on account over turnover $(2,500 - 1,600)$	(900)
Current liability	(350)

3   *Emmerdale plc*

	£'000
Costs incurred to date	4,000
Cost of sales (W4)	(3,875)
Long term contract balance	125
Turnover (W4)	4,050
Payments on account	3,000
Amounts recoverable on contracts	1,050

4   *Profit and loss account*

	Emmerdale £'000		Archers £'000		Neighbours £'000	Total £'000
Turnover						
	$(45\% \times 9)$ 4,050	$(20\% \times 150)$	30	$(25\% \times 6.4)$	1,600	5,680
Cost of sales						
	$(45\% \times 7.5)$ 3,375	$(20\% \times 120 - 20^*)$	20	$(25\% \times 5)$	1,250	4,645
Additional costs						
	$(8 - 7.5)$ 500		20			520
	(3,875)		(40)		(1,250)	(5,165)
Profit (loss) on						
long term contracts	175		(10)		350	515

   * *Note.* Because the machine is being written off in one year, its total cost, rather than a percentage, is allocated to that year.

5   *Balance sheet*

	Emmerdale £'000	Archers £'000	Neighbours £'000	Total £'000
Current assets				
Stocks				
Long term contract balances	125 (W3)	12.5 (W1)		137.5
Debtors				
Amounts recoverable on contracts	1,050 (W3)			1,050
Current liabilities				
Payments on account			(350) (W2)	(350)

9   **CORAX**

(a)   CORPORATION TAX (20X5) ACCOUNT

	£		£
Bank	16,300	Balance b/f	16,300

CORPORATION TAX (20X6) ACCOUNT

	£		£
Profit and loss a/c over provision	1,200	Balance b/f	5,000
Balance c/d	3,800		
	5,000		5,000

CORPORATION TAX (20X7) ACCOUNT

	£		£
		Profit and loss a/c	36,000
Balance c/d	36,000		
	36,000		36,000

DEFERRED TAXATION ACCOUNT

	£		£
		Balance b/f	29,400
		Profit and loss a/c	
Balance c/d	36,400	(increase in provision)	7,000
	36,400		36,400

(b)   PROFIT AND LOSS ACCOUNT
      FOR THE YEAR ENDED 31 DECEMBER 20X7 (EXTRACT)

	Note	£
Profit for the year on ordinary activities		100,000
Tax on profit for the year	1	(41,800)
Profit for the financial year		58,200
Dividends paid and proposed	2	(52,500)
Retained profit for the year		5,700
Unappropriated profits brought forward*		43,000
Unappropriated profits carried forward		48,700

* Movements on the profit and loss account may be shown separately in a note to the accounts.

BALANCE SHEET AS AT 31 DECEMBER 20X7 (EXTRACT)

	Note	£
Note		
Creditors: amounts falling due within one year	3	
Other creditors including taxation		
(£3,800 + £36,000 + £31,500)		71,300
Provisions for liabilities and charges		
Taxation, including deferred taxation	4	36,400
Capital and reserves		
Called up share capital - 700,000 ordinary shares of 50p each, allotted		
and fully paid		350,000
Profit and loss account		48,700

The notes referred to in the left margin form an integral part of these accounts.

NOTES ON THE ACCOUNTS (EXTRACTS)

		£
1	The tax on profit for the year comprises:	
	UK corporation tax (provided at X% on taxable profits for the year)	36,000
	Less over provision on profits of previous year	1,200
		34,800
	Transfer to deferred taxation account	7,000
		41,800

		£
2	Dividends for the year on the allotted ordinary share capital are:	
	Paid: 3p on 700,000 shares	21,000
	Proposed: 4.5p on 700,000 shares	31,500
		52,500

3   The figure for creditors includes a proposed dividend of £31,500 payable on the ordinary shares.

		£
4	Deferred tax balance at 31 December 20X6	29,400
	Charge for the year	7,000
	Balance at 31 December 20X7	36,400

10   CHER

> *Tutorial note.* The calculations involved in this question are not particularly complicated. However, a large number of marks are available for explanations and understanding. Part (d), particularly requires you to think very carefully about the implications of merger accounting for EPS.

(a)   Earnings per share (EPS) is one of the most frequently quoted statistics in financial analysis. Because of the widespread use of the price earnings (P/E) ratio as a yardstick for investment decisions, it became increasingly important.

It seems that reported and forecast EPS can, through the P/E ratio, have a significant effect on a company's share price. Thus, a share price might fall if it looks as if EPS is going to be low. This is not very rational, as EPS can depend on many, often subjective, assumptions used in preparing a historical statement, namely the profit and loss account. It does not necessarily bear any relation to the value of a company, and of its shares. Nevertheless, the market is sensitive to EPS.

EPS has also served as a means of assessing the stewardship and management role performed by company directors and managers. Remuneration packages might be linked to EPS growth, thereby increasing the pressure on management to improve EPS. The danger of this, however, is that management effort goes into distorting results to produce a favourable EPS.

The ASB believed that undue emphasis was being placed on EPS, and that this led to simplistic interpretations of financial performance. Consequently, in issuing FRS 3 *Reporting financial performance*, the ASB attempted to de-emphasise EPS by requiring it to be calculated after extraordinary items. Because of this, and other changes, EPS became volatile and, arguably less useful for analysis; many companies provided additional EPS figures, prepared on what they saw as a more meaningful basis.

The introduction of FRS 14 *Earnings per share* has helped to reduce the subjectivity of EPS and also covers these alternative EPS disclosures.

(b) CHER (HOLDINGS) PLC
EARNINGS PER SHARE FOR THE YEAR ENDED 30 JUNE 20X4

Earnings		£460,000
Number of shares		
In issue for full year		800,000
In issue 1.7.X3 - 30.9.X3		
$200,000 \times {}^3/_{12} \times 60\%$	30,000	
In issue 1.10.X3 - 30.6.X4		
$200,000 \times {}^9/_{12} \times 100\%$	150,000	
		180,000
		980,000

$$\text{Earnings per share} = \frac{460,000}{980,000} = 46.9\text{p}$$

(c) (i) *Theoretical ex rights price per share*

	£
Value of 4 shares before rights issue (4 × 1.90)	7.60
Value of 1 rights issue share	1.30
Value of 5 shares after rights issue	8.90

$$\text{Theoretical ex rights price } \frac{8.90}{5} = £1.78$$

Adjustment factor

$$\frac{£1.90}{£1.78} = 1.067$$

Earnings		£1,310,000
Number of shares in issue		
1.7.X4 - 28.2.X5		
	711,610	
$1,000,000 \times \dfrac{8}{12} \; 1\text{-}067$		
1.3.X5 - 30.6.X5		
$1,250,000 \times {}^4/_{12}$	416,667	
		1,128,277

$$\text{EPS } \frac{1,310,000}{1,128,277} = 116.1\text{p}$$

Revised EPS calculation for 20X4

$$\frac{46.9}{1.067} = 43.9\text{p}$$

CHER (HOLDINGS) PLC
EARNINGS PER SHARE FOR THE YEAR ENDED 30 JUNE

	20X5	20X4
	116.1p	43.9p

(ii) A rights issue is a popular method through which public companies are able to access the stock market for further capital. Under the terms of such an issue, existing shareholders are given the opportunity to acquire further shares in the company on a pro-rata basis to their existing shareholdings.

The 'rights' shares will usually be offered at a discount to the market price. In such cases, the issue is equivalent to a bonus issue combined with an issue at full market price. Bonus issues are treated as though they have been in issue for the whole year and are also taken into account in the previous year's EPS calculation to give a comparable result. FRS 14 states that it is necessary to adjust the number of shares in issue before the rights issue to reflect the bonus element inherent in the issue. The notes to the financial statements should preferably refer to the adjustments made to the comparative EPS figure to reflect the bonus element of the rights issue.

The bonus element of the rights issue is given by the following fraction, which gives the appropriate adjustment factor.

$$\frac{\text{Fair value of current shares}}{\text{Theoretical ex rights price per share}}$$

The 'cum rights price' is the *actual* price at which the shares are quoted inclusive of the right to take up the future shares under the rights issue.

The 'ex rights price' is the *theoretical* price at which the shares would be quoted, other stock market factors apart, after the rights issue shares have been issued.

In order to calculate earnings per share with a rights issue, the shares are time apportioned before and after the date of the rights issue. The number of shares is calculated in two stages as follows.

Before rights issue

Number of shares before rights issue	× Adjustment factor ×	Fraction of year before rights issue

After rights issue

Number of shares after rights issue × Fraction of year after rights issue

The two figures produced by the above calculations are added together to give the denominator for the fraction required in calculating earnings per share.

When calculating the revised earnings per share for the previous year, the latter has to be adjusted to take account of the bonus element by **dividing** it by the **adjustment factor**.

This makes the previous year's figure comparable with that of the current year.

(d) *Current year*

Earnings	£1,520,000

Number of shares		
As at 1 July 20X5	1,250,000	
2 Sonny for 1 Cher	×2	2,500,000

$$\text{EPS} = \frac{1,520,000}{2,500,000} = 60.8\text{p}$$

Note. We are told in the question that the principles of merger accounting have been adopted. This means that the shares in issue at the end of the year are assumed to have been in issue for the whole of the year. There is therefore no need to time apportion as we had to with the rights issue. The previous year's EPS figure will have to be adjusted to reflect the number of shares deemed to have been in issue in that year, ie twice as many as were in fact in issue.

Previous year

EPS = 116.1p × ½ = 58.05p

SONNY (HOLDINGS) PLC
EARNINGS PER SHARE FOR THE YEAR ENDED 30 JUNE

	20X6	*20X5*
	60.8p	58.05p

11 **SPICE**

(a) SPICE PLC
CASH FLOW STATEMENT
FOR THE YEAR ENDED 31 MARCH 20X6

Reconciliation of operating profit to net cash inflow from operating activities

	£m
Operating profit	280
Depreciation	76
Profit on sale of fixed asset (42 – 38)	(4)
Decrease in stocks	30
Increase in debtors	(40)
Increase in creditors (426 – 258)	168
Premium on cancellation of preference shares 40 × 20p to be included in finance costs	8
	518

CASH FLOW STATEMENT

	£m
Net cash inflow from operating activities	518
Returns on investments and servicing of finance (note 1)	(4)
Taxation (W1)	(44)
Capital expenditure (note 1)	(152)
	318
Equity dividends paid (W3)	(48)
	270
Management of liquid resources (note 1)	(160)
	110
Financing (note 1)	(86)
Increase in cash	24

Reconciliation of cash flow to movement in net debt (note 2)

	£m	£m
Increase in cash in the period	24	
Cash inflow from increase in finance lease	36	
Cash used to repurchase debentures	40	
Cash used to increase liquid resources	160	
Change in net debt resulting from cash flows		260
New finance lease		(56)
Movement in net debt in the period		204
Net debt at 1 April 20X5		(168)
Net funds at 31 March 20X6		36

NOTES TO THE CASH FLOW STATEMENT

1   *Gross cash flows*

	£m	£m
Returns on investments and servicing of finance		
Interest received (6 + 4 − 2)	8	
Interest paid (14 + 4 − 6 − 6)	(6)	
Interest element of finance lease	(6)	
		(4)
Capital expenditure		
Purchase of tangible fixed assets (W2)	(194)	
Sale of tangible fixed assets	42	
		(152)
Management of liquid resources		
Purchase of short term investments	(160)	
		(160)
Financing		
Issue of share capital	20	
Share premium	20	
Cost of share capital issue	(2)	
Cancellation of preference shares	(40)	
Premium on cancellation of preference shares	(8)	
Repurchase of debentures	(40)	
Capital element of finance lease (W4)	(36)	
		(86)

2   *Analysis of changes in net debt*

	At 1 April 20X5	Cash flows	Other changes	At 31 March 20X6
	£m	£m	£m	£m
Loan notes repayable on demand (190 − 160)	-	30		30
Cash	42	(30)		12
Bank overdraft	(40)	24		(16)
	-	24		
Debt due within one year	-	-	-	-
Debt due after one year				
Debentures	(80)	40		(40)
Obligations under finance leases	(90)	36	(56)	(110)
Current asset investments	-	160	-	160
	(168)	260	(56)	36

Workings

1   *Taxation*

TAX

	£m		£m
Cash paid (bal fig)	44	B/d 1.4.X5	
C/d 31.3.X6		Corporation tax	20
Corporation tax	32		
		Deferred tax	16
Deferred tax	24	P&L charge	64
	100		100

BPP PUBLISHING

2   _Purchase of tangible fixed assets_

TANGIBLE FIXED ASSETS

	£m		£m
Bal b/d 1.4.X5	400	Depreciation	76
Finance leases	56	Disposals at NBV	38
Revaluations	14	Bal c/d 31.3.X6	550
Cash purchases (bal fig)	194		
	664		664

3   _Dividends_

DIVIDENDS

	£m		£m
Cash paid (bal fig)	48	Balance b/d 1.4.X5	16
Bal c/d 31.3.X6	8	P&L charge	40
	56		56

4   _Capital element of finance lease_

OBLIGATIONS UNDER FINANCE LEASES

	£m		£m
Capital repayment (bal fig)	36	Bal b/d 1.4.X5 (3 + 42)	90
Bal c/d 31.3.X6 (5 + 50)	110	Additions	56
	146		146

(b)   _Movement on share capital and reserves_

	Ordinary £m	Preference £m	Share premium £m	Capital redemption reserve £m	Revaluation reserve £m	Profit and loss account £m
Balance at 1.4.X5	180	40	70	-	-	162
Issues of shares for cash	20		18			
Bonus issue	20			(20)		
Redemption		(40)				
Transfer to CRR				40		(40)
Revaluation					14	
Profit for year						208
Dividends						(40)
Balance at 31.4.X6	220	-	88	20	14	290

(c)   Under the direct method, the operating element of the cash flow statement is shown as follows.

	£m
Operating activities	
Cash received from customers	X
Cash payments to suppliers	(X)
Cash paid to and on behalf of employees	(X)
Other cash payments	(X)
Net cash flow from operating activities	X

The direct method is, in effect, an analysis of the cash book. The information it shows is not found elsewhere in the financial statements and it may be useful in assessing future cash flows relating to the items in question. It can also be argued in favour of the direct method that the indirect method does not provide new information.

There are problems with the direct method, however. Many companies might find it difficult to collect the required information. The cash book may need to be re-analysed to collate results from different cash sources. A further problem is that the figures in the cash book generally include VAT. The indirect method is easier as it draws on figures which can be obtained from the financial statements fairly easily.

FRS 1 (revised) does not require the direct method, and in practice it is rarely used. Marks & Spencer is an example of a company which has opted for the direct method, possibly because the nature of its business is such that its information systems collect the information in any event. It could be argued that _all_ companies ought to monitor their cash flows carefully enough on an ongoing basis to be able to use the direct method at minimal extra cost.

12 JUSTIN CASE

FRS 12 states that an entity should **never recognise** a **contingent liability** in the financial statements. The FRS requires a contingent liability to be **disclosed unless** the possibility of any **outflow of economic benefits to settle it is remote**.

In **this case** the contingent liability would merely be **disclosed** in the **notes** to the accounts as follows.

(i)   The **nature** of the contingency

(ii) The **uncertainties** which are expected to **affect** the **ultimate outcome**

(iii) A **statement** that it is **not practicable** to make an **estimate** of the **financial effect**

The employee's claim should be included in contingent liabilities, since it is likely that a payment will have to be made.

13 MULTIPLEX

(a) To calculate the finance charge:

	£'000	£'000
Total proceeds £80m × 90%		72,000
Total payments made		
Interest £80m × 8% × 5 years	32,000	
Redemption £80m × 112%	89,600	
Issue costs: direct only	400	
		122,000
Total finance cost		50,000

This is apportioned (straight line per the question) over 5 years of the loan stock life:

Profit and loss charge = £10m

BALANCE SHEET

	£'000
Proceeds received	72,000
Less issue costs	(400)
Less payments made £80m × 8%	(6,400)
Add finance charge	10,000
Balance at 31 March 20X1	75,200

Shown in creditors due after more than one year.

(b) The impairment losses are allocated as required by FRS 11 *Impairment of fixed assets and goodwill*.

	Asset at 1.1.20X1 £'000	1st provision (W1) £'000	Assets at 1.2.20X1 £'000	2nd provision (W2) £'000	Revised asset £'000
Goodwill	200	(200)	-	-	-
Operating licence	1,000	(300)	700	(100)	600
Property: stations/land	250	-	250	(50)	200
Rail track/coaches	250	-	250	(50)	200
Steam engines	1,000	(500)	500	-	500
Other net assets	300	-	300	-	300
	3,000	(1,000)	2,000	(200)	1,800

Workings

1   *First provision*

£500,000 relates directly to an engine and its recoverable amount can be assessed directly (ie zero).

FRS 11 then requires goodwill to be written off. Any further impairment must be written off intangible assets.

2   *Second provision*

The first £100,000 of the impairment loss is applied to the operating licence to write it down to NRV.

The remainder is applied pro rata to assets carried at other than their net selling prices.

(c) At the year end of 31 March 20X1, the company has committed itself to a **binding decision** to close the engineering operation. The expected losses on closure **must** therefore **be provided** for and, as they are **material**, they will be classed as **exceptional**. FRS 3 *Reporting financial performance* requires **separate disclosure** of losses on the closure of an operation on the face of the profit and loss account.

However, again under FRS 3, the closure of the division appears to meet **only three** of the four criteria for it to be treated as a discontinued operation, ie:

(i) The activities have **ceased permanently**.

(ii) The closure has a **material effect** on the nature and focus of Multiplex's operations.

(iii) The results are **separately distinguishable**.

(iv) But the closure will *not* be completed **within three months** of the year end.

The provision must therefore be shown as part of **continuing operations**, although it can be disclosed separately in the notes as discontinuing.

		£m
The amount will be:		
Loss on sale of net assets (46 – 30)		16.0
Other costs:	redundancies	2.0
	Professional costs	1.5
	Penalty costs	3.0
		22.5

FRS 12 *Provisions, Contingent Liabilities and Contingent Assets* does not permit future operating losses to be recognised as a provision unless they relate to 'onerous contracts' (which is not indicated in this question).

(d)

Profit and loss account	£m
Turnover (W2)	18.0
Cost of sales (balancing figure)	(14.1)
Profit (W3)	3.9

Balance sheet:	£m
Current assets	
Long-term contract balances (W5)	6.0
Debtors: amounts recoverable on long-term	
Contracts (W6)	5.0

Workings

1 *Percentage completion*

$$\text{Percentage completion} = \frac{\text{Work certified}}{\text{Contract price}}$$

20X0	*20X1 (including variation)*
$\dfrac{£12m}{£40m} = 30\%$	$\dfrac{£30m}{£45m} = 66.7\% \text{ (ie } {}^2/_3)$

2 *Turnover*

Accumulated turnover to 31 March 20X1 = £45m × ²/₃ = £30m

In 20X1 turnover = £30m – £12m (20X0) = £18m

3 *Profit*

Revised estimated total profit = £45m – £30m = £15m

Accumulated to 31 March 20X1 = £15m × ²/₃ = £10m

Total profit for year ended 31 March 20X1:

	£m
Accumulated to date	10.0
Less 20X0 profit taken (W4)	(3.6)
Less rectification costs	(2.5)
	3.9

4   *Profit for 20X0*

	£m
Turnover	12.0
Cost of sales (bal fig)	(8.4)
Profit = (£40m − £28m) × 30%	3.6

5   *Long-term contract balance*

		£m
Costs incurred to 31 March 20X1		28.5
Cost of sales charged:	20X0 (W4)	(8.4)
	20X1	(14.1)
		6.0

6   *Debtors: amounts recoverable*

	£m
Value of work certified 31 March 20X1	30.0
Payments on account	(25.0)
Amounts due	5.0

14   DIVIDEND DISTRIBUTION

(a)   (i)   This statement of principle is now expressed in a statutory rule (s 263 CA 1985) that a distribution (a dividend) may only by made out of profits available for that purpose, namely, accumulated realised profits less accumulated realised losses (so far as the losses have not already been written off). However, 'realised' profits have been defined by the Act only in rather obscure terms, and this leaves a query over such items as profits on long-term contract work in progress.

(ii)   A public company is subject to the additional requirement that it may only distribute a surplus of its net assets over the aggregate of its called-up share capital and undistributable reserves (s 264 CA 1985). The statement that profits shall be 'accumulated' requires a company to make good losses of past years out of profits. In effect, this means that any surplus of unrealised losses over unrealised profits must be deducted from realised profits less realised losses in determining the maximum amount available for distribution.

(iii)   The requirement that profits shall be realised prevents a company from distributing a revaluation surplus on retained assets.

(iv)   Provisions made in the accounts, for example for depreciation, are generally treated as realised losses which must be deducted in computing profits available for dividend: s 275(2), but this rule does not apply to an increased provision for depreciation made necessary by revaluation of fixed assets.

(v)   There is no objection to payment of dividends out of capital profits (that is, surplus over book value of fixed assets) but such profits must have been realised by sale. An unrealised capital profit arising from revaluation of retained fixed assets may only be distributed by a bonus issue of shares, not as a dividend: s 263 (2) CA 1985.

(vi)   The amount of profit available for distribution is determined by the 'relevant accounts' which are in a typical case the latest audited accounts (provided that the auditor has not qualified his report).

(b)   (i)   The revaluation represents an unrealised holding gain of £20,000. The net difference between unrealised profits and unrealised losses would thus improve, thereby providing a greater 'safety margin' for a public company under s 264 CA 1985. Depreciation is usually regarded as a realised loss, but this does not apply to additional depreciation arising as a consequence of an asset revaluation, therefore the extra depreciation charge would not be treated as a realised loss in computing the maximum amount available for distribution.

(ii)   The company had an unrealised gain of £(440,000 − 150,000) = £290,000 prior to the sale. This would have been included in the 'safety margin' under s 264, as described in (a) above, but it disappears when the sale occurs, because a realised profit of £350,000 is now made, and this is a distributable capital profit.

15 REVENUE RECOGNITION

(a) In revenue recognition, the 'critical event' is the point in the earnings process or operating cycle at which the transaction is deemed to have been **sufficiently completed** to allow the **profit** arising from the transaction, or a distinct component part of it, to be **recognised** in income in a particular period. This has to be addressed in order to allocate transactions and their effects to different accounting periods and is a direct result of the episodic nature of financial reporting. For most companies the **normal earnings cycle** is the purchase of raw materials which are transformed through a manufacturing process into saleable goods, for which orders are subsequently received, delivery is made and then payment received.

In the past the approach has been to **match costs with revenues** and record both once the critical event has passed; in most systems this critical event has been full or near **full performance of the transaction**, so that no material uncertainties surround either the transaction being completed or the amounts arising from the transaction. This is encompassed in the notion of prudence, so that revenue is recognised only in cash or near cash form. However, any point in the cycle could be deemed to be the critical event. This approach leaves the balance sheet as a statement of uncompleted transaction balances, comprising unexpired costs and undischarged liabilities.

In contrast, the *Statement of Principles* defines gains and losses (or income and expenses) in terms of **changes** in assets and liabilities other than those arising from transactions with owners as owners, not in terms of an earnings or matching process. The balance sheet thus assumes primary importance in the recognition of earnings and profits. A gain **can only be recognised** if there is an **increase** in the **ownership interest** (ie net assets) of an entity not resulting from contributions from owners. Similarly, a loss is recognised if there is a **decrease** in the ownership interest of an entity not resulting from distributions to owners. Thus gains arise from recognition of assets and derecognition of liabilities, and losses arise from derecognition of assets and recognition of liabilities. The Statement explains that it is not possible to reverse this definitional process, ie by defining assets and liabilities in terms of gains and losses, because it has not been possible to formulate robust enough base definitions of gains and losses (partly because the choice of critical event can be subjective). Nevertheless the two approaches are linked by the Statement, which says that **'sufficient evidence'** for recognition or derecognition will be met at the critical event in the operating cycle.

(b) *On the acquisition of goods*

This would be **unlikely** to be a critical event for most businesses. However, for some the acquisition of the raw materials is the most important part of the process, eg extraction of gold from a mine, or the harvesting of coffee beans. Only where the goods in question could be **sold immediately in a liquid market** would it be appropriate to recognise revenue, ie they would have to have a **commodity value**.

During the manufacture or production of goods

This is also **unlikely** to be the critical event for most businesses because **too many uncertainties** remain, eg of damaged goods or overproduction leading to obsolete stock. An **exception** would be **long-term contracts** for the construction of specific assets, which tend to earn the constructing company revenues over the length of the contract, usually in stages, ie there is a **series of critical events** in the operating cycle (according to the *Statement of Principles*). It would **not** be appropriate to recognise all the revenue at the end of the contract, because this would reflect profit earned in past periods as well as the present period. Profit is therefore recognised during manufacture or production, usually through certification of a qualified valuer. Some would argue that this is not really a critical event approach, but rather an 'accretion approach'.

On delivery/acceptance of goods

Goods are frequently sold on **credit**, whereby the vendor hands over the inventory asset and receives in its place a **financial asset of a debt** due for the price of the goods. At that point legal title passes and **full performance** has taken place. In general, the bulk of the risks of the transaction have gone and the only ones remaining relate to the creditworthiness of the purchaser and any outstanding warranty over the goods. Many trade sales take place in this way, with periods of credit allowed for goods delivered, eg 30 days. This therefore tends to be the critical event for many types of business operating cycles.

Where certain conditions have been satisfied after the goods have been delivered

In these situations the customer had a right of return of the goods without reason or penalty, but usually within a time and non-use condition. A good example is clothes retailers who allow **non-faulty goods to be returned**. Another example is that the goods need only be paid for once they are sold on to a third party. Traditionally, recognition of revenue is delayed until, eg the **deadline to allowed return passes**. However, in circumstances where goods are never returned, it might be argued that the substance of the transaction is a sale on delivery.

Receipt or payment for credit sales

Once payment is received, only warranty risk remains. A company may wait until this point to recognise income if receipt is considered uncertain, eg when goods have been sold to a company resident in a country that has **exchange controls**. It would otherwise be **rare** to delay recognition until payment.

On the expiry of a guarantee or warranty

Many businesses may feel unable to recognise revenue in full because of **outstanding warranties**, eg a construction company which is subject to fee retention until some time after completion of the contract. Other businesses, such as car manufacturers, may make a **general provision** for goods returned under warranty as it will not be possible to judge likely warranty costs under individual contracts.

(c) (i) This agreement is worded as a **sale**, but it is fairly obvious from the terms and assessed substance that it is in fact a **secured loan**. Jensen should therefore continue to recognise the stock on balance sheet and should treat the receipt from Wholesaler as a loan, not revenue. Finance costs will be charged to the profit and loss account, of £35,000 × 12% × 9/12 = £3,150.

(ii) Years 2 to 5 of the franchise contract would be **loss making** for Jensen and hence part of the initial fee of £50,000 should be **deferred over the life of the contract**. Since Jensen should be making a profit margin of 20% on this type of arrangement, revenues of £10,000 will be required to match against the costs of £8,000. The company will receive £5,000 pa and so a further £5,000 × 4 = £20,000 of the initial fee should be deferred, leaving £50,000 – £20,000 = £30,000 to be recognised in the first year. However, this may not represent a liability under FRS 12 *Provisions, contingent liabilities and contingent assets*, where a liability is defined as an obligation to transfer economic benefits as a result of past transactions or events. It will be necessary to consider the terms of the initial fee and whether it is returnable.

(iii) The cost of the first 6 months' publications is £192,000 ÷ 24 × 6 = £48,000. On an accruals basis, income of £240,000 ÷ 24 × 6 = 60,000 should be recognised. This would leave deferred income of £240,000 – £60,000 = £180,000 in Jensen's balance sheet (ie as a liability). As in (ii), however, this may not represent a liability. In fact, the liability of the company may only extend to the cost of the future publications, ie £192,000 – £48,000 = £144,000. This would allow Jensen to **recognise all the profit** on the publications **immediately**. In want of an accounting standard on revenue recognition, it will be necessary to consider the extent of Jensen's commitments under this arrangement.

16 RELATED PARTY TRANSACTIONS

(a) Disclosure is required for all material related party transactions. Related party transactions are required to be disclosed whether or not a price is charged. The following are examples of related party transactions that require disclosure by a reporting entity in the period in which they occur:

(i) Purchases or sales of goods (finished or unfinished)
(ii) Purchases or sales of property and other assets
(iii) Rendering or receiving of services
(iv) Agency arrangements
(v) Leasing arrangements
(vi) Transfer of research and development
(vii) Licence agreements
(viii) Provision of finance
(ix) Guarantees and the provision of collateral security
(x) Management contracts

(b) Financial statements should disclose material transactions undertaken by the reporting entity with a related party. Disclosure should be made irrespective of whether a price is charged. The disclosure should include:

(i)   The names of the transacting related parties

(ii)   A description of the relationship between the parties

(iii)   A description of the transactions

(iv)   The amounts involved

(v)   Any other elements of the transactions necessary for an understanding of the financial statements

(vi)   The amounts due to or from related parties at the balance sheet date and provisions for doubtful debts due to such parties at this date

(vii)   Amounts written off in the period in respect of debts due to or from related parties

Transactions with related parties may be disclosed on an aggregated basis (aggregation of similar transactions by type of related party) unless disclosure of an individual transaction, or connected transactions, is necessary for an understanding of the impact of the transactions on the financial statements of the reporting entity or is required by law.

17   SEGMENTAL REPORTING

SSAP 25 requires larger companies (ie plcs, banking and insurance companies or those meeting ten times the medium sized company criteria) to provide, where applicable, an analysis of turnover and operating profit attributable to different classes of business and an analysis of turnover attributable to each geographical market.

Segmental net assets are also required to be disclosed.

The purpose of **SSAP 25 disclosures** is **to provide users with information as to which classes of business**:

(1)   **Earn the best rate of return**
(2)   **Have a lower degree of risk**
(3)   **Show the best growth rates**
(4)   **Demonstrate the best potential for future development.**

18   GROUP ACCOUNTS

The object of annual accounts is to help shareholders exercise control over their company by providing information about how its affairs have been conducted. The shareholders of a holding company would not be given sufficient information from the accounts of the holding company on its own, because not enough would be known about the nature of the assets, income and profits of all the subsidiary companies in which the holding company has invested. The primary purpose of group accounts is to provide a true and fair view of the position and earnings of the holding company group as a whole, from the standpoint of the shareholders in the holding company.

A number of arguments have been put forward, however, which argue that group accounts have certain limitations.

(a)   Group accounts may be misleading.

(i)   The solvency (liquidity) of one company may hide the insolvency of another.

(ii)   The profit of one company may conceal the losses of another.

(iii)   They imply that group companies will meet each others' debts (this is certainly not true: a parent company may watch creditors of an insolvent subsidiary go unpaid without having to step in).

(b)   There may be some difficulties in defining the group or 'entity' of companies, although the Companies Act 1989 has removed many of the grey areas here.

(c)   Where a group consists of widely diverse companies in different lines of business, a set of group accounts may obscure much important detail unless supplementary information about each part of the group's business is provided.

19 ARLENE AND AMANDA

Stage 1. Amanda Ltd has accounted for a proposed dividend of £10,000, but Arlene plc has not yet accounted for its share of the dividend receivable. Arlene's draft balance sheet is therefore adjusted as follows.

		£	£
DEBIT	Dividends receivable (90% × £10,000)	9,000	
CREDIT	Revenue reserve		9,000

The adjusted balance on Arlene's revenue reserve is £199,000.

Stage 2. There are no current accounts to be agreed.

Stage 3. There are two part-cancelling items: Amanda Ltd's share capital and the dividend receivable/payable.

Stage 4. Minority interests

	£
Ordinary share capital (10% × 150,000)	15,000
Revenue reserves (10% × 99,000)	9,900
Capital reserves (10% × 15,000)	1,500
	26,400

Stage 5

Goodwill

	£	£
Cost of investment		190,000
Share of net assets acquired as represented by:		
Ordinary share capital	150,000	
Revenue reserves on acquisition	20,000	
Capital reserves on acquisition	10,000	
	180,000	
Group share 90%		162,000
Goodwill		28,000

Consolidated revenue reserve

	£
Arlene plc (adjusted balance)	199,000
Share of Amanda Ltd's post acquisition reserves	
(99,000 – 20,000) × 90%	71,100
	270,100

Consolidated capital reserve

	£
Arlene plc	60,000
Share of Amanda's post-acquisition reserve	
(15,000 – 10,000) × 90%	4,500
	64,500

ARLENE PLC
CONSOLIDATED BALANCE SHEET AS AT 31 DECEMBER 20X5

	£	£
Intangible fixed assets: goodwill		28,000
Tangible fixed assets		560,000
Current assets		
Stocks	125,000	
Debtors	150,000	
Bank and cash	56,000	
	331,000	
Current liabilities		
Trade creditors	127,000	
Proposed dividend to members of Arlene plc	30,000	
Minority proposed dividend (10% × £10,000)	1,000	
	158,000	
Net current assets		173,000
Total assets less current liabilities		761,000
Capital and reserves		
Ordinary shares of £1 each		400,000
Reserves		
Revenue reserves	270,100	
Capital reserves	64,500	
		334,600
		734,600
Minority interest		26,400
		761,000

20   PUCCINI

Key points for discussion include:

(a)   FRS 6, Appendix 1 specifies that where a dividend is paid to the acquiring company out of pre-combination profits, it would appear that it need not necessarily be applied as a reduction in the carrying value of the investment in the subsidiary undertaking.

(b)   Such a dividend received should be applied to reduce the carrying value of the investment to the extent necessary to provide for the diminution in value of the investment in the subsidiary undertaking as stated in the accounts of the parent company.

(c)   To the extent that this is not necessary, it appears that the amount received will be a realised profit in the hands of the parent company.

(d)   Although this requirement refers specifically to the accounts of the parent company, some practitioners believe this provides some guidance as to how pre-acquisition dividends should be treated in consolidated accounts.

(e)   The impact of the above is that if the subsidiary recovers in value after the distribution, the loss in value is temporary and no amount need be deducted from the cost of the investment (only permanent diminutions should be provided).

(f)   Where the investment is carried at fair value, however, it is likely that a dividend which represents a return of pre-acquisition profits would give rise to a diminution in the value of investment and thus should be applied in reducing the cost (carrying value) of that investment.

(g)   If this diminution is not permanent, this treatment is not mandatory. Thus companies could distribute all the subsidiary's pre-acquisition profits as long as the subsidiary could replace them in the future.

(h)   This practice may be legal but if offends good accounting practice. The pre-acquisition dividend is usually regarded as a return of the purchase price and it therefore seems right to deduct it from the cost of the investment.

> **Tutorial note:** For examination purposes, ACCA has indicated that any questions they set on this area will indicate the company's policy on pre-acquisition dividends.

21 HAND

Note. This is quite a complex question which brings together a number of complications. It is important in dealing with such questions to be methodical in following the recommended five-stage approach.

Stage 1. All dividends have been accounted for by both companies, but Hand Ltd has treated its share of Finger Ltd's 20X0 dividend incorrectly. The dividend comes from pre-acquisition profits of Finger Ltd and should be credited not to profit and loss account, but to the 'investment in subsidiary' account. The following adjustment is therefore necessary to Hand Ltd's draft balance sheet.

DEBIT	Revenue reserves (40/60 × £6,000)	£4,000
CREDIT	Investment in Finger Ltd	£4,000

Hand Ltd now has a balance of £(90,000 - 4,000) = £86,000 on revenue reserve, while its investment in Finger Ltd is stated at cost less amounts written down £(50,000 - 4,000) = £46,000.

Stage 2. The current accounts differ by £2,000, being cash in transit from Finger Ltd to Hand Ltd. £2,000 cash in transit will appear in the consolidated balance sheet as an asset.

Stage 3. The only cancelling items, apart from the current accounts, are Hand Ltd's investment in subsidiary and Finger Ltd's share capital. These will be dealt with in the goodwill calculation.

Stage 4

	£
Share capital ($^1/_3$ × £60,000)	20,000
Reserves ($^1/_3$ × £38,700)	12,900
Minority interest	32,900

Goodwill	£	£
Cost of investment		50,000
Less dividend from pre-acquisition profits		4,000
		46,000
Share of net assets acquired, as represented by		
Share capital	60,000	
Reserves (W)	30,000	
	90,000	
Group share ($^2/_3$)		60,000
Capital reserve		14,000

Reserves	£
Hand Ltd (see stage 1)	86,000
Share of Finger Ltd's post acquisition retained reserves	
£(38,700 −30,000) × $^2/_3$	5,800
Revenue reserve	91,800

BPP PUBLISHING

Working: reserves of Finger Ltd

	£	£
Pre-acquisition		
Balance at 31.12.X0	18,000	
Profit for 6 months to 30.6.X1 ($^6/_{12} \times$ £18,000)	9,000	
Consolidation adjustment: revaluation surplus *	3,000	
		30,000
Post-acquisition		
Profit for 6 months to 31.12.X1 ($^6/_{12} \times$ £18,000)	9,000	
Consolidation adjustment: increase in dep'n charge		
($^1/_5 \times$ £3,000 $\times$ $^6/_{12}$)*	(300)	
		8,700
		38,700

* These consolidation adjustments are necessary so that the assets of Finger Ltd are revalued to their fair value on acquisition.

HAND LIMITED
CONSOLIDATED BALANCE SHEET AS AT 31 DECEMBER 20X1

	£	£
Intangible fixed assets: goodwill		(14,000)
Tangible fixed assets		178,700
Current assets		
Sundry	257,000	
Cash in transit	2,000	
	259,000	
Current liabilities	199,000	
Net current assets		60,000
		224,700
Capital and reserves		
Ordinary shares of £1 each		100,000
Revenue reserve		91,800
		191,800
Minority interest		32,900
		224,700

22   WAR

> *Tutorial note.* This question may look intimidating because it involves an acquisition part of the way through the year, some FRS 7 issues and both the consolidated profit and loss account and balance sheet. It is, however, fairly straightforward. You should not have overlooked FRS 3 aspects in the consolidated profit and loss account.

(a)   FRS 7 *Fair values in acquisition accounting* states that quoted shares should be valued at market price on the date of acquisition. However, the standard acknowledges that the market price may be difficult to determine if it is unreliable because of an inactive market. In particular, where the shares are not quoted, there may be no suitable market. In such cases the value must be estimated using:

(i)   The value of similar quoted securities
(ii)   The present value of the cash flows of the shares
(iii)   Any cash alternative which was offered
(iv)   The value of any underlying security into which there is an option to convert

It may be necessary to undertake a valuation of the company in question should none of the above methods prove feasible.

(b) WAR GROUP PLC
CONSOLIDATED BALANCE SHEET AS AT 30 JUNE 20X7

	£'000	£'000
Fixed assets		
Tangible assets (1,750 + 500)		2,250
Goodwill (W3)		151
		2,401
Current assets		
Stocks	600	
Debtors	451	
Cash at bank and in hand	299	
	1,350	
Creditors: amounts falling due within one year	(650)	
Net current assets		700
Total assets less current liabilities		3,101
Creditors: amounts falling due after one year		(1,225)
		1,876
Capital and reserves		
Ordinary share capital		750
Share premium (W6)		250
Profit and loss account (W5)		621
		1,621
Minority interests (equity) (W4)		255
		1,876

WAR GROUP PLC
CONSOLIDATED PROFIT AND LOSS ACCOUNT
FOR THE YEAR ENDED 30 JUNE 20X7

	£'000	£'000
Turnover		
Continuing operations	3,150	
Acquisitions $(^2/_{12}) \times 1,770)$	295	
		3,445
Cost of sales		(1,788)
Gross profit		1,657
Distribution costs	638	
Administrative expenses (W7)	348	
		(986)
Operating profit		
Continuing operations	606	
Acquisitions	65	
		671
Interest payable		(75)
Profit on ordinary activities before taxation		596
Tax on profit on ordinary activities		(306)
Profit after tax		290
Minority interests (equity) (W8)		(11)
		279
Dividends paid		(38)
Retained profit for the financial year attributable to the group		241

Workings

1   *Revaluation surplus*

	£'000
Peace Ltd: tangible fixed assets at market value	500
Carrying value	350
Revaluation surplus	150

FRS 7 *Fair values in acquisition accounting* states that open market values should be used to value tangible fixed assets, and it is this figure which is compared with the carrying value here, rather than the net realisable value. The latter is lower because the costs of realisation are deducted. However, as the group does not intend to dispose of the asset, the market value is more appropriate.

2   *Pre-acquisition dividend*

Dividend paid by Peace to War: £42,000
Pre-acquisition element $^{10}/_{12} \times £42,000 = £35,000$

3   *Goodwill*

	£'000	£'000
Cost of investment		800
Less pre-acquisition dividend (W2)		(35)
		765
Share capital	100	
Share premium	150	
Revaluation surplus	150	
Profit and loss account		
Prior year: 450 – 165	285	
Current year: $^{10}/_{12} \times 165$	138	
	823	
Group share: 70%		576
Goodwill		189

4   *Minority interests (balance sheet)*

	£'000
Share capital	100
Share premium	150
Revaluation surplus	150
Profit and loss account	450
	850

MI = £850,000 × 30% = £255,000.

5   *Profit and loss account*

	£'000	£'000
War plc		625
Less goodwill written off ($189 \times ^1/_5$)	38	
Less pre-acquisition dividend	35	
		(73)
		552
Add back issue costs		50
		602
Peace Ltd $165 \times ^2/_{12} \times 70\%$		19
		621

6   *Share premium account*

	£'000
War plc	300
Less issue costs	(50)
	250

7   *Administrative expenses*

	£'000
War plc	325
Peace Ltd ($^2/_{12} \times 210$)	35
Goodwill written off	38
	398
Less issue costs	(50)
	348

8   *Minority interests (p & l)*

$225 \times ^2/_{12} \times 30\% = £11,250$

23   CHIGWELL

Tutorial note. This question tested in detail your understanding of the differences between acquisition and merger accounting.

The question does not, therefore, contain as many of the complications such as unrealised profit or intercompany sales, usually associated with consolidation questions. You would not have scored highly if you ignored some of the fundamental differences such as the treatment of goodwill.

BPP PUBLISHING

(a) CHIGWELL PLC
CONSOLIDATED PROFIT AND LOSS ACCOUNT
FOR THE YEAR ENDED 31 DECEMBER 20X2

	£'000
Group turnover ($80{,}946 + (17{,}194 \times {}^{8}/_{12}) + (3{,}420 \times {}^{4}/_{12})$)	93,549
Cost of sales and expenses ($62{,}184 + (13{,}592 \times {}^{8}/_{12}) + (2{,}560 \times {}^{4}/_{12})$)	72,099
Group operating profit	21,450
Share of operating profit in associate	143
Interest receivable ($120 + (50 \times {}^{8}/_{12})$)	153
Goodwill written off (W3)	(1,063)
Profit before tax	20,683
Taxation ($6{,}740 + (1{,}525 \times {}^{8}/_{12}) + (390 \times {}^{4}/_{12}) + (390 \times 25\% \times {}^{8}/_{12})$)	7,952
Profit after tax	12,731
Ordinary dividends	
Interim	550
Final	50
Preference dividend	12
Retained profit for the year	12,119

(b) Of the group retained profit of £12,119,000

	£'000
Retained by Chigwell plc (W4)	10,495
Retained by Sharon plc (W4)	1,398
Retained by Tracy Ltd (W4)	226
	12,119

(c) CHIGWELL PLC
CONSOLIDATED PROFIT AND LOSS ACCOUNT
FOR THE YEAR ENDED 30 DECEMBER 20X2

	£
Turnover ($80{,}946 + 17{,}194 + 3{,}420$)	101,560
Cost of sales and expenses ($62{,}184 + 13{,}592 + 2{,}560$)	78,336
Operating profit	23,224
Interest receivable ($120 + 50$)	170
Profit in ordinary activities before taxation	23,394
Taxation ($6{,}740 + 1{,}525 + 390$)	8,655
Profit after tax	14,739
Interim dividend to outside interests ($75\% \times 12$)	9
Profit for the year	14,730
Ordinary dividends: interim	550
final	50
Preference dividend	12
Retained profit for the year	14,118

(d) Of the group retained profit of £14,118,000

	£'000
Retained by Chigwell plc	11,575
Retained by Sharon plc	2,091
Retained by Tracy Ltd	452
	14,118

(e)   RECONCILIATION OF RETAINED PROFIT FIGURES

	£'000	£'000
Retained profit under acquisition method		12,119
Add goodwill		1,063
		13,182
Pre-acquisition profits to be included under merger accounting		
Sharon		
$^4/_{12} \times 2,127$	709	
Less pre-acquisition dividend (W2)	16	
		693
Tracy		
$^8/_{12} \times 75\% \times 452$		226
Add pre-acquisition dividend		17
		14,118

(f)   INVESTMENT IN SUBSIDIARIES UNDER THE MERGER METHOD

	£'000	£'000
Investment using acquisition method		
Sharon	960	
Less pre-acquisition dividend	(16)	
		944
Tracy	280	
Cost of previous holding $280 \times {}^{25}/_{75}$	93	
Less pre-acquisition dividend	(1.5)	
		372
Add back pre-acquisition dividend		18
		1,334
Reserve (excess of market value of shares over nominal value)		
Sharon	573	
Tracy	80	
		(653)
Investment using merger method		681

Workings

1   *Group structure*

1.4.X2	00%		25%	
			75%	1.9.X2
			100%	

Sharon — Subsidiary for $^8/_{12}$ months

Tracy — Associate for $^8/_{12}$ months / Subsidiary for $^4/_{12}$ months

2   Dividends receivable

	Associated Co £'000	Subsidiary pre-acquisition £'000	Subsidiary post-acquisition £'000	Total £'000
From Sharon				
Interim				
$24 \times 100\% \times {}^4/_6$		16.0		16.0
$24 \times 100\% \times {}^2/_6$			8.0	8.0
Final				
$12 \times 100\% \times {}^6/_6$			12.0	12.0
	-	16.0	20.0	36.0
From Tracy				
Interim				
$12 \times 25\% \times {}^6/_6$	3.0			3.0
Final				
$6 \times 25\% \times {}^2/_6$	0.5			0.5
$6 \times 75\% \times {}^2/_6$		1.5		1.5
$6 \times 100\% \times {}^4/_6$			4.0	4.0
	3.5	1.5	4.0	9.0
Total	3.5	17.5	24.0	45.0

3   Goodwill

	£'000
Sharon	
Per question	986
Pre-acquisition dividends	
to be deducted from cost of investment (W2)	16
	970
Written off to P & L	(970)
	0

	£'000
Tracy	
Per question	95.0
Pre-acquisition dividends (W2)	1.5
	93.5
Written off to P & L	93.5
	0.0

∴ Total to be written off to P & L = £(970,000 + 93,500) = £1,063,500

4   Profit retained by each company

	£'000	£'000
Sharon		
Profit after tax ($^8/_{12} \times 2,127$)	1,418	
Less post acquisition dividends (W2)	20	
		1,398.0
Chigwell		
Retained profit	11,575.0	
Less pre-acquisition dividends	(17.5)	
Less goodwill	(1,063.0)	
		10,494.5
Retained by Tracy (bal. fig.)		226.0
		12,118.5

(g)   FRS 6 *Acquisitions and mergers* has heightened the requirements for merger accounting by concentrating on the *spirit* of the transactions, rather than on mechanical aspects such as levels of shareholding. The following criteria are set out in FRS 6 to determine whether a transaction is a merger.

Criterion 1

Neither party is portrayed, by either its management or any other party, as either acquirer or acquired.

Criterion 2

All parties take part in setting up a management structure and selecting personnel for the combined entity on the basis of consensus rather than purely by exercise of voting rights.

Criterion 3

The relative sizes of the parties are not so disparate that one party dominates the combined entity by virtue of its relative size.

Criterion 4

A substantial part of the consideration for equity shareholdings in each party will comprise equity shares; conversely, non-equity shares or equity shares with reduced voting rights will comprise only an 'immaterial' part of the consideration. This criterion also covers existing shareholdings.

> 'Where one of the combining entities has, within the period of two years before the combination acquired shares in another of the combining entities, the consideration for this acquisition should be taken into account in determining whether this criterion has been met.

Note that this criterion states in general terms what is laid out in the Companies Act 1985 in terms of specific shareholdings.

Criterion 5

No equity shareholders of any of the combining entities retains any material interest in the future performance of only part of the combined equity.

Note that, for the purpose of Criterion 4, the consideration should not include:

'(a)   an interest in a peripheral part of the business of the entity in which they were shareholders and which does not form part of the combined entity; or

(b)   the proceeds of the sale of such a business, or loan stock representing such proceeds.

A peripheral part of the business is one that can be disposed of without having a material effect on the nature and focus of the entity's operations.'

It should be apparent that Chigwell's purchase of the remainder of Tracy's share capital obeys the letter of the Companies Act and the old SSAP 23 rules, but is against the spirit of merger accounting. It is not clear when Chigwell acquired its original 25% holding in Tracy. If it was within the last two years and was for cash rather than equity shares, the combination would fail on criterion 4. The sale to a merchant bank and subsequent re-purchase of 20% of the original holding is clearly an attempt to circumvent the old rule on the minimum shareholding to be acquired (90%).

Criteria 1, 2 and 3 are concerned with whether the combination is in the spirit of an acquisition or a merger. The transaction would certainly fail on criterion 3 and probably on 1 and 2. Criterion 5 is less relevant.

It is apparent from the above that the combination of Chigwell and Tracy would not qualify as a merger; in fact it is exactly the kind of transaction that FRS 6 was intended to outlaw.

24   ENTERPRISE AND VULCAN

Step 1

Calculate the goodwill in the investment in Vulcan Ltd. This will be needed in order to calculate the 'Investment in associated undertakings' line on the balance sheet since goodwill is being amortised, and is not yet fully amortised.

Goodwill

	£'000	£'000
Cost of investment		2,000
Share capital	2,000	
Revaluation reserve	200	
Profit and loss reserve	900	
	3,100	
	× 30%	(930)
		1,070

£1,070,000 ÷ 5 = 214,000 amortised per year
3 years amortised already £214,000 × = 642,000

Add this year's amortisation of £214,000:

£
856,000   amortised to date
214,000   unamortised
1,070,000   total goodwill

Step 2

Complete the top half of the balance sheet including the 'Investments in associates' line as below, and insert the share capital of Enterprise plc.

	£'000
Investment in associate's net assets	
(30% × 7,940,000)	2,382
Unamortised goodwill (see Step 1))	214
	2,596

Step 3

Calculate the balance sheet reserves.

1   *Revaluation reserve*

	£'000	£'000
Enterprise plc		2,000
Vulcan Ltd: at balance sheet	1,000	
at acquisition	(200)	
	800	
× 30%		240
		2,240

2   *Profit and loss reserve*

	£	£
Enterprise plc		5,100
Vulcan Ltd: at balance sheet	4,940	
at acquisition	(900)	
	4,040	
× 30%		1,212
Less goodwill amortised to date (see Step 1)		(856)
		5,456

Step 4

Complete the consolidated P&L account up to the group operating profit line, and calculate the share of operating profit in the associate. Any adjustments to the P&L account for the amortisation of goodwill should be charged now to reduce this figure.

Share of operating profit in associate

	£'000
Operating profit × 30% (£2,120,000 × 30%)	636
Amortisation for the year (see task one)	(214)
	422

Step 5

Complete the balance sheet and profit and loss account.

ENTERPRISE PLC
CONSOLIDATED BALANCE SHEET AS AT 30 JUNE 20X8

	£'000	£'000
Fixed assets		
Tangible assets		8,000
Investments:		
Investments in associates		2,596
		10,596
Current assets		
Stock	1,340	
Debtors	1,000	
Cash	260	
	2,600	
Creditors (due within one year)	(1,500)	
Net current assets		1,100
		11,696

ENTERPRISE PLC GROUP
CONSOLIDATED PROFIT AND LOSS ACCOUNT
FOR THE YEAR ENDING 30 JUNE 20X8

	£'000	£'000
Group turnover		10,000
Cost of sales		(6,000)
Gross profit		4,000
Expenses		(1,500)
Group operating profit		2,500
Share of operating profit in associates	636	
Amortisation in associate	(214)	
		422
		2,922
Interest payable:		
Group		(100)
Associates (30% × 20,000)		(6)
Profit on ordinary activities before tax		2,816
*Tax on profit on ordinary activities**		(1,010)
Profit on ordinary activities after tax		1,806
Equity dividends		(600)
Retained profit for the group and its share of associates		1,206

* Tax relates to the following:

Parent and subsidiaries	£800,000
Associates (30% × £700,000)	£210,000

Note: As the share in the associates is equal to more than 25% of the group figure (before associates) for operating profit, additional disclosures required under FRS 9 would need to be given, if not specifically excluded from the question requirements.

25 HEPBURN AND SLATER

(a) HEPBURN PLC
CONSOLIDATED PROFIT AND LOSS ACCOUNT
FOR THE YEAR ENDED 31 MARCH 20X1

	£'000
Turnover (W1)	1,600
Cost of sales (W2)	(890)
Gross profit	710
Operating expenses (W3)	(184)
Debenture interest (12 × 6/12)	(6)
Operating profit	520
Taxation (100 + (40 × 6/12)	(120)
Profit after tax	400
Minority interest (200 × 20% × 6/12)	(20)
Profit after tax and minority interest	380
Dividends: interim	(40)
final	(40)
Retained profit for the year	300

HEPBURN PLC
CONSOLIDATED BALANCE SHEET
AS AT 31 MARCH 20X1

	£'000	£'000
Fixed assets		
Intangible: goodwill (W4)		
Tangible fixed assets		180
Land and buildings (400 + 150 + 125)		675
Plant and machinery (220 + 510)		730
Investments (20 + 10)		30
		1,615
Current assets		
Stock (240 + 280 – 10 (W2))	510	
Debtors (170 + 210 – 56)	324	
Bank (20 + 40 + 20)	80	
	914	
Creditors: amounts due < 1 year		
Trade creditors (170 + 155 - 36)	289	
Taxation (50 + 45)	95	
Dividends	40	
	424	
Net current assets		490
		2,105
Creditors: amounts due > 1 year		
8% Debentures		150
Net Assets		1,955
Capital and reserves		
Ordinary shares £1 each (400 + 300 (W4))		700
Share premium account (900 – 300 (W4))		600
Profit and loss account (W5)		460
		1,760
Minority interests (W6)		195
Shareholders' funds		1,955

Workings

1	*Turnover*	£'000
	Hepburn	1,200
	Salter (1,000 × 6/12)	500
	Less: intercompany sale	(100)
		1,600

BPP
PUBLISHING

2	*Cost of sales*		£'000
	Hepburn		650
	Salter (660 × 6/12)		330
	Less: intercompany sales		(100)
	Unreaslied profit in stock (100 × 50% × 25/125)		10
			890

3	*Operating expenses*		£'000
	Hepburn		120
	Salter (88 × 6/12)		44
	Goodwill amortisation (W4)		20
			184

4	*Goodwill*	£'000	£'000
	Cost of investment in Salter		
	150 × 80% × 5/2 (= 300) × £3		900
	Fair value of net assets acquired		
	Share capital	150	
	Profit and loss account		
	At 1 April 20X0 (700 - 200)	500	
	Profit to 1 Oct 20X0 (200 × 6/12)	100	
	Fair value adjustment	125	
		875	
	Group share (80%)		700
	Goodwill		200
	Amortisation (200 ÷ 5 × 6/12)		20
	Unamortised		180

5	*Profit and loss account*	£'000
	Hepburn	410
	Unrealised profit in stock (W2)	(10)
	Salter	
	Share of post-acquisition profits 80% × (200 × 6/12)	80
	Goodwill amortisation (W4)	(20)
		460

> Profit sit: books of parent, hence eliminate from gro profits

6	*Minority interest*	£'000
	Share capital: 20% × 150	30
	Profit and loss account: 20% × 700	140
	Fair value adjustment of land: 20% × 125	25
		195

(b) In **voting rights**, Hepburn's interest in Woodbridge Ltd is **60%**; however it is correct that it is only entitled to 6,000/24,000 = 25% of any dividends paid.

The approach taken by Hepburn to its investment in Woodbridge seems to be based on the view that, with a **25% equity holding**, the investment would normally be treated as an associate and equity accounting applied. However, Hepburn does not exert any significant influence over Woodbridge and hence under FRS 9 *Associates and joint ventures* it can rebut the presumption of associate status.

This overlooks the fact that FRS 2 *Accounting for subsidiary undertakings* bases the treatment of an investment in another entity on the notion of control rather than **ownership**. Hepburn can control Woodbridge by virtue of its holding the **majority of the voting rights** in the company.

> Key poin

Woodbridge is thus a **subsidiary** and should be **consolidated in full** in Hepburn's group accounts, **from the date of acquisition**.

Hepburn's directors may wish to avoid consolidation because of Woodbridge's **losses**. But these **losses** may indicate that the **value of the investment** in Woodbridge in Hepburn's own individual accounts may be **overstated**. A test for **impairment**, as required by FRS 11 *Impairment of fixed assets and goodwill* may reveal that the **recoverable amount** of the investment has fallen below £20,000, thus requiring a write down in Hepburn's own accounts and a write down of Woodbridge's assets in the consolidated accounts.

26 CPP AND CCA

(a) In accounting, the value of income and capital is measured in terms of money. In simple terms, profit is the difference between the closing and opening balance sheet values (after adjustment for new sources of funds and applications such as dividend distribution). If, because of inflation, the value of assets in the closing balance sheet is shown at a higher monetary amount than assets in the opening balance sheet, a profit has been made. In traditional accounting, it is assumed that a monetary unit of £1 is a stable measurement; inflation removes this stability.

CPP accounting attempts to provide a more satisfactory methods of valuing profit and capital by establishing a stable unit of monetary measurement, £1 of current purchasing power, as at the end of the accounting period under review.

A distinction is made between monetary items, and non-monetary items. In a period of inflation, keeping a monetary asset (eg debtors) results in a loss of purchasing power as the value of money erodes over time. Non-monetary assets, however, are assumed to maintain 'real' value over time, and these are converted into monetary units of current purchasing power as at the year end, by means of a suitable price index. The equity interest in the balance sheet can be determined as a balancing item.

The profit or deficit for the year in CPP terms is found by converting sales, opening and closing stock, purchases and other expenses into year-end units of £CPP. In addition, a profit on holding net monetary liabilities (or a loss on holding net monetary assets) is computed in arriving at the profit or deficit figure.

CPP arguably provides a more satisfactory system of accounting since transactions are expressed in terms of 'today's money' and similarly, the balance sheet values are adjusted for inflation, so as to give users of financial information a set of figures with which they can:

   (i)   Decide whether operating profits are satisfactory (profits due to inflation are eliminated)

   (ii)   Obtain a better appreciation of the size and 'value' of the entity's assets

(b) CPP and CCA accounting are different concepts, in that CCP accounting makes adjustments for general inflationary price changes, whereas CCA makes adjustments to allow for specific price movements (changes in the deprival value of assets). Specific price changes (in CCA) enable a company to determine whether the operating capability of a company has been maintained; it is not a restatement of price levels in terms of a common unit of money measurement. The two conventions use different concepts of capital maintenance (namely operating capability with CCA, and general purchasing power with CPP).

In addition CPP is based on the use of a general price index. In contrast, CCA only makes use of a specific price index where it is not possible to obtain the current value of an asset by other means (eg direct valuation).

(c) In CCA, holding gains represent the difference between the historical cost of an asset and its current cost. If the asset is unsold, and appears in the balance sheet of a company at current cost, there will be an 'unrealised' holding gain, which must be included in a current cost reserve. When the asset is eventually sold, the profit (equal to the sale price minus the historical cost) may be divided into:

   (i)   An operating profit which would have been made if the cost of the asset were its current value

   (ii)   A *realised* holding gain which has arisen because of the appreciation in value of the asset between the date of its acquisition and the date of its sale

The handbook's method of CCA excludes realised holding gains from the calculation of current cost operating profit, and the implication is that realised holding gains should not be made available for distribution as a dividend, because to do so would result in a loss of 'business substance' or 'operating capability' by the business.

(d) (i)   The cost of sales adjustment is the difference between the historical cost of goods sold and their current cost. In a CCA statement, the COSA is therefore used to adjust 'historical cost profit' towards 'current cost profit' by, in effect, changing the cost of sales from an historical cost to a current cost basis.

    (ii)   The COSA does not allow for the fact that purchased goods are acquired on credit and finished goods are likewise sold on credit. In a period of inflation, a company benefits from creditors (because payments are made at 'yesterday's prices') but loses with debtors, because a delay in the receipt of cash means that more money is required to purchase replacement assets (at 'tomorrow's prices') in order to maintain the operating capability of the business. The MWCA is therefore a charge, if the company has positive, rather than negative, monetary working capital (MWC defined roughly as debtors minus creditors) which takes account of the effect of deferred payments on business substance in arriving at the current cost operating profit.

(iii)   The depreciation adjustment is the difference between the depreciation share based on the historical cost of fixed assets and the charge based on their current cost. In a CCA statement, the depreciation adjustment is therefore used to adjust 'historical cost profit' towards 'current cost operating profit' in order to reflect the current value of fixed assets 'consumed'.

(iv)   The gearing adjustment is calculated after the current cost operating profit has been determined. A company is financed not only by share capital, but also by debt capital, which falls in 'real' value over time in a period of inflation. There is no need to maintain the operating capability of the business with respect to assets financed by debt capital. The more usual 'type 1' gearing adjustment is the amount of holding gains (ie a proportion of the three adjustments described in (i) to (iii) above) which is attributable to assets financed by debt capital rather than equity. These gains, because they will never be paid to the holders of debt capital, are 'free' to the equity shareholders, and the gearing adjustment is therefore added to the current cost operating profit in order to arrive at a value for 'current cost profit attributable to shareholders' of the company.

27   STATEMENT OF PRINCIPLES

The merits of the ASB's *Statement of Principles* should, ideally, be summarised in its objective, which is given in the *Foreword to Accounting Standards*:

'to provide a framework for the consistent and logical formulation of individual accounting standards (and to provide) a basis on which others can exercise judgement in resolving accounting issues.'

The following points may be made in favour of the *Statement of Principles*.

(a)   The principles have in fact been used in the formulation of standards, for example its definitions of assets and liabilities have been used in FRS 5 *Reporting the substance of transactions*.

(b)   The *Statement* helps reduce scope for individual judgement and the potential subjectivity that this implies.

(c)   Financial statements should be more comparable because, although alternative treatments will still be available, there will be a consistent and coherent framework on which to base one's choice of a particular alternative.

(d)   The *Statement* puts forward a consistent terminology and consistent objectives, for example in the definitions and the qualitative characteristics.

It could be argued that the *Statement of Principles* is too theoretical. It is certainly general rather than particular. However, as has been seen with FRS 5, the general principles can be applied to very specific issues in accounting standards. Moreover, in areas not at present covered by accounting standards, the statement can give general guidance. Nevertheless, in the short term, the principles in the *Statement* may conflict with some accounting standards which had already been issued before it was written.

24   XYZ

(a)   To: Managing director
        From: Company Secretary
        Date: 3 June 20X6
        Subject: *XYZ Group performance 20X5/X6*

In accordance with your instructions, I have prepared a report on the XYZ Group. The report is presented under the 'criteria for a healthy company' suggested by you. Appropriate ratios are listed in the appendix.

Asset base

The fixed assets are in each case covered by the shareholders' funds. The asset base of company X appears adequate, although substantial investments in intangible assets appear in the balance sheet. The freehold property is reported at cost and is therefore likely to be undervalued. Plant is on average half-way through its useful life. Company Y does not own its own property and rental agreements should be examined to check on security of tenure. Again plant is approximately half-way through its useful life. Company Z has a substantial asset base and its plant has been purchased fairly recently. However, the term of the lease appears to have almost expired and details of arrangement for renewal or replacement need to be investigated.

Control of working capital

There are unexpectedly large variations in the stock holding period, in view of the fact that all three companies are engaged in the same trade. The reason why Y and X, respectively, carry stocks for twice and three times the period of Z needs to be examined. Similarly the debt collection periods of X (14 weeks) and Y (19 weeks) appear excessive. Systems of stock and debtor control in companies X and Y require investigation.

Liquidity

All three companies are engaged in manufacturing. The current and liquid ratios of X appear adequate for this type of operation. The liquidity position of Y is weak, which may be the reason why it takes 14½ weeks to pay suppliers. Also the company has a large bank overdraft in relation to its scale of operations. The solvency ratios of Z appear excessive and, with suppliers representing 2½ weeks purchases, it does not seem as if maximum credit is being taken. The possibility of transferring resources from Z to Y should be explored.

Borrowing capacity

The gearing of both X and Y is high. At X, the amounts due to suppliers and providers of loan finance (£2,166,000) exceed the equity interest; at Y, there is a substantial balance of liabilities due within one year. In neither of these cases is a great deal of borrowing capacity apparent. Z has no borrowings, low creditors and cash at the bank; its borrowing capacity is therefore more promising.

Operating performance

Again there are substantial unexplained variations in performance. The net profit ratio of Z (18.4%) is well above the average for the group (10.3%). The negative net margin of Y requires careful investigation.

Commercial return for shareholders

The return on shareholders' funds earned by Z appears adequate, that of X is low while Y produces a negative return on the shareholders' investment.

Appendix: accounting ratios

Ratio	Calculation	X	Y	Z	Group
Stock turnover *	$\frac{\text{Closing stock}}{\text{Cost of goods sold}} \times 52$ (weeks)	18	11	5½	11
Debt collection *	$\frac{\text{Closing debtors}}{\text{Sales}} \times 52$ (weeks)	14	19	7	12
Payment of creditors	$\frac{\text{Creditors}}{\text{Cost of sales **}} \times 52$ (weeks)	15½	14½	2½	9¾
Current ratio	$\frac{\text{Current assets}}{\text{Current liabilities}}$:1	2.5:1	1.1:1	6.4:1	2:1
Liquid ratio	$\frac{\text{Debtors + bank}}{\text{Current liabilities}}$:1	1.3:1	0.7:1	4:1	1.2:1
Gearing ratio	$\frac{\text{External finance}}{\text{Total finance}} \times 100$	50%	52%	4%	44%

Net profit ratio	$\dfrac{\text{Net profit} ***}{\text{Sales}} \times 100$		8.9%	(4%)	18.4%	10.3%
Return on capital employed	$\dfrac{\text{Net profit} **}{\text{Shareholders equity}} \times 100$		7.3%	(8.2%)	18.7%	14.7%

*   Closing balances used as insufficient data provided to calculate averages.

**   Cost of goods sold used as an approximation of purchases.

***   Net profit after interest and before tax.

(b) *Items requiring further investigation*

Company X. Research and development of £180,000 needs to be investigated to check that the requirements of SSAP 13 are satisfied. According to this standard, and the Companies Act, research expenditure should be written off immediately it is incurred. Development expenditure may only be capitalised where stringent conditions are met, including the requirement for a clearly defined project where commercial viability is reasonably certain.

Freehold property, £300,000. FRS 15 and the Companies Act require fixed assets to be written off either immediately or over its useful economic life. There is no evidence that this is being done.

Company Y. Customer prepayments of £106,000. The nature of this item should be investigated. Is the company able to supply the goods at the agreed price?

Company Z. Goodwill £200,000. FRS 10 and the Companies Act require purchased goodwill to be written off over its useful economic life. Non-purchased goodwill should not appear in the accounts. The accounting policy followed should be investigated to ensure compliance with these regulation.

Freehold property at valuation £800,000. Again a check needs to be made to ensure that the asset is being depreciated over its estimated useful life.

Extraordinary item £73,000. FRS 3 contains regulations regarding the treatment of rare, unusual items. Only extraordinary items may be reported 'below the line' and evidence must be produced to prove that this item has been properly classified.

(c) A company may, legally, pay a dividend out of accumulated realised profits less accumulated realised losses. The available balance is £20,000 and so the company is clearly unable to make the proposed payment of £60,000. The capital redemption reserve is, for all purposes, to be treated as share capital, and is therefore not available to back the proposed payment. Apart from legal regulations, cash availability is the crucial practical constraint on proposals to pay a dividend. The company's bank overdraft of £172,000 suggest that even a dividend payment of £20,000 would be ill-advised at this stage.

29 WEBSTER

(a) PROFIT AND LOSS ACCOUNTS (Restated)

	Cole Ltd		Darwin Ltd	
	£'000	£'000	£'000	£'000
Sales (W1)		2,875		4,400
Opening stock	450		720	
Purchases (W2)	2,055		3,080	
	2,505		3,800	
Closing stock	(540)		(850)	
		(1,965)		(2,950)
Gross profit		910		1,450
Operating expenses (W3)	520		844	
Debenture interest	80		-	
Overdraft interest	15		-	
		(615)		(844)
Net profit		295		606

BALANCE SHEETS (restated)

	Cole Ltd		Darwin Ltd	
	£'000	£'000	£'000	£'000
Fixed assets (W4)				
Premises		1,900		1,900
Plant		1,200		720
		3,100		2,620
Current assets				
Sales	540		850	
Debtors (522 + 375)	897		750	
Bank (W5)	-		60	
	1,437		1,660	
Current liabilities				
Creditors (438 – 275)	163		562	
Overdraft (W5)	795		-	
	958		562	
Net current assets		479		1,098
		3,579		3,718
10% debenture		(800)		-
Net assets		2,779		3,718
Share capital and reserves				
Ordinary shares £1 each		1,000		500
Revaluation reserve (800 – 40)		760		700
Profit and loss account		1,019		2,518
(684 + 295 + 40)/(1,912 + 606)		2,779		3,718

Workings

1	*Cole's sales*	£'000
	Per P&L account	3,000
	Over-priced intra group sales (500 – 375)	(125)
		2,875

2	*Cole's purchases*	£'000
	Per P&L account	2,030
	Under-priced intra group sales (300 – 275)	25
		2,055

3	*Operating expenses*	£'000
	Cole: as if property is revalued	
	Per P&L account	480
	Additional depreciation (2,000 – 1,200) ÷ 20	40
		520

	Darwin's as if plant not yet acquired	£'000
	Per P&L account	964
	Less depreciation on plant (600 × 20%)	(120)
		844

4	*Fixed asset balance*	Cole	Darwin
		£'000	£'000
	Property	2,000	2,000
	Depreciation	(100)	(100)
		1,900	1,900
	Plant	1,200	1,200
	Less plant not on stream (600 – (600 × 20%))	-	(480)
		1,200	720

5	Bank balances	£'000
	Cole	
	Per balance sheet	20
	Intra group sale	(500)
	Intra group purchase	(300)
	Overdraft interest	(15)
		(795)
	Darwin	
	Per balance sheet	(550)
	Plant purchase reversed	600
	Overdraft interest reversed	10
		60

6   Ratios

	Cole Limited		Darwin Limited	
	Original	Restated	Original	Restated
ROCE (W1)	19.4%	10.5%	13.3%	16.3%
Asset turnover (W2)	1.01 times	0.80 times	1.23 times	1.18 times
Gross profit margin (W30)	35.3%	31.7%	33.0%	33.0%
Net profit margin (W4)	16.7%	10.3%	10.8%	13.8%
Debtors collection period (W5)	64 days	114 days	62 days	62 days
Creditors payment period (W6)	79 days	29 days	67 days	67 days

Workings

1   ROCE

$$\text{Cole} = \frac{295 + 80}{2,779 + 800} = 10.5\%$$

$$\text{Darwin} = \frac{606}{3,718} = 16.3\%$$

2   Asset turnover

$$\text{Cole} = \frac{2,875}{3,579} = 0.80 \text{ times}$$

$$\text{Darwin} = \frac{4,400}{3,718} = 1.18 \text{ times}$$

3   Gross profit margin

$$\text{Cole} = \frac{910}{2,875} = 31.7\%$$

4   Net profit margin

$$\text{Cole} = \frac{295}{2,875} = 10.3\%$$

$$\text{Darwin} = \frac{606}{4,400} = 13.8\%$$

5   Debtors collection period

$$\text{Cole} = \frac{897}{2,875} \times 365 = 114 \text{ days}$$

6   Creditors payments period

$$\text{Cole} = \frac{163}{2,055} \times 365 = 29 \text{ days}$$

The general effect of the restatement is to **improve Darwin's results** in comparison to Cole's. Once the impact of the **beneficial intra-group purchases** and sales are removed, Cole is shown to have a **poorer gross profit margin** than Darwin. This has fed through to the net margin, which is also affected in Cole's case by the impact of a **higher depreciation charge**. The **cash flow** situation for Cole is significantly **worse**, thus increasing interest payable which also impacts on net profit margin.

Darwin's **return on capital** has been **improved** by removing the asset that had yet to make a contribution to the company's profitability. It is significant that the revaluation of Cole's property along the same lines as Darwin has **failed to compensate** for the increase in depreciation and the decrease in gross margin caused by the adjustments to the intra-group transactions.

These adjustments have also had a marked effect on **Cole's collection periods**; whereas these are evenly matched between debtors and creditors by Darwin; Cole's figures indicate an **imbalance**, with far longer taken to pay by debtors than Cole can take to pay its own debts to creditors.

In summary, **Darwin** looks much the **better investment opportunity**. However, Webster will also have to consider:

(i)   The relative **asking prices** of the companies.

(ii)   The likelihood that the **historical results** are a **true reflection** of future profitability (eg what is the likely effect of Darwin's new machinery coming on stream?).

(c) **Some** but **not all** of the **information** is likely to be available, although each company may disclose voluntarily beyond that required by legislation or standards.

Items (i) and (ii)

FRS 8 *Related party transactions* requires the disclosure of transactions and balances, between **related parties**. These would be included, but may be aggregated with other similar transactions, as permitted by the standard. Further, if Cole is 90% + owned by Velox, then an exemption from disclosure is permitted.

Item (iii)

Companies that do not follow a policy of revaluation are **not required** to state **market values**, other than in the Directors' Report, where considered significant. However, those that **do revalue** are required to give **historical cost information**; in any case, the additional depreciation would appear in the note of historical cost profits and losses.

Item (iv)

The company's **depreciation policy** would be disclosed, but not necessarily that a certain asset is yet to come on-line, nor how the purchase had been financed.

Item (v)

Without the information in (i) and (ii), it would **not** be possible to work out how much overdraft interest Cole would have to pay.

Index

Note: **Key Terms** and their references are given in **bold**

A true and fair view, 51

Abstract 4 Presentation of long-term debtors
   in current assets, 27

Abstract 5 Transfers from current assets to
   fixed assets, 27

ACCA, 29

Accounting concepts, 4

Accounting policies, 4, 44, 62, 532

Accounting records, 52

Accounting reference period, 51

Accounting standard, 9, 10, 26

Accounting Standards Board (ASB), 10, 23

Accounting Standards Committee (ASC), 5,
   10, 22

Accruals and deferred income, 69

Accruals, 40

Acquisition accounting, 340, 400, 405

Acquisition expenses, 383

Acquisition v merger accounting, 401

Acquisition, 219, 384, 405

Advanced financial accounting, 454

Advantages and disadvantages of current
   cost accounting, 488

Advantages of cash flow accounting, 245

Advantages of current exit value accounting,
   472

Advantages of replacement costing, 468

Agency theory, 489

Allocation of impairment, 139

Allotted share capital, 279

Alternative accounting rules, 79

Alternative Investment Market (AIM), 144

Amortisation, 124, 125

Analysis of cash flow statements, 244

Application notes, 268

ASB, 267

Assets, 267, 269, 501

Associate, 426

Associated undertaking, 333, 421

Associates, 421

Attributable profit, 165

Atuarial method, 150

Auditors' report, 51

Authorised share capital, 278

Balance sheet, 51, 56, 57, 61, 503

Banks, 247

Big GAAP/little GAAP, 28, 29

Bonus shares, 298

Borrowings, 285

Business combination, 384, 405

Business income, 463

CA 1985, 15, 196, 298, 318, 330, 338, 404

CA 1989, 52, 330, 336

Calculating ratios, 516

Called up share capital, 69

Capital grants, 109

Capital instruments, 279

Capital maintenance, 454, 473

Capital measurement, 455

Capital redemption reserve, 299, 305

Cash flow based forecasts, 247

Cash flow risk, 287

Cash flow statement, 428

Cash forecasting, 247

Categories of ratios, 512

CCA profits, 481

Central assets, 138

Chairman's report, 75, 513

Chambers, R J, 470

Change in accounting policy, 224

Check list for report writing, 537

Class of business, 319

Class of fixed assets, 94

Class of intangible assets, 122

Classification of companies, 53

Close family, 314

Common costs, 320

Companies Act 1985, 9, 55, 72, 106, 158, 197,
   340, 350

Companies Act 1989 (CA 1989), 9

Companies Acts, 49

Conceptual framework, 13

Consignment stock, 272

Consistency, 39

Consolidated balance sheet, 432

Consolidated profit and loss account, 429

Consolidation, 333, 504

Constructive obligation, 253

Consultative Committee of Accountancy
   Bodies (CCAB), 10, 23, 29

Contingencies, 31, 385

Contingent assets, 259

Contingent liabilities, 69, 259

Contributions from owners, 501

Control, 314, 332, **426**

Convertible loan stock, 208

Corporate report, 4
Corresponding amounts, 59
Cost of acquistion, 386
Cost of sales adjustment (COSA), 482
Cost of sales, 60
Cost, 81
Co-terminous accounting periods, 338
CPP (current purchasing power accounting),
     463, 475
CPP, 475
Credit risk, 287
Credit sale, 147
Creditors, 262
Creditors: amounts falling due after more
     than one year, 68
Creditors: amounts falling due within one
     year, 68
Criteria, 406
Criticisms of FRS 10, 130
Currency risk, 287
Current cost accounting, 480
Current cost reserve, 487
Current entry value accounting, 463
Current entry values, 460
Current exit value accounting, 470
Current exit values, 460
Current operating gains, 462
Current purchasing power (CPP) accounting,
     475
Current purchasing power (CPP), 473
Current tax, 181
Current value accounting, 460

Date of acquisition, 384
Debt, 279
Debtors, 68
Deferred taxation, 186
Department of Trade and Industry, 29
Depreciation, 88
Deprival value, 480
Derecognition, 270
Derivative financial instrument, 285
Derivatives and financial instruments, 132
Diminution in value, 131
Directly attributable finance costs, 84
Directors' report, 51, 72, 513
Disclosure of subsidiaries, 339
Disclosure requirements for lessees, 156
Disclosure requirements for lessors, 157
Disclosure requirements of FRS 15, 94
Disclosures, 129
Discontinued operations, 219

Discount rate, 139
Distributable profits, 298
Distributions to owners, 501
Distributions, 300
Dividend yield, 531
Dividends and pre-acquisition profits, 375
Dividends payable by a subsidiary, 353
Dividends, 66, 294
Dominant influence, 332
Dsclosures for associates and joint ventures,
     443
Dsclosures required by FRS 9, 443
Dscounting, 190
Duties of directors, 301

Earnings yield, 532
Earnings, 203
Economic income, 450
Economic value (EV) , 460, 480
ED 47 Accounting for goodwill, 120
Edwards & Bell (The theory and
     measurement of business income 19, 461
Edwards and Bell, 463
Efficient market hypothesis, 490
Efficient market, 491
Elements of financial statements, 498, 501
Employee information, 65
Employment Act 1982., 73
Entity and proprietary concepts of capital,
     456
Entity concept of capital, 457
Entity, 426
Entry and exit values, 460
Equity accounting, 421
Equity instrument, 202, 285
Equity shares, 405
Equity, 279
Estimation technique, 44
Euity accounting, 334, 420, 421
European Union, 9
Exceptional items, 215, 428
Exemption of subsidiary undertakings from
     preparing group account, 336
Exercise of significant influence, 427
Exit values, 470
Exposure draft FRS for smaller entities, 29
Extraordinary items, 216

Factoring of debts, 273
Factors affecting depreciation, 89
Fair value adjustments, 381

Fair value of purchase consideration, 386
Fair value, 123, **148**, **202**, 294, 340, **384**
Filing exemptions for small and medium-
sized companies, 70
Finance cost, 281
Finance lease, 148
Financial asset, 286
Financial instrument, 202, 286
Financial liability, 286
Financial Reporting Council (FRC), 10
Financial Reporting Exposure Draft
(FRED), 23
Financial Reporting Standards (FRSs), 10,
12, 23
Financial Reporting Standards (FRSs), 9
Financial Services Act 1986, 9, 70
Fixed assets, 78, 464
Fixed assets: disclosure, 80
Fnance cost, 281
Foreseeable losses, 165
Foreword to Accounting Standards, 9, 25
Foreword to UITF Abstracts, 28
Format of reports, 538
Format of the accounts, 53
Framework for the preparation and
presentation of financial stat, 13
FRED 13 Derivatives and other financial
instruments: disclosure, 285
FRED 15 Impairment of fixed assets and
goodwill, 85
FRS 1 Cash flow statements, 31, 51, 229, 230,
244, 410
FRS 2 Accounting for subsidiary
undertakings and FRS 7 Fair values in
acquisition accounting, 411
FRS 2 Accounting for subsidiary
undertakings, 263, 330, 335, 339
FRS 3 Reporting financial performance, 30,
206, 215, 429
FRS 4 Capital instruments, 29, 30, 279
FRS 5 Reporting the substance of
transactions, 30, 157, 267
FRS 6 Acquisitions and mergers, 383, 400,
405
FRS 7 Fair values in acquisition accounting,
380, 383
FRS 8 Related party disclosures, 263, 314
FRS 9, 438
FRS 10 Goodwill and intangible assets, 129,
132, 433
FRS 11 Impairment of fixed assets and
goodwill, 93, 131

FRS 12 Provisions, contingent liabilities and
contingent assets, 82, 252
FRS 13, 285
FRS 14 Earnings per share, 202
FRS 15, 88
FRS 18 Accounting policies, 39
FRS 19 Deferred tax, 185, 187, 189
FRSSE, 30
Full provision, 187
Functional (or local) currency, 286
Fundamental errors, 224
Fungible assets, 47
Fxed asset investments, 428

G A Lee Modern financial accounting, 457
GAAP, 13, 15
Gains, 501
Gearing adjustment, 484
General price inflation, 475
Geographical analysis, 319
Geographical segment, 319
Going concern concept, 472
Going concern, 40
Goodwill adjustments, 386
Goodwill and intangible assets, 141
Goodwill and pre-acquisition profits, 358
Goodwill, 119, 428
Gross equity method, 438, 439
Group reconstruction, 405

Headline' EPS, 206
Hire purchase agreement, 148
Historical cost accounting, 461
HM Customs & Excise, 182
'holding company', 330
Holding gain, 460, 472
HP Agreement, 147
Hundred Group, 387
Hybrid instruments, 280

IAS 1 Disclosure of accounting policies, 263
Ias 18 revenue, 294
Identifiable assets and liabilities, 122, 384
Identification of income generating units,
137
Impairment review, 126, 132
Impairment, 132
Income and capital, 450
Income and value measurement\:Theory and
practice, 454

Income measurement, 455
Income, 450, 452, 454
Inherent goodwill, 119
Institute of Investment Management and
    Research (IIMR), 206
Intangible assets, 115, 123, **134**, 385
Intangible fixed assets, 66
Inter-company sales of fixed assets, 368
Inter-company trading, 393
Interest held on a long-term basis, 332, **427**
Interest payable and similar charges, 66
Interest rate implicit in the lease, 148
Interest suspense account, 152
Interest, 294
Interest, royalties and dividends, 297
Internally generated goodwill, 123
International Accounting Standards
    Committee (IASC), 12
International Accounting Standards, 12
Investment property, 104
Investment, 144
Issue costs, 283
Issued ordinary shares, 203

Joint arrangements, 440, 422
Joint control, 421, **437**, 440
Joint venture, 437, 440
Joint ventures, 421

Kaldor (An expenditure tax 1955), 452
Key management, 314

Laying and delivery of accounts, 52
Lease term, 148
Lease, 147
Lee, T A, 454, 471, 480
Level spread method, 150
Liabilities, 253, **267**, 501
Limitations of ratio analysis, 534
Linked presentation, 270
Liquidity risk, 287
Listed companies, 71
Loan transfers, 275
Long-term contract, 163
Long-term interest, 421, 427
Losses, 501

Market price risk, 287
Measurement in financial statements, 498,
    503

Measurement of revenue, 295
Merge, 406
Merger accounting, 400, 405
Merger relief, 413
Merger, 406
Minimum lease payments, 148
Minority interest, 349, 373, 393, 413, 437
Minority interests in unrealised
    inter-company profits, 366
Modified accounts, 71
Monetary assets and liabilities, 385
Monetary item, 476
Monetary working capital adjustment
    (MWCA), 483

Negative goodwill, 121, 128
Net realisable value (NRV) , 134, 480
Net realisable values for assets, 470
Net replacement cost (NRC), 480
New parent company, 407
Nil provision approach, 187
Non-depreciating assets, 466
Non-equity shares, 406
Non-monetary assets, 128
Non-monetary item, 128, **476**
Non-purchased intangibles, 123
Normative accounting concepts, 494
Normative theory, 494
Notes to the accounts, 60, 62

Objective of financial statements, 498
**Obligation to transfer economic benefits,
    280**
Off balance sheet finance, 266
Offset, 271
Oerous contract, 256
Operating and Financial Review (OFR), 75,
    535
Oerating lease, 148
Operating profit, 63
Oportunity cost, 471
Options, 208
Ordinary activities, 215
Ordinary shares, 202
Other creditors including taxation and social
    security, 68
Other market price risk, 287
Ownership interest, 501

P/E ratio, 531

Parent undertaking, 330
Partial provision, 187
Participating interest, 331
Participating interest, 331, 421, **426**, 440
Payments on account, 165
Pendrill and Simon, 454
Pensions and other post-retirement benefits, 385
Permanent differences, 186, 190
Persons acting in concert, 314
Positive accounting concepts, 494
Positive purchased goodwill, 123
Post balance sheet events, 252
Potential ordinary share, 203
Potential problems with FRS 3, 226
Pre-acquisition losses of a subsidiary, 375
Pre-acquisition losses, 375
Pre-acquisition profit, 373, 395
Preference dividend, 355
preference shares, 208
Preparing a cash flow statement, 237
Presentation of financial information, 499, 503
Prior period adjustments, 224
Problems with SSAP 19, 108
Profit and loss account, 51, 55, 58, 61, 197, 413, 503
Profit smoothing, 253
Profitability, 519
Proportion consolidation, 438
Proprietary concept of capital, 457
Provision, 253, 262
Provisions for liabilities and charges, 262
Prudence, 39
PSSAP 7, 477
Public Sector Liaison Committee (PSLC), 23
Published accounts, 51
Purchased goodwill, 119, **122, 134**

Qualitative characteristics of financial information, 498, 500
Quasi subsidiary, 263, **272**
Quoted investments, 385

Ranking dilutive securities, 212
Ratio analysis, 512
Readily ascertainable marekt value, 123
Realisable income, 470
Realisable values, 460
Rebuttable presumption, 125
Recognition in financial statements, 498, 501

Recognition, 269
Reconciliation of movements in shareholders' funds, 222
Recoverable amount, 84, 134, **384**
Redemption of shares, 302
Registrar of Companies, 51
Registrar, 52
Regulatory system of accounting, 9
Related party transactions, 53, 313
Rendering of services, 296
Replacement cost, 460, 480
Reporting entity, 499
Reports on financial performance, 536
Repossessions, 153
Repurchase of own debt, 283
Reserves, 69, 262, 265
Residual value, 122, 125
Restructuring, 257
Revaluation reserve, 79, 265
Revenue, 294
Reversal of impairment, 127
Reversal of past impairments, 140
Review Panel., 10, 11
Royalties, 294
Rule of 78, 150

S 131 CA 1985, 413
Sale and leaseback transactions, 273
Sale of goods, 295
Sandilands Committee, 454
Schedule 4, 54
Scrip dividends, 284
Securitised assets, 275
Segmental reporting, 318
Share capital, 278
Share options, 209
Share premium account, 299, 304
Shareholders' investment ratios, 531
Shares not yet ranking for dividend, 208
Shares, 283
Shearer v Bercain Ltd 1980, 304, 404
Short term debtors and creditors, 286
Short-term work in progress, 160
Significant influence, 421, 440
Small and medium-sized groups, 337
Small companies and the Companies Act, 33
Small companies, 70, 71
Solomons report, 14
Solomons, 13
Specific price inflation, 475
SSAP 1, 264, 333

SSAP 2 Disclosure of accounting policies, 38

SSAP 3 Earnings per share, 215, 531

SSAP 5 Accounting for value added tax, 182

SSAP 9 Stocks and long term contracts, 163, 263, 292

SSAP 12, 104, 265

SSAP 16 Current cost accounting, 467, 480

SSAP 17, 252

SSAP 18, 252

SSAP 19 Accounting for investment properties, 104

SSAP 20, 50

SSAP 21 Accounting for leases and hire purchase contracts, 31, 147, 263

SSAP 21, 156, 158

SSAP 22 Accounting for goodwill, 360

SSAP 25 Segmental reporting, 318

SSAP The treatment of taxation under the imputation system in the accounts of companies, 197

SSAPs, 23, 49

Statement of Aims, 15, 24

Statement of Principles for Financial Reporting, 498

Statement of Principles, 8, 12, 15, 41, 267, 279

Statement of total recognised gains and losses, 30, 503

Statements of Standard Accounting Practice (SSAPs), 9, 10

Sterling, R R, 470

Stock Exchange, 318

Stocks and work in progress, 385

Stocks, 160

Structure of the profit and loss account, 217

Subsidiary undertaking, 330

'subsidiary', 330

Substance over form, 263

Substantial acquisitions, 410

Summary financial statements, 71

Sum-of-the-digits method, 150

Tangible assets, 385

Tangible fixed assets, 134

Tax credit, 181

Tax on profits on ordinary activities, 66

Taxation, 194

The auditors' report, 74

The making of accounting standards, 10

The Royal Institution of Chartered Surveyors, 108

The Stock Exchange, 13

The theory of interest 1930, 452

Timing differences, 186

Total recognised gains and losses, 429

Trading in financial assets and financial liabilities, 286

True and fair view, 49

Turnover, 59, 62

UITF Abstract 15 Disclosure of substantial acquisitions, 410

Undistributable reserves, 299

Unrealised losses, 299

Unrealised profits, 299

Urgent Issues Task Force (UITF), 11, 27

Useful economic life, 122, 125

Users of corporate reports, 5

Users of financial statements, 499

Valuation of fixed assets, 78

Value and capital 1946, 453

Value in use, 134, 384

Value of capital, 454

Value to the business (deprival value, 480

VAT, 182

Warrants or options, 203

Warrants, 208, 284

Withholding tax, 181

Yellow Book, 13

REVIEW FORM & FREE PRIZE DRAW

All original review forms from the entire BPP range, completed with genuine comments, will be entered into a draw on 31 January 2003 and 31 July 2003. The names on the first four forms picked out will be sent a cheque for £50.

Name: _____   Address: _____
_____

How have you used this Text?
(Tick one box only)
☐ Home study (book only)
☐ On a course: college _____
☐ With 'correspondence' package
☐ Other _____

Why did you decide to purchase this Text?
(Tick one box only)
☐ Have used complementary Ki
☐ Have used BPP Texts in the past
☐ Recommendation by friend/colleague
☐ Recommendation by a lecturer at college
☐ Saw advertising
☐ Other _____

During the past six months do you recall seeing/receiving any of the following?
(Tick as many boxes as are relevant)
☐ Our advertisement in *ACCA Student Accountant*
☐ Our advertisement in *Pass*
☐ Our brochure with a letter through the post

Which (if any) aspects of our advertising do you find useful?
(Tick as many boxes as are relevant)
☐ Prices and publication dates of new editions
☐ Information on Text content
☐ Facility to order books off-the-page
☐ None of the above

Which BPP products have you used?

Text	☑	MCQ cards	☐	i-Learn	☐
Kit	☐	Tape	☐	i-Pass	☐
Passcard	☐	Video	☐	Virtual Campus	☐

Your ratings, comments and suggestions would be appreciated on the following areas.

	Very useful	Useful	Not useful
Introductory section (Key study steps, personal study)	☐	☐	☐
Chapter introductions	☐	☐	☐
Key terms	☐	☐	☐
Quality of explanations	☐	☐	☐
Case examples and other examples	☐	☐	☐
Questions and answers in each chapter	☐	☐	☐
Chapter roundups	☐	☐	☐
Quick quizzes	☐	☐	☐
Exam focus points	☐	☐	☐
Question bank	☐	☐	☐
Answer bank	☐	☐	☐
List of key terms and index	☐	☐	☐
Icons	☐	☐	☐
Mind maps	☐	☐	☐

	Excellent	Good	Adequate	Poor
Overall opinion of this Text	☐	☐	☐	☐

Do you intend to continue using BPP Products?   ☐ Yes   ☐ No

Please note any further comments and suggestions/errors on the reverse of this page. The BPP author of this edition can be e-mailed at: philfontbin@bpp.com

Please return to: Katy Hibbert, ACCA Range Manager, BPP Publishing Ltd, FREEPOST, London, W12 8BR

REVIEW FORM & FREE PRIZE DRAW (continued)

TELL US WHAT YOU THINK

Because the following specific areas of the text contain new material/cover tricky topics/cover highly examinable topics etc, your comments on their usefulness are particularly welcome.

- Fixed assets
- Interpretation of accounts
- Long-term contracts

Please note any further comments and suggestions/errors below.

See overleaf for information on other
BPP products and how to order

ACCA Order

To BPP Publishing Ltd, Aldine Place, London W12 8AW
Tel: 020 8740 2211   Fax: 020 8740 1184
email: publishing@bpp.com   online: www.bpp.com

Mr/Mrs/Ms (Full name) _____

Daytime delivery address _____

Postcode _____

Daytime Tel _____   Date of exam (month/year) _____

	6/02 Texts	1/02 Kits	9/01 Passcards	MCQ Cards	Tapes	Videos	7/02 i-Learn	7/02 i-Pass	Virtual Campus
PART 1									
1.1 Preparing Financial Statements	£20.95 ☐	£10.95 ☐	£5.95 ☐	£5.95 ☐	£12.95 ☐	£25.00 ☐	£34.95 ☐	£24.95 ☐	£90.00 ☐
1.2 Financial Information for Management	£20.95 ☐	£10.95 ☐	£5.95 ☐	£5.95 ☐	£12.95 ☐	£25.00 ☐	£34.95 ☐	£24.95 ☐	£90.00 ☐
1.3 Managing people	£20.95 ☐	£10.95 ☐	£5.95 ☐		£12.95 ☐	£25.00 ☐	£34.95 ☐	£24.95 ☐	£90.00 ☐
PART 2									
2.1 Information Systems	£20.95 ☐	£10.95 ☐	£5.95 ☐		£12.95 ☐	£25.00 ☐	£34.95 ☐	£24.95 ☐	£90.00 ☐
2.2 Corporate and Business Law	£20.95 ☐	£10.95 ☐	£5.95 ☐		£12.95 ☐	£25.00 ☐	£34.95 ☐	£24.95 ☐	£90.00 ☐
2.3 Business Taxation FA 2001 (for 12/02 exam)	£20.95 ☐	£10.95 ☐	£5.95 ☐		£12.95 ☐	£25.00 ☐	£34.95 ☐	£24.95 ☐	£90.00 ☐
2.4 Financial Management and Control	£20.95 ☐	£10.95 ☐	£5.95 ☐		£12.95 ☐	£25.00 ☐	£34.95 ☐	£24.95 ☐	£90.00 ☐
2.5 Financial Reporting	£20.95 ☐	£10.95 ☐	£5.95 ☐		£12.95 ☐	£25.00 ☐	£34.95 ☐	£24.95 ☐	£90.00 ☐
2.6 Audit and Internal Review	£20.95 ☐	£10.95 ☐	£5.95 ☐		£12.95 ☐	£25.00 ☐	£34.95 ☐	£24.95 ☐	£90.00 ☐
PART 3									
3.1 Audit and Assurance Services	£20.95 ☐	£10.95 ☐	£5.95 ☐		£12.95 ☐	£25.00 ☐			
3.2 Advanced Taxation FA 2001 (for 12/02 exam)	£20.95 ☐	£10.95 ☐	£5.95 ☐		£12.95 ☐	£25.00 ☐			
3.3 Performance Management	£20.95 ☐	£10.95 ☐	£5.95 ☐		£12.95 ☐	£25.00 ☐			
3.4 Business Information Management	£20.95 ☐	£10.95 ☐	£5.95 ☐		£12.95 ☐	£25.00 ☐			
3.5 Strategic Business Planning and Development	£20.95 ☐	£10.95 ☐	£5.95 ☐		£12.95 ☐	£25.00 ☐			
3.6 Advanced Corporate Reporting	£20.95 ☐	£10.95 ☐	£5.95 ☐		£12.95 ☐	£25.00 ☐			
3.7 Strategic Financial Management	£20.95 ☐	£10.95 ☐	£5.95 ☐		£12.95 ☐	£25.00 ☐			
INTERNATIONAL STREAM									
1.1 Preparing Financial Statements	£20.95 ☐	£10.95 ☐	£5.95 ☐	£5.95 ☐					
2.5 Financial Reporting	£20.95 ☐	£10.95 ☐	£5.95 ☐						
2.6 Audit and Internal Review	£20.95 ☐	£10.95 ☐	£5.95 ☐						
3.1 Audit and Assurance Services	£20.95 ☐	£10.95 ☐	£5.95 ☐						
3.6 Advance Corporate Reporting	£20.95 ☐	£10.95 ☐	£5.95 ☐						
Success in your Research and Analysis Project – Tutorial Text (8/02)	£20.95 ☐								
Learning to Learn (7/02)	£9.95 ☐								

Subtotal £ [ ]

POSTAGE & PACKING

Study Texts

	First	Each extra	
UK	£3.00	£2.00	£ [ ]
Europe*	£5.00	£4.00	£ [ ]
Rest of world	£20.00	£10.00	£ [ ]

Kits/Passcards/Success Tapes

	First	Each extra	
UK	£2.00	£1.00	£ [ ]
Europe*	£2.50	£1.00	£ [ ]
Rest of world	£15.00	£8.00	£ [ ]

MCQ cards   £1.00   £1.00   £ [ ]

CDs each

UK	£2.00	£ [ ]
Europe*	£2.00	£ [ ]
Rest of world	£10.00	£ [ ]

Breakthrough Videos

	First	Each extra	
UK	£2.00	£2.00	£ [ ]
Europe*	£2.00	£2.00	£ [ ]
Rest of world	£20.00	£10.00	£ [ ]

Grand Total (incl. Postage)   £ [ ]

I enclose a cheque for (Cheques to BPP Publishing)

Or charge to Visa/Mastercard/Switch

Card Number [ ][ ][ ][ ]

Expiry date [ ]   Start Date [ ]

Issue Number (Switch Only) [ ]

Signature _____

We aim to deliver to all UK addressess inside 5 working days; a signature will be required. Orders to all EU addresses should be delivered within 6 working days. All other orders to overseas addresses should be delivered within 8 working days.
* Europe includes the Republic of Ireland and the Channel Islands.